Social Studies in Elementary Education

Thirteenth Edition

Walter C. Parker
University of Washington

Allyn & Bacon
is an imprint of

Boston • New York • San Francisco
Mexico City • Montreal • Toronto • London • Madrid • Munich • Paris
Hong Kong • Singapore • Tokyo • Cape Town • Sydney

Vice President and Executive Publisher: Jeffery W. Johnston
Acquisitions Editor: Meredith D. Fossel
Editorial Assistant: Maren Vigilante
Senior Project Manager: Linda Hillis Bayma
Production Coordinator: Norine Strang, S4Carlisle Editorial Services
Design Coordinator: Diane C. Lorenzo
Interior and Cover Design: Candace Rowley
Photo Coordinator: Valerie Schultz
Cover Images: Corbis
Operations Specialist: Susan Hannahs
Electronic Composition: S4Carlisle Publishing Services
Director of Marketing: Quinn Perkson
Marketing Manager: Darcy Betts Prybella
Marketing Coordinator: Brian Mounts

For related titles and support materials, visit our online catalog at www.pearsonhighered.com

Between the time website information is gathered and then published, it is not unusual for some sites to have closed. Also, the transcription of URLs can result in typographical errors. The publisher would appreciate notification where these errors occur so that they may be corrected in subsequent editions.

Library of Congress Cataloging-in-Publication Data

Parker, Walter C.
Social studies in elementary education/Walter C. Parker—Thirteenth ed.
    p. cm.
Includes bibliographical references and index.
ISBN-13: 978-0-13-233707-6
ISBN-10: 0-13-233707-X
1. Social sciences—Study and teaching (Elementary)—United States. I. Title.
 LB1584.J3 2009
372.83′0440973—dc22   2008000328

Printed in the United States of America

10 9 8 7 6 5 4 3 2   **EB** 12 11 10 09 08

Allyn & Bacon
is an imprint of

For my parents, Martha McClurg and Chalmerse Parker—
kind people, good citizens.

About the Author

Walter Parker teaches in the College of Education at the University of Washington in Seattle where he chairs the Social Studies Education Program. Earlier he taught at the University of Texas at Arlington. He studies K–12 social studies education generally and, in particular, civic education and the new international education movement. His other books include *Renewing the Social Studies Curriculum* (1991); *Educating the Democratic Mind* (1996); *Education for Democracy: Contexts, Curricula, and Assessments* (2002); and *Teaching Democracy: Unity and Diversity in Public Life* (2003). He is the editor of the Research and Practice column for *Social Education*, the flagship journal of the National Council for the Social Studies.

Walter was born and raised in Englewood, Colorado, on Denver's south side, and taught school for many years in Adams County on Denver's north side. He earned the B.A. in Political Science (University of Colorado, Boulder), the M.A. in Social Foundations of Education (University of Colorado, Denver), and the Ph.D. in Curriculum and Instruction (University of Washington, Seattle). He lives in Seattle with his wife, Sheila Valencia.

Preface

I have three goals for this new edition. First, to present the most powerful social studies content and pedagogy for children in elementary and middle schools. (This is not social studies "lite.") Second, to offer this material in simple and accessible ways, keeping always in mind the readers of this book who are new to teaching as well as those for whom English is a second or third language. Third, to write in a first-person active voice, not third-person passive. Readers are getting this material through a "real person" who loves this subject matter and has beliefs about how children can best be helped to learn it. To summarize, powerful material, accessible writing, and active voice guided this revision.

Purposes

The purpose of *social studies education* is twofold: to help students develop social understanding (knowledge of the social world—history, geography, government, economics, etc.) *and* the ability to think and act as democratic citizens in a multicultural society. Neither social knowledge nor democratic competence materializes out of thin air. Both have to be created continually, and that is why we have social studies education in the schools.

The purpose of *this book* is to introduce new teachers to the world of social studies teaching and learning in elementary and middle schools, and to help them unleash their intelligence and creativity on this vitally important subject area. Geography, history, government, and the other social sciences are delivered into the palm of the new teacher's hand, along with a suite of tools and ideas for bringing authentic social studies to life in the elementary and middle school classroom.

Text Organization

The book has three major sections: the first orients readers to the mission of social studies education and to the increasingly diverse children we teach; the second concentrates on the curriculum—*what* we want these students to learn; the third deals with instruction—*how* we plan and teach this curriculum. There are 13 chapters, including one (ch. 10) that focuses squarely on *resources* for teaching and learning social studies. I have always believed that good teaching is utterly dependent on good resources. Excellent teachers certainly are not writing all those lessons and materials themselves; there's just no time for that. Rather, they know where to find them and how to adapt them, and they don't hesitate to borrow good ideas and resources from others.

With this new edition, I reorganized Chapter 10 into "Four Great Resources," which is the new chapter title. Lots of resources are reviewed throughout the book, but these are the "core four," so to speak. They are the school's library (resource center/media center), the community, the computer, and the social studies textbook.

In the previous edition I moved the assessment chapter forward to Chapter 7 so that it comes *before* the planning and teaching chapters. Readers were happy with that move, so it stays put. I did it for what is now a widely accepted reason, called "backward design." This means that the primary purpose of assessment is not to score students' work after teaching, but to improve both teaching and learning. This requires thinking about assessment sooner, not later; that way, teacher and students alike have a clear and shared focus on what is to be learned and are gathering information about how teaching and learning are progressing.

Chapter 8 and 13 are the two unit-planning chapters in the book. While it might be logical to have one follow right after the other, that wouldn't actually make sense in this book. The reason is that Chapter 13 relies on the material presented in the intervening Chapters 9 through 12. Chapter 8, then, is an *introduction* to unit planning, whereas Chapter 13 is more advanced and presents two sophisticated models of integrated unit plans.

New to This Edition

The book has been thoroughly revised. Much has been updated to reflect current scholarship, much has been clarified, and I present new material, too. Also, redundancies that had crept in during prior revisions were removed.

It is a more practical book than ever, with more ready-to-use applications. As always, the book blends theory and practice: The emphasis is constantly on the *practices* of teaching social studies, but also on *understanding* them—how they work and why they matter. Because readers understand them, they are able to adapt these practices and invent their own. That's the whole idea: being creative professionals who know what we are doing and why. Now, let me highlight the key revisions.

- *Reflections.*   Each chapter has a sidebar called "Reflection" that is placed alongside what I believe is the most important material in the chapter. This lets readers know what the author of the book takes to be the key content of the chapter, and asks them to stop and ponder it. Also, the first Discussion Question at the end of the chapter asks readers to think about it some more. When I am reading a chapter in a textbook, I like to know what the author would point to as the material that would remain in the chapter if all the rest were forced out. This reflection sidebar, once in each chapter, plus Discussion Question 1, is my way of pointing.

- *Trends.*   Chapter 1 takes stock of strong currents that are washing over schools today. At the center is the high-stakes testing frenzy that got underway in the late 1990s and has resulted in both "curriculum standards" and "curriculum narrowing." Also central is globalization and the increasing pressure to educate U.S. students about the world—global education.

- *Pledging Allegiance.*   As pressure for global education mounts, so does nationalism. More states are requiring students to recite the *Pledge of Allegiance.* Cosmopolitanism and patriotism are crossing paths in interesting ways. Chapter 3 delves into democratic citizenship education, and a new section on the Pledge provides a brief history of those 31 words along with two activities—a seminar and a simulation— that will help children *think* about the Pledge rather than merely memorize it. Also, there are historical and contemporary photos of "pledging allegiance" from the United States and Singapore.

- *Maps and Google Earth.*   Chapter 5 focuses on teaching with and about maps, globes, charts, and graphs. The four full-color pages now feature an illustrated "dictionary of geographic terms" in addition to, as before, a cross-section landform map and the Dymaxion world map projection. Also, Google Earth is now presented along with a powerful teaching procedure that takes advantage of its 3-D graphic capabilities. The children's own school is at the center, and this software's ability to zoom out from there and back is highlighted.

- *Controversies.* Each school subject has controversial issues that teachers love to talk with one another about. There is the "phonics versus whole language" debate in language arts, "drill versus problem solving" in math, and so forth. In social studies, too, there are plenty of professional controversies, and this new edition invites you to participate in these debates. Here are several:
  - Patriotism (ch. 3)—Should children recite the Pledge of Allegiance daily?
  - Capital punishment (ch. 5)—Should children memorize the states and their capitals?
  - Political views (ch. 6)—Should teachers leave their political opinions at the classroom door?
  - Pluto's demotion (ch. 9)—How and why does knowledge change?
  - The technology solution (ch. 10)—Is a laptop for every child a boon or a waste of money?
  - Curriculum integration (ch. 13)—When should subjects be integrated and when is it better for them to be kept apart?
- *Field Trips and Fieldwork.* The thorough three-phase field trip planning guide is back by popular demand, and now it is supported with photographs of Singapore's unique approach to "fieldwork."
- *Deep Conceptual Learning.* In Chapter 9 the treatment of the powerful strategy *concept formation* now incorporates the story of Pluto's demotion from planetary status. The case clearly illustrates how concepts are made by humans, not nature. The concept *planet* was revised at a meeting of astronomers in the summer of 2006, and Pluto was asked to leave. Because concepts are constructs, teachers need to understand that teaching them means helping students construct them themselves. This is what *concept formation* is all about: deep conceptual learning rather than superficial "coverage."
- *Manipulatives.* The full-color manipulatives section of hands-on construction activities is again included in the planning chapter (ch. 8). These folded paper graphics are featured in other chapters, too, as aids to concept formation and inquiry in Chapter 9, for example. These kinesthetic activities tap into a different kind of intelligence, scaffold students' understanding of social studies topics, encourage creativity, and are ready to use in a beginning teacher's first classroom.
- *Web-Based Inquiries.* These are featured as one of two uses of the Internet in Chapter 10. The teacher pre-identifies the websites students encounter, and in this way keeps children safe while modeling wise *inquiry-oriented* Internet use. And back by popular demand is the *virtual field trip.* Now students can "visit" not only the seven ancient wonders of the world, but the seven new wonders recently chosen by voters around the globe.
- *Time and Chronology.* The section called "Developing a Sense of Time and Chronology," which includes developing the vocabulary of chronology as well as the ability to read and make time lines that show the relative amount of time between events, was moved from Chapter 5 to Chapter 4. Note the three time lines here.

- *Children's Literature.* Dozens of carefully selected (and often award-winning) children's literature suggestions are given throughout the book. Chapter 12 ("The Literacy–Social Studies Connection") considers how to use these trade books for maximum effect in social studies instruction, especially for teaching multiple perspectives on a single historical event. By popular demand, the *Socratic Seminar,* which is a powerful approach to literature circles in social studies, is included in this chapter as well.
- *Lesson Plans.* Twenty-three model Lesson Plans are again provided throughout the text. Each has been carefully updated and features important content, a sensible procedure, assessment, and ideas for curriculum integration. And now, each objective is keyed to one or more of the NCSS standards.
- *NCSS Standards.* The national and state curriculum standards movement is thoroughly introduced in Chapter 1 and, as always, a selection of the curriculum standards of the National Council for the Social Studies are provided in the NCSS standards *Sampler* that comes free with every new copy of this text. Discussion Question #4 at the end of each chapter asks readers to examine a particular teaching example from the *Sampler* that is related to the material in that chapter.
- *Resources.* As mentioned at the outset, Chapter 10 zeros in on resources for teaching and learning social studies. With this edition it emphasizes just four sets of core resources.
- *End-of-Chapter Questions.* These have been systematized. The first question at the end of every chapter asks readers to delve further into the Reflection sidebar that appeared once earlier in the chapter. The second and third questions focus on additional key material in the chapter. The fourth directs readers to connect the chapter to one of the illustrative teaching vignettes (lesson examples) that appear in the NCSS standards *Sampler.*

Supplements

Instructor's Manual

An instructor's manual is available to instructors using this textbook. It includes a sample course outline, suggested activities and assignments, and, for each of the book's 13 chapters, the following:

1. A list of key ideas and skills to be developed in the chapter
2. Suggestions for using the figures, photos, and charts
3. Suggestions for using the 23 Lesson Plans throughout the text
4. Assessments of students' understanding of the material in each chapter

PowerPoint Slides

A set of PowerPoint slides was created for instructors' use with each of the 13 chapters in the book. They can be downloaded from the Instructor Resource Center at the Pearson Higher Education website (www.pearsonhighered.com).

Acknowledgments

I am grateful first and foremost to John Jarolimek for the invitation to assume responsibility for this book nearly 20 years ago. John was the book's first author. I joined him as co-author of the 9th (1993) and 10th (1997) editions, and I became sole author as of the 11th edition (2001). John and I remain dear friends, and he is surely the book's closest reader.

I am especially indebted to Simone Schweber of the University of Wisconsin and Bruce Larson of Western Washington University for tremendously helpful feedback. Their suggestions pervade this new edition. I also want to thank the following professors who made numerous helpful suggestions for this new edition: Ernest Barnett of Georgia Southwestern State University; Karen Ivers of California State University, Fullerton; Deborah C. Johnson of Holy Family University; Claire Mamola of Appalachian State University; and Carolyn F. Riley of Northern Illinois University.

I want to express my gratitude as well to a number of scholars who gave generously of their time, whether reading drafts, offering suggestions, or challenging my thinking and setting me straight. These include my wife and literacy scholar Sheila Valencia; my sister and social work scholar Lynn Parker; multicultural education scholars James A. Banks and Audrey Osler; geographers Katharyne Mitchell and Matt Sparke; literacy educator Regie Routman; democratic education researchers Carole Hahn, Diana Hess, Patricia Avery, and Ian Davies; special education scholars Gene Edgar and Ilene Schwartz; history education scholars Linda Levstik and Keith Barton; classroom technology guru Joseph Braun; poet and literary activist Frances McCue; Washington state social studies leaders Caleb Perkins and Wendy Ewbank; NCSS president and former teaching partner Gayle Thieman; and my dear colleague at the National Institute of Education in Singapore, Ee Moi Kho, whose work and good sense have been deeply inspiring. My friend and colleague Joe Jenkins, one of the most skillful educational researchers on the planet, helped me work through the implications of Pluto's demotion (from planetary status) for teaching and learning key concepts in any field (see especially Chapter 9).

Also, I've been privileged to work with another fantastic group of graduate students including Carol Coe, Khodadad Kaviani, Steve Camicia, and Caleb Perkins. I'm grateful as well to my former and current deans, Allen Glenn and Patricia Wasley, who have supported my work in many ways.

Thanks also to a number of individuals who assisted in securing photographs, artwork, and other materials. Special thanks go to Raymond Bong who teaches at Rosyth School in Singapore and is the school's head of social studies. Photos of Rosyth students appear in Chapters 3 (pledging allegiance) and 10 (engaged in fieldwork). Thanks also to John Ferry of the Buckminster Fuller Institute, Bob Abramms of the Peters map, Michael Simpson of the National Council for the Social Studies, Robert Leming of the Center for Civic Education, Lee Arbetman and Deborah Foster of Street Law, Karen Limbacher of the Macmillan/ McGraw-Hill School Division, and Kelly Aramaki, principal of John Stanford International School in Seattle.

I was most fortunate as well to have the creativity and commitment to quality of my team at Pearson: Meredith Fossel, Linda Bayma, Carol Sykes, and Valerie Schultz, and Norine Strang of S4Carlisle Editorial Services.

Walter C. Parker

PEARSON
myeducationlab
Where the Classroom Comes to Life

"Teacher educators who are developing pedagogies for the analysis of teaching and learning contend that analyzing teaching artifacts has three advantages: it enables new teachers time for reflection while still using the real materials of practice; it provides new teachers with experience thinking about and approaching the complexity of the classroom; and in some cases, it can help new teachers and teacher educators develop a shared understanding and common language about teaching. . . ."[1]

As Linda Darling-Hammond and her colleagues point out, grounding teacher education in real classrooms—among real teachers and students and among actual examples of students' and teachers' work—is an important, and perhaps even an essential, part of training teachers for the complexities of teaching today's students in today's classrooms. For a number of years, we have heard the same message from many of you as we sat in your offices learning about the goals of your courses and the challenges you face in teaching the next generation of educators. Working with a number of our authors and with many of you, we have created a website that provides you and your students with the context of real classrooms and artifacts that research on teacher education tells us is so important. Through authentic in-class video footage, interactive simulations, rich case studies, examples of authentic teacher and student work, and more, **MyEducationLab** offers you and your students a uniquely valuable teacher education tool.

MyEducationLab is easy to use! Wherever the MyEducationLab logo appears in the margins or elsewhere in the text, you and your students can follow the simple link instructions to access the MyEducationLab resource that corresponds with the chapter content. These include:

Video: Authentic classroom videos show how real teachers handle actual classroom situations.

Homework & Exercises: These assignable activities give students opportunities to understand content more deeply and to practice applying content.

Case Studies: A diverse set of robust cases drawn from some of our best-selling books further expose students to the realities of teaching and offer valuable perspectives on common issues and challenges in education.

Simulations: Created by the IRIS Center at Vanderbilt University, these interactive simulations give hands-on practice at adapting instruction for a full spectrum of learners.

Student & Teacher Artifacts: Authentic student and teacher classroom artifacts are tied to course topics and offer practice in working with the actual types of materials encountered every day by teachers.

Readings: Specially selected, topically relevant articles from ASCD's renowned *Educational Leadership* journal expand and enrich students' perspectives on key issues and topics.

[1]Darling-Hammond, L., & Bransford, J., Eds. (2005). *Preparing Teachers for a Changing World.* San Francisco: John Wiley & Sons.

Other Resources:

Lesson & Portfolio Builders: With this effective and easy-to-use tool, you can create, update, and share standards-based lesson plans and portfolios.

MyEducationLab is easy to assign, which is essential to providing the greatest benefit to your student. Visit www.myeducationlab.com for a demonstration of this exciting new online teaching resource.

Brief Contents

Contents

Note: Every effort has been made to provide accurate and current Internet Information in this book. However, the Internet and information posted on it are constantly changing, so it is inevitable that some of the Internet addresses listed in this textbook will change.

Lesson Plans

Orientation to Social Studies Education

Social Studies Education: What and Why

CHAPTER ONE

Chapter Outline

- Goals for Social Studies: Social Understanding and Civic Efficacy
- Curriculum Scope and Sequence
- Curriculum Standards: National, State, and Local
- Trends
- Conclusion

Key Concepts

- Social studies
- Social understanding
- Civic efficacy
- Curriculum goals
- Scope and sequence
- Curriculum standards
- Grade and unit topics
- Conceptual themes
- Trends

MAIN IDEA

The purpose of social studies education is to help students develop social understanding (i.e., knowledge of people and places near and far [geography] and now and then [history]) and civic efficacy (i.e., the ability to think and act as a democratic citizen in a diverse society).

PICTURE THIS

As they enter the classroom, the kindergarten children are excited to find a large strip of paper going down the middle of the floor. Their teacher, Jacob Stern, tells them to hang up their coats and come sit beside the paper strip. The strip, he tells them, is a highway connecting two distant towns. Mr. Stern takes a toy car and starts driving it along the highway. "What might happen as someone drives along?" he asks. The children suggest a number of possibilities: running out of gas, getting tired, and being hungry. "What services might be necessary for people as they drive from town to town?" Tanisha suggests a gas station. A milk carton is placed along the highway and named "Tanisha's Gas Station."[1]

When I was in elementary school in Englewood, Colorado, just south of Denver, I loved social studies. I had brilliant teachers, and they taught us social studies every day, every week, and every month. It was serious social studies, not social studies "lite." They introduced us to the knowledge and skills of the social sciences while preparing us to hold the highest office in the land: citizen. It was challenging, it was fun, and it was with social studies material that my reading and writing skills developed.

Those of us from Lowell Elementary School appeared to our middle school teachers to be the smart kids, which was not the case; we were just well taught. Prior knowledge always makes a student look smart. Our elementary teachers gave us that gift: By the time we got to middle school, we already knew something about what these new teachers wanted to teach us. We had a foundation they could build on. Best of all, the teachers at Lowell didn't simply load us up with facts and skills. They taught us *ideas* and ignited a lifelong interest in them.

My experience in elementary school fueled more than my love of social studies subject matter. It also fueled my interest in how children can develop a solid foundation in social studies *before* they go on to middle and high school. I think of that often, and it pervades this book. In the primary grades (kindergarten–3rd), what should children be learning about social studies? And then how can they best build on that in the intermediate grades (4th–5th)? And then in the middle grades (6th–8th)? Simply put, social studies education is powerful, and not having access to it, for whatever reason, is disabling intellectually, socially, and morally.

Without historical understanding, there can be no wisdom; without geographical understanding, no cultural or environmental intelligence. Without economic understanding, there can be no sane use of resources and no rational approach to decision making and, therefore, no future. And without civic understanding, there can be no democratic citizens and, therefore, no democracy.

This is why social studies education matters. When children are empowered by knowledgeable and skillful teachers with the information, ideas, skills, and attitudes and values that compose the social studies curriculum, their *judgment* is improved. Consequently, they can reason historically, help solve community problems, embrace diversity, fight intolerance and bigotry, protect the environment, and, with deep understanding, empathize with the hopes, dreams, and struggles of people everywhere.

GOALS FOR SOCIAL STUDIES: SOCIAL UNDERSTANDING AND CIVIC EFFICACY

There are two primary goals of social studies education, and they are the guiding lights of most social studies curriculum standards. "Standards," as we will see later in this chapter and throughout the book, are statements that describe what students are supposed to learn—the desired results of instruction—also called objectives. But curriculum standards—whether national, state, or local school district standards—are not to be confused with the broad goals or purposes of curriculum and instruction. *Standards make no sense unless we know the goals they are aiming to achieve.* To get at the goals of social studies, let's begin with a definition.

According to the National Council for the Social Studies (NCSS), social studies education can be defined as follows:

> Social studies is the integrated study of the social sciences and humanities to promote civic competence. The primary purpose of social studies is to help young people develop the ability to make informed and reasoned decisions for the public good as citizens of a culturally diverse, democratic society in an interdependent world.[2]

On one side of this definitional coin is the subject matter that is studied. "Subject matter" is the *what* of teaching and learning—the curriculum. It includes the facts (also known as information or data), ideas, skills, issues (short for "controversial issues"), and methods of inquiry drawn from the seven social sciences: history, geography, civics and government (political science), economics, sociology, psychology, and anthropology. The humanities—philosophy, ethics, literature, religion, music, and the visual and performing arts—are involved as well.[3] These fields of study or "disciplines" serve as *resources:* The social studies curriculum draws on them, blending and integrating them with two additional ingredients—students' lived experience and society's needs—in order to provide children with meaningful learning experiences about the human condition. But to what ends? What is the purpose?

On the other side of the coin is the purpose, "civic competence" or democratic citizenship: "the ability to make informed and reasoned decisions for the public good as citizens of a culturally diverse, democratic society in an interdependent world."

To locate your state social studies standards, go to MyEducationLab and search under "Resources."

When we turn to the "vision statement" of the NCSS, we see both sides of this definition stated as goals: "Powerful social studies teaching helps students develop social understanding and civic efficacy."[4] *Social understanding* is knowledge of human beings' social worlds drawn from the social science disciplines plus the humanities, from our students' lives, and from society's needs. *Civic efficacy* is the readiness and willingness to assume citizenship responsibilities and the belief that one can make a difference. These responsibilities include more than just voting. In a democracy, it is also one's responsibility to serve on juries and to be just and lawful; one is expected to be tolerant of political and cultural differences; it is one's duty to participate in creating and evaluating public policy; and it is one's duty to be civic-minded—to think not only of oneself and one's rights and freedoms but also of the good of the whole community.

In a nutshell, then, social studies education has two goals: social understanding (i.e., knowledge of human societies) and civic efficacy (i.e., democratic citizenship). When reading any set of curriculum standards for social studies, keep an eye on the goals.

Schools typically approach these two broad goals by way of three subgoals: knowledge, attitudes and values, and skills. More specific objectives (or "standards") are typically listed under each subgoal. When readers examine their state and local social studies curriculum standards, they will most likely find that the standards take this form or one that is similar. Please take some time now to find out.

Knowledge

Which social knowledge is most important? We can answer this question in three ways: disciplines, themes, and topics.

One way is to refer to the *fields* of study—the seven social science disciplines and the humanities—where this knowledge is created, interpreted, and revised continually in a never-ending process of disciplined (i.e., it's not random or without rules of inquiry) knowledge construction. But these are large fields containing huge amounts of ideas, information, and methods of inquiry.

Another approach to determining which social knowledge is most important is to identify a set of basic content *themes*. Themes help curriculum planners and teachers narrow the scope somewhat and give them a better idea of *which* social knowledge deserves the most attention. The *Curriculum Standards for Social Studies* created by the National Council for the Social Studies identifies 10 such themes. They have become the best-known knowledge themes for social studies instruction in the elementary and middle grades and have been incorporated into a number of state and local social studies standards frameworks:

1. Culture
2. Time, Continuity, and Change
3. People, Places, and Environments
4. Individual Development and Identity
5. Individuals, Groups, and Institutions
6. Power, Authority, and Governance
7. Production, Distribution, and Consumption
8. Science, Technology, and Society
9. Global Connections and Interdependence
10. Civic Ideals and Practice

Please take a minute now to skim the little book that came with this textbook called *A Sampler of Curriculum Standards for Social Studies*. Find the brief descriptions of each of the 10 themes toward the beginning of the book. The remainder of the *Sampler* spells out each of these 10 standards and gives teaching examples for both early grades and middle grades. This will be a very helpful resource for you as you plan lessons and units. At the NCSS website (www.socialstudies.org) you can get still more details on each theme, order the complete book, and find links to teaching resources.

A third way to answer the "Which knowledge is most important?" question is to identify *topics*. There is no shortage of topics, and of course they cannot all be taught and no one would want to learn them. One scholar, E. D. Hirsch, Jr., produced a list of over 5,000 topics that he thought elementary school children in the United States should learn in order to give them a common knowledge base.[5] Without this, he argued, there can be no common culture that bridges our many cultural differences. But most educators, while sympathetic to Hirsch's thesis that shared knowledge is important, found his list too long and too fragmented to be of much help in curriculum development. A more typical and manageable set of topics for unit development in each of the elementary grades appears in the next section on curriculum scope and sequence. For example, elementary students should know:

- Great rivers of the world
- Desert cultures and forest cultures
- Food, clothing, and shelter (now and then, near and far)
- Geographic regions of the United States
- The American Revolution
- Rights and responsibilities of citizens

Attitudes and Values

The second subgoal of social studies learning—attitudes and values—is directed less at rational knowledge and more at the realm of emotion, feeling, and beliefs about what is right and wrong. Particular attitudes (also called dispositions, traits, and virtues) and values are essential to democratic citizenship. Sometimes these are divided into two categories and listed separately, as we will see in Chapter 3, but for now we can lump them together in order to distinguish them from knowledge and skills. Without them, like a car with no steering wheel, democratic government and civic life would be impossible. The following are typical of what is listed in state and local curriculum guidelines.

1. Being committed to the public values of this society as suggested in its historical documents, laws, court decisions, and oaths (e.g., from the Pledge of Allegiance, "liberty and justice for all")
2. Being able to deal justly and effectively with value conflicts that arise when making decisions about the common good (public policy)
3. Developing a reasoned loyalty to this nation and its form of government. (Note that the Pledge of Allegiance is made not to a person, but to a form of government: a "republic," that is, a constitutional democracy)
4. Developing a feeling of kinship to human beings everywhere—to the human family
5. Taking responsibility for one's actions and fulfilling one's obligations to the community

Skills

The third subgoal—skills—identifies what students should know how to do. Of course, doing involves knowing; skillful behavior is skillful to a great extent because of the knowledge that supports it. A child is skillful at something because he or she *knows* how to do it well. A skill, then, is also called *know-how* or *procedural knowledge*. Skills are often subdivided as follows:

I. Democratic Participation Skills
    A. Listening to and expressing opinions and reasons
    B. Participating in classroom, school, and community decision making, especially, participating in group discussions of public issues (classroom, community, international) with persons with whom one may disagree; leading such discussions; mediating, negotiating, and compromising
    C. Working cooperatively to clarify a task and plan group work
    D. Accessing, using, and creating community resources

II. Study and Inquiry Skills
    A. Using and making time lines, maps, globes, charts, and graphs
    B. Locating, reading, and analyzing information from a variety of resources, such as books, encyclopedias, the Internet, newspapers, and libraries
    C. Writing reports and giving oral presentations
    D. Distinguishing between primary and secondary sources
    E. Forming and testing hypotheses

III. Intellectual Skills (higher-order thinking)
　A. Comparing and contrasting
　B. Making and evaluating conclusions based on evidence
　C. Identifying and clarifying problems and issues
　D. Distinguishing fact from opinion
　E. Inferring cause-effect relationships

CURRICULUM SCOPE AND SEQUENCE

So far we have been considering the goals of social studies teaching and learning. Before jumping further into the curriculum standards, we need also to understand the idea of "scope and sequence." After all, this is what the standards are giving expression to, and understanding this is the key to understanding any given set of standards.

Building a firm foundation in an earlier grade to support learning that should occur in a later grade is the reason curriculum directors and standards authors carefully plan the scope and sequence of a social studies program. The *scope* of the program refers to the subject matter—the knowledge, values and attitudes, and skills—that the program is to include. The *sequence* is the order in which the various subject matters are to be presented.

As for scope, it is not the purpose of the elementary school to teach the social science disciplines apart from their relevance to children's lives or society's problems and needs. Disciplinary knowledge should be taught in ways that will help children gain insight into the social and physical world in which they live. When children are making islands and mountains on the classroom floor or learning to draw maps of the playground, they are dealing with geography in simple ways. When they are asked to explain what they already know about the need for agreed-upon rules in games, and then dramatize the signing of the U.S. Constitution, and are then helped to create a classroom constitution—a rule book they agree to follow—they are having their first brush with history and self-government. Moreover, the teacher is connecting the social studies curriculum to students' lived experience. Likewise, when they compare and contrast the playground bully to the elected classroom president, they are beginning to understand basic ideas from political science (law and legitimate authority). In these ways, the subject matter is connected to what the children already know and do. But the curriculum also broadens their horizons, taking them to distant places and times—to the signing of the Constitution, the life of a scribe in Cleopatra's court, the sisters and their cousins who carry drinking water from the well to their village in the Sahara desert, and village life in one of the first farming communities thousands of years ago. So, the social studies curriculum is connected to the child's life, *and* it enlarges that life outward to include the less familiar, the far away, and the long ago. Of course, role-playing and simulations—playing, pretending, and imagining—help to make all this vivid and concrete. Being asked what really happened and how they know that to be true, again and again, familiarizes them with the "disciplined" ways of knowing that mark the social sciences.

REFLECTION

Many school subjects are comprised of knowledge and skills, but social studies makes room for attitudes and values, too. Thinking about the two goals of social studies presented earlier, why is that?

Dramatizations with simple sets bring geography to life. *(Anthony Magnacca/Merrill)*

As for sequence, ordinarily topics that have a concrete and familiar focus for children are included in the primary grades, topics such as homes and houses, schools and stores, local rivers and lakes, the clothes (what anthropologists call "costume") the children are wearing and the foods they are eating and where these come from and how. Topics that are more remote in space and time, such as the nation, the United Nations, and regions of the world, are focal points in the intermediate and middle grades. *It must be emphasized, however, that this does not mean that first-graders spend a year studying their own families, or that second-graders study only the local neighborhood or third-graders only the local community.* Rather, a compare-and-contrast approach should be used, for it builds intellectual strength and conceptual power. For example, children should learn how local houses and apartments are similar to and different from shelters long ago and far away. The same is true for families, neighborhoods, and communities.

Here is a scope-and-sequence plan published by the National Council for the Social Studies.[6]

Kindergarten—Awareness of Self in a Social Setting
Grade 1—The Individual in Primary Social Groups: Understanding School and Family Life
Grade 2—Meeting Basic Needs in Nearby Social Groups: Neighborhoods
Grade 3—Sharing Earth-Space with Others: Communities
Grade 4—Human Life in Varied Environments: Regions

Grade 5—People of the Americas: The United States and Its Close Neighbors

Grade 6—People and Cultures: The Eastern Hemisphere

Grade 7—A Changing World of Many Nations: A Global View

Grade 8—Building a Strong and Free Nation: The United States

Grade 9—Systems That Make a Democratic Society Work: Law, Justice, and Economics

Grade 10—Origins of Major Cultures: A World History

Grade 11—The Maturing of America: United States History

Grade 12—One-year course or courses required; selection(s) to be made from the following:

> Issues and Problems of Modern Society
>
> Introduction to the Social Sciences
>
> The Arts in Human Societies
>
> International Area Studies
>
> Supervised Experience in Community Affairs

Now, let's draw all this together. Look again at the 10 themes identified in the *Curriculum Standards for Social Studies* (see page 5 and the accompanying *Sampler*). How might such themes be used with a scope-and-sequence plan of this kind? It is important to note that the 10 themes are ideas or, more precisely, concepts. Furthermore, as the *Curriculum Standards for Social Studies* make clear, these themes are recommended as the basis for instruction in each grade, kindergarten through 12th. What we can do is select a grade level from the scope-and-sequence plan here (or one provided by a local school district) and use the 10 themes to help plan conceptually rich units and lessons. For example, let us select the grade 3 emphasis—communities—and think of some focus questions that will engage children with each of the 10 themes.

What does this involve? In the example on the next page we use two resources to create a powerful third-grade social studies curriculum. We took the third-grade topic "Communities" from the NCSS scope-and-sequence recommendation, and then we elaborated the *scope* of that topic by using the 10 conceptual themes from the NCSS curriculum standards.

Take some time now to draft a similar example for another grade level. This will provide experience in thinking conceptually about the social studies topical emphasis of a given grade level. We applied the 10 conceptual themes to the topic of communities, but the same process can be followed for the second-grade emphasis—neighborhoods—or the fourth-grade emphasis—geographic regions—the fifth-grade emphasis—United States history—and so on. You may need the accompanying *Sampler* to bolster your understanding of the 10 themes.

This is one of the most important curriculum-planning habits any teacher can develop. Its gist is to apply the 10 NCSS conceptual themes to the subject matter topics emphasized at a given grade level. *In so doing, the scope of the topic is expanded and deepened so that a student's understanding is also expanded and deepened.* Without this kind of planning, the teacher may be limited to skating across the thin surface of a topic, communicating facts about it perhaps, but not helping students to organize the facts into big ideas that they can then apply to the next topic, and the next, and so on.

GRADE 3   SHARING EARTH-SPACE WITH OTHERS: COMMUNITIES

1. *Culture.* How does life in our community differ from life in our sister cities in Japan and Russia?

2. *Time, Continuity, and Change.* What were the turning points in our community's history?

3. *People, Places, and Environments.* How did our community come to be located where it is, and how would our lives be different if it were located on the edge of the sea, in a desert, or high in the mountains?

4. *Individual Development and Identity.* How does learning in school differ from learning that takes place elsewhere in our community—on the job, on the playing field, at home, at a city council meeting?

5. *Individuals, Groups, and Institutions.* What after-school clubs do young people belong to in our community, and how do they differ from those in our sister cities in Japan and Russia?

6. *Power, Authority, and Governance.* What are the three branches of government in our community and who serves in them?

7. *Production, Distribution, and Consumption.* What things do people in our community want and need? What do we make in our community and what do we have to import? How are these different from the wants and needs in our sister cities in other countries?

8. *Science, Technology, and Society.* How do our values influence the use of buses and cars in this community?

9. *Global Connections and Interdependence.* What three products are imported in the greatest quantities to our community? Are any products exported?

10. *Civic Ideals and Practice.* Who is eligible to vote in this community? Where can they register to vote? What percentage of them voted in the last presidential election? In the last local election? What can our class do to encourage eligible voters to vote?

With this kind of curriculum planning, students not only learn the topic that is currently emphasized, but they learn it in a way that will help them grasp more about subsequent topics in the curriculum *sequence*. What results is a snowball effect that empowers students in each subsequent grade. Researchers call this the Matthew effect, named after the idea expressed in the Christian Bible's Book of Matthew: the rich get richer and the poor get poorer. In modern terms, the rich get richer because they are able to invest their surplus, earning still more, which they can reinvest, and so on. The analogy to education is that the knowledgeable become more knowledgeable. The knowledge they already possess enables them to learn still more. *Children become more knowledgeable because their prior knowledge serves as a fertile seedbed in which subsequent knowledge can take root.*[7] A mind furnished with powerful concepts is fertile ground for the germination of new ideas.

"My" neighborhood, school, and house. Maps reveal the spaces of our lives.
(Silver Burdett Ginn)

Unit Topics by Grade Level

This section provides examples of unit topics taught in grades K–8 in schools across the nation. These examples should not be construed as a model curriculum; they will not be precisely the same as those found in any specific school program. Rather, the intention here is to help readers gain a better idea of what subject matter may actually be taught at different grade levels.

Kindergarten

Kindergarten programs ordinarily deal with topics that help to familiarize children with their immediate surroundings. The home and school provide the setting for these studies. With some kindergarten children it is possible to include, in a simple way, references to the world beyond their immediate environment.

Rules for Safe Living	Our Earth
America the Beautiful	People Change the Land
Working Together at School	Hooray for Holidays

Grade 1

Grade 1 studies are based in the local area, such as the school and neighborhood, but the local area is connected to the larger world. Basic work with history and geography begins.

Units should provide for easy transition from the near at hand to the far away and back again at frequent intervals.

Who We Are and Where We Live	Our Country Now and Long Ago
Families at Work	Explorations Near and Far
Families Around the World	Cities, Islands, Jungles

Grade 2

The grade 2 program provides for frequent and systematic contact with the world beyond the neighborhood. By studying transportation, communication, food distribution, and travel, children begin to learn how their part of the world is connected to other places on Earth.

Comparing Holidays	Food, Clothing, and Shelter (cultural universals)
Exploring Our Past	Transportation and Communication
We the People: Elections	How Neighborhoods Change

Grade 3

The grade 3 program often emphasizes the larger community concept: what a community is, types of communities, how communities provide for basic needs, how they are governed, their history, and their variety around the world. A comparative approach is recommended.

Rural and Urban Communities	Community Workers
Native and Newcomer Communities	Our City's Government
Washington, DC: Our Nation's Capital	Tokyo: Japan's Capital

Grade 4

In grade 4 the geographic regions of the United States are often stressed. Home-state history is also common (often by legislative requirement). A comparative approach is recommended: comparing the home state with other states and the home region with other regions.

History and People of the Home State
Regions of the United States: The West, Southwest, Midwest, Northeast, and South
Deserts and Forests of the World (world regional comparisons)
Rivers of the World (world regional comparisons)
The Three Branches of Democratic Government

Grade 5

Almost all schools include the geography and history of the United States in the grade 5 program. The program may focus on the United States alone or the United States plus Canada and Latin America. The 5th-grade emphasis should be coordinated with the 8th- and 11th-grade programs in order to revisit difficult concepts (e.g., colony, constitutional democracy, slavery, civil war, culture, pluralism, region, justice, civil rights). Commonly, units coincide with historical eras. In some states, students are introduced to all eras in grade 5; in others, coverage extends only through the topics in the left-hand column below. The final unit of the school year may focus on one of the United States' neighbors, Canada or Mexico. In other districts, this unit occurs in grade 6.

The American Land	The Institution of Slavery
The Native Americans	The Civil War
European-Native Encounters	The New Nation's Westward Expansion
The American Colonies	The Industrial Revolution
War for Independence	The World Wars
Creating a New Nation	The Civil Rights Movement

Grades 6 and 7

Sixth-grade programs may include the study of Latin America and Canada, the history and geography of the Eastern Hemisphere, ancient civilizations, or world geographic regions. Each of these patterns is common. A major limitation of grade 6 programs is that they attempt to deal with too many topics, often resulting in a smattering of exposure an inch deep and a mile wide. Not only is this not powerful learning, it's boring! The same criticism applies to the seventh grade. Stronger programs emerge if teachers carefully select a few units representative of basic concepts that have wide applicability. For example, a class need not study each poor nation to gain some understanding of the problems of developing countries. An in-depth study of two would provide both depth and contrast.

The content of the grade 7 program depends on that of grade 6. The Eastern Hemisphere and world regions are popular choices for this grade. World geography is also included in some districts, as are studies of the home state. California schools shift from ancient civilizations in the sixth grade to medieval and early modern times in the seventh. Note below that the term *hemisphere*, not *civilization*, is used. To the extent that these terms still have meaning in a rapidly globalizing world, Europe is a continent located in the Eastern Hemisphere *but* Western civilization, and Asia is a continent located in the Eastern Hemisphere *and* Eastern civilization.

Western Hemisphere Emphasis

Cooperation and Conflict in the Americas	The Prairie Provinces
Three Incan Countries	The Amazon
The Organization of American States	Canada and Mexico

Eastern Hemisphere Emphasis

The Birthplace of Three Religions	The World Wars
Ancient Civilizations	The Holocaust
The Dark Ages and the Renaissance	Collapse of the USSR
Empires and Revolutions	Africa Today

Ancient Civilizations

Early Humans	The Agricultural Revolution
Mesopotamia, Egypt, Kush	India and China
Hebrews, Greeks, and Their Legacy	The Rise and Fall of Rome

World Geography (comparative regional study)

The Five Themes of Geography	Map Projections (Mercator, Peters, Fuller, etc.)
Africa	South America
Asia	Oceana
Europe	North America

Grade 8

The study of the United States is widespread in grade 8. The program usually stresses the development of U.S. political institutions and consists of a series of units arranged chronologically. A biographical approach (lots of details in Chapter 13) effectively integrates social studies and language arts.

Natives and Colonizers: Cultures and Conquest	Creating a Democracy
The Institution of Slavery	A Divided Nation
Birth of an Industrial Giant	Immigration
The United States and the World	Globalization

CURRICULUM STANDARDS: NATIONAL, STATE, AND LOCAL

To locate your state social studies standards, go to MyEducationLab and search under "Resources."

You have probably noticed in this class and others that there is much talk about curriculum standards. This is because there has been over the past two decades a concerted effort to "raise standards" in American education. As a consequence, curriculum standards have been written by national, state, and local educational authorities, and testing has increased dramatically—the latter to find out if the new standards are being met. Caution is needed: The flurry of activity around standards and testing has become like a blizzard on the high Colorado plains of my childhood. It's difficult to see clearly in any direction. Here, in brief, is the story.

Curriculum standards are statements that describe what students need to learn. They try to answer one of the most controversial questions of all time for all peoples: What kind of people do we want our children to become? What should they know and be able to do? Not surprisingly, people disagree over the answer to this question, for the answer depends on what they value and how they are positioned relative to other people. Do they value historical knowledge or only practical know-how? *Whose* history and *which* know-how?[8]

A number of national curriculum standards committees in a variety of subject areas were convened across the nation in the 1990s. For the subject of social studies, there are five sets of national standards. These are *voluntary* standards; no state or school district is required to implement them, yet most have drawn on them to some degree as they prepare state and district curriculum frameworks. But why might they be important to you? *They are a rich source of ideas for planning your social studies lessons and units.* Sometimes you will see an objective that you will want to copy directly into your plan. (Feel free to do this; they are written to be used. But remember to credit your source.) At other times you will get good ideas for student learning activities. The *Sampler* that accompanies this textbook has numerous real-life examples of such activities.

These voluntary national standards are most likely found in the curriculum library of school district offices or in your college or university library. Or you can find them on the Internet. At the top of the list that follows is the best single set of standards for elementary and middle school teachers of social studies because it draws on and integrates the other four, which were developed for the separate disciplines of history, geography, civics/government, and economics.

Social Studies (Integrated)

Curriculum Standards for Social Studies. Developed by the National Council for the Social Studies (www.socialstudies.org/standards). Your textbook came with a *Sampler* of these standards. Please take time now to familiarize yourself with this booklet and read several of the learning activities.

History

National Standards for History. Developed by the National Center for History in the Schools, University of California, Los Angeles (www.nchs.ucla.edu/standards). See especially the history standards for grades K–4 and the standards for grades 5–12. There is also a "basic" revised version, but it contains less useful information for classroom teachers.

Geography

Geography for Life: National Geography Standards (www.ncge.net/geography/standards). Developed by the National Council for Geographic Education, Washington, DC.

Civics/Government

National Standards for Civics and Government (www.civiced.org). Developed by the Center for Civic Education, Calabasas, CA.

Economics

Voluntary National Standards in Economics (www.ncee.net). Developed by the National Council on Economic Education, New York.

The chapters that follow, especially Chapters 3 through 5, highlight each of these sets of standards. And don't forget: A *Sampler* of the first set, the integrated social studies standards developed by the National Council for the Social Studies, accompanies this text.

In addition to these *national* standards, each of the 50 *states* and most of the school *districts* within them have curriculum standards of their own. "How," you might ask, "have state and district curriculum standards been influenced by the various sets of *national* curriculum standards?" (This would be a good question to ask at an interview for a teaching position.) Anything is possible. There may have been no influence at all, or the state or district may have adopted a set of national standards verbatim. Something in between is more likely. Most states view the national standards documents as resources, with teachers and curriculum directors pondering them but not adopting them wholesale. According to most reports, few states feel obliged to use them. (The U.S. Constitution makes education a state-by-state project, not a national one.) As one Texas official put it, "If there is a conflict between the Texas standards and the national standards, this is Texas. And, by God, we would choose Texas standards."[9]

Most important, find the social studies standards for your state and local school district, and read them. To help make sense of what you read, please keep in mind the preceding discussion in this chapter about curriculum *goals* and *scope and sequence*.

TRENDS

A social trend is a social force. Like any force, a social force has power—the power to carry people, their thinking, beliefs, and identities, in one direction or another. The dictionary defines a trend as a prevailing direction or current. Trends are sometimes hard to see but they are also hard to ignore. When you step into a river's current, you are moved by it, and moved not just anywhere but in the particular direction the river is flowing. Trends shape our values and beliefs, our costume and diet, our courtship rituals and consumer habits, and a thousand other things. They shape our treatment of one another and our attitudes toward ourselves. Trends even shape our bodies, for physical beauty, too, is a cultural invention that changes from place to place and time to time.

Unique trends are influencing teachers who are beginning their careers today. Had you applied for a teaching position in the late 1950s, the successful launching of the Soviet satellite *Sputnik* would have loomed over your interview with the personnel director. You may have been carried away by the strong current of "beating the Soviet Union to the moon." You may have replaced your classroom supply of fingerpaints with beakers and microscopes as so many teachers did. Had you applied to teach in 1970, the war in Vietnam and antiwar protests might have shaped the interview. You may have been asked to take a loyalty oath—a statement swearing your loyalty to the United States and its laws. You may have sewn a peace symbol on your tie-dyed shirt.

Today the currents are different. Teachers are being asked to take the vision of the public school more seriously than ever before, offering high-quality education to each child, welcoming children of all cultures, and closing the achievement gap between White students and students of color (trend 1 below). Teachers also are being held accountable more than before, especially for teaching reading and mathematics, with "high-stakes" tests. This is affecting the teaching and learning of social studies, sometimes crowding it to the outskirts of the curriculum (trend 2). Meanwhile, it is a post-9/11 world and globalization surrounds us—at once exciting, disorienting, and dangerous. Accordingly, global education (trend 3) is taking on new importance and new definition. At the same time, education for democratic citizenship has taken on new meaning and urgency (trend 4). Democracies are fragile, after all; on this the historical record is clear. Typically they are short-lived and replaced by some kind of tyranny, either religious or secular. Teachers are expected to be democracy educators—educators of "we the people." As well, they are expected to be computer educators, capable both of using technology as an instructional resource and of teaching children to use it wisely (trend 5). Moving comfortably among the school subjects, knowing when and when not to integrate them, is another expectation (trend 6); especially, knowing how to integrate reading and writing instruction with social studies instruction. Finally, teachers are increasingly paying attention to the communication system of the classroom—to discourse (trend 7). These trends are introduced here and revisited throughout the book. During an interview for a teaching position, you most likely will be asked about one or more of them.

Trend 1: Closing the Achievement Gap

The public school movement of the mid-1800s was geared to getting children into schools at public expense (private schools for the wealthy were already well established). That public-school movement was quite successful. But once access to schools was extended to all our children, access to good *curriculum and instruction* within them depended largely on the social class, race, and gender of the child. To varying degrees, it still does.

The U.S. Supreme Court ruled in 1954 that the segregated school system was failing to provide equal education for all children, and communities were forced to racially integrate their schools. Yet, the curriculum standards to which African American children were held and the instructional support they received inside the newly integrated schools sometimes were, and still are, lower than those for White children. Today, schools are *re*-segregating, which is making matters worse by separating the urban poor—mainly Black and Latino families—from the suburban middle class—mainly White families. As a result, there are what Jonathan Kozol famously named "savage inequalities" between schools within the same metropolitan area.[10]

As we will see in Chapter 2, social-class status complicates the picture. Poor children are often held to lower standards, and students of color (especially Native American, African American, and Latino students) are disproportionately from poor families. Moreover, middle-class children of whatever race or ethnic group do not have access to the same curriculum and instruction that generally are available to children from wealthy families who attend exclusive private schools. As a result, an achievement gap persists between White and non-White students and between students of low-income parents and other students of whatever race or ethnic group.

Today's teachers are expected to work diligently to educate the diverse children of today's classrooms and to create more successful ways of doing so than have been developed thus far. Access to (i.e., inclusion in) high-quality curriculum and instruction is the goal. To this end, today's teachers are expected to know the content and skills they are teaching—from world geography to reading-comprehension skills—as well as instructional methods that will help children learn these things. They are also expected to acknowledge and root out their own prejudices and stereotypes—which all of us have—and thereby to recognize the intelligence and strengths in each child. They are expected to set challenging expectations and provide a strong and supportive instructional environment for all students. As we shall see in the next chapter, this means not only that teachers must examine their own attitudes about racial, gender, and cultural differences, but also that they must learn about the home cultures of their students, which in some cases may be markedly different from their own and the culture of the school.

Trend 2: Testing, Accountability, and Curriculum Narrowing

By 2001, there was a high-stakes testing frenzy in the schools. Today, many parents and educators believe it has gotten out of hand. America's public schools currently administer more than 100 million standardized exams each year, and it is expected that most states will more than double the number of tests they give now. Any teacher will tell you that the pressure is on to raise children's scores on these tests.

As we will see in Chapter 7, there are three main purposes of testing: (1) to improve teaching and learning; (2) to sort and place students in special programs; and (3) to hold schools accountable to parents and the public. Trend 2 is all about the third purpose of assessment. But why? Why this pressure for accountability?

The pressure comes from many sources. The effort to close the achievement gap is one. An African American school principal said to me, "If it wasn't for this testing, I wouldn't be able to get my teachers to teach the kids of color with the same high expectations they have for the White kids." Pressure also comes from a new law. In 2002, then President George W. Bush signed the No Child Left Behind Act (NCLB), the guiding principle of which is *accountability for results:* "All states must implement statewide accountability systems that will set academic standards in every subject and identify strengths and weaknesses in the educational system." Simply put, the 50 states must now do three things. First, they must set curriculum standards for what a student should know and learn in every grade in three curricular areas: reading, math, and science. Second, states must test every student's progress toward those standards by using tests that are aligned with them. Third, schools and school districts must publicly report their performance on these tests. And here is the pressure point of the act: "If the district or school continually fails to make adequate progress toward the standards, then they will be held accountable."

As a consequence, testing time has increased dramatically. Just a few years ago, yearly testing in elementary schools may have taken only one week. According to a third-grade teacher in California, yearly testing has lengthened to three weeks. "Although learning did take place during this time through the review of subject matter," she reports, "the school felt like it was in 'suspended animation' until all tests were completed. And, teachers were encouraged to give test reviews when students were not actually taking tests."[11]

It is not only the administration of such tests that concerns teachers—the time and energy they spend on them—it is how the results will be used to influence *what* is taught to children and *how*. Evidence shows that teachers reallocate instructional time so as to teach to the test, and their principals often demand it. The result is called *curriculum narrowing*, which is the intense focus on reading and math to the exclusion of social studies, science, art, and music (other terms are "marginalization" or "sidelining"). And you can be sure it doesn't happen equitably. Poor children in urban schools are subjected to more curriculum narrowing than well-off children in suburban schools.[12]

Some teachers are joining with parents and community leaders to take action against the testing frenzy. "It is destroying the curriculum," they protest. "Only what is tested is taught, and what's tested is reading and math." Twenty-seven busloads of parents from New York City caravanned to the state capital in Albany to protest "an overreliance on state tests to gauge student achievement." They were concerned that the testing frenzy would "undermine innovative instruction and zap students' intrinsic motivation to learn."[13] Other parents have protested by keeping their children home during testing or enrolling them in private schools.

Trend 3: Global Education

Globalization is not new (Columbus and Marco Polo were key players in globalization), but it is intensifying. It has many dimensions, all interesting, some bad, some good. One kind of globalization is widening the rich-poor gap around the world in the name of new markets, "free trade," and cheap labor. A new report warns that "workers in virtually every sector must now face competitors who live just a mouse-click away in Ireland, Finland, China, India, and dozens of other nations whose economies are growing."[14] Another kind of globalization—humanistic rather than economic—is spreading human rights. Pressure is being put on oppressive governments for liberal reforms such as freedom of speech and religion and gender and racial equality. Airplane travel, email, Internet-based video games, and cell-phone technology are fueling a communications revolution that is, in turn, fueling just about everything else.

How are educators responding? One way is by strengthening math and science education, for these are viewed as central to American competitiveness in the global economy. Another is by strengthening world language instruction in the elementary grades. In an increasing number of schools, *all* children (not only the children of immigrants whose mother tongue is something other than English) are studying a second language beginning in kindergarten. In other words, students whose mother tongue is English are increasingly expected to learn a second language, and schools are being transformed for language immersion. At Stanford International Elementary School in Seattle (pictured in Chapter 3's photo collection), for example, instruction is provided in English, Japanese, and Spanish starting in kindergarten. At another elementary school, the languages may be English, Mandarin, and Arabic. At another, English, Tamil, and French. This trend is taking the monolingual, English-only-speaking portion of the U.S. population in a very different direction from where it has been; it is taking this group toward, like much of the world, multilingualism.

Leaving aside the world languages curriculum, instruction about the world and its peoples has long been a central feature in the social studies curriculum. World geography (societies near and far) and world history (humanity now and then) have always been at the core of the social studies curriculum. As we saw in the unit topics earlier, grade 1 often features "Families Around the World," grade 2 has "Transportation and Communication," and grade 3 features communities around the world. Grade 4 has "Deserts and Forests of the World." Grades 6 and 7 are aimed squarely at learning about the world and its peoples. The trend now is to look again at these core aspects of the social studies curriculum and strengthen them. This means making sure that, to take one example, in grade 3 students don't study only their own community but instead compare and contrast it to three or four communities around the world.

Trend 4: Democracy Education

The democratic ideal celebrates government "of, by, and for the people," as President Lincoln said in his speech at Gettysburg, and it does not tolerate repression or discrimination. Political scientists call this *liberal democracy*. If democracies are political systems in which the people govern, usually by electing representatives who govern, then liberal democracies (as opposed to illiberal ones) add to elections something else: individual liberties and rights—such as the rights specified in the Bill of Rights of the U.S. Constitution or the United Nations' Universal Declaration of Human Rights. The idea is that people can practice any religion they choose, or none, and they have the freedoms of speech, press, association, and protest. "I disapprove of what you say," goes the saying attributed to Voltaire, "but I will defend to the death your right to say it." This is a core principle of liberal democracy.

Students gather data at online history collections. *(Masterfile Royalty Free Division)*

Accordingly, democracy is much more than a political system; it is a way of life—a way of being with one another, and not just friends and family but *strangers*, whether in the city hall, a faculty meeting, or the classroom. It is certainly not a perfect path; in fact, it is frustrating, contentious, and exasperating. The only thing worse than democracy, the saying goes, is all the alternatives.

That democracies fall short of these aspirations is a plain fact, and it is the chief motive behind social movements that struggle to close the gap between the actual and the ideal. Thus, Dr. Martin Luther King, Jr., demanded in his 1963 March on Washington address not an alternative to democracy, but its *fulfillment.* Standing on the steps of the Lincoln Memorial in Washington, DC, he said:

> (W)e have come to our nation's capital to cash a check. When the architects of our republic wrote the magnificent words of the Constitution and the Declaration of Independence, they were signing a promissory note to which every American was to fall heir. . . . We have come to cash this check, a check that will give us upon demand the riches of freedom and the security of justice.[15]

If democracy is to be the vision that holds our diverse society together, then the people must be educated for it. The simple truth is that there can be no democracy without democratic citizens. This is because the people themselves, as Lincoln and King said, create and sustain democratic governments. Furthermore, these citizens don't fall from trees. People aren't born already grasping basic principles of democracy, such as liberty, equality, justice, and the separation of church and state. They aren't born knowing why so many democracies fail and so few last. They aren't born able and willing to talk with strangers about the common good. These things are not, as history makes very clear, born into our genes. Rather, they are social, moral, and intellectual achievements—the products of a planned curriculum.

Teachers, therefore, need to see themselves as democracy educators, and this education, as we shall see in Chapter 3, should begin in kindergarten. These five-year-olds are experiencing their first sustained emergence from the private worlds of home and family into the public world of citizens. Research has been clear that if we expect democratic behavior from adults—tolerance of diverse religions, for example, and knowing how to participate in government—then we must begin their democratic education in the primary grades and build from there.

Trend 5: Information and Communication Technology

New information is being produced more rapidly than ever before; that is, the *rate* at which it is being generated has increased. There is more of it, and its availability has flourished. An information superhighway—the World Wide Web (WWW)—runs through the middle of most schools and the homes of many students. People under 25 swim in a new ocean of information and communication technology (ICT) whether they know it or not (as the saying goes, the last thing the fish sees is the water it is swimming in). People over 25 struggle to keep up and learn from their kids. Video games and a rush of digital music products are teaching new ways of thinking and knowing to the students in your classroom.

New teachers are expected to be somewhat tech-savy themselves, familiar with their students' ICT habits and able to serve as trustworthy Internet guides. Additionally, new teachers reasonably can be expected to

- Access the online history collections at great libraries and museums, such as the Library of Congress and the Smithsonian Institution, as well as state and local collections
- Evaluate curriculum software, video games, and Internet sites, and help students use them wisely
- Use and troubleshoot desktop computers, laptop and handheld computers, LCD projectors, portable scanners, and digital cameras
- Keep attendance and achievement records on spreadsheets
- Scan and photograph student work samples and maintain an electronic classroom portfolio
- Maintain a classroom website where students' projects can be collected and presented, and that parents and students can access from home
- Use digital-image, email, and word-processing programs to send newsletters home
- Make visually rich classroom presentations using digital technology, and teach students to do likewise
- Access the online resources at organizations such as the United Nations, local and international newspapers, and foundations (e.g., George Lucas's Edutopia)

There is much debate about the causes, consequences, and utility of the technology trend in schools. A tremendous amount of "hype" (exaggerated claims) clouds the picture. Millions of dollars are spent on computer labs, simulations, laptop and handheld computers, Smart Boards, video cameras, and LCD projectors that teachers and students can use for electronic presentations. Millions more are spent on technical support and software for word-processing, presentation, email, and Internet facilities. Is this a wise expenditure? Would other curriculum resources be more helpful? Some say that technology is *the* solution to failing schools and an old-fashioned education system; others argue that corporate-sponsored technology is only making matters worse and costing taxpayers more. Some say that less testing, less computer time, and more teaching is the answer. "But look at all that information that is brought right to students' fingertips!" others respond.

Computer resources are featured throughout this book. Chapter 10 describes several that are particularly helpful to new teachers. My favorites are taking students, via the Internet, on virtual field trips—to the Seven Wonders of the Ancient World and to geographically mind-bending extremes such as the capes of Good Hope and Horn at the southern tips of Africa and South America, the North Pole, the Amazon, and the tops of the world's highest mountains. However, on the "low-tech" side of the coin, see lesson plan 6 in Chapter 5 called "Dance of the Solar System." It is a simulation for primary grades that uses a floor lamp for the sun, a globe for Earth, and balloons for the other eight . . . er, make that seven, planets.

Trend 6: Integrated Curriculum

The high-stakes testing and accountability trend is now fueling a new integrated curriculum trend. Curriculum integration, also known as interdisciplinary education, comes and goes as a pressing concern of American educators and the public. It was trendy in the 1930s, faded out of the picture until the 1950s, and then faded out again until the late 1980s.[16] Each time it fades, the academic disciplines return to the forefront of the school curriculum with renewed vigor, along with the suspicion that attempts to integrate the school subjects, in spite of good intentions, lower standards and produce mediocre results. There are signs today that the pendulum is swinging again. The latest flurry of interest in integrated education is moderating somewhat, and disciplinary thinking is once again being advanced as the best way to introduce children to the great questions, knowledge, and know-how of humankind. Howard Gardner, the renowned psychologist whose popular theory of multiple intelligences (presented in the next chapter) has revolutionized the way educators think about children's ability and potential, has titled a recent book *The Disciplined Mind*. He argues that the disciplines are indispensable in any good educational endeavor because they represent the highest achievements of talented human beings, toiling in concert across generations, always critiquing one another's work, and striving toward explanations of enduring importance. True, the best work of these talented individuals is interdisciplinary, but they are capable of this only because of their deep knowledge within the separate disciplines. Genuinely interdisciplinary education "is simply not feasible for most youngsters," Gardner concludes, because youngsters do not (and developmentally cannot) have the necessary foundation in the disciplines that would make such interdisciplinary work possible.[17]

Gardner does, however, favor what he calls "commonsense" integration in the elementary grades. The key to using curriculum integration in the classroom to increase the quality of education is to remember that *integration is a strategy, not a goal*. It must be aimed not at itself (i.e., integrated education for its own sake), but rather at particular understandings and skills that we want children to build.

Because reading and writing achievement are subjected to high-stakes testing, the newest "commonsense" trend is to teach social studies through the language arts curriculum. At Rosyth Elementary School in Singapore, for example, teachers like to say "Language Arts for skills, Social Studies for content." Accordingly, students at Rosyth read and write to build and express what they are learning in social studies; put differently, their language arts learning enables their social studies learning, and their social studies learning gives content and substance to their language arts learning. Rosyth students are pictured in Chapters 3 and 10.

Readers can evaluate how successful I have been in this text at providing models of commonsense integration. Each of the 23 lesson plans spread throughout this text contains integration suggestions; the literacy–social studies connection is treated explicitly in Chapter 12; and two models of integration—writing biographies and forming generalizations—are presented in detail in Chapter 13.

Trend 7: Classroom Discourse

I conclude this section with a trend that is having a sweeping impact on integrated reading, writing, and social studies teaching and learning. More and more teachers and researchers are paying attention to the communication system of classrooms. For example, a common communication pattern in classrooms—a common "discourse"—is called IRE. First, the teacher asks a question; that is, the teacher Initiates an exchange with students. Some number of students raise their hands, and the teacher calls on one of them for a Response to the question. Next, the teacher Evaluates this response, and then Initiates another exchange.[18] This discourse, also called *recitation*, has advantages and disadvantages: the teacher controls the speech traffic in the classroom; only a few students participate; the teacher can provide specific one-on-one feedback as to the correctness of a few students' responses; students address the teacher rather than one another.

Are there alternatives? Indeed there are. Discussion is the main alternative to IRE. In discussions, the teacher initiates just one main question and then lets the students respond and exchange views for the duration of the discussion, often without initiating another main question. Students address one another rather than the teacher, and the teacher doesn't evaluate each student's statement. Students learn to jump in during pauses in response to what another student has said and to suggest additional ideas. This classroom discourse is more like a conversation than an oral quiz. Two forms of discussion highlighted in this book are decision-making discussions called "deliberation" (Chapter 3) and literature-focused Socratic seminars (Chapter 12).

Conclusion

Why is there a social studies curriculum in the schools? Because without it there can be no wisdom, no cultural or environmental intelligence, no democratic citizens, and, therefore, no democracy. The goals of the social studies curriculum are social understanding and civic efficacy. Social understanding is knowledge of human beings' social worlds drawn from the social sciences and the humanities along with students' lives and society's needs. Civic efficacy is the readiness and willingness to assume citizenship responsibilities. The purpose of this introductory chapter was to examine these goals and various scope-and-sequence plans for achieving them. It showed how to use the 10 themes from the NCSS curriculum standards to elaborate the scope of the social studies curriculum emphasis for any grade. The chapter ended with trends that will shape at least the beginning years of your teaching career.

Of course, teachers don't only teach curriculum; they teach children. The children themselves are the concern of the next chapter. Although a science textbook might take a biological approach to such a chapter, it is appropriate that a social studies textbook take a demographic approach, as readers shall see.

Discussion Questions and Suggested Activities

Go to MyEducationLab and select the topic "NCSS Standards," then read the article "The Values Manifesto Project" and complete the activity.

1. Look back at the *Reflection* sidebar near the opening Goals section of the chapter and at your response to the questions asked there. Then, with a partner reread the definition and the two goals of social studies education given earlier and the explanation that follows. Work together to clarify the distinction between *social understanding* and *civic efficacy,* and discuss the ways knowledge, values and attitudes, and skills are each involved.

2. What are your "sister cities" in the world? Called "town twinning" in Europe, the idea is to pair geographically distinct communities for the purpose of global understanding and fostering cultural links, student exchanges, pen pals, and the like. They are useful resources in elementary social studies units because they provide meaningful comparisons to the local community. The relationship affords opportunities for class-to-class writing and video conferencing, collaborative projects, and exchanges. Visit *Sister Cities International*'s website to find out how to request a sister city or to learn which cities are already paired with yours. If necessary, email a city council representative and ask. Then sketch with a partner a unit in which children at a particular grade level compare their own town with two or three "sisters." What should they compare? (food, clothing, and shelter? longitude and latitude? sports, games, and household pets?) Remember to consult the scope-and-sequence section of this chapter.

3. Go online to locate a copy of the social studies curriculum framework for the state in which you reside or to which you plan to move. How is it organized? Is the goal statement divided into knowledge, attitudes and values, and skills, as presented in this chapter? Is the curriculum scope and sequence similar to what was presented in this chapter? If not, how do they differ?

4. NCSS Standards. Examine the fourth-grade classroom vignette for standard #10 on page 25 of the standards *Sampler* that accompanies this book. How well does it express the spirit of the "civic efficacy" goal you read about in this chapter?

Selected References

Banks, James A. (2008). *An introduction to multicultural education* (4th ed.). Boston: Allyn & Bacon.

Bennett, Linda, & Berson, Michael J. (Eds.). (2007). *Digital age: Technology-based K–12 lesson plans for social studies.* Silver Spring, MD: National Council for the Social Studies.

Brophy, Jere, & Alleman, Janet. (2006). A reconceptualized rationale for elementary social studies. *Theory and Research in Social Education, 34*(4), 428–454.

Evans, Ronald W. (2006). The social studies wars: Now and then. *Social Education, 70*(5), 317–321.

Levstik, Linda, & Tyson, Cynthia A. (Eds.). (2008). *Handbook of research on social studies education*. Mahwah, NJ: Lawrence Erlbaum.

McGuire, Margit E. (2007). What happened to social studies? The disappearing curriculum. *Phi Delta Kappan, 88*(8), 620–624.

Merryfield, Merry, & Wilson, Angene. (2005). *Social studies and the world: Teaching global perspectives*. Silver Spring, MD: National Council for the Social Studies.

Parker, Walter C. (2003). *Teaching democracy: Unity and diversity in public life*. New York: Teachers College Press.

MyEducationLab is a collection of online tools for your success in this course, your licensure exams, and your teaching career. Go to www.myeducationlab.com to utilize these extensive resources including videos from real classrooms, Praxis and licensure preparation, a lesson plan builder, and materials to help you begin your teaching career.

Knowing the Children We Teach

CHAPTER TWO

Chapter Outline

- Guidelines and Teaching Examples
- Understanding Changing Demographics
- Conclusion

Key Concepts

- Diversity
- Demography
- Cultural deficit model
- Cultural difference model
- Individualized instruction
- Culturally responsive instruction
- Race
- Social class
- Ethnicity
- Culture
- Gender
- Sexual orientation
- Language and dialect
- Gifts and challenges
- Multiple intelligences

MAIN IDEA

Good teachers have always tailored social studies instruction to individual children. Today, however, the diversity within a single classroom is of a different kind, number, and range than in the past. The *demographics* of the classroom have changed. Today's teachers need to understand the changes and teach in ways that ensure a caring environment for all and an equal opportunity to learn.

PICTURE THIS

Each spring, the students in Ginny Simpson's fourth-grade class conduct the "Citizenship Simulation." They simulate the ceremony at which people who have immigrated to the United States become citizens of this country. One child, playing the mayor, gives a welcome speech. Another, playing a federal judge, asks everyone a few questions from the citizenship test: "What is the Constitution?" "Who is eligible to vote?" "What colors are in the U.S. flag?" Then the citizens-to-be take the Oath of Allegiance, followed by the Pledge of Allegiance. Afterward, there is a party with congratulatory speeches and songs.

Thinking back on the new class of children she greeted today, the first day of school, Ginny Simpson could hardly believe the diversity. There were boys and girls, of course, and tall and short, outgoing and shy. They were born in Mexico, Russia, Ethiopia, Korea, and the United States. Four languages other than English, and even more dialects, were spoken at home. There were Blacks, Whites, Asians, and Hispanics. There were Muslims, Christians, Jews, and Buddhists. How did she know these things? She observed and she asked some questions, beginning with "Let's find out who we are and where we are from, what we like to do at recess, and how we spend our time on the weekends." One little boy had a physical disability, and two children had been classified as intellectually gifted.

The children in today's classrooms are similar in many ways, too. They like to play and pretend, and they will sit transfixed for a good story. Cartoons enchant them, and they are hurt when teased or excluded from other children's play. They keenly observe the subtlest physical details in other children: their breath, skin tone, sweaty palms, the works. They scribble before printing and print phrases before paragraphs, and they will not master the five-paragraph essay or the written report for many years—maybe never. Anyone who has spent time with young children knows they often talk to themselves while at play, and as they grow a little older this speech shifts to the "inside." Their physical, personal, social, and cognitive development progresses in fairly orderly ways.

As recently as two generations ago, Ms. Simpson would have faced a classroom in which the children were remarkably similar in appearance, too. Children were required to attend their neighborhood school, and because neighborhoods were not racially integrated, neither were schools. Children with learning disabilities, physical challenges, and mental challenges often were not a part of the regular classroom.

All of this has changed in recent years for six key reasons: federally mandated racial desegregation of schools, immigration, changing birth rates, increased mobility, increased integration of housing within (but generally not between) social classes, and inclusion of students with disabilities. Together these reflect the changing demographic pattern in the nation's schools, which can be summarized as *rapidly increasing diversity.* Examine the bar graph in Figure 2–1 and you'll discover that immigrants are decreasing from Europe and increasingly from Latin America and Asia.

Partially because of immigration, but also for the other reasons just given, the ratio of White to non-White *students* is rapidly changing. Students who are White decreased from 78% of students in the United States in 1972 to 58% of students in 2005. Students who are considered to be part of a racial or ethnic minority group increased from 22% in 1972 to 42% in 2005. Looking ahead, demographers estimate that by 2026 the White student population will be down to 30%. In the 100 largest school districts in the United States, this is roughly the proportion today.[1] Remember that these figures apply to children and youth, not adults or the population as a whole. Teachers, meanwhile, are mostly White and female (75% and 83%, respectively).

New teachers need to be aware of and plan for this diversity. Three reasons stand out. First, teachers need to teach social studies subject matter to every one of their students. Without understanding the changing demographics of the classroom, without knowing their students, teachers can fall into the habit of teaching well only those students who are culturally similar to themselves. Quoting a native Alaskan teacher: "If there's someone who doesn't understand what I'm teaching, I try to understand who they are." Notice that she does not change her curriculum; rather, she works to increase her knowledge of the child. Similarly, an African American teacher remembered: "My instructors knew what you knew because they talked to you. . . . Teaching is all about telling a story. You have to get to know

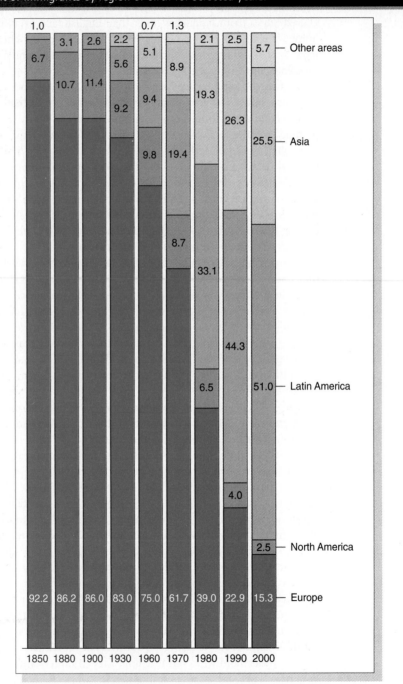

FIGURE 2–1 Changing demographics: Immigration now, and since 1850. Percent of immigrants by region of birth for selected years.

Source: U.S. Census, 2000 (www.census.gov).

kids so you'll know how to tell the story."[2] In other words, teachers need to learn about the cultural characteristics of their students and adapt instruction accordingly. This is called "culturally responsive instruction," as we'll see below.

Second, demography and diversity are key social studies concepts that teachers need to understand in order to teach well. *Demography*, a subfield of geography, is the study of human populations, especially their size, growth, migrations, living conditions, and birth and death rates. *Diversity* is variability—differences—within populations, especially with reference to ethnicity, race, culture, language, religion, gender, sexual orientation, and social class.

Third, schoolteachers are expected to be stewards of democracy. Democracy requires the peaceful and respectful living together of groups and individuals who are different from one another. In a highly diverse nation like the United States, these differences exist in all their glory and difficulty right there in the classroom. Teachers must demonstrate that they *recognize* the differences and *respect* them. In so doing, they are showing students how to behave in public places as democratic citizens.

In one sense, the challenge posed by changing demographics and increasing diversity is not new. Good teachers have always tailored instruction to individual children, not ignoring differences, but recognizing them and helping all children learn the curriculum. But, make no mistake about it, the diversity in the classroom today is of a different kind and magnitude.

GUIDELINES AND TEACHING EXAMPLES

Because children are different, they cannot possibly benefit equally from identical educational experiences. If everyone is treated the same, we simply institutionalize and perpetuate inequality. How? A school typically has a culture—a way of doing things, of speaking and thinking, and of relating to others. This school culture may or may not match the children's home cultures. For some children the cultural match between home and school will be a good one: the language matches, the dialect matches, and the customs and beliefs match those already practiced at home. The school doesn't seem a strange or foreign place—new, perhaps, but basically a continuation of the same ways of thinking, valuing, and behaving. The match gives these children a head start, enabling them both to learn more and to learn more quickly. The effect is similar to having a red carpet rolled out to welcome them; they are "advantaged" by the match of home and school culture. Children for whom the home-school match is not so good are similarly "disadvantaged." The teacher's style and instructional strategies are not as comprehensible to them, nor are the curriculum materials or guest speakers. The classroom customs may be foreign and sometimes unfathomable. Identical instruction for unidentical children, then, is not the best course. Gloria Ladson-Billings puts it this way in her book *The Dreamkeepers*, which details the work of successful teachers of African American children: "Different children have different needs and addressing those different needs is the best way to deal with them equitably."[3]

Two Extremes and a Middle Way

Well-intentioned teachers have disagreed on how to teach children from diverse backgrounds. At one extreme is the belief that it is best to ignore differences among children. "I don't see color, I just see children," we have often heard. Or, "I don't care if they're red, green, or polka dot, I just treat them all like children."[4] Teachers who think this way may well understand that children are, after all, children, and alike in so many ways. But these teachers often are members of the majority culture, and they may be uncomfortable talking about cultural differences or race and may have little or no knowledge of the concepts of demography, diversity, ethnicity, culture, and second-language acquisition. On the other side are teachers who are so knowledgeable about and sensitive to individual and cultural differences that they are nearly paralyzed in their role as teacher. They shy away from teaching core subject matter to the whole class, partly due to anxiety about selecting the content and skills that all children should learn and partly due to anxiety about selecting appropriate instructional strategies. "Who am I to choose?" we have heard such teachers say. "I just let the children choose. That seems the safest route."[5]

A middle way is needed. Good teachers walk a sensible path between ignoring diversity and being immobilized by it. They see both similarities and differences among the children in their classroom, and they hold high learning standards for all of them—boys and girls, native born and immigrant, rich and poor, working class and middle class, gifted and challenged, Asian American, African American, Latino, and White.

Different or Deprived?

This middle way is individualized instruction. Individualized instruction means that children are given personally meaningful learning experiences that will help them to achieve curriculum goals. Traditionally, this has meant that learning experiences should be tailored to each child's capabilities. This definition emerged in an era when educators were concerned mainly with ability, development, and intelligence differences among White, European American, Christian children of the majority language and culture. The contemporary definition of individualized instruction encompasses not only children's *capabilities* but also the array of *cultural* differences they bring to class because of their diverse group memberships—ethnic, racial, class, gender, religious, and linguistic—and the different social statuses that are attached to these differences.

Accompanying this definitional change is a shift in how educators view cultural differences. There are two distinct views. One is the *deprivation* (or cultural deficit) model; the other is the *differences* (or pluralistic) model. According to the cultural deprivation view, children who are culturally different are thought to be deprived—worse off because of their home cultures. Their nonmainstream languages, values, behaviors, and beliefs are viewed as less developed, less important, and less attractive when compared to the cultural attributes of the majority mainstream culture. Teachers holding this view might make comments, such as "If only we did not have to send the children home at night" and "What can we expect of kids with parents like that?" This is not a helpful attitude because, as Christine Bennett observes, "it focuses on where our students aren't and blinds us to where our students are."[6]

The cultural differences model, in contrast, assumes that schools need to teach children of all groups. This is the American dream that has attracted people to the United States from all over the world. It means that people of all cultures and creeds are free to be themselves while getting the best education possible. *Rather than arguing that culturally diverse children are unready for school, the cultural differences model argues that schools too often are unready for children.* It is the schools' responsibility to teach, and teach effectively, all children. Teachers need to view cultural differences as strengths—as resources, or what Luis Moll famously has called "funds of knowledge"[7]—and always be on the lookout for ways to incorporate and build on those strengths. One way to begin learning about the demographic characteristics of the classroom with your students is to conduct a class census (see Lesson Plan 1).

WHO ARE WE? TAKING A CLASS CENSUS

Grades	3–7
Time	One class period
NCSS Standards	1 (culture) and 4 (individual identity and development)
Objectives	Students will learn about one another and develop an initial understanding of a basic social studies concept: *demography* (demographic information about people; characteristics of populations).
Interest Building	Ask the students, "How many of us are in our classroom population?" Then, "How are we alike? Different?"
Lesson Development	

1. *Assessment.* Ask students what they know about the meaning of the word *population.*

2. *Build Background Knowledge.* Provide information about the U.S. Census as needed. (A census is required by the U.S. Constitution. It is taken every 10 years to provide information that helps us know who "we"—the people of the United States—are.) Take students to the U.S. Census Bureau's website at www.census.gov. There, students will see the U.S. population updated every five minutes, and they can click on their state and get a state census profile. They will find all sorts of demographic data at this site: the state population, predictions for population growth or decline in the future, the percentages of young and older people in the state, birth and death rates, and the number of doctors, schools, and the like.

3. *Activity.* Ask students to complete the Census Survey. Then, select two or three surveys each day and ask the respondents to read theirs aloud. Keep a running tally of responses on the chalkboard. After everyone has shared aloud, the class can post the information on a bulletin board display, "Our Class Census," such as the following sample. This is a good opportunity to apply math skills.

Our Class Census, September 20

Population	Gender	Average age	Average pets at home	Average family size	Cookie preference
27	Girls: 14 Boys: 13	9	1.5	3.5	Chocolate chip

Census Survey: Mr. Albright's Class

(Note: Adjust question #6 to grade level and interests of the class.)

1. What is your name?
2. What is your age?
3. Check one: male _____ female _____.
4. Do you have pets at home? If so, how many?
5. How many people are in your family?
6. What is your favorite kind of cookie?

Assessment/ Follow-up	Ask students what a census is. Ask students to guess (hypothesize) how other classrooms in the same school building will differ in census results from their own class. Then select and survey two additional classes, and compare and contrast the results. Help children display these data on a pie graph (see Chapter 5).
Materials	Copy of census survey for each student. U.S. Census Bureau website.

Integration   *Mathematics:* The class cannot tally at step 3 or develop the pie graph during the Follow-up without mathematical reasoning. The concept of average (i.e., the mean) is challenging. And rounding is a controversial issue with averages. Should "1.5" pets be rounded up to 2 or down to 1? Ask your students and listen carefully to their reasoning.

Six Guidelines for Teaching in Diverse Classrooms

Here are six guidelines for teaching in ways that respect all the children in the class and help them learn the social studies curriculum. Each guideline is followed by a number of examples and applications. The guidelines in brief:

1. Culturally responsive instruction
2. Know your "knapsack"
3. Multimedia/multiple entry points
4. High expectations for learning
5. Multicultural curriculum
6. Flexible grouping

Guideline 1. Culturally Responsive Instruction

Learn about the cultural and linguistic characteristics of the children in your class and adapt instruction accordingly. Teach in ways that bridge the gap between children's home cultures and the school culture.

The purpose of culturally responsive instruction is to help children maintain their cultural identities while learning the school curriculum. Doing so helps them learn what you want them to learn because they are not required to hide or feel bad about who they are. Curriculum scholar Geneva Gay defines culturally responsive teaching as "using the cultural knowledge, prior experiences, frames of reference, and performance styles of ethnically diverse students to make learning encounters more relevant to and effective for them. It teaches to and through the strengths of these students."[8] Kathryn Au, a University of Hawaii literacy scholar who worked many years with native Hawaiian children at the Kamehameha Elementary Education Program (KEEP), clarifies this idea: "The approaches teachers use to work with students of diverse backgrounds should allow students to retain and feel pride in their own ethnic and cultural identity. . . . Too often, students of color and students from working-class homes find themselves in the position of having to choose between school success and their cultural identity."[9] This is an unfair choice for any child in a diverse, democratic society, and it systematically stunts the academic development of non-White and Latino students and poor working-class students of any color. One of the reasons many children from the majority ethnic and racial groups do better in school than many children from minority groups is that they do not face this choice. *The school, typically, is already culturally responsive to majority, middle-class children.*

What to do? The general approach is to abandon the way we usually "do school" that requires children to make such a choice, and in its place to teach in ways that leverage the children's knowledge and customs learned at home, using them as resources for learning.

Teaching Examples

- A fifth-grade teacher begins her unit on the U.S. Constitution by asking students what they know about the bylaws and articles of incorporation of groups to which they belong in the community. Members of scouting groups and 4-H often are familiar with the rule books and oaths of these organizations. Students who are involved in religious organizations might know a little about their bylaws as well. African American children, who may be the most deeply involved in church activities of all the children in class, "learn the significance of such documents in forming institutions and shaping ideals while they also learn that their own people are institution-builders."[10]

- Native Hawaiian students often are raised in families that practice sibling caretaking. At school, they might feel just as comfortable learning from peers as from an adult teacher. Accordingly, their teachers often pair them for practice and for teaching one another the meaning of what they are reading in their social studies books.

- The teacher learns to say "please" (e.g., *por favor*), "thank you" (*gracias*), "good morning" (*buenos días*), and "see you tomorrow" (*hasta mañana*) in the home languages of each of her language-minority children. She often uses these phrases when working individually with the children, when greeting them in the morning, and when saying good-bye in the afternoon. She publicly admires them for already being at work on a second language, and she cajoles the English-only speakers to learn a second language.

- A fourth-grade class is planning a classroom newspaper, which will be sent home to parents and to a fourth-grade partner classroom in another school. Their teacher brought in copies of weekly newspapers from local ethnic-minority communities, rather than only the mainstream newspaper, to serve as models.

- Noticing that the rural children in her class are picked on and called names by the town children, Ms. Jenkins (herself a "townie") goes to the county fair and rodeo each year, tries hard to learn about farm life, and praises these activities publicly in the classroom.

- The teachers at Evergreen Heights Elementary School near Seattle decided at a faculty meeting that they would learn about their students' communities. Based on their experiences, they recommend the following activities:

   1. Collaborate with the ethnic-minority communities in your area. Volunteer at youth centers and adult literacy programs.

   2. Ask the parents of immigrant children if their children are attending a Saturday language and culture school. Volunteer to share maps, globes, and other social studies materials.

   3. Find out what churches, mosques, and temples your children attend. Talk with them about this. Go to a religious service or an open house, choir concert, or picnic.

Guideline 2. Know Your "Knapsack"

History begins at home. Teachers need to study their own family history—its ethnic and linguistic characteristics, social class, religion, social values, gifts, and disabilities.

This country's leading multicultural education scholar, James Banks, writes,

Teachers are human beings who bring their cultural perspectives, values, hopes, and dreams to the classroom. They also bring their prejudices, stereotypes, and misconceptions to the classroom. Teachers' values and perspectives mediate and interact with what they teach and influence the ways that messages are communicated and perceived by their students.[11]

Banks then gives a classic example: Teachers who unreflectively ask their students questions like "When did Columbus discover America?" send a different message to students than teachers who know that America was already populated by major indigenous (native) civilizations and ask, simply, "When did Columbus come to America?"

Peggy McIntosh of the Wellesley College Centers for Women calls this bundle of cultural perspectives, values, hopes, and dreams a cultural "knapsack." Everyone, including teachers, carries one on his or her back, so to speak, because everyone is born into a cultural group or a combination of cultural groups. One teacher's knapsack is bound to be at least somewhat different from another's, yet there will be similarities. Teachers who occupy roughly the same *social position*—a particular location in society's social hierarchy—may have similar knapsacks; teachers who occupy different social positions probably will not. This is because social power and privilege are not equal across social positions. For example, McIntosh realized that as a woman and a feminist she had seen very clearly her disadvantaged social position relative to men. But as a White person she had not seen, or had denied, her own privilege relative to non-Whites. She reflects:

> I think whites are carefully taught not to recognize white privilege, as males are taught not to recognize male privilege. So I have begun in an untutored way to ask what it is like to have white privilege. I have come to see white privilege as an invisible package of unearned assets which I can count on cashing in each day, but about which I was "meant" to remain oblivious. White privilege is like an invisible weightless knapsack of special provisions, maps, passports, codebooks, visas, clothes, tools, and blank checks.[12]

Each of us is located in one or more already-existing social positions ("already-existing" because we didn't create them; rather, they preceded us—we were born into them). I was born of working-class, English-speaking, White, Anglo-Saxon, Protestant (WASP) parents in Englewood, Colorado; brought up in the Sunday school classes, summer camps, and youth groups of a United Methodist church; and schooled in my neighborhood's public schools. All this contributes to my knapsack. I *chose* none of it (knapsacks are not voluntary).

Furthermore, a social position locates us in some social groups but not others, thereby placing us closer to some individuals (my fellow WASPs in the church youth groups of which I was a member) and, simultaneously, farther from others who are positioned differently (e.g., wealthy WASPs living in other neighborhoods, poor Whites, African Americans or Muslims of any social class). In other words, all of us are positioned closer to persons similarly positioned, and therefore *we tend to share similar knapsacks—social perspectives*. Of course, we don't share exactly the same identity. Social position *influences* our identity but doesn't *determine* it (each of us deals differently with the situations in which we find ourselves—we respond uniquely to the "hand of cards we were dealt," as the saying goes).[13]

Teaching Examples

- All teachers carry their invisible knapsacks into the classroom. Try to see yours a little more clearly each day. One way is to research your family tree or narrate a family history. Share this with other teachers who have done the same. Think about how your own race, gender, linguistic characteristics, social class, and ethnicity shapes your interaction with students.

- Examine one or two first-grade social studies textbooks published since 2000. "Families around the world" is a common theme. Search for representations of your family. Do you see yourself there? Are others there? Who is not?
- Visit culturally different neighborhoods in your own town or city and, if you can, in other nations. Such experiences provide a reflective mirror in which you can better "see" your own customs and values. (Self-knowledge is difficult for all of us without comparisons.)
- Read the histories of different American ethnic groups and compare them to your own.

Guideline 3. Multimedia/Multiple Entry Points

Provide variation in the ways children acquire social studies information, think about it, and express what they are learning.

The intake of new information is an essential requirement of social studies education. The conventional information sources have been the textbook, primary documents, children's trade books, other literature, videos, and the teacher. It is important to broaden the array of information sources with computer software, films, songs and speeches, paintings and photographs, interviews, class discussions, and so forth. Psychologist Howard Gardner calls these "entry points."[14] Different students will prefer and profit from different entry points. Similarly, the ways in which children are asked to manipulate and express the information they have gathered need to be expanded. Children can translate information heard in a film to a bar graph or time line. They can organize information on charts, write plays and songs about it, compose narratives, and draw and reason mathematically about it.

Teaching Examples

- Teach children how to read and make charts and graphs depicting geographic or economic data they have gathered about their community. (See the folded paper graphics in Chapter 8.)
- Create multimedia presentations using the school or classroom document camera and scanner, download music and images from the Internet, and use good multimedia software (e.g., PowerPoint).
- Build plenty of opportunities to sing and move into your lessons. (See www.songsforteaching.com)
- Teach children to retell a historical narrative as a play, song, or dance (e.g., dramatize the events of the Boston Tea Party or the Underground Railroad).
- Create self-contained learning centers that feature multimedia presentations on an important topic: hospitals in our community, our state capital, goods and services in our community, food and shelter in China, or regions of the United States, for example.

Guideline 4. High Expectations for Learning

Expect, assist, and cajole all students to learn the social studies curriculum.

Children tend to perform according to their teachers' expectations. Teachers in the past often have expected less achievement from girls, students whose home language is not English, African American and Hispanic children, children with learning disabilities, and poor children. Sometimes teachers have lowered curriculum standards for these children or created an altogether different curriculum for them, thereby teaching them less important subject matter. In her wonderful book, *Other People's Children: Cultural Conflict in the Classroom* (1995), Lisa Delpit calls this, simply, "teaching less."

Attached to low expectations are behaviors. A teacher who expects boys but not girls to develop sharp intellects may praise girls for neat work while praising boys for thoughtful work, or drill limited-English students on skills while helping language-majority children learn the powerful ideas of geography, civics, and history. Based on unconsciously held stereotypes, a White teacher may expect Asian American children to do well in math while expecting African American children to misbehave.

Teaching Examples

- Call on girls as often as boys. Praise them for intellectual work—their reasoning and understanding—and provide constructive criticism. Be attentive to the misbehavior of both boys and girls. Use a checklist to help keep track of your feedback patterns. Ask a colleague to videotape your interaction, and then return the favor.
- Make every effort to teach limited-English-speaking children the social studies curriculum, not only language skills. Place the language instruction in the context of the social studies curriculum. Use drama, art, simulation games, construction, and music activities to lighten some of the language burden. For limited-English-speaking students, especially poor minority children in urban schools, there is too often a grueling regime of remedial drills on basic skills. Missing is a rich curriculum of engaging and enriching content, such as history, geography, and civics.
- Monitor carefully your nonverbal behavior. Take care not to shy away from culturally different children; *they will feel it.* Children notice if their teacher genuinely cares that they learn and the extent to which their teacher requires them to learn and helps them to learn. Like you, they remember it long enough to talk about it when they are grown.

Guideline 5. Multicultural Curriculum

Help children understand key concepts, events, issues, and historical figures from diverse viewpoints.

Paying attention to how we teach is an important dimension of teaching in diverse classrooms. Paying attention to *what* we teach is another. Teachers should enrich students' learning of social studies topics by including multiple viewpoints or perspectives. Multicultural

Praise girls' intellectual work—their *reasoning*.
(© *iStockphoto.com/lijlexmom*)

education is good education because it is more comprehensive. It places one perspective on a historical event or character alongside others so that students can compare them and try to draw defensible conclusions.

Teaching Examples

- Have children in the fifth grade examine the American Revolution from the perspectives of Loyalists as well as rebels, men and women, and slaves and free persons. They should study the westward movement of European immigrants from the viewpoints of native groups as well as pioneer families. When setting up a classroom store, help third-grade children plan for employees and customers who have disabilities and religious and language differences.

- Take care not to teach only the Anglo-American perspective on United States history. European conquerors came from Spain as well as England, and their history involves the American southwest more than the northeast. Asian immigrants came through San Francisco while European immigrants were lining up on Ellis Island in New York City. The popular term *westward expansion* refers to the Anglo-American immigrant movement from the northeast toward the already occupied (by natives) lands to the west. *El Norte* would better capture the movement of Spanish-speaking immigrants from the south.

- When teaching any social studies concept, include multiple viewpoints. See Chapter 12 for examples using children's tradebooks.

- When teaching about the children's neighborhoods, emphasize both cultural diversity and the laws, values, and customs that bind us together as one people. We may be culturally many, but we are politically one (our constitutional democracy).

Talk with children about the classroom rules, such as listening carefully to one another and respecting diversity, that "make us all one people."

- Teach directly about prejudice, racism, discrimination, and stereotyping. These are central social science concepts that children need to understand and act upon. Chapter 9 presents a time-honored strategy for teaching any concept. Learning any concept requires three or four vivid examples and a teacher who helps students do the necessary intellectual work of comparing, summarizing, and applying.

- Have children write biographies about people who have courageously displayed toleration and insisted on the rights not just of themselves but of others. Hold them high as heroes. (See Chapter 13 for a powerful biography-writing strategy.)

- Post the famous saying by the French philosopher Voltaire, "I disapprove of what you say, but I will defend to the death your right to say it."

- Invite to the classroom historians, geographers, political scientists, economists, anthropologists, and sociologists—both men and women, people with disabilities, and members of racial or ethnic minority groups. This helps break stereotypes while teaching social studies content.

Guideline 6. Flexible Grouping

Group children in various ways, always with a clear purpose, and change the groups often.

During social studies instruction, groupings of children should be temporary and task oriented. Often these groups are formed on the basis of a common interest, for example, working together on a display, construction project, play, or report. Other groups are formed on the basis of a common need. For instance, a teacher may work with a small group on reading a text, developing a map skill, or learning to use the materials in a learning center while other children are working independently. Avoid fixed groups in which children are separated permanently for whatever reason, such as reading ability, prior knowledge, or behavior.[15]

Teaching Examples

- Use whole-class grouping when children should have a shared experience— a discussion of a classroom problem, for example, dramatizing a story about Abraham Lincoln, or being introduced to time lines or different kinds of maps, charts, and graphs.

- Needs-based groups should be used at times to remediate students who need this kind of assistance but generally to help students achieve beyond what they normally do—both children with specific disabilities as well as gifted children. This kind of assistance is called *instructional scaffolding* because, like an actual scaffold erected next to a building, it lifts children up to where they can reach a higher level of performance than otherwise would be possible. And it's adjustable: Different learners can be lifted more or less, as needed, and the structure can be taken down when it is no longer of use, that is, when learners can reach high without it.

- Use cooperative pairs when you want children to practice with information they have heard, give one another explanations, share responses to a reading, or test one another on material that has been studied. Pairs also can be used to coach one another if they are taught to ask good questions—questions that seek clarification, elaboration, a summary, or a prediction. Pairs are easier to form and disband than small groups.

- Use peer-tutoring pairs when a student who is more knowledgeable can help a student who is less so.
- Use cooperative learning in small groups of three to five children for tasks that are complex and require division of labor and group planning. Examples include making different kinds of maps (political, landform, vegetation, highway) of the same area, writing a multichapter "book" on Mexico or Canada, or creating a model of a Pueblo village. These groups should mix children of different abilities, social status, and ethnicity. (See Chapter 11 for details for making cooperative learning effective.)

UNDERSTANDING CHANGING DEMOGRAPHICS

Now that we have considered six guidelines for teaching and learning in diverse classrooms, let's look more closely at some of the demographic characteristics of children in classrooms. Why? Because key social studies concepts are involved, and because it is not enough only to "celebrate diversity." Teachers need to *understand* diversity and understand it more deeply than professionals in just about any other field. We will examine these:

1. Ethnicity
2. Social Class
3. Race
4. Culture
5. Gender
6. Sexual Orientation
7. Language and Dialect
8. Giftedness, Disability
9. Multiple Intelligences

Ethnicity, Race, Class, and Culture

A child's ethnic group membership matters to the child and to others. Ethnic groups have different values and different ways of seeing the world. Children from different ethnic groups do not behave in the same ways, do not organize or experience the world in the same ways, and do not necessarily learn in the same ways. The content of one's "knapsack" is strongly influenced by ethnic group memberships. Mexican American children in your classroom often have been exposed to traditional family values and role models; Nicaraguan American children, however, may have experienced a more modern home life. This difference is due to the culture and politics of each homeland. The European American children in your classroom may very well reflect that ethnic group's valuing of individualism and independence. Filipino and Japanese immigrant children may have seen vastly different sex-role behavior—more gender equity in the Philippines, less in Japan.

Although teachers must be aware of ethnic differences, they must also be careful not to overgeneralize—to stereotype—on the basis of ethnicity. Asian American children clearly are not all alike, as anyone who has had Hmong, Japanese, and Chinese (Han) American children in class will tell you. Nor are European American children all alike, or Arab or

African American children. Differences in religion and, especially, social class can have an enormous impact on the behavior and values of children who share a similar ethnic background. Middle-class Whites generally share more cultural characteristics with middle-class Blacks than with poor Whites, for example. Native American children raised in families that emphasize acculturation to the mainstream American culture, which is heavily influenced by European American ethnicity generally and Anglo-Saxon ethnicity specifically, may view classroom and playground situations very differently from those who have been encouraged to maintain traditional values.

Each of these variables—ethnicity, social class, race, and culture—is complicated *and connected*. James Jones wrote of the connection between race and social class in his popular text, *Prejudice and Racism*:

> One of the big difficulties we have is disentangling race from class. . . . Blacks, in particular, and ethnic minorities in general, are found disproportionately in the lower economic strata. To what extent are the examples of racism cited merely vestiges of racist disadvantage that now manifest themselves in class-related processes?[16]

David Berliner, an educational researcher, wrote of it this way:

> Our children live nested lives. Our youth are in classrooms, so when those classrooms do not function as we want them to, we go to work on improving them. Those classrooms are in schools, so when we decide that those schools are not performing appropriately, we go to work on improving them, as well. But both students and schools are situated in neighborhoods filled with families. And in our country the individuals living in those school neighborhoods are not a random cross section of Americans. Our neighborhoods are highly segregated by social class, and thus, also segregated by race and ethnicity.[17]

Let us define a few terms. *Social class* is the rung on the social ladder—the place in the social hierarchy—where individuals find themselves. Economic power largely determines one's rung on the ladder today whereas, to draw a simple comparison, physical prowess was more important in premodern hunting-and-gathering societies. Today, the amount of education one has—some high school, high school diploma, some college, college diploma, advanced degree—is a good predictor of economic power, as shown in Table 2–1. But it is also more or less the consequence of the parents' economic power. Accordingly, education, occupation, income, and class are tightly linked. One's job influences one's choice of friends and life partners; one's income affects one's political views and religious beliefs. (These are generalizations based on evidence—they are *generally* true—but there are, of course, exceptions.)

TABLE 2–1	Education and annual income.			
	No high school diploma	High school graduate	Bachelor's degree	Advanced degree
Median personal income in 2005	$18,734	$27,915	$51,206	$74,602

Source: U.S. Census Bureau (www.census.gov).

Race and class are linked, too, as we saw in Jones's and Berliner's statements. According to the U.S. census, Asian Americans have the highest yearly income, then Whites, then Latinos, and then African Americans. Also linked are *gender* and class. While U.S. culture remains generally male-centered or patriarchal, gender roles do differ by social class. This is due in large part to the mediating impact, again, of *education*. Sociologist Dennis Gilbert explains that "college life, generally a prologue to upper-middle class careers, delays marriage and encourages informal, relatively egalitarian association between men and women."[18] Egalitarian gender roles are not as common in the working class.

Culture can be defined as the values, beliefs, and customs—in brief, the way of life or lifestyle—shared by a group of people or society. Culture is learned. You can belong to several groups, each with distinct cultural characteristics. For example, one is a member of a gender group (women), regional group (southerner), racial group (African American), religion (Baptist), occupation (schoolteacher), social class (middle), ability (hearing impaired), and ethnic group (southern, rural African American). The cultural characteristics of each of our (and our students') several social positions overlap, making for a complex cultural identity and social perspective.

An *ethnic group* is a particular kind of culture group. Everyone is a member of one or more ethnic groups. Members of an ethnic group share a common history, a sense of peoplehood and fate, and values and beliefs. Moreover, they usually view their group as distinct and separate from other cultural groups within a society. A major exception to this last statement is that members of the majority ethnic group may not "see" their ethnicity and, therefore, may not view themselves as distinct and separate (e.g., WASPs in the United States; Han in China). This is why my parents (WASPs themselves) would say "Let's go *out* for ethnic food," not seeing that the dinner of baked ham, green beans, and boiled potatoes we were eating at home was, indeed, ethnic food: the food of our ethnic group. Logically, then, no one can say "Let's go out for ethnic food." To be accurate, we would have to say: "Let's go out for *different* ethnic food than the ethnic food we usually eat at home."

More broadly, an ethnic group is a group of people who are distinguished by race, religion, language, or national origin, and often a combination of these. Many ethnic groups live in the United States, more than in most other nations. There are, for example, Vietnamese Americans, Anglo Americans, Mexican Americans, German Americans, African Americans, Russian Americans, Arab Americans, and Native Americans (e.g., Lakota Sioux). Irish Catholics are sometimes considered an ethnic group, as are Mormons, midwesterners, southern Baptists, and west Texans. The Pilgrims and Puritans of American colonial times were ethnic groups, as were the native peoples they encountered.

An *ethnic minority group* has characteristics, usually both physical and cultural, that make its members identifiable to members of other groups. Very often, ethnic minorities suffer discrimination and subordination within a society. Arab Americans, Filipino Americans, Jewish Americans, African Americans, and Mexican Americans are a few of the examples of ethnic minority groups in the United States. Latino (also called Hispanic) Americans demonstrate powerfully that within-group variation can be very large indeed. A combination of Spanish conquistadors and indigenous peoples created this ethnic group, and the differences among its very diverse members (e.g., they are members of different races) are artificially obscured by the fact that they share a common language—Spanish.

Ethnocentrism is the habit of judging other ethnic groups' beliefs and behaviors by one's own ethnic group's standards: comparing a "them" unfavorably to an "us" because "they" are not like "us" in ways that are important to "us." "Their" language sounds like gibberish.

TABLE 2–2	Projections of the U.S. population by race and Hispanic origin, 2000–2025 (Numbers in thousands).			
	2000		2025	
	Number (thousands)	% of Total	Number (thousands)	% of Total
Total Population	275,306	100.0	337,814	100.0
By race				
White	226,265	82.2	265,305	78.5
Black	35,332	12.8	47,089	13.9
American Indian	2,433	0.9	3,399	1.0
Asian and Pacific Islander	11,275	4.1	22,020	6.5
By Hispanic origin				
Hispanic	32,478	11.8	61,433	18.2
White, non–Hispanic	196,669	71.4	209,339	62.0
Black, non–Hispanic	33,490	12.2	43,527	12.9
American Indian, non–Hispanic	2,047	0.7	2,668	0.8
Asian and Pacific Islander, non–Hispanic	10,619	3.9	20,846	6.2

Source: U.S. Census Bureau Population Projections Program (www.census.gov).

Their religion isn't a religion at all. And so on. During geography lessons focusing on societies that have customs quite different from the children's own, the teacher will sometimes hear ethnocentric statements. These are good opportunities—teachable moments—to teach about human diversity, to provide instruction on the concept of ethnocentrism, to encourage respect and empathy for people everywhere, and to inquire seriously into why a seemingly odd behavior can make complete sense to the people doing it. For example, when hamburger-eating American students learn that hungry families in rural India do not eat a readily available food (a cow), they may be incredulous.

Race is a contested term that is rapidly losing useful meaning for social and natural scientists alike (see Table 2–2). Race, like any concept, is a social invention, but it is one that has been used to divide people and, very often, to discriminate, conquer, and subjugate. "The race concept," write the authors of a helpful new book on race, culture, and biology,

> has historically been associated with the idea that there are "natural" divisions of the human species, that there are clear-cut, discrete, homogenous, and easily distinguishable subgroups or "races," and that people can be easily categorized into these racial groups.[19]

While this idea probably originated with early 18th-century European scientists, racial categories (e.g., Black and White, African American and European American, negroid and caucasian, Asian) have constantly changed across time, place, and cultural context. At the time of the large Irish migration to the United States in the early 20th century, when Anglo Saxons were clearly the dominant ethnic group in the United States, the Irish were considered non-White by other Whites of Anglo-Saxon ethnicity. Today, the Irish are commonly regarded as White and generally designate themselves as such in surveys such as the U. S. Census. Italians and Jews, similarly, were considered by some Anglo Saxons to be racially different (not White) at the time they immigrated in large numbers from Europe. Today, all these groups are generally considered White.[20]

Ethnicity is gradually replacing race as a useful category for understanding demography and human similarities and differences. Still, many people believe that race is a distinct and useful concept as it refers to genetically transmitted visible characteristics. Race and ethnicity are often confused because they overlap. For example, the Japanese have physical characteristics that identify them as an Asian racial group. At the same time, the Japanese people have a language, tradition, common heritage, and history that give them an ethnic identity distinct from other Asians such as the Han (the dominant ethnic group within China). Imagine: A blond European baby boy who, at the moment of birth, is adopted and raised by a Japanese family will, as an adult, be ethnically Japanese in spite of the physical (racial) characteristics that he inherited from his European ancestors. Perhaps this boy will not be fully accepted by the Japanese society because of his distinguishing physical characteristics. If so, this is because negative social values are being associated with the physical characteristics. This is *racism,* which is the practice of attaching nonphysical characteristics to physical qualities of human beings. This practice has been and continues to be quite common in the United States and many (probably most) other societies. Race and racism are problems not because of the reality of physical differences among human beings, but because there are social values—prejudices and negative stereotypes—attached to those differences.

During the past four decades, dramatic changes have occurred in the racial, ethnic, and cultural composition of school populations. Inside our classrooms—as in U.S. society generally—the term *minority group* is quickly becoming factually inaccurate. Traditionally, the term has been used loosely to refer to non-White and Latino people in the United States, but among the student population, the numerical minority will be the numerical majority in a matter of decades. In the largest school districts in the nation, this is already the case.

Gender

In 1920 the Nineteenth Amendment to the Constitution became the law of the land. Women won the right to vote, a right enjoyed by most free White men since the founding of the Republic in 1788, the year the Constitution became law. Discrimination against women, however, did not end with the Nineteenth Amendment.

School programs of the past contributed to discrimination against women because they reinforced conventional notions of male superiority. Where this can be studied with a degree of objectivity, as, for example, in analyzing school textbooks, the evidence is overwhelming that males had a clear advantage. They were consistently represented in positions of greater prestige and as being more courageous and more skillful than women. Women tended to be represented in subservient positions in social-service roles or in roles that require serving men, as, for example, secretarial service and nursing. Thus, discrimination against women became *institutionalized:* Both boys and girls came to believe in the superiority of the male. Such blatantly sexist material generally does not appear, with a few exceptions, in recently published textbooks and other instructional materials.

Nevertheless, during the preschool, elementary, and middle-school years, students continue to experience gender bias. Though sex-role stereotyping in curriculum materials has diminished significantly, it remains a serious problem in children's interactions with one another and their teacher. Three aspects of gender bias have been well documented:

- Girls receive less attention from classroom teachers than do boys.
- African American girls have fewer interactions with teachers than do White girls, despite evidence that they attempt to initiate interactions more frequently.
- Sexual harassment of girls by boys—from innuendo to assault—is increasing.[21]

Research on this problem suggests that too often there are two academic worlds in the classroom: one of active boys, the other of inactive girls. One study concluded: "Male students control classroom conversation. They ask and answer more questions. They receive more praise for the intellectual quality of their ideas. They get criticized. They get help when they are confused."[22]

Consider this example from a fifth-grade classroom that is getting out of hand. Before this exchange, the teacher had quieted down the commotion and reminded students of the rule to "raise your hand." She told students the reason for the rule: "There are too many of us here to all shout out at once." Order was restored. Soon, Stephen shouts out.

Stephen: I think Lincoln was the best president. He held the country together during the war.

Teacher: A lot of historians would agree with you.

Mike (seeing that nothing happened to Stephen, calls out): I don't. Lincoln was okay, but my dad liked Reagan. He always said Reagan was a great president.

David (calling out): Reagan? Are you kidding?

Teacher: Who do you think our best president was, Dave?

David: FDR. He saved us from the Depression.

Max (calling out): I don't think it's right to pick one best president. There were a lot of good ones.

Teacher: That's interesting.

Kimberly (calling out): I don't think the presidents today are as good as the ones we used to have.

Teacher: Okay, Kimberly. But you forgot the rule. You're supposed to raise your hand.[23]

REFLECTION

This vivid classroom scene is based on ground-breaking research done in the early 1990s. Based on your experience in classrooms, as a student, observer, or teacher, is this sort of gendered interaction (a) still common today? (b) frequent but not common? (c) rare? How would you advise this teacher to be gender-fair?

As a result of interactions like these, boys may receive more instruction and better instruction than girls. When boys are praised, for example, it is more often for the kind of learning and thinking they are doing at the moment; consequently, it serves as valuable feedback that will affect achievement. When girls are praised, it is often less specific and, therefore, less instructive. Furthermore, when girls receive praise or criticism in a more helpful, specific way, they are twice as likely as boys to receive it for following or breaking the rules of interaction, form, and appearance, as Kimberly was, rather than for the substance of their thinking and their work. "I like how quiet you are" is one message the girls get. "You are so neat" is another. "I love your margins" is another.

Doonesbury

The major goal of gender equity in the classroom is equal opportunity to learn. Sex discrimination prevents children from having an equal chance to get attention, praise, constructive criticism, and, in general, *instruction*. Over the years, this lack of helpful attention adds up. By one estimate, girls receive 1,800 fewer hours of instruction than boys between preschool and college. The main theme of the studies on gender in the classroom is that girls are taught less often and less constructively than boys.

As for sexual harassment, the upper elementary grades become increasingly difficult for girls, and in middle school touching and grabbing in a sexual way becomes somewhat common.[24] "When I was in middle school," writes Kimberly Palmer, "boys grabbed girls' breasts in the stairwells and cafeteria as casually as they would say 'hello.'"[25] These overt sexual advances were usually overlooked by teachers, she reports. "Teachers let it slide like the other dumb behavior that happens among adolescents. They shouldn't have."

Boys suffer gender bias, too. Consider how strictly the boundaries of sexual identity are policed in the elementary and middle school. The taunts "sissy" and "tomboy" announce that a boundary has been crossed, a gender norm violated. The label "sissy" suggests that a boy has strayed too far into the forbidden "feminine,"

> while "tomboys" are girls who claim some of the positive qualities associated with the "masculine." The images condense many cultural messages about gender, in part through their striking asymmetry: "tomboy" holds mixed, and often quite positive meanings, while "sissy" is an unmitigated word of contempt."[26]

Sexual Orientation

Imagine this. You open a social studies textbook or trade book and find that the worth of every individual in the book is judged against the standard of being male, Protestant, and Anglo Saxon. Females are of less worth as are Catholics, Mexicans, and a host of others. Further, imagine that the typical American was assumed to be male, Protestant, and Anglo Saxon. You would be outraged by this, of course, not only because that representation of *American* is factually wrong, but also because the *belief* that it is true, or that it ought to be true, is racist, sexist, and ethnocentric.

Strangely, however, the belief that the typical American is heterosexual persists. Social scientists call this *heteronormativity*: The belief that the archetypal human being (American, Cambodian, Iranian, Nigerian, whatever) is heterosexual. While diversity is increasingly becoming a legitimate idea in many societies—witness all the "celebrate diversity" banners hanging in U.S. schools today—at least one major exception remains. Stephen Thornton writes,

> It is still tacitly assumed everyone is heterosexual until proven otherwise. Despite striking growth in social, political, legal, and media presence of gays in American life, especially in the last decade, few social studies materials appear to have substantive treatment of gay history and issues. Indeed many of these materials fail to even mention such words as "homosexual," "straight," and "gay." It is as if the millions of gay inhabitants of the United States, past and present, did not exist.[27]

Millions? Indeed. The number of gay and lesbian people in the U.S. population is hotly debated but is probably between 5% and 10% (15–30 million). So it is curious that heteronormativity typically goes unchallenged in social studies curriculum materials. "Unless children are raised in a limited number of locales or have teachers who go beyond what the textbook provides," Thornton continues, "they may graduate from high school being none the wiser that heteronormativity paints an inaccurate picture of social life and perpetuates intolerance, sometimes with tangibly destructive consequences such as harassment and physical violence."

As a first step, teachers need to acknowledge that differences in sexual orientation exist in the United States and in the world. Beyond simple recognition of the facts, teachers can also point out discrimination against homosexuals just as they point out discrimination against other groups—religions, races, languages, or women. The Taliban men of Afghanistan, for example, not only denied basic human rights to women, but to gay men as well. Some popular music is not only sexist, but heterosexist.

Beyond acknowledging the facts and teaching against discrimination, it is every schoolteacher's responsibility to protect and nurture children. In hallways and classrooms, few taunts are more common than "gay" and "fag." On playgrounds, the name calling can turn meaner, into physical violence. Teachers must not ignore these taunts or actions any more than they would ignore racial slurs, sexual harassment, or other forms of humiliation. It has long been recognized that depression and suicide are far more common among youngsters who are homosexual than among their straight peers. If teachers or other building leaders are silent, they teach an important lesson to children: "This is okay. We need not care for one another. We can be cruel." Silence is not neutral; it quietly condones the persecution. The grown-ups at school—the teachers and administrators—are usually the only responsible adults to whom these at-risk children can turn for support as well as equal educational opportunities.

Language Differences in the Classroom

Over 100 distinct language groups are present in the United States. "English language learners" (ELL) is probably the most popular term used in schools today to describe students—many but not all of them immigrants—who are learning English as their second (or third or fourth) language. Approximately 76% of ELL students in the United States speak Spanish as their primary language; in contrast, about 4% speak Vietnamese or Hmong. Of course,

Gaining academic proficiency in a second language is a huge accomplishment.
(Anne Vega/Merrill)

this varies widely state by state. You can obtain information on the primary languages spoken in your state by calling the state education office or by searching the state-by-state information at the U.S. Census Bureau's website.

When children come to school in most communities in the United States today, they find that most of the adults and classmates speak one language at school, English, and that one dialect, standard English, is preferred. Depending on whether their home language matches the school's, students might face an awesome communication and learning barrier. If the match is perfect, however, the effect is like having a red carpet rolled out for them. Many of the directions and explanations given in classrooms and on the playground are verbal; most reading materials are in English; and a child's social contacts with peers, which are crucial for social development, depend heavily on linguistic expression. The impact on a child who speaks little or no English can be enormous. Consider this reflection by a Chinese American student:

> I started to hate myself when I failed to answer the teacher's questions . . . because I couldn't express my answers in English. Then I began to hate everything in the world, including my parents because they took me to this country.[28]

Or this one:

> I just sat in my classes and didn't understand anything. Sometimes I would try to look like I knew what was going on; sometimes I would just try to think about a happy time when I didn't feel stupid. My teachers never called on me or talked to me. I think either they forgot I was there or else wished I wasn't.[29]

Certainly not all English language learners react this way. Some respond eagerly to the task of learning the new language, have a relaxed attitude toward the difficulties that inevitably arise, and make good progress learning English and academic content and skills.

Such children most likely are those who are provided content-based instruction in their home language, supplemented with English lessons and practice. The children who do especially well are often those whose command of the home language is excellent for their age, who are highly motivated to learn the new language, and whose family support for second-language acquisition is warm and unambiguous. Some of these children's parents and teachers may themselves be multilingual and move smoothly between languages and dialects, depending on the social situation.

Even then, there is nothing easy about it. In the picture book called *My Name is Yoon* (Helen Recorvits & Gabi Swiatkowska, 2003), a little girl's difficult adjustment to the English language is beautifully portrayed. Yoon, whose parents emigrated to the United States from Korea, thinks her name looks much happier written in Korean than in English. "I did not like YOON," she says. "Lines. Circles. Each standing alone."

Research shows that it takes about two years to learn a second language well enough to engage in face-to-face conversation (conversational proficiency). It takes three times as long, or longer, to develop the skills needed to learn subject matter in a second language (academic proficiency). Readers of this book who are themselves bilingual will know well this distinction. It is one thing for an English-speaking student of French (as a second language) to engage in conversational French with a classmate or a waiter in a café. It is quite another to go to a French school where it is necessary to comprehend textbooks written in French and to grasp concepts from lessons delivered in French.

Finally, we arrive at the term *dialect,* which is a variation of a language spoken by members of a regional or ethnic group. Each variation has somewhat different rules of speech and meaning. Educators disagree on how best to deal with dialect variations in the classroom. Most seem to agree that speakers of nonstandard dialects should learn to speak standard English[30] because if they do, social rewards, such as higher paying jobs and status, generally will follow. *Teachers, however, should encourage students to retain and use the home dialect as well.* The point is *not* to replace it. Like a first language, a first dialect is, and should be regarded as, a strength, not a deficit. It should be validated and affirmed. Not only are language and dialect important to our students' identities (as they are to our own identities), but teachers and children who are bilingual and bidialectic clearly have the advantage—the competive edge—in a modern, global society.

The single most important thing a teacher can do is to not confuse the lack of proficiency in the new language or dialect with a lack of knowledge or a learning disability.

Children with Special Needs

The logic of individualizing—knowing individual children and their cultures and seeing differences as differences, not deficits—extends to children with special needs. Children with special needs have abilities and disabilities that are exceptional—beyond the usual. Educators and parents often believe these children require what is traditionally called "special education," the purpose of which, simply, is to help these children reach their potential.

It is important that children with disabilities not be denied access to the academic curriculum (also called the general curriculum). For this reason, the teacher can expect one or more children with varying types of disabilities to be present in the classroom. This practice is popularly called mainstreaming or inclusion, and it is the school's response to laws requiring that such children be educated with their nondisabled peers to the maximum extent possible. Figure 2–2 describes the *Individuals with Disabilities Education Act* (Public Law 105-17).

FIGURE 2–2   Know the law.

The *Individuals with Disabilities Education Act* (IDEA), known as PL 105-17, was signed into law by President Bill Clinton in 1997. Formerly known as the Education for All Handicapped Children Act of 1975, this legislation is based on a philosophy of inclusion rather than exclusion. It embraces the "zero-reject" principle and shatters long-held assumptions about who is educable. PL 105-17 assures that students with disabilities receive free appropriate public education (FAPE) in the least-restrictive environment and the related services and support they need to achieve. IDEA was enacted to help states and school districts meet their legal obligations to educate children with disabilities, and to pay part of the extra expense of doing so.

Main points of the legislation:

1. The availability of a free and appropriate public education for all children with disabilities between the ages of 3 and 21; school districts are obliged to search for and identify such children.
2. The maintenance of an Individualized Education Program (IEP) for all children with disabilities, prepared in cooperation with the parent or guardian, the teacher, and the school principal.
3. The guarantee of complete due-process procedures, including parental participation. Parents must be informed of their children's rights and can participate in all decisions affecting their child.
4. The provision of special education and related services as needed in the "least-restrictive" environment (LRE).
5. Nondiscriminatory testing, evaluation, and placement.
6. Placement in regular public school settings with nondisabled peers to the maximum extent appropriate and feasible.

What the teacher can and will do with children with disabilities in the classroom depends on the individual child's knowledge, experiences, and needs, and the kinds of support services that are available. But it also depends on teachers' own attitudes toward children with special needs. "One of the main, if not the main, causes of inequality in special education," Herbert Grossman writes, "is prejudice. . . ."[31] He is referring to prejudice by teachers and administrators toward children with special needs generally, and especially when they are Black, Native, or Latino children: "they are still misplaced in programs for the developmentally disabled and denied access to programs for students with gifts and talents." Here again we see that race, language, ethnicity, social class and, now, special education in schools are connected.

It is quite clear that a child who has a physical disability but who is intellectually gifted will be taught differently than a child whose physical development is typical but whose mental development is retarded in some way. If the classroom has an instructional assistant who can work with such a child for part of the time, it becomes easier to effectively integrate that child into the day-to-day life and activities of the classroom.

An Individualized Education Program (IEP) will be prepared for each child who qualifies for special education. The IEP is prepared by a team that includes a teacher trained in special education, the regular classoom teacher, the student's parents or guardian, and, if appropriate, the student. The classroom teacher may be responsible for only a small part of the implementation of the IEP, but his or her collaboration is essential because it is the classroom teacher who represents the general curriculum to which access is being arranged via the IEP. It is imperative for the classroom teacher, the special education teacher, and other support personnel to communicate and cooperate to ensure a coordinated program of instruction for the child.

Because the Individualized Education Program must take into account the child's present level of attainment or development, an assessment will be done. Based on that assessment, the IEP will stipulate the long-range goals to be met by the end of the year and the short-term objectives to be achieved in order to attain the long-range goals. Although the classroom teacher may exercise some initiative in preparing the IEP, the program planning and development must include, on a firsthand basis, the principal or other school representative and the child's parent or guardian. (Teacher-prepared IEPs that are merely sent to the child's parent or guardian for signature are not acceptable under federal legislation.)

The actual format of the IEP varies from district to district, although the substance of what is included remains much the same. The sample form provided in Figure 2–3 illustrates some of the major components of an IEP.

Gifts and Talents

Harvard psychologist Howard Gardner notes that we are all gifted and challenged simultaneously.[32] Perhaps you are a gifted violinist, but when your car breaks down on the highway you are utterly mystified and do not even bother to look under the hood. Or you are mechanically talented but cannot carry a tune. Even still, though each child is unique or exceptional in her or his own way, some children are singled out as exceptional. Children with special gifts or talents have a remarkable degree of general ability, extraordinary specific abilities, or both. Furthermore, they display advanced creativity and are highly motivated to achieve in the areas of their ability and talent. They will often persevere on a problem far beyond the point at which other children lose interest or give up. Such children in the elementary grades usually handle subject matter easily because of their capacity to use language and understand abstract relationships. Their work is sometimes "over the top"—very advanced for their age. Here is the gifted pianist or poet in the fourth grade, and the third-grade child who not only plants kernels of corn in milk cartons at the plant table, but captivated by the fact that beans are an inexpensive and plentiful source of protein, brings to class the next week a well-worked-out plan for cultivating beans in greenhouses attached ingeniously to homeless shelters. She has attended to the details of light and moisture, researched the necessary building permits, and is asking how to raise the funds.

Recognizing giftedness is not always this easy. The state department of education or the local school district establishes criteria that teachers and administrators are asked to use. They usually are derived from a child's school achievement history, teacher observations, and scores on intelligence tests. Sometimes schools define as gifted any child who scores in the top 2% or 3% of their age group. Guidelines may be distributed to teachers with questions such as these: Who among your children has an extraordinary vocabulary? Who is remarkably (and perhaps annoyingly) observant? Who seems to know about many things the other children do not? Who tackles problems that other children do not even see?

Regardless of the availability of special programs for children with special gifts and talents, the regular classroom teacher will need to make provisions for them. Social studies is a curriculum area that is ideally suited to make such adjustments because of its open-ended subject matter. A few suggestions are given here, and readers wanting more will find helpful the popular work of Carol Tomlinson.[33]

- *Tiered (differentiated) assignments.* All children will be learning to understand what maps are and how to make them, but the teacher may ask children with higher abilities to examine the mapping problems faced by cartographers working in the field today, perhaps in space or on the ocean floor.
- *Independent study.* Follow the interests of the high-ability child and encourage independent studies in those directions. Perhaps the teacher has led an interpretive discussion of an entry in the Lewis and Clark journals (see Chapter 4). A student with remarkable spatial gifts might then independently create a relief map of the entire journey, and this could be the centerpiece of a submission to the state's History Day competition. Another child with a talent for writing or an unusual insight into the human condition might compare the journals of renowned journal authors (e.g., Anne Frank and Meriwether Lewis).

Disabilities and Challenges

Just as some people are exceptionally gifted, other people are exceptionally challenged. In America's elementary and middle schools are children who have mild or profound mental retardation, physical disabilities (e.g., epilepsy, hearing impairment, cerebral palsy), emotional and behavioral disorders, and communication disorders (e.g., delayed language development, stuttering). Other children (sometimes the same ones) have learning disabilities. Learning disabilities (LD) pose challenges in specific aspects of functioning, for example, reading, writing, or thinking abstractly. Dyslexia is one well-known learning disability. Nearly half of all school-aged children in special education are identified as LD.

It is important to note that *learning disability* is a much-overused term, and dangerously so. No doubt too many children are made to endure this label. For example, limited-English-speaking students do not have a learning disability; they just do not know the second language well enough to understand their teacher. Children who belong to ethnic minority groups, especially African American boys, are disproportionately labeled learning disabled. This was especially true before a federal law was passed that prevented this sort of segregation, but it persists today. Some African American parents have created separate schools for their children to protect them from racist practices like these.

Two cautions: First, learning challenges are not disadvantages unless the child is in a situation where the disability or disorder gets in the way. A child with a hearing impairment, for example, is not necessarily at a disadvantage when making a map of the classroom or playground. The violin-playing driver above, the one with a mechanical "disability," is not disadvantaged when eating dinner with friends.

Second, educators' conversations about exceptionality are loaded with labels that are double-edged swords. On the one hand, labels help educators speak precisely about teaching and

FIGURE 2–3 Sample IEP form.

PIEDMONT PUBLIC SCHOOLS
INDIVIDUALIZED EDUCATION PROGRAM

Student _____ Birthdate _____
C.A. _____

Address _____ (include zip) Lives With _____ Relationship _____ Home Phone _____ Work Phone _____

Home School _____ Grade _____ IEP Conference Date _____ Projected Review Date _____

Teacher _____ Program _____ School _____ Date Enrolled _____ Terminated _____

PLACEMENT OFFICE ONLY:

Program Assigned _____
Building _____
Teacher _____
Date Enrolled _____

I. SUMMARY OF PRESENT LEVELS OF PERFORMANCE
(Include statements of progress in each area from last reporting period)

ACADEMIC:

PHYSICAL:

SOCIAL:

II. ANALYSIS OF ASSESSMENT DATA
(Report of significant changes since initial IEP)

ELIGIBILITY CRITERIA: _____

PROGRAM AND/OR REPLACEMENT CHANGE:

Team Leader: _____ Date: _____
Parent: _____ Date: _____

PROGRAM RECOMMENDATION:

Psychologist: _____ Date: _____
Parent: _____ Date: _____

III. STUDENT GOALS & OBJECTIVES

Academic Year _____

Special Classroom Teacher _____

Support Services _____

(Specify Service)

Name of Student	Age	Grade	Program	Building	Teacher	Date Enrolled

Goals:	Initial Objectives:	Evaluation Criteria & Progress Notes (include pre-test, post-test data, and grades)	Date Started	Date Completed

_____
Signature of person or persons responsible for reporting progress on goals and objectives

_____
Parent Signature

_____
Date

learning; on the other, labels can be attached to children and stick. When that happens, children may not be helped to achieve their potential, which, recall, is the purpose of special education. Rather, the label may be used as an excuse by teachers, administrators, and parents not to bother teaching children what they actually may be capable of learning.

Multiple Intelligences

Q: Are you gifted or are you challenged?

A: You are both.

I conclude this demographic tour of today's diverse classrooms by taking a closer look at a fascinating idea mentioned earlier: Each person is simultaneously gifted and challenged. Howard Gardner's theory of multiple intelligences has become popular with teachers across the nation, especially teachers who are eager to individualize instruction for each child. Gardner (among others) rejects the unitary concept of intelligence, of which each of us has more or less, and proposes instead a plural concept of intelligence. There are, Gardner says, at least seven intelligences—seven ways to be smart—and maybe more. The seven are linguistic, musical, spatial, logical-mathematical, bodily-kinesthetic, interpersonal understanding, and intrapersonal understanding. Additional candidates are naturalist, spiritual, existential, and moral intelligence. But the real point here is not to identify every possible intelligence but, Gardner writes, "to make the case for the *plurality* of intellect."[34] Each of us probably has all of them to one degree or another. Most people eventually develop all the intelligences to a fairly competent level, but some people are gifted in one or more areas and disabled in others. Readers who wish to read about the basic seven as well as the additional "new candidate intelligences" (Gardner's term) are referred to his book, *Intelligence Reframed* (Basic Books, 1999), and Thomas Armstrong's brief *Multiple Intelligences in the Classroom* (ASCD, 2000).

There are many ways to be intelligent in each category. The purpose of gearing activities to multiple intelligences is to tap into each child's current strengths so as to help him or her learn the curriculum, and also to encourage each child to develop strengths in new areas. Traditionally, activities emphasizing linguistic and logical intelligence have predominated in many classrooms. As a consequence, children with these strengths may have been advantaged while other children were not given sufficient opportunities to learn. Remember the red-carpet effect? Here is yet another way to roll out the metaphorical red carpet for each child. Table 2–3 describes eight kinds of intelligence (the basic seven plus one new candidate) and suggests related learning activities in which children might participate.

By individualizing, teachers can help more children achieve greater understanding of the curriculum. The third-grade child who loves to dramatize can be put in charge of a short play about the first meeting of Spaniards and Pueblo Indians in what is today New Mexico, and the child who has not participated much in dramatics can be encouraged to take a role. Another child can head the team that writes (and revises again and again) the script. Second-graders assembling the classroom store can be measuring, writing, and counting. Others can be planning the grand opening ceremony, complete with songs and interviews, with local officials played by classmates.

TABLE 2–3	Teaching students with multiple intelligences.	
Intelligence	**Characteristics**	**Entry Points**
Linguistic	Sensitivity to words, their meanings and functions.	Read and write about it, discuss it.
Musical	Appreciation of musical expression and ability to produce music.	Sing or hum it, drum it or rap it, listen quietly to it, compose it, find out what music has been written to express it.
Spatial	Keen perception of the visual-spatial world and ability to change initial perceptions into other forms.	Map it, draw it, visualize the whole procedure.
Logical–mathematical	Sensitivity to and ability to perceive logical and numerical patterns.	Quantify it, identify the lines of reasoning used, classify it.
Bodily-kinesthetic	Sensitivity to one's body movements and ability to control them.	Dance it, get your hands in it, build it, dramatize it.
Interpersonal	Sensitivity and capacity to respond to other persons' way of being (feelings, moods).	Tutor someone, collaborate with others, discuss it, conduct "oral history" interviews.
Intrapersonal	Access to one's own feelings and moods and the ability to discriminate among and draw on them.	Write about it in a response journal, find personal analogy to it.
Naturalist	Appreciation of the natural world— plants and animals, oceans, the universe.	Observe it closely; put it under a microscope (literally or figuratively); imagine the life of plants and animals.

Source: Adapted from Howard Gardner, *Frames of Mind: The Theory of Multiple Intelligences* (New York: Basic Books, 1983); *Multiple Intelligences: The Theory in Practice* (New York: Basic Books, 1993); *The Disciplined Mind* (New York: Simon & Schuster, 1999); and *Intelligence Reframed* (New York: Basic Books, 1999).

Two cautions about multiple intelligence (MI) theory must be mentioned: trivializing the curriculum and stereotyping children. First, Gardner himself is chagrined to learn that his theory is often "invoked to convey trivial examples, or to present important examples in an offbeat or anecdotal way ('Let's sing our times tables, children!' says the teacher . . .)." MI theory should be invoked instead to present "ideas that are consequential."[35] His worry is that MI theory becomes an end in itself rather than a means to an end. Choose a powerful, mind-expanding curriculum first, he urges. Then think of the multiple intelligences as multiple *entry points* for helping individual students engage and achieve that curriculum. Every child should learn, for example, to use the methods of scientific inquiry to formulate and test hypotheses about the social and natural world. Some children might enter this domain of knowledge through discussion in which they can hear the ideas of one classmate expressed alongside the ideas of another. Other children might enter it by audiotaping war veterans in their family or neighborhood and then interpreting and writing an oral history (see Chapter 4). Others might research the songs of war and peace—both the marches and the laments—while others delve into the mathematics of food production and distribution. The point is this: keep your eye on the prize (a worthy curriculum) and use MI theory (a means) to help children achieve it.

A second caution: MI theory shouldn't be used to peg a child as this or that. "He is a musical learner, she is linguistic, he is kinesthetic, she is a naturalist" and so forth. Quite to the contrary, Gardner emphasizes that we are all gifted and challenged simultaneously. All of us have strengths and weaknesses across the plurality of intelligences in us, to be sure, but nearly all of us become fairly competent in each intelligence area in our lifetimes.[36]

Conclusion

As David Berliner put it, "our children live nested lives." In the formal education system, children are nested in the social role called "student," and in this role they are further nested in classrooms and schools. Outside school, they are nested in the role called "children" and further nested in families and neighborhoods, and places of worship. Across these contexts children are positioned socially in racial and ethnic groups, social class and gender, language and dialect, giftedness and disability, "majority" and "minority" group, and so on. As we have seen, these social classifications are both complicated and connected. I provided six guidelines for teaching in diverse classrooms and emphasized the crucial difference between two views of diversity: understanding and treating children as different and understanding and treating them as deprived.

When teaching in today's diverse classrooms, you will be called on to continually add to your inventory of professional knowledge and skills. As a result, your work should steadily become more rewarding and fulfilling. This makes for a satisfying professional life, and it is just the sort of thing people are leaving other kinds of work to find. You will be stimulated to keep learning about your students and yourself. You will come to better understand your own cultural knapsack. Your students will benefit because they have a teacher who genuinely appreciates them and sees them, who does not shy away from their cultural and individual differences, who does not see their differences as deficits, and who has high expectations for each of them.

When we look into a U.S. public school, one thing we can be sure of is that the children do not share a common ethnic identity, home language, or set of abilities and talents. At parent night, we do not encounter families with a common set of political party preferences, religions, or experiences. With all this diversity is there nothing that unites us? There is. Our most essential common ground is a civic partnership: our shared commitment to the values and principles of constitutional democracy. First among these are the freedoms of religion, speech, and the press, and the commitments to equality and fairness. These stand alongside our commitment to rule by law and the expectation that each person will take seriously the rights and obligations of citizenship, for the alternative is what the ancient Greeks called *idiocy*. This is the focus of the next chapter.

Discussion Questions and Suggested Activities

Go to MyEduca-tionLab and select the topic "Diverse Learners," then analyze the artifact "Winter Break" and complete the activity.

1. Look back at the classroom scene portrayed on page 44 and the question that was asked in the *Reflection* sidebar. Also look again at the Doonesbury cartoon nearby. In both cases, the teacher is female, not male. A female teacher is discriminating against girls and giving more instructional attention to boys. How do you explain this? How typical or atypical do you believe it is, and what is your evidence?

2. Which of the six guidelines for teaching in diverse classrooms will be most useful to you in your first couple of years of teaching? Least?

3. Do you agree with the following statements? Take a position on each one and discuss your reasons with a partner.
   a. "The problem is not that some children are unready for school. Rather, schools too often are unready for children."
   b. "Teachers sometimes treat cultural differences in children as deficits. This is not right, and it is ethnocentric."
   c. "You shouldn't treat a child with a special gift as 'gifted' any more than you would treat a child with a learning disability as 'disabled.'"
   d. "I don't care if they're red, green, or polka dot. I just treat them all like children."

4. NCSS Standards *Sampler*. Examine the first-grade classroom vignette for standard #1 on page 7 of the standards *Sampler* that accompanies this book. How does it compare to the Lesson Plan, "Who are We?," in this chapter? Which do you prefer?

Selected References

American Association of University Women. (2007, March). *Separated by sex: Title IX and single sex education* (position paper on single-sex education). Washington, DC: Author.

Armstrong, Thomas. (2000). *Multiple intelligences in the classroom*. Alexandria, VA: Association for Supervision and Curriculum Development.

Au, Kathryn. (2006). *Multicultural issues and literacy achievement*. Mahwah, NJ: Lawrence Erlbaum.

Banks, James A., & Banks, Cherry A. M. (Eds.). (2007). *Multicultural education: Issues and perspectives* (6th ed.). Hoboken, NJ: John Wiley.

Bayly, Michael J. (2007). *Creating safe environments for LGBT students: A Catholic perspective*. New York: Harrington Park.

Gardner, Howard. (1999). *Intelligence reframed: Multiple intelligences for the 21st century*. New York: Basic Books.

Gay, Geneva. (2000). *Culturally responsive teaching*. New York: Teachers College Press.

Gay, Lesbian, and Straight Education Network (link at www.glsen.org).

Moll, Luis C., Amanti, Cathy, Neff, Deborah, & Gonzales, Norma. (1992). Funds of knowledge for teaching: Using a qualitative approach to connect homes and classrooms. *Theory into Practice 31*(2), 132–141.

Mukhopadhyay, Carol, Henze, Rosemary C., & Moses, Yolanda T. (2007). *How real is race? A sourcebook on race, culture, and biology*. Lanham, MD: Roman & Littlefield.

Pang, Valerie O., & Cheng, Li-Rong L. (Eds.). (1998). *Struggling to be heard: The unmet needs of Asian Pacific American children*. Albany: State University of New York Press.

Sadker, David M., & Silber, Ellen S. (Eds.). (2007). *Gender in the classroom*. Mahwah, NJ: Lawrence Erlbaum.

Shearer, Branton. (2004). Multiple Intelligences theory after 20 years. *Teachers College Record 106* (1), 2–16.

Tatum, Beverly Daniel. (2007). *Can we talk about race?—And other conversations in an era of school resegregation*. Boston: Beacon Press.

Tomlinson, Carol Ann. (2001). *How to differentiate instruction in mixed-ability classrooms* (2nd ed.). Alexandria, VA: Association for Supervision and Curriculum Development.

Ukpokodu, O. (2006). Essential characteristics of a culturally conscientious classroom. *Social Studies and the Young Learner 12* (2), 4–7.

MyEducationLab is a collection of online tools for your success in this course, your licensure exams, and your teaching career. Go to www.myeducationlab.com to utilize these extensive resources including videos from real classrooms, Praxis and licensure preparation, a lesson plan builder, and materials to help you begin your teaching career.

Democratic Citizenship Education

CHAPTER THREE

Key Concepts

- Democratic citizenship
- Allegiance
- Deliberation
- Voting
- Community service and action
- Citizenship knowledge
- Democratic values
- Democratic dispositions and virtues

MAIN IDEA

There can be no democracy without the "we the people" who create it day by day. These people are called democratic citizens, and producing them is a central mission of social studies curriculum and instruction. There are six dimensions of citizenship education. Attending to each will help nurture citizens who can create a better world.

PICTURE THIS

Ms. Paley gathered the kindergartners at the rug area where they have their best discussions. She put up a poster that read, YOU CAN'T SAY "YOU CAN'T PLAY" and asked the children, "Do you think we need this rule in our classroom?" They greeted the idea with disbelief. Hands shot into the air, and here began a long-term inquiry into public life—democratic life beyond family and friendship groups. With two additional questions that she asked often (Will the rule work? Is it fair?), Ms. Paley guided the discussion to issues at the heart of democratic citizenship in a diverse society. These kindergartners are engaged in the supreme act of popular sovereignty, the same as legislators: deliberating public policy.

I magine that you are stranded on a desert island. Having realized that help may never come, you and your shipwrecked friends, acquaintances, and strangers are going to draw up the blueprints for a new society. A number of gatherings are held and gradually you develop some knowledge of the whole group, enough to know that there are significant ethnic, linguistic, and religious differences. Eventually, deliberations turn on three questions: How virtuous (or not) can everyone be expected to be? What arrangements are needed for living together cooperatively and settling the conflicts that inevitably will arise? And how can these arrangements be changed as conditions and beliefs change? Sorting out these issues together, you eventually create a civic partnership—a social contract, a constitution.

Readers who have studied political science will recognize these three questions as the core issues of that field. What they reveal is that democracy is not a perpetual motion system that runs on its own internal fuel supply. Quite the opposite, it is a human invention that must continually be reinvented, one generation instructing the next on how to live together freely and fairly. People become democratic citizens not when they are born in, or move to, a democratic society, but when they participate in this ongoing reinvention of democracy. This is an active—hands, feet, hearts, and minds—definition of democratic citizenship.

Democratic citizenship is the opposite of what the Greeks of ancient Athens called *idiocy*. They defined idiocy to mean selfish. *Idiots* were citizens who paid no attention to the common good. These were people who legally and officially were citizens—they had attained privileged membership in the political community—but then shunned the responsibilities of that role. Instead, they concerned themselves only with themselves: their private lives. They placed personal concerns (their own and their families' needs and wants) far out in front of community concerns and, in this lethal act of imbalance, threatened the freedoms and rights they were so eager to enjoy.

Democratic citizenship education aims to combat "idiocy" by nurturing democratic citizens. It aims to prepare children for a particular kind of civic partnership. Although students will identify with their own ethnic communities, religious beliefs, and family backgrounds, they will share one political identity: democratic citizen. This common political identity exists alongside their multiple cultural identities. This is the meaning of the motto on our coins, *e pluribus unum:* alongside the many, the one.[1] But this co-relationship between diversity (of culture and belief) and unity (common good) is not easy for people to understand. Accordingly, education is critically important. As Thomas Jefferson said in 1787, "their minds must be improved to a certain degree,"[2] and he championed public education for as long as he lived.

The *Sampler* of the NCSS standards that accompanies this text includes "civic ideals and practices" as one of the 10 standards. The first sentence of this standard (#10) reads, "An understanding of civic ideals and practices of citizenship is critical to full participation in society and is a central purpose of the social studies." As this is the central focus of this chapter, please take a moment to read the related performance expectations and classroom vignettes for both the early and middle grades in the *Sampler*.

The first section of this chapter delves into the purpose of democratic citizenship education. The second illustrates the active approach—hands, feet, hearts, mind—to citizenship education favored in this book by looking closely at the normally passive ritual of reciting the

Pledge of Allegiance at school. Two powerful learning activities are provided, one a seminar and the other a simulation. The third section identifies and explains the six dimensions of democratic citizenship education: deliberation, voting, service learning and community action, democratic knowledge, democratic values, and democratic dispositions.

WHY CITIZENSHIP EDUCATION?

Without democratic citizens, there can be no democracy. They are the force that creates and sustains it. But these citizens don't materialize out of thin air. Accordingly, the motivating vision of the public school movement back in the 1840s, stemming in no small way from Jefferson's pleas, was to create these citizens at school and thereby cultivate a public—a "we the people"—that could meet the challenge of self-government. Schools were understood to be ideal places for this work because they are public places to which students come from diverse private worlds.

In democracies the people themselves are expected to be the governors: solving problems and making policy, protecting civil rights, and ensuring the liberty of people to express even unpopular views. This is "government of the people, by the people, and for the people," as Lincoln said at Gettysburg. With each new outbreak of "ethnic cleansing" somewhere in the world, however, with each new hate crime committed in our own communities, with each new poll showing increased apathy and cynicism among the electorate, with each new incursion of private religious doctrine into public government—with each such assault on the democratic ideal we are reminded that democracy is a fragile social system. In fact, so many democracies over the past 2500 years have slipped back into the grip of tyranny (military dictatorship, theocracy, plutocracy, kingdom, police state, etc.) that political scientists are famously pessimistic about its prospects.

It may seem obvious, therefore, that education for democratic citizenship is a worthwhile educational goal. Indeed, most school districts in the United States include it in their mission statements. Yet citizenship education is often overlooked amid the pressure to increase students' scores on academic tests. Also, it is sometimes assumed that the knowledge, values, attitudes, and skills citizens need are by-products of the study of other school subjects. But this is wishful thinking.

In a talk to teachers some years ago, writer and social critic James Baldwin, who was African American and gay, warned that if children are not educated to live democratically, they may well become apathetic or worse: They could become the next generation of people to commit a Holocaust such as the one in Germany in the 1930s and 1940s. Baldwin observed that the perpetrators of these crimes against humanity were very well educated and knew a great deal about reading, writing, literature, math, and science, but in spite of their education, they could not live democratically. They used their knowledge and skill to build not only great works of art and architecture, but concentration camps and a human nightmare. They swore allegiance to a tyrant and committed unimaginable atrocities against humanity. "The boys and girls who were born during the era of the Third Reich," Baldwin said, "when educated to the purposes of the Third Reich, became barbarians."[3]

Democracy requires that we educate children to the ideals of democracy and encourage them to work steadily to transform those ideals into realities. These ideals involve the commitment to democratic values such as limited government, the rule of law, and "liberty and justice for all." They require citizens who can think critically, resolve disputes in nonviolent ways, cooperate with persons they may not like, tolerate religious and political views different from their own, and insist on the free expression of those views— their own and others.

This is a tall order! What can elementary and middle school teachers do? They can do plenty. As Polly Greenberg wrote in the journal *Young Children,* "Democracy is full of problems waiting to be solved." Teachers can encourage children continually to solve small problems cooperatively. They can form the habit of saying to a group of young children, "How can we solve this problem?" "What should we do?" "What's your idea?"[4] Such questions nurture cooperative discussion, decision making, and civic responsibility, which, together, are the basic labor of democracy. Each primary grade classroom should have "the rug." The rug, as elementary school principal Ethel Sadowsky describes it, is "a spot where children gather on the first day of school to formulate the rules that will govern the classroom."[5] Metaphorically, the rug is a town hall—the meeting point for community planning and action. The rug is used throughout the year as a place not only to talk about books, but also *to discuss current problems and concerns.* Below, we call this kind of talk *deliberation.* It is the first of the six dimensions of democratic citizenship education. Listening to what students are complaining about will suggest some problems for deliberation. During playtime: "She never lets me play with them." Teamwork problems: "He never lets anybody else talk!" Justice issues: "It's not fair that the row closest to the door always gets to the playground first." Curriculum issues: "Can we study something else?"

Aside from deliberations on classroom and playground problems, there is a great deal to be learned *about* democracy, as we shall see. A substantial focal point occurs in the fifth grade when children typically are introduced to the *Constitution of the United States.* Many teachers incorporate the Constitution into their teaching and classroom management systems long before the fifth grade, but it is usually in this grade that children are helped to read and interpret the Constitution. This is an important moment in the political socialization of the next generation, for the Constitution spells out the nation's partnership— our formal agreements about how to cooperate and settle conflicts, our social contract.

A paraphrased version of the U.S. Constitution is usually included in fifth-grade textbooks and is included here on the following pages. Readers will note that it contains all the parts: the preamble, the 7 articles containing the rules by which citizens agree to live, and 27 changes or additions, called amendments. The first 10 amendments together are called the Bill of Rights.

ACTIVE AND PASSIVE CITIZENSHIP EDUCATION: THE CASE OF THE PLEDGE

There is general consensus in constitutional democracies that citizens need to be educated to understand and participate in majority rule, respect minority rights, care for the common good, protect one another's freedoms, and limit the size and reach of government. Still,

Summary of the Constitution of the United States

PREAMBLE

We, the People of the United States, in Order to form a more perfect Union, establish Justice, insure domestic Tranquility, provide for the common Defense, promote the general Welfare, and secure the blessings of Liberty to ourselves and our Posterity, do ordain and establish this Constitution for the United States of America.

This is the meaning of the Preamble:

The people of the United States made the Constitution for the following reasons: (1) to set up a stronger government and a more united nation than the one that existed under the Articles of Confederation: (2) to ensure peace and justice among the people: (3) to defend the nation against enemies: (4) to help ensure the well-being of all the people, and (5) to make sure that the people of this nation will always be free.

ARTICLE 1 LEGISLATIVE BRANCH

Section 1: The Congress

The legislative branch, or Congress, makes the nation's laws. It is made up of two houses—the Senate and the House of Representatives.

Section 2: The House of Representatives

Members of the House of Representatives are elected for two-year terms. A representative must be at least 25 years old, a citizen of the United States for at least 7 years, and live in the state he or she represents.

The number of representatives a state has depends on the state's population. In order to find out how many people live in each state, the government must do a count of the population every ten years. This count is called a census.

Section 3: The Senate

The Senate is made up of two senators from each state. Each senator is elected for a six-year term. A senator must be at least 30 years old, a citizen of the United States for at least 9 years, and live in the state he or she represents.

The Vice President of the United States is in charge of the Senate but may vote only if there is a tie.

Sections 4–6: Rules

The houses of Congress set their own rules for their members. Each house must keep a record of its meetings and how each member voted.

To make sure that there is complete freedom of discussion in Congress, senators and representatives cannot be arrested for things they say while doing their jobs.

Section 7: How a Bill Becomes a Law

A suggested law, or bill, becomes a law when both houses of Congress agree to it by a majority vote and when the President signs it. If the President vetoes, or rejects, the bill, it can still become a law if both houses of Congress approve it again by a two-thirds vote.

Section 8: Powers of Congress

The powers of Congress include the power to: collect taxes; borrow money; control trade with other countries and among the states; decide how foreigners can become citizens; coin money; set up post offices; set up courts; declare war; set up an army and a navy; make all laws necessary to carry out powers granted to the government.

Section 9: Powers Denied to Congress and the States

There are certain powers that Congress and the states do not have. Congress cannot, for example, spend money without telling how the money will be spent. The states cannot make treaties with other countries or coin money.

ARTICLE 2 EXECUTIVE BRANCH

Section 1: President and Vice President

The President and Vice President head the executive branch. Along with the people who work with them, their job is to carry out the laws made by Congress. They are elected for four-year terms.

The President and Vice President must be natural-born citizens and at least 35 years old, and must have lived in the United States for at least 14 years.

Sections 2–4: Power and Duties

The President's powers and duties include: commanding the armed forces; appointing government officials; reaching agreements with other countries; and pardoning crimes. At least once a year, the President must tell Congress how the nation is doing. This is called the President's State of the Union message.

A President who commits a serious crime may be removed from office.

ARTICLE 3 JUDICIAL BRANCH

Section 1: Federal Courts

The judicial branch is made up of the Supreme Court and all other federal, or United States, courts. Federal judges are appointed for life.

Section 2: Duties

The judicial branch has the power to decide the meaning of the Constitution. It may decide if the actions of the other two branches are unconstitutional, or go against the Constitution.

Federal courts have a say in many cases, such as those having to do with the Constitution, federal laws, or disagreements between citizens from different states.

Section 3: Treason

Treason is a crime committed when a citizen of the United States betrays the country, especially in wartime.

ARTICLE 4 THE STATES

Sections 1–4: Dealings Among the States

All states must accept the actions, records, and court decisions of other states. When citizens visit another state, they must be given the same rights as citizens of the states they are visiting.

New states may be added to the United States. The United States government promises to protect the states from enemies.

ARTICLE 5 AMENDMENTS

The Constitution may be amended, or changed, if Congress and three fourths of the states agree.

ARTICLE 6 SUPREME LAW, OATHS OF OFFICE, DEBTS

The Constitution of the United States is the supreme law, or the highest law, in the nation. Government officials must promise to support the Constitution. In addition, the government promised to pay back all debts owed before the Constitution was adopted.

ARTICLE 7 APPROVING THE CONSTITUTION

The Constitution was to become law when 9 of 13 original states ratified, or approved, it. Special conventions were held for this purpose, and the process took nine months to complete.

AMENDMENTS TO THE CONSTITUTION

(The first 10 are called The Bill of Rights)

AMENDMENT 1

Freedom of Religion, Speech, Press, Assembly, and Petition (1791)

Congress cannot make a law setting up an official religion. It cannot stop people from practicing any religion they choose. Congress cannot take away freedom of speech or of the press. Congress cannot stop groups from assembling, or meeting together, peacefully. It cannot stop people from petitioning, or asking the government, to end an injustice.

AMENDMENT 2

Right to Keep Arms (1791)
  The people have the right to keep and carry arms, or weapons.

AMENDMENT 3

Quartering Soldiers (1791)
  During peacetime, people cannot be forced to quarter soldiers, or let them stay in their homes.

AMENDMENT 4

Search and Seizures (1791)
  People's homes and other property cannot be searched and seized unless the police have a search warrant.

AMENDMENT 5

Rights of Accused Persons (1791)
  People who are accused of a crime cannot be forced to testify, or give evidence, against themselves. Their lives, freedom, or property cannot be taken away from them unfairly. The government may take a person's property for public use only if the person is paid for it.

AMENDMENT 6

Jury Trial in Criminal Cases (1791)
  People accused of crimes have the right to a public and speedy trial with a jury. They have the right to be told the charges against them. They have the right to have a lawyer.

AMENDMENT 7

Jury Trial in Civil Cases (1791)
  In most civil, or noncriminal, cases, people have the right to a jury trial.

AMENDMENT 8

Excessive Bail or Punishment (1791)
  Bail must be reasonable for people accused of a crime. Punishments may not be cruel and unusual.

AMENDMENT 9

Other Rights of the People (1791)
  The people have rights in addition to those listed in the Constitution.

AMENDMENT 10

Powers of the States and the People (1791)
  Powers that are not granted to the national government and not forbidden to the states are left to the state governments or to the people.

AMENDMENT 11

Suing the States (1798)
  A state government can be sued only in its own courts.

AMENDMENT 12

Election of President and Vice President (1804)
  Electors vote for President and Vice President on separate ballots.

AMENDMENT 13

Abolition of Slavery (1865)
  Slavery is abolished, or made illegal, in the United States.

AMENDMENT 14

Rights of Citizens (1868)
  Every citizen of the United States is also a citizen of the state in which he or she lives. No state may pass a law limiting the rights of citizens or take away a person's life, liberty, or property unfairly. Every person must be treated equally under the law.

AMENDMENT 15

Voting Rights
　　No person may be denied the right to vote because of race.

AMENDMENT 16

Income Tax (1913)
　　Congress has the right to tax people's incomes.

AMENDMENT 17

Direct Election of Senators (1913)
　　United States senators are elected directly by the people of their states.

AMENDMENT 18

Prohibition (1919)
　　The manufacture or transport of liquor is prohibited, or banned, in the United States.

AMENDMENT 19

Women's Voting Rights (1920)
　　Women cannot be denied the right to vote.

AMENDMENT 20

Terms of Office (1933)
　　The President and Vice President take office on January 20. Senators and representatives take office on January 3.

AMENDMENT 21

Repeal of Prohibition (1933)
　　Amendment 18 is repealed, or ended.

AMENDMENT 22

Two-Term Limit for Presidents (1951)
　　A President may serve only two terms in office.

AMENDMENT 23

Presidential Elections for District of Columbia (1961)
　　People who live in Washington, D.C., have the right to vote for President and Vice President.

AMENDMENT 24

Poll Tax (1964)
　　No citizen may be made to pay a tax in order to vote for President, Vice President, senator, or representative.

AMENDMENT 25

Presidential Succession and Disability (1967)
　　If a President leaves office before the end of term, the Vice President becomes President. If the Vice President leaves office, the President suggests a person to fill the job and Congress must approve. If the President becomes too ill to do the job, the Vice President becomes Acting President until the President recovers.

AMENDMENT 26

Voting Age (1971)
　　Citizens who are at least 18 years old have the right to vote.

AMENDMENT 27

Congressional Salaries (1992)
　　Congress cannot change its salary until after the next congressional election.

Source: Reproduced with the permission of the McGraw-Hill Companies from *The United States and Its Neighbors*, J. A. Banks et al., Macmillan/McGraw-Hill, 1995.

wide leeway is left to teachers. Some conceptualize the citizen role mainly as one of compliance with authorities. Accordingly, they teach courteousness and obedience. Other teachers define the role in broader, more active and political terms. They teach students that it is their civic duty to vote regularly and only after informing themselves, to participate in civic decision making, and to engage in public service.

This book recommends the second, more active approach. In this section, we examine a very ordinary civic ritual that occurs in thousands of schools daily: reciting the Pledge of Allegiance. We contrast the passive memorization and recitation of the Pledge with an active, shared inquiry into its meanings. But first, a brief history of the Pledge.

When schoolchildren in the United States recite the *Pledge of Allegiance*, they are immersed in a powerful civic ritual. They are standing, they are facing the flag, and they are (nowadays—see the historical photos) placing their right hand over their heart. Then they say aloud some words in which loyalty is promised to a symbol (the flag), a nation (the United States of America), a democratic way of living together (a "republic"), and certain ideals ("liberty and justice for all"). That's a big promise! This pledge was formally recognized by the federal government in 1942 and amended with "under God" in 1954. The recitation of the Pledge in schools is required by law in most of the 50 states, and the number increased after the terrorist attacks of September 11, 2001.

The U.S. Pledge of Allegiance has a long history that reflects the changing hopes and fears of the nation. It was penned in 1892 by a former Baptist minister from Boston named Francis Bellamy. When he wrote the Pledge, Bellamy was working for a popular magazine called *Youth's Companion,* which was busily selling flags to schools across the country. The 400th anniversary of Columbus's landing was at hand and was to be commemorated in a nationwide Columbus Day public school celebration at which students would raise the U.S. flag over their school. A suitable oath was needed, and Bellamy wrote these 23 words.

> I pledge allegiance to my flag and to the republic for which it stands—one nation indivisible—with liberty and justice for all.

The oath and the schoolhouse flag movement were immediately controversial. Critics found such flag-raising and flag-waving to be a dangerous combination of superficiality and chauvinism. An editorial in the *Nation* magazine in 1906 expressed this view:

> The truth is that love of country, in the high and proper sense, cannot be taught. It is commanded by the country which deserves it. Give men justice, freedom, and equal treatment before the law, and you do more than all possible schools and schoolmasters to intensify their national love for land and kind. Try to stimulate this by hothouse methods, and you make patriotism artificial and false, an idle name; you stifle the noblest kind of love for country.... It is not shouting for the old flag ..., it is doing justice and loving mercy.[6]

The Pledge has taken two additional forms since the 1892 version was published by *Youth's Companion.* Each change increased the length of the Pledge from the original 23 words and altered its meaning in interesting and historic ways. Both alterations were made during periods of high national anxiety. The first was made after World War I when the nation was still traumatized by that horrific war and gripped by fear of communists and new immigrants. This first change clarified the object of allegiance by changing "my flag" (critics complained it could mean any flag) to "the flag of the United States of America."

The second change occurred during the post–World War II period called the "cold war" between the United States and its wartime ally, the U.S.S.R. (Union of Soviet Socialist Republics). Again, the nation was gripped by fear of communism and immigration, but now also of atheism and nuclear war. On Flag Day, June 14, 1954, a new Pledge with the controversial "under God" clause was rolled out. As Richard Ellis tells us in his fascinating history, *To The Flag: The Unlikely History of the Pledge of Allegiance,* President Eisenhower signed a bill early that day making the new wording the law of the land. Later that morning, a new flag donated by the American Legion was raised over the Capitol building. Assembled House and Senate officials recited the new Pledge of Allegiance, and then "a bugle rang out with the familiar strains of 'Onward, Christian Soldiers!' The 'stirring event,' in the words of Walter Cronkite, was televised live by CBS and broadcast nationwide on the network's morning show."[7]

A Changing Pledge

I pledge allegiance to **my flag** and to the republic for which it stands—one nation indivisible—with liberty and justice for all.	*1892*	23 words
I pledge allegiance to **the flag of the United States of America** and to the republic for which it stands, one nation, indivisible, with liberty and justice for all.	*1924*	29 words
I pledge allegiance to the flag of the United States of America and to the republic for which it stands, one nation **under God**, indivisible, with liberty and justice for all.	*1954*	31 words

This particular pledge is only one of many promises of civic loyalty that can be imagined. Notice that across its changes it has remained a *national* pledge—a promise of loyalty to a nation. But now that globalization is making the world steadily more interdependent, and now that global warming is making clear the shared fate of humans, the idea of teaching students that they are world citizens (what the ancient Greeks and Romans termed *cosmopolitans*) is gaining adherents. Why should we be more inclined to pledge allegiance to people who dwell in a certain nation, namely *our* nation, but not when they dwell in another nation, say Nigeria, Peru, or China? "What is it about the national boundary," asks the philosopher Martha Nussbaum, "that magically converts people toward whom we are both incurious and indifferent into people to whom we have duties of mutual respect?"[8] Don't we undercut the case for multicultural respect when we fail to make the case for a broader, worldwide respect? Don't we also undercut humanity's ability to solve worldwide problems when we train children to draw the boundary of their loyalty so close to home? Educators are increasingly asking *to which portion of humanity should teachers encourage students' allegiance?* Should students in school learn that they are, above all, citizens of a particular nation (the United States or Canada or Chile), or should they learn instead that they are, above all, citizens of the world? (We will revisit this question in the second end-of-chapter question.)

Seminars on the Pledge

One way to help your students to be actively thoughtful about the Pledge rather than only recite it passively is to lead a "seminar" on it. A seminar is a mind-expanding discussion of a text of some sort (e.g., a story, letter, oath, photo, painting). Its purpose is to help children achieve a bigger and better understanding of its meanings than they could reading it alone and without discussion. Readers will find more details on how to lead seminars in Chapter 12, "The Literacy–Social Studies Connection." But for now suffice it to say that the teacher opens a seminar by stating the purpose, clarifying the rules of participation, and asking an interpretive question—one that gets participants to *think* about the text. Unlike a literal question, it has no one correct answer. Instead, interpretation is needed and, consequently, different students will have different things to say. Seminars accomplish their purpose because one's own view of the text is placed alongside the views of other participants and, in this way, each participant's thinking is "fertilized" by the thinking of others. If the seminar proceeds in a diverse group of students and with a teacher who is a skilled discussion leader, so much the better: Each child's interpretation is likely to grow more complex.

I have led nearly 100 seminars on the Pledge with students and with teachers, administrators, and professors. Typically my opening interpretive question—with all ages—is this one: When people say this, what are they pledging their allegiance to?

I learn something new in each seminar. Mainly, I have learned that while many natural-born citizens have recited it daily in school and may even know it "by heart," few have seriously given thought to its meaning or evaluated the whole idea of promising loyalty to one group of people but not another. Participants typically say they've not done this before; they have been putting their hands to their hearts and promising something they have not thought much about. Three arguments typically unfold in seminars on the Pledge, some philosophical and others semantic.

First, and most important to many adult participants, is the phrase "under God" and what it does to the text when it is present or (as before 1954) absent. The mixing of theism and nationalism—God and country—evokes a torrent of opinion among older students and adults. They not only disagree about what the phrase does to the Pledge but whether it belongs in a national oath in a democracy where church and state are separate versus a theocracy, such as Iran, where they are joined.[9]

Second, to *what* are we pledging allegiance when we recite it? To the flag, say some. "It says so right there in the first line." To the nation, say others. No, "to the republic," say others, pointing both to the "and" and to the words "for which it (the flag) stands." Does this argument matter? It does, because only one of these is an idea about how to live with one another. Nazis and Romans pledged allegiance to a person (Heil Hitler, Hail Caesar), countless others have pledged allegiance to a plot of land ("land where my fathers died"). But "to the republic" signals something different: loyalty to the ideals of constitutional democracy.

Then there's that final phrase, "with liberty and justice for all." Now the argument turns on what *kind* of statement this is. Is it a *description* or an *ideal*? Does the phrase point to a reality or an aspiration? On this question the argument runs deep, and for good reason: One side suggests that the citizen's job is to *protect* democracy (because it has been accomplished); the other, that the citizen's job is to *achieve* it (because it has not). "These are our hopes for the future," a fifth-grade girl said. "We aren't there yet."

Listening to these discussions, it has become clear to me that rote recitation without interpretative discussion is a ritual but not an *education*. I am not making a case for or against reciting the Pledge, but for thinking about its meanings and the issues it raises, and for doing so with others. Beginning in about the third or fourth grade, seminars on the Pledge can be mind-expanding opportunities for students and wonderful assessment opportunities for teachers.

Simulating a Naturalization Ceremony

Another creative way for the class to think about the meaning of allegiance and democratic citizenship is to simulate a naturalization ceremony. When newcomers to the United States decide they want to become citizens, they must apply to the U.S. government. The process is called *naturalization,* and its culminating event is a swearing-in ceremony at which the applicants formally become citizens. At this ceremony, they make two promises: the first is the Oath of Allegiance. This is an even more difficult vow to comprehend than the Pledge— its vocabulary is technical and rare. In it, they formally renounce their loyalty to the country they are leaving. The second is the Pledge of Allegiance. Here they promise loyalty to the new country. Before this ceremony takes place, each applicant is required to pass a number of tests—of reading and writing ability, ability to understand English, and knowledge of some basic facts about democratic citizenship.

Children should attend a public naturalization ceremony, if at all possible, and prepare for it with seminars on the Oath and the Pledge and by practicing the citizenship test. In advance of the field trip or afterward, the ceremony can be simulated in the classroom.

1. *Preparing for the simulation.* The teacher explains that the class is going to simulate (pretend to have) the ceremony in which immigrants become citizens of the United States. The purpose is to better understand the naturalization experience from the perspective of participants, to learn what they must learn in order to become citizens, and to think about the meaning of democratic citizenship. The teacher then assigns and clarifies everyone's role: judge, citizenship test-giver, citizens-to-be, family members present as spectators and supporters. Some training and practice will be needed for each role. Props are distributed to make the simulation both fun and realistic: a gavel and robe for the judge, for example, and small flags for the new citizens. Some of the audience members are holding babies (dolls) and others are costumed in the traditional clothing of their native lands.

    Students will need to practice for the citizenship test. Make a copy of a portion of the practice test for your students. (Note: The citizenship test is occasionally revised. Check the U.S. Citizenship and Immigration Services website at www.uscis.gov for updates and study materials.) The teacher can invite a recently naturalized citizen to class and have this guest tell about studying for the test and lead a practice session with students.

2. *Simulating the ceremony.*
    a. The presiding "judge" asks the applicants to introduce themselves and tell where they are from and why they want to become U.S. citizens.
    b. The judge calls on another student who is playing the role of the test giver, who administers the citizenship test orally. This can be done in teams (as in a spelling

bee), in writing, or in a large group where the test giver asks one question of each applicant. For example:

- Why does the U.S. flag have 13 stripes?
- What do the colors mean?
- What is the Constitution?
- What are the three branches of government?
- How old must you be to vote?

   c. "Applicants" who pass the test proceed to reciting the Oath of Allegiance and then the Pledge of Allegiance. The judge should read a few words, and then the participants repeat them, until both loyalty statements have been recited.

3. *Debriefing the simulation.* The teacher ends the simulation and debriefs it with students. "Tell me one thing you learned in our simulation" is a good prompt. Listen carefully. This is an important assessment opportunity.

Take a minute now to examine the photos, pledges, and oaths on the color pages in this chapter. Both historical and comparative views are provided.

CITIZENSHIP EDUCATION: SIX DIMENSIONS

We turn now to six facets of a proper education for living together freely and fairly. The first is deliberation. In the early elementary grades, children are brought often to the rug to discuss shared problems and concerns and to help decide the rules by which they will agree to live in the classroom. In intermediate and middle grades, the rug is replaced with a class meeting. It is the shared decision making about something that matters to each person in the group—civic discourse about a rule that will be binding on all—that teaches the citizenship lessons in this case.

This approach means also that young persons are taught about voting (dimension 2). Voting is a powerful public act, both symbolically and literally. It connects the voter to the broader political community that lies beyond one's smaller cultural communities (religious and ethnic groups, racial and linguistic groups, family and occupational groups, one's neighborhood, etc.). The act of voting helps create and sustain the citizen identity that must exist alongside these other identities. And, of course, one's own vote has literal consequences for everyone else: legislators and presidents are elected or defeated; conservative or liberal Supreme Court justices are appointed; ballot initiatives are voted up or down; schools get more or less funding.

The power a citizen exercises in the act of voting, however, should be guided by knowledge (dimension 4), democratic values (dimension 5), democratic dispositions (dimension 6), and the voter's own experiences in community action (dimension 3). Children need to begin developing all of these in kindergarten. Even community action, such as participating in canned food drives, simple as it is, gives children the opportunity to care for people they do not know, yet to whom they are related as members of the same community.

These, then, are the basic dimensions of democratic citizenship education, six fronts in the battle against the cruelty of which Baldwin reminded us (see Figure 3–1). We explore each in the following sections. The first—deliberation—gets the most attention because it is the most basic and because so much of its foundation can be laid in the primary grades and then elaborated in the intermediate and middle grades.

FIGURE 3–1   Dimensions of democratic citizenship education.

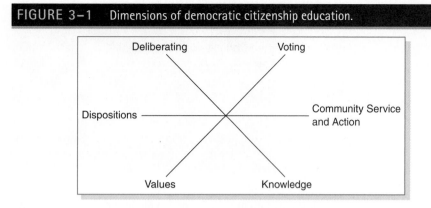

Deliberation: Discussion and Decision Making

> "After lots of talk, we decide on our rules."
> —*Gretchen Calkins, third-grader*

Deliberation is discussion for the purpose of making a decision that will be binding on everyone. From the Latin *libra*, for "scale," deliberation means "to weigh," as in weighing all the alternatives to make the best decision. Deliberation involves discussion because the alternatives are weighed with other people. That way, one's own opinion about the alternatives can be examined alongside others' opinions and, if participants are open- and fair-minded, the group can challenge one another's views and, in time, forge a decision about what to do. Deliberation, then, relies on discussion, but not just any discussion; the discussion is about what "we" should do. For example, a classroom decides on a playground rule, a community decides where to locate a park, or a play group decides how to share toys more fairly.

Deliberation is probably the most important foundation of democratic citizenship. Contrary to sayings such as "talk is cheap" or "actions speak louder than words," deliberation should be appreciated as a wonderful and constructive alternative to violence. Compared to fighting—whether over toys, territory, taunts, or friends—talking things over is the nonviolent bridge of choice. When children learn to talk through their disagreements on the playground and in the classroom, and later at work and on committees, by explaining, listening, negotiating, compromising, and forgiving, they are making significant progress toward democratic citizenship. The ancient Greeks, who were the first to experiment with democratic living, were in awe of the power of discussion. Athenian leader Pericles said, "Instead of seeing discussion as a stumbling block in the way of action, we think it an indispensable preliminary to any wise action at all."[10] Discussion is not merely better than fighting; discussion leads to *wise action*.

Deliberation skills do not necessarily develop on their own; they need to be taught, practiced, and learned. Teachers can let children know that when they are brought to the rug, they need to practice the skills of good discussion. These can be posted:

DISCUSSION SKILLS

Listen as well as talk.

Encourage others to participate.

Criticize ideas but not people.

Support opinions with reasons.

Weigh alternatives.

These skills can be taught using a good skills-teaching procedure involving instruction and role-playing, such as the one presented in Chapter 9. Let us look now at two well-known teachers of social studies in the elementary school and how they make deliberation a regular part of classroom life. In brief, they orchestrate their students' deliberations around classroom rule making.

Rather than posting rules, they opt for a more active approach: These teachers prefer to elicit them (draw them out) from students. Tarry Lindquist, for example, describes her method of elicitation:

> I often start out in September by asking the class to brainstorm all the things we could do to make our classroom a terrible place, a place where no one would want to come, a place where we could guarantee no learning would occur.
>
> As we list the surefire ways to kill a classroom, each suggestion more outrageous than the last, we begin to build a community. Eventually, when we have exhausted our efforts, most sincere and many hilarious, I ask the class to picture a room like the one we've just described. I ask them, "What would you know if you stayed in a classroom like that one all year? What would you be able to do? How would you feel?" After that discussion, it doesn't take long to reverse the list, identifying what needs to happen to make our classroom a place of joy where all students want to be and where all students can learn.[11]

Ms. Lindquist goes on to create with her students a sort of constitution—a social contract, an action plan for a peaceful classroom. After much discussion and decision making, the plan is finalized. Each child signs it, as does Ms. Lindquist. She sends a copy home. When misbehavior occurs, she can communicate with children and parents with the rule book in mind. "Do you recall the action plan we signed at the beginning of the year?" she might say to parents. "I am concerned that Nancy doesn't seem to be able to help the class reach this goal. Specific things about Nancy's behavior that have prompted my concern are. . . ." Ms. Lindquist can now describe the behavior problem by referring to specific agreements written in the plan, such as "we are respectful of others" and "we listen and pay attention."

Another mentor on the art of conducting rich discussions with even the youngest children is the renowned Chicago kindergarten teacher Vivian Paley. Ms. Paley's approach is sometimes to post a rule for interaction, sometimes to elicit it from students, but most often to *propose* a rule. She tells her children a rule she is considering, not one she has decreed, and then engages them in an ongoing deliberation about the rule. The inquiry may last for months and focuses on two questions: Will the rule work? Is it fair? These questions are compelling ones for the children. They have memories and opinions immediately.

Classroom democracy at work. *(Anthony Magnacca/Merrill)*

My favorite example of this process is when Ms. Paley informed her class that she was considering a new classroom rule. She put up a poster that read, YOU CAN'T SAY "YOU CAN'T PLAY." It was greeted with disbelief, she recalls. "Only four out of twenty-five in my kindergarten class find the idea appealing, and they are the children most often rejected. The loudest in opposition are those who do the most rejecting. But everyone looks doubtful. . . ."[12]

Ms. Paley's approach to classroom discussion of rules is an elegant combination of two techniques: (1) she brings her students to the circle often to discuss a new rule she is considering; (2) she interviews older children to ascertain their views and then brings these views back to her kindergartners who, of course, are terribly impressed that their issues are of such interest to the older children.

Ms. Paley began one discussion with her students this way: "I just can't get the question out of my mind. Is it fair for children in school to keep another child out of play? After all, this classroom belongs to all of us. It is not a private place, like our homes."[13] Notice here that Ms. Paley discourages "idiocy" directly. She communicates that the classroom is a civic or public place and that how we conduct ourselves in such a place is different. *In public places, we have to be concerned with the common good, not just private interests.* We are obliged to act with civility, to be civic-minded. "The children I teach are just emerging from life's deep wells of private perspective: babyhood and family," she says. Selfishness and jealousy are natural to both conditions. "Then, along comes school. It is the first real exposure to the public arena."[14]

Indeed, this is why deliberation is important. Discussion is a civic practice that introduces children to ways of behaving that are imperative if we are to have, as the Constitution calls it, "domestic tranquility," or what Ms. Lindquist's class calls, simply, "peace."

Ms. Paley: Should one child be allowed to keep another child from joining a group? A good rule might be: "You can't say 'You can't play.' "

Ben: If you cry, people should let you in.

Ms. Paley: What if someone is not crying but feels sad? Should the teacher force children to say yes?

Many Voices: No, no.

Sheila: If they don't want you to play, they should just go their own way and you should say, "Clara, let's find someone who likes you better."

Angelo: Lisa and her (Sheila) should let Clara in. . . .[15]

REFLECTION

Ms. Paley is *proposing* a new rule to her kindergartners, which she leverages into a serious civic discussion lasting many days. On what other rules could a discussion be sustained over many days with such interest and immediacy?

Soon, Ms. Paley trades classes with a second-grade teacher for a little while. She asks those children's opinions about her class's plan. "I've come to ask your opinions about a new rule we're considering in the kindergarten. . . . We call it, YOU CAN'T SAY "YOU CAN'T PLAY." These older children know full well the issue she is talking about. Examples and some vivid accounts of rejection spill from their mouths. They are fully engaged in the discussion because it is a problem that they both recognize and feel. Many children believe it is a fair rule, but that it just will not work: "It would be impossible to have any fun," offers one boy.

Later, while interviewing a fourth-grade class, she hears these students conclude that it is "too late" in their lives to give them such a rule. "If you want a rule like that to work, start at a very early age," declares one fourth-grader. "Yeah, start it in kindergarten," someone says. "Because they'll believe you that it's a rule. You know, a law."[16]

Ms. Paley takes these views back to the discussion circle in her own classroom. Her children listen, enthralled, to her retelling of the older children's thinking. They often revise their opinions as a consequence of hearing one another's arguments. In the Socratic spirit, gently, Ms. Paley is forever challenging them to develop their own opinions, to support their views with reasons, and to *listen carefully and respond to the reasoning of other children, classmates, and older children alike.*

Listening to Diverse Views

This last detail is important: children must listen carefully to the *reasoning* of classmates. Why does this matter? A good discussion about an engaging problem with a diverse group of children stimulates cognitive growth (growth in children's ability to *reason*), and it is more likely to have this effect if each child (a) encounters and (b) listens to and grapples

The old salute, 1899.

(Photo by Frances Benjamin Johnston, courtesy of the Library of Congress)

The newer salute, 1941.

(Photo by John Vachon, courtesy of the Library of Congress)

Today's salute, 1942, prior to incarceration of Japanese American children.

(Photo attributed to Dorothea Lange, courtesy of the Library of Congress)

I pledge allegiance to the Flag
of the United States of America
and to the Republic for which it stands,
one Nation under God,
indivisible,
with liberty and justice for all.

Today's salute, 1958, segregated classroom.

(Photo by Dick DeMarsico, courtesy of the Library of Congress)

In Singapore, the salute is a closed fist placed over the heart. Notice the differences between the two pledges.

(Photos by Raymond Bong, Rosyth School, Singapore, 2007)

We,
the citizens of Singapore,
pledge ourselves
as one united people,
regardless of race,
language or religion,
to build
a democratic society
based on justice
and equality
so as to achieve happiness,
prosperity and progress
for our nation.

The daily raising of the national flag at Rosyth School.

PLEDGING ALLEGIANCE

"International schools" are cropping up across the United States today. Pictured here is John Stanford International School, a public elementary school in Seattle. From the outside, the appearance of this old but well-maintained building is normal. But on the inside, the look and feel of the school are something different: Flags of many nations hang in the hallways, and guests are welcomed in many languages. Every student studies at least two languages. What else would you like to see happening in an "international school"?

(Photos by Steven Camicia)

"LET'S FACE IT, WE'RE NOTHING BUT A PUPPET GOVERNMENT."

(Reprinted with permission of Dave Carpenter)

with reasoning that is different from and, in comprehensible ways, challenges his or her own.[17] Teachers, therefore, should encourage all children to speak during discussions, giving both their opinions (i.e., a decision or position) and reasons (i.e., a justification for that decision or position). Just as important, teachers should help all children listen carefully to one another's opinions and reasons. Asking children regularly to paraphrase what others have said is a good way to build the listening habit. "Brandon, what was Neetha saying to the group?" "Jamal, were you listening as Myrna gave her reasons? Will you restate them for us, please?" Also, when two children share the same opinion but have different reasons, help the class notice this: "You two seem to agree that we should create a map of the cafeteria, not the library, but for different reasons. Who else agrees, but for a still different reason?"

Discussions of this sort help children develop their capacity to reason about moral issues. This is extremely important because democratic life requires a well-developed sense of what adults call justice (children call it fairness). To treat others as you yourself would wish to be treated if you were in their situation is hailed as the supreme level of moral maturity in the world's religions. One way to help children move in this direction is to engage them in discussions of fairness issues of all sorts, especially those involving rules that apply to all class members, as did Lindquist and Paley. Within these deliberations, teachers can help children listen to and grapple with reasoning that is different from their own. This is the kind of discussion that helps to produce wise action.

Assessing Discussion

An entire chapter is devoted to assessment later in this book, but it should be helpful to look at this matter now in the context of deliberation and citizenship education. As teachers plan how they will find out (assess) what students have learned about a topic or skill, they must think about levels of proficiency, or the *criteria* by which a performance can be judged. These criteria also serve as the objectives of instruction. Let's see what this means.

Social studies educators in Michigan have carefully examined this issue and developed a guide for assessing the quality of a child's participation in discussions of civic issues.[18] A civic issue is a public issue—an issue that "we the people" face in common. Public issues range from simple matters, such as how we behave toward one another in a classroom and whether we have a rule that you can't exclude classmates from your play, to major policy issues that confront our communities today: Who is responsible for the poor? Are affirmative action policies fair? How much individual freedom, and whose, should be limited for the sake of national security? Should students be tested for drug use before they can play team sports? What can be done about hate crimes? Teenage pregnancy? Homelessness?

The Michigan assessment emphasizes two sets of criteria for teaching and assessing discussion, one substantive (the "what") and one procedural (the "how"). The substantive dimension refers to what children contribute to the discussion—the knowledge and information they bring to it and their ability to support opinions with reasons and analogies. The procedural dimension indicates how children participate—whether they invite others to contribute, for example, or make negative statements that inhibit others from participating. Figure 3–2 lists the substantive and procedural guidelines, and Table 3–1 arranges these into four levels of quality. An unacceptable performance in a discussion would mean that on the substantive dimension a child remained silent or made only irrelevant comments, and on the procedural dimension, the child made no comments to help the conversation along or made statements that lacked civility—they were negative in character.

A highly skillful contribution to the group discussion, on the other hand, is characterized by a child's making no comments that inhibit other students' participation and intervening if others do this. Moreover, the child engages in sustained dialogue with others, both talking and listening. On the substantive side, the skillful deliberator weighs multiple perspectives and considers what is best for everyone—*the common good*. Moreover, this child uses higher-order participation skills, such as drawing analogies and summarizing what has been said.

Teachers use this scoring guide to assess their students' current discussion abilities and, just as important, to help plan instruction. Perhaps a teacher will decide to teach the difference between positive and negative comments, followed by a lesson on how to encourage other children to participate and how to respond constructively to ideas they offer. Assessment guides of this sort, called scoring rubrics or rating scales, can be enormously helpful in planning instruction.

A much simpler discussion rating scale is shown in Figure 3–3. Teachers in the primary grades may wish to use this scale as may teachers in the intermediate grades until they become more adept at clarifying with children the more ambitious discussion guidelines used in Figure 3–2. In Chapter 7, "Assessing Student Learning," you will learn to use such guides as *both* a tool for assessing (measuring, determining) the discussion skills of your students *and* a tool for teaching them precisely what good discussion "looks like." By clarifying the target (the objective or goal) of teaching and learning, both teachers and students know what they are aiming for. Sometimes this is called "backward design." It means that good

FIGURE 3–2   Performance criteria for discussing public issues.

THE SUBSTANTIVE DIMENSION
+ States and identifies issues
+ Brings knowledge to the discussion
+ Specifies claims or definitions
+ Elaborates statements with explanations, reasons, and
  evidence
+ Recognizes values or value conflict
+ Argues by analogy

THE PROCEDURAL DIMENSION
Positive
+ Acknowledges the statements of others
+ Challenges the accuracy, logic, relevance, or clarity of
  statements
+ Summarizes points of agreement and disagreement
+ Invites contributions from others

Negative
− Makes irrelevant, distracting statements
− Interrupts
− Monopolizes the conversation
− Engages in personal attack

Source: David Harris, "Classroom Assessment of Civic Discourse," in *Education for Democracy: Contexts, Curricula, and Assessments* (pp. 211–232), ed. Walter C. Parker (Greenwich, CT: Information Age, 2002). Used with permission.

teaching begins with having the target clearly in mind, including the criteria by which students' performances will be evaluated, and then planning the instruction that will help students hit the bull's eye. (Please look ahead to Figure 7–4 on page 228.)

Teaching Decision Making

Many teachers already engage students in discussions of classroom rules and problems as well as community and world events. These discussions naturally revolve around decisions: Which rule is fairest? Which plan of action is wisest? What should we do? Teachers can and should take it further, however, to include teaching the decision-making process directly and explicitly.

There are three reasons for recommending this. First, as we saw in Chapter 2, teachers must provide explicit instruction on the topics and skills they expect their students to demonstrate. To withhold instruction merely gives an advantage to children who already learned the skills at home or elsewhere while creating a disadvantage for children who did not. Second, the decision-making process offers many opportunities for higher-order thinking. When children ferret out all the alternatives for a particular decision and predict the consequences of each alternative, they are engaged in several important intellectual processes that will enable them to be more thoughtful citizens. Third, the decision-making process offers opportunities for

TABLE 3–1	An ambitious scoring guide for assessing students' participation in discussions of public issues on two dimensions, grade 6.			
	Exemplary (3)	Adequate (2)	Minimal (1)	Unacceptable (0)
Substantive	Weighs multiple perspectives on a policy issue and considers the public good; uses relevant knowledge to analyze an issue; employs a higher-order discussion strategy, such as argument by analogy, stipulation, or resolution of a value conflict.	Demonstrates knowledge of important ideas related to the issue; explicitly states an issue for the group to consider; presents more than one viewpoint; supports a position with reasons or evidence.	Makes statements about the issue that express only personal attitudes; mentions a potentially important idea but does not pursue it in a way that advances the group's understanding.	Remains silent; contributes no thoughts of his or her own; makes only irrelevant comments.
Procedural	Engages in more than one sustained interchange, or summarizes and assesses the progress of the discussion. Makes no comments that inhibit others' contributions and intervenes if others do this.	Engages in an extended interchange with at least one other person, or paraphrases important statements as a transition or summary, or asks another person for an explanation or clarification germane to the discussion. Does not inhibit others' contributions.	Invites contributions implicitly or explicitly, or responds constructively to ideas expressed by at least one other person. Tends not to make negative statements.	Makes no comments that facilitate dialogue, or makes statements that are primarily negative in character.

Source: David Harris, "Classroom Assessment of Civic Discourse," in *Education for Democracy: Contexts, Curricula, and Assessments* (pp. 211–232), ed. Walter C. Parker (Greenwich, CT: Information Age, 2002). Used with permission.

values education. Groups and individuals choose an alternative typically because they value its consequences more than those of the others; similarly, conflicts can arise when values differ. Budding citizens in a diverse society need many opportunities to wrestle with value conflicts, which are an inevitable and necessary part of democratic life.

Children can be taught the decision-making process in four phases: awareness, analysis, modeling, and practice. Older children may not need to begin with the first phase.

First, the teacher helps children become aware of decisions and decision making. The children themselves make many decisions each day, as does their teacher. Decisions are being made throughout the school and community. Some of the decisions are political, that

FIGURE 3–3   Rating scale for discussion in the primary grades.

(Primary Grades)	Always	Sometimes	Not Often
1. Helps make plans			
2. Listens to what is said			
3. Takes turns			
4. Gives own ideas			
5. Considers what others have said			

is, they are decisions about rules and laws by which "we the people" agree to live. Others are social, concerning fund-raising for charities or welcoming new students to school. Still others are personal: What shall I wear? How should I spend my allowance?

Second, the teacher helps children unpack a decision and make a visual representation of it—a decision map. Decision maps show all the parts of a decision in relationship to each other: the occasion for the decision (a problem), the array of alternatives that could be considered, and the consequences of each alternative.

Third, the teacher models good decision making for children. Standing in front of a "decision tree" (see Figure 3–4) sketched on the chalkboard or posted on the wall, the teacher can talk about how he or she decided on the next unit of study, for example, or how to handle a difficult class problem. With this think-aloud demonstration, children witness a decision being made thoughtfully and can then practice the process themselves.

Fourth, the teacher provides opportunities for students to practice decision making. The opportunities are too numerous to list here, but key areas are decisions about classroom rules and issues; decisions about classroom management (cleanup, playtime, cooperative group work, work habits); and decisions about subject matter: Which reference resources will be best for this project? Will students use the tools to build a tower or a bridge? Make a model of Mt. Everest or Pikes Peak? Write about Rosa Parks or Susan Anthony?

Lesson Plan 2 is geared to the first and second phases of decision-making instruction. Notice that it teaches the design of a basic decision map, shaped as a tree, while building children's awareness of the decisions they and others make.

When it is time in the second phase to introduce children to the skill of predicting consequences, two focus questions are helpful for organizing the lessons. First, what might be the consequences (effects) of each alternative on all the persons involved? This question focuses students' attention on each alternative and its possible consequences. It challenges students to think of *everyone's* interests, not just their own. Second, will the alternative help or hinder the realization of democratic values, such as liberty, equality, and fairness? This question asks students purposefully to bring the ideals of democracy into the heart of decision making. These values can act as powerful screening tools, causing children to reject an alternative because it unnecessarily curtails someone's liberty, because it treats people unequally, or because it fails to consider the welfare of the whole community.

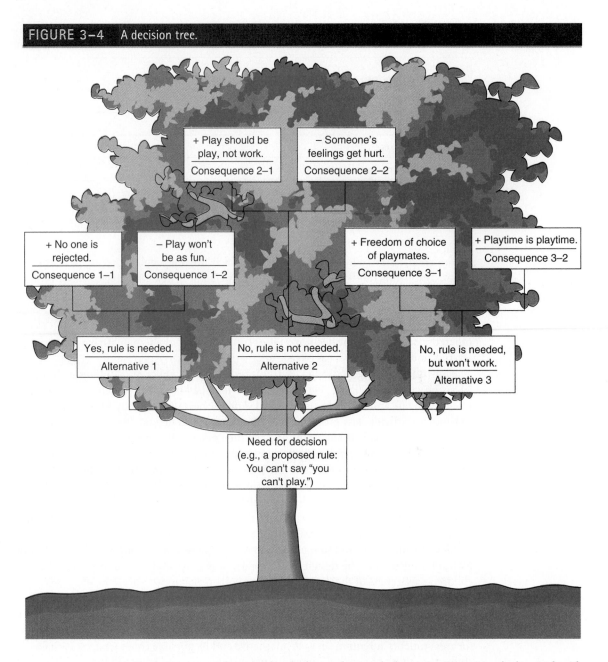

FIGURE 3–4   A decision tree.

Student teams can be created to do this work on each alternative. Team 1 is asked to work with Alternative 1, Team 2 with Alternative 2, Team 3 with Alternative 3, and so on. As readers can see, decision making is challenging intellectual work, especially when students take seriously the task of predicting consequences. An elaborate decision map in the form of a decision tree is shown in Figure 3–4.

Lesson Plan 2

MAKING A DECISION TREE

Grades	1–3
Time	One class period
NCSS Standards	6 (power, authority, and governance) and 10 (civic ideals and practices)
Objectives	Children will become aware of the numerous decisions they make every day and the alternatives that are considered in each decision. They will learn a way to map, or portray, such decisions.
Interest Building	Remind students of a lively discussion they had recently about a rule, such as deciding on a rule for sharing books or playground equipment. Ask them to recall what was decided. Help them remember the alternatives (choices, options) that were considered. As they recall the alternatives, record them on the board using a decision map such as this:

Need for decision _____   alternative #1 _____
                                          alternative #2 _____
                                          alternative #3 _____

Lesson Development	1. Ask students to think of all the decisions they have made so far today: whether to get up early or late; whether to eat cereal, toast, or something else; what to wear; what to do on arriving at the school building; whether to get to class early or just when the bell rang; and so forth. Record these on butcher paper and post.
	2. Explain that decision making means choosing among alternatives. Select a few decisions that will not invade anyone's privacy, such as what to do on arriving at school and whether to get to class early. Have the class help you map one of these decisions on the chalkboard, as you did yourself in the introduction. Then put children in pairs and ask them to map one or two more of these decisions. Ask the pairs to share their maps with the class.
	3. Build awareness of decisions that others make. Ask one pair of children to list the decisions they think the school principal might make in a typical day; to other pairs, assign the librarian, an athletics coach, an orchestra conductor, a police officer, a firefighter, an ambulance driver, a newspaper delivery person.
Summary and Assessment	Ask each pair to decide on one decision to share from step 3. As each pair shares, listen for misunderstandings and provide explanations. Diagram each decision on a decision map. Post these on a bulletin board labeled "Decisions in Our Community."
Follow-up	Ask the children to tell brief stories about courageous decisions that someone has had to make. Probe for the alternatives that person may have considered. Make decision maps for the decisions and alternatives.
Materials	Posters and marker for decision maps in summary. Also, if children have difficulty coming up with stories of courageous decision makers, you may want to have some ready. You can draw on literature the children are reading and exciting historical examples: Harriet Tubman's decision to continue the Underground Railroad despite great dangers; the Pilgrims' decision to sail for America.
Integration	Writing: As the weeks go by, have children make more decision maps based on material they are studying in math, science, and literature. As students work through math problems, they must decide, for example, whether to add or subtract. Writing also requires an endless stream of decision making.

Voting and Elections

Learning about voting is the second dimension of a proper education for democracy. Elementary teachers should miss no opportunity to involve their students in deliberation and voting. These two dimensions of democratic citizenship education go hand in hand: Deliberation informs voting. Voting should be seen as a culminating activity that comes after thinking with others about the issues and candidates. Without study and deliberation, children (and adults) vote without having thought together about the power they are exercising.

Participating in real and mock elections—whether as voter, candidate, member of the press, delegate, representative, or campaign worker—affords students opportunities to learn many concepts that will travel with them into subsequent school years and into adulthood. Some of these are listed in Figure 3–5. Historical study is important, too, for voting rights did not come easily. The struggle for the vote can teach children a good deal about the American struggle for democracy and equality. Overall, it is important to help children understand that voting is a civic duty, that it was hard won, and that it should not be done casually, but after study and deliberation.

The Long Struggle for Voting Rights.   The words of Elizabeth Cady Stanton and Martin Luther King, Jr., can be posted in the classroom to help children grasp the importance of voting and the long battle their ancestors had to wage for voting rights. Older children can write biographies of these and other voting rights activists (see the example in Chapter 13). Stanton and King were amazing. Stanton founded the American Equal Rights Association in 1866 and 20 years earlier had organized the Seneca Falls Convention, the birthplace of the women's suffrage movement. One of the convention's resolutions read: "It is the duty of the women of this country to secure to themselves

---

FIGURE 3–5   Voting-related concepts.

Instructions: Determine which of these you can readily define and exemplify. Then, spend a few minutes with a dictionary to find definitions of the others.

Concept	
Campaign	Poll watcher
Candidate	Polling place
Civil rights	Press conference
Delegate	Public issue
Democracy	Representative
Dictatorship	Secret ballot
Electoral college	Suffrage
Fairness (justice)	Voter eligibility
Majority rule	Voter registration
Political party	Voting
Politician	

their sacred right to the elective franchise." Note the words *duty* and *sacred* used in connection with voting. A century later, women had won the fight for the vote but African Americans still had not—at least, not actually in many places. The Fifteenth Amendment to the U.S. Constitution in 1870 made it illegal to deny the right to vote to anyone because of race, but then Whites invented poll taxes and other means to keep Blacks from voting. Poll taxes were not made illegal until the passage of the Twenty-fourth Amendment in 1964. But even this did not solve the problem of actually registering Black voters, particularly in the deep South. Freedom Riders flocked to southern states to help register African American men and women, and many of them were imprisoned; some were shot. In a speech delivered at the Lincoln Memorial in Washington, D.C., Dr. King demanded: "Give us the right to vote. . . . Give us the ballot. . . ." He knew that getting involved in the voting rights campaign was risky business that required great courage. "I realize that it will cause restless nights sometimes. It might cause losing a job; it will cause suffering and sacrifice. It might even cause physical death for some."[19] But he knew it was worth it.

Your students—the people in "we the people"—need to know it, too! There are more ways to involve children in voting than there is room here to present. So let us focus on a few powerful ways: holding real elections, holding mock elections, and preparing for these elections.

Holding Real Elections

Hold elections for one or two classroom delegates to the school's Student Advisory Council. If your school doesn't have one, help get it started. Cottage Lane Elementary School provides an excellent model. At Cottage Lane, these elections involve the whole student body in school governance, grades 1 through 6. There are two student advisory councils (SACs): "Little SAC" is for students in the primary grades; "Big SAC" is for students in grades 4 through 6. The school principal presides over both. "Our one purpose here," she always tells them, "is to identify problems and try to solve them."[20]

Each class elects two of its members to serve on the council. These students are delegates, not representatives, and consequently must vote at SAC meetings as instructed by their classmates. One student, Douglas, clarifies the distinction: "We are delegates. We can't just say what we want or tell only about our own problems. We must bring notes from the class and talk about the class's problems at SAC meetings." Therefore, the elections matter to the class, and class meetings at which delegates are given instructions are a critical part of the program. The deliberation in these meetings can be authentic and lively. With this kind of program, even primary-grade children gain experience with electing and being elected, with majority rule, with the distinction between delegate and representative, and with deliberation on issues that are important to them.

Elections can also be held to decide on any number of classroom roles. When a committee is formed, members can be asked to elect a chairperson. The same applies to students in charge of watering plants and feeding classroom pets, guiding the class to the lunchroom, and welcoming a guest speaker in the main office.

Caution: An election at school can be nothing more than a popularity contest in which students are elected on the most irrelevant criteria—gender, physical appearance, and athletic ability, for example. You can point out this problem to students and encourage them to identify relevant criteria for doing the job. "What knowledge or skills will our delegate to the student advisory council need?" Listen carefully as students respond, and you will learn how they are thinking about the job to be done. Ask one or two students to record the list on the board. Then help students prioritize items on the list. Then hold the election.

Holding Mock Elections

Every four years in November is a presidential election; every two years is a congressional election. City, county, state, and school district elections often coincide with these, but sometimes are held at other times. Each election is an opportunity to hold a mock election.

A mock election is and is not a real election. It is not an actual election because one need not be a citizen or a registered voter or at least 18 years of age to participate, and the votes cast in mock elections do not actually elect anybody. It is a real election, however, because voting does occur, and so do all the learning activities that lead up to and prepare children for the voting; namely, deliberation, press conferences, speech writing, research on candidate positions, and so forth.

Tennessee teacher Carole Hamilton Cobb routinely conducts mock elections with her kindergarten children. They vote in local and presidential elections. But first they learn about the candidates and discuss some of the issues. Then they register to vote and receive a voter registration card, which they take to the polling place (in the hallway) on voting day. Meanwhile, they help make polling booths from refrigerator boxes, such as the one shown in the photo on the next page.

Preparing for an Election

All sorts of learning activities help prepare children for an election, real or mock. Here are several.

Children's Literature About Elections.   Incorporate books about voting and elections into your regular reading instruction:

- Eileen Christelow's *Vote!* (Clarion, 2004) is a nonfiction book with loads of information on campaigning, registering to vote, volunteering, and ballot boxes. Ages 6–10.
- Elinor Batezat Sisulu's *The Day Gogo Went to Vote* (Little Brown, 1994) tells the story of Thembi who accompanies her great-grandmother, Gogo, to vote for the first time in the new South Africa after apartheid. Ages 4–8.
- Emily Arnold McCully's *The Ballot Box Battle* (Dragonfly/Random House, 1998) tells the story of young Cordelia whose neighbor is none other than Elizabeth Cady Stanton, the heroic suffragist. Ages 5–9.
- Catherine Thimmesh's *Madam President* (Houghton Mifflin, 2004) is another nonfiction book with lots of facts and a good narrative about the roles women have played in politics. Ages 10 and up.

Making a Polling Place.   In the photo of the kindergartner voting, note the polling place itself. These can be constructed by parent aides or older students, but the children should have design input. Ask them why voting should be done secretly. What is the reason? Listen to what they say, and ask them how a voting place could be made to ensure secrecy. "We can all close our eyes," one student will suggest. "Or put our heads down," offers another. It will

When children participate in mock or real elections, it is best to ensure a secret ballot. Here, a refrigerator box is transformed into a polling booth. *(Carol Hamilton Cobb)*

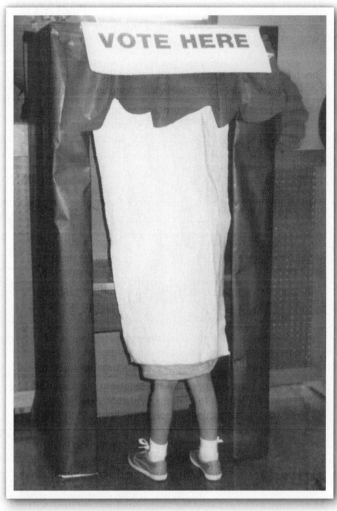

help if they can see a real polling place—a terrific field trip experience—to figure out how secrecy is.

Tell them that there is a history to the secret ballot, that it was used sometimes in Greece a very long time ago and, much more recently, was specified in modern democratic movements in France and England. Voting, according to a 19th-century political reform movement in England called Chartism, was "to be exempt from the corruption of the wealthy and the violence of the powerful," and therefore had to be secret. Kindergartners will not be able to relate to the "corruption of the wealthy," perhaps (the fact that people's votes can be bought by outright payments or costly media blitzes) but the "violence of the powerful" is not so far from their experience with bossy classmates and playmates.

Mock Press Conferences.   Mock press conferences provide terrific opportunities for role-playing and learning about elections. A committee can be formed to plan a press conference, gather information, and assign the roles (candidates, press, moderator, audience). Every student in class should have a role. Many can be members of the press—reporters representing television stations and newspapers. Tape recordings of press conferences can be made from television news programs and shown to students to give them a clearer idea of the real thing.

Guest Speakers.   Invite members of the press to share information and personal experiences on covering elections and campaigns. Invite winners and losers of local elections to share their experiences with students.

Speech Competitions.   Here is another good opportunity to infuse language arts instruction. Help students study the general concept of speech writing and speech giving with some famous examples (e.g., Patrick Henry's "Give Me Liberty or Give Me Death"; Martin Luther King, Jr.'s "I Have a Dream"; Sojourner Truth's "Ain't I a Woman?"; and Abraham Lincoln's Gettysburg Address). Some will be found on video- and audiotapes and CDs. These speeches can be read aloud then dramatized by the class. Next, help students form the more specific concept of campaign speeches. These examples can be drawn from the speeches reprinted in the newspaper and seen on television. With this background knowledge, students are ready for a speech-writing competition of their own. Attend to these things: choose judges, determine criteria for judging speeches, select topics, establish due dates and length (e.g., five minutes), decide on location and time, invite an audience, and prepare the audience.

Deliberation.   Elections—real and mock—are another opportunity for students to practice the democratic skill of deliberating controversial issues with one another. Prior to an election, the issues should be identified, studied, and then deliberated. Here is a good opportunity to teach newspaper-reading skills (using the directory to find the editorials, skimming the letters to the editor, or interpreting political cartoons), to help students form the attitude that voting is one's duty, and to show students that voting should always be preceded by study.

In addition to the specific issues of the election, general voting issues can be discussed:

- What difference does one vote make?
- Are secret ballots really necessary?
- Should voting be required or voluntary?
- Should convicted criminals be allowed to vote?
- Should the voting age be lowered? Raised?

Issues-finding Discussions.   Before the election or press conference, the teacher can lead the class in several issues-finding discussions. The purposes of such discussions are to:

- Help children develop the concept of a *public issue*—a controversial, shared problem on which reasonable people have different positions but must nevertheless reach a decision that will be binding on all. Public issues can be classroom, school, local, national, or world issues.
- Assess what the children perceive to be the public issues that candidates should be addressing (drugs, crime, poverty, homelessness, parks and recreation facilities, global warming, etc.).
- Decide what issues should be included in deliberative forums, covered in press conferences (the issues about which candidates will be questioned), and voted on

in the election. In preparing for a press conference, the teacher might ask: "What should the members of the press ask our candidates about?" Students can be prompted with reminders of local issues, for example: "Several of you have been concerned about the homeless people you see lying on streets. Do you want to ask the candidates for their ideas about that?" Or "The city council is trying to decide where to put the new park. Shall we ask the council candidates about that?" And "On what other public issues do you want to know their positions?"

Once issues have been identified, a data-retrieval chart such as the one shown in Figure 3–6 can be used during and after the press conference to help organize and record candidates' positions on the issues.

Visiting Candidate Websites.   Candidates in national elections now typically have websites. Create a data-retrieval chart with students, similar to the one in Figure 3–6, to help them organize the information they collect from several candidates' webpages.

Bulletin Boards.   Fill the boards with candidates' photos, issues, speeches, bumper stickers and campaign buttons, yard signs, editorials, and political cartoons—created by students and found in the newspaper, at party headquarters, and elsewhere.

Writing the Classroom Newsletter.   So much reading and writing goes on in conducting an election, whether real or mock, it would be a shame for it not to be featured in a special election day issue of the classroom newsletter.

Newspapers in the Classroom.   Children can learn a good deal about the organization and contents of daily newspapers during mock elections that coincide with actual national or local elections. Here is the teachable moment for distinguishing between news stories, editorials, Op-Ed (opposite the editorial) page columns, and letters to the editor, and between the literary genres of narrative (sometimes news stories are in narrative form), exposition (laying out the facts of the matter), and persuasive argument (in editorials and letters). Can your students find the lead in a news story? Children can be assigned to follow the press coverage of different candidates and to watch for the day when the city newspapers endorse one candidate over another and advise readers on how to vote on ballot initiatives. Contact your local newspaper to find out about its Newspapers in Education program.

FIGURE 3–6   Comparing candidates on the issues.

	Public issue # 1 Location of new park	Public Issue # 2 Park play equipment	Public Issue # 3 Regulating dogs in the park
Candidate #1			
Candidate #2			

Voting Websites

- Kids Voting USA is a nonprofit, nonpartisan, grassroots organization dedicated to securing democracy for the future by involving youth in the election process today. Visit the website (www.kidsvotingusa.org) and look at the classroom activities, educator e-bulletin, and more.
- At Project Vote Smart (www.vote-smart.org), hundreds of volunteers and student interns have labored "to provide their fellow citizens with the most crucial tool to citizens in a democracy: abundant, relevant information on those who govern us, or wish to replace those who already do." Students can enter their home or school zip code and find their elected representatives. There are lesson plans and many links to other good voter-education resources.

Service Learning and Community Action

The real test of a social studies program comes in the out-of-school lives of children. If the school has provided new insights, improved skills, and increased civic-mindedness, such learning should be apparent in students' out-of-school behavior now as children and later as adults. One way to help bridge citizenship learning in school with citizenship experiences in the community and the world is through community-service activities.

Participation can be social or political in nature. If children are concerned with vandalism of school property, for example, they might volunteer to clean up and repair some of the damage. This is social action. But if they propose new rules to officials or request stronger enforcement of existing rules, this is political action. Both social and political action by citizens are important for the health of democratic communities. As Supreme Court Justice Louis Brandeis said, "The greatest menace to freedom is an inert people."

Community-service activities can be spontaneous and short-lived, such as when children learn of a fire at a nearby house and collect canned goods and clothing for the family. Activities can also be planned systematically and sustained over a longer period of time, such as the adoption of a creek or a section of the school grounds.

Examples of Community Service

The following projects have been done by real kids in real communities. Note that some are social, some are political, and some are both.

Saving a Creek.   The children at an elementary school near Everett, Washington, decided to do something about a dirty little stream named Pigeon Creek. The children were alarmed that Pigeon Creek had become so dirty that salmon stopped coming there to lay their eggs, so they "adopted" it.

The first thing the children did was to get an aquarium for their classroom and raise thousands of salmon eggs. Meanwhile, they worked with people in their community to clean up the creek. Litter was removed, and the children put up "DON'T DUMP" signs. When the eggs hatched, the students released them in Pigeon Creek and monitored the creek to keep it clean.

Getting Out the Vote.   One elementary school teacher from Salt Lake City, Barbara Lewis, has a unique way of impressing on her students the importance of voting. In her book for children about social action, she tells them:

> Do you know that a lot of adults are numb? They're numb from filling out forms, balancing checkbooks, changing diapers, and changing tires. In the process, many have forgotten the principles our country was founded upon. Many don't think their votes count for anything. . . . Imagine what could happen if kids attacked their communities in a campaign to shake adults out of the mothballs.[21]

Children can be influential participants in get-out-the-vote campaigns. Distributed door-to-door, their flyers can read: "We can't vote yet. You can. Please do." By urging adults to register and vote, children learn about voting eligibility, voting rates, and the role voting plays in representative democracies. Hopefully, the experience will encourage them to become regular voters themselves. Take care to be nonpartisan (neutral): Encourage citizens to register and to vote, but don't tell whom to vote for. Help students understand the difference.

Giraffes Stick Their Necks Out.   Ask your students if they want to form a Giraffe Club in the classroom or schoolwide. Giraffes make this vow: "I promise to stick my neck out to make a difference. I will help people, animals, and my environment to make the world a better place to live." The little giraffes do all manner of things to help people. Visit www.giraffe.org. (Giraffe and other organizations appear in Figure 3–7.)

Other Community Projects

Good Neighbor Club.   Middle-grade students formed a Good Neighbor Club to help elderly residents in the neighborhood with yard work and errands.

Peer Tutoring for Citizenship.   Your students can help welcome new children from other lands, not only into the classroom social system, but also into the processes of democratic citizenship. An immigrant child can be paired with an especially good citizen in your classroom—or one who needs to learn to be a better citizen. This tutor helps the new student learn to participate in class discussions and consider all alternatives when making a decision. Ask a resourceful parent to obtain a copy of the citizenship test preparation booklet from the Internet. The peer tutor can go over the items with the new student and explain ideas, people, and places (e.g., national and local elections, representatives, and Washington, D.C.).

Adopt a Part of the School.   Frustrated by vandalism and litter on school grounds, fifth-grade children surveyed other students in the school to determine how many regarded this as a pressing problem. Results in hand, they wrote a proposal to the principal. On its approval, the children divided up the grounds by the number of

---

FIGURE 3–7   Community-service resources.

American Bar Association, www.abanet.org

American Red Cross, www.redcross.org

American Society for the Prevention of Cruelty to Animals, www.aspca.org

Boys and Girls Clubs of America, www.bgca.org

Center for Civic Education, www.civiced.org

Close Up Foundation, www.closeup.org

Constitutional Rights Foundation, www.crf-usa.org

Educators for Social Responsibility, www.esrnational.org

4-H, www.4husa.org

Giraffe, www.giraffe.org

National Association for the Advancement of Colored People, www.naacp.org

Rethinking Schools, www.rethinkingschools.org

Volunteers of America, www.voa.org

classrooms in their school. Then they mounted a campaign to persuade each class to adopt one section of the school grounds as its own, regularly picking up the litter and painting over vandals' marks.

Civic Letter Writing.   On a walk around the school, a third-grade class noticed that a sidewalk was so badly damaged that children on their way to and from school had to walk into the street to avoid it. The class had practiced writing five kinds of letters: letters of support, letters giving information, letters requesting something, letters disagreeing with an action or opinion, and persuasive letters. They deliberated which kind was best for the current situation, eventually deciding to draft a letter to the city council informing it of the problem and requesting a repair.

Public Information Campaigns.   Students can create posters and flyers for the school and neighborhood. These should be informational in nature, educating readers about a problem and suggesting possible or proven solutions the students think others should know about. Possibilities are fire safety in the home and at campgrounds, poisonous products in the home, and pet safety.

One group of fourth-graders was studying pollution problems in each region of the United States as part of their U.S. geography curriculum. One student brought to class a newspaper article about things that can pollute their front yards—weed killers and chemical fertilizers. Children playing in the yard and pets rolling in the grass can come into contact with these chemicals and track them into the house. They may develop rashes and become ill. These students produced a flyer that described the problem, listed information resources, and suggested remedies:

1. After using weed killers and fertilizers, water the lawn once a day for two days before allowing people or pets on it.
2. Take your shoes off before entering the house.
3. Don't use "weed and feed" products. They fertilize grass while spreading weed killer even where there are no weeds. Instead, pull weeds or use a spot sprayer.

The children printed the flyers and distributed them to the houses or apartments near their homes. Children, of course, should never go door-to-door without an adult supervisor. When this poses a difficulty, teachers rely on the classroom newsletter to get the word out to parents, school board members, and others on the class's mailing list.

Citizenship Knowledge

We have examined three categories of participatory democracy: discussing and deciding what to do about public problems (in the classroom, the community, and beyond), voting, and community service and action. If children learn to be good deliberators, well-prepared voters, and generous community servants, that would be terrific. But there is something better: knowledgeable deliberators, knowledgeable voters, and knowledgeable community servants. When participants possess a rich storehouse of knowledge about democracy and social life near and far, their discussions and decisions are more intelligent and their service projects more effective. As James Madison, one of the leading minds behind the U.S. Constitution and fourth president of the United States, wrote in 1788, "A people who mean to be their own governors must arm themselves with the power knowledge gives."

Informed participants have a keen respect for the facts. They are disposed to listen to evidence rather than prejudices, stereotypes, or the first thought that jumps into mind. Moreover, they have learned ideas, examples, and analogies from their studies of other peoples' experience—people who may have lived long ago and far away. History is one of democracy's best teachers. Knowing, for example, that other democracies have collapsed into hatred and tyranny when the people became apathetic or afraid is powerful information. Or knowing the history of the struggle for voting rights may motivate some children to mount a voter-registration campaign in the school neighborhood.

Core Citizenship Ideas

Ideas, or what we shall know more precisely as *concepts* in Chapter 9, are the cornerstones of social studies education generally and of democratic citizenship in particular. *Democratic* is an idea, as is *citizenship*. Ideas are the basic mental tools that human beings think with. Without them, problem solving, reflection, and living could not proceed. Imagine going to the grocery store without the benefit of such concepts as *nutrition, cost,* or *fresh.* Or imagine being stranded on a remote island with persons who did not carry in their minds the ideas *cooperation* or *sense of humor.*

Identifying the key ideas that children should develop for democratic citizenship is a task to which teachers need to devote a good deal of time. Fortunately, good advice is available. As we saw in Chapter 1, several sets of voluntary national curriculum standards have been published. As we have seen, those published by the National Council for the Social Studies include "civic ideals and practices" as one of 10 subject-matter themes for the social studies curriculum. Examining the expectations for the early grades related to this theme (see the standards *Sampler* that accompanies this textbook), we see that emphasis is given to several ideas:

- Democratic government
- Common good
- Actions that influence public policy
- Rights and responsibilities of citizens

Another helpful source of citizenship concepts is the book *National Standards for Civics and Government.* Some of the ideas this resource emphasizes are featured in the citizenship glossary in Figure 3–8. Teachers can help children develop such ideas first by providing examples of them drawn from children's literature, the newspaper, local and national elections, mock elections held in the classroom and school, and the social studies textbook, and then by helping children see similarities among the examples. This teaching procedure, called concept formation, is detailed in Chapter 9.

The Internet has helpful resources as well. Ben's Guide to U.S. Government for Kids (see page 97) has been a favorite of elementary teachers for years. Not only is Ben Franklin the friendly host at this website, but there is a separate set of pages for grades K–2, 3–5, and 6–8.

This is not to say that knowledge of democracy needs to be learned first, before democratic participation experiences begin. As anyone who spends time with young children knows, this would never work, even if it were a good idea (which it is not). *Children need to "learn as they go," experientially:* identifying problems, discussing and debating them, defining them further; doing research and listening to stories to answer questions that were raised;

FIGURE 3–8   A glossary for democratic citizenship.

Bill of Rights. First 10 amendments to the Constitution. Ratified in 1791, these amendments limit governmental power and protect basic rights and liberties of individuals.

Citizenship. Status of being a member of a state; one who owes allegiance to the government and is entitled to its protection and to political rights.

Civil rights. Protection and privileges given to all U.S. citizens by the Constitution and Bill of Rights.

Civil rights movements. Continuing efforts to gain the enforcement of the rights guaranteed to all citizens by the Constitution.

Common or public good. Benefit or interest of a politically organized society as a whole.

Constitutionalism. Idea that the powers of government should be distributed according to a written or unwritten constitution and that those powers should be effectively restrained by the constitution's provisions.

Democracy. Form of government in which political control is exercised by all the people, either directly or through their elected representatives.

Due process of law. Right of every citizen to be protected against arbitrary action by government.

Equal protection of the law. Idea that no individual or group may receive special privileges from nor be unjustly discriminated against by the law.

Founders. People who played important roles in the development of the national government of the United States. Framers are delegates to Philadelphia in 1787 who wrote the Constitution.

Freedom of expression. Refers to the freedom of speech, press, assembly, and petition that are protected by the First Amendment.

Freedom of religion. Freedom to worship as one pleases.

Government. Institutions and procedures through which a territory and its people are ruled.

Justice. Fair distribution of benefits and burdens, fair corrections of wrongs and injuries, or use of fair procedures in gathering information and making decisions.

Limited government. Constitutional government; a government created by the people to protect their individual rights and promote the common good. The opposite is totalitarian government.

Loyal opposition. Idea that opposition to a government is legitimate; organized opponents to the government of the day.

Politics. Process by which a group of people, whose opinions and interests are divergent, reach decisions that are binding on the group and enforced.

Representative democracy. Form of government in which power is held by the people and exercised indirectly through elected representatives who make decisions.

Rule of law. Principle that every member of a society, even a ruler, must follow the law.

Separation of powers. Division of governmental power among several institutions that must cooperate in decision making.

Suffrage. Right to vote.

Source: Adapted from *National Standards for Civics and Government* (Calabasas, CA: Center for Civic Education, 1994), 151–156. Used with permission.

then returning for more discussion, then more learning, and so on. In the midst of decision making, for example, when children realize they can identify only two alternatives, they are driven to do more research until they can describe several alternatives and how each affects various people in a diverse society. Participation skills and knowledge go hand in hand.

Citizenship Values

Children need to understand that democratic ideas and practices as they have developed in the United States rest on a foundation of democratic values. But what are values? They are a special kind of idea. They are ideas about the *worth* of something—some behavior, person, place, or thing. Values define for us what is worth striving for, what is right and desirable, what is important, what is preferred, what constitutes worthy life goals, what may be worth sacrificing one's life for. Like other ideas, values are abstract conceptions (mental phenomena) and, therefore, cannot be observed directly. But they can be inferred from our decisions and our actions.

Basic democratic values include the individual rights to life, liberty, and the pursuit of happiness; the public or common good; justice; equality of opportunity; diversity; and responsibility. There is general agreement among Americans that such things are valuable. They are judged positively and are widely believed to be worth nurturing in our children.

But can the school teach values in a democratic society? After all, this is a diverse society, and we don't wish to force our values on one another. The answer is simple: Yes, the schools can teach democratic values and they must. Democratic values are what we hold in common alongside our many differences. Democratic values are public or general values. They are expressed in our great public documents, such as the *Declaration of Independence,* the *Constitution of the United States,* the *Bill of Rights,* the *Seneca Falls Resolution,* and the speeches of Martin Luther King, Jr., Abraham Lincoln, and many others. Individuals who lead exemplary lives that reflect these general values are extolled as national heroes.

If children are to be socialized in accordance with these general values of society, they must be provided with examples of behavior that illustrate these values in action. That is, young people need to have encounters with idealized models—persons who illustrate by their way of life the values that society rewards and likes to see in its citizens. Because these values are internalized by the majority of citizens, orderly social life can take place. We expect our fellow citizens to behave in ways that are predictable and consistent with the basic premises inherent in those values on which there is general consensus. Law enforcement agencies are provided to protect society from the minority of persons who cannot or will not live in accordance with the general values embraced by the majority. But no police force could possibly monitor the behavior of all citizens if they were not willing to comply voluntarily with the accepted rules of the society.

Lesson Plan 3 provides a good example of a lesson based on public or general values. These values are promoted through social studies in the following ways:

1. Daily life in the classroom that stresses consideration for others, freedom and equality, independence of thought, individual responsibility for one's actions, and the dignity of individual human beings
2. The study of the history and development of this country, stressing the ideals that inspired it and showing that a continuing effort is needed to overcome hypocrisy and bridge the gap between reality and those ideals

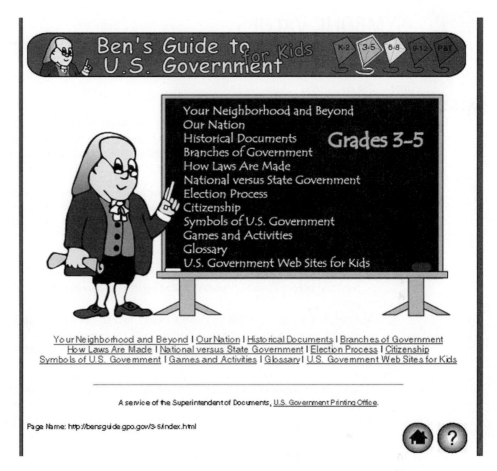

3. The study of biographies of individuals whose lives reflect the general values of the nation
4. The study of law, the justice system, and the U.S. Constitution
5. The celebration of holidays that reinforce values and ideals associated with the holiday (e.g., Veterans Day, Fourth of July, Martin Luther King, Jr.'s birthday)
6. Thoughtful analyses of the meaning of such statements as the Pledge of Allegiance, the Preamble to the Constitution, the Bill of Rights, and the Declaration of Independence (here is another good opportunity to integrate language arts and social studies instruction)
7. Building awareness of situations that violate values to which this society is committed
8. Cross-cultural studies to illustrate differences in values from one society to another

As we move from public values to personal values, the role of social studies becomes considerably different and, to some extent, less clear. Personal values are those values that influence the decision making of individuals in their own personal lives. To some extent, they represent individual interpretations of general values, that is, the integration of general values in the personal life of each individual. However, they also refer to cultural values and

SYMBOLIC VALUES

Grades   4–6

Time   One class period

NCSS Standards   1 (culture) and 10 (civic ideals and practices)

Objectives   Children will infer information about a country's civic values from symbols placed on its coins.

Interest Building   Placing a penny in each child's hand should build interest. Also, using the Internet, display the "kid" homepage of the United States Mint (www.usmint.gov/kids/). Focus students' attention on the slogan, "Coins are history in your pocket!"

Lesson Development   **Teacher:** Boys and girls, for the past few days we have been studying the use of signs and symbols. At the close of our discussion yesterday we came to an important conclusion. What was it?

Tess: We said that we could tell what people considered important to them by the symbols and signs they use on their buildings and clothing.

Teacher: Yes. What was an example?

Kim: I liked the flag example. The stars stand for states, and that shows that in our country people think it is important that the states have power. It's not only the national government that has power.

Teacher: Thank you. Today you will have a chance to test that idea in a slightly different way. Each of you has a coin to use for a reason. Study the coin carefully, as you did the flag yesterday, and see how many things you can tell about the country just from what you see on the coin.

Ask children to examine very closely the coin in their hands. After they have had time to make their observations, ask the children what they have concluded. As their ideas are presented, write them on the board. Have each child tell why the conclusion was made. Some of the following ideas may surface in this discussion:

These people believe in God.

They believe in liberty.

Men are more important than women in this country.

They build large buildings.

They speak more than one language.

They like birds.

They are a peace-loving people.

They are proud of their war heroes.

Now extend study to the 50 state quarters. The U.S. Mint released 5 new state quarters per year until all 50 had been printed in 2008. (The release sequence was the order in which the states entered the union.) Place one of your state's quarters in each child's hands and repeat the procedure above.

Assessment   Imagine that the United States is planning to issue a new two-dollar coin and there is a contest for the best design. You decide to enter the contest. The rules are these:

- Write down two ideas that best describe what people in the United States think are important to them.
- Think of and draw symbols that could be used on a coin to show these two values.

Materials   At least one penny and one commemorative quarter from your state for each child.

Follow-up   *Literature/Internet:* (1) Read aloud a children's literature selection that will deepen students' understanding of civic values and culture. For example, Elinor Batezat Sisulu's *The Day Gogo Went to Vote* tells the South African story of Thembi who accompanies her great-grandmother, Gogo, to vote for the first time after apartheid. What does Gogo value? Why? (2) Now, go online and take the class to the South African mint at www.samint.co.za. They will be curious to see what symbols have been placed on these coins. Is there something about voting? What are those animals? (wildebeest, kudu, springbok) Interested students can follow up with other countries' coins.

Math and Economics: In another direction, students may have questions about coins. What is their function? Compare the worth of different coins (penny, dime, quarter). Ask students what they think people did before there were coins or paper money. Good resource: Timothy A. Keiper and Bruce E. Larson's "The Fifty State Quarters: Art and Historical Inquiry," *Social Studies and the Young Learner, 13*(2), P5–P8, Nov./Dec. 2000.

---

customs—for example, beliefs and practices that Catholics may have but Methodists do not, or that Buddhists may have that Jews do not, or that (some) Mexican Americans may have that (some) Cambodian Americans do not.

Personal values also refer simply to what individuals like or want to do—preferring films to television, blue to yellow, bicycling to jogging. Modern life in affluent, industrialized societies involves an incredible amount of choice: how to spend our time, what career to choose, what clothes to buy and to wear, where to live, what brand products to buy, what hobbies and leisure-time activities to pursue, and how to spend our money. Each decision is an expression of individual preferences. It should be obvious that the social studies program cannot promote personal values in the same way that it can promote general values.

Citizenship Dispositions and Virtues

Dispositions, also known as attitudes, character traits, and virtues, are closely related to values. *They are habits or inclinations that summarize a person's behavior and values.* One may value honesty and courage and decency, for example, but only rarely behave honestly, courageously, and decently. On the other hand, if we describe a person as honest, courageous, or decent, we mean that *routinely* he or she exhibits these traits. It is one thing to be honest now and then; it's something quite different to be honest generally. Such behavior has become a habit, a part of this person's character. If such habits were not widely formed by people, life would be chaotic and living together democratically, with our differences intact, would be impossible. The authors of the U.S. Constitution knew this. James Madison often said that if the people are not virtuous, then no amount of law, government, or police power will protect us from one another.

Teaching children to develop positive dispositions is what many today call character education. Others call it moral or values education, terms often used interchangeably. Whatever we call it, it is a long-standing tradition in American education. It has been called the "great tradition" not only in the United States, but everywhere, for "the transmission of moral values has been the dominant educational concern of most cultures throughout history."[22] Let us look a little more closely at six democratic virtues (Figure 3–9).

Responsibility and Civility

What virtues are important to democratic citizenship? Thinking back to the desert island exercise at the beginning of the chapter, which virtues do you hope your shipwrecked partners

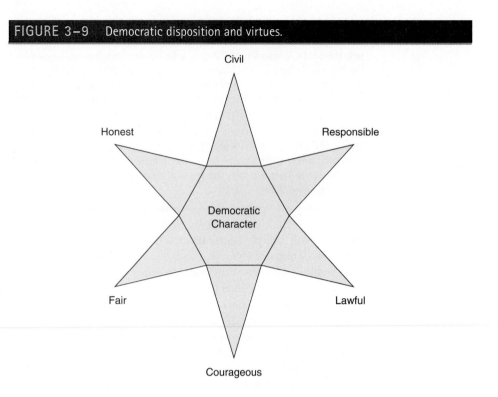

FIGURE 3–9 Democratic disposition and virtues.

already amply possess? Perhaps the most important are individual **responsibility** and **civility**. *Individual responsibility* is the habit of fulfilling one's obligations to family, friends, teachers, and other citizens in one's community, nation, and world. *Civility* is the habit of treating other persons courteously and respectfully, regardless of whether one likes them, agrees with their viewpoints, or shares their cultural or religious beliefs. Uncivil behavior is summed up by terms such as *rude, snotty, bigoted, ill-mannered, criminal,* and *hateful.* The willingness to listen generously to others, asking for clarification and elaboration, especially to persons one may not know well or not want especially to be friends with, is a hallmark of civility. If people are to walk the democratic path together, they must behave with civility toward one another.

The virtues of responsibility and civility combine to mean something that is greater than the sum of the parts: *civic-mindedness.* Recall, this is the opposite of what the ancient Greeks called *idiocy.* More recently, the brilliant French visitor to America, the sociologist Alexis de Tocqueville, observed that Americans were at a "dangerous passage" in their history. They were at a point where they "are carried away and lose all self-restraint at the sight of the new possessions they are about to obtain." Getting "carried away" like this is dangerous, he warned, because it can cause people to lose the very freedom they are enjoying: "The more they look after what they call their own business, they neglect their chief business, which is to remain their own masters."[23] What did he mean by this—that our chief business is to remain our own masters? He meant that we need to maintain the kind of community that secures our freedom. Without democratic community—without civic life—there is no freedom. This is why the Greeks said it was "idiotic" to ignore civic life.

Children must be taught to enjoy the rights democracy affords them in such a way that their enjoyment does not become an obsession that harms the common good and ruins the very system that protects those rights. This means they must be taught to pay attention to the common good, nurture it, and not become so self-centered as to become, well, idiotic.

Courage

Courage is the habit of standing up for one's convictions when conscience demands. For younger and older children alike, courage is required when everybody is doing it, but one knows in one's heart that it is wrong. This applies to cheating, stealing, teasing, lying—all the very real temptations of social interaction. Bringing children to the circle for a discussion of courage can be a wonder-filled event for the teacher who is curious about children's character development. Ask children to give examples of courageous behavior and courageous persons. Listen carefully to their conceptions of courage.

Fairness (Justice)

Even kindergartners have a keen sense of what is and isn't fair. But it is not necessarily a well-developed sense, for that will take time, experience, maturation, coaxing, a stimulating social environment with good models, and intellectual development.

As we saw in the discussion of deliberation and decision making, moral philosophers tend to agree that the highest development of the sense of fairness is expressed as the commitment to treat others as you yourself would want to be treated if you were in their situation. This is the Golden Rule in the Judeo-Christian faith, and the Mahayana doctrine of compassion in the Buddhist tradition.

Other Virtues

Other democratic dispositions, such as being lawful, respecting the rights of others, being a critical thinker, and being patriotic, are surely important. And no list of democratic dispositions is complete without honesty. Honest Abe Lincoln is an honored figure in American history, largely due to his reputation for truth telling; and whether or not George Washington actually chopped down that cherry tree, the famous line "I cannot tell a lie" resonates in the American citizen's value system. The mere thought that a politician is corrupt or that a military academy cadet has cheated is sufficiently jarring to be featured in the news. Teachers can help children develop the habit of honesty by exhibiting it themselves, pointing it out in those who model it, and giving children plenty of opportunities to discuss with one another, in the style of Ms. Paley earlier in this chapter, the challenge of being honest when nobody else is or when it is easier to avoid punishment by lying or cheating.

RELIGION AND SOCIAL STUDIES

Any discussion of values education and dispositions inevitably takes us to religion, because religions, if they have anything in common, are concerned with the inculcation of particular values and dispositions. Religions at their best are, in Huston Smith's phrase, "the world's *wisdom traditions*. They look like data banks that house the winnowed wisdom of the human race."[24]

Yet, in keeping with the mandate of the First Amendment, schools in the United States have been diligent in their effort to maintain what Jefferson called "a wall of separation" between church and state. Ours is not a Christian nation, an Islamic nation, or a Jewish, Hindu, or Buddhist nation. Rather, it is a constitutional democracy where "we the people" created a government that would protect our liberties, not force a common way of life—a common culture—on us. John F. Kennedy, when running as the Democratic candidate for president in 1960, had to assure Protestants that he, a Catholic, would not "take orders from the Pope." In doing so, he had to remind them of Jefferson's wall of separation:

> Because I am a Catholic, and no Catholic has ever been elected President, the real issues in this campaign have been obscured. . . . So it is apparently necessary for me to state, once again, not what kind of church I believe in, for that should be important only to me, but what kind of America I believe in. I believe in an America where the separation of church and state is absolute, where no Catholic prelate would tell the President, should he be Catholic, how to act, and no Protestant minister would tell his parishioners for whom to vote.[25]

But for teachers, this can be cause for confusion. Some observers, both liberal and conservative, believe that schools have been overly zealous in removing religion from the classroom. As a result of this omission, a distorted understanding of history has been fostered. It is as though religion does not exist as an important force in shaping the affairs of human beings and their cultures, as if people's wisdom traditions didn't matter to them. Of course, nothing is further from the truth. Religion has had and continues to have a tremendous impact on history and human affairs, from the wars between Protestants and Catholics that plagued Europe before the Enlightenment to the forced conversion of American Indians to Christianity by the conquistadors and the jihadist terrorism of the 21st century.

But it is a complex and varied picture, which is precisely why teaching *about* religion is necessary. Faith and belief are what churches, temples, and mosques can offer; *education* is what schools can do.

History on every continent is loaded with examples of religious hope giving comfort to oppressed peoples and religious hate causing wars and persecutions. Also, there are persons with deep religious convictions who intervened to prevent wars and to halt persecutions. Think of the Hindu Mahatma Gandhi in India, the Christian Martin Luther King, Jr., in the United States, and the Buddhist Thich Nhat Hanh in Vietnam. All led major nonviolent political movements that rested squarely on religious values. Religion also plays a key role in migrations (e.g., the Pilgrims) and the formation and maintenance of cultures (think of Shintoism in Japan, Judaism in Israel, Catholicism in Mexico, Islam in Iraq, and Protestantism in the African American community in the United States). Religion plays a central role also in conquests (e.g., the Crusades) and in the transformation of individual character (e.g., the practices of Christian or Muslim prayer or Buddhist meditation).

Modern industrialized peoples are generally less defined by church doctrine than were premodern agricultural peoples, and they generally are taught at school to value pluralism and toleration, which permit persons of different religions to live and work and educate their children in the same community. In fact, this is a defining attribute of modernity in general and modern constitutional democracy in particular. Still, religion is an enormous historical force to be reckoned with. Historians who study the past and sociologists and anthropologists who study the present typically make much of it. It is at best strange, then, for the school curriculum to ignore it.

Where does this leave the teacher? Most important, the teacher should understand that the First Amendment prohibition is against teaching doctrinal religious beliefs; it in no way disallows the *study* of religion—that is, teaching *about* religion as a powerful phenomenon of history and culture. Therefore, the study of religion as a social phenomenon constitutes a legitimate area of inquiry for social studies. Children cannot possibly understand historical events, such as the European colonization of the Americas or the Civil Rights movement, without understanding the role of religion on all sides. Nor can they appreciate the fact that democracy, with its guarantee of religious liberty and its insistence on religious tolerance, is infinitely better than the alternative: religious hatred, warfare, and persecution.

The challenge to teachers is to make religion a natural part of the social studies topics studied. Just as it is common to have children study the geography, government, and history of a selection of communities around the world, it should also be common for them to gather information about the religions practiced in these communities. Lesson Plan 9 in Chapter 6, for example, capitalizes on students' interest in a nation that is dominating the news and has them study its culture, *including its religions*, along with its government, economy, and geography.

Closer to home, teachers need to learn about the religions embraced by the families of the children in their classrooms. As noted in Chapter 2, a teacher can display genuine respect for children's home cultures in many ways; attending a special event at a child's mosque, temple, or church is one way that is sure to be remembered by the child and the family for many years. This simple act of kindness is good pedagogy as well—referred to in Chapter 2 as culturally responsive instruction.

Conclusion

Democracy is an exasperating form of living together. But, as Winston Churchill put it, democracy is the worst form of government *except for all the others.* It means not only enjoying the rights and freedoms of democracy but also the responsibilities. It means cooperating with strangers and with people we are not particularly fond of, and it means tolerating beliefs—religious beliefs, political beliefs, and so on—that we may find strange and untrue.

There can be no democracy without the democratic citizens who create it day by day. Educating these citizens is the primary mission of the social studies curriculum. This chapter favored active *and* informed approaches to realizing this goal. We began with activities for helping children wrestle with the ideas in the Pledge, and then presented the six dimensions of democratic citizenship education. Each should be part of the classroom life teachers create for students: deliberating classroom rules and problems, voting in real and mock elections, taking action on school and community problems, developing the knowledge citizens need, understanding the values expressed in the documents and speeches that anchor our democracy, and developing the virtues that make democratic life possible.

Discussion Questions and Suggested Activities

Go to MyEduca-tionLab and select the topic "NCSS Standards," then read the article "When Children Make Rules" and complete the activity.

1. Look back at Ms. Paley's classroom deliberation and the question that was asked in the *Reflection* sidebar on page 76. She conducts a lively and ongoing deliberation centered on two questions: *Will the rule work? Is the rule fair?* Do you think it would be better if she simply posted the rule? After all, we don't let children deliberate whether to look both ways before crossing the street; rather, we simply train them to do so. What's to be gained by having children discuss a rule such as You Can't Say "You Can't Play?"

2. If it were your decision to make, would you have students recite the Pledge of Allegiance at the beginning of each school day? Explain your position. And, are there any changes to the Pledge that you would recommend, such as making it a pledge to Earth or to all humanity?

3. Develop a reading lesson on the U.S. Constitution. For example, a lesson to teach pre-viewing and skimming skills, using the entire document, is featured in Chapter 12. Or you might try leading a literature circle on the Preamble or the First Amendment. Or. . . .

4. NCSS Standards *Sampler.* Examine the third-grade classroom vignette for standard #6 on page 17 of the standards *Sampler* that accompanies this book. How does it compare to the deliberative rule-making strategies of Paley and Lindquist featured in this chapter?

Selected References

MyEduca-tionLab is a collec-tion of online tools for your success in this course, your licensure exams, and your teaching career. Go to www.myeducationlab.com to utilize these extensive resources including videos from real classrooms, Praxis and licensure preparation, a lesson plan builder, and materials to help you begin your teaching career.

Alleman, Janet, & Brophy, Jere. (2006). Introducing children to democratic government. *Social Studies and the Young Learner, 19,* 17–19.

Allen, Danielle S. (2004). *Talking to strangers: Anxieties of citizenship since Brown v. Board of Education.* Chicago: University of Chicago Press.

Avery, Patricia G. (2002). Teaching tolerance: What research tells us. *Social Education, 66* (5), 270–275.

Banks, James A., Banks, Cherry A. M., Cortes, Carlos E., Hahn, Carole L., Merryfield, Merry M., Moodley, Kogila A., Murphy-Shigematsu, Stephen, Osler, Audrey, Park, Caryn, & Parker, Walter C. (2005). *Democracy and diversity: Principles and concepts for educating citizens in a global age.* Seattle: Center for Multicultural Education, University of Washington.

Hahn, Carole L. (2002). Education for democratic citizenship: One nation's story. In Walter C. Parker (Ed.), *Education for democracy: Contexts, curricula, assessments* (pp. 63–92). Greenwich, CT: Information Age.

Jefferson, Thomas. (1954/1787). *Notes on the State of Virginia.* New York: Norton.

Paley, Vivian Gussin. (1992). *You can't say you can't play.* Cambridge, MA: Harvard University Press.

Parker, Walter C. (2005). Teaching against idiocy. *Phi Delta Kappan, 86*(5), 344–351.

Parker, Walter C. (2006). Talk isn't cheap: Practicing deliberation in school. *Social Studies and the Young Learner, 19* (1), 12–15.

Parker, Walter C. (2003). *Teaching democracy: Unity and diversity in public life.* New York: Teachers College Press.

Schweber, Simone A. (2006). "Holocaust fatigue" in teaching today. *Social Education, 70* (1), 44–50.

Wade, Rahima C. (2007). *Social studies for social justice: Teaching strategies for the elementary classroom.* New York: Teachers College Press.

Westheimer, Joel (Ed.). (2007). *Pledging allegiance: The politics of patriotism in America's schools.* New York: Teachers College Press.

History, Geography, and the Social Sciences

CHAPTER FOUR

Chapter Outline

- Teaching History
- Teaching Geography
- Teaching Political Science
- Teaching Economics
- Teaching Anthropology
- Teaching Sociology
- Conclusion

Key Concepts

- History
- Historical reasoning
- Primary source
- Absorbing and doing history
- Geography
- Political science
- Economics
- Anthropology
- Sociology

MAIN IDEA

The main sources of subject matter for the social studies curriculum, in addition to society's needs and the children's own lives, are the social science disciplines. The social studies curriculum in the elementary school often integrates these, typically leading with history or geography, and steers students toward becoming democratic citizens. The key to teaching these subject matters well is to help children *do* them—engage in the kinds of thinking and action associated with each—as well as learn *about* them. Like the two wings of an airplane, neither works alone.

PICTURE THIS

A small group of fourth-graders was working on a script for a reenactment of the meeting of Lewis and Clark with Sacagawea, who was a Shoshone, and her French Canadian husband. Each time they learned something new, their teacher encouraged them to revise their script. At the Public Broadcasting Service's Lewis and Clark website, they discovered that the explorers had developed a ceremony they used when meeting a new people. The children made the ceremony a part of their drama. Other small groups dramatized the day Lewis and Clark's team set out on the Missouri River in 1804, the day they sighted the Pacific Ocean in 1805, and the day they returned to St. Louis in 1806. Lewis and Clark were good observers, and they kept journals, which students also obtained from the website.

The subject-matter banquet table of the social studies curriculum in the elementary and middle schools is loaded with offerings, each more tempting than the next. The center-pieces traditionally have been history and geography. These are taught together usually, but sometimes, for increased clarity, they are taught separately. Children typically are introduced to the history and geography of their community, state, nation, and the world in grades 3 through 6, respectively. Geography is easily integrated into historical study because historical narratives cannot be comprehended or composed apart from their geographical settings. For every when there's a where, and vice versa.

This chapter introduces the fields of history and geography, along with political science, economics, anthropology, and sociology. These are major sources of information, ideas, and issues for social studies lessons and units. History receives the most attention in this chapter, and geography is the central focus of the next chapter. As political science was the subject of the previous chapter on citizenship education, it receives only brief coverage here.

Beware, dear reader: This is one of the longest chapters in the book. So as not to lose sight of the forest for the trees, it is advisable to preview and skim the six major sections of the chapter before reading them more closely. Also, read the conclusion and the four questions for discussion.

TEACHING HISTORY

History is the subject in which students learn stories about the past, learn how these stories are created, learn that these stories are created differently by different people, *and learn to create these stories themselves, as historians do, using historical reasoning*. The key to teaching history to children is to do two things, not one. Like the two wings of an airplane, these two work together and neither works alone. One is exposing children to historical narratives that others have written or told. The other is helping children to write and tell historical narratives of their own making.

If children are to do either of these things well and to understand the difference between them, their teachers need to understand what history is and why they should bother with it in the elementary and middle grades. After all, the school principal may be waving copies of reading and math tests at the faculty before addressing the importance of historical knowledge and historical reasoning. Accordingly, this chapter begins with the "why" and "what" of history and then returns to the two wings of the airplane: absorbing and doing history.

Rationale

The famous child psychologist Bruno Bettelheim argued that elementary school children need "rich food for their imagination, a sense of history, how the present situation came about."[1] What is at stake here is wisdom. Without historical knowledge and know-how there can be no wisdom. Here, briefly, are five reasons for history instruction throughout the elementary school years and into adulthood.

1. *Judgment.* The first reason for history teaching and learning is that historical knowledge and know-how help people develop better judgment, especially the

judgment needed for what is called *political intelligence*. Here is what the National Standards for History say:

> Knowledge of history is the precondition of political intelligence. Without history, a society shares no common memory of where it has been, of what its core values are, or of what decisions of the past account for present circumstances. . . . Without history, one cannot move to the informed, discriminating citizenship essential to effective participation in the democratic processes of governance and the fulfillment for all our citizens of the nation's democratic ideals.[2]

Just how do historical knowledge and know-how give us political intelligence? Mainly, they help us learn from others' experiences. Martin Luther King, Jr., for example, learned from the experience of another social activist: Indian revolutionary Mahatma Gandhi (1869–1948). As Dr. King wrote, "Christ furnished the spirit and motivation, while Gandhi furnished the method."[3] What method? King is referring to the method of social action and protest that he and others used successfully during the Civil Rights movement. That method was a version of Gandhi's *satyagraha:* nonviolent civil disobedience. King watched and read Gandhi closely, as did many in the movement, for Gandhi's nonviolent protests in India had helped free the Indian people from British rule. Some of the same methods were then used in Montgomery, Birmingham, and Selma, Alabama, in the 1950s and '60s to challenge racist laws and customs. When I visited the King Center in Atlanta, Georgia, I found that the bookstore was loaded with books by and about Gandhi. King's judgment, then, was nurtured by his historical knowledge. Indeed, one way to help children celebrate the life and work of Dr. King is to study Gandhi's life and work. This becomes an inspiring study of interfaith respect as well, because King was Christian and Gandhi was Hindu.

2. *Empathy and self-knowledge.* A second reason for history instruction is that history builds children's knowledge of the world's peoples and the inclination to understand their struggles and appreciate their humanity. By learning about the diversity of the world's societies and their histories, children see that many people live differently from how they do. Simultaneously they learn about themselves—that their own way of life is "different," too. Respect for the tapestry of human similarities and differences is a virtue that distinguishes the intolerant bigot who loves to hate from the good neighbor who seeks friendship and peace with people alike and different. Interestingly, understanding of others and understanding of oneself develop in tandem.

3. *Imagination.* A third reason for history teaching and learning is that, as Bettelheim says, it is rich food for the imagination. History enlarges and excites children's imagination. It gives them experiences they have not actually had. In some cases, one is thankful for having been spared the actual experience; in others, one longs to have been there. History, like other kinds of good literature, is by its nature expanding and liberating. It takes children to faraway places and faraway times and to unknown destinations close to home. It puts them into the shoes of both the queen and the queen's slaves, the president and the pauper. It introduces them to decent people and horrible people, to inspiring ideas and despicable ones, and to remarkable events and ordinary life—all this around the world and across decades, centuries, and millennia. These people, ideas, issues, and values fuel the imagination as gasoline does an automobile engine; without it, there may be a spark, but there is no combustion.

4. *Agency.* Agency means the power to take action, to do something about personal and public problems. History shows us that people are shaped by their circumstances; they are acted on by social forces that often are beyond their control. Yet, history teaches us also that people make a difference. "Don't mourn, organize!" goes the activist's familiar slogan. It's true: people make a difference. They can create organizations of like-minded people, they can form protest movements, they can discover cures for diseases, they can treat others fairly, they can write letters and make laws, they can make speeches that rouse people to action for good (think of King) or ill (think of Hitler). Teachers should expose their students to many examples of people making a difference in their neighborhoods, the nation, and the world: men and women, boys and girls, famous and not. Historical study, then, helps children to see that just as they have been shaped by the past, so will they shape the future. Change *is* possible, and they can make it happen. Whether by their actions or their inaction, they will do it. How do they want to shape the future? For what contribution do they want to be remembered? Ask them these questions often.

5. *The long view.* There have been about 10,000 years of human civilization. Before that, for 10 times longer, humans were hunters and gatherers who roamed for food and shelter. About 8000 BCE, a major change occurred in how people lived: agriculture. Agriculture triggered the beginning of settled village life and, with that, the beginnings of civilization. Since then, humanity has had two major lifestyles: agricultural (or traditional) and, very recently (about 1900 CE), industrial (or modern). The biggest difference between the three lifestyles is the amount of time individuals and groups spend on food production. Securing food was the main event in agricultural societies; not so in industrial societies, where advances in science and technology allowed most people to do other things. Families became smaller, students went away from home to school, and parents went away to work at things other than food production. Every facet of social life—from politics to religion—was transformed.

```
                                                             Industry
                                                             1900 CE
   |----------------------------------------------------------|-|‖
   80000 BCE Hunters + Gatherers                      8000 BCE    Today
                                                      Agriculture
```

Humanity now shares a web of stories reaching all the way back to the first farming villages and stretching all the way forward through the Industrial Revolution to the space age and the global marketplace. Feeling this connection going all the way back and forward, sensing it, knowing it, having it pervade one's judgment—this is having the long view. This is long-term thinking.

The fifth reason for teaching and learning history, then, concerns the chief problem humanity faces today. Biologist-inventor Stuart Brand captures it well: "How do we make long-term thinking automatic and common instead of difficult and rare? How do we make the taking of long-term responsibility inevitable?"[4] The bizarre speed of current events, information overload, and consumption and production gives even adults a pathologically short attention span. They are acting more and more like children, showing too little inclination to serve the long-term interests of the family, the community, and the planet. Historical study is one, partial solution, for it introduces people to a crucially important perspective: the long view.

To summarize the five reasons for history instruction, I return to the single word *wisdom*. Students' encounters with distant times and places become part of who the children are. These encounters, and the meaning students make of them, are added to the inventory of knowledge they take with them to new situations and problems. History helps liberate us from the blinders placed on our vision by the circumstances of our lives. It broadens our horizons and extends our time frame back to those first villages, forward to the next 10,000 years, and outward to people everywhere.

Developing a Sense of Time and Chronology

Children learn much about time through ordinary living outside school. Undoubtedly, most children learn how to tell time and identify the days of the week and months of the year, and they become familiar with terms ordinarily used in referring to units of time, such as *noon, midnight, afternoon,* and *morning.* The school program can ensure that these concepts are learned correctly, however, and concentrate study on those aspects of time and chronology that are not likely to be learned outside school. These include (1) the more technical concepts of time and chronology, such as *century, decade, fortnight, fiscal year, calendar year, generation, score, millennium,* A.M., P.M., BCE, and CE; (2) placing events in chronological order; (3) developing an understanding of the time spans that separate historical events; and (4) developing what in the previous chapter was called the *long view* and with it, the capacity for long-term thinking. References to *indefinite* units of time—"many years ago," "several years had passed," "in a few years"—need special attention because they are apt to mean almost any amount of time to young children. Definite references to time can be made meaningful by associating them with units of time that are known to the children: their own ages, the length of time they have been in school, when their parents or grandparents were their age, and so on. The teaching of these relationships can and should take place within the context of social studies units, especially those that focus on history and current events.

The development of time concepts should begin with time situations that are within the children's realm of experience. Children should be given help in learning to read clock time and in understanding references to the parts of the day, days of the week, months, seasons, and the year. Even though primary-grade children make statements about things that happened "a hundred years ago," they have little comprehension of the real meaning of the expression and simply use it as a vague reference to something that happened in what seems to them a long time ago.

A time line is a continuum that shows how related events are arranged in chronological order *and* the relative amount of time that separates them in time. Teachers can help children make their first time lines by first arranging events that the children experience firsthand. They can make time lines that show things that happened to them yesterday, today, or are being planned for tomorrow. The five days of the school week can be represented on a time line divided into five equal segments, and children can see how many segments separate Monday from Friday. The amount of time included on the line can gradually be expanded to cover several months and then years, decades, centuries, and millennia.

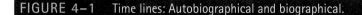

FIGURE 4–1   Time lines: Autobiographical and biographical.

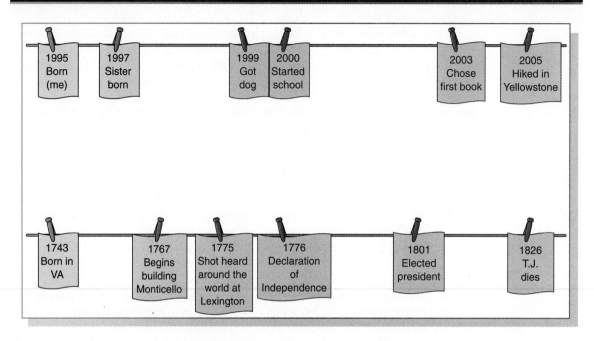

Of course, time lines are more interesting to children if events are shown pictorially rather than simply as dots and dates. With third- and fourth-grade students, frequent use can be made of time lines in connection with historical studies of their home state and nation. One third-grader's illustrated time line of her hometown appears in Chapter 8. Figure 4–1 shows two simple time lines, one of events in the child's own life and one of Thomas Jefferson's life.

A "Living Wall"

Software programs such as *TimeLiner* (Tom Snyder Productions) allow teacher and students to create, store, edit, merge, and print time lines. This is a wonderful tool. The time line, once created, can be represented in various forms—as a banner that stretches around the classroom or a list that runs down the classroom door. As students learn to use this program, their oral and written reports and their autobiographies and biographies should be expected to contain helpful and accurate time lines. A time-line banner can be stretched around the classroom, with children adding new events and persons as the year progresses. Joseph Braun and his colleagues recommend that butcher paper be stretched below the time line and used to create a mural of key events. "Thus a living wall can be created, providing a visual record of any period of study."[5]

What History Should Be Taught?

Learning history is much, much more than learning to make time lines. Let's turn to the matter of choosing themes and topics. The school district curriculum guide will probably list themes (e.g., the NCSS historical standard "time, continuity, and change") and topics (e.g., the

FIGURE 4–2   Historical topics for study in the early grades.

1. Family life now and in the recent past; family life in various places long ago.
2. History of students' local community and how communities in North America varied long ago.
3. The people, events, problems, and ideas that created the history of their state.
4. How democratic values came to be, and how they have been exemplified by people, events, and symbols.
5. The causes and nature of various movements of large groups of people into and within the United States, now and long ago.
6. Regional folklore and cultural contributions that helped to form our national heritage.
7. Selected attributes and historical developments of various societies in Africa, the Americas, Asia, and Europe.
8. Major discoveries in science and technology, their social and economic effects, and the scientists and inventors from many groups and religions responsible for them.

Source: National Standards for History for Grades K–4: Expanding Children's World in Time and Space (Los Angeles: National Center for History in the Schools, 1994), 29–30.

American Revolution; the Lewis and Clark expedition). Figure 4–2 lists eight curriculum topics suggested for study in grades K–4 in the National Standards for History. For grades 5–12, this group suggests the chronological study of both United States and world history.

Although this is a powerful and comprehensive list of topics, another piece of curriculum advice should also prove helpful. Table 4–1 summarizes the U.S. history knowledge on which 4th-, 8th-, and 11th-graders are assessed by the National Assessment of Educational Progress (NAEP)—the only *national* test of American students' historical knowledge. The group that produced this curriculum included teachers and historians, liberals and conservatives, and members of both majority and minority ethnic groups. Especially interesting here is what was *agreed* to: eight chronological eras and four themes for emphasis in each era. Here is a brief elaboration on the four themes:

1. **Democracy:** *Change and Continuity in American Democracy:* the development of American political democracy from colonial times to the present; this includes basic principles and core civic ideas developed through the American Revolution, the U.S. Constitution, the Civil War, and the struggles over slavery and civil rights.
2. **Culture:** *The Gathering and Interactions of Peoples, Cultures, and Ideas:* the gathering of people and cultures of many countries, races, and religious traditions that have contributed to the American heritage and the development of American society.
3. **Technology:** *Economic and Technological Changes and Their Relation to Society, Ideas, and the Environment:* the transformation of the American economy from rural frontier

TABLE 4–1	U.S. History content outline by periods and themes.			
Periods	**Democracy**	**Culture**	**Technology**	**World Role**
Beginnings to 1607				
Colonization, Settlement, and Communities (1607 to 1763)				
The Revolution and the New Nation (1763 to 1815)				
Expansion and Reform (1801 to 1861)				
Crisis of the Union: Civil War and Reconstruction (1850 to 1877)				
The Development of Modern America (1865 to 1920)				
Modern America and the World Wars (1914 to 1945)				
Contemporary America (1945 to Present)				

Source: U.S. History Framework for the 2006 National Assessment of Education Progress (NAEP) (Washington, DC: National Assessment Governing Board, 2006).

to industrial superpower and its impact on society, ideas, and the environment. This includes the influence of geography; the development of business and labor; and the impact of science and technology, a market economy, and urbanization.

4. **World Role:** *The Changing Role of America in the World:* the movement from isolation to worldwide responsibility. The evolution of relationships between the United States and other nations, including American foreign policy and the nation's participation in world and regional wars. Students will consider the influence of geography, economic interests, and democratic ideals in evaluating the role of the United States in foreign affairs.[6]

Historical Reasoning

Passive absorption of this material is certainly not the point. Recall the opening snapshot of this chapter: A fourth-grade class was divided into small groups, and each was studying and dramatizing an event in the Lewis and Clark expedition from 1804 to 1806. Each time they encountered some new facts about their event (e.g., that Lewis and Clark enacted a standard ceremony whenever they met a new people), their teacher encouraged them to revise their script for the dramatization. Here is the point: The script students were writing and revising—what writers call "drafting"—was *a historical narrative of their own construction.* They were using historical reasoning to figure out what happened and to decide how to portray it.

Historical reasoning is interpretive reasoning. Because the past is over with, it must be interpreted. But what exactly is interpreted? There is a makeshift record of the past left to us in the form of what historians call "sources," and these are what gets interpreted. They contain the evidence in historical interpretation. Historical narratives must be pieced together from this evidence. The evidence is found in three kinds of sources: primary sources, artifacts, and secondary sources.

Primary sources are materials created (written, spoken, filmed, painted, etc.) during the time under study. These are eyewitness accounts, such as those contained in the journals of Lewis and Clark. *Artifacts* are objects made by persons during the time under study, such as a medicine pouch carried by Sacagawea. *Secondary sources* are interpretations of these primary sources and artifacts. The Ken Burns PBS film of the Lewis and Clark expedition and Stephen Ambrose's best-selling book about it, *Undaunted Courage,* are both secondary sources. When you conduct a lesson or unit on the Lewis and Clark expedition, your students will need to work with primary and secondary sources as they compose a narrative description (a story) of what happened. When they do this, they are engaging in historical reasoning. Lesson Plan 4 suggests a way to teach the difference between primary and secondary sources.

Some primary sources will be collected for you in the textbook program and its ancillaries and some are available online. Local museums will often lend a few artifacts, and a field trip to a museum may be arranged. Biographies (which are secondary sources) are probably in the school library or multimedia center, along with photo collections and paintings.

Interpretive reasoning, then, is investigative reasoning. The historian—whether a child or a professional—conducts an *inquiry,* an *investigation.* It is a question-driven search for evidence and answers. There is a problem to be solved (e.g., Were Lewis and Clark kind to the American Indian peoples they encountered?). Information must be collected and evaluated and a conclusion drawn. This conclusion is difficult to draw because, among other things, *there are gaps in the record.* Plenty of them. Furthermore, not all the information that is available is altogether credible. (Who said it? What was his or her agenda? In what direction did the person's bias run?) And that's not all. The author—whether your student or a professional—makes choices about what to pay attention to. "No historian tries to write a 'complete' account, and no one would have time to read one."[7]

Understandably, then, one student's interpretation will differ from another's, just as do the interpretations of professional historians. Historians disagree about almost everything, even such basics as the causes of the American Revolution, the meaning of Lincoln's Gettysburg Address, Dr. King's role in the Civil Rights movement, and the reasons for the U.S. invasion of Iraq. Consequently, *teaching history is not a simple matter of teaching children "what happened."* It is, rather, helping children, using evidence and argument, to *figure out* what happened: to reconcile competing primary and secondary accounts of the same event, to make sense of an old artifact, to bridge gaps in the record, to produce a credible and fair-minded account.

Readers wanting to delve further into historical reasoning are referred to the national standards for history (www.nchs.ucla.edu) where, in addition to topical guidelines, they will find a good discussion of five sets of skills that together add up to historical reasoning: chronological thinking, historical comprehension, historical analysis and interpretation, historical research capabilities, and historical issues-analysis and decision making.

Lesson Plan 4

PRIMARY AND SECONDARY SOURCES

Grade 5 or 6

Time One class period

NCSS Standards 2 (time, continuity, and change) and 10 (civic ideals and practices)

Objectives Students will form an initial concept of what historians call *primary* and *secondary sources* and learn how to interpret conflicting primary sources.

Interest Building Send a committee of students on an errand to the school library or multimedia center (e.g., to borrow the "best" dictionary). While they are gone, stage an event to which the students remaining in the classroom will be eyewitnesses. It should surprise students but not upset or disturb them. Two that have been used successfully rely on an unexpected classroom visit: (a) Ask the principal to come into your class unexpectedly, sneak up behind you, and say, "Boo!" Surprised, you spill a cup of water. (b) Ask a colleague to come into your classroom unexpectedly and recite a short poem very dramatically while you look on in surprise. Then, the unexpected visitor leaves.

Lesson Development 1. Explain to the class that this was a pretend event for the purpose of teaching an important idea about history.

2. *Primary source.* Ask students immediately to write down legibly an eyewitness account of exactly what happened. Tell them not to talk with one another, but to rely only on their memory. They should be sure to record all the details: the time at which the person came into the room, what he or she was wearing, saying, and doing; what the teacher did in response, the expression on the teacher's face, any words that were spoken, and all physical movements.

3. Congratulate students on having just written what historians call a primary source. When the committee returns with the dictionary, ask one of them to open it and read aloud the definition of primary (e.g., "first in time or order of development"). Explain that a primary source is one that is written at the time the event occurred by someone who was there.

4. *Secondary source.* Explain that secondary sources are accounts of an event written by a person or persons not present but who use primary sources as the basis for interpreting what happened. The committee that had been out of the room now is welcomed back and given the task of composing a brief written account of what happened. They have nothing to rely on but their classmates' primary accounts. Have each student read aloud his or her primary account and instruct the committee to listen carefully. After each eyewitness has spoken (and inevitably there are differences), the committee members confer with one another and write a secondary source, which is read to the class.

5. *Critique.* Ask the eyewitnesses to judge the quality of the secondary account. This should create some lively discussion.

Summary Lead a discussion on this question: How and why did our primary sources differ from one another? Then, review the difference between primary and secondary sources.

Assessment 1. Ask students to write down the definition of primary and secondary sources and to contrast the two. Ask several students to read their definitions aloud. Collect them to read later.

2. Ask students to decide whether a diary is a primary or a secondary source. (This will be difficult, allowing the teacher to assess where the difficulties lie.) Have them hold up one finger for primary, two for secondary, a closed fist if they are not sure. Then listen carefully to their reasons and any confusions. These will indicate what you need to clarify and whether the distinction needs to be retaught.

Materials   Cup of water if you choose scenario (a) as described under "Interest Building."

Integration   *Reading and writing*: Following this lesson, concentrate your reading and writing instruction on primary documents. Letters and journals (of Columbus, of Abigail Adams, of Anne Frank, of abolitionists, of soldiers and nurses at battlefields, etc.) are especially interesting to children. Martin Luther King, Jr., wrote his most famous letter from a jail cell in Birmingham, Alabama. Lewis and Clark's journal entries appear on pages 116 and 117. Students can write their own journal entries in response to these, or write a letter back to Abigail Adams, Martin Luther King, Jr., Columbus, or whomever's primary sources they read.

Teaching Suggestions

Now what was said at the outset should make more sense: The key to teaching history to children is to head in two directions, not one. Using the airplane analogy again, these two "wings" work well together but not at all alone. In one direction, children are exposed to historical narratives that others have constructed; in the other, children are engaged face-to-face with historical reasoning: they are helped to construct their own narratives. Put in the simplest way, one is absorbing history, and the other is doing history. One is comprehending a historical account; the other is creating a historical account. The first is reading history; the other is writing history. The first is listening to stories; the second is storytelling. In the first, the student is the recipient; in the second, the student is the author.

Absorbing: Exposure to Narratives Others Have Constructed

Good historical stories (narratives) abound. They have already been composed by someone else—a professional historian, a grandparent, a children's book author, or ancestors. They may be cherished stories that date back hundreds or thousands of years. They include the basic civic stories of the founding and growth of this nation (e.g., the stories of the American Revolution, the Civil War, and the Civil Rights movement). One wing of the history-teaching airplane emphasizes exposing students to such stories.

Students listen to the teacher or others read these historical narratives aloud or tell them from memory. Or students read these accounts themselves, discuss them with classmates, and tell them from memory. They are assisted in doing this with before, during, and after reading or listening activities, which together aid children's comprehension of the story. Depth of understanding is encouraged, as with any good literature instruction. Exposure should not be dismissed as passive or superficial, for considerable intellectual effort is needed to really comprehend and interpret any story. Like music appreciation, story appreciation requires an active listener who is intellectually and emotionally awake.

Doing: Constructing Historical Narratives Themselves

REFLECTION

Absorbing and doing are the two wings of history education: What experiences have you had, in school or out, with either?

The other wing of history teaching helps students do the historical work themselves. On this wing, students are helped to compose (author, construct) historical interpretations using primary sources, artifacts, and secondary sources. Again, lots of assistance is needed. The teacher provides instruction on the inquiry process, teaching students about hypotheses, evidence, and drawing tentative conclusions. The teacher also helps them formulate good questions for their inquiries, teaches them about the different kinds of sources, helps them judge the quality of the evidence they find, and teaches them to draft, revise, and publish their interpretations.

Table 4–2 gives examples from each wing of history learning, and these are fleshed out in the following sections.

Absorbing History

Let us examine several ways to help students learn about history. As the following examples show, learning about history is loaded with opportunities to improve students' comprehension skills.

Discussing the Meanings of a Primary Document

March 30, 1806, journal of Meriwether Lewis:

> They have also a very singular custom among them of bathing themselves allover with urine every morning.

Can't you just imagine students reaction to hearing this? Ask them, *Who* is bathing? (From this account alone, we don't know. Members of his corps? Members of a people he encountered? We have to search backward in the journal for evidence.) Ask them, *Why?* Do they know why anyone would bathe with urine? Elicit hypotheses from students, and ask them what sources would help them find out which hypothesis is most likely true.

TABLE 4–2 The two wings of history learning: Absorbing and doing history	
Absorbing History **(exposure; knowing about)**	**Doing History** **(construction; composition)**
Listening to someone else read: • a primary document • a secondary source narrative • historical fiction Reading and examining: • a primary source document (e.g., diary, photo, newspaper editorial, speech) • a secondary source document • historical fiction Discussing the possible meanings of: • an artifact (e.g., a cave painting or other artwork) • a primary source document • a secondary source document • historical fiction Communicating the story to others by: • telling • dramatizing • singing • dancing	Using artifacts and primary and secondary sources, students will compose: • an autobiography • a biography • an oral history • an interpretative narrative (a story) of a current event in the school or local community • an interpretative narrative of an event in the recent past (e.g., the Montgomery Bus Boycott), the distant past (e.g., Boston Tea Party), or ancient times (the Trojan Horse) • a dramatic reenactment of an event • time travel

April 1, 1806, journal of Meriwether Lewis:

I purchased a canoe from an Indian to day for which I gave him six fathoms of wampum beads; he seemed satisfyed with his bargain and departed in another canoe but shortly after returned and canceled the bargain, took his canoe and returned the beads. This is frequently the case in their method of trading and is deemed fair by them.

How admirable that Lewis tries to understand what to him must have been a very annoying behavior. Ask your students if they would consider this fair today and why. Ask them to empathize with this custom—to assume it is intelligent—and see if they can imagine why it would be "deemed fair by them."

Listening to Historical Narratives (Fiction or Nonfiction) and Discussing Their Meaning

Young children can be gathered at the rug area to hear the story of "the shot heard round the world" at Lexington Green, which began the War for Independence. Older children can read it themselves or, taking turns, aloud to one another. Or there's the story of the Underground Railroad—the network by which enslaved Africans living in southern states were able to move, well hidden, to the north. There's the story of the women who, against all odds, fought for and won the right to vote long after men had fought for it and won it for themselves. There is the American patriots' hard winter at Valley Forge, the coronation of Cleopatra, the assassination of Lincoln, the murder of Sitting Bull, and Custer's "last stand." There are the extraordinary stories of countless immigrants, both infamous conquistadors and anonymous stowaways, seekers of fortune and seekers of freedom. There are the stories of individuals who have died in wars defending their nations and of the innocent children caught up in them. There is the story of Martin Luther King, Jr., a pastor who rose to the leadership of the Civil Rights movement, his learning from Gandhi, his relationship with his children, his wife, and Malcolm X. And, there is the story of Rosa Parks.

Ms. Paley, the kindergarten teacher we met in the prior chapter was reading aloud to her students from Rosa Parks's autobiography about the Montgomery bus boycott. The boycott was inspired by the now-famous incident in which Rosa Parks refused to give up her seat to a white man. The children were riveted to the story. Afterward, they were eager to retell it, dramatize it, and talk about the consequences. Consider this excerpt from a discussion in which Ms. Paley's kindergartners are considering the morality of segregating people by race. We can see them trying to distinguish between good and bad reasons for separating people from one another.

Wally: Martin changed all the rules.

Lisa: All the bad rules.

Fred: But not the one for the bathroom. The girls still have to separate from the boys.[8]

Role-Playing

There may be no activity more powerful for developing historical empathy than to role-play the characters involved in a real historical happening. Display a photo, painting, or other visual representation of a historical event to help children imagine being there, and read aloud a vivid description of the event from a piece of historical fiction, textbook, magazine, or encyclopedia. Assign children the roles of key persons in the scene. Coach them into the appropriate postures, expressions, and feelings. In this way, children can reenact Paul Revere's ride, the signing of the Declaration of Independence, or the coronation of Cleopatra. They can march for women's rights, conduct a sit-in at a segregated lunch counter, land on the moon, or surround Custer's troops at the Battle of the Little Big Horn. More ideas can be found in Vivian Paley's work with kindergartners in her book, *Wally's Stories,* and in Douglas Selwyn's *Living History in the Classroom.*

Children's Literature

The four themes and eight periods of U.S. history shown in Table 4–1 may take some readers of this book aback. "I don't know this material very well" is likely the first reaction of some readers who themselves may not have taken a course in history since high school. Teachers must know the material they want to teach, and it is well documented that teachers' knowledge of a subject shapes their teaching of it, often dramatically. Nonetheless, it is true that teachers themselves sometimes learn much of the material they will teach as they plan it. The children's social studies textbook and its teacher's guide are major sources of information for teachers. Trade books written for children are another source. Reading aloud Jean Fritz's stirring *China's Long March: 6000 Miles of Danger* during a unit on China will teach children and teacher alike much about China's geography, Mao's struggle against Chiang Kai-shek, and the horrendous march. Reading aloud from Fritz's *Where Was Patrick Henry on the 29th of May?* and then having the children dramatically reenact Henry's famous speech on liberty will teach children and teacher alike about both the orator and the events of 1775. The following children's trade books, geared to the four themes in Table 4–1, suggest the range of possibilities.

Theme 1: Democracy

Madam President, Catherine Thimmesh (Houghton Mifflin, 2004).
Shh! We're Writing the Constitution, Jean Fritz (J. J. Putnam & Sons, 1987).
I Am Rosa Parks, Rosa Parks and James Haskins (Dial, 1997).
Freedom Summer, Deborah Wiles (Atheneum, 2001).

Theme 2: Culture

La Línea, Ann Jaramillo (Roaring Brook, 2006).
Building a New Land: African Americans in Colonial America, James Haskins and Kathleen Benson (Amistad/HarperCollins, 2001).
Tales from Gold Mountain: Stories of the Chinese in the New World, Paul Yee (Groundwood, 1999).
The Pilgrims of Plimouth, Marcia Sewall (Aladdin, 1996).

Theme 3: Technology

Now and Ben: The Modern Inventions of Benjamin Franklin, Jean Barretta (Henry Holt, 2006).
To Fly: The Story of the Wright Brothers, Wendie Old (Clarion, 2002).
Who Came Down That Road?, George Ella Lyon (Orchard, 2004).
Titanic: The Disaster That Shocked the World, Mark Dubowski (DK, 1998).

Theme 4: World Role

Patrol: An American Soldier in Vietnam, Walter Dean Myers (HarperCollins, 2002).
The White Swan Express: A Story About Adoption, Jean Davies Okimoto and Elaine M. Aoki (Clarion, 2002).
A World in our Hands: In Honor of the 50th Anniversary of the United Nations, Young People of the World (Ten Speed Press, 1995).
Sadako, Eleanor Coerr (Putnam, 1994).

Guidelines for selecting literature.   Here are three basic guidelines for selecting historical narratives (both fiction and nonfiction) for the classroom:

1. Does it tell a good story?
2. Is the story accurate in its historical detail, including the setting and the known events? (Remember, a good story is not necessarily an accurate story, that is, based on sound evidence.)
3. Whose voices are missing? No narrative can include every perspective (no narrative is complete). But because narrative can be a powerful genre, it is important to bring voices that are missing in one story to the forefront in another.[9]

But, as we shall see in Chapter 12, multiple perspectives are better than one. Even though one book can represent one perspective quite well, sometimes brilliantly, providing rich contextual detail, two books on the same event dramatically enrich the study.

Examining Artifacts

Children love to examine historical objects closely and handle them. A monthly "artifact day," when children bring objects from home or their parents' workplaces, can be planned. An item of traditional clothing, a great grandparent's family Bible or Koran or prayer beads, an old butter churn, photo, rice steamer, or tortilla press—any of these might be shown to classmates, placed on a time line, and stories told about them. Arrowheads from a native group, an army recruitment poster, a spinning wheel or spittoon, a manual typewriter or rotary telephone, a quill pen or piece of fool's gold—any of these could be related to the instructional unit at hand. If an item is brought from home and highly valued, it is best for the adult owner to bring it to school to show the children and tell them of its significance.

Local museums often have permanent displays of historical materials significant to the local community, state, and region. Increasingly, they package materials in a "museum treasure chest" that is loaned to the school. A phone call should provide needed information about this service. Also, artifacts can be viewed online. At the Smithsonian Institution's "Spotlight Biography" website, click on "inventors," then on Ben Franklin's printing press where you will see the press Franklin used in London as a young man in 1725. The disadvantage to such online artifacts, of course, is that students cannot touch them or see them from different angles.

Using Song and Dance

Collect folk songs, patriotic songs, and dances of various eras of history. These will help children absorb the feeling of the era through a different "entry point," as Howard Gardner describes multiple intelligences (see Chapter 2). Present to another class "A Musical Pageant of American History."

Speechifying

Depending on the event you or the children select for role-playing, there may be a terrific speech that can be memorized and reenacted. Patrick Henry's famous speech before the House of Burgesses, for example, is the one that ends, "But as for me, give me liberty or give me death!" And there is Sojourner Truth's "And, Ain't I a Woman?", Lincoln's "government of the people, by the people, and for the people," King's "I Have a Dream," and Chief Joseph's "I Will Fight No More Forever."

Doing History

We turn now to the other wing of history teaching and learning, where the students them-selves learn to investigate the past and compose histories using the material tools of histo-rians: primary and secondary sources and artifacts, as well as the mental tools of historical reasoning. Teachers who plan to help their students work toward this objective will want to collect work samples along the way. A sample portfolio is shown in Figure 4–3 (and see Chapter 7, "Assessing Student Learning," for details). The following are examples of doing history.

Composing a Dramatic Reenactment

Returning to our chapter-opening classroom snapshot, recall that the students were not only retelling an episode from the Lewis and Clark journey that would help them absorb this moment in history. Beyond this, they were trying to get it just right, trying to figure out what really happened at that moment when Lewis and Clark met up with Sacagawea. Doing so required students to construct an understanding of that meeting. They had to gather and judge evidence and draw a conclusion. Their conclusion would be "published" as a drama-tization before classmates, and this in turn would be filmed.

Noticing that they were relying on just two sources of information—the journals of Lewis and Clark and a fictionalized trade-book narrative—their teacher encouraged them to find a third source. They returned to the PBS website that has the journals and found, in another section, this secondary source description of the meeting ceremony.

> Over the course of the expedition, Lewis and Clark developed a ritual that they used when meeting a tribe for the first time. The captains would explain to the tribal leaders that their land now belonged to the United States, and that a man far in the east—President Thomas Jefferson—was their new "great father." They would also give the Indians a peace medal with Jefferson on one side and two hands clasping on the other, as well as some form of presents [often trade goods]. Moreover, the Corps members would perform a kind of parade, marching in uniform and shooting their guns. (From the PBS website of the Ken Burns film)

Some students will be saddened and angered by this information, believing it wrong for the expedition to claim the land for the United States. "That's stealing," one might say. The teacher can ask, "Well, *is it even true?* What's your evidence? Who wrote this description? Go find out before you put it in your drama." Eventually, they revise their script to incorporate this ceremony, judging that it was enacted at the Sacagawea meeting just as it routinely was enacted elsewhere.

FIGURE 4–3   A "Doing History" portfolio.

Contents of My "Doing History" Portfolio		Name _____
Type of History	**Topic**	**Date/My Comments**
Autobiography	My life	_____/_____ _____ _____
Oral history	A veteran's stories	_____/_____ _____ _____
Oral history	A classmate's move	_____/_____ _____ _____
Biography	President Lincoln	_____/_____ _____ _____
Cooperative Biography	Sojourner Truth	_____/_____ _____ _____

Time Travel

These dramatic reenactments can be spiced up when framed as "time travel." A "time machine" made from boxes and chicken wire or a "time curtain" made with a shower curtain suspended from a wooden dowel can serve as "portals" through which students pass on their way back in time. In Linda Bailey's fun and fact-filled picture books (e.g., *Adventures in Ancient Egypt, Adventures in the Ice Age*), the Binkerton family visits the Good Times Travel Agency, which specializes in time travel.

Oral History

Structured interviews or informal conversations with local persons of historical significance can be preserved as "oral history" by using tape recorders. Children are fascinated when

Dramatic reenactments are fun and informative. *(Charles Gatewood/PH College)*

old-timers talk of their experiences in the early community. They are surprised to hear that the person now speaking to them marched in the Civil Rights movement, bicycled across a desert or mountain range, sailed across an ocean, fought in Afghanistan or Iraq, or helped change a law. This procedure has the added value of *involving children firsthand in gathering historical data*. The taped interviews, therefore, need to be planned, with questions written out and practiced first with classmates. After the data have been gathered, they need to be interpreted. Where does the story really begin? Where does it end? What is the chain of causation? Who influenced whom and how? Why did people act as they did? How did geography (climate, landforms, culture) influence events?

Painting

Paint a mural of some aspect of the history of the local community or state. Help students narrow in on a single aspect of the community's history, and then assemble resources that will enable them to learn a great deal about that. Then, help them decide what to include and exclude and how to know what is true. These are all decisions that involve students in historical reasoning.

Making Models

Models can be made of many things: communities (the children's town as it looked 50 or 100 years ago, Mesa Verde, Tokyo, Plimoth), shelters (hogans, igloos, tepees, high-rises, and longhouses), transportation (oxcarts, wagon trains, rockets, ships, and canoes), and means of long-distance communication (Pony Express, telegraph, radio, television, telephone, and Internet). Whether model building belongs to *doing* history rather than only *absorbing* it depends on whether the teacher involves the students in interpreting artifacts and primary and secondary sources. This is the evidence base with which students compose their model and defend it as fair and accurate—something every historian must be prepared to do. "How do you know that's true?" is a question the teacher must ask again and again, gently, until students themselves begin to ask it of one another and themselves. See the section in Chapter 8 called "Incorporating Construction Activities."

Writing and Drawing Snapshot Autobiographies

A rich yet simple place to begin teaching the youngest students about the tools of historical inquiry is with the autobiography. The "snapshot" autobiography approach is my favorite. It has students think of just four or five events that happened in the last two or three years. A special birthday, the first day in a new school, a move, a pet. A drawing of each makes the "snapshot." Students should begin by making a time line of the events, showing the relative time between them. Then, as shown in Figure 4–4, the events are strung together, accordion

---

FIGURE 4–4   A snapshot autobiography.

My Last Three Years

1. ... My Dog
2. ... Our Move
3. ... The Fire
4. ... Relatives

We got Spotty when he was one month old and I was four. He chewed everything.

One and one-half years later we moved to Northeast 123rd street. Then I was five and one-half.

That first month, we had a fire in the kitchen! Mom put it out with the red fire extinguisher.

The next year our relatives came for Thanksgiving. There were lots of us.

style, in sequence, with a very brief written narrative description of each. The narrative description tells what is happening in the drawing. Add a title page and table of contents, and the child has a complete autobiography. The children should be taught the vocabulary of chronology and asked to use it in each snapshot description, thereby locating it in time (e.g., "when I was four," "one-and-one-half years later," "that same month," "the following year"). As appropriate for the developmental level of the children, encourage them to think more deeply about their audience, the events they will choose, and the interaction of the two; also, have them search for an *artifact* that provides evidence for each event. For example, if a child has featured a move from one home to another, a good artifact would be an addressed and delivered envelope showing that mail was forwarded from the old to the new address.

Writing and Drawing Snapshot Biographies

After building some experience with autobiographies, children are ready to write snapshot *biographies.* Normally, the subjects are the historical figures they are studying. These might be biographies of courageous citizens, labor and business leaders, explorers, presidents, framers of the U.S. Constitution, women's suffrage and civil rights activists, heroes, villains, and other persons of historical significance. These could also be biographies of persons in their own lives: an aunt or uncle, a pastor or rabbi, a club leader, a brother or sister. Snapshot biographies focus on just four or five events with an illustration and brief description of each. Again, work with students on the vocabulary of chronology and deepen their understanding of the idea of primary and secondary sources. Chapter 13 explains how teams of children can together compose elaborate biographies. Be sure children *read* biographies before trying to *write* them. This way, they learn first about the genre.

Constructing a Classroom or Library Museum Exhibit

Children can engage in a major act of historical interpretation when they create a museum exhibit as the culminating project of a historical inquiry. The exhibit can be placed in the classroom, a showcase in the main office, or the school multimedia center. A curator from a local museum might come to talk with the children about the process of selecting topics, artifacts, and documents for exhibits and teach them how to write the brief description that will be placed alongside each. Visitors need these to understand what they are seeing. Fourth-graders in Colorado constructed an exhibit on the history of that state. At Parent Night, students served as docents (museum guides) while others appeared in costume. The docents introduced parents to a gold miner, banker, sheriff, cavalry officer, and a group of Plains Indians. One or two field trips to museums will help students' exhibits become more authentic, and virtual field trips on the Internet (see Chapter 10) to the Smithsonian and other collections will provide additional food for thought.

Linda D'Acquisto has given lots of thought to the museum project idea. Her book, *Learning on Display: Student-Created Museums that Build Understanding* (2006), tells readers how to do it, from A to Z, including helpful details on planning and assessment. Figure 4–5 displays her vision of the instruction process for student-created museums.

Simulations

In the simulation game *Pilgrims* (grades 2–4, Interact), children re-create the Plymouth colony in 17th-century Massachusetts. Older students (grades 4–8, Interact) will enjoy

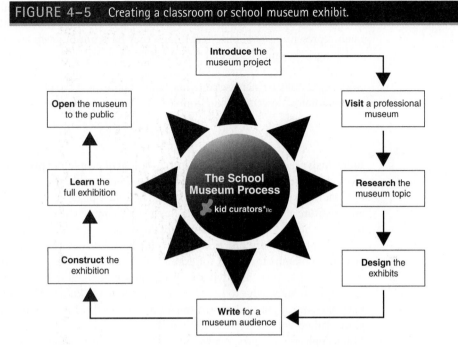

FIGURE 4–5   Creating a classroom or school museum exhibit.

Source: © Kid Curators, LLC, 2001, 2006; Linda D'Acquisto; www.kidcurators.com. Used by permission.

Debating the Documents: The Pilgrims, in which traditional stories about the Pilgrims are compared with primary and secondary sources.

TEACHING GEOGRAPHY

Not only astronauts but all of us live in space. Geography's vantage point is not so much historical as spatial, although these certainly overlap. The word *geography* derives from a Greek word meaning "writing about Earth." When we engage in geographical study, we learn about the arrangement and interaction of people and places on Earth. Geography brings the physical (e.g., landforms, climate, regions) and the human (culture, migration, politics) together, and shows how they influence one another, back and forth. You've heard of global warming? That is humans influencing Earth's climate, which, in turn, influences human behavior. You've heard of floods? That is Earth shaping people's lives, but perhaps the flood occurred *after* people prevented water absorption by cutting down a forest, building a suburb, and paving much of the land with asphalt.

Maps help us know where we are in space, and they represent various characteristics of that space—its roads or elevations or populations. Accordingly, maps are probably the most common kind of *graphic representation* found in geographical study. Maps represent real things (a map of Japan is based on the actual physical image of Japan), which makes them easier for children to read than other kinds of graphics, such as bar graphs and pie graphs.

Still, map reading is challenging for children because, first, they are only just at the beginning of learning about representations (symbols) and, second, even if they understand that maps represent or symbolize real things, they have not built up an adequate inventory of real things! They may learn that ∧ ∧ ∧ symbolizes a mountain range, but they may not have formed the concept of mountain range. Elementary and middle school teachers need to work continually to increase students' understandings of the graphics and the real things—the mountains, deserts, climate zones, crops, and regions—to which they refer.

Purposes

Individuals need to understand the spatial settings of people and places on Earth for many reasons. The most basic reason is existential: People everywhere want to make sense of their lives; they want to know the nature of the world and their place in it. Great religions, philosophy, and literature of all sorts grapple with this uniquely human need. Humans want to understand the world they're in, and geography helps them know where they are, literally and figuratively.

There are also very practical reasons for having geographical knowledge and abilities: getting from home to school, for example. Travelers, explorers, generals, and entrepreneurs would be at a great loss without geographical tools and information. All of us need geographical knowledge to get where we want to go, to know where we have been, to locate natural resources, to understand the wants and needs of people in different places, and to grasp daily events in relation to their settings—a picnic in July in Phoenix, a flat tire in Minneapolis in February, a subsistence farmer on the horn of Africa, the American rebels' winter at Valley Forge, Southeast Asian refugees settling in Oakland, California.

From a child's point of view, the practical needs for geographical knowledge spring to life when his or her parents decide to take a road trip or to move their home from one place to another, whether they are refugees fleeing a war, a working-class family moving to another town in search of employment, or suburbanites who decide to move to the city to be close to museums, galleries, and theaters.

The Geography Curriculum: The Thematic Approach

Is there any way a teacher can grasp the Earth-sized body of knowledge and skill called geography, at least well enough to do a good job of teaching it? There is. A set of curriculum guidelines was developed jointly by the National Council for Geographic Education and the Association of American Geographers. This group identified five themes, and they have since provided teachers and publishers of curriculum materials with a meaningful framework for getting a grip on this sprawling field *and* enriching geography learning for children beyond memory work alone. The five themes of geography are described briefly in the following list. My students developed an acronym to help them remember all five: MR. HELP.

1. *Movement: Humans Interacting on Earth.* Human beings occupy places unevenly across the face of Earth. Some live on farms or in the country; others live in towns, villages, or cities. Yet these people interact with one another, that is, they travel from one place to another, they communicate with one another, or they rely on products, information, and ideas that come from beyond their immediate environment. The most visible evidences of global interdependence and the

People everywhere strive to know the world. *(Tom Watson/Merrill)*

interaction of places are the transportation and communication lines that link every part of the world. Most people interact with other places almost every day of their lives, even in an action as simple as a resident of Georgia eating an apple grown in the state of Washington and shipped to Atlanta by rail or truck. On a larger scale, international trade demonstrates that no country is self-sufficient.

2. *Regions: How They Form and Change.* The basic unit of geographic study is the region, an area that displays unity in terms of selected criteria. There are many kinds of regions. Some are defined by one characteristic, such as a language group (e.g., the Cantonese-speaking region of China) or, more typically, a landform type (e.g., the Midwest or the Pacific Northwest in the United States). It is typical in the fourth grade for the social studies curriculum to concentrate on regions of the United States and in the sixth or seventh grade to focus on world regions.

3. *Human-Environment Interaction.* All places on Earth have advantages and disadvantages for human settlement. High population densities have developed on floodplains, for example, where people could take advantage of fertile soils, water resources, and opportunities for river transportation. By comparison, population

densities are usually low in deserts. Yet floodplains are periodically subjected to severe damage, and some desert areas, such as Israel, have been modified to support large population concentrations.

4. *Location: Position on Earth's Surface.* Absolute and relative location are two ways of describing the positions of people and places on Earth's surface. One of the great dramas in Europe's age of exploration was keeping sailors from being lost at sea as soon as they lost sight of land. "Launched on a mix of bravery and greed, the sea captains of the fifteenth, sixteenth, and seventeenth centuries relied on dead reckoning to gauge their distance east or west of home port. . . . Long voyages waxed longer for lack of longitude and the extra time at sea condemned sailors to the dread disease of scurvy."[10] So writes the author of *Longitude,* Dava Sobel, telling the story of John Harrison, who developed the device that helps sailors locate their ships at sea. As you will see in the next chapter, there is much that children need to learn about location, both relative (Taiwan is off the coast of China) and absolute (Taiwan is where 120 degrees longitude meets the Tropic of Cancer).

5. *Place: Physical and Human Characteristics.* All places on Earth have distinctive characteristics, some tangible and some intangible, that give them meaning and character and distinguish them from other places. Geographers generally describe places by their physical or human characteristics. Your classroom, for example, is a place with both physical and human characteristics. Chapter 2 emphasized the latter—the demographic makeup of the classroom. The physical characteristics all can be represented on maps.

Each theme is a concept that students form gradually as they work with multiple examples. Progress toward this goal can be made in every grade level of elementary and middle school. As they study classmates' immigration from points around the world, Lewis and Clark's movement westward followed by the development of wagon trains and loco-motives, the Native American movement eastward into America thousands of years before, the construction of interstate highways, and Mexican migration northward today, students are gathering the building blocks for geographic understanding.

Readers should be aware that the National Council for Geographic Education also developed 18 standards for geography education, published in an outstanding book called *Geography for Life.* Those 18 standards can be grouped as follows:

1. The world in spatial terms
2. Place and regions
3. Physical systems
4. Human systems
5. Environment and society
6. Uses of geography

Advice on working with these standards is provided in a free pamphlet, *Making the Standards Work for You,* available from the Council's website (www.ncge.org). Nonetheless, in my own work with new and experienced elementary and middle school teachers, the five themes discussed on pages 126–128 have proven to be more readily understandable and, because of that, of lasting value than the new 18 standards. Readers should decide for them-selves, however, and I do highly recommend both the book that contains the new standards and the pamphlet that accompanies it.

Teaching Suggestions

The next chapter has many teaching suggestions for geography, so we will discuss only a few basics here.

Moving

Every year, tens of millions of Americans load their possessions into cars and trucks and move to new neighborhoods, near and far. A class can help orient a newly arrived classmate to the geography of the school grounds and community by creating maps, conducting guided tours, and preparing a "Welcome" brochure. Questions and answers in the brochure can be geared to the five themes of geography.

1. *Movement.* How did the earliest native groups get to this place? How did newcomers arrive? How many arrive each year, and by what means of transportation? How many leave? Is there an interstate highway near?
2. *Region.* What region is our town a part of and what are the regions in our town? What things do nearby towns have in common? What kinds of jobs do people in this region have? What are the highest and lowest average temperatures in this region?
3. *Human-Environment Interaction.* What natural resources can be found here? How have people here changed the environment? Do we recycle anything? Where does our food and drinking water come from? How much waste (human and material) do we produce and where does our waste go? Where is the water purification plant?
4. *Location.* Where is our school in our community? Why is it located there? Where is it relative to the park and city hall? Where is our community in the state? In the country?
5. *Place.* What is it like here? What are this community's most notable natural and human-made features? What do kids do here for fun? What languages are spoken here? If you wanted to draw this place, what color crayons should you bring? How does the rest of the world look from this vantage place?

Water—at School and in the Neighborhood

Help build students' awareness of water—our most precious natural resource. Earth is the "water planet." Yet, the coming water shortage will be among the world's most serious crises.

Have children observe firsthand how fresh drinking water comes into the school building, then appears in sinks, toilets, and drinking fountains. Then have them observe in the school's neighborhood various bodies of water and their relation to landforms—lakes, creeks, ditches, islands, hills, gullies, slopes. Younger children can draw these; older children can draw them to scale and locate them on maps they create themselves. It is especially helpful if children can safely see firsthand the joining of a creek with a stream, or a stream to a river, or the confluence of two rivers. Where are the headwaters located? Where do they end up? Also, children should study water purification procedures and take a field trip to a water purification plant. Many primary-grade children will be able to read *A Cool Drink of Water* by Barbara Kerley (National Geographic Society, 2002). Readers may wish to jump ahead to the environmental unit called "Explore" in the final chapter of this book. The third lesson there helps children form the concept—*survival needs of living things.*

Seminar on *The View from the Oak*

A stunning book by Judith and Herbert Kohl called *The View from the Oak: The Private Worlds of Other Creatures* (New Press, 2000) can be read independently by many children aged 10 years and up and can stimulate the imaginations of younger children when read aloud. Teachers can gather children and read just the first chapter, then discuss it. Students will learn that each animal has its own unique vantage point in the world—its own place and way of experiencing it that is unique to that species. The authors call this unique view an *umwelt*. In the first chapter, readers get a feel for how the authors' golden retriever experiences the world, then an ant and a bee. A good interpretive question for the discussion might be: What do the Kohls want us to know about animals? A second question might be: What is the *umwelt* of children? This book won the National Book Award for children's literature in 1977 and has been recently reprinted. (Please see the section on conducting seminars in Chapter 12.)

School-Yard Geography

Divide the class into five teams and the school grounds into five spaces. Each team studies its space through the five themes of MR. HELP.

Drawing the World Map in 30 Seconds

Help children get to the point where they can draw a world map from memory. This is for them and their parents a notable achievement. The task is not as difficult as it might seem! Children must be provided ample opportunity to study world maps and to practice drawing their own. One helpful technique is to begin with circles (Figure 4–6). Chapter 5 goes into detail on how the world is viewed depending on which projection is used. With second- and third-grade children it is unnecessary to get into projections, but fourth-graders and up will find it an intriguing problem. See especially Lesson Plan 8 in Chapter 5.

Making Maps with Clay

Visualizing the size and shape of land masses relative to one another is the aim of the preceding activity. Zooming in on one local area *within* a land mass is the aim of making maps with clay. Now students represent the local features—both natural and human-made—in three dimensions. A full-color photo of a third-grade girl's map of Seattle, Washington, appears in the learning activities section of Chapter 8. Please look ahead now.

Orienteering in the Library/Multimedia Center and Elsewhere at School

Have children start this activity by mapping the classroom. Then have teams of children make maps of the school's library or media center. They will learn where the catalog, the biography section, and the CD and DVD collections are located while symbolizing them on the map and in the map key. Polar directions should be included, and the maps should be drawn to scale. Then have students map the cafeteria, the playground, and the rest of the school grounds. See the lesson plan in Chapter 10 on orienteering in the library/multimedia center.

Weather and Climate

Weather and climate present another area of exploration. Children will have seen weather forecasts on television, and weather will have affected them in many ways that they will have noticed and cared about. They will have heard about global warming, may know nothing or quite a lot about it, and want to know more. In primary-grade classrooms, children will want to chart various weather data they observe each day. The teacher reads the daily temperature,

FIGURE 4–6   Steps for drawing a world map.

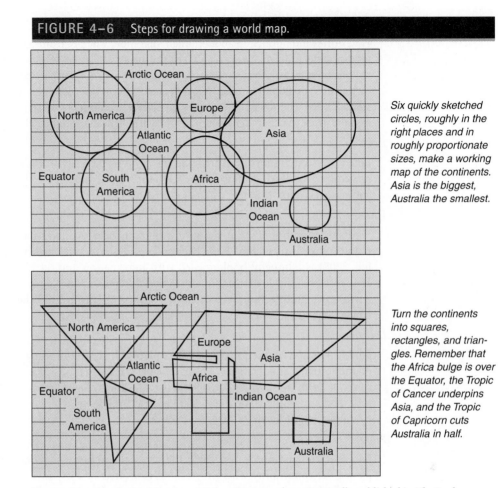

Six quickly sketched circles, roughly in the right places and in roughly proportionate sizes, make a working map of the continents. Asia is the biggest, Australia the smallest.

Turn the continents into squares, rectangles, and triangles. Remember that the Africa bulge is over the Equator, the Tropic of Cancer underpins Asia, and the Tropic of Capricorn cuts Australia in half.

Source: Mapping the World by Lovett Johns Cartographers. Originally published in *The Real World,* 1991 © Marshall Editions, London; and reprinted in *Geography for Life: National Geography Standards* (Washington, DC: National Geographic Research and Exploration, 1994), 65. Reprinted by permission.

or the children report the official daily temperature that they have heard over an early morning radio broadcast. These temperatures can be shown graphically, thereby applying knowledge of numbers and graphs. Over a period of several weeks or months the graph will show the changes occurring in temperatures and seasons of the year. Children can also record data about wind velocity, cloud formations, precipitation, and similar subjects. They can even make their own predictions based on the data they have collected. Sensitivity to weather changes will again call attention to the changes in native plant and animal life as well as to the adaptations people make to changing seasons. Here the teacher can apply another technique of the geographer: recording data and using simple charts.

Children's Literature

The five themes of geography have been widely used as reference points for selecting children's trade books while teaching them some of the fundamentals of geography. Let the themes be your guide as you search the school media center and the public library.

Movement

Find stories and nonfiction about human migration, whether from one continent or country to another or from one side of the river or forest to the other. Also locate stories and nonfiction about transportation—the planes, trains, boats, and trucks that move people, mail, earth, junk, goods, and supplies. *Night Boat to Freedom* (Margot Theis Raven, 2006) tells the story of a boy who rowed slaves across the river to freedom in Ohio. *Tonka: If I Could Drive a Dump Truck* (Michael Teitelbaum, 2001) will delight the youngest children.

Region

Find stories and nonfiction that vividly display the characteristics of one or more regions of a country or Earth. A classic story set in the United States is *Sarah, Plain and Tall* (Patricia MacLachlan, 1985).

Human-Environment Interaction

Find stories and nonfiction about how human societies shape and are shaped by the physical environment. *This Is My Planet: The Kid's Guide to Global Warming* (Jan Thornhill, 2007) is a hopeful book, loaded with information and terrific photographs. *The Hoover Dam* (Elizabeth Mann, 2001) vividly conveys this gigantic feat of human-environment interaction. A comparative unit on dams around the world—from the United States to China to Egypt—would be great fun to develop.

Location

Find stories and nonfiction about where places can be found using both absolute ("It's on the corner.") and relative ("It's near the big lake.") methods. *The Librarian Who Measured the Earth* (Kathryn Lasky, 1994) is a public library favorite that combines math, history, and geography. The "librarian" is Eratosthenes of Cyrene who estimated the circumference of Earth in the year 200 BCE.

Place

Locate stories and nonfiction about the physical and human characteristics of specific places: the community where the school is located or a place far away. *Cactus Hotel* (Brenda Guiberson, 1993) is a charming example. "On a hot, dry day in the desert, a bright-red fruit falls from a tall saguaro cactus. . . ."

TEACHING POLITICAL SCIENCE

Political science is a field of study that is concerned with questions dear to children's hearts: power, authority, and fairness. Can we all get along? How shall we deal with the conflicts and problems of learning and playing together? Should the strongest rule over the less strong? Does might make right? Do we have to have rules? Should they be written down or can they exist only in our minds? Should rules be binding on everyone, even the leader or boss? What is the fairest way to make and enforce rules? To choose leaders?

When students are building knowledge about people and places on Earth (geography) and about the past (history), it is important that they ask these political questions, too. In this way, they construct a fuller understanding of a society—they gather more pieces of the puzzle. And the political piece is crucial; without it, they are ignorant of the political system holding that society together. Is there a tyrant who won power by force and uses the police and military to keep everyone in line, jailing or executing those who disagree? Are the people afraid to speak out? Can they practice only the leader's religion? Are they prevented from joining clubs because the leader fears that opposition to his or her power will grow in them? There are plenty of tyrants in the world today. Ask your students whether this is right. Does might make right? If not, why not?

Ms. Paley, recall, discusses these topics with her kindergartners. She begins by proposing (not posting) a rule for their consideration: "Should we have a rule that goes, You Can't Say 'You Can't Play'?" The students discuss this over several months; consequently, 5-year-olds are doing the work of legislators—deliberating public policy. When her kindergartners get to the third grade, where they study a set of communities on Earth, they are ready to begin looking at the political systems of these communities by asking questions:

- Who is the leader? How did he or she become the leader?
- Does the government rule the people or do the people rule the government? Do the people vote? How often?
- Do they have a democracy or a dictatorship?
- What are the rights of citizens in this place?
- What are the responsibilities of citizens in this place?
- What are the public values expressed on their coins, in their anthems, in their pledges of allegiance?
- Is there discrimination toward cultural and racial minorities? Are minorities treated fairly? Are women treated equally to men?
- Is there freedom of religion? Language?
- Are the laws written down? Is there a constitution?
- Is government power divided up (e.g., judicial, legislative, executive, local, national)?

Teaching Suggestions

Chapter 3 was devoted entirely to teaching suggestions related to political science. Here is a brief review of the six dimensions of citizenship education presented there.

Six Dimensions of Citizenship Education

Deliberation. Give students opportunities to engage in sustained decision-making discussions about classroom life and problems. The decision is one that will be binding on all—a rule or law. Accordingly, keep prodding them, as did Ms. Paley, with two questions: Is the decision fair (just)? Will it work?

Voting and Elections. Teach about elections and engage students in elections—real and mock.

Service Learning and Community Action. Communities are inevitably filled with problems. As students come across them on their own, or learn about them as part of current events instruction, help them think of ways to study them and take action (see Chapter 6).

Knowledge. To think well about community problems, students need to think with a knowledgeable mind. Look back to Chapter 3 at the glossary for citizenship (Figure 3–8). It contains key concepts citizens need to learn (e.g., civil rights, constitution, democracy, rule of law).

Values. Revisit the distinction in Chapter 3 between personal values and public values. Public values, such as tolerance, are the glue that holds a diverse society together and forms the basis of community life. Personal values, such as religious beliefs, are removed from the public realm in democracies for the sake of religious freedom and peace.

Dispositions and Virtues. Citizens without virtues (right habits, dispositions) are "idiots" in the Greek sense noted in the previous chapter because they are a threat to their own and others' liberty. We concentrated on six in Chapter 3: civility, courage, lawfulness, fairness (justice), responsibility, and honesty.

TEACHING ECONOMICS

Economics is the study of the production, distribution, exchange, and consumption of the goods and services that people need or want under conditions of scarcity. You may want to read that sentence again, for it contains key concepts of this field. In a modern, industrialized, capitalistic (or "market") economy such as in the United States, Canada, Europe, and, increasingly, in Asia, Africa, and South America, needs and wants are many because individuals expect a high standard of living *and* because an incessant stream of corporate advertising continually lengthens the list of wants—creating them from thin air. Supplying needs and wants involves production, distribution, exchange, and consumption, all connected in a web of relationships and laws. When the teacher flips the classroom lights on and off, she can ask students to think of all the people and resources that make possible this sudden illumination, then darkness, then illumination again. "We are consuming it, but who is producing and distributing it? How much money do they make? Who pays them? What kind of job is it? Do you think most of the world's people have electricity? Only a few?" These are good questions for a unit, "Who Produces What We Consume in Our Classroom?"

Ideas like these are the central subject matter of economics. The group that has been working most diligently on what teachers can do to help students learn them is the National Council on Economic Education (NCEE). This group identified 20 content standards for economics teaching and learning, and its website (www.ncee.net) features sample lessons for each. The website also can connect you to your state's own council for economic education, which may be a good source for workshops and guest speakers. In 2007, NCEE developed an interactive tool, *Virtual Economics.* This is a lesson-planning CD containing over 12,000 standards-based plans keyed to grade level and more.

One key idea that elementary and middle school children need to develop corresponds to the first of 20 standards. Its central concepts are *scarcity, choice,* and *opportunity cost:*

> Productive resources are limited. Therefore, people cannot have all of the goods and services they want; as a result, they must choose some things and give up others.

Students who understand this idea should be able to know when choices are needed and what they gain and what they give up when they make choices. NCEE provides specific grade-by-grade "benchmarks" related to this idea, such as the fourth-grade examples below. Next to each benchmark is a performance standard that suggests how students will be able to use that knowledge.

Benchmarks	Performance Standards
People make choices because they can't have everything they want.	Identify some choices they have made and explain why they had to make a choice.
Economic wants are desires that can be satisfied by consuming a good, service, or leisure activity.	Match a list of wants with the correct example of a good, service, or leisure activity that satisfies each want.
Goods are objects that can satisfy people's wants.	Create a collage representing goods that they or their families consume.
Services are actions that can satisfy people's wants.	Create a collage representing services that they or their families consume.
People's choices about what goods and services to buy and consume determine how resources will be used.	Explain why a choice must be made when given some land and a list of alternative uses for the land.
Whenever a choice is made, something is given up.	Choose a toy from a list of four toys and state what was given up.
Productive resources are the natural resources, human resources, and capital goods available to make goods and services.	Identify examples of natural resources, human resources, and capital goods used in the production of a given product.
Natural resources, such as land, are "gifts of nature"; they are present without human intervention.	Use a resource map of this state to locate examples of natural resources.
Human resources are the quantity and quality of human effort directed toward producing goods and services.	Draw pictures representing themselves as workers. Also, identify examples of human resources used in the production of education at their school.
Capital goods are goods that are produced and used to make other goods and services.	Draw a picture representing a capital good used at school. Also, identify examples of capital goods used to produce a good or service in their community.

Teaching Suggestions

Are such ideas beyond the reach of elementary school children? Definitely not. Economics education scholars James Laney and Mark Schug sum up the research: "Many studies have been conducted over the years that provide evidence that children can learn economics when it is taught."[11] The problem is that it is often not taught.

The elementary and middle school program of economics instruction should concentrate on basic economic ideas such as those given here, and situate them in broader units and in learning-by-doing experiences.

1. *Create comparative units such as "Farm and Factory Life in Canada and Mexico" and "Needs and Wants in the Years 10, 1010, and 2010."*
2. *Examine ways that people depend on each other in their families, neighborhoods, and communities.* Relate this to the need for many different kinds of jobs in a community and to the concept called *division of labor.*
3. *Familiarize children with goods and services produced locally through field trips and guest speakers.*
4. *Help students distinguish between spending and saving.* Children are fascinated by money—that magic that satisfies their wants for toys and candy. Ask them, "What is money?" and follow up with clarification and elaboration questions: "What do you mean?" "Tell us more about that." "What do you others think?" A simple, informal

assessment of this sort will reveal your students' knowledge and misconceptions around which you can then plan instruction.

Continue the assessment with such questions as these:

a. What are credit cards? (Many young people do not know that credit cards are a form of borrowing money.)

b. What is the difference between cash, checks, and credit cards? (Most young people cannot explain the difference.)

c. Does television advertising create your wants or do you already have them?

Then, you may want to ask students, "What shall we do with the money we are making from our classroom chores other than spending it all in the market?" Suggest to them that four classroom banks be created. Don't just do it, however; share the idea and lead them in discussions about it. Let them decide whether and how to do it. One is a spending bank for *money to be used soon.* Second is a saving bank for *money to be used later.* Third is an investing bank for *money that will grow on its own.* Fourth is a bank for donating *money to help others.* More ideas can be found at www.themint.org.

5. *Raise students' awareness of advertising.* Help them see its ubiquity and its effects on them. Begin by asking students what they want that they don't now have, and help them trace these wants back to their origins. "Where did you learn about that?" Show a videotape of some ads from Saturday morning television programs. See the inquiry lesson in Chapter 9 on advertising.

6. *Use children's literature to introduce or deepen students' understandings of economic ideas.* Just as there are children's trade books geared to history, geography, and citizenship education, so are there books geared to basic economic ideas. Delightful books for primary-grade children are *When the Bees Fly Home* (Andrea Cheng, 2002) and my favorite, *Uncle Jed's Barbershop* (Margaret King Mitchell, 1993).

7. *Build awareness of inequality and poverty.* Children need to learn that over half the people in the world are hungry. Readers will find in Chapter 6 an outline for a unit on the question, "Who is responsible for the poor?" But before children will think to wonder about this, they must become aware of the enduring problem of poverty. Then they'll want to know *why.* Here the issue is not why *goods and services* are distributed as they are (to whom, where, when, and why) but why *income* is distributed as it is (why so much to so few and so little to so many). Canned and dry foods campaigns for the hungry are a caring and helpful place to start, but they do not by themselves teach students why there is so much poverty in a rich nation like ours (the United States has the highest poverty rate among industrialized nations) or why over half of the world's people are always hungry even though *there is plenty of food to go around if it were divided evenly.* There is no shortage of food.

A simulation. An organization called United for a Fair Economy operates an informative website and has developed teaching materials. Polly Kellogg has adapted one of them in a teacher resource book called *Rethinking Globalization.*[12] Ask 10 students to line up in the front of the room, seated in chairs that are facing the rest of the room. Explain that each chair represents 10% of the wealth of the United States and each occupant represents 10% of the population. Accordingly, when each chair is occupied by one student, wealth is *evenly distributed.* Explain that actually in the United States, 10% of the population has 70% of the wealth (more or less). Now ask, "How can we show that?" Have one of the students recline across seven of the chairs while the other nine students cram themselves onto the remaining three chairs. Ask questions to determine what sense students are making of this simulation and how it feels. Clarify as needed. Lead a discussion on the question, "What is a fair way to distribute wealth (money)?"

8. *Simulated and "real" marketplace and miniature society experiences.* Whenever possible, economic ideas should be introduced with real-life experiences that actually engage students in economic decision making and require them to live with the consequences of their decisions. The "MicroSociety" approach is deservedly popular, and the organization's website (www.microsociety.org) will introduce readers to its history and classroom materials. MicroSociety was launched by a struggling 22-year-old teacher named George Richmond. As you can read in his book, *The MicroSociety School: A Real World in Miniature,* he finally figured out how to transform his classroom into a fully functioning miniature society—complete with bank, wellness center, plant place, museum, and much more. Researchers who have studied MicroSociety and similar programs recommend that in first-grade and up, teachers begin by setting up a "real" classroom marketplace.[13] This requires four things.

   a. *Money.* First, inject money into the classroom by paying play money daily to children for all the normal classroom chores and learning tasks (e.g., $1 for each book read, $2 for cleaning up, $1 for attending school).

   b. *Goods.* Second, inject goods into the classroom by opening a "factory warehouse" operated by the teacher. Students "buy" paper, pencils, crayons, toys, and other supplies from the warehouse.

   c. *Markets.* Third, inject market life into the classroom for 20 minutes each day. The children engage in dramatic play in which they buy and sell the goods they have purchased from the warehouse as well as other goods and services they may produce. This will require them to set up "stores," "employees," "partners," and the like.

   Beyond setting up a marketplace, a whole society can then be established with a court, bank, city government (complete with a mayoral election), Department of Environmental Protection, library, post office, and so forth.

   d. *Debriefing.* Fourth, in classroom simulations such as MicroSociety and the others described in this book, debriefing is crucial, for without it learning and retention are sacrificed. Debriefing means reflecting on what has been done so far and planning what to do next. A debriefing strategy is needed. Here are four steps that should work well with most classroom simulations:

   1. *Description.* Have students describe in their own words a teacher-selected event from their work that day. The teacher should choose an event related to a key concept he or she wants students to learn (e.g., opportunity cost, division of labor, government).

   2. *Problem framing.* Ask students, "What is the problem here?" Help them identify and articulate the problem in the selected event. For example, there were fewer units of a toy than the students wanted.

   3. *Instruction.* Teach students new information about this problem. For example, teach the concepts of scarcity and opportunity cost.

   4. *Application.* Help students use this new information as they think through the problem and plan for the next day's activities. For example, "Will toys still be scarce tomorrow?" And, "How can you fairly distribute the toys that are available?"[14]

The World of Work

The world of work is a subset of economic education, and elementary and middle schools have for many years included it in their social studies programs. In teaching about the work world, a systematic, integrated approach is probably more effective than special units spaced throughout the grades. Most who have been involved in curriculum work in this field suggest that *awareness building* should be a major goal in the elementary school. Children should not be encouraged to make occupational choices when they are in elementary school, but they can begin to build a background of knowledge about a broad spectrum of occupations that will one day help them make intelligent career choices. The major components of such a program follow.

Opportunity to Explore Work Values

Children need to see the connection between values that are stressed in school, such as responsibility, civility, honesty, cooperation, and courage, and the world of work. They need to develop a sense of appreciation for a job that is well done. They need to learn what it means to take pride in one's work. It may be difficult for children who dislike doing chores to realize, but hard work done well is an important source of happiness for humans.

Workplace Cooperation

Part of awareness building for the world of work is learning to work cooperatively and productively with persons with whom one may not have chosen to work. This reflects the reality of most job settings. For this reason, an important attribute of the instructional method called cooperative learning (Chapter 11) is teacher-assigned work groups. In this way, children gain experience at working well and solving interpersonal problems with classmates who are not necessarily their friends.

Workplace Competencies

Assign children to small groups and ask each group to brainstorm a list of skills and dispositions that, if developed, would help them get and keep the kind of work they want. Second, have the groups share their lists on butcher paper with the whole class. Third, share with the class two economic trends: the internationalization of production, distribution, and consumption (i.e., globalization), and the changing technological skills required on the job. Give examples from your community to help the children understand the trends. Fourth, ask the groups to revise their lists as needed, based on these trends. Fifth, share with the class the list of workplace skills and dispositions shown in Figure 4–7.

Activities for Studying the World of Work

- *Inquiry*. Brainstorm a list of reasons people might have selected particular occupations. This list should include such things as "It provides me with a chance to be my own boss" or "I earn a good salary." Use the list as the basis for a survey the children distribute to working adults in your community. Have the adults choose three reasons from the list and rank them from most important to least important. Then help students organize and analyze these data and prepare reports.

| FIGURE 4–7 | Workplace competencies. |

Resources	Know how to allocate time, money, materials, space, and staff.
Interpersonal Skills	Know how to work on teams, teach others, serve customers, lead, negotiate, and work well with people from culturally diverse backgrounds.
Information	Know how to acquire and evaluate data, organize and maintain files, interpret and communicate, use computers to process information.
Systems	Know how to understand social, organizational, and technological systems; monitor and correct performance; design and improve systems.
Technology	Know how to select equipment and tools, apply technology to specific tasks, and maintain and troubleshoot equipment.

Source: *Learning a Living: What Work Requires of Schools* (Washington, DC: U.S. Department of Labor, 2003).

- *More Inquiry.* Conduct interviews to find out how adults in the community earn money. Have the children compile a list of categories for their questionnaire, such as:

  People who produce things

  People who fix things

  People who study things (social scientists, naturalists)

  People who provide services (dentists, lawyers, teachers, veterinarians)

  People who govern (people who work for any branch of government)

  Help students organize and analyze these data and prepare reports for the classroom newsletter.
- *Awareness.* Here is a good assessment activity from which the teacher can determine students' conceptions of occupations and the world of work. Have them brainstorm a list of 25 to 50 jobs and occupations. In groups, have the children organize the data into only four categories, using any system they wish to devise. Have each group explain its system. The teacher can work with students on important categories such as manufacturing jobs (the declining industrial age) and information jobs (the ascendant post-industrial age).
- *More Awareness.* After completing the previous activity, use the categories students devised to analyze the classified sections of local newspapers. What types of work are most available? Help them revise their categories as needed.
- *Gender Equity.* To sensitize children to sex-role stereotyping, have them generate lists of occupations that are associated with males, those associated with females, and those that are neutral. Discuss these in terms of equality of job opportunity and whether a person's gender has anything to do with performance of the jobs listed in

the male and female categories. Then have students analyze television commercials and newspaper and magazine advertisements to detect evidence of sex-role and racial stereotyping in certain occupations.

- *Division of Labor*. This is a concept best formed through actually doing it. Teachers often create a division-of-labor simulation in the classroom, such as the assembly-line simulation presented in Chapter 8. Lesson Plan 5 illustrates how a primary-grade teacher helped the class become familiar with the concept of division of labor.

TEACHING ANTHROPOLOGY

Anthropology is often thought of as a unifying social science because it is the study of human beings in their cultures and environments. In the elementary grades, anthropology is typically folded into geography. Geography, as we have seen, is concerned not just with the environment (climate, land and water forms), but also with human-environment interaction and culture. Anthropology is unique in its steadfast concentration on the idea of *culture*. Culture (like ethnicity) is a uniquely human creation and, in addition to human physiology, it is the primary distinguishing attribute of humans from other animals. Ants live in groups, like humans, and have complex social organizations, like humans, but they don't have culture. This means they don't learn. They don't need to learn because all the information they require for living is contained in their physical makeup.

Unique to anthropology, too, is its method of inquiry. Called ethnography, the method requires anthropologists to live within a culture other than their own and there to do fieldwork: observe, write detailed notes on these observations, observe some more, write more notes. "The ethnographer," writes renowned anthropologist Clifford Geertz, "inscribes social discourse."[15] That is, he or she writes it down. The emphasis is on descriptive detail. Geertz calls this "thick description." Ethnographies try to capture the stream of social happenings completely, both what was said and how, and what wasn't said and how. Ethnographies, therefore, often make for wonderful reading. If you haven't done so, look into classics such as Margaret Meade's *Coming of Age in Samoa* (1928), Ruth Benedict's *Patterns of Culture* (1934), or Shirley Brice Heath's *Ways with Words: Language, Life and Work in Communities and Classrooms* (1983). Heath's book is especially relevant to elementary school teachers who work with children's diverse "ways with words" every day.

Anthropological studies are often comparative. Cross-cultural studies show the wide range of capabilities of human beings: the modern surgeon and the tribal shaman; preliterate and literate lifestyles; affluence and poverty; humanitarian behavior and cruelty and war; urban living and rural life; life in extremely cold areas and life in hot desert regions. People are highly adaptive in their behavior. They can, within limits, control and shape their environment and rebuild the culture they were born into. To solve problems they rely on their ability to think, stand, manipulate objects with their hands, imagine, and innovate. These characteristics result in great diversity among the people of the world in how they live, what they believe, and how they conduct their affairs. Nonetheless, people are all part of the human family; all are a part of the animal group *Homo sapiens*, and all have a number of common physical and social needs (food, shelter, work, and love).

DIVISION OF LABOR

Grade	2 or 3
Time	Two class periods
NCSS Standards	7 (production, distribution, and consumption) and 8 (science, technology, and society)
Objectives	Children will form an initial concept of what economists call *division of labor* and build their awareness of jobs in the community.
Interest Building	Distribute an apple to each child and invite children to eat their apples at recess later. Read aloud a story that shows in a child-friendly way an example of *division of labor*. For example, in *Apple Picking Time* by Michele Benoit Slawson a girl named Anna helps her family with the harvest. Anna expects to be paid for her work at the end of the day (the concept *employment*) and we see that hers is only one of a number of interdependent jobs involved in getting apples from the orchard to our lunchboxes *(division of labor)*.

Have children discuss jobs they know about in their family or neighborhood by responding to these questions: Do you have a job at home? What do you do? Who else at home has a job? Do you know of any jobs that it takes more than one person to finish?

Explain that during the next few days they are going to learn about different kinds of jobs in the community and the idea of division of labor.

Lesson Development   Have the children make a chart with the headings like the following:

Name of Job	Reasons for the Job
1. _____	_____
_____	_____
2. _____	_____
_____	_____
3. _____	_____
_____	_____

Instruct the children to take the chart home with them and complete it with the help of a parent, naming three different jobs in the community.

The next day, have the children compare and discuss their lists with one another.

Compile a list of as many different jobs as possible on the chalkboard. Children should pick one from their individual lists until everyone has had a turn to name one. Keep going as long as different jobs are named.

Have children discuss the need for a variety of jobs by responding to these questions:

1. Why do we have so many different jobs in our community?
2. Why couldn't each family do all these jobs itself?
3. Why do you suppose people in a community divide the work the way they do?
4. Do you think people can do their jobs better when each person has a special job?

Tell the children that when people divide work so that each one does something special, we call that division of labor. Write this term on the chalkboard. Have students discuss this term using these questions:

1. Does anyone know another word for *labor?* (Children suggest *work* as a synonym for labor. This is discussed and examples are provided.)
2. Can anyone tell us in his or her own words what "division of labor" means? (Children respond that division of labor means dividing the work.) This is discussed and examples are elicited.

<table>
<tr><td>Assessment and
Summary</td><td>Have children tell in their own words how they see the division of labor in these places or others they know:</td></tr>
</table>

their school	the shopping center
their families	a hospital
the supermarket	the airport or bus station
the post office	church or temple

Materials One copy of *Apple Picking Time* or any one of many stories that depict *division of labor.*

Follow-up Arrange a field trip to see division of labor at a supermarket.

Integration *Art*: Have students make an accordion book on a division of labor they decide to study. Each illustration of the book should show, in correct sequence, a different job (e.g., picking grapes, processing grapes, wholesaling grapes, retailing grapes).

The following are sample generalizations from anthropology that have been used as objectives when developing social studies units:

1. Every society has formed its own system of beliefs, knowledge, values, traditions, and skills that can be called its culture.
2. Culture is socially learned and serves as a guide for human behavior in any given society.
3. Although people everywhere are confronted with similar psychological and physiological needs, the ways in which they meet these needs differ according to their culture.

Teaching Suggestions

The central concept of anthropology, *culture,* is so complex and comprehensive that it cuts across all the social science disciplines and takes years to master. Thus, social studies units in every grade often contain a substantial amount of information that could be defined as anthropological even though it may not be made explicit in the curriculum.

Activities such as the following have been used by elementary and middle school teachers in studies having an anthropological emphasis. The essence of each activity is observation—to observe those things that we may no longer even notice because they have become familiar and mundane.

1. *Children's Literature.* As you will learn in Chapter 9 in the section "Concept Formation," concepts are formed by noting similarities across examples of the concept. Culture is no different. Children need to absorb multiple examples of this complex idea before they can begin to construct the idea itself. Many children's trade books are available on specific cultures. After the children have at least three distinct cultures in mind, ask them how the cultures are alike and different. List their responses on butcher paper and post it on the wall. Keep adding to the list after additional cultures are studied. Examples include *The Maori of New Zealand* (Steve Theunissen, 2002), *The Navajo Year: Walk Through Many Seasons* (Nancy Bo Flood, 2006), *The North Pole Was Here: Puzzles and Perils at the Top of the World* (Andrew C. Revkin, 2006), *Salaam: A Muslim American Boy's Story* (Tricia Brown, 2006).

2. *Make the Familiar Strange.* Ask students to observe something familiar—the lunchroom, the playground, or artifacts such as a postage stamp or coin. Ask them to see it as though for the first time so that it actually seems strange rather than familiar. This takes lots of practice. It may help if they pretend they are from outer space or from the distant past or future. The key questions then are, "What do you see?" "What is happening here?" Like anthropologists, they should take field notes. (See Lesson Plan 3 in Chapter 3, in which students examine a coin, such as a penny, and attempt to infer what is valued in the society that made this coin.)

3. *Fieldwork.* Divide the class into five fieldwork teams. On each day of the week, a different team takes field notes on what its members see in the cafeteria. On Friday afternoon, field notes are compiled and a "thick" description called "Life in Our Cafeteria" is attempted. Following this activity, read aloud a thick description from an actual ethnography. (Or read one or two of the Lewis and Clark journal excerpts from pages 116 and 117 and ask students to judge whether they are adequately detailed to count as a "thick description.")

4. *Tools.* Trace the development and use of certain everyday human tools: pencil, backpack, lawn mower, hammer, computer. Again, make the familiar seem strange.

5. *New Tools.* Study ways that inventions have changed civilizations (e.g., clocks, cell phones, video games, television, backpacks).

6. *Charts.* Prepare data-retrieval charts to compare different cultures on a variety of dimensions: the use of tools, care for the young, family roles, food, shelter.

7. *Music.* Have students listen to music that is culturally different from what most of them are accustomed to. Japanese and Chinese melodies, for example, can seem strange from the perspectives of Europeans, South Americans, or Africans.

8. *Art.* Show slides of artwork that is culturally different from what most students are accustomed to. Art museums, particularly on college campuses, usually have slides to lend.

9. *Dig.* In the upper grades, participate in a simulated archaeological dig. A committee of students can "bury" on the school grounds artifacts that they believe represent life in your town today (current coins, stamps, bottles, fork, chopsticks, etc.—remind them that theirs is a culturally diverse town). The rest of the class then simulates an archaeological dig. They excavate the artifacts and must make sense of what they find by trying to get inside the minds of the people who used them.

10. *Simulations. Dig* is a popular commercial (Interact) simulation of an archaeological dig with a nice twist. Competing teams create a culture and bury representative artifacts on the school grounds for each other. Each team then excavates and analyzes the other team's artifacts, using them to reconstruct its culture.

TEACHING SOCIOLOGY

Someone once quipped that economics is about how people have to make choices, and sociology is about how they don't really have any choices to make. There's truth here.

Sociology is a broad social science that is especially concerned with social organization—the way people organize themselves into (and sometimes are forced into) groups, subgroups, social classes, and institutions. According to sociologists, humans are *completely situated* in these organizations. Even one's supposedly private thoughts and fantasies utilize language and concepts derived from these organizations. That doesn't mean that we don't each deal uniquely with the "hand of cards," so to speak, that we were "dealt," but that *which* hand we are dealt depends largely on *which* groups, subgroups, social classes, and institutions—*the social organizations*—we belong to. Social organizations shape even deviants, or so-called nonconformists, because they are defined by the norms of these organizations. One cannot even be nonnormal, then, without reference to what is normal, and nonconformists are products of their society.

The following are major generalizations from sociology that have been used as organizing ideas to develop social studies units with a sociological emphasis.

- The social environments in which a person is raised and lives have a profound effect on the personal growth and development of that individual.
- Racism, sexism, language, body image, and political beliefs all are learned from these social environments. This learning process is called *socialization*.
- The family is the basic social environment in most cultures and the source of some of the most fundamental socialization. Yet, families are themselves nested within social classes.
- Social classes exist in every society although the bases of class distinction and the degree of rigidity of the class structure vary widely. Social-class membership shapes much of an individual's behaviors, values, and beliefs.
- Every society develops a system of roles, norms, values, and sanctions to guide and control the behavior of individuals and groups within the society. Deviancy is identified and dealt with in reference to this system.

Teaching Suggestions

Just as anthropology is steadfast in its concentration on the concept of culture, sociology is steadfast on the concept *group membership*. The first three grades of school typically focus on three groups: family, neighborhood, and community.

In actual practice, the study of these groups is integrated with the study of geography, history, and political science. And a comparative approach is strongly recommended. Comparison is the gateway to higher-order thinking and in-depth, sophisticated knowing. Comparison allows students to grasp the similarities among as well as the variety of—differences among—families, neighborhoods, and communities around the world. The two basic teaching suggestions regarding sociology, then, are to integrate it with the other social sciences and organize learning activities that require comparison.

Take the first-grade topic "The Family." Children learn about the variety of forms this basic group has in our society and elsewhere on Earth. They can also learn some of its functions and the roles of various members. A data-retrieval chart (like the one in Figure 4–8) posted on the bulletin board can support students' comparisons. *Note:* While data-retrieval charts of this sort can look simple and ordinary to adults, it is important not to underestimate their strength as aids to children's learning. They capture, in their simplicity, the power of *comparing and constrasting multiple examples.* This is the essence of the concept-formation strategy, which adds depth and richness to learning that otherwise can be superficial, trivial, and boring. Concept formation is explained in Chapter 9 and then exemplified in Lesson Plans 11, 15, 21, and 22.

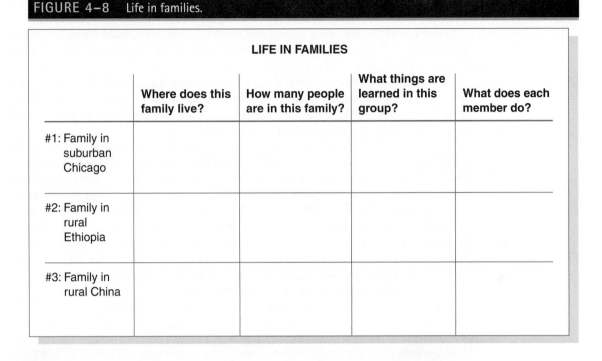

FIGURE 4–8   Life in families.

LIFE IN FAMILIES				
	Where does this family live?	How many people are in this family?	What things are learned in this group?	What does each member do?
#1: Family in suburban Chicago				
#2: Family in rural Ethiopia				
#3: Family in rural China				

Of course, controversy swirls around the definition of family and the roles of family members. Is an unmarried couple a family? What about a married couple without children? Are gay and lesbian couples families? Presently in the United States, something called "family values" is a political hot potato. Family life and the social norms and political debates that surround it are ripe research subjects for professional sociologists. Most elementary school social studies curriculum materials, meanwhile, generally teach that there is no *typical* family. A photo of grandparents and a child will be placed next to a mother and three children and, next to this, a traditional-appearing family with a mother, father, two or three children, and a dog. All are labeled, "Families in Our Community." Next to this set of photos will be other photos of diverse families from around the world, large and small, rural and urban, agricultural and industrial. This set might be labeled "Families Around the World."

A child's own family will no doubt differ from those represented in texts as well as those represented in story and picture books. Ethnic, racial, religious, and social-class differences will make a difference. Perhaps the school media specialist will collect trade books on Latino families, Chinese American families, Arab American families, or rural and urban families. One of my favorite trade books about family life (maybe because I love tamales) is *Too Many Tamales* (Gary Soto, 1993). It shares a Latino family's preparation for Christmas dinner, with a hilarious incident involving a lost diamond ring thought to be in the tamale batter, the *masa*. If the data-retrieval chart shown in Figure 4–8 is too difficult for the youngest children, or if information on families around the world is not readily available, a single storybook can be used. In this case, the chart might look like the one developed by Mary Hurlbut Cordier and Maria A. Perez-Stable in Figure 4–9.[16]

In the second grade, another group—the neighborhood—is featured. Again, a comparative approach is recommended to show both differences and similarities. Now the data-retrieval chart might look something like Figure 4–10.

Note that the questions at the top of the chart are essentially geographic: location, place, movement, and place again (from the five themes of geography). Again, if this approach is too difficult for young children, or if information on diverse neighborhoods is not readily available, a data-retrieval chart could look like Figure 4–11.

Peer groups and *peer pressure* are topics of great interest to upper elementary and middle school students, and a tremendous amount of sociological research has been done on them. Children's literature can be used to introduce these concepts to your students while building on their own experiences. Readers no doubt have their own favorites (one of mine is *Best Friends* by Loretta Krupinski, 1998). But fascinating inquiries can be conducted as well on such questions as "Does peer pressure exist in all cultures?" (NCSS standards 1 and 4). And "How do power and authority work in peer pressure situations?" (NCSS standards 4 and 6). The key is to raise students' awareness of peer pressure, give them knowledge about it, express genuine curiosity about how they understand the phenomenon, and introduce new vocabulary that they can use to deepen their understanding.

FIGURE 4–9   Life in families.

	My Family	Storybook Family
Homes and family members		
Food, for every day and for special events		
Clothing, for every day and for special events		
Recreation, home, school, community		
School, grade levels, size, special features		
Jobs, adults and children		
Contributions to America, as good neighbors		

FIGURE 4–10 Life in neighborhoods.

	Where is this neighborhood located?	What is life (work? play?) like here?	How do people and goods get around?	How does climate influence life here?
#1: A suburb in New York				
#2: A city in the Midwest				
#3: A farm town in New Mexico				

FIGURE 4–11 Life in neighborhoods.

	Where is this neighborhood located?	What is life (work? play?) like here?	How do people and goods get around?	How does climate influence life here?
My neighborhood				
The neighborhood in our book				

Conclusion

Major sources of subject matter for the social studies curriculum are the social science disciplines. The social studies curriculum integrates these, usually giving the bulk of time to history and geography, and aiming them toward the development of democratic citizens. The key to teaching history, geography, and the other social sciences to younger and older children alike is to help them build both knowledge and know-how. They must not only absorb history, but also learn to do history: drawing conclusions based on evidence. The same is true of geography and the other social sciences. The learning/doing of history, geography, economics, and so forth naturally requires reading and writing of all sorts; accordingly, a good portion of the language arts curriculum can be folded into the social studies curriculum. Whether helping children write snapshot biographies or detailed ("thick") descriptions of everyday events, or helping them read children's trade books or make maps, charts, and folded 3-D graphics, it is not surprising that for many gifted teachers, the language arts curriculum is achieved alongside the social studies curriculum. The next chapter looks more deeply into social science teaching and learning, concentrating on the tools of geography.

Discussion Questions and Suggested Activities

Go to MyEducationLab and select the topic "History," then watch the video "Local History" and complete the activity.

1. Look back at the absorbing/doing distinction that was drawn in the history section of this chapter and your response to the question asked in the *Reflection* sidebar. Reading a biography of a key historical figure is a good example of *absorbing* history. Producing such a biography alone or as part of a writing team is a good example of *doing* history because students must decide—as must "real" historians—what story to tell and how, what to leave out, what sentiments to invoke in readers, and so on. With a partner, select another pair of activities for history, geography, or another social science that vividly illustrates the absorbing/doing distinction drawn in this chapter.

2. History is (choose one or more): (a) the recorded past, (b) the story of the past, (c) a set of methods for figuring out what happened in the past, (d) a set of sources for interpreting what happened in the past, (e) all of the above. [*Note*: I choose (e). The first option helps us understand that *prehistoric* does not mean before anything happened, but before written records were kept. The second is quite true except that it would be more accurate to say that a history is *a* story of the past, not *the* story of the past. The third and fourth answers make good sense.]

3. In the *Curriculum Standards for Social Studies Sampler* that accompanies this text read the performance expectations and the teaching examples given for history (theme 2), geography (themes 1, 3, and 9), economics (theme 7), sociology (theme 5), and anthropology (theme 1).

4. NCSS Standards *Sampler*. Examine the third-grade classroom vignette for standard #4 on page 13 of the standards *Sampler* that accompanies this book. How does it compare to the Lesson Plan on primary and secondary sources in this chapter?

Selected References

History

Curriculum advice: National Center for History in the Schools. (1994). *National standards for history.* National Center for History in the Schools: (www.nchs.ucla.edu/standards).

Read a good history book written for adults: James W. Loewen. (1996). *Lies my teacher told me: Everything your American history textbook got wrong.* New York: Simon & Schuster.

Read a good history book written for children: Jennifer Armstrong. (2006). *The American story: 100 true tales from American history.* New York: Random House.

Research on history education: Keith C. Barton & Linda S. Levstik. (2004). *Teaching history for the common good* (2nd ed.). Erlbaum.

Geography

Curriculum advice: National Council for Geographic Education. (1994). *Geography for life: National geography standards.* National Council for Geographic Education: (www.ncge. net/standards).

Read a good geography book written for adults: Dava Sobel. (1996). *Longitude: The true story of a lone genius who solved the greatest scientific problem of his time.* New York: Penguin.

Read a good geography book written for children: Gail L. Karwoski. (2006). *Tsunami: The true story of an April Fool's Day disaster.* Plain City, OH: Darby Creek.

Read a good geography book written for parents: National Council for Geographic Education. *The power of geography.* (Available at the Council's website: www.ncge.net/ geography/power/family). Suggests ways for parents and caregivers to develop children's geographic literacy.

Research on geography education: Sarah Bednarz et al. (2006). Maps and map learning in social studies. *Social Education, 70,* 398–404.

Political Science

Curriculum advice: Center for Civic Education. (1994). *National standards for civics and government.* Center for Civic Education: (www.civiced.org).

Read a good political science book written for adults: Danielle S. Allen. (2004). *Talking to strangers: Anxieties of citizenship since Brown v. Board of Education.* Chicago: University of Chicago Press.

Read a good political science book written for children: Senator Edward M. Kennedy. (2006). *My senator and me: A dog's-eye view of Washington, DC.* New York: Scholastic.

Research on civic education: Center for Information and Research on Civic Learning and Engagement (CIRCLE). (2003). *The civic mission of schools.* New York: CIRCLE and the Carnegie Corporation of New York.

Economics

Curriculum advice: National Council on Economic Education. (1998). *Voluntary national content standards in economics.* (www.ncee.net).

Read a good economics book written for adults: Steven D. Levitt & Stephen J. Dubner. (2006). *Freakonomics: A rogue economist explores the hidden side of everything.* New York: William Morrow.

Read a good economics book written for children: Andrea Cheng. (2002). *When the bees fly home.* Gardiner, ME: Tilbury House.

Research on economics education: James D. Laney & Mark C. Schug. (1998). Teach kids economics and they will learn. *Social Studies and the Young Learner, 11,* 13–17.

MyEducationLab is a collection of online tools for your success in this course, your licensure exams, and your teaching career. Go to www.myeducationlab.com to utilize these extensive resources including videos from real classrooms, Praxis and licensure preparation, a lesson plan builder, and materials to help you begin your teaching career.

Powerful Tools: Maps, Globes, Charts, and Graphics

MAIN IDEA

Making sense of physical and cultural space—spatial reasoning—requires tools. Elementary school children can and should learn to use a good number of them as they are extremely useful, both practically and intellectually. From wall maps and globes to charts and graphs, the social studies curriculum can teach children powerful ways to read and organize the world. Teacher favorites are included: multiple wall maps showing different "projections," Google Earth, the high-tech maps at the National Geographic Society's website, students' own hand-made paper pie graphs, and a simulation for the primary grades called "dance of the solar system" in which a birthday child gets to carry Earth around the sun.

PICTURE THIS

Three wall maps were taped side by side to the chalkboard at the front of the room. One is a Mercator projection, one a Winkel, and one a Peters. "This is the United States," the teacher said, pointing to the United States on the first map. "Right?" she asked. "Right!" the children cheered. "And so is this and this," she said as she pointed to the other maps. "Right?" "Right!" "But the shape of the United States is different in each," she continued. "So is Africa. And Greenland. Why is that? Come have a closer look and tell us what you think." The next morning, she handed a fresh orange to each student. "Peel this orange, like you were peeling the globe, then try to flatten out the peel on your desk. Tell us what happens."

This chapter presents hands-on and minds-on tools that children can use to learn about the world around them. By learning them in the elementary school, these students will look "smart" to their middle school teachers. And deservedly so. These tools promote in students an attitude of thoughtfulness about social data by requiring them to organize and analyze rather than merely memorize.

The social studies curriculum operates within a space–time matrix that might be represented very simply as follows:

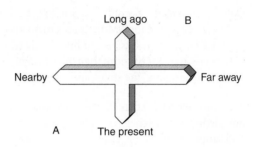

Experiences that could be charted at point A would be the least abstract and would usually be found in the primary grades. Experiences at point B would be more difficult to make concrete for children because they are remote not only in space but also in time. But because many children today have firsthand experiences—and secondhand via the media—that acquaint them with places beyond their immediate environment, it is not necessary to confine the social studies program to the local area. There can be movement from the near at hand to the far away even in the early grades—from the local river to the Amazon, the local mountains to the Himalayas, from the local prairie to the Great Steppe, from the island in the local lake to the only island that is also a city and a country, Singapore, located at the southern tip of Malaysia. In this way, the far away is anchored to the nearby, allowing a compare-and-contrast approach while connecting the lesser known to the somewhat better known.

Globes and maps are indispensable tools for understanding and acting on social phenomena. But so is the chart that helps us compare several families or neighborhoods, as we did at the end of the previous chapter. Meanwhile, graphs make quantitative relationships vivid. Hand-made paper graphs like those at the end of this chapter can make those relationships kinesthetic and concrete. The point of view in this chapter is that children need to learn to read such tools for representing data but also to *make* them with their own hands. *Frequent*—not necessarily daily but weekly—experiences with globes, maps, charts, and graphs is the key.

 CAPITAL PUNISHMENT?

Is there a place for old-fashioned memorization? A perennial controversy in social studies is whether to require students to memorize the fifty states and their capital cities. Let's begin this chapter with pro and con arguments. When the social studies curriculum standards for California made states-and-capitals a requirement, the editor of the newsletter of the

California Council for the Social Studies wrote an editorial opposing it. His essay, in turn, provoked letters to the editor both supporting and opposing the requirement:

Pro: "Some teachers testify to tedium and failure, but in the instances with which I am familiar, states and capitals were taught and learned with felicity. . . . There is no reason why any teacher should apologize for having students learn the names and location of the 50 states. The value of learning capitals is perhaps less tangible . . . (but it) does give students a vocabulary of U.S. cities they would never know otherwise."

Con: "In each class I ask all of my students how many of them learned the states and capitals in elementary school. More than a majority of students in each class say they memorized those facts. Then I ask them how many of them can recite today what those states and capitals are. Out of more than 300 students, only three replied that they could. . . . Those three could 'sing' the states and capitals."[1]

The "pro" writer is correct: Memory work can pay off in vocabulary development and, as any elementary teacher will tell us, vocabulary development is an enormously important and empowering achievement. Furthermore, parents are proud when their students can rattle off the states and capitals (or the rivers and mountain ranges of the world), and children themselves report a feeling of accomplishment. Additionally, even when students forget the particular capitals, they remember that every state has a capital city. But the "con" writer makes a good point, too. We can memorize but in a year's time not remember, and we can memorize *without understanding*. Readers need only to recall the Pledge of Allegiance discussion in Chapter 3.

The National Council for Geographic Education enters the debate this way: "Geography is often identified with memorizing facts about rivers, capitals, products, and other seemingly trivial things. Geographers, however, are more concerned about understanding *why* things are located where they are and *how* they are related to the location of other features. . . ."[2] On my interpretation, the Council does not rule out memorizing, and note the adverb "seemingly" before "trivial." But it does put a higher priority on knowing why and how. Maybe there is room for both.

At the end of this chapter, you will be asked to take a stand on the states-and-capitals controversy. Perhaps the material between this opening section, glibly called "Capital Punishment," and the final section, "Conclusion," will sway your opinion one way or another.

MAP AND GLOBE SKILLS ESSENTIAL TO THE SOCIAL STUDIES CURRICULUM

Maps and globes are tools for representing space and place symbolically. The essential features of all maps and globes are a *grid, color, scale, symbols,* and a *legend* that explains the symbols used. The ability to read and interpret maps and globes, like conventional reading, is a composite of several subskills. These can be inferred by analyzing the behavior of someone reading a map skillfully. The following are essential map-reading skills:

1. Orient a map and note directions.
2. Use the scale and compute distances.

3. Locate places on maps and globes.
4. Express relative location.
5. Interpret map symbols and visualize what they mean.

Directional Orientation

To deal with directional relationships on maps and globes, the child must first understand them in reality. The easiest directions to use are those that express relative location, such as *close to, near, over here,* and *over there.* These can be learned in the primary grades. The *cardinal directions* (the four main points of the compass) are also learned in the primary grades. Teachers can point out and refer to places that are known to children as being north of, east of, south of, and so on. Placing direction labels on the various walls of the classroom is a must. It helps remind children of cardinal directions. They can associate east and west with the rising and setting of the sun. They can learn how a compass is used to find the cardinal directions in any place. While on field trips, children should be given practice in using the compass, noting directions, observing especially the directions of streets and roads. Gradually, they learn the purpose of the poles, the meridians of longitude, and the parallels of latitude in orienting a map and noting directions.

Using Map Scales

In making a map, the cartographer tries to reproduce as accurately as possible that portion of Earth being represented. Because globes are models of Earth, they can represent Earth more correctly than can maps. No map can altogether faithfully represent Earth simply because it is round and maps are flat. The flattening process inevitably results in some distortion.

Scaling is the process of reducing everything by the same amount. Mathematical reasoning is involved, and here is a good opportunity for math and social studies curricula to overlap. When one works with children in the primary grades, scaling should be done in the relative sense. Some things are larger or smaller than other things, and the maps should show their *relative* size as accurately as possible. For example, a 50-foot-high tree in the schoolyard should be about five times larger than the 10-foot-tall playground set. On conventional maps, three types of scales are used:

1. The graphic scale

0   100   200   300   400   500   600

2. The inches-to-miles scale

0   300   600   900

3. The representative fraction   1 : 250,000

Of these, the graphic scale is the easiest to use and can be taught at about third grade. The inches-to-miles scale is more complex. It can be taught in the fourth or fifth grades. The representative fraction is usually considered beyond the scope of the elementary school program.

As children's experiences become more global in nature, or when they participate in their first "5K fun run," they will encounter metric vocabulary and map scales. If metric measurement is used, the distance on a graphic scale will be recorded in kilometers. Likewise, rather than as inches-to-miles, the scale will show the relationship as centimeters-to-kilometers. The following graphic scale illustrates the same distance expressed in miles and in kilometers.

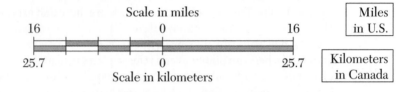

Locating Places

Location, recall, is one of the five themes of geography (the L in MR. HELP). The ability to locate places on maps and globes and to verbally express locations comes with a familiarity with these devices cultivated over a period of several years. Children first learn to locate places that are known to them on simple maps and layouts that they make in the classroom. In the early grades, too, children can learn the names and shapes of some of the major geographic features, such as continents, oceans, the equator, and the poles. Commercially prepared maps and globes designed for the lower grades are quite plain, showing only a few features. Gradually, children increase the repertoire of known places they can find on the map and globe because of frequent references to the location of important cities, countries, rivers, mountains, and other physical features.

In the intermediate grades, children are taught to use *coordinates* to locate places. Local highway maps are well suited for use in teaching this skill because they deal with an area familiar to the children. One set of lines of the grid—perhaps the east–west lines—is identified with letters; the other set of lines is numbered as in Figure 5–1. The teacher can have the children find several places located on or very near to a north–south line, say 2. Then several places can be found on an east–west line, say C. If the teacher picks coordinates that intersect on a major point of interest, the children will discover that some city or other important feature is located at the point where C and 2 intersect. Figure 5–1 is an example of an exercise of this kind. This experience provides readiness for the use of meridians of longitude and parallels of latitude in locating places on wall maps and the globe. At this age, children can understand why reference points such as poles, the equator, and the prime meridian are essential in locating places on a sphere.

Expressing Location

The teacher needs to understand that there are two ways to indicate the location of any place: relative and absolute. *Relative location* is indicated by real estate agents when they tell you that the home is located "near schools and restaurants." They have told you where it is—sort of. They could add, "It is south of the university campus." Or, "It is northeast of

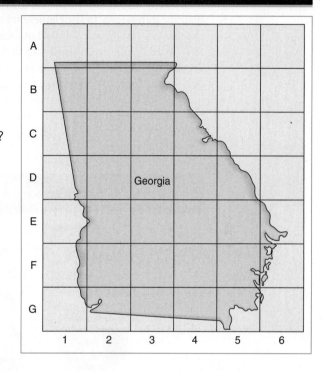

FIGURE 5–1 Intermediate-grade children can learn to use a grid in locating places by using road maps that have coordinates of the type shown on this map.

Test your own memory of place locations by responding to these questions:

1. What major city is located in square C2?
2. What major city lies near the intersection of the squares D1, D2, E1, and E2?
3. Describe the location of Savannah by using the coordinates provided on this map.

Check your answers by consulting a map of Georgia that shows cities.

the city, across the river." In each case, they are locating the house relative to other places. *Absolute location,* in contrast, is indicated by such statements as these: "The house is at the corner of Maple and Third"; "Most of Australia lies between 120°E and 160°E," which places it between two lines of longitude.

Ask your students, "Where is our classroom?" and help them understand the two ways of answering this question (e.g., "in the middle of the hall" versus "room 115"). As homework, ask them to locate their home, relatively and absolutely. Have them choose three additional places, too, and express their relative and absolute locations. For example:

A park

A grocery store

A theater

A stop sign at an intersection

A river or stream

Reading Map Symbols

Maps use symbols to represent real things: dots of varying sizes stand for cities of different populations; color is used to represent elevation; stars indicate capital cities; and lines are used to show boundaries, coastlines, and rivers. Naturally, readers will not comprehend the messages of maps unless they know what these symbols represent. Children begin to learn their meanings early in the elementary school social studies program. The development of this subskill closely parallels that of locating places on maps.

Map and globe symbols vary in their abstractness. Indeed, some simple maps for children in the primary grades use symbols that are pictorial or semipictorial. These symbols either look like the object being represented or provide a strong clue as to its identity, as shown in Figures 5–2 and 5–3. It would not take much imagination, for example, to differentiate water areas from land areas on a globe simply on the basis of their color.

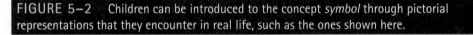

FIGURE 5–2　Children can be introduced to the concept *symbol* through pictorial representations that they encounter in real life, such as the ones shown here.

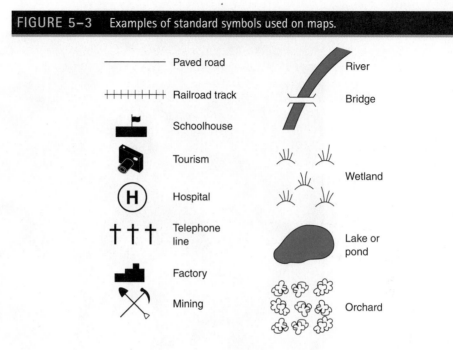

FIGURE 5-3   Examples of standard symbols used on maps.

The instructional sequence to be followed in teaching the symbol system of maps is to move gradually from pictorial and semipictorial symbols on maps made by children to the abstract symbols used on conventional wall maps, globes, and maps that are included in the textbooks of the intermediate and middle grades. It is essential that children learn to consult the map legend or key to confirm which symbols are being used. In most cases, children in the middle and upper grades will be dealing with maps that use conventional map symbols, but special-purpose maps, such as those showing vegetation, rainfall, population density, and so on, often use symbols that are unique to the particular map.

It is always a good idea to make generous use of images of the areas shown on a map to help children associate the map symbol with what the place actually looks like. Similarly, when children go on field trips, they should be encouraged to observe the appearance of landscapes, rivers, bridges, railroad tracks, and other features shown on maps. In time, they will be able to visualize the reality that the abstract map symbols represent.

TEACHING THE GLOBE

Every social studies classroom should have one or more globes and use it often. A well-equipped school will have a class set of globes on a rolling cart that can be shared by all the classrooms. In grades 1, 2, and 3 a simplified, 12-inch globe is generally recommended because small children find it easier to handle than the larger, 16-inch globe. For these grades, the globe should display a minimum amount of information. It should use no more

Globes invite inspection. *(Anne Vega/Merrill)*

than three colors to represent land elevation or more than two colors to represent water depth. Only the largest cities, rivers, and bodies of water should be shown. In the intermediate and middle grades, a 16-inch globe is recommended because of its easy scale of one inch to 500 miles. Moreover, its larger size allows more detail to be shown without the globe becoming a confused collection of symbols.

The chief value of the globe in grades 1, 2, and 3 is to familiarize children with the roundness of Earth and to begin to develop a global perspective. Parents speak of places in the news, and the children wonder where those places are. They hear of wars and famines and wonder about their location. Perhaps a girl has just joined the class; her family has moved from another part of the world, and she wants to show the class the location of her former home. The teacher will use situations such as these, and dozens more like them, to acquaint children with the globe.

The teacher should help children discover other things about the globe—differences between water and land areas and that these are represented by different colors; the line that separates the water and the land is called the seacoast or coastline. Children may be shown images to help them visualize different kinds of seacoasts. Similarly, the teacher extends their understanding of other concepts—cities, rivers, lakes, and mountains. Children learn that most of the brown areas that represent land are on the half of Earth that has the North Pole and that it is here that the majority of the people of the world live.

In addition to making incidental references to the globe, the teacher uses the globe frequently when teaching social studies, science, and literature. For instance, in a reading lesson, children might find where their book friends live. Thus, the globe can be used in a variety of ways to lay a good foundation for more formal aspects of the teaching of these skills later on. The following experiences can be planned with the globe for children in the lower grades. It is best if every child has a globe at hand that can be manipulated during these activities. Or, pairs can share a globe or, if there is only one, the teacher can use it and, later, children can take turns with it.

1. Explain that the globe is a very small model of Earth, and that Earth is our home—where all of us live. Good models look exactly like the real thing but are smaller. The globe is a good model of Earth.
2. Show the children how land areas and water bodies are represented on the globe. Have them find the big land areas (continents) and water bodies (oceans). Names of these need not be taught at this level, but it is good for children to begin hearing the names. Explain that all water bodies and land areas have names.
3. Help children see that there is considerably more water than land shown on the globe. Ask them if they have any hunches about why that is. Tell them that Earth is sometimes called the "water planet."
4. Show children the location of the North Pole. Show that most of the land of the world is on the same half of the globe as the North Pole. We call this the Northern Hemisphere, or northern half.
5. Show children the location of the South Pole. Show that most of the water areas of the world are on the same half of the world as the South Pole. We call this the Southern Hemisphere.
6. Explain that our Earth is a planet, one of eight spinning around the sun. (Indeed, Pluto was demoted. Read how this happened in the concept-formation section of Chapter 9.) This can be simulated in the splendid activity called "Dance of the Solar System" in Lesson Plan 6.
7. Show children how they can find their country, their continent, their state, and their city on the globe.
8. Use the globe to find places that are familiar to the children—places they have visited on vacations, places in the news, homes of book friends and visitors from other countries, or places in the world from which some circus or zoo animals are brought.
9. Encourage children to handle the globe and to find places on it themselves.
10. Visit a map collection on the Internet. The National Geographic Society's "map machine" is good. And, see the online maps lesson (Lesson Plan 16) in Chapter 10, "Resources."

Lesson Plan 7 is an example of a plan used by one teacher to familiarize primary-grade children with geographic concepts and skills using the globe.

As children move into the intermediate and middle grades, instruction in using the globe should take two forms. First, the teacher takes time from regularly scheduled unit activities to teach skills needed in reading and interpreting the globe. Second, in unit work and other classroom activities, there are frequent references to the globe and maps. Both of these aspects of instruction are important, and one should supplement the other. To hope that children will become skillful in using a globe or maps simply by making incidental references to them is wishful thinking. The best approach is to provide explicit instruction on the use of map- and globe-reading skills as a part of unit activities in which these skills will be *used*. (Readers may want to look ahead to the skill-teaching strategy in Chapter 9.)

DANCE OF THE SOLAR SYSTEM[3]

Grades	K–3
Time	One class period
NCSS Standards	3 (people, places, and environments) and 9 (global connections)
Objective	Children will develop an initial sense that they live on Earth, and that Earth is moving. They will experience Earth moving in conjunction with her sister planets—around the sun. They will gain an appreciation for, and a desire to care for, Earth.
Preparation	In the library, cafeteria, gym, or other room with a large, empty floor space, use masking tape to mark on the floor the orbits of the eight planets around the sun. This is a good task for a student committee (see the section in Chapter 11 titled "Getting Started with Cooperative Groups") or parent volunteers. There will be eight ellipses (ovals) to mark out with tape. (*Note:* The tape doesn't need to be continuous—a "dotted line" suffices and is easier to make.)
Interest Building	Tell children that in the next activity they will simulate (pretend to be) Earth and the other planets spinning around the sun. Then walk them to the cafeteria (or other room being used).
Lesson Development	

1. Give an overview of the activity. Tell students they will pretend to be the planets spinning around the sun. The purpose, tell them, is to see that all the planets are moving around at once while at the same time spinning, but that the sun stands still in the middle of the solar system. It will appear to be a dance. Explain that *solar* means sun. These eight planets belong to the sun. Together they are the sun's system, its family.

2. Eight students are needed to simulate the planets. Place the sun, symbolized by a floor lamp, in the middle. Say something simple about the sun: "The sun is at the center of our solar system. It's a great ball of fire that keeps burning and doesn't move." Ask, "Who wants to be the sun in our solar system?" Now for the planets: "Who wants to be the planet farthest from the sun—very cold?" and so forth to Mercury, closest to the sun and very hot. *When Earth is named, make it very special.* If today is a child's birthday, honor that child by pronouncing him or her Earth. "Earth is our home. This is where we live with all our parents going way back and all our children going way forward, and the whole human family living all around Earth, and all the birds, plants, and animals, all the lakes and mountains, the rivers and streams, the clouds and snow, the palm trees and the pine trees. . . ." When a child takes the role of Earth, tell him or her that this is a special responsibility. Hand the child the globe. This child is holding Earth. This child is Earth's protector. This is a serious responsibility.

3. Ask Earth to take its place first—on the third ellipse from the sun. Ask this child to hold the globe carefully and to slowly walk Earth's orbit around the sun. During this, tell the class that this takes one year. Ask the child carrying the globe "How old are you?" When the child answers, add that Earth has orbited the sun that same number of times in his or her lifetime—it takes a whole year to orbit once.

4. When Earth completes its orbit, ask it to stop. Then have Mercury take its place on the ellipse closest to the sun. Place a red balloon in this child's hands. Tell students that because Mercury is closest, it moves more quickly than any other planet. Ask Mercury to walk its orbit. Next have Venus take another balloon and walk its orbit with the other planets stopped. Now begin the dance: have Mercury, Venus, and Earth orbit the sun at the same time. Ask them to stop while Mars takes its place, then Jupiter, then Saturn, Uranus, and, finally, Neptune, each with a balloon. When all eight planets are in orbit, clarify what is happening. "Now all the planets of our solar system are orbiting around our sun. All the planets are here. There's Neptune on the outside, then Uranus. . . . This is our solar system."

5. Ask another seven students to take balloons and for Earth, the globe, and repeat the dance, and so on until all students have participated.

Summary and
Assessment

1. Find out what sense children have made of this. "What did we do in the solar system activity?" might be a good opening question. Simply listen and ask occasional follow-up questions to find out more. Remember that primary children are not ready to fully understand the solar system. The objective, recall, is to "develop an initial sense."

2. Summarize briefly. The Earth moves around the sun once each year. The other planets also move around the sun, but at different speeds (two faster, five slower) and on different paths, called orbits. The sun is a big ball of fire and doesn't move. The planets spin while traveling around the sun.

Materials

Masking tape, a globe (Earth), floor lamp (sun), balloons for the other planets or photos or paintings of the planets mounted on wooden sticks (like campaign signs).

Follow-up

As children have their birthdays, the first part of this dance can be repeated. Give the birthday child the globe and have him or her circle the sun the same number of times as years.

Integration

Science: See the smart, interdisciplinary "Explore" unit in Chapter 13. Its lessons help children understand what the living things on Earth—animals, plants, people—need in order to thrive, and the things humans can do to help the other living things thrive. An appreciation for the plants and animals of Earth should go hand-in-hand with an appreciation for humanity.

Maps may be used to find distances between points only under some conditions, due to the projection problem (below), but the globe represents distances accurately and true to scale at all points on the surface of Earth. It is easy to place a flexible ruler or tape measure on the globe and directly measure the distance between two points in question. Then refer to the scale and determine the actual distance between the two places. The airplane routes of the world use "great circles" because these are the shortest distances from place to place on Earth's surface. A great circle is any line that divides any sphere into two halves. If nothing but flat maps are used, it is difficult to understand the concept of great circle routes. The globe can help clarify this concept (see Figure 5–4).

Globes are helpful, too, in establishing concepts of direction. It is not difficult to think of north as being in the direction of the North Pole when using a globe. On the other hand, this concept may be confusing if only a flat map is used. Furthermore, the relative direction of various parts of Earth can be better understood through the use of a globe. Many Americans are surprised, for example, when they learn that Great Britain lies to the north of all the 48 midcontinental states of the United States; that Boston has nearly the same latitude as Rome; that our most westerly state is not Hawaii but Alaska; that our most southerly state is not Florida but Hawaii; and that Antarctica is not only the coldest continent on Earth, in part because it has the highest average elevation, but also the largest desert, because it has so little precipitation.

TEACHING MAPS AND MAPPING

Eui-kyung Shin and Marsha Alibrandi provide a good summary of how children learn map skills:

> Students experience place and space through their interaction with the environment, during which they construct "mental maps" of their world. Like the learning of language, the development of mapping abilities proceeds in a predictable manner, is age-related, and involves

Lesson Plan 7
USING THE GLOBE TO LEARN ABOUT EARTH

Grades K–2

Time One class period

NCSS Standards 3 (people, places, and environments) and 9 (global connections)

Objective Children will develop some familiarity with concepts relating to the globe.

Interest Building Give the children free time to manipulate a globe and explore it on their own.

Lesson Development The teacher directs the following questions to the children:

What shape is a globe?

Can you find the North Pole? Place your finger on it.

Where is north on a globe?

Where is south on a globe?

Is south the opposite direction of north?

What divides the north from the south?

Have any of you lived near the equator?

Is the equator really a line?

How much of the globe is north?

How much of the globe is south?

What is half of a sphere?

Does anyone know what we call the northern half of the globe?

Does anyone know what we call the southern half of the globe?

How can we tell water from land on the globe?

Does anyone know what we call these large pieces of land?

Can you find a continent in the Northern Hemisphere?

Can you find a continent in the Southern Hemisphere?

Are there any continents that are in both hemispheres?

Summary and Assessment How is the globe divided?

Can you name the parts of the globe we talked about?

Can you point to the Northern Hemisphere?

Can you point to the Southern Hemisphere?

Can you point to a continent?

Materials As many globes as are available so that each child can easily explore and manipulate a globe.

Integration *Math:* Use flexible rulers (or pieces of string) to measure the distances between the students' home state and places on the globe they want to visit. Develop the relative vocabulary of *nearer* and *farther.*

FIGURE 5–4   Notice how differently the map and globe portray global relationships.

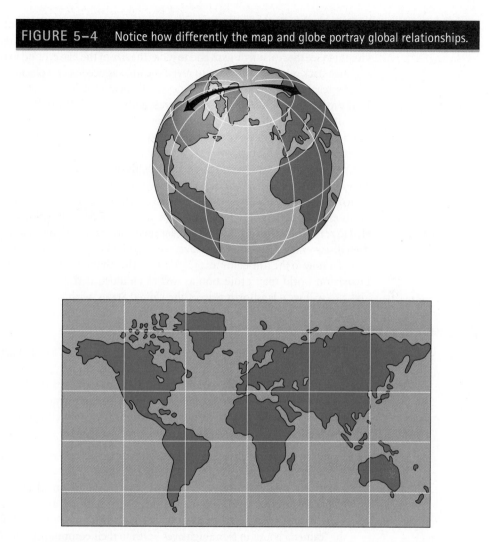

repetitious behavior. Their map skills will improve if we provide more challenging situations in the classroom as they develop intellectually.[4]

Students *already* have in their minds these mental maps of their homes, neighborhoods, the school, and other places and vicinities in their daily life. What teachers can do is help them develop their spatial competencies beyond these naïve understandings. Early experiences with maps should be kept simple. This can best be done by using diagrams and maps that the teacher and the children make of their immediate vicinity. Students begin to see how familiar places can be represented using *grid, color, scale, symbols,* and a *legend.* These early experiences may take the form of a layout on the classroom floor, using blocks and milk cartons for houses and public buildings, strips of paper for streets, paper leaves on sticks in dough for trees. Masking tape can be placed on the floor itself to represent seacoasts, borders, streets, or roads. The school grounds might be the subject of the first map laid out on the classroom floor, with big blocks standing for the school building, a small milk carton for the jungle gym, and the playground marked off with string or tape. The school's street number can be written on a yellow sticky and affixed to the front of the "building." The class can then be taken outside to the front of the school to see the real street number near the main door, and to count the number of trees, then to the playground to see the real jungle gym and to judge the size of the playground in relation to the building, then back into the classroom to revise the map as needed and placing an "N" for north.

The teacher can then show Google Earth (below) using the classroom computer and LCD projector. By entering the school street address in the "fly to" box, children watch as the software zooms in on their school grounds. With the advantage of this aerial view, students can better judge the scale of their floor map—the relative sizes and shapes of playground, parking lot, and buildings.

Opportunities to teach and apply these skills often arise in the everyday life of the classroom. For instance, children in one class learned about map direction when a new student joined the group. Soon after the child arrived, the teacher used a map to show the class the location of the child's previous home. They determined the direction the child's family traveled to reach their new home. The teacher then used a map of the local area and had the children discover the direction they travel when going from their homes to school each day.

Refer now to the full-color images found in this chapter. You will see Buckminster Fuller's Dymaxion world map projection as well as an illustrated dictionary of geographic terms. You also will see a landform map of the United States, with an interesting cross section.

Zooming In and Out with Google Earth

If the classroom computer is up to speed, so to speak, then Google Earth can be a visually vivid resource for teaching about maps and mapping. Google Earth can be downloaded for free and, after experimenting with it, the teacher can model its use for the class. (In the upper grades, a student committee can be appointed for this purpose.) A procedure such as the following would make a good introductory activity, after which students will be eager to try it themselves.

1. Using the compass direction in the corner of the screen, rotate the globe. Amazingly, Earth rotates in the direction you choose. I like to rotate northward and southward, eventually looking at the Arctic and Antarctic straight-on, placing them in the middle of the perspective rather than at the "top" and "bottom" as on most world maps.

2. Enter in the "fly to" box the city or town where the school is located. The children will see the "camera" zoom in from high over Earth to their community. Enter another nearby city or town, and by clicking on Roads the connecting streets or highways will appear.

3. Using the zoom button, identify the streets near the school and identify familiar places and landmarks. Click on various categories in the Layers section of the screen: Roads, Community Services, Parks and Recreation, etc. Build directional and relative vocabulary to locate them ("What is south of the school?" "What parks are farthest away from the school? Nearest?" "Where is the shopping center?" etc.).

4. Using the Tilt button, the horizon can be adjusted thanks to 3-D graphic capabilities.

5. Use these satellite images to introduce students to spatial distribution patterns. Shin and Alibrandi recommend teaching students why some places in their community are located close to each other (e.g., major retail stores and lodging), while others are more dispersed (e.g., golf courses and ski resorts). Ask why the stores were built next to the highway rather than the park? Why are the schools generally in residential areas rather than commercial areas? The point is to develop students' understanding—both the vocabulary and the concepts these terms name—about *why* human constructions are located where they are.

6. Zoom back out to the global perspective. Ask students what far-away place they would like to visit. Enter that into the "fly to" box and watch the "camera" zoom into it. Take them to icy Antarctica where, by clicking on Geographic Features, something surprising will be shown on Earth's coldest continent: volcanoes.

This online service is regularly updated. Some locales are still blurry for lack of more precise digital imagery. Road maps and driving directions are not available for all places yet, and other information, too, is more precise for certain areas than others.

The Projection Puzzle—From Globe to Map

When teaching about maps with students of any age, try to motivate a sense of fascination with what maps *are.* The problem of turning a round globe into a flat map is an excellent place to start.

A definite advantage that globes have over world maps is that they show the size and shapes of areas exactly as they appear on Earth's surface. Maps inevitably distort Earth's surface because they are flat, whereas the space they represent is round. No flat map can be accurate; each distorts space in a different way. In the chapter opening "Picture This" (p. 150), teacher and students are working on this very problem. To spark students' curiosity about this problem, the teacher has them each peel an orange carefully so as to not tear the skin too much. She asks them to try to flatten the peel and then talk about what happens. Why does the skin need to break in many different places?

From round to flat: the projection puzzle. *(Anthony Magnacca/Merrill)*

Professional mapmakers—cartographers—have a name for the process of transferring information from the round globe to a flat map: *projection*. Imagine a translucent globe sitting on the floor in the center of the classroom; then place a lightbulb in the center of the globe and turn out the room lights. The image projected onto the flat walls would be one kind of projection. A variety of projections using mathematical formulas have been developed by cartographers. From the available projections, geographers, hikers, sailors, pilots, and families on road trips select whichever projection will provide the least distortion to the area shown *and serve the purpose for which the map is to be used.*

The Mercator projection, invented by a Flemish cartographer and craftsman named Gerardus Mercator in the late 16th century, is still popular despite the fact that it grossly distorts the size of land and water masses—enlarging those near the poles (North America, Europe) and shrinking those near the equator (South America, Africa). Was this nothing but a 16th-century European prejudice manifested in a cartographer's handiwork? Somewhat, to be sure. But the story is more complex. European conquest and colonization fueled the ocean-going navigation craze of that era, which, in turn, required the best maps there were—maps for the purpose of navigating great distances. Never mind the hopes and dreams of Europe's rulers for glory and gold, *sailors* knew the advantage of the Mercator map. Gerardus developed it for navigation purposes. The compass-bearing direction of sea travel is consistent on this projection. Navigators of wooden sailing ships in the 16th and 17th centuries and thereafter could trust that compass directions between two points on the Mercator map were accurate. In their enlightening book, *Seeing Through Maps: The Power of Images to Shape Our World View,* Ward Kaiser and Denis Wood tell us that the Mercator projection "is a map for a world of sailors. It should not surprise us, then, that the way the map shows the world should reflect the interests of sailors too."[5]

But sizes of landmasses are distorted on the Mercator. Greenland appears much larger than its true area—larger than South America and about the same size as Africa! In fact, Africa is nearly 15 times larger than Greenland. Europe also appears to be larger than South America, though on a globe it is only half as big. North America appears to be larger than Africa, but on a globe it is the other way around: Africa's area is greater than that of the United States and Russia combined. The same goes for Alaska and Mexico: Alaska *appears* larger; Mexico *is* larger. And Antarctica, at the bottom of the map, is enormously distorted. It appears to be a giant continent that encircles the lower part of Earth. Notice the different shapes of North America on the three projections illustrated in Figure 5–5.

Arno Peters thought North Americans and Europeans needed a projection that corrected the distorted view of the world that Mercator had instilled in their (nonsailing) minds. The Peters projection, published in 1974, strives to show Earth's landmasses in accurate *proportion* to one another. On the Peters Equal Area Projection (see Figure 5–6), Africa is much larger than the United States, as is South America. No longer do nations far from the equator appear larger than nations nearer to it; if they are bigger, they *look* bigger. Still, to achieve this effect, shapes on the Peters map are distorted. Comparing the Mercator and Peters projections, Kaiser and Wood reiterate that every map has a purpose and advances particular interests.

Another cartographer, Buckminster Fuller, wanted desperately to create a projection that got the sizes (land areas in proportion to one another) right *and* the shapes, too. The Fuller projection, also known as the Dymaxion map, has no visible distortion in the shape or relative size of any landmass when compared to the globe. And, do you remember the orange-peeling activity?

FIGURE 5-5   Projections of North America.

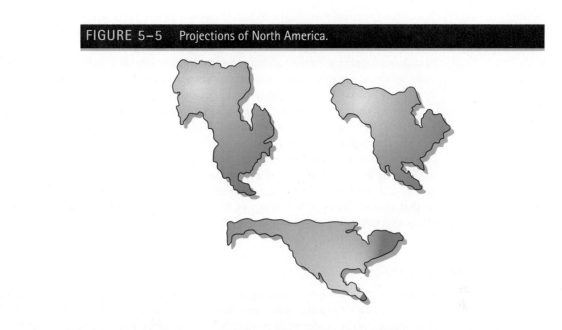

FIGURE 5-6   Peters Equal Area Projection.

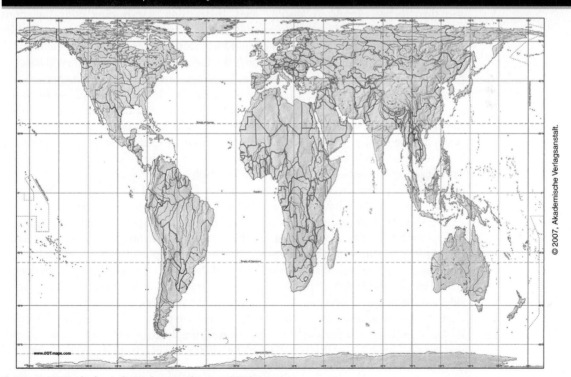

Source: © 2007, Akademische Verlagsanstalt. www.ODTmaps.com

The skin needs to break if it is to be laid flat. One of Fuller's nifty ideas was to put those breaks into the ocean as much as possible. Uniquely, this projection provides a worldview in which the landmasses are almost connected, not separated by giant oceans as in the Mercator and Peters. Fuller's purpose was to urge people in different corners of the world to see the whole human family together and to take responsibility for the family home, Earth, before it is too late.[6]

In the 1980s, the National Geographic Society and other geographic organizations began to prefer a projection that was developed by Arthur Robinson in 1963. Another change took place in 1998 when the Society replaced the Robinson with the Winkel projection.

Lesson Plan 8 allows students to see a number of these projections and presents a challenging lesson for teacher and students alike. It aims to introduce students to world maps—not innocently, but in full view of the projection problem. It is an online lesson so that teachers without wall maps of the various map projections can share them with students on the Internet.

Teaching Map Symbols

A fundamental skill in map reading is to learn that a symbol represents a real thing. The symbol may be arbitrarily chosen and bear no resemblance to the object represented, or it may suggest to the reader what is intended. A post office might be represented by a small circle or by a small square with a flag placed on top. It is easier to associate the flag and square with a post office than to associate the circle with it. The flag and square are, therefore, less abstract. With young children, it is better to use pictorial or semipictorial symbols of this sort than to use completely abstract ones. In teaching map-reading skills, one must remember that both reading and interpretive skills are involved, and the interpretive skills depend heavily on maturity and background knowledge. For example, when children are constructing a map of the neighborhoods in their own community, they should be prompted to represent the various religious buildings. But deciding how to appropriately symbolize a Christian church, a Jewish or Buddhist temple, a mosque, and so forth will require more background knowledge than young children will have. Still, it is extremely important that the cross typically used to represent a Christian church not also be used to symbolize the worship places of other faiths. A committee of children might be appointed to do research on religious symbols. Or a parent aide could be asked to make a few phone calls. Showing this sort of respect for the various faith communities in town should win the admiration of parents and school-board members. Similarly, if a square with a flag is used for the post office, then how should a school and a courthouse be represented?

The idea of objects representing other objects, people, or things is not new to the children; they have substituted symbols for the actual things many times in imaginative play. The teacher can begin by explaining that they are going to draw a map of the schoolroom, schoolyard, or some segment of the immediate vicinity. It is best if this can be done on the classroom floor so the layout can be oriented exactly as it appears in relationship to the classroom. This practice sidesteps the matter of orientation to directions at this early stage. Trees, doors, playground equipment, parking areas, and so on appear in relation to other objects; only the major ones should be included. The purpose of this experience is simply to show that *it is possible to represent space symbolically, and that symbols stand for real things.* Their maps should have a title and a key to tell what the symbols stand for. This is the first experience in developing the skill of comprehending map symbols, and it will be continued and extended as long as maps are used.

Lesson Plan

8

EXPLORING MAP PROJECTIONS

Grades	4–8
Time	Two class periods
NCSS Standards	3 (people, places, and environments) and 9 (global connections)
Objective	Students will develop curiosity about maps; learn that globes cannot be made into flat maps without distorting shapes or sizes of landforms and water bodies; learn that different projections get different aspects of the globe right: Mercator gets the compass bearings for sailors right, Peters gets the proportions of landmasses to one another right, and Fuller gets the landmass sizes (relative to one another) right while creating a provocative view of the world.
Interest Building	Point to three wall maps that have been placed close together in the front of the room, and engage students with the problem of flattening out a sphere by using the orange-peeling exercise from this chapter's opening Picture This.

Lesson Development

1. Explain to students that every *projection* (introduce this term) has distortions and why this happens. Explain that *cartographers* (introduce this term) solve the projection problem in different ways.

2. Show the three wall maps and, using an LCD projector, display websites that provide a clear image of each of these projections: Mercator, Peters, Winkel (or Robinson), and Fuller (Dymaxion). At the time of writing, the following websites were some of the best (but keep searching, as websites change).

   Mercator
   www.liftoff.msfc.nasa.gov/academy/rocket_sci/orbmech/mercator.html

   Peters
   www.petersmap.com/table.html
   www.diversophy.com/petersmap.htm

   Dymaxion
   www.bfi.org/map.htm

   Winkel (also Winkel Tripel)
   Use a trusted search engine to find a good illustration of this projection.

Summary and Assessment

Ask students to jot down responses to the following questions. Then, call on several students to read what they wrote for question 1, a different set of students for question 2, and so on. Don't correct or provide feedback; just listen. (This is assessment, not instruction.)

1. Think for a minute about our attempt to flatten the orange skin. How is that like the problem cartographers face when they make a world map?
2. How does the Mercator map distort (change) Earth?
3. How does the Peters map distort (change) Earth?
4. What did Fuller try to do?
5. Which projection do you prefer and why?
6. What do you want to know now about maps?

After assessing, provide feedback and correction to the whole class as needed. Summarize by repeating the main point: Maps inevitably distort Earth's surface because they are flat whereas the space they are representing is round. Each projection has a different *purpose*.

Materials

Internet access, computer and a computer projector for showing a website on a large screen for all to see, and websites bookmarked for easy access during the lesson.

Follow-up   1. Create a map-projections learning center on a table beneath a bulletin board. Pose the problem in the title. For example, "Which View of the World?" Place copies of the Peters, Mercator, Dymaxion, and Winkel world maps on the bulletin board. (The school or district should provide these, or they can be purchased at many home stores, bookstores, pharmacies, or online. Shop around; it is unnecessary to buy expensive versions.) Make a photocopy of Figures 5–4 and 5–6 and place them upright on the table on a bifold poster board about 12″ × 16″. Place a globe on the table, too. Supply students with a stack of grid paper. Directions can read: 1. Study the world maps and the globe and notice the differences between the projections. 2. Practice drawing freehand a simple world map using one of the projections. Get ideas from the two small posters on the table. 3. Put your name, the date, and the name of the projection on the map and leave it in the "Cartographer's Work" basket.

2. Ask a small committee of students (see tips in Chapter 11, "Cooperative Learning in Social Studies") to search the Internet for websites that feature map projections. Their mission is to find good examples of projections for *younger* students to study—say, one grade below. This will help them find vivid visuals and clear, simple explanations—precisely what's needed. As these websites are discovered, ask the committee to share them with the class.

Integration   *Mathematics:* Working with the north–south (longitude) and east–west (latitude) grid on a map involves mathematical reasoning; using language to distinguish one projection from another involves still more. Peters emphasizes landmasses in relation to one another (proportions). Proportions are what Mercator so strangely distorts.

Teaching Map Directions

For reasons of simplicity, orientation to direction may be avoided in the children's first attempts at making diagrams or maps. But the need to orient a map properly for direction will become apparent to them if their classroom map is rotated. Being able to note and read directions is a prerequisite to serious map study, and this skill should be introduced fairly early, perhaps in the second grade. Children can learn the *cardinal directions* (the four main points of the compass) by having the directions pointed out to them. They learn which wall of the room is north, south, east, or west because the teacher has placed labels on the walls. They learn that if one knows the direction of north, the other directions can be determined, for if one faces north, the direction of south will be to one's back, east to the right, and west to the left. To extend their ability to orient themselves, children should be taken outdoors and the directions pointed out to them. If this is done at noon on a sunny day, the children's shadows will point in an approximate northerly direction. After the children have this basic orientation to direction, subsequent map-work should include reference to direction and should become increasingly more complex.

Finding directions on conventional wall maps can be facilitated with the aid of a globe and perhaps it should not be taught much below the fourth grade. When this concept is introduced, it should be done through reference to north–south and east–west *grid lines.* Thanks to these grid lines, *every place on Earth has an absolute address.* Children are taught that north is in the direction of the North Pole and that south is in the direction of the South Pole. The poles can be easily found by following the *meridians of longitude.* The east–west directions can be found by following the *parallels of latitude.*

Generalizations such as "north is at the top of the map" and "south is at the bottom of the map" should *not* be taught because they are not correct and because they may be confusing when children use a variety of map projections. Similarly, references to north as up and south as down should not be taught in connection with either maps or globes. When we speak of Earth, the term *down* means toward the center of Earth and *up* means away from the center of Earth. The matter of associating up with north introduces many instructional problems as children learn more of the geography of Earth. For example, if north is up, how can so many of the world's rivers flow north? The children will invariably ask why we say "down south" for Alabama or "the Land Down Under" for Australia; these can be explained as being colorful expressions and figures of speech similar to "out west" or "out at sea" that have crept into our language but have nothing at all to do with direction itself (see Figure 5–7).

FIGURE 5-7   This map illustrates why statements such as "north is at the top of the map" are incorrect. Here, north is in the middle. East–west lines or parallels of latitude have been omitted to draw attention to north–south meridians of longitude. What questions might you pose to students studying this map?

Teaching Map Scale

Children can be helped to understand the need for map scales by pointing out that world maps must be small enough to bring into the classroom or carry in backpacks. State and national road maps must fit in the glove compartment of the car. Trail maps need to fit in a pants or jacket pocket. We cannot make maps as big as the area we wish to show, and who would want one that big? A map must be made smaller than the place it represents, and everything on the map must be made smaller in the same amount. This is scaling. Just as a photograph of the family shows everyone smaller in the same amount, so must the map; otherwise, it would not give a true picture. Children should learn that maps are precise and accurate tools. In primary grades, the scaling is not done in the mathematical sense, but the reductions are correctly made in the relative sense. That is, lakes would be larger than houses, streets longer than driveways, cars smaller than buildings, and so on. In intermediate grades, when children have had sufficient background in mathematics, they can deal with graphic reductions—scaling—more precisely. They learn that wall maps have the scale printed on them and are taught how to read the various ways by which scale can be indicated.

Teaching Map Interpretation

When children have learned the meaning of map symbols, are skillful in orienting a map to direction, and can recognize and use map scales, they are well on their way toward an understanding of the language of maps. This does not mean, however, that they find maps especially useful or that they regard them as a valuable source of information. Proficiency in interpreting maps will vary considerably among the children. One who is skillful in map use has developed the ability to visualize what an area actually looks like when it is seen on the map. Looking at the map color, one in a sense "sees" the rugged Rocky Mountains of our West, the waving grainfields of western Montana, the rich farmlands of the Midwest, and the rolling countryside of Virginia. Because children cannot visualize places not actually seen except in an imaginative way, *the generous use of additional visual material along with maps is suggested.* Good-quality pictures are especially important, and the class should see several pictures of an area to avoid fixing a single impression of the area in their minds. Films and television are excellent aids. Chapter 10, "Four Great Resources," suggests several websites where students can see an array of maps as well as photographs of everything from the pyramids of Egypt to the Pilgrim settlement at Plymouth. Stories and other narrative accounts are also useful in helping children visualize areas represented on maps.

The following activities can be used to relate the abstractions of maps to the reality they represent.

1. Observing local landscapes and geographical features, preferably from a high point.
2. Using three-dimensional models of the areas mapped; using blocks and models to represent buildings.
3. Making maps of the local area with which children are familiar.
4. Making generous use of pictures, films, and drawings of the areas shown on maps.
5. Relating aerial photographs to maps of the same area.

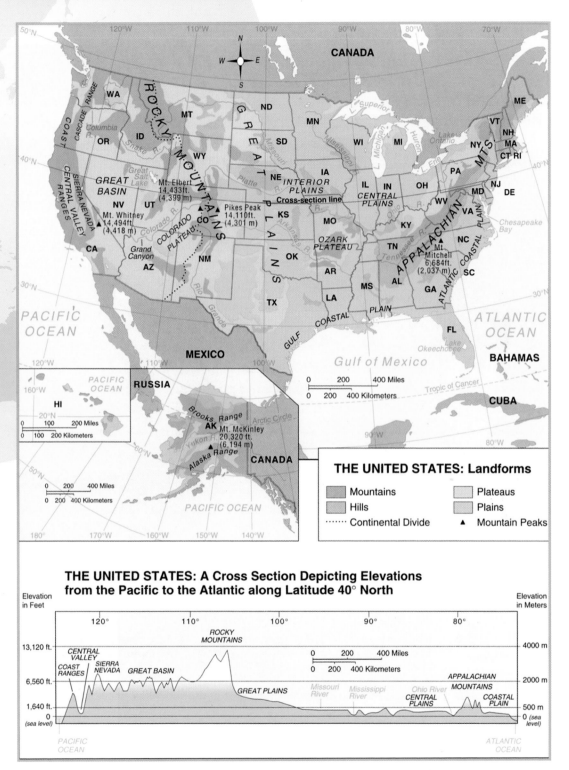

THE UNITED STATES: Landforms

- ■ Mountains
- ■ Hills
- ⋯⋯ Continental Divide
- ■ Plateaus
- ■ Plains
- ▲ Mountain Peaks

THE UNITED STATES: A Cross Section Depicting Elevations from the Pacific to the Atlantic along Latitude 40° North

Source: Reproduced with the permission of the McGraw-Hill Companies from *The United States and Its Neighbors*, J. A. Banks et al., Macmillan/McGraw-Hill, 1995.

Dictionary of Geographic Terms

1 **BASIN** A bowl-shaped landform surrounded by higher land

2 **BAY** Part of an ocean or lake that extends deeply into the land

3 **CANAL** A channel built to carry water for irrigation or transportation

4 **CANYON** A deep, narrow valley with steep sides

5 **COAST** The land along an ocean

6 **DAM** A wall built across a river, creating a lake that stores water

7 **DELTA** Land made of soil left behind as a river drains into a larger body of water

8 **DESERT** A dry environment with few plants and animals

9 **FAULT** The border between two of the plates that make up Earth's crust

10 **GLACIER** A huge sheet of ice that moves slowly across the land

11 **GULF** Part of an ocean that extends into the land; larger than a bay

12 **HARBOR** A sheltered place along a coast where boats dock safely

13 **HILL** A rounded, raised landform; not as high as a mountain

14 **ISLAND** A body of land completely surrounded by water

15 **LAKE** A body of water completely surrounded by land

16 **MESA** A hill with a flat top; smaller than a plateau

Source: Banks, Colleary, Greenow, Parker, Schell, Zike. *The United States*, © 2009 Macmillan/McGraw-Hill. Reproduced by permission of the McGraw-Hill Companies.

#	Term	Definition	#	Term	Definition	#	Term	Definition
17	MOUNTAIN	A high landform with steep sides; higher than a hill	23	PLATEAU	A high, flat area that rises steeply above the surrounding land	28	VALLEY	An area of low land between hills or mountains
18	MOUNTAIN PASS	A narrow gap through a mountain range	24	PORT	A place where ships load and unload their goods	29	VOLCANO	An opening in Earth's surface through which hot rock and ash are forced out
19	MOUTH	The place where a river empties into a larger body of water	25	RESERVOIR	A natural or artificial lake used to store water	30	WATERFALL	A flow of water falling vertically
20	OCEAN	A large body of salt water; oceans cover much of the Earth's surface	26	RIVER	A stream of water that flows across the land and empties into another body of water			
21	PENINSULA	A body of land nearly surrounded by water	27	SOURCE	The starting point of a river			
22	PLAIN	A large area of nearly flat land						

FULLER PROJECTION
Dymaxion™ Air-Ocean World

Source: The Fuller Projection Map design is a trademark of the Buckminster Fuller Institute © 1938, 1967, & 1992. All rights reserved. www.bfi.org

DO-IT-YOURSELF MAP

This exercise can be used in the intermediate and middle grades for teaching and/or assessing map skills. The teacher can have everyone in class do the exercise as the directions are read, one step at a time. When the maps are completed, the exercise should be discussed and, if appropriate, the maps posted for all to see. Children can be invited to walk around the room to see maps drawn by their classmates.

1. On a clean sheet of paper, draw an outline map of an imaginary *continent*. You may make it any shape you wish, but you must include at least one peninsula and one bay.
2. Show a scale of miles in your legend for the map.
3. Draw east–west and north–south lines on your map.
4. Draw a mountain range running east and west across your continent, but include at least one mountain pass. Place the symbol you use for your mountain range in your legend.
5. Show a city in the northern half of your continent and one in the southern half. Make each one a seaport.
6. Show a railway joining the two cities.
7. Show three rivers on your continent; show a lake and a wetland. Place all the symbols you use for cities, rivers, lakes, and wetlands in the legend.
8. Place a third city somewhere on your map where you think a city should be. On the bottom of your map tell why you think a city should be where you have placed it.
9. Show boundary lines that divide your continent into three large countries and one small country.
10. Next to the legend draw a compass rose.

The types of information that can be read directly or inferred from map study can be classified as follows:

Land and water forms—continents, oceans, bays, peninsulas, islands, straits, wetlands

Relief features—plains, mountains, hills, rivers, deltas, deserts, plateaus, mesas, valleys

Direction and distance—cardinal directions, distance in miles or kilometers, relative distance, scale, compass rose

Demographic data—population density, size of communities, location of major cities, birth and death rates

Economic information—industrial and agricultural production, soil fertility, trade routes

Political information—political boundaries such as a city's and county's, capital cities, county seats, legislative districts

Human projects—cities, canals, railroads, highways, dams and reservoirs, bridges, nuclear power plants

Comparing Maps

Comparing different maps of the same place can be an insightful experience. In the fourth and fifth grades, teachers often have children compare transit and political maps with physical maps and, within the latter category, resource maps and elevation maps. They also have them compare maps showing the location of important resources, such as iron and water, with maps showing the location of industrial centers, population densities, and so on. It is quite common to find special-purpose maps of the same region in the children's textbook, making comparisons easy. These provide excellent settings for critical thinking as the children study the data presented on two or more maps.

Google Earth can be a helpful online tool for comparing different maps of the same place. By clicking on Roads, streets and highways are superimposed on a physical map. By clicking on Parks and Recreation Areas, these places are highlighted. By clicking on Community Service, schools, hospitals, and museums are shown and named.

Being able to interpret and draw different kinds of maps is valuable know-how, and it is tested carefully on the fourth-grade National Assessment of Educational Progress for geography. Below are the 10 most difficult items on that test.[7]

Interpret a resource map to determine the likely location for a large city to develop.	Use multiple maps to compare conditions for farming in two countries.
Draw a map based on written description of its features.	Interpret the information given on a transit map.
Identify the mountain range in which Switzerland is located.	Find and draw a specified route on a transit system map.
Use multiple maps to locate states where crops grow year around.	Identify a megalopolis on a population map.
Use a map to determine which countries might have a conflict over resources.	Determine the elevation of a region on a physical map.

Teaching Map Color

The use of color causes confusion for children trying to visualize elevations. Children seem to believe that all areas represented by one color are precisely the same elevation, not recognizing that variations in elevations occur within the limits of the interval used by the color representation (see Figure 5–8). Moreover, children develop the mistaken idea that changes in elevations occur abruptly where colors change. Conventional color symbols give no impression of gradual elevations or depressions and create the illusion that changes are abrupt. The use of a relief map helps show that changes in elevation occur gradually. Comparing colors of a wall map with elevations on a relief map helps children gain a better understanding of map color used to represent elevations.

Landform maps are often used in social studies textbooks. The usual landforms shown are *plains, plateaus, hills,* and *mountains;* each is represented by a different color. Misconceptions arise when children mistakenly think of the colors as representing elevations in absolute amounts. For example, there are high mountains (the Himalayas in Asia) and low mountains (the Olympics in North America), yet on a landform map they may appear in

FIGURE 5–8   This diagram shows two methods of illustrating keys to colors, used to express elevations on classroom maps. Some teachers find it helpful to construct a three-dimensional papier-mâché model of the key to help students associate elevation with the color code.

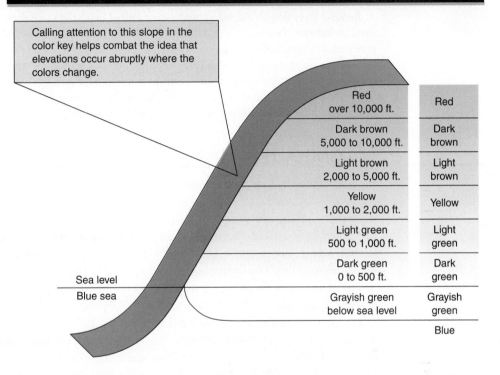

Calling attention to this slope in the color key helps combat the idea that elevations occur abruptly where the colors change.

Red over 10,000 ft.	Red
Dark brown 5,000 to 10,000 ft.	Dark brown
Light brown 2,000 to 5,000 ft.	Light brown
Yellow 1,000 to 2,000 ft.	Yellow
Light green 500 to 1,000 ft.	Light green
Dark green 0 to 500 ft.	Dark green
Grayish green below sea level	Grayish green
	Blue

Sea level
Blue sea

the same color. Some high plateaus are actually higher in absolute elevation than some low mountains. Some hills may be lower in elevation than plateaus and plains. Children need to learn that landform maps show only where the plains, plateaus, hills, and mountains are located, not how high they are above sea level. A landform map is shown in combination with a *cross-section elevation map* in this chapter's full-color pages. The cross-section map can dispel misconceptions. For example, in the eastern United States are the Appalachian Mountains and in the west are the Rocky Mountains. Both are mountains, but note the striking difference in elevation.

Applying Map and Globe Skills

Map- and globe-reading skills are learned through direct teaching and by application in situations in which the skill is normally used. In many instances, these processes can be combined. Let us say, for example, that children in a fourth-grade class read, "Permafrost is a condition found only in high latitudes." The teacher can use this encounter with "high latitudes" to teach map reading in connection with that concept. Class time can be taken to teach the meaning of high, low, and middle latitudes on maps and globes, and this teaching would occur in what is referred to as a functional or authentic setting. Teachers are encouraged to teach as many map and globe skills as possible in this way rather than to isolate the skills from their relevant subject matter. After direct teaching there must be a generous application and use of the skills if proficiency is to be developed and maintained.

Because these skills are developmental, one cannot expect to teach them once and assume that they have been learned. Most skills are introduced in the early grades and then are retaught, reviewed, or expanded later on. We expect that children will show increased proficiency and maturity in using these skills each year they are in school. Such development comes through continued teaching and use, not automatically through the natural process of maturation.

The following map and globe activities can be used to stimulate interest and at the same time teach important concepts and thinking skills related to map and globe reading.

MAKING A TRIP MAP

The teacher showed children color photographs of several states and discussed the many interesting things that can be seen and done in them. Children shared some of their own travel experiences. The teacher provided the class with road maps of several different states and asked them to find places that might interest someone visiting those states. These places of interest were discussed briefly. Children were then asked to think about and select a state they would enjoy visiting. Choices were to be made by the next day.

The following day the children selected the states they wanted to "visit." Using a road map of their chosen state provided by the teacher and using resources available in and outside the classroom, they were to plan a route of travel through the state of their choice, making at least five stops at places that would interest a visitor. The teacher demonstrated Google Earth, entering city names in the "fly to" box. Then students gave it a try, entering the city names that they might include on their tours. By clicking on Roads, they could see the highways connecting cities. By clicking on Travel and Tourism, they could see new possibilities for trip stops. Once they had decided, they were to mark these stops with a sticky label and write a short narrative description to accompany the map telling about the travel route, state or national parks, historical landmarks, zoos, and other items of interest.

The children responded to the teacher's encouragement to be creative in describing their imaginary trips, and they revised their narrative descriptions, eventually producing travel brochures and recorded travelogues. They began a classroom exhibit of their trip maps and narratives, and in a week the room resembled a make-believe travel agency. This generated a considerable amount of discussion and sharing of ideas, as well as numerous opportunities for revision of the maps and brochures. The children acquired lots of geographical information, developed and applied important skills, and gained an appreciation for a several states.

A professionally prepared curriculum unit resembling this activity, but more elaborate and involving the students' own state, is a "storypath" unit called *State Studies: The Visitors' Center.* Developed by Margit McGuire (www.teachstorypath.com) for grades 3 through 5, students create a visitors' center for their state and then a state tourism brochure. Also, they must deal with a number of unexpected events, such as a drop in tourism revenues.

1. After an on-the-spot observation of the school grounds or the immediate vicinity, construct a three-dimensional floor map of the area.
2. Locate the places where stories about children in other lands take place or where news events are occurring.
3. Find pictures in magazines and the textbook that illustrate various landforms: plains, plateaus, hills, and peninsulas.
4. Make multiple maps of the same area, such as the playground or local county, using different scales for each map.
5. Plan a pretend trip to a distant place. Teach the needed vocabulary to describe the destination's location in relative and absolute terms. Have small groups each develop a different route, one group heading east, another going west, another south, another southeast, and so on.
6. Develop a classroom exhibit of maps found in current newspapers and periodicals. Place captions under each that describe its unique features, errors, and projection.
7. Secure an outdated political map of the world and have the class compare it with a current one. Point out countries that have changed names (e.g., Congo, Burma) and countries that no longer exist (e.g., Soviet Union, Yugoslavia).
8. Hold a regular Monday morning geography bee. Teacher-assigned teams rehearse and compete, vying to spell and define the terms correctly. Figure 5–9 contains more than 50 terms. The teacher can select terms the children are ready for, and the children can

FIGURE 5–9   The Monday morning geography bee.

Select easier or more difficult terms from this list as appropriate.

absolute location _latitude_	flora	mesa
barrier island _longitude_	forest	metropolis
bay _exact location_	globe	migration
biosphere _earth's fancy name_	groundwater	monsoon
canal	hemisphere	mountain range
cartographer	hill	nonrenewable resource
channel	hurricane	peninsula
climate	industrialization	plateau
contour map _3d map built from clay_	infant mortality rate	population density
creek	inlet	rain shadow _the rain dumping on the mountain_
culture	interdependence _being dependent on others_	region
deforestation _getting rid of the forest_	island	relative location _how far is Issaquah from Seattle_
desert	lake	river system
developing country	landform	scale
ecology _study of the environment_	latitude	settlement pattern _the way in which people settled_
ecosystem	legend (key)	sustainable development
equator _invisible line that goes around the earth_	longitude	terrace _like steps_
ethnocentrism _you think your ethnic group is the best_	map	terrain
fauna	map projection	urbanization
fertility rate	megalopolis	wetland

work on the definitions, using the textbook, dictionary, Internet, and other sources, as they compile an illustrated glossary in item 9 below.

9. Develop an illustrated dictionary of geographic terms.

10. Use computer software such as *Mapmaker's Toolkit* by Tom Snyder Productions (grades 4 and up). Hundred of maps are available and students can add names of rivers or highways, illustrate crop harvests or droughts, color-code nations or regions, and create legends that define the symbols used. *Neighborhood MapMachine* (grades 1–5), also from Tom Snyder Productions, scaffolds younger students into making and manipulating maps and introduces them to key concepts (coordinates, legend, scale, etc.). Readers can see brief videos of these tools at www.tomsnyder.com.

And be sure to look at *Where in the World Is Carmen Sandiego?* This is one of the most exciting and useful pieces of computer software available for learning geography. It is a game that can be played alone, in small groups, or by the entire class. Carmen, you will discover, is the thief of some of the world's great treasures. Students play the role of detectives hot on her trail across six continents and innumerable cities. Each on-site investigation produces clues that lead them on to the next city. Lots of geographical data are involved, all requiring interpretation and organization. The game is played using a database from *The World Almanac and Book of Facts*.[8]

Resources

Teaching map and globe skills requires some special resources and equipment. To access online maps and the features of Google Earth, one or more classroom computers and an LCD projector are needed. The computers need to have the necessary memory and speed to for quick displays. Every classroom should have a globe and wall maps appropriate to the curriculum content of the grade. In third grade and above, all classrooms should have at least one wall map of the world. It is better to have two or three, showing different projections. Outline maps are needed on which students can draw and write, and it helps to have available a three-dimensional relief map of the United States and of the home state. A class set of globes should be available in the resource center, shared by all classrooms. Additional equipment might include individual student desk maps, charts showing conventional map symbols, and special-purpose maps showing vegetation, crops, and natural resources. When children engage in mapmaking, they will need to have available essential construction materials: boxes, blocks, butcher paper, black tape, tracing paper, colored pencils, pens or crayons, paints and brushes, papier-mâché, plaster, salt and flour, or another modeling material.

A Summary of Map and Globe Skills

Elementary and middle school children should develop map and globe skills associated with the following concepts and generalizations:

1. Primary Grades
   - A map is a drawing or other representation of all or part of Earth.
   - On maps and globes, symbols are used to stand for real things.
   - Earth is a huge sphere, and we live on it. It is our home.
   - A globe is a small model of Earth and is the most accurate representation of Earth.
   - Half of Earth is called a hemisphere.

- Earth can be divided into several hemispheres. The most common ones are the Eastern, Western, Northern, and Southern Hemispheres; land hemisphere and water hemisphere; and day hemisphere and night hemisphere.
- Any part of the globe can be shown on a map.
- Large bodies of land are called continents.
- Large bodies of water are called oceans.
- Terms such as *left, right, near, far, above, below, up,* and *down* can be useful in expressing relative location.
- A legend or key on a map tells the meaning of colors and symbols used on the map.
- Directions on a map are determined by the poles: to go north means to go in the direction of the North Pole; to go south means to go in the direction of the South Pole.
- North may be shown any place on a map; north is not always at the top of a map.
- The scale on a map or globe makes it possible to determine distances between places.
- Maps are drawn to different scales; scale ensures that all objects are made smaller in the same amount.
- Maps and globes use legends, or keys, that tell the meaning of the symbols used on the map.
- The cardinal directions are north, south, east, and west; intermediate directions are northeast, northwest, southeast, and southwest.
- All places on Earth can be located on maps and globes. Different maps provide different information about Earth.

2. Intermediate and Middle Grades
   - The larger the scale used, the larger each feature appears on the map.
   - The same symbol may mean different things from one map to another; the legend tells what the symbols stand for.
   - The elevation of land is measured from sea level; some maps provide information about elevation.
   - Physical maps can be used to determine land elevations, slopes of land, and directions of rivers.
   - Parallels of latitude can be used to establish east–west direction and are also used to measure distances in degrees north and south of the equator.
   - All places on the same east–west line (parallel of latitude) are directly east or west of one another and are the same distance north or south of the equator.
   - All places north of the equator are in north latitudes; all places south of the equator are in south latitudes.
   - The tropic of Cancer and the tropic of Capricorn are imaginary lines of latitude lying north and south of the equator. The part of Earth between them is known as the Tropics.
   - The Arctic and Antarctic Circles are imaginary lines that define the polar regions.
   - The low latitudes lie on either side of the equator; the high latitudes surround the poles; and the middle latitudes lie between the low and high latitudes.
   - Parallels of latitude, parallel to the equator, get shorter as they progress from the equator to the poles.

- Knowing the latitude of a place makes it possible to locate its north–south position on Earth.
- Meridians of longitude can be used to determine north–south direction and are also used to measure distances in degrees east and west of the prime meridian.
- The zero or "prime" meridian passes through Greenwich, a suburb of London.
- Meridians of longitude are imaginary north–south lines that converge on both poles.
- Meridians of longitude are "great circles" because they divide Earth into two hemispheres.
- The shortest distance between any two places on Earth follows a great circle.
- West longitude is measured to the west of the prime meridian from zero to 180°; east longitude is measured to the east of the prime meridian from zero to 180°.
- All places on the same north–south line (meridian of longitude) are directly north or south of each other and are the same distance in degrees east or west of the prime meridian.
- The latitude and longitude of any place determine its exact location on a globe or map.
- Longitude is used in determining the time of day at places around the world. Earth rotates through 15° of longitude every hour; Earth is divided into 24 time zones.
- Globes give such information as distance, direction, relative and exact location, and sizes and shapes of areas more accurately than flat maps can.
- Maps and globes often use abbreviations to identify places and things.
- An imaginary line through the center of Earth, running from pole to pole, is called Earth's axis; Earth rotates on its axis from west to east.
- Night and day are the result of the rotation of Earth.
- Maps and globes provide data about the nature of areas by using color contour, visual relief, and contour lines.
- All flat maps contain some distortion because they represent a round object on a flat surface. This is a map's projection.
- Different map projections provide different perspectives on the sizes and shapes of areas shown.

TEACHING CHARTS AND GRAPHS

Because of the widespread use of graphs and charts in social studies and in printed material outside school, it is imperative that children develop the skills needed to read and interpret them.

Charts

Like graphs, charts are widely used to present ideas in a vivid and forceful way. *Data-retrieval charts,* as they are called, are widely used in social studies teaching, especially as aids to concept formation. They are employed throughout this text.

Note that data-retrieval charts are two-way charts, otherwise known as two-dimensional charts. Across the top are focus questions that guide students' examination of the places, people, or things that run down the left side. Look back at the data-retrieval charts in the "Sociology" section of the prior chapter—Figures 4–8 through 4–11.

In concept learning especially, this sort of chart helps students to keep track of and organize a large quantity of information across several examples. It scaffolds understanding. Without it, the task of comparing and contrasting examples would be too difficult for too many students. Teachers who are able to get more students to learn more (note the two uses of "more") rely on such tools as this.

There are other kinds of charts, which can be categorized as follows:

1. *Tabulation Chart:* Lists data in table form to facilitate making comparisons. *Examples:* data placed in tabular form to show infant mortality rates, illiteracy rates, or per capita income among nations of the world.
2. *Classification Chart:* Groups data into various categories. *Examples:* types of communities (urban, rural), categories of food (vegetables, juices), or modes of transportation (animal-powered, engine-powered).
3. *Organization Chart:* Shows the structure of an organization. *Examples:* the three branches of government, the structure of a corporation, or the organization of a city government or a school district.
4. *Flow Chart:* Shows a process involving change at certain points. *Examples:* how an ear of corn becomes a tortilla, how a bill becomes a law.

The frequent use of charts in children's books provides a good basis for learning. In the process, children not only learn how to read and interpret the chart, but also broaden their understanding of associated concepts.

Graphs

Graphs are used to illustrate relationships among quantities. They are so widely used that readers will find them in every section of a daily newspaper, from Sports to Business to Weather and Today's News. The most commonly used graphs are the *bar graph,* the *pie graph,* and the *line graph.* Any of these graphs may include pictorial representations, thereby making them more interesting to young children and making the content more real and concrete, that is, less symbolic and abstract. For instance, with primary-grade children, stick figures can be used to represent children in a bar graph showing the number absent from class each day. Or two paper chains can be hung side by side to represent the results of a class vote on some issue, say, whether as part of a unit on food processing to take a field trip to a dairy or to a cannery (Figure 5–10).

It is easy to visualize the relationships of the parts to the whole in a pie graph, but to construct one accurately requires the ability to compute percentages, which will be difficult for children in the elementary school grades. But visualizing proportions is a significant achievement in its own right, even if children do not yet have the vocabulary: two-thirds, 66%, 2/3. In fact, having the visual creates a need for the vocabulary. Children can be taught to make simple pie graphs with cut paper, as shown in Figure 5–11. Using safety scissors, children cut two circles using a bowl, paper plate, or other pattern. Then they cut one radius line in each circle. Now the circles can be slipped one into the other and then moved around to show different proportions: voilà, a manipulable pie graph! (See the section on folded three-dimensional graphic organizers and the full-color insert in Chapter 8 for more ideas.)

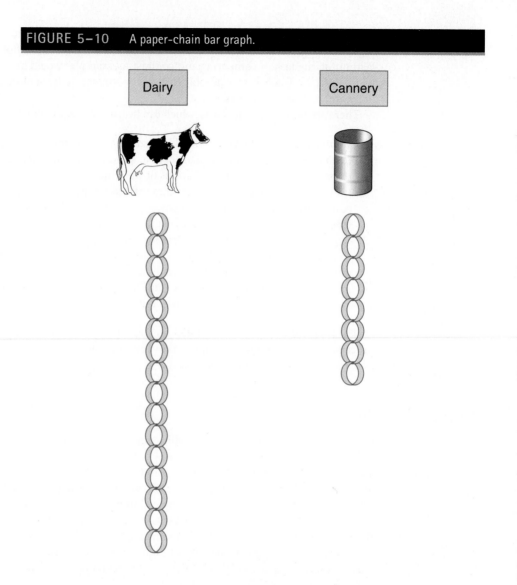

FIGURE 5–10   A paper-chain bar graph.

Children can learn much about graphs and how to read them by constructing their own. Here again are the two wings of the pedagogical airplane introduced in Chapter 4. Just as *reading* a history is one thing and *writing* one is another, reading graphs that others have made is one thing and making your own is quite another. Learner-made graphs should be encouraged as visual aids when students make oral written reports. These can be collected for bulletin-board displays. All sorts of information can be graphed in ways that are meaningful to children (see Figure 5–12).

Elementary school textbooks make liberal use of graphs in presenting data, but children need to be instructed in how to read and interpret them. Because graphs can be designed to present distorted pictures of data, children in the intermediate and middle grades should be taught how bias can be introduced in a graph (see Figures 5–13 and 5–14).

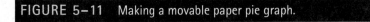

FIGURE 5–11 Making a movable paper pie graph.

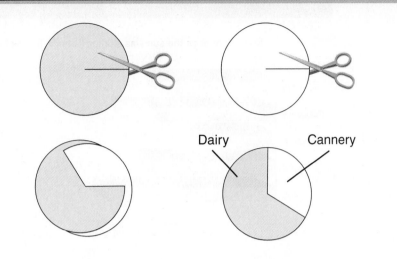

Conclusion

Making sense of space and place requires all sorts of tools, both physical and intellectual. From wall maps and globes to charts and graphs, a good social studies curriculum teaches children a wide variety of ways to read and organize the world around them. These tools promote in students an attitude of thoughtfulness about social data while dramatically expanding their vocabulary and skills.

Discussion Questions and Suggested Activities

Go to MyEducationLab and select the topic "Geography," then watch the video "Salt Maps" and complete the activity.

1. Look back at the Projection Puzzle section and think back to your response to the question asked in the *Reflection* sidebar. The classroom environment—the visual images, banners, and learning centers you have created on the walls, tables, ceiling, and floor—helps achieve your teaching and learning goals, but only if you use it. How could a teacher who wanted more than anything for her students to develop into *world citizens* provision this environment? What about the flags, banners, and learning centers?

2. Review the opening section called "Capital Punishment?" and take a stand on this longstanding controversy.

3. Using scissors and paper, make a paper pie graph as shown in Figure 5–11. Then manipulate it to show various forms of social data (e.g., the proportion of your day that is spent in school on an *average* day, and then on unusual days; the amount of time you have lived at your current address in relation to the amount of time you lived at a prior address; the percentage of the world's people who are always hungry; the proportion of the world's people who live north of the equator; the proportion of men and women in your class.)

4. NCSS Standards *Sampler*. Examine the K–2 classroom vignette for standard #3 on page 12 of the standards *Sampler* that accompanies this book. How does that area-by-area study of the children's city compare to the Google Earth activity presented in this chapter?

Number of days the sun was shining at noon for the first five months

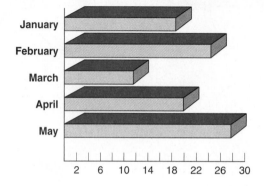

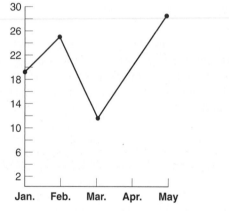

A class kept a record of the number of days the sun was shining at noon from the first of January through May. In January there were 19 days when the sun was shining at noon; in February there were 25; in March there were 12; in April there were 20; and in May there were 28 days. These graphs show three different ways of showing these data. Graphs of this type can be constructed and used for study purposes by elementary school children. What inquiry questions might be based on these graphs?

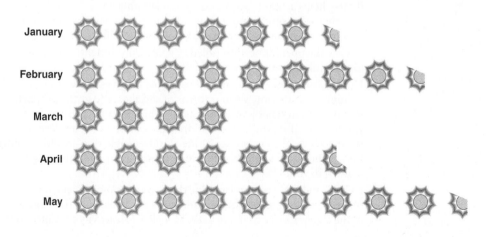

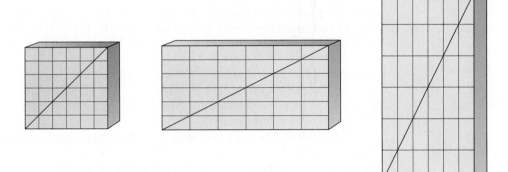

Growth in profits over a 4-year period

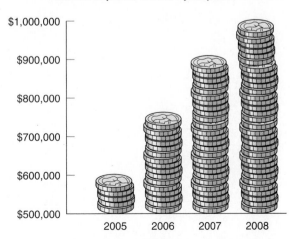
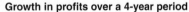

Selected References

Alibrandi, Marsha. (2003). *GIS in the classroom.* Portsmouth, NH: Heinemann.

Bednarz, Sarah W., Acheson, Gilian, & Bednarz, Robert S. (2006). Maps and map learning in social studies. *Social Education, 70,* 398–404.

de Blij, H. J., & Muller, Peter O. (2006). *Geography: realms, regions, and concepts* (12th ed.). Hoboken, NJ: Wiley.

Carroll, Terry C., Knight, Cheryl, & Hutchinson, Ed. (1998). Carmen Sandiego: Crime can pay when it comes to learning. In Joseph A. Braun, Jr., Phyllis Fernlund, & Charles S. White (Eds.), *Technology tools in the social studies curriculum* (pp. 77–86). Wilsonville, OR: Franklin, Beedle & Associates.

Kaiser, Ward L., & Wood, Denis. (2001). *Seeing through maps: The power of images to shape our world view.* Amherst, MA: ODT, Inc.

National Council for Geographic Education. (2000). *How to help children become geographically literate.* Indiana, PA: Author.

Segall, Avner. (2003). Maps as stories about the world. *Social Studies and the Young Learner, 16,* 21–25.

Shin, Eui-kyung, & Alibrandi, Marsha. (2007). Online interactive mapping: Using Google Earth. *Social Studies and the Young Learner, 19,* P1–P4.

Sobel, Dava. (2005). *The planets.* New York: Viking.

Sobel, David. (1998). *Mapmaking with children: Sense of place education for the elementary years.* Portsmouth, NH: Heinemann.

Social Studies and the Young Learner. (November/December, 2007). Entire issue on "Geography: It's a small world."

 MyEducationLab is a collection of online tools for your success in this course, your licensure exams, and your teaching career. Go to www.myeducationlab.com to utilize these extensive resources including videos from real classrooms, Praxis and licensure preparation, a lesson plan builder, and materials to help you begin your teaching career.

Current Events and Public Issues

CHAPTER SIX

Key Concepts

- Current events
- Public issues
- Controversy

MAIN IDEA

A deliberate program of teaching and learning about current events and controversial issues is required in each classroom each year. Such a program will help rouse the children's civic-mindedness and develop the knowledge they need in all spheres of life, including holding "the office of citizen."

PICTURE THIS

While the national news was focused on the economy, local television news and daily newspapers were dominated by the whale capture story, and Mr. Bower's students were upset. He asked them, "What do you want to do?" Their responses indicated that they didn't understand the matter well enough to choose an action. He suggested that they study it daily, using the same five-part decision-making process they used earlier in the year on another local controversy. They began by identifying the facts of the case and the controversial issues of the case, going back and forth between these. Finally, they selected one of the issues for decision making, role-playing, and citizen action.

A 10-year-old named Michael wondered what to do with his life. Seeking advice, he wrote to Buckminster Fuller, the philosopher, architect, engineer, poet, social activist, and inventor of the geodesic dome and the Dymaxion map pictured in Chapter 5. "Bucky's" response to Michael was direct:

> Thank you very much for your recent letter. The things to do are the things that need doing; that *you* see need to be done, and that no one else sees need to be done.

Bucky then tells Michael that doing what *he* sees needs to be done will naturally bring out his own unique brilliance. He encourages Michael, closing the letter with this:

> You have what is most important in life—initiative. Because of it, you wrote to me. I am answering to the best of my capability. You will find the world responding to your earnest initiative.[1]

The point of view in this chapter is that a program of teaching current events and social problems is a must in elementary and middle school classrooms. Such a program must be planned carefully and taught well. Without it, children are not likely to form citizenship dispositions that are critically important to the health of their communities, such as civic-mindedness and initiative. Without it, they may not have adequate opportunities to see the things that need doing, to respond, and, in turn, to develop their own talents.

Included in this chapter are strategies and activities for increasing children's awareness of current events and for teaching children about current events. The chapter also addresses a sampling of the enduring social problems—public issues—that make so many current events controversial: poverty, environmental degradation, crime, war and peace, and prejudice. When tailored appropriately to the ages and experiences of children and linked to social studies education, these events and issues can and should be taught in the elementary school. Readers concerned that young children are too young for current events and social problems need only look back to Chapter 3, where Ms. Paley leads a month-long deliberation with her kindergartners on a controversial issue that concerns them deeply: Should we have a rule that says you can't tell someone else that he or she can't play with you? Furthermore, current events are what any group of children in any historical era *live in and are shaped by*. Not to be aware of and thoughtful about them is to be clueless of the forces that are affecting us.

Purposes

The first major purpose of teaching current events and public issues at the elementary school level is to promote the habit of *awareness and interest* in current events and social problems. This is no small undertaking. A market-driven, individualistic, affluent society encourages children to think of themselves and their families sometimes to the exclusion of minding the public square. This, recall, is what the ancient Greeks called "idiocy." Civic-mindedness is a virtue—a habit—that must be cultivated, and one way elementary and middle school teachers can do that is by developing a regular, ongoing program of instruction involving daily news and issues.

Rational analysis of current events requires the use of a variety of skills and abilities:

1. Interpreting the news
2. Discriminating between important and less important news items

Teaching current events connects school learning to life outside school.
(Tom Watson/Merrill)

3. Taking a position on issues based on knowledge and critical evaluation of the facts
4. Predicting likely consequences of different positions

Promoting the *growth of these skills* is the second major purpose of current-events instruction at the elementary school level. These skills evolve over several years through the study of current events under the guidance of capable teachers. It is unrealistic to hope for an adult population that can exercise critical judgment regarding social problems and issues unless individuals have at their command the fundamental abilities such action demands.

The third major purpose of teaching current events is to help children *relate school learning to life outside school*. The constant reference to current events is good insurance against the separation of school activities from the nonacademic life of the child. Good teachers recognize that there is always a gap between the information contained in books and changing developments in the world. A generous use of current events materials helps to close this gap. Because textbooks and supplementary books usually are not revised each year, teachers must depend on newspapers, magazines, radio, television, and the Internet (including streaming audio and video) for the latest information on some topics.

BUILDING A CURRENT EVENTS PROGRAM: THREE APPROACHES

The three most common approaches to including current events in the elementary school program are (1) teaching current events in addition to social studies, (2) using current events to supplement or reinforce the regular social studies program, and (3) using current events as the basis for social studies units. As we examine these approaches, readers can weigh their advantages and disadvantages and decide which suits them.

Teaching Current Events in Addition to Social Studies

Ms. Hansen, who teaches fourth grade, plans to spend a few minutes each morning during the sharing period for the discussion of important news stories. She encourages children to bring news clippings from daily newspapers or from weekly magazines for the class bulletin board. Children are encouraged to bring news stories related to classroom work, and Ms. Hansen helps interpret these stories for the children by her comments and leading questions, such as "Do you suppose the new highway will help our town?" "What are the astronauts looking for on these expeditions?" "Why do you suppose the animals died when they were brought here?" "Can you show the class on the map the exact location of the war?"

Ms. Hansen uses a classroom news periodical, *Scholastic News*, and plans to spend one hour on it with the children each week reading the material or portions of it and then discussing it. She varies the procedure from week to week and uses the suggestions provided in the teacher's edition that accompanies the periodical. During presidential election years, she involves students in the debates and mock elections that are always featured. (*Scholastic News* is a newsweekly for grades 1–6. A sample issue may be requested online.)

This method has the advantage of providing a regularly scheduled time for news each day and for the classroom periodical each week. Such periods can be useful in building awareness and interest in current events and in teaching the skills of reading and interpreting news stories. When the bundled stack of newsweeklies is delivered to the classroom, students may be delighted by the change of pace that is soon to follow. This method has the disadvantage of isolating current affairs from the remainder of the school program, most especially from social studies.

Using Current Events to Supplement Social Studies

Mr. Hsiao schedules his social studies period immediately following morning opening activities for his fifth-grade class. As a part of the opening activities, he gives students time to share news items. He often suggests parallels or analogies between events that happened long ago and events that they bring up during this time, thereby illustrating recurrent problems in the conduct of human affairs. For example, one student reported on a civil war in a European nation, and Mr. Hsiao asked whether that civil war was similar to our own in this country in the middle of the 19th century. Another student read aloud a news story on a terrorist incident at a military base abroad. Mr. Hsiao reminded students of the Boston Tea Party and asked if there was any connection between the two incidents. When the class was studying early European exploration, Mr. Hsiao related this study to present-day exploration in space. In addition to drawing these historical parallels, Mr. Hsiao brings in news stories that he reads to students and interprets within the context of the topic under study. He seizes upon these stories as an entry point for applying social studies skills, such as map, graph, or chart reading. Because he integrates language arts and social studies instruction, he makes frequent use of editorials and news stories as writing samples.

The difference between this method and the one used by Ms. Hansen is that Mr. Hsiao is more explicit in making the connection between current events and the social studies (and language arts) curriculum. He is concerned mainly with news stories that can support this curriculum. This method has the advantage of motivating greater student interest in the curriculum and displaying the relevance of the curriculum for understanding the current world scene. It has the disadvantage of restricting the range of news stories that are appropriate. Therefore, if this approach is used, the teacher should provide some opportunity to examine news items that are significant and timely, yet may not directly relate to the social studies unit under study at the time.

Using Current Events as the Basis for Social Studies Units

Ms. Diaz likes to develop social studies units with her sixth-grade class around topics that are currently in the news. She schedules these between the regular units she is required to teach. During her years as a teacher, she has found that units of this type must be carefully selected because it is not always possible to find enough instructional material suitable for children that deals with topics in the news. Units that she has taught successfully in this way have dealt with gun control legislation, gangs, terrorism, contemporary explorers, new developments in science, current elections, and world organizations, such as the United Nations. When Ms. Diaz selects the unit topics carefully, she finds it possible to include much of the subject matter ordinarily included in her social studies curriculum under other unit titles. She believes that the use of current news happenings as a starting point for units does much to stimulate interest and discussion in her class.

Lesson Plan 9 ("A Nation in the News") illustrates this third approach. A current event happening in another country—a tsunami, a war, the Olympic Games—has captured the interest of students, and this is used as the springboard for learning a good deal about that country, spanning its cultures, history, geography, economy, government, and civic ideals. This method has the advantage of being highly motivating because it deals with subject matter that is of immediate interest. It also bridges school learning with life outside school. But most important, it provides students with information that they very likely do not have and helps them build a knowledge base for understanding current and future events. As students construct knowledge about history and politics, peoples and places, climate and environment, each new current event is a little less surprising and a little more comprehensible. Building that knowledge base, little by little, can be enormously helpful when "the next big thing" happens.

Any of the three current events programs described here can be used successfully. Good programs devote time during the school day to study and discussion of current affairs that may be entirely unrelated to topics under study in the social studies units, and perhaps unrelated to any other curricular area as well. At the same time, in guiding unit work, the teacher will seek the current events that will add strength and excitement to the unit. From time to time, too, the teacher and children can plan an entire social studies unit from current news developments. Units dealing with the concepts of energy, poverty, the environment, safety, warfare, peace-making, ethnicity, law and justice, housing, food production and distribution, elections, and discoveries frequently grow out of current events. When the social studies program includes one or more of these three methods, the teacher and class will use any or all of the procedures described in the following sections.

A NATION IN THE NEWS

Lesson Plan 9

Grade	6 or 7
Time	Seven class periods
NCSS Standards	3 (people, places, and environments) and 9 (global connections)
Objectives	Students will learn about the country behind the current event—its geography (people, places, climate, landforms, resources), history (major turning points and pivotal people), government, economy, and social life (religion, music and dance, family life, education, holidays and festivals). Also, they will refine their research and social skills and learn to present a group oral report.
Interest Building	Seize upon students' interest in a current event that is happening in another nation. They may be interested in a famine that is reported in the news, a foreign policy crisis for the United States, a civil war somewhere, a natural disaster, or a terrorist incident. Use the daily newspaper to enlarge their understanding of the event (including news articles, editorials, cartoons, and letters to the editor). Use the five-step procedure presented in this chapter for helping students make a decision on what should be done about the event (e.g., Should the United Nations send money? Troops?). Hold a debate. Invite a guest speaker.
Preassessment	Ask students to write down in their response journals three facts they know about the country in the news. Prompt them as needed, for example, with location questions (On which continent? In which hemisphere? Near what other countries?) and historical questions (What happened earlier in this country?).
Lesson Development	Tell students that they need to understand the country behind the event—that any current event needs to be placed in its historical and geographical setting. Brainstorm a list of topics that would be suitable for small-group information-gathering projects. Have a student list the topics on butcher paper (see classroom poster). Divide the class into teams of six students each. Teams meet and elect a leader; discuss, agree on, and sign up for a topic. Help students divide their topics into subtopics. Each team member is responsible for one subtopic, except for the chair, who also helps each team member search for information. Tell students they will have five class periods to gather information and two class periods to plan a team presentation. One team will present each day after lunch until all teams have presented. Give each student a copy of the assessment form and clarify (see sample scoring guide). Review the procedure for taking notes and for properly citing the sources of information. Assign report dates. Monitor and guide the teams during the research days and the planning days.
Summary	Groups give their oral reports with each member contributing to the presentation. They field questions and comments from the audience.
Assessment	The scoring guide is used to judge the quality of the team presentations.
Materials	• Textbook: *World Regions* • Reference books: almanacs, atlases, encyclopedias • Recordings: speeches, television specials • Internet: use Google Earth to locate the country and its region • Trade books will depend on the country selected.
Integration	*Literature:* Help students find biographies about political leaders, scientists, artists, and inventors from the nation under study, as well as the literature suggested in the "Materials" section. *The arts:* If students don't themselves suggest dance, film, and fine arts, show videos or use the document camera to show photos that will stimulate interest in these things.

Classroom poster: A nation in the news.

Topics	Names of team members	Presentation date
Culture Food, shelter, clothing, festivals, ethnic groups, religions, health care, arts		
History Key turning points, key people, civil rights' struggles, economic development		
Geography Land and water forms, climate, natural resources, major cities, transportation		
Economy Goods and services, production and consumption, poverty and wealth, industrialization, scarcity		
Government Type of political system, rule of law, key documents, political controversies		
Civic ideals Rights and responsibilities of citizens, social justice		

Scoring guide: Team presentations.

Criteria	Exemplary	Adequate	Minimal	Absent
Introduction				
Main ideas				
Conclusion				
Visual aids				
Teamwork				

FOUR STRATEGIES FOR TEACHING CURRENT EVENTS

Strategy 1: Daily Discussion of News

Children enjoy discussing the news and should be given the opportunity to do so within the school program. It is fairly common for classes to have a morning meeting or sharing period at the beginning of each school day, during which students can report news items. Children in the primary grades frequently report only news that affects them directly: Mom took a business trip, the family has a new baby, the pet cat had kittens, or other similar items of "news." As people mature, they move away from news items of concern only to them personally to news of more general interest.

When the news is terrible—a terrorist attack, an accident or shooting that killed or injured students or teachers at the school, a hurricane or famine—the principal of the school will most likely initiate a schoolwide plan so that teachers are not left to care for children alone. Counselors may be made available to the school to help children share their feelings and talk with one another and with adults about what happened.

Use of Daily Newspapers

Some teachers in the intermediate and middle grades find a daily newspaper helpful in promoting the goals of current-events instruction. In units dealing with aspects of communication, the newspaper is an important learning resource. Students will profit from classroom instruction on the use of newspapers that focuses on items such as these:

- The organization of the newspaper; the purpose of various sections; where to look for certain kinds of information
- The nature of news stories; why some appear on the front page and others elsewhere
- The purpose and use of headlines
- Illustrations, photos, maps, charts, graphs, and cartoons
- The editorial page and its function
- Detecting bias in news stories
- How to read a newspaper

From time to time the teacher can devise practice exercises such as those described in this chapter to help students develop their skills in using a daily newspaper.

Many teachers have found the Newspaper In Education (NIE) program sponsored by the Newspaper Association of America (NAA) to be a useful resource in teaching current events and, more specifically, in using the newspaper. For information about the NIE program and the several materials available through it, contact your local newspaper. The NIE program provides many teaching and learning resources.

The World's Newspapers and Television Networks on the Internet

Your local newspapers and television stations have Internet home pages as do newspapers and TV stations around the world. Both media typically provide news updates online plus (and this is important to the students' study) online editorials and letters to the editor.

Students must search for these opinions if they are to grasp the multiple perspectives that attend a current event or issue.

Older students can be helped to find newspapers and television sites *in other countries*. Several can be found in English and the many other languages your students may speak. At the British Broadcasting Company (BBC) website (www.bbc.co.uk/worldservice), students not only get a different perspective from that of the American press, but they can choose to read it in any number of languages! This will make for a special way to connect with students whose most comfortable language is not English. Also, audio clips of breaking news stories can be played for the whole class.

At www.newseum.org, students can find "today's front pages" from all over the world. Another good source is www.worldpress.org. The key advantage of introducing students to worldwide news sources is that *comparison of multiple perspectives* is made possible. The comparative approach is especially effective for dealing with a breaking news story or crisis with which the children and community are intensely concerned.

Use of Political Cartoons

Cartoons are a widely accepted and influential form of social commentary. Responding to the cartoon's dramatic visual format, the reader projects meaning by virtue of his or her own experience. Cartoons are often humorous because they exaggerate, they present subjects in caricature, and they are designed to show the vices or virtues associated with a particular character. Cartoons are especially effective in calling attention to the ironies that surround our lives. They use humor to make a serious point, and they provide additional opportunities to teach "reading" in a more visually engaging way.

Ordinarily, we do not get new information from political cartoons. The cartoonist relies on what we already know—our *prior* knowledge. What makes one cartoon more difficult to interpret than another is generally the amount of prior knowledge students must have to make sense of it. Figure 6–1 presents two cartoons for comparison.

In the case of cartoons with words, the teacher can mask them out before displaying the cartoon on the document camera or overhead projector, and ask students what words they would add. Only after students have had a chance to interpret the cartoon themselves should they be shown the cartoon with the cartoonist's words included. This is an effective way to teach cartoon interpretation.

Editorial cartoons are not necessarily funny. They are often biting in their criticism of a government policy or social fad. Political cartoons usually deal more with irony, hypocrisy, and cynicism than they do with humor. Recognition of the fact that only one point of view is represented in cartoons is important in their interpretation. Older children need to be taught the general makeup of cartoons that deal with social and political problems and need the experience of evaluating their message critically. It is good for the children to imagine, then draw, an opposite point of view from the one depicted in the cartoon.

Strategy 2: Decision Making on Controversial Issues

There can be no doubt that the social studies teacher has a responsibility to include controversial issues in the current events and social studies curriculum. In so doing, the teacher has a strong ally in the National Council for the Social Studies. According to an NCSS

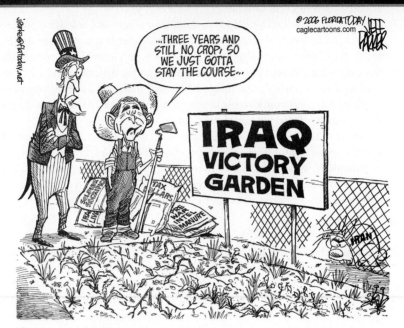

Source: Reprinted with permission of Cagle Cartoons Inc.

Source: Reprinted with permission of North American Syndicate.

policy statement on the subject, it is the prime responsibility of the schools to help students assume the responsibilities of democratic citizenship. To do this, education must impart the skills needed for intelligent study and orderly resolution of the problems inherent in a democratic society. Students need to study issues on which there is disagreement and to practice analyzing problems, gathering and organizing facts, discriminating between facts and opinions, discussing differing viewpoints, and drawing tentative conclusions. *It is the clear obligation of schools to promote full and free study and deliberation of controversial issues and to foster appreciation of the role of controversy as an instrument of progress in a democracy.* Otherwise, how will children become an intelligent "we the people"? Certainly not by avoiding the people's work.

When teaching a controversial issue, the teacher has a special responsibility to help children develop the disposition to be civil and tolerant of the expression of various opinions, to evaluate sources of information, and to pursue multiple perspectives on a single issue. Young children are impressionable, and the habit of insisting on hearing all sides of an issue before taking a stand can be taught to youngsters by the teacher's example. The professional obligation remains to not attempt to impose a personal point of view on the children concerning issues that are unsettled and on which there may be honest differences of opinion among well-informed persons. Instead, the teacher should encourage children to discuss the matter with other adults whom they respect whose views may be different. The child thus learns that there are honest differences of opinion among reasonable persons who consider problems in good faith.

Daily discussion of the news is bound to expose students to controversial issues of all kinds. The news story in Figure 6–2 is a good example of the types of controversial issues that can be found in nearly all communities, large and small. It is a current event because it is happening now. But it also involves enduring public issues—in this case, protecting the natural environment and deciding how best to navigate the perennial value conflict between individual liberty and the common good. Enduring public issues, also called social concerns or social issues, are what turn a current event into a controversial issue. *Controversial* can be taken to mean that reasonable people will disagree over what needs to be done.

Not all current events are controversial. Many current happenings around the school and the community arouse little disagreement and debate: the school halls are swept nightly, parents go to work, the town garbage is picked up once each week, children go to school during the day, rice or potatoes are eaten in many homes each evening, schools are often closed for the summer, children are not allowed to run for the state legislature, people water their gardens. Perhaps no one makes an issue of these humdrum events of daily life. Until someone does, they are not controversial issues. Once someone does, however, the issue becomes controversial.

One of the best ways to teach current events is to select those that are controversial. In addition to the whale capture in Figure 6–2, here are several other current events that involve controversy.

- Establish citywide curfew for persons under 18 years of age.
- Test school athletes for illicit drug use.
- Choose new equipment for the playground.
- Allow animals to be used for medical research.
- Prevent a new sports stadium (or concert hall or jail) from being built.

FIGURE 6-2   A sample controversial issue in the newspaper.

Whale Capture Creates Wail

Seattle– Six killer whales are being held inside the Aqua Life, Inc. nets at Cook Inlet while Bill Holberg decides which ones, if any, will be kept for aquarium exhibits. Hundreds of people watched the capture from boats and shore yesterday afternoon.

The huge mammals swam slowly round and round inside two purse seine nets today, surfacing to "blow" for only moments. They stayed under for five minutes at a time.

GOVERNOR RECONSIDERING

Meanwhile, a political storm was gathering over the capture operation. The governor today interrupted her skiing vacation long enough to say that she was "reconsidering" the state's position on making the inlet a sanctuary for killer whales. The state's senior senator in Washington said that a declaration of support from the governor for a whale sanctuary would clear the way for protection of the sea animals. The senator also said, "Apparently this man [Holberg] had a valid permit. But there aren't going to be any more. This is the end!"

DEPTH CHARGES USED

Raul Santana, an assistant to the State Game and Fisheries director, watched the capture from about 50 feet away. Santana said Aqua Life, Inc. boats used "sonar, radar, and 'depth' charges" to drive the whales into smaller and smaller coves and finally into the nets. He said he watched three men in power boats racing across the water atop the whale school, "dropping 'depth charges' as fast as they could light them. I've never seen anything so disgusting in all my life," he said today. "This ought to be stopped right now."

A federal enforcement officer who supervised yesterday's operation said, "there is nothing in the permit that prohibits the use of such explosives."

USE OF CHARGES DENIED

Many citizens complained about the capture operation. An automobile dealer from South Harbor said he saw an airplane dropping "tomato can"-size cannisters that apparently exploded as the plane herded the whales. Sheila Moss, veterinarian for Aqua Life, Inc. said no such charges were used. She said the whale chasers used "firecracker"-type explosives thrown from boats to herd the whales. Holberg himself was aboard the Aqua Life, Inc. boat, KANDU, and was unavailable for comment.

COURT ACTION THREATENED

Environmentalists and others bitterly opposed the capture of the whales. Fred Russell, president of the state's largest environmental protection group, PROTEX, demanded that the whales be released. He said his group was prepared to take the matter to court if necessary to prevent Aqua Life, Inc. from keeping the creatures. "This is an outrage," he said, "and we are not going to sit by and let it happen."

Russell cited a Canadian biologist who found that only 65 killer whales remain in the Straits of Georgia and Juan de Fuca and Puget Sound. Earlier data had placed the number of whales at about 300.

OVERLAPPING JURISDICTION

The power to create a whale sanctuary rests with the federal government, but federal law says the governor of a state that contains the sanctuary may veto its creation. This overlapping jurisdiction sometimes creates confusion or results in no action being taken.

Until today, federal officials thought the governor opposed creation of a killer whale sanctuary in this area. The governor's staff said that no record could be found of the governor's . ever having opposed such a proposal.

- Remove a park for a shopping center.
- Remove a tree for a sidewalk.
- Place metal detectors at school entrances.
- Serve only low-fat and low-sugar foods in the school cafeteria.
- Outlaw cell-phone use by drivers of automobiles.
- Ban text-messaging anywhere on school grounds.
- Ban sports utility vehicles from school parking lots.
- Require public school students to wear uniforms.
- Permit organized prayer in schools.
- Pass a dog-leash ordinance.
- Ban the sale of cigarettes throughout the city.
- Close swimming pools to save water for farmers.

These current events present good opportunities for teaching children how to deal constructively with controversy. The following decision-making procedure, based on the decision-making model presented in Chapter 3, is recommended. Using a decision-making framework, teaching current events and social concerns serves a citizenship purpose: educating "we the people" to participate more thoughtfully in community decision making. The procedure has five parts: (1) learning the facts of the matter, (2) identifying the controversial issues, (3) deliberating on one of the issues, (4) dramatizing the issue, and (5) sharing (publishing) the decision and reasons.

1. Have the children identify the facts of the case. In an examination of the captured whales news story in Figure 6–2, some of the facts are these:
   - Six killer whales were captured.
   - The governor said she was reconsidering the state's policy.
   - Raul Santana said he saw three men dropping depth charges.
   - Sheila Moss said they used firecracker-type explosives.
   - The state and federal governments both have jurisdiction over whale sanctuaries.

   When identifying the facts, it is important not to confuse them with opinions. Though the distinction is often fuzzy, children can develop a working understanding of the difference between facts and opinions. In the whale story, one would need further documentation that the explosives were of the firecracker type and that they were thrown from the hunters' boats, not dropped from an airplane.

2. Have students identify the issues in the case. Help them to identify a broad range of issues. Usually, issues involve conflicting values. In the whale case, the following are some of the issues. Notice that the issues are stated as questions. People disagree on how to answer these questions, and this is why they are called controversial issues.
   - Should the capture of wild animals for uses in aquariums, zoos, and circuses be permitted? If so, to what extent, and why?
   - Should animal hunters be allowed to use explosives?
   - Was Holberg's permit valid?
   - Should the captured whales be freed?
   - Should governments, state or federal, protect wildlife? Or does this violate the constitutional principle of limited government?

3. With the students, select one of the issues. Make it an issue that requires a decision that the children can deliberate in the following way (see Chapter 3):
   a. Identify a range of alternatives.
   b. Predict the consequences for each alternative.
   c. Discuss which is the best alternative.

   There is no need to rush toward a decision: The process of identifying alternatives and consequences, discussing them, and learning more about the issue is the primary objective. Indeed, *slowing* children's inclination to jump to a conclusion (a decision about what the community should do) is precisely what is needed here. As discussed in Chapter 3, we want them to grow in their ability and disposition to be thoughtful and reflective citizens, not reckless, uncivil, or ill-informed.

   a. *Identify alternatives.* Let us assume that a group of children selects the fourth issue, Should the captured whales be freed? Using a decision tree (Figure 3–4), the children can then be helped to identify alternatives. One group suggested these:
   - Free the whales immediately and arrest Holberg.
   - Free the whales immediately and pay Holberg for them with public tax money.
   - Make courts decide if Holberg was acting lawfully.

   b. *Predict consequences.* After identifying alternatives, the teacher helps the children predict consequences for each. The following consequences might be suggested:
   - Holberg takes "we the people" to court, claiming that he was acting lawfully.
   - The whales return to open sea and live happily ever after.
   - Zoos across the United States close down because no one will collect zoo animals after reading what happened to Holberg.

   c. *Deliberation.* After completing a decision tree on the issue, the teacher leads a discussion resulting in a decision about what should be done. The teacher might push students in the direction of a consensus, though this really is not necessary. The children may agree to disagree on the issue. (See Chapters 3 and 11 for specific ideas for conducting discussions with children.) Structured Academic Controversy (Chapter 11) is a brilliant strategy for small-group discussions of controversial issues. Roundtable and panel discussions are additional alternatives to whole-group discussions.

4. Issues such as these lend themselves well to role-playing and dramatic play. Children can play the roles of Holberg, the governor, the senator, Santana, the federal enforcement officer, the automobile dealer, Moss, and Russell. Doing this helps make the event and the issues more concrete for children. Additional questions will be raised (this is inevitable), and the information can be secured by the students from the point of view of the role they are playing. Children can gather this additional data from the community by interviewing individuals and reading local news stories.

5. Publish. Something must be done with the students' deliberation on the issue. After all, this deliberation by children in the community is news! A report can be written for the classroom newsletter, of course, and a copy sent to the relevant government office and to the local newspaper. An accompanying letter from the teacher should tell the audience that the main objective of this work is to help students learn a key democratic skill: taking and defending a position on an issue. Other objectives may involve the writing process, such as in the "Follow-Up Activities" on the next page and "Strategy 4: Writing About Issues" on page 203.

Follow-Up Activities

This decision-making strategy should not be limited to the use of newspaper articles. It is equally useful when the current event is a classroom or playground incident on which a decision is needed. It is also useful when children are considering the adoption of a new rule, such as Ms. Paley's "you can't say 'you can't play'" rule (see Chapter 3).

A decision-making procedure used to examine a current event can generate a great deal of student interest. The teacher may wish to channel this enthusiasm into follow-up activities. These learning activities need to be related to the same event, yet they should expand the learning outward to incorporate additional ideas and skills. Several categories of follow-up activities are widely applicable.

Biography. Study the lives of individuals related to the event studied (e.g., people who have dedicated themselves to the preservation of wildlife and other aspects of the natural environment: Rachel Carson, Bill McKibben, John Muir, and local environmentalists). Then write a brief biography of one of these persons.

Organizations. Find out about the purposes and activities of organizations concerned about the event (e.g., the Sierra Club, the National Wildlife Federation, the Environmental Protection Agency, and Greenpeace). Then write a comparison of these organizations.

Government/Jurisdiction. Study the authority of federal, state, local, and voluntary associations in relation to the current event (e.g., the whale capture event should lead students to local and state regulations concerning wildlife, conservation, and hunting). Then write a report called "Who's in Charge?"

Community Service/Action. Use the event to build interest in developing a community service or action project (e.g., a project dealing with ecology or conservation).

Strategy 3: Teaching About Different *Kinds* of Controversy

Discussions of controversial issues foster healthy disagreements, which in turn foster more discussion, more higher-order thinking, and more effort to *apply* what students know. Consequently, disagreements should not be discouraged; rather, students should be prepared to take advantage of them—to learn more about the topic and one another and to practice reaching a consensus. An extremely helpful way to teach intermediate- and middle-grade students to learn from disagreements is to teach them to stop for a moment in the middle of a disagreement and think about the kind of disagreement they are having. Doing so creates some distance from the disagreement and provides an opportunity to analyze the issue at hand. The three most common kinds of disagreements, together with suggested methods for dealing with them, follow.

Factual Controversies

These disagreements over the facts of the case are sometimes called informational disagreements or disagreements over the data. Children may disagree about what Holberg was planning to do with the whales, whether depth charges were actually used, and so on.

Methods.   To help children deal with factual disagreements, they can be taught to (1) reread the source of information, searching for relevant facts; (2) go to a reference resource, such as an almanac or encyclopedia; and (3) ask a credible authority for a judgment (e.g., ask the teacher, call the journalist who covered the story, ask the librarian).

Definitional Controversies

These are disagreements over the meaning of a term. Even these can be quite heated. Children might disagree about whether Holberg was a "hunter," for example. Some children will argue that animal hunters kill whales for food or sport, whereas Holberg was searching for whales in order to sell them to an aquarium. When discussing homelessness, water pollution, poverty, crime, and other social problems, children will disagree over basic terms.

Methods.　　To help children deal with definitional disputes, they can be taught to (1) get a dictionary; (2) agree to accept the dictionary definition; or (3) tentatively agree to define the term in a particular way. Called *stipulation*, this last method is used in everyday situations when someone suggests, "Let's say that (a term, e.g., poverty) means (a definition, e.g., not having enough money to eat three nutritious meals a day)," and the others involved in the conversation agree.

Value Controversies

These are disagreements about what is most important, right, best, or worthwhile. Typically, value conflicts arise as children (and adults) are trying to decide the question, "What should

Teachers help students learn to scrutinize, not watch passively, television news programs. *(Scott Cunningham/Merrill)*

the community do?" In the captured whales example, value disagreements will arise as children discuss which alternative course of action is best.

Methods.   To help children deal constructively with value disagreements, they can be taught to (1) clarify the values at stake, which involves asking one another questions such as "What do you mean?" and "What is important to you in this issue?"; (2) give reasons for arguing that one alternative is more valuable than another; or (3) agree to disagree, meaning that they realize there is a disagreement and it has not yet been settled. In the latter method, everyone involved will continue to be friendly toward one another just as citizens in a community or nation often disagree and must remain civil toward those with whom they disagree.[2]

Strategy 4: Writing About Issues

Controversial issues present many authentic opportunities to improve children's writing. Writing letters to the editor of the classroom, school, or community newspaper is one good way to work with children on brief persuasive writing. Another way is to send to local and national officials (the mayor, the school principal, a senator) an analysis of an issue and a suggested course of action. Letters can be sent conventionally (always appreciated) or by email. This involves students in the planning and making of a documentary film about a current event or controversy. The teacher leads them through the writing process, not to produce an essay but a screenplay. The Digital Directors Guild at www.ddguild.org gives K–6 (and up) teachers the opportunity to explore digital moviemaking.

A favorite writing technique for helping children think more deeply and creatively about current events and social problems is called the dialogical essay. As the name implies, the writer creates a dialogue about the choices that need to be made. This dialogue occurs inside the writer's mind, but only after the student has explored the issue orally with the class using the decision-making strategy detailed earlier. Writing in this way helps the child sort out the opposing arguments on a controversial issue. This is far better than merely giving one's own opinion again and again, for it encourages students to examine multiple perspectives on the issue. For this reason, it is preferable to the common persuasive essay.

One short-essay format has been found especially effective for this purpose.[3] Most children in the intermediate grades will have the necessary writing skills to compose such an essay, but clear directions are needed. The essay format, with directions, follows.

- *Paragraph 1.* Tell your reader that you are going to write an essay on this issue. Then tell your reader your position on the issue. Do not give any reasons yet.
- *Paragraph 2.* Give your reasons for your position. In other words, give good arguments that support your position.
- *Paragraph 3.* Give good reasons against your position. In other words, give good arguments that support the opposing position on the issue.
- *Paragraph 4.* Come to a conclusion. Now that you have thought about the reasons for and against your position, what is your position?

Writing persuasive letters to editors of newspapers and public officials is, of course, a time-honored method of helping students to write persuasively while giving them the opportunity to learn about government and influence public policy as a young democratic citizen. Once students have had the opportunity to clarify the issues and their own position and reasoning—for which the dialogical essay is a powerful tool—then a more authentic writing task is in order, such as a persuasive letter. Teachers need to take care that first drafts of such letters are not sent, but that the letters have been "fully processed" using the writing process procedures of repeated drafting, editing, and revising.

It is especially important when making letter-writing assignments related to controversial issues that students be encouraged to develop their own position and rationale after study and discussion with others, and not be required to argue for a particular side. This may seem obvious, but the latter is what some parents thought teachers were doing at an elementary school in Madison, Wisconsin, in the autumn of 2005. The Iraq war was fully underway then, and a team of teachers developed a letter-writing project for the school's five classes of third-grade students. Students were to write letters to fellow students and public officials urging "an end to the war in Iraq." A parent protested this assignment, and then a legislator wrote to the school principal calling for an end to the assignment. The superintendent of schools said that the assignment was a direct violation of school board policy, which prohibits teachers "from exploiting the institutional privileges of their professional positions to promote candidates or parties or activities."[4] The teachers defended the project as one intended to involve citizen action, which is one of the district's curriculum standards for social studies. One teacher added,

> We saw peace as a common good. We were just advocating that people keep working toward peace.

Soon, the school sent a letter to parents apologizing for the assignment and informing them that it had been canceled. The school board president clarified that teachers were required to withhold the expression of personal opinion unless asked a direct question when dealing with controversial issues.

While it is important that teachers not shy away from teaching about controversies for the reasons already stated, it is just as important to handle controversial issues appropriately: fairly and with respect for differing views on the matter; and making sure that students are learning to develop their own positions and not simply mimicking the views of their teachers.

TEACHING ENDURING PUBLIC ISSUES

We turn now to enduring public issues. These are controversial issues that do not simply go away when the current event ends. Rather, the current event is the most recent incident in a long stream of incidents related to the enduring issue. As we have seen, children can learn to deliberate these issues—discuss them, make decisions, plan service or action projects, and send their advice to officials.

Issue-centered, also known as problem-centered, unit planning has been one of the most popular approaches to social studies education in the 20th century. The central focus of an issue-centered unit is an enduring public controversy that is sure to be as controversial tomorrow as it is today and was yesterday. It should be an issue that has challenged people throughout history and in many cultures. For example:

1. *Poverty*. Who is responsible for the poor?
2. *Human–Environment Interaction*. How much environmental harm, if any, should be allowed for the sake of human economic productivity? How much pollution should be permitted for the sake of providing jobs?
3. *Justice*. How should society punish lawbreakers? Are there better responses than "an eye for an eye"?
4. *Peace*. How can war be prevented? What can individuals do to increase peace and harmony among people?

A food drive is a direct, compassionate action a class can undertake while studying the enduring issue of poverty. *(Mary Kate Denny/PhotoEdit Inc.)*

5. *Diversity/Unity.* How can we keep our individual and cultural differences and be one people? How can we achieve *e pluribus unum?*

Note that the issues are stated as questions, and that the questions are mighty. They are recurring (also called perennial) issues: People have grappled with them for years but never have answered them once and for all. One of the responsibilities of being a member of the public—a citizen—is to tackle such problems. They are, of course, the sort of questions on which reasonable people will disagree; they lend themselves, therefore, to discussion and decision making.

With such a question as the unit's centerpiece, the teacher plans learning activities that rely on iterations of discussion, writing, and reading. Discussion is especially important because it brings out into the open the diverse opinions and perspectives people have on the issue. Writing occurs *after* discussion, because discussion produces interpretations that students can then grapple with in their writing. (Recall the richness of Ms. Paley's discussions with kindergartners.) And, a need to know is created that motivates information searches; students can then read with purpose.

Poverty

Let us consider a sample unit that was built around the central focusing question, "Who is responsible for the poor?" Figure 6–3 shows that the children will endeavor to gather information from various disciplines to inform their decisions on this matter. The suggested

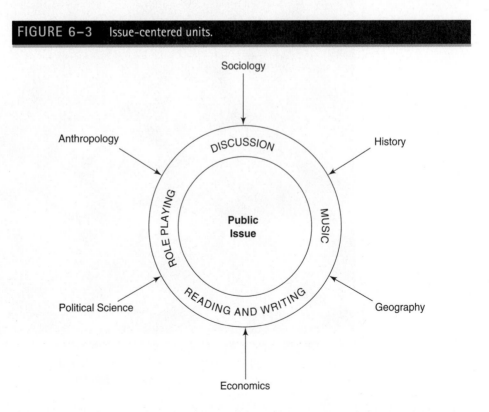

FIGURE 6–3   Issue-centered units.

procedure that follows can be altered considerably to suit a teacher's knowledge of the issue, particular interests (e.g., homelessness, hunger, health care), and related curriculum materials. Its setting can be shifted from the United States to another country or to the children's own state. The essence of the plan is an iterative cycle of *study* and *discussion*. There should be plenty of both. There also needs to be ample opportunity for students to reflect on the quality of their discussions and the quality of their investigations.

WHO IS RESPONSIBLE FOR THE POOR?
(An Outline for an Integrated Issue-Centered Unit)

1. *Initial discussion of* the *unit question* followed by writing on the question in a discussion journal or learning log.

2. *Instruction on the characteristics of good discussion* (see the scoring rubric in Chapter 3).

3. *Historical study.* Using a time line that has been drawn on the board, the teacher describes for children several historical eras in which poverty was a problem and who did what about it.

   a. Enslaved Africans living on plantations
   b. Poor immigrants
   c. Poor unemployed workers or farmers during the Great Depression and Dust Bowl
   d. A current, local example (rural or inner-city poverty, homelessness)

4. *Additional data gathering.* The class is divided into four committees. Each is assigned to one of the four examples listed in item 3. The committee's job is to find out more about its example and to give children a sense of the era by providing interesting facts about society at that time. The teacher adds information about how poverty is *defined,* the difference between "poor" and "poverty," and how the official poverty "line" or "threshold" is determined.

   Option: If the children are too young to conduct small-group research, the teacher can provide the additional information on each example using the same material the small groups would use—films, stories, guest speakers, the textbook, primary documents, and references.

5. *Second discussion of the question,* now informed by historical information. This discussion is followed by reflection on the quality of the discussion.

6. *Second writing in journals on the unit question.* Revise and share with peers.

7. *Additional data gathering.* Again using a small-group research format (*option:* teacher provides the data), the children divide group members among four social sciences: economics, sociology, political science, and anthropology. Each is given

(continued)

WHO IS RESPONSIBLE FOR THE POOR? (continued)

study questions and works with others from the other groups assigned to the same topic. (This technique, called Jigsaw, is explained in Chapter 11.) Study questions should be designed with the capabilities of students and available curriculum materials in mind. Examples:

Economics: For two or three of the examples, describe (a) who else in society was poor and (b) who was rich.

Sociology: For two or three of the examples, find out (a) what conflicts occurred and (b) how families were affected by poverty.

Political Science: For two or three of the examples, find out (a) whether government helped the poor and, if so, how, and (b) who else helped.

Anthropology: For two or three of the examples, describe (a) how the lifestyle of the poor people—their culture—was different from that of nonpoor people and (b) an example of poverty in another nation.

8. *Third discussion of the unit question.* Informed by the additional data.

9. *Third writing in journals on the unit question.* Share, revise, and publish.

(Note: *See the poverty curriculum at the United Nations website. Click on "cyber schoolbus."*)

Human–Environment Interaction

Another enduring public issue, and one for which children have much natural concern, can be stated something like this: How can humans best live with the natural environment? Human consumption, especially in the affluent nations of Europe and North America, has already overwhelmed many ecosystems, and the developing nations of Asia, South America, and Africa are close behind. At the present rate, Earth will be overwhelmed by its human residents in the not too distant future.

Perhaps no topic is related more directly to the day-to-day lives of citizens than is energy production and consumption. One thing that distinguishes a modern, economically developed nation such as the United States, Japan, or Canada from a less developed nation is its use of and dependence on various forms of energy. Modern nations have taken burdens off the backs of human beings and animals and have substituted inanimate sources of power and energy. The dependence on various forms of such energy—in huge and escalating amounts—is absolute in modernized nations. Their economic systems cannot survive without it. They could not sustain their present standards of living if their energy sources were curtailed.

Energy, of course, is related to the natural environment. The relationship occurs at all stages of the energy production-distribution-consumption sequence. Looking back to Chapter 4's section on economics, it becomes quite obvious that the central concept of that discipline, scarcity, which requires choice making and sacrifice, applies perfectly to a study of energy. Extracting energy sources such as coal, gas, and oil from the earth either scars or pollutes the environment. Processing the raw materials of energy into usable forms and delivering the finished products also harm the environment. Similarly, the consumption of energy in most instances has some environmental impact. Americans' love affair with energy-consuming automobiles and even higher-consuming passenger trucks called by the euphemism "sports utility vehicle" makes a hypocrisy of their supposed love of the great outdoors. Thus, one of the profound social issues of our time is that of providing for the vast energy needs of our modern industrial society while at the same time preserving an environment that can sustain human and other forms of life at an acceptable level of quality. This brings to mind another enduring public issue: What limitations should be made on individual liberty in order to sustain life for humans and other living things? (See the final Lesson Plan.)

When European settlers first came to North America, the incredible abundance of resources they found produced no concern in their minds for the environment or conservation. There was fresh water aplenty. Forests and trees were in such abundance that they were perceived as obstacles to land use. There was no shortage of places to dispose of solid wastes. There were no internal combustion engines or other devices creating large quantities of hydrocarbons to pollute the air. The forests and streams were well stocked with wildlife and fish. What happened in the 300 years that followed provides us with a case study of exploitation and waste.

Serious efforts to reverse this trend got under way about three decades ago. National and state leadership, combined with publicity in the popular press and, most important, concerned citizen groups, raised the consciousness of the general public to the damage being done to the ecosystem. More than that, these forces were successful in securing state, national, and local legislation that slowed somewhat the pace of environmental abuse. Scientific data relating to the use of certain energy-producing fuels raised the frightening possibility that the planet could experience something in the way of an "eco-catastrophe" in the foreseeable future. The most significant danger signals seemed to be those associated with (1) the use of fertilizers and pesticides, (2) the mass consumption of beef and pork and the associated animal waste and grain consumption, (3) the disposal of solid wastes, (4) air pollution, (5) water pollution, (6) global warming, (7) the proliferation of radioactive substances and radioactive waste, and (8) overpopulation.

As with the study of poverty and other public issues, a program of energy and environmental studies should concern itself with three types of broad goals.

1. *Awareness and Knowledge.* It should provide children with an opportunity to develop a basic understanding of the problems surrounding energy production and consumption and the natural environment, the causes and consequences of ecological disaster, the remedial measures already under way, and the need for additional corrective action.
2. *Caring.* It should help children develop an attitude of responsible concern for energy use and the quality of the environment. It should leave them with the feeling that they have a personal investment in their natural surroundings—that energy and the environment truly are everybody's business and that their own behavior matters.
3. *Action.* It should provide children with the opportunity to do something themselves and with others about improving the environment and not harming it further.

Chapter 13 presents a truly exemplary interdisciplinary environmental studies unit. Readers may wish to read ahead at this point. This section, however, provides simple learning activities, not whole units, that are related to issues of human–environment interaction. Beginning teachers have used these successfully with elementary school children.

Population

1. Using a checkerboard or other similar squares and kernels of corn, try doubling the number of kernels in each square, starting with one. How many kernels can be used before there is no longer room to double again? Discuss how this relates to population growth and its implications.
2. Encourage children to suggest problems that would be caused by an increase of twice as many persons in their environment.
3. Become familiar with the webpage of the U.S. Census Bureau, especially the section with information about your own state (click on "select a state"). See Lesson Plan 1 in Chapter 2, "Taking a Class Census."
4. Construct a map showing areas of heavy population in the city, state, nation, or world. Identify sparsely populated areas. Have children give reasons for both conditions.

Air Pollution

1. Construct a map of the local region showing places of highest pollution. Explain why these areas have a high level of pollution.
2. Discover the major sources of air pollution. Compare these on charts and graphs.
3. Relate air pollutants to health problems.
4. Have the class gather data associating smoking with lung cancer and other respiratory ailments.

Water Supply

1. Learn about drinking water—what it is and where it comes from. Learn the difference between fresh and salt water, and how salt water can be made into drinking water. Learn that Antarctica has 70% of the world's fresh water supply. Learn that Earth is the "water planet."
2. Take a field trip to a water treatment plant (e.g., where lake water is "washed" to make it potable), then to a sewage treatment plant, then to a garbage dump.
3. Discover major sources of water pollution in the local area. Prepare a chart showing those sources. Present the chart to local government officials.
4. Select a water body in the local area that is not available for recreation because of contamination. Plan a strategy to have it rehabilitated. Present the plan to local officials. Begin a movement to mobilize public opinion in support of such action.

Energy Use

1. Through discussion, establish the relationship between increasing wants and needs and increased energy consumption. Find pictures from magazines to illustrate points. Advertisements for sport utility vehicles can be examined.

2. Develop a class project to encourage energy conservation in the children's homes (turning off lights, turning down thermostats, shutting off televisions and appliances not in use, and so on).
3. Prepare a bulletin-board display of energy-related news stories and political cartoons. Through discussion, establish the importance of energy to the daily lives of everyone.
4. Make a survey of children's homes to identify energy uses that would not have been in homes 50 years ago or 100 years ago. Discuss in terms of new demands on energy resources.

Crime and the Rule of Law

We turn now from poverty and human–environment interaction to a third group of public issues. The United States has long held the distinction of being the most violent and lawless of all industrialized nations. Moreover, in every category of violent crime—rape, murder, robbery, assault—the number of offenses committed by youngsters (children and teenagers) has increased substantially in the past decade. As well, youngsters increasingly are the victims of violent crime.

What is causing this? That is a very good question to put to older students. As Chapter 9 will show, such an inquiry teaches children to hypothesize at the same time that it teaches them to gather relevant data (information) and revise hypotheses as the data require. A planned program of law-related education (LRE) can help children focus on the problem of lawlessness and the idea of rule by law. Such a program should concern itself with broad goals such as these:

1. Develop an understanding of concepts that are basic to the legal system, such as liberty, justice, fairness, toleration, power, honesty, property, equality, and responsibility
2. Develop an understanding and appreciation of the constitutional basis of the American legal system
3. Develop a functional knowledge of how the institutions of the legal and justice systems operate
4. Develop an understanding of and respect for the need for a system of law and justice as prerequisites for orderly and harmonious living

In addition to inquiry-oriented units on crime, such simple activities as the following can make a difference in children's attitudes toward and knowledge of this enduring social concern.

- Invite a local police officer to talk to the class about law enforcement, drug traffic, youth gangs, or some other real or potential problems in the community.
- Bring in news clippings describing acts of vandalism; discuss the effects and costs of such behavior.
- Discuss rights versus responsibilities along lines familiar to children, such as, "Can we go to the movies and talk out loud?"
- Research the latest legislation on drugs (upper grades). Find out if the legal penalties for drug abuse are the same for adults as for juveniles.

- Take a field trip to a court, the state legislature, or a city council meeting.
- Find out how a jury is selected. Invite someone who has recently served on a jury to speak to the class about the responsibilities and duties of jurors.

Peace and Global Perspective

We live in a world fraught with danger, which is likely to increase as modern weapons become available to more and more nations. Even a minor power without a nation, as Americans saw on September 11, 2001, can pose a serious threat and cause havoc. Perhaps through educational programs directed toward the understanding of others and toward a search for world peace, a more satisfactory method of resolving international disputes can be found than the oldest and most destructive method, war. Many believe that a tolerant global perspective is essential if humankind is to survive. Others, using the slogan "Peace and Justice," believe that a fair sharing of resources is a prerequisite for peace. There is no shortage of food to feed the people of Earth, for example; rather, food is unequally divided. Some have way too much; others have way too little.

Teachers will need to be imaginative in exploring and discovering new paths to peace. But there is plenty of help. The award-winning Second Step program teaches preschool and kindergarten children (and up) the social and emotional skills for violence prevention. Sponsored by the Committee for Children (www.cfchildren.org), the program has good curricula and many ideas for teacher and parent education.

The most basic and productive teaching plan is to extend each social studies unit in such a way that it includes global comparisons and a global perspective. For example, when children in the primary grades are studying homes and home life, that is the time to begin developing the understanding that people all over the world need homes and that they build them in a variety of ways. Or when the food market is studied, time might be spent examining food markets around the world. Units on transportation and communication can, likewise, be expanded to familiarize students with these functions on a global basis rather than only in the local community. Almost any topic has within it such possibilities for global comparison.

Many other activities also have been used successfully. A sampling follows.

Take teaching ideas from the United Nations. The UN operates a good website. Click on "cyber schoolbus" at cyberschoolbus.un.org for curriculum ideas for teaching and learning about peace. The "peace education" page is especially good.

Use experiences from the everyday lives of children as a springboard for global studies. Take blue jeans, for example. Here we have a fashion fad that began in the United States during the 1960s and spread worldwide. Responding to this demand, blue jeans factories were established in South Korea, Mexico, the Philippines, China, and elsewhere. Or take chocolate. What is it? How and where is it produced? Trace it from the candy counter to its roots.

Guests. Invite to the classroom former members of the Peace Corps, immigrants, diplomats and ambassadors, and other persons who have lived at least a year abroad.

Make direct contact. iEARN (International Education and Resource Network [www.iearn .org]) is an increasingly popular organization with thousands of participating schools in over one hundred countries. A creative source of collaborative projects, online school-to-school relationships, and face-to-face meetings, iEARN emerged in the 1980s with projects between educators in the United States and the former Soviet Union that used telecommunications technology to enhance learning and create online global communities. Clearly, one of the best learning experiences for children who are studying the people of other lands is to have direct contact with someone from that country, especially a child their own age, who can answer questions about the clothes they wear, their schools and games, their celebrations, and their homes. With help from the teacher and their parents, students can correspond with children abroad, exchanging photos, news, and stories.

Diversity, Fairness, and Prejudice

It is one thing to teach about differences around the world and another to teach about differences right here at home. The latter often is called *ethnic heritage studies* or *multicultural education*. As we saw in Chapter 2, the children in our classrooms come increasingly from diverse home cultures (defined broadly to include ethnicity, race, language, religion, and social class). Thanks to the trend toward inclusion of special-needs children in the regular classroom, the children we teach will become even more diverse. This gives teachers a tremendous opportunity to teach children firsthand about the meaning and value of diversity. Teachers can engage children in projects in which they play and work together and thereby develop habits of friendliness, cooperation, and appreciation for one another.

Prejudice means prejudging people and places; that is, judging them before they are known, before the facts are gathered. It is a type of ignorance. Before we meet someone, we might believe we know quite a bit about him or her based, perhaps, on stereotypes we hold about that person's group membership. Actually, we may know nothing at all about this person. When combined with fear, greed, and anger, prejudice has played a central role in all sorts of social problems and all manner of hate crimes—even the atrocities called crimes against humanity, such as genocide. Prejudice has made slavery, the extermination of native populations, apartheid, the Holocaust, and the Japanese American internment possible. It is a deep and pernicious problem that humans historically have had an extremely difficult time avoiding or overcoming. On the bright side, prejudice is a concept that children can learn, and they can learn it well enough to recognize it when they see it or read it. With the help of caring teachers and other adults in their lives, they may learn to courageously take a stand against it.

In Chapter 9, strategies for teaching any concept, such as prejudice, are explained. Many teaching suggestions related to diversity were also given in Chapter 2. Accordingly, only a few additional activities are suggested here.

Vocabulary

Teach children the meaning of the terms *prejudice, respect, stereotype, race, customs, religion,* and *tolerance.* Then read selections from newspapers, the textbook, children's trade books, and other resources in which these terms are used.

Perspectives

The most powerful form of multicultural study for children in the intermediate and middle grades is to compare the perspectives of various cultural groups on a single event, historical or current. Newer social studies textbook programs often give multiple views on events. For example, both Native American and European perspectives on westward expansion are given. Children's trade books can also be a great help. See the trade book examples for teaching multiple perspectives given in Chapter 12.

Cooperative Groupwork

Create small, diverse working groups of children. Each group should contain as much diversity as the composition of the class allows. During groupwork, help children cooperate on a meaningful and challenging task. The task will help take the attention off one another, placing it instead on the work to be done. The children will gradually get to know one another as a natural result of completing the task. The problems they have working together will be the usual ones of sharing, communicating, participating, listening, keeping agreements, and so forth, each of which is an opportunity to provide instruction on cooperation. Cooperative learning techniques are explained in Chapter 11.

Guest Speakers

Invite representatives of various ethnic and racial groups in the community to your class. Ask them about their cultural roots. Be sure to include European Americans; otherwise, children might develop the misconception that Whites are somehow neutral (not ethnic).

Music and Art

Encourage children and their parents to share music and art that has distinct ethnic origins or particular meaning to the family. Invite an ethnic musicologist to the class to share information about music's cultural roots. Model for children that regardless of your own ethnic or racial identification, you value many different forms of music and art.

Languages

Value multilingualism. Conduct a survey of the school or local area to find out the number of different languages spoken and identify each. To show that multilingualism is valued, develop an award for the person who speaks the greatest number of languages.

Conclusion

This chapter began with a genius's letter to a fifth-grade boy named Michael. "Bucky" Fuller urged Michael to do the things that need doing, "that you see need to be done, and that no one else sees need to be done." This advice captures the soul of a current-events curriculum. Help children develop an eye and an ear for current events and a heart for caring about the community.

A current-events program is a must in elementary and middle school classrooms, because without it children are not likely to form the citizenship dispositions that are vital to the health of their communities. Without it, they may not have adequate opportunities to see the things that need to be done or to respond and, in turn, to develop their own talents. There are three *purposes* for building a current events program, three *approaches* to it, and four main *strategies* for teaching current events. Remember that there is an important distinction between current events and controversial issues, and that some controversies are short-lived while others are enduring. Five enduring controversial issues were identified. These and others can be the focus of integrated issue-centered units that rely on discussion, writing, and reading.

Discussion Questions and Suggested Activities

Go to MyEducationLab and select the topic "Current Events/Controversial Issues," then watch the video "Teaching with Current Events" and complete the activity.

1. Look back at the four strategies for teaching current events and your response to the question in the *Reflection* sidebar. Discuss with classmates the strategies you and they prefer and why. Also discuss the letter-writing assignment that went awry in Madison, Wisconsin. What does it suggest to you about teaching controversial issues?

2. Three approaches to current events teaching were given in the examples involving Ms. Hansen, Mr. Hsiao, and Ms. Diaz. The latter featured a lesson plan for studying the nation behind the current event. Compare and contrast the three approaches. Which is the strongest?

3. Select a public issue other than "Who is responsible for the poor?" Then, revise the issue-centered unit plan as needed for teaching that unit.

4. NCSS Standards *Sampler*. Examine the first- and second-grade classroom vignette for standard #9 on page 23 of the standards *Sampler* that accompanies this book. How does this heritage unit, especially later in the year when students are gathering news stories, compare to the Lesson Plan, "A Nation in the News," in this chapter?

Selected References

Banks, James A., et al. (2005). *Democracy and diversity: Principles and concepts for educating citizens in a global age.* Seattle: Center for Multicultural Education, University of Washington.

Ehrenreich, Barbara. (2001). *Nickel and dimed: On (not) getting by in America.* New York: Henry Holt.

Hess, Diana. (2004, April). Controversies about controversial issues in democratic education. *PS: Political Science & Politics, 37* (2), 253–255.

Johnson, David W., & Johnson, Roger T. (Guest Editors). (2005). Peace education. *Theory Into Practice, 44* (4).

Passe, Jeff. (2006). Sharing the "current events" in children's lives. *Social Studies and the Young Learner, 19* (1), 4–7.

Rose, Steven (2002). Using current events media in the classroom. *Social Studies and the Young Learner, 14* (3), P1–P2.

Swan, Kathleen Owings, Hofer, Mark, & Levstik, Linda S. (2007). Camera! Action! Collaborate with digital moviemaking. *Social Studies and the Young Learner, 19* (4), 17–20.

MyEducationLab is a collection of online tools for your success in this course, your licensure exams, and your teaching career. Go to www.myeducationlab.com to utilize these extensive resources including videos from real classrooms, Praxis and licensure preparation, a lesson plan builder, and materials to help you begin your teaching career.

PART THREE

Planning and Teaching Social Studies

Assessing Student Learning

CHAPTER SEVEN

Chapter Outline

- Assessment Is Natural
- Purposes of Assessment
- Principles of Assessment
- Methods of Assessment
- Conclusion

Key Concepts

- Purposes, principles, and methods of assessment
- Formal and informal assessment
- Diagnostic, formative, and summative assessment
- Performance standards and scoring guides

MAIN IDEA

Assessment goes on continually in the classroom and is both a natural and an essential part of a learning environment. The primary purpose of assessment is not to sort children or to compare schools; it is to improve teaching and learning. For this reason, this chapter has been placed *before* the planning and teaching chapters.

PICTURE THIS

Mr. Bailey introduces his students to the concept democracy as part of the fourth-grade social studies–language arts curriculum. But he thought he would find out what the students already know about dictatorships and democracies. He asks a few questions: "Are our classroom meetings democratic? Thumbs up if you think so, down if you think not, sideways if you're not sure." He counts thumbs. "Thank you. Now let's hear your reasons." Their decisions tell him little about their understanding of democracy, but listening to their reasoning he learns that they have very little understanding, only something vague about elections. The next week, he launches the unit on democracy. At the end, he will revisit this question and listen again to their reasons.

I begin with a rather long story about classroom assessment. If you read it thoroughly, you will find it a helpful introduction to the main idea of this chapter.

Ms. Rivera is a new fourth-grade teacher who plans to teach children to read and make maps of their state and the United States. The school district curriculum guide states that fourth-grade teachers should achieve the following objectives. The first specifies under-standings, the second skills.

> Knowledge: At the end of the fourth grade, pupils should understand (1) the difference between state and national maps and (2) the differences and similarities among different kinds of maps: political, landform, and shaded relief maps.
>
> Skills: Pupils at the end of fourth grade should be able to (1) use map symbols and directions, (2) make different kinds of maps of the school grounds, and (3) locate places on the U.S. map using longitude and latitude.

Before she begins planning a unit of instruction, Ms. Rivera decides to find out what these children presently know about maps. She considers asking the whole class several questions: "What is a map? Have you ever used a map? What kinds of information do maps give us? What things make a map a really good map? Who knows what a map legend is?" She also contemplates listing key map terms on the board and asking students to define each of them on a sheet of paper. These are fine ideas. After weighing these alternatives, Ms. Rivera decides to create a brief pencil-and-paper test so she can maximize the amount of informa-tion she obtains from each child. Using ideas from her college methods course, she finds a map-skills practice exercise in the students' social studies workbook (Figure 7–1) and makes a copy for each child.

The next day, Ms. Rivera informs the children that she wants to find out what they know about maps so she can plan instruction accordingly. She warms them up to the task by ask-ing them about their experiences using and making maps. Then, she hands them the prac-tice sheet and directs them to take 15 minutes or so to answer the 10 questions below the map. After they finish, to find out their immediate reactions, she asks the class which items were the most and least difficult for them. She jots down a few notes on what they say.

Later that day, she looks over her notes and scores the assessment. She notes that two thirds of her students marked 4 or 5 of the 10 items correctly. Two students answered none correctly, and two answered 9 of the 10 items correctly. No one got all 10. Examining re-sponses item by item, she observes that no students correctly answered the question about due north, and nearly all the children identified the railroad. This is good information, and she figures it will help her plan instruction on maps.

She goes back to school the next day eager to gather more information. She decides to lead a class discussion of the same 10 items. She makes a transparency of the map and ques-tions, and displays it on the overhead projector. This time, she asks the class to respond to each question out loud. Her questioning procedure goes something like this: She directs her students' attention to the first question and asks the children which responses they selected yesterday. She uses the "fingers" technique to maximize participation: "Hold up one finger if you said it was a swamp, two if you said it was a desert, and three fingers if you said it was mountainous." Then she calls on a student to give reasons for his or her choice. After listen-ing, she asks another child for his or her reasoning, and then another child. This way, she is able to hear their reasoning—something that yesterday's exercise did not allow. As she moves through the 10 items, she is able to hear each student reason aloud at least once. Children are able to hear one another's reasoning, too. Ms. Rivera is careful to call on as many girls as boys.

FIGURE 7–1 Assessing map skills.

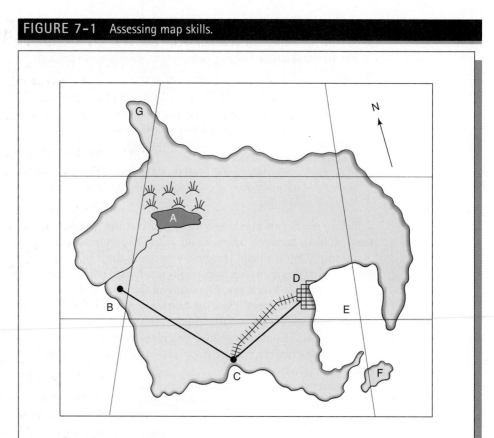

Use the map above to decide the correct answers. Then underline the correct answers.

1. The land north of A is (a wetland), (a desert), (mountainous).
2. The mouth of a river is located near letter (A), (B), (C).
3. The city at D is perhaps a (capital), (seaport), (mining town).
4. The river flows (from southwest to northeast), (from northeast to southwest), (from east to west).
5. An island is marked by the letter (A), (B), (F).
6. A railroad runs between (B and C), (D and B), (D and C).
7. The letter E marks (a bay), (a peninsula), (an island).
8. A peninsula is shown on this map at (B), (G), (C).
9. A delta might be found just north of (C), (A), (B).
10. The letter G is due north of (C), (A), (B).

Hungry for still more information, she turns to a different kind of assessment procedure on the following day. She places a blank sheet of paper in front of each student and asks them individually to try to draw from memory a map of the United States. She tells them to sketch very roughly the nation's general outline, add the Rocky Mountains and the Mississippi River, and draw in their own state, locating it as best they can. She asks them to indicate compass directions as well and to create a legend or key to explain any symbols used. Her students are nervous and a little embarrassed at the prospect of drawing. Ms. Rivera calms them with a little humor and impresses upon them how important it is for her to find out what they now can do so she can plan the very best instruction for them.

She has a hunch, based on the prior assessment, that several children will do very well on this map-drawing exercise, but mainly she is genuinely curious to see what they will draw, where they will draw the Mississippi River, whether they will use symbols, and where they will say north is.

After mulling over all the information she has gathered, Ms. Rivera plans a unit. The learning activities begin with conversations about road maps found in automobile glove compartments, which several students bring from home, and she displays well-worn trail maps that she has used on summer hikes. During the unit, pairs of children learn to make maps of the classroom and playground, and they search for explorers' routes on CDs and the Internet. Assigned to cooperative teams, the class develops expertise on different regions of the United States, making political and landform maps of each region. Each day, they practice drawing an outline map of the United States from memory, after studying once more the map hanging in the front of the room. Global comparisons are made between each U.S. region and a geographically similar region on another continent; for example, the Rockies are compared to the Swiss Alps, Death Valley to the Sahara, the Great Plains to the steppes of Russia, and so forth.

When introducing the unit, Ms. Rivera (with great flourish) informs the class that "by winter vacation this year, each of you will be able to place in your portfolio a landform map of the United States drawn from memory, and it will include our own state mapped correctly."

ASSESSMENT IS NATURAL

Assessment means finding out what students know and are able to do. Like a detective trying to get the facts, assessment's emphasis is on observation of what is happening now. Evaluation, by contrast, involves value judgment: comparing what is—the facts about the child's present understanding—with what ought to be—the desired outcome of instruction. This distinction is often blurred. When teachers assess children's present understanding of a landform map or map legend (or citizenship or immigration), they usually do so with a desired level of understanding—a standard—in mind. Indeed, assessment and evaluation often occur in one breath. In this chapter I will follow common practice and use the terms *assessment* and *evaluation* almost interchangeably, making the distinction where necessary for clarity. But first let's reflect on Ms. Rivera's assessments.

She was assessing her students' map knowledge and skills. But *why*? To help her plan an effective unit of instruction. Was she doing anything out of the ordinary? Not really. Teachers assess their students almost continually, observing them at their desks, checking their homework, and looking over their shoulders as they make models, paint lakes and mountains, read about deserts of the world, and write stories about historical events. They notice when children raise their hands higher and higher, hoping to be called on, and when they slump down in their chair, avoiding the teacher's gaze. They notice when children are rejected from one another's play and observe how they negotiate tasks in small cooperative groups. Teachers, because they are *teachers*, are constantly assessing.

Ms. Rivera is a model of curiosity. She loves to learn what her children already know and can do. She is able to make them feel comfortable as she gathers information. They know she has much to teach them and that *she diagnoses their present knowledge and skills so she can properly plan instruction.*

Note the variety of assessment procedures she used. First, there was the paper-and-pencil assessment. She pulled an activity from the workbook and adapted it to her assessment purpose. This paper-and-pencil assessment was of the selection, or multiple-choice, type because students were asked to select the best response from several given. The next day, she asked the whole class which items they found difficult and easy. Informal questioning of this sort is probably the most common kind of assessment conducted by teachers. Ms. Rivera then placed the same map and questions on the overhead projector and conducted a sort of group interview—using a planned sequence of questions and the "fingers" technique to get all of her students involved—so that she could gather information about how they puzzled their way through these items. She did not provide correction or instruction; these would come later, during the unit. For now, she was only trying to find out what they knew and how they thought about these things. Finally, she used a production (also called supply) assessment when she had students sketch the U.S. map. When Ms. Rivera introduced the unit to students, she informed them of a key performance expectation or target.

These are only a few of the kinds of assessment commonly carried on in classrooms, and Ms. Rivera's purpose—to plan instruction—is only one purpose. This chapter will explore these and other kinds and purposes of assessment. First, it is important to emphasize that assessment goes on continually in classrooms. And it ought to. Assessment "ought to become part of the natural learning environment," writes Howard Gardner. "As much as possible it should occur 'on the fly,'" as part of a teacher's or learner's "natural engagement in a learning situation."[1] What is to be avoided is a view of assessment as a formal procedure that occurs only at the end of an instructional unit for the purpose of reporting a score or grade. That is one purpose of assessment, and a necessary one. But it is a narrow purpose and not one that helps teachers plan or children learn.

 PURPOSES OF ASSESSMENT

This section and the next invite you to think carefully about purposes and principles of assessment. The following sections explain the main kinds of assessment techniques, from simple observation to self-assessment checklists, scoring guides, and portfolios. First, though, consider three general purposes of assessment (Figure 7–2).

Ms. Rivera's assessments were serving the purpose of diagnosing her students' knowledge and skills, which in turn served the purpose of planning effective instruction. This—instructional planning—is the primary purpose of assessment as far as the teacher is concerned. Instructional decision making without assessment data would be subject to considerable error. Not only does assessment information allow teachers to tailor instruction to individual students, it also helps them decide on the instructional objectives themselves and monitor students' progress. If Ms. Rivera knows, for example, that her children's oral reports on the geographical regions of the United States will be graded on organization, accuracy, voice clarity, and use of visual aids, then these become major performance objectives of the unit. I will discuss this in detail in the next section.

FIGURE 7-2 Purposes of assessing student learning.

Instructional Planning

Assess in order to
- diagnose students' understanding of maps before developing a map unit
- provide feedback to students on their progress and problems
- decide how to modify a unit plan
- identify cultural differences
- identify ability strengths and weaknesses
- provide evidence of success to students; therefore, motivate them to persevere

Public Accountability

Assess in order to
- report student progress to the community
- compare students across schools, school districts, states, and nations
- discuss with parents students' progress and problems

Student Placement

Assess in order to
- assign students to pairs and cooperative groups or ability groups
- decide which students require an IEP
- place profoundly retarded and extraordinarily gifted children in special programs

---

Public accountability and program evaluation is a second purpose of assessment. Most states in the United States have developed social studies assessments that are administered to students statewide, and the U.S. Congress funds assessments of students' knowledge in history, geography, and civics.[2] Assessments such as these are typically administered to students in grades 4, 8, and 12, and the results are used by parents and public officials to compare education programs and student achievement within districts, across states, and among nations. Assessments designed for this purpose are usually standardized and norm-referenced. *Standardized* means that the test is designed to be administered and scored in the same way wherever it is given. *Norm-referenced* means that the results will be used to compare one student or group of students (e.g., those in your school or state) to another (students in the nation as a whole).

A third purpose of assessment is placement, that is, the selection of students for particular schools and programs. IQ tests and the Scholastic Aptitude Test (SAT), introduced in 1926, are perhaps the best-known tests used for this purpose. IQ and similar tests are frequently used to determine placements of exceptional children. The SAT has determined college and university admission for millions of high school students. In the elementary grades, standardized reading and math tests are often used to determine ability-group placement, and other assessments of social competence, intelligence, and language proficiency are used to place students in special programs.

Critics of testing for this purpose have called attention to some of its abuses, one of which is to sort children into categories from which there may be no escape. As was noted in Chapter 2, once a child is labeled, the label often sticks long after its supposed benefits to the child have worn off. It may generate negative effects as a self-fulfilling prophecy: Teachers' expectations of the child may be lowered in a way that is not warranted, the child's self-perceptions may be lowered accordingly, and, making matters worse, he or she may be permanently (rather than only temporarily) separated from other children. As a result of the separation, the child may experience a less challenging and less empowering curriculum. As a consequence, he or she will know and be able to do less than his or her peers. Labels have been misused especially with racial-, ethnic-, and language-minority children. For these reasons, teachers are urged to use extreme caution when using test results for placement purposes.

PRINCIPLES OF ASSESSMENT

When teachers plan to assess their students' learning, they should also be thinking about curriculum objectives and alternative ways to provide instruction. Similarly, when teachers plan curriculum objectives and think about how they will teach to them, they need also to consider how they will assess student achievement of these objectives. They are, in effect, thinking about three things at once. For this reason, it has become popular to say that the boundaries between assessment, curriculum, and instruction are blurred. This brings us to the first principle of good assessment practice.

Principle 1: Assessment Is an Integral Part of Curriculum and Instruction

Assessment planning should not be tagged onto the end of a unit, after the curriculum has been planned and instruction delivered. Good assessment is not an add-on or an afterthought. If assessment is to facilitate student learning, it must be woven into the fabric of curriculum and instruction. It must be done before, during, and after instruction.

Assessments conducted before instruction are *diagnostic* assessments. Ms. Rivera developed her unit to address the geographic knowledge and skills she found wanting in the assessments she conducted before planning the unit. Assessments conducted during instruction are *formative* assessments. These assessments help teachers decide what to do next in a lesson or unit. They are called formative because they help teachers "form" or modify instruction to help children achieve the objectives. These are certainly the most common kinds of assessment. Often they are nothing more than observations made of students while they are engaged in project or committee work, or while they are working independently at their desks, but they may also be brief paper-and-pencil tests given periodically through a unit of instruction. Such tests help teachers to check students' understanding of the topic at hand and then to alter the lesson as needed. They also give students knowledge of the results of their work and a sense of making progress, which can be of tremendous help in motivating learners of all ages to carry on with the task at hand. Frequent formative assessment provides both teachers and students with the feedback they need to teach and learn better.

Assessments conducted after instruction are *summative* assessments. These are used to judge students' overall achievement at the end of instruction. They sum up the learning that has taken place and may incorporate many quizzes, work samples, performances, and other evidence of learning. Chapter and unit tests are the most common kinds of summative assessments, along with the grade given at the end of the school term.

Whether before, during, or after instruction, assessments facilitate student learning by helping student and teacher alike *find out* what is and isn't being learned. This information is then used to plan further teaching and learning.

Principle 2: Devote Time to Essential Learnings

Teachers should spend their assessment time on a relatively small number of essential subject matters or skills. Key themes and topics of citizenship, history, geography, and the other social sciences were discussed in Chapters 3 through 6, and the teacher should direct assessment in social studies primarily to these. It is more important, for example, to develop assessments related to ideas such as democracy, cultural pluralism, poverty, human–environment interaction, and the enduring tension between individual freedom and the common good than it is to spend time listing Civil War battlefields, the governors of your state, or the sequence of Chinese and English dynasties. Of course, these latter subjects may have their place in a well-conceived curriculum, but school time is precious. Thoughtful teachers spend most of their instruction and assessment energies on the knowledge, skills, virtues, and values that matter most.

Take a moment to contemplate Figure 7–3, "What's worth knowing?" The question asks teachers to set priorities—to engage in the thoughtful task of content selection: From the universe of possible topics, which few should we spend time teaching and assessing? Try to

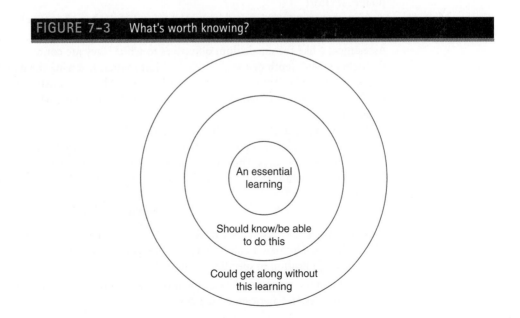

FIGURE 7-3   What's worth knowing?

An essential learning

Should know/be able to do this

Could get along without this learning

think of examples that might fall within each circle. For example, "list the governors of our state" might be placed in the outer circle and "understand why democracies sometimes collapse" in the inner circle. In between might be "identify the beginning and ending dates of three past democracies." These distinctions are not necessarily easy to make. Different teachers, students, and parents will certainly disagree on where to draw the lines. Content selection (in social studies especially) is a deeply value-laden procedure. It is political as well as pedagogical. The decision tree in Chapter 3 (Figure 3–4) may come in handy.

But help is available. The members of the committee that developed the curriculum standards for social studies (see the accompanying *Sampler*) debated this question continually. The 10 standards represent their advice to beginning and experienced teachers alike.

Principle 3: Set High Standards for Teaching and Learning

The minimum competency movement of the 1970s and 1980s was an attempt by the educational community to restore public confidence in American education. Test data indicated a downward trend in scores on tests of basic school subjects over a period of several years. It was widely believed by the public—rightly or wrongly—that the achievement of American schoolchildren was falling behind that of their counterparts in other industrialized nations. Out of this concern came the idea that schools should identify minimum levels of competency for basic school subjects that presumably all students would be expected to master. Teaching for these minimum competencies would be followed by minimum competency tests. This movement had great appeal and received strong support from public officials. Several states developed programs to implement minimum competency testing. What was not anticipated in this process was the detrimental effect of foreshortening achievement by focusing on minimum requirements. Minimum expectations gave no hint of the kinds of targets toward which students and teachers should put forth their best effort.

"Social studies teaching and learning are powerful when they are challenging," according to the vision statement developed by the National Council for the Social Studies.[3] Assessments, like the curriculum objectives to which they are connected, need to capture the richness and depth of social studies subject matter. Knowing the names of those who signed the U.S. Constitution falls short of knowing why the Constitution has the content it does, grasping the principles on which it relies, and knowing what democracy requires of citizens.

To set high standards for children's learning and to assess their attainment in relation to these standards, teachers need to be familiar with the several sets of curriculum standards developed in recent years. These were addressed in Chapters 1, 3, 4, and 5. Consider the two following curriculum standards for social studies learning developed for children in the early grades.

By the end of the fourth grade, students should be able to:

- Identify key ideals of the United States' democratic form of government, such as individual human dignity, liberty, justice, equality, and the rule of law, and discuss their application in specific situations.[4]
- Explain the purposes of rules and laws, and identify the most important values and principles of American democracy.[5]

Teachers who teach to these standards in the early grades are aiming high. But there is more. To assess student achievement of these standards, it is necessary to envision the levels of achievement that students must reach to receive particular scores, awards, or certificates. These levels are called *performance standards* or *performance criteria*. They define levels of achievement—degrees of mastery or proficiency—from high to low. Teachers often define three levels: good, fair, and poor. When a fourth level is added, it usually specifies a still higher level: excellent, superior, commendable, highly proficient, and distinguished. Sometimes five or six levels are specified. Below is a set of performance criteria that spell out three levels of achievement. These performance criteria were developed to assess the quality of short essays that fifth-grade students write about important events in American history, such as the signing of the Declaration of Independence or the Emancipation Proclamation.

- Level 3—Proficient: Response shows considerable knowledge of the time period and geographic factors, as appropriate, and frequently demonstrates insight. It usually supports ideas and conclusions with specific historical examples. Response is well reasoned and organized and is largely historically accurate.
- Level 2—Adequate: Response contains adequate information about the event. It demonstrates some knowledge of the time period and geographic factors, as appropriate. Response demonstrates some understanding, but reasons and evidence are in limited depth.
- Level 1—Minimal: Response addresses the question, but shows minimal understanding. It may lack historical and geographical context. It may contain numerous historical errors. It may simply rephrase the question but includes at least a word or phrase showing historical knowledge.[6]

Principle 4: Clarify Targets (Objectives) Early

Teachers need to clarify for students early in the instructional unit the targeted level of performance. In other words, they should let students in on the objectives of instruction and try to describe those objectives as clearly as possible, specifying what students will know and be able to do if they achieve the objective. If teachers want children to develop their skills and knowledge to a high degree of proficiency—if they want children to hit the target—then the children must know the target well in advance. Just as an archer cannot shoot an arrow to the bull's-eye if she cannot see the target, children cannot become proficient if they have no idea of the level of performance they are striving for. Skillful teachers, therefore, clarify the goals of instruction at the beginning of the year and state specific objectives and performance criteria at the beginning of the unit. How to frame these objectives is central to unit planning, as the next chapter will reveal.

For example, Ms. Paley's kindergartners know in advance that their dramatizations of historical events must be rich in detail. Consequently, each time she repeats to them the story of Rosa Parks's bus ride or of Squanto, the Pilgrims' friend, it is with the expectation that their retellings of the story will evolve. And they do.[7] Likewise, Mr. Smith tells his seventh-grade class in September that by June they will draw a world map beautifully from memory on a blank piece of tagboard. "When they arrive here, I tell them they'll end up with 150 countries, and they tell me, 'No way.'" But they do, confidently. "I used to hear about

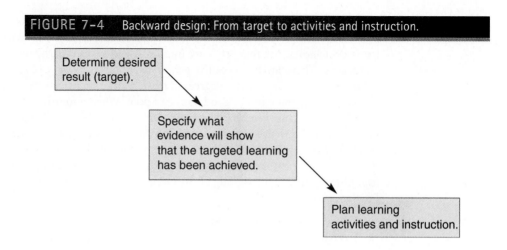

FIGURE 7-4   Backward design: From target to activities and instruction.

countries on television and think they were over there somewhere," admitted one student. "I hadn't heard of half of them. Now I can figure out better what's going on in the world. I'll always know that Angola is in Africa and not just over there somewhere."[8]

Teachers like Ms. Paley and Mr. Smith make clear for children the "destinations" of their efforts. Ms. Paley's specification that dramatizations are to be "rich in detail," and Mr. Smith's that their world maps will be drawn "beautifully" and "from memory," let children in on the performance criteria by which their work will be judged and toward which their work should be aimed. This is tremendously important. This can be called "backward design"[9] because the end point (the arrow hitting the target) is envisioned first, and then specified ("in rich detail," "drawn beautifully from memory"), and only then are learning activities planned (see Figure 7–4).

Teachers assess continuously, in large and small ways, formally and informally, within learning activities and between them. Teachers then can provide additional instruction and experiences as needed, calibrating them to student progress toward the desired results. In this way the first principle of assessment is realized: improving teaching and learning.

Principle 5: Aim for More Authentic Assessments

Assessments should be geared to finding out students' ability to apply knowledge and skills successfully in meaningful or "authentic" tasks. These tasks are exhibitions of children's ability to *use* what they have learned—to apply it. Such tasks are meaningful because they are goal directed, and these goals have a real-world quality; hence, they are not school-bound tasks that have no bearing on what people do in their lives as citizens, workers, family members, and neighbors. Rather than focusing only on what children have memorized, they require children to use information, to analyze, manipulate, or interpret it in some way; consequently, higher-order thinking is incorporated into the assessment.

Grant Wiggins clarifies: "Authentic assessments require students to be effective performers with acquired knowledge. Traditional tests tend to reveal only whether a student can recognize, recall, or 'plug in' what was learned out of context. This may be as problematic as inferring driving or teaching ability from written tests alone."[10]

One way students can display the depth of their understanding of the U.S. Constitution is to create, democratically, a classroom constitution. Lots of deliberation should precede voting on rules. *(Anthony Magnacca/Merrill)*

Examples of authentic tasks in social studies are plentiful. Teachers can assess students' ability to

- Participate in deliberations on classroom, playground, and community problems as part of maintaining a healthy civic life
- Use reference books and the Internet as part of social studies inquiry projects
- Work cooperatively as part of a team that's completing a challenging task
- Display historical reasoning by creating a classroom museum exhibit of an ancient community (e.g., Mesa Verde)
- Read and make charts and graphs showing food supply, election results, census data, and economic data
- Write and illustrate a travel brochure of the community

Principle 6: Collect Multiple Indicators of Learning—An Array of Evidence

Teachers should collect multiple indicators of student achievement. A score on a lone chapter test or a summative performance assessment does not go far enough to tell what a child knows and is able to do in relation to the most important learning objectives, and it gives no indication of progress. In this sense, a single score can be said to lack *validity:* it doesn't really capture the learning it claims to be capturing. Teachers can remedy this problem by having students collect numerous work samples into a portfolio that documents their work over the course of a unit. The portfolio might contain a chapter test from the social studies textbook program along with two or three other paper-and-pencil tests and quizzes. There might also be a team-written biography to which the student contributed a chapter, letters to the editor about current events, self-assessments of the student's reading and thinking skills, and several drawings and maps. In this way, students have much to show for their work, and teachers can justify the grades they give by pointing to an array of evidence.

Principle 7: Provide Ample Opportunities to Learn

Students should not be held accountable for learning subject matter on which they have not been provided adequate instruction. Therefore, schools should not only provide targets for learning, but also the means of achieving them—teachers, curriculum materials, classrooms, wall maps, libraries, stimulating environments. Children must be provided support or assistance if they are to reach the targets. School buildings in poor physical condition, outdated curriculum materials, school administrators who deny teachers the assistance of knowledgeable curriculum coordinators, unsupportive citizens, and teachers who have little professional competence or are not themselves readers and learners all combine to deny children sufficient opportunities to learn. Clearly, some of these problems are larger than what individual teachers can deal with in their own classrooms. Nonetheless, what teachers can do is assess what is taught, teach what will be assessed, and assure the community that what is taught and assessed are essential learnings. Figure 7–5 summarizes the seven principles.

FIGURE 7-5   Principles of good assessment.

Principle 1:   Treat assessment as an integral part of curriculum and instruction.

Principle 2:   Direct assessments toward essential learnings.

Principle 3:   Set high standards for teaching and learning.

Principle 4:   Clarify targets early.

Principle 5:   Assess student performance in authentic tasks.

Principle 6:   Collect multiple indicators of learning.

Principle 7:   Provide ample opportunities for students to learn.

METHODS OF ASSESSMENT

We turn now to a variety of methods of assessment, beginning with informal techniques and then moving to more formal methods of paper-and-pencil tests, performance assessment, and portfolios. The latter are more formal because they are less likely to be done on the fly, require more planning, and require the development of materials such as scoring guides.

Informal Assessment Techniques

Much of the evaluation of learning in social studies is done informally by the teacher. Many times each day the teacher observes learners and judges the quality of their work. The teacher notices what problems individual children are encountering or what kind of help they need to progress. The teacher then decides what deficiencies are apparent in children's work, whether the instruction is proceeding too rapidly or too slowly, what materials are required, how well concepts have been understood, or how proficient children are in their use of skills. Of course, formal tests have a place in this process, but most of the assessing a teacher does involves informal methods and simple observation. This means that careful records must be kept if the progress of each child is to be reported accurately. Some of the more commonly used informal assessment techniques are described on the pages that follow.

Observation

Observation is among the best techniques the teacher can use to learn about children, appraise their progress, and determine areas for improvement. Although all teachers use this method of learner appraisal, not all teachers are skillful in its application. The teacher who makes the most of observation knows what to look for, systematizes observations, and tries to objectify the information so obtained. To this end, some suggestions follow.

1. Spell out what is to be evaluated in terms of child behavior. For example, if the teacher is looking for progress in historical reasoning, it would be important to determine whether the student asks where a primary document came from and wants to know who wrote it rather than just reading it and believing it without question. Or, if the teacher wants to observe growth in democratic virtues, the following questions would be appropriate. Two virtues, civility and individual responsibility, can be combined into one: consideration for others. Does the child
   a. Show respect for the ideas and feelings of classmates?
   b. Refrain from causing disturbances that make it impossible for others to do their best work?
   c. Carry a fair share of the workload in a small group?
   d. Enjoy helping a classmate when needed?
   e. Display sensitivity to injustices that may occur in the course of life in and out of the classroom?
   f. Return borrowed materials? Obtain permission to use materials that belong to others?
   g. Observe group rules?
   h. Fulfill responsibilities on time?

2. Select certain children for intensive observation and study rather than observing in general. This intensive observation might be limited to specific situations. For example, just what happens to David when he is placed on a committee to accomplish some task in connection with a social studies unit? The purpose of observations of this type is to gain insight into the child's behavior in the context of a specific set of circumstances.

3. Record observations in writing and do not depend on memory. Keep a written record of information obtained through observation and maintain this record over a period of time. Here are six entries in one teacher's anecdotal record on a child:

Sara Larsen

9/24	Difficulty in getting going in independent choice work; ignored all suggestions of activities. . . . "It's boring."
9/26	Found a fiction book related to unit for Sara. Read during work time. Took it home today.
9/27	Finished book . . . took suggestion to make a poster showing main characters.
10/1	Asked for time to show class the poster and to tell about the story.
10/2	Showed work. Is she a budding artist? Received lots of compliments/support from classmates.
10/3	Sara asked for another book; suggested biography to her; also suggested she draw a map showing the area in which the person lived.

Group Discussion

The teacher should reserve some time near the end of every social studies period for the class to discuss its progress and to make plans for the next day's work. This discussion reminds students of all the things they are learning in social studies and gives the teacher an opportunity to identify their emerging understandings and stubborn misconceptions.

Asking Basic Questions

Asking questions is perhaps the most widely used assessment technique of all time. Parents could not get along without it, and skillful teachers turn it into an art form. For example, Janet Alleman and Jere Brophy have developed a brilliant set of questions for diagnosing primary-grade students' understandings of *cultural universals* before beginning units on them. Cultural universals are dimensions of human life that can be found in all human cultures, past and present. The assessment questions Alleman and Brophy developed are basic because they get right to the bottom of a child's understanding of, in this case, the concepts *food*, *clothing*, and *shelter*.[11]

Food

- People all over the world eat food. Is that just because they like to, or do they need food? . . . Why? . . . What does food do for us?
- What is food? . . . How is food different from other things that are not food?

Clothing

- People all over the world wear clothes. Is that because they need to, or just because they want to? . . . Why? . . . (If a child's response only mentions keeping warm) Do they wear clothes in warm places like Hawaii? . . . Why?
- Our clothes are made out of cloth. What is cloth made from?

Shelter

- Do people live in homes just because they want to, or do they need homes? . . . Why?
- What about in places like Hawaii where it's warm all year? Do people still need homes there? . . . Why?

Additional examples of basic questions can be found in the culminating integrated unit plan of this book—the plan called "Explore," in Chapter 13. Again, these are basic because they go to the core of children's present understandings (and misunderstandings) of important ideas.

- What is the scientific way of learning? (lesson 1)
- What is true of all living things? (lesson 2)
- What do all living things need to survive? (lesson 3)
- What decisions and plans do people have to make to see to it that living things have what they need to survive and develop? (lesson 4)

Asking Classifying Questions

Classifying questions may be the most useful for purposes of assessment, and for this reason they are worth learning well. Classifying questions are perfect for assessing students' understanding of a concept. You will learn in greater detail in the concept learning section of Chapter 9 that there are four types of classifying questions. Briefly, the first asks students whether something that the teacher is displaying is or is not an example of the concept being studied. The second asks students to sort a number of things into two sets: examples and nonexamples of the concept. The third asks students to produce an example of that concept, and the fourth asks students to correct a nonexample. Here a teacher uses two of these types: the first, then the third, and then the first again. The concept is *transportation*.

- "Children, I want to ask a few questions about what you think transportation is. Hold up one finger if you think walking from the cafeteria to the playground is an example of transportation. Hold up two fingers if you think it is not an example. Hold up a closed fist if you aren't sure."
- "Good. Now let's hear some of your reasons. Rosa? Tom?"
- "Let's get lots of examples of transportation on the board. Who will give us the first example? Okay, Sara? Rick?"
- "Good. We have 15 suggestions on the board. Now let's hear the thinking behind them. Nicole, you suggested covered wagons. What makes you think covered wagons are an example of transportation?"
- "Thank you. No one mentioned the space shuttle. Is it an example of transportation? Think about it for a minute and then jot down your decision and your reasons. In a minute, I'll ask several of you to share your response with the class."

Note that this teacher is not providing instruction on the defining attributes of transportation. She is not *teaching* the concept *transportation*. Rather, she is using classifying questions to assess what her students already know about this concept. Their decisions and the reasons they give will both provide the teacher with ample information to decide what sort of instruction the students need on this concept. Do they think transportation means simply movement? If so, a cloud and a worm are both examples of transportation. Or do they think one thing is being moved by another? The teacher will find out as she listens to their decisions and reasons.

Readers may wish to read again the opening vignette of this chapter, now paying attention to how Ms. Rivera uses classifying questions as she diagnoses her students' knowledge of the concept *map*.

Conferences

Conferences with children should teach them how to assess their own work, thereby leading to increased self-direction. The teacher–learner conference can help identify particular learning problems and difficulties that children may be having, provide insight into students' feelings about schoolwork, and help the teacher become aware of special personal or social problems the children may be having. The conference is a method of assisting every child individually in a personal way. Teachers need to budget their time to allow regular 10-minute conferences with individual children. Children need the personal contact with their teacher that a conference can give.

A conference will be of little value if the teacher does all the talking and the child all the listening. A friendly, helpful approach is needed, one that results in greater feelings of personal worth and accomplishment on the part of the child along with some constructive and concrete help for improvement. This close working relationship with children is critical to good education, especially in the social studies.

Paper-and-Pencil Tests

Paper-and-pencil tests in the classroom usually are constructed by the teacher or selected from the collection of tests that accompany textbook programs. Even though they can be used successfully with primary-grade children (assuming they are designed appropriately), their value increases as the child moves into the third and fourth grades and beyond. Such tests can help teachers gather data about how well students understand the concepts they are learning, their ability to write and to reason, their ability to recall key information, and their ability to use skills.

Ms. Rivera's diagnostic exercise relied on a paper-and-pencil test of map symbols and directions (Figure 7–1). It assessed both knowledge and skill. The classifying test shown in Figure 7–6 is a straightforward way to assess students' understanding of economic concepts concerning the theme of production. Note that it is a variation of the third type of classifying in which children are asked to produce one or more examples. In this case, the test provides one example and then asks the student to produce a second. Students' understanding of any concept, from climate to culture, government to religion, ecosystem to rain shadow, sentence to paragraph, can be assessed in this simple way.

FIGURE 7-6   Understanding concepts.

UNDERSTANDING CONCEPTS

One example is given for each of the terms listed. Your job is to write down *another* example.

1. Raw material   *Wood* is a raw material for making furniture; another raw
   material is _____
   used in making _____

2. Fuel   *Oil* is a fuel used for heating; another fuel is _____
   used for _____

3. Grain   *Corn* is a grain used for feed; another example of a grain is _____
   used for _____

4. Industry   *Dressmaking* is an industry; another example of industry is _____
   that makes   _____

5. Natural   *Water* is a natural resource necessary for life; another natural
   resource   resource is_____
   used for _____

6. Manufactured   A *rocket booster* is a manufactured product used for space exploration; another
   product   example of a manufactured product is _____
   used for _____

Even a complicated skill such as using the encyclopedia can be assessed, at least in part, using a paper-and-pencil format. Figure 7–7 suggests a test in which students find topics in one encyclopedia and then locate the same topics in another. A benefit of this particular test is that children find their way around not one, but two encyclopedias. From the standpoint of *concept formation*, the teaching strategy discussed in Chapter 9, two examples are always better than one. Locating the same items in an online encyclopedia would make a good third example for older students, once they have completed this task.

Paper-and-pencil tests lend themselves to both formative and summative assessment. Short matching and true–false quizzes can be written and scored quickly, and these can help students feel successful if they are purposefully made to be somewhat easy. One suggestion for giving these formative tests is to put children in teams of four. Hand the team two sheets of paper. One has the questions only; the other has the answers filled in. Of course, the material on the test has been taught to students over the previous one or two days. Explain that the reason you have given students both the questions and the answers is that the team's job is to make sure that each person on the team understands *why* these are the answers. Inform them that they will have 20 minutes for this review. Appoint a timekeeper and chairperson for each team. Explain that this review will be followed by a quiz on the same material and that the teams that do well will earn a certificate. After the time has expired, administer the same test to each individual. Robert Slavin, who conducts research on cooperative learning,

FIGURE 7-7   Using the encyclopedia.

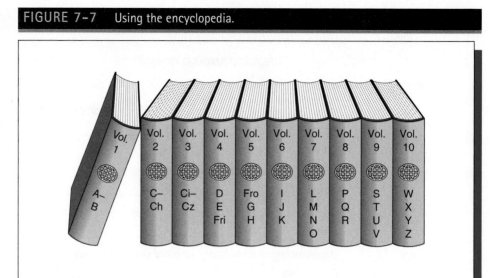

Directions: Using the ten-volume *Our Own Encyclopedia* shown in this diagram, select the number of the volume in which you would find information about each of the items listed below. Write the number of the volume you select in the spaces on the left side of the sheet. Then list the volume number of *World Book* in which the same items are found in the spaces on the right side of the sheet.

Our Own		*World Book*
1. _____	1. Earthquakes in Japan	1. _____
2. _____	2. The Mexican leader Zapata	2. _____
3. _____	3. The history of rocketry	3. _____
4. _____	4. The People's Republic of China	4. _____
5. _____	5. The U.S. Constitution	5. _____
6. _____	6. Apple-growing in Washington State	6. _____
7. _____	7. The Pony Express	7. _____
8. _____	8. Countries that are members of the United Nations	8. _____
9. _____	9. Confucius	9. _____
10. _____	10. The history of computers	10. _____

has shown that this assessment technique has many positive benefits, which are examined in Chapter 11, "Cooperative Learning in Social Studies." Not the least of these benefits is that children learn the material on the test.[12] This is good news, reflecting the primary purpose of assessment: to improve teaching and learning.

Of course, more challenging and authentic assessments are needed as well. Two kinds of paper-and-pencil test items are becoming increasingly popular. Both are challenging, and both require higher-order thinking. One uses multiple-choice items; the other requires short essay responses. Remember that multiple-choice tests require students to select the best response of those given. The major shortcoming of such tests is that too often they are not authentic tasks; that is, people rarely engage in multiple-choice tasks outside school settings. But this shortcoming can be offset when the questions (1) deal with essential social studies learning and (2) require higher-order thinking: analysis, interpretation, application, or manipulation of information. The multiple-choice test items shown in Figure 7–8 accomplish both. How?

These are multiple-choice-with-justification items. Such items present students with more than one reasonable correct answer. The student's task is to choose the response that can best be supported with reasons based on knowledge. In other words, the child has to justify his or her selection. The emphasis, therefore, is on the reasoning children bring to the choices they make. "By justifying their answers, students must go beyond mere rote learning. The answers they give provide teachers with greater insight into the knowledge and thinking patterns of individual students."[13]

Turning to short essay assessments, Figure 7–9 shows a short essay item used to assess fifth-grade students' understanding of historical events. There are several impressive features here. First, it deals with essential learning, events leading to the American Revolution. Second, it presents students with something for them to examine—a stimulus—in this case, a time line. Other possibilities are a map, photo or painting, or a brief quote from a primary document, such as the Declaration of Independence or an eyewitness account of the Boston Tea Party. Third, the directions for student writing are given in one, very clear sentence. Fourth, assistance or scaffolding is provided in the form of several "be sure to" prompts. These are intended to help students to reason with facts (in this case, explain the relationship between two events) rather than only to recall facts. Applying these four attributes, teachers can construct similar items for other historical events. Try this now with one of the following events: the Cherokee Trail of Tears, Columbus's first voyage, the first women's rights convention at Seneca Falls.

FIGURE 7–8   Multiple-choice with justification.

Example #1

I. Which of these was a cause of the Declaration of Independence?

a. The Intolerable Acts.
b. The king sent troops to force the colonists to obey.
c. Americans wanted to keep their wealth rather than share it with England.
d. The way the English treated the colonists.

II. Give your reasons.

Example #2

I. Which of these is an example of the idea *culture*?

a. The life of the people living in a Lakota Sioux village.
b. The rules of cooperation and interaction in our classroom.
c. The way kittens in a litter are raised by cats.
d. The animals and plants living together in a forest.

II. Give your reasons.

Source: Steven L. McCollum, *Performance Assessment in the Social Studies Classroom. A How-To Book for Teachers* (Joplin, MO: Chalk Dust Press, 1994).

FIGURE 7-9 Short essay item.

EVENTS LEADING TO THE AMERICAN REVOLUTION

(Suggested time: 30 minutes)

In history, important things happen that cause other things to happen. This is very plain when we talk about the events leading to the American Revolution.

Study the time line below.

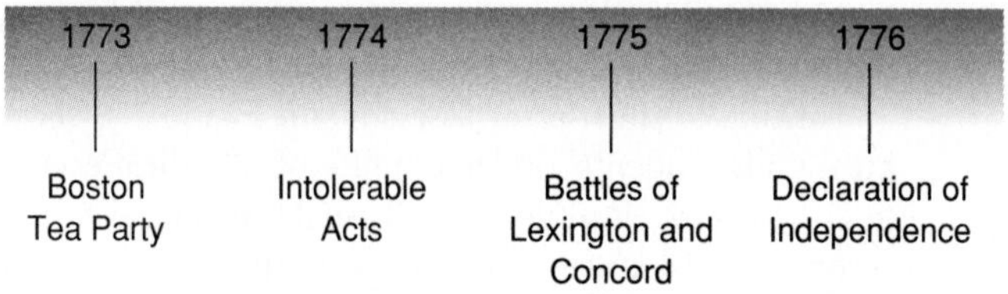

1773	1774	1775	1776
Boston Tea Party	Intolerable Acts	Battles of Lexington and Concord	Declaration of Independence

Circle two events on the time line and write a short essay about them, using your knowledge of history.

Be sure to:

• Describe each event.
• Explain how the two events are related to each other.
• Explain how the events are related to the American Revolution.

_____

_____

_____

_____

_____

_____

_____

_____

_____

_____

_____

Source: *A Sampler of History–Social Science Assessment, Elementary* (1994), 35. Reprinted by permission of the California Department of Education, CDE Press, 1430 N. Street #3207, Sacramento, CA 95814.

Performance Assessment

Figures 7–8 and 7–9 actually are performance assessments. Why? Performance assessments are assessments that help teachers find out how well students can translate knowledge into action. In the multiple-choice justification assessment (Figure 7–8), children are required to use the knowledge they have acquired to defend the choice they make. In the short historical essay assessment using the time line (Figure 7–9), students are required to use their knowledge of cause and effect to explain the relationship between two events on the time line. Both are authentic tasks, too. Using one's knowledge to defend a position or explain a choice one has made is a valuable and necessary life skill; being able to determine what caused what, and how, is another.

Performance Criteria

If students are to aim high in their responses, performance criteria are needed. These performance criteria serve also as instructional objectives, and this is why performance assessment truly blurs the boundary between instruction and assessment. The performance criteria are the behaviors we want students to learn. On a scoring guide (also called a scoring rubric or rating scale), these criteria are identified and sequenced from high to low proficiency. As mentioned in the discussion of the third principle of good assessment, these criteria can be arranged on a three-level rating scale with descriptors such as proficient, adequate, and minimal. Doing so helps students to aim high, toward proficiency, and to want to know just what a proficient performance will look like. Look again at the short historical essay item (Figure 7–9). A rating scale needs to be created that spells out for students and teachers the criteria that will help them distinguish between a proficient short essay and one that is merely adequate or only minimally competent. Suggested criteria were given earlier in the chapter in the explanation of principle 3. That was a 3-point scale,

The construction of time lines can be used to assess students' knowledge of symbols and chronology and their ability to display graphically the amount of time between events. *(Anthony Magnacca/Merrill)*

and while it certainly will be more helpful to students and teachers than a simple "yes/no" checklist, a 5- or 6-point scale can make for a still more powerful instructional tool and scoring guide.

A 6-point scoring guide for teaching and assessing short-essay historical writing is found in Table 7–1. California teachers field-tested this rubric with fourth- and fifth-grade students. Its advantage over the 3-point scale is that it has greater explanatory power: More distinctions are made, and thus the quality of students' performances can be refined. Just as pianists at a recital or divers at a tournament are not judged merely "good," "fair," and "poor," historical reasoning—even in the elementary grades—can be advanced beyond the 3-point scale. Of course, the 6-point scale is more difficult than the 3-point scale—difficult both to comprehend and to use. Teachers can start students out on the simpler scale and graduate them, as they become able, to the more complex one. (Different scales can be used with students of different ability.) A good illustration of this difference can be found in Table 3–1 and Figure 3–3 in Chapter 3. In that chapter the point was made that discussion competence is one of the most important of all citizenship behaviors. Two rating scales were presented for assessing students' discussion abilities: one that might be more appropriate for children in the primary grades, the other for students in the fourth grade and higher (or students with greater discussion ability in the primary grades). The latter was field-tested in the Oakland County, Michigan, schools with sixth-grade students.

How to Create a Scoring Guide

Remember, the 3-point scoring guide is a terrific place to begin. It is easy to develop because children's work so easily falls into three categories: the good, the bad, and the in-between. Creating a scoring guide, whether 3-point or more, is a fairly direct procedure with five steps.

Step 1. *Objectives/curriculum standards.* Determine the desired results of instruction— what students are to learn. Refer to state and school district curriculum guidelines, the curriculum standards published by professional organizations (e.g., the NCSS curriculum standards; the History, Geography, and Civics standards), and the suggestions in this book. Be sure to think in terms of skills (intellectual skills, study skills, reading and writing skills, social skills) as well as knowledge (ideas and information). Also consider democratic values and attitudes. Here is an illustrative list of social studies objectives.

By the end of the fifth grade, children should
- Know the history, government, and geography of their home town/state
- Know why the American colonists declared independence from England
- Know the parts and principles of the U.S. Constitution
- Know the differences between the geographic regions of the United States
- Know how and why so many different ethnic groups have come to the United States
- Be able to distinguish between goods and services, and production and distribution
- Be able to develop different kinds of maps to represent the same physical space
- Be able to participate competently in deliberations of classroom and community policy controversies
- Be able to draw cause–effect conclusions based on evidence (historical thesis)
- Value liberty, equality, fairness, and the rule of law

TABLE 7–1 Short-essay scoring guide for elementary–middle school historical writing.

Development of Historical Ideas	Historical Accuracy	Organization and Communication
A "6" short essay Always stays on the historical topic. Uses many important historical facts and reasons to support ideas, and makes detailed conclusions. Shows understanding of the historical time period by • comparing and contrasting ideas, events, and people, or • showing cause and effect between events, or how past and present connect.	**A "6" short essay** Has no historical mistakes.	**A "6" short essay** Is very well organized. Has very clear beginning, middle, and end. Makes excellent sense. Responds to all parts of prompt.
A "5" short essay Same as a "6," but doesn't use as many important historical facts and reasons to support ideas.	**A "5" short essay** Has minor historical mistakes.	**A "5" short essay** Is well organized. Has clear beginning, middle, and end. Makes good sense. Responds to all parts of prompt.
A "4" short essay Mostly stays on the historical topic. Uses some important historical facts and reasons to support ideas, and makes conclusions. Shows some understanding of the historical time period and tries to: • compare and contrast ideas, events, or people, or • show cause and effect between events, or how past and present connect.	**A "4" short essay** May have a big historical mistake, but most information is correct.	**A "4" short essay** Is organized. Has beginning, middle, and end. Makes sense. Sometimes responds very well to part of prompt, and not very well to other part of the prompt.
A "3" short essay Sometimes stays on the historical topic. Shows some knowledge of the historical time period with a few facts and reasons. Makes a few connections between events or people. Describes an event but doesn't analyze it.	**A "3" short essay** Has some correct and some incorrect information about history.	**A "3" short essay** Does not have beginning, middle, and end. May respond only to parts of prompt. Makes some sense, but sometimes writing and grammar make it hard to read and understand.
A "2" short essay Often goes off the historical topic and describes events or people that are not correct for the prompt. Lists historical facts with little description.	**A "2" short essay** Has serious historical mistakes.	**A "2" short essay** Has very little organization. Doesn't make much sense, and often writing and grammar make it very hard to read and understand.
A "1" short essay Mentions historical topic with very few facts. Describes mostly events or people that are not correct for the prompt.	**A "1" short essay** Has very little knowledge of history and may have many serious mistakes.	**A "1" short essay** Doesn't make any sense.

Source: *Sampler of History—Social Science Assessment, Elementary* (1994), 31. Reprinted by permission of the California Department of Education, CDE Press, 1430 N. Street #3207, Sacramento, CA 95814.

- Routinely consider evidence rather than jump to conclusions
- Routinely respect cultural differences
- Routinely work cooperatively with other students in small-group work

Step 2. *Performances.* Determine how children might exhibit or demonstrate what they have learned. That is, what *evidence* could they give to show that they have learned and how could they show (exhibit, perform) it for all to see? Brainstorm performances with colleagues and ask your students for their ideas. Pianists usually have recitals, artists exhibit their work in galleries, athletes perform in tournaments. What about your students? Earlier, you learned about two kinds of performances, both using paper-and-pencil formats. Later, you will encounter others that do not rely on writing.

Step 3. *Criteria/performance standards.* Create a relevant scoring rubric. It should provide students, teachers, and parents with indicators, or actual descriptions, of the behaviors at different levels of mastery.

Step 4. *Share.* After creating the rubric, discuss it with students. Listen carefully to the questions they raise about these performance criteria and watch for confusion. Typically, teachers will learn enough from this experience to revise the rubric somewhat before trying it. Naturally, students will not understand these criteria very well, for they have not yet received instruction on them. The point is to provide students a reasonably clear idea of the target so they will be able to marshal their efforts accordingly.

Step 5. *Revise the rubric.* Explain the performance criteria and provide the instruction that should help children develop proficiency. Use what you learn to revise the rubric before using it again.

REFLECTION

It's obvious how a scoring guide helps teachers assess student learning. But how does it help students learn?

Checklists

Scoring guides come in all sizes and shapes. The simplest are checklists that specify how often a desired behavior (the learning target or objective) occurs. A 4-point scale might read: "Always," "Usually," "Rarely," "Never." Figures 7–10 and 7–11 present two checklists. The first lists behaviors called "consideration for others" that were given under the informal technique of observation. Using a checklist, teachers can assess each student periodically and record the observations directly on the checklist. This is much preferred to relying on memory. At conference time, checklists can be shared with parents.

Children also can be taught to assess their own behavior using the same 4-point scale. Figure 7–11 shows a self-assessment checklist that can be used during the unit (formatively) as well as at the end (summatively). Both formative and summative assessments can be gathered into students' portfolios.

Portfolios

The practice of saving samples of children's work in a portfolio has become increasingly popular in recent years. Begun with the literacy instruction in the late 1990s,[14] it rapidly expanded to all the subject areas and in some schools has become a major way to assess students' progress both through a single school year and across several years. This practice

FIGURE 7-10 Checklist: Consideration for others.

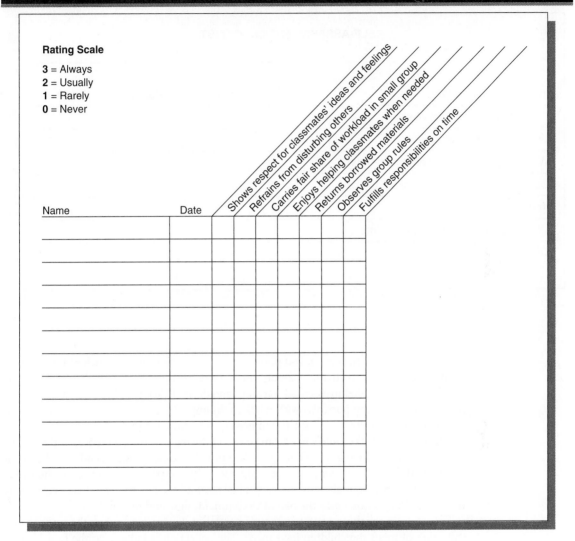

is similar to that of the parent who cuts notches on the inside of a closet door recording the height of a child at various ages. Both the parent and the teacher know that changes are occurring, but, because of their continuous, day-to-day contact with the child, changes are sometimes imperceptible. They need, therefore, a specific sample of the child's work at one point to compare with his or her work later.

Work samples saved for this purpose are usually written material and may include a biography, a story, a classroom test, an explanation, a booklet, and a conclusion drawn after a research project. The teacher will also want to save a child's map work, artwork done in

FIGURE 7–11   Checklist: Student self-assessment.

SELF-ASSESSMENT CHECKLIST

DATE _____   NAME _____

In this unit I was able to:	Always	Usually	Rarely	Never
Choose appropriate activities				
Use my work time efficiently				
Work cooperatively with another person				
Use materials from the Resource Center				
Keep my work area clean				
Use suggestions that others gave me				

Comments:

connection with social studies, and photos of a construction project, such as the museum exhibit the children created for parents' night. Care must be taken that the work samples saved are closely related to essential learnings and desired social studies outcomes. There is no need to clutter the portfolio with relatively unimportant work when so many learning outcomes are critically important and in need of continuous assessment.

The portfolio of the child's work can be useful during parent conferences at the regular reporting periods during the school year. Additionally, some teachers send samples of the child's work home from time to time simply to keep the parents informed of the child's progress in school. To make sure the parent has received the material, teachers may want to use a message sheet that asks the parent to comment, sign, and return.

This chapter concludes with two sample portfolios. Figure 7–12 shows the contents of a collection of maps the children have made. The collection is tailored to the fourth-grade mapping objective that Ms. Rivera was working with in the chapter-opening snapshot. Ms. Rivera's students, after much instruction and practice, eventually became proficient at creating three different kinds of maps, and six different places were mapped, ranging from the playground to the North American continent. The second collection (Figure 7–13) contains children's written responses to social studies literature. This collection displays students' ability to integrate literacy skills and social studies subject matter. Note the categories of responsive writing (paraphrasing, composing a new verse, interpreting) and the variety of social studies literature—from trade books and textbooks to songs. Other portfolios can capture students' sustained work over time on other important social studies objectives. A teacher who takes seriously the objective to teach children to do history rather than only absorb the history written or told by others (see Chapter 4, Figure 4–3) can begin this

FIGURE 7–12   A map portfolio.

Contents of My Map Portfolio		Name _____
Type of Map	**Place**	**Date/My Comments**
landform	our community	_____/_____
landform	North America	_____/_____
political	United States	_____/_____
political	counties in our state	_____/_____
shaded relief	playground	_____/_____
shaded relief	state	_____/_____

portfolio with the snapshot autobiographies his or her students composed at the beginning of the school year. Next might come their oral histories based on interviews with old-timers in the community, and then the oral histories conducted with students who have moved from one neighborhood, state, or nation to another. Next might come their first brief biography written about a U.S. president, followed by a more extensive cooperative biography

---

FIGURE 7-13 A response to literature portfolio.

**Contents of My Social Studies
Literature Response Portfolio**

_____
Name

Response Type	Selection (genre)	Date/My Comments
paraphrase	Paul Revere's ride (poem)	_____/_____
compose new verse	"Oh Freedom" (song)	_____/_____
memorize	"I Have a Dream" (speech)	_____/_____
book review	*Aekyung's Dream* (book)	_____/_____
explain	The Pledge of Allegiance (oath)	_____/_____
short story	climate of Sahara (textbook)	_____/_____

---

written with a team of classmates. In this way, a body of work is collected that displays, first, that historical reasoning is being attempted (itself an ambitious endeavor) and, second, that progress is being made.

Finally, the assessment glossary in Figure 7–14 should assist readers as they try to make sense of the specialized vocabulary that describes assessment procedures in social studies.

FIGURE 7-14 Assessment glossary.

Assessment
The process of gathering and interpreting information about students in order to plan instruction and evaluate achievement.

Authentic Assessment
Assessing students' ability to succeed in meaningful (goal-directed, "real-world") tasks. For example, observing students' participation in a discussion of a classroom problem or their use of reference books while drawing maps.

Criteria
The aspects of a performance task that are most important to its successful completion and are used by judges to evaluate the quality of the performance.

Curriculum (or Content) Standards
Statements that describe what students are supposed to learn; they specify the knowledge, skills, and values that students should learn.

Evaluation
The process of making judgments about the quality of a performance.

Formative Assessment
Assessment conducted during a unit of instruction for the purpose of improving student learning; providing feedback to students to help them improve their performance (see *Summative Assessment*).

Grade
A symbol (usually a letter, word, or number) that represents a student's level of achievement of one or more curriculum standards.

Objective
A statement that describes what students are expected to learn; in performance assessment, the behaviors they will learn to perform (see *Criteria*).

Performance Assessment
Assessing students' ability to translate knowledge into action—that is, to *demonstrate* their knowledge and skills.

Performance Standards
Levels of attainment that students must reach to receive particular grades, awards, or certificates. They are based on criteria and define what degree of mastery is "good enough."

Portfolio
A collection of a student's schoolwork that can be used to document achievement over time.

Reliability
The extent to which an assessment procedure will produce the same information about a student each time it is used.

(Continued)

FIGURE 7-14 Assessment glossary. (Continued)

Scoring Rubric
A rating scale that describes levels of attainment in relation to an assessment task. Used to score performances and to focus curriculum and instruction.

Summative Assessment
Assessment conducted at the end of a unit of instruction for the purpose of determining a grade (see *Formative Assessment*).

Task
An *authentic* assessment activity within which a student is asked to demonstrate his or her knowledge and skills.

Validity
The extent to which an assessment procedure measures what it claims to measure and is appropriate for making decisions.

Conclusion

Assessment simply means *finding out* what students know and can do. It goes on continually in the classroom and is a natural part of the learning environment. Sometimes it is used to place children in this or that group (in the "gifted" class or a "special education" program, in this or that reading group, in this or that college). And sometimes it is used to compare schools, school districts, states, and nations. *But the overarching purpose for classroom teachers and students is to improve teaching and learning.*

Like all of teaching, assessment is a principled activity: One has to know what one is doing and for what purposes. Then the various methods can be implemented wisely. Ms. Rivera used a paper-and-pencil test and informal questioning. She conducted a group interview and watched while students sketched a map of the United States—all this to find out what they already knew about maps and map reading. This is diagnostic assessment, and its purpose is to help the teacher plan instruction: what *this* group of children needs *now*. There are other purposes and other methods, including performance assessment and the development of scoring guides. The popularity of performance criteria and scoring guides ("rubrics") in the past 10 years has helped countless teachers and students clarify the targets of learning—helping everyone know exactly what target they are aiming at. Portfolios in social studies have been of tremendous help, too. They can be used to encourage students to develop a body of map work, a body of literature, a body of historical interpretation, a body of persuasive writing to legislators and newspaper editors, and so forth, making these efforts not mere hit-or-miss occasions, but sustained, continuous work at objectives worth achieving.

Fortunately, teachers teach for more than one school year! This means that the assessments they develop in one year can be revised and used again the following year. In this way, teachers, too, develop a body of work consisting of well-honed assessments, scoring guides, teaching strategies, and resources. This teacher portfolio represents the development of expertise over time.

Discussion Questions and Suggested Activities

Go to MyEducationLab and select the topic "Assessment," then analyze the artifact "Dear Queen Isabella" and complete the activity.

1. Look back at the five steps for creating a scoring guide and your response to the question in the *Reflection* sidebar. Another way to ask that question is this: How does "backward design" (assessment principle 4) help students learn? Discuss the matter with classmates, and please be candid (e.g., if you do not think it helps students learn, say so and explain why). For additional examples of rubrics, visit these two websites: (a) Several of Washington state's classroom-based assessments for the fifth grade are available online at www.k12.wa.us/assessment/WASL/socialstudies/. There are assessments for history, geography, civics, and economics, and each has a field-tested rubric. (b) As you will learn in Chapter 10, WebQuests are inquiry-oriented Internet searches. The sample WebQuests posted at this website (www.webquest.org) typically feature fully developed scoring rubrics.

2. Examine the portfolio examples featured in Figures 7–12 (maps), 7–13 (responses to literature), and 4–3 (doing history). Then sketch a fourth example that targets a social studies learning you care a great deal about.

3. Item construction: (a) Construct two multiple-choice-with-justification items similar to the ones given in Figure 7–8. Focus the first item on an important *event* in American history; focus the second on an important *concept*. (b) Then, construct a related short-essay item with the same four attributes as those in the item in Figure 7–9.

4. NCSS Standards *Sampler*. Examine the 4th-grade classroom vignette for standard #2 on p. 9 of the standards *Sampler* that accompanies this book. What sort of assessment does it include? What sort of *formative* assessments could the teacher add?

Selected References

Popham, W. James. (2002). *Classroom assessment: What teachers need to know*. Boston: Allyn & Bacon.

Sleeter, Christine E. (Ed.). (2007). *Facing accountability in education: Democracy and equity at risk*. New York: Teachers College Press.

Social Education. (1999, October). Guest editor Pat Nickell created a wonderful issue of the journal called "Authentic Assessment in Social Studies."

Taylor, Catherine S., & Nolen, Susan B. (2008). *Classroom assessment: Supporting teaching and learning in real classrooms* (2nd ed.). New York: Prentice Hall.

Wiggins, Grant, & McTighe, Jay. (2005). *Understanding by design* (2nd ed.). Alexandria, VA: Association for Supervision and Curriculum Development.

MyEducationLab is a collection of online tools for your success in this course, your licensure exams, and your teaching career. Go to www.myeducationlab.com to utilize these extensive resources including videos from real classrooms, Praxis and licensure preparation, a lesson plan builder, and materials to help you begin your teaching career.

Planning Units, Lessons, and Activities

CHAPTER EIGHT

Chapter Outline

- Teachers' Knowledge and Goals
- Planning the Unit
- Teaching the Unit
- Planning Lessons Within Units
- Five Ways to Enrich Any Unit
- Conclusion

Key Concepts

- Unit
- Lesson
- Teaching/learning objective
- Learning activity
- Dramatic play
- Higher-order thinking
- Construction activity
- Simulation activity

MAIN IDEA

Unit planning is the heart of social studies instruction. Within units are lessons and activities, which require planning, too, and are always aimed at the unit's objectives and assessments. Social studies units typically are integrated (interdisciplinary) because they incorporate two or three of the social sciences (e.g., history and geography) and provide a content focus for the development of reading and writing skills.

PICTURE THIS

For a manufacturing simulation in the unit "Jobs in Our Community," the second-graders decided to make envelopes. Mr. Allison wanted the activity to deepen the children's understanding of the concept division of labor. One half of the class became assembly-line workers, the other half became custom workers. When all the preparations were completed, Mr. Allison gave the signal to start. Both groups began making envelopes. The assembly-line workers divided the labor, each student doing just one task. The custom workers each did everything. In 30 minutes, Mr. Allison stopped production. Students were asked to think about both the process and the results, and then to draw conclusions. To test their conclusions, they repeated the process and interviewed both sets of workers.

Dear Dr. Hahn:

This is a fan letter. We think Mr. Allison is the best thing that ever happened to Lori. He was clearly the most creative, imaginative, and effective teacher she had during the seven years she attended your school. He always had the most unusual things going on in that room that would so hook the kids that they spent hours of unsupervised study on what they were doing. Schoolwork seemed to be a sheer delight, strange as that may seem. They simulated law and justice procedures (Lori was a juror twice); they made butter churns and other pre-electricity technology and collected water in rain barrels; they went on a field trip to watch immigrants become citizens; there were art, music, and dramatic activities galore. Once they constructed a whole set of models of Native American villages from different regions of the country. This involved the children in an incredible amount of research. And there were always inquiries ("history mysteries," he called them)—tremendous interest grabbers. Children had to be told to go home after school. If not, they would stay until dinnertime working on that butter churn.

And through all this he taught reading and writing. In our other daughter's classrooms, reading and writing lessons were for some strange reason separated from social studies lessons; with Mr. Allison, however, Lori developed her reading skills by reading history, maps, plays, encyclopedias, folk songs, and speeches.

When we asked him how he did it, he looked sideways as though telling a secret. "Planning," was his reply. "Planning." We would have said it was charm or charisma or that he was a natural born teacher. But he set us straight. Please extend our thanks to him (again) for all the time he spent "planning."

Sincerely,

Joe and Erna Montoya

How do teachers like Mr. Allison develop stimulating programs of study for students in social studies? Planning.

Such planning comes partly from a knowledgeable teacher who is able to select powerful social studies unit topics that also will require the development of children's literacy skills. Social studies units, when planned well, are almost always integrated or interdisciplinary units because, first, social studies learning almost always requires reading and writing. Children need to be taught to read maps, expository text material, primary documents, newspapers, reference books, and so forth. Second, social studies itself is already an integrated school subject. Social studies integrates history and the social science disciplines and, at times, the humanities. Third, many social studies units are animated by the same way of knowing what animates the science curriculum: inquiry (i.e., the scientific method of problem solving). When a unit centers on inquiry, the children are immersed in a problem or event (e.g., Why did the *Titanic* tragedy occur? Where did all the buffalo go? Are the poles melting? How much is the Disney Pocahontas like the real Pocahontas?). Then they formulate and test hypotheses, sift through evidence, and, finally, draw conclusions. We take a close look at inquiry teaching in the next chapter, taking the *Titanic* tragedy as one example.

Such planning also comes from an attentive and imaginative teacher who is able to listen, watch, and respond to children—to capitalize on their interests, curiosity, and home cultures. The teacher selects the topics of learning from the curriculum guide in combination with his or her own priorities, knowledge, and creativity and then encourages the children to raise questions and suggest activities. In this way the child, teacher, and curriculum meet.[1] Unit planning, then, is a social process (you, your colleagues, the curriculum supervisors, your students, and sometimes their parents). Also, unit planning involves the writing process. A unit is not planned in a single draft any more than a story or report is written in one draft. Revision is involved, and the unit is "published" when it is finally implemented. After it is implemented, it is revised again before being implemented again the following year.

In this chapter, we turn our attention to planning social studies units, lessons, and activities. You will frequently be referred to prior and subsequent chapters in this text. This can be annoying, but it is unavoidable because social studies unit planning builds on all your knowledge of children, social studies, and teaching.

Social studies planning asks teachers to be four planners at once: a curriculum planner, an assessment planner, an activity planner, and a resource planner. The curriculum planner asks, "Which social studies subject matter is essential? That is, what do I want my students to know and be able to do?" The assessment planner asks, "What evidence would indicate whether the essentials have been learned, and how good is 'good enough'?" The activity planner asks, "What activities will engage my students' interest—both physically (hands-on) and intellectually (minds-on)—for a sustained period of time?" The resource planner asks, "What resources do I need and what resources do my students need? Where are they and how do I get them?" Figure 8–1 depicts these as four terms in an equation that adds up to social studies unit planning.

Teachers are not free to teach any topic they choose; rather, in most instances, the school district will supply a curriculum guide, district and state assessment expectations, a textbook for each student, some additional instructional resources, and a resource person such as a social studies curriculum coordinator or, more generally, a curriculum director. It is typical to find some subject matter required by the curriculum guide, some optional, and some to be chosen by the teacher. Subject matter chosen by the teacher is often within a general topical area that is required by the curriculum guide. The guide may read,

FIGURE 8–1   Being four planners at once.

Curriculum Planner	+ Assessment Planner	+ Activity Planner	+ Resource Planner	= UNIT PLANNER
What social studies knowledge, skills, attitudes, and values are essential?	What evidence will assure us that the essentials have been learned?	What activities will engage my students, both hands-on and minds-on, for a sustained period of time?	What resources do I need, what resources will students need, where are they, and how do I get them?	Choosing and organizing subject matter, planning lessons and assessments, designing related activities, and securing resources.

Grade 5 Social Studies

One-year study of American history from pre-Columbian times through the U.S. Civil War. The year will conclude with a unit on either "Canada: Our Northern Neighbor" or "Mexico: Our Southern Neighbor."

Individual teachers or teams of teachers then select and organize subject matter within the general topical area. We will walk through examples later in this chapter.

TEACHERS' KNOWLEDGE AND GOALS

Let us be careful not to skirt the importance of the teacher's own knowledge and professional goals. Clearly, elementary school teachers need to develop their own subject matter understanding so that they are capable of teaching to the broad curriculum goals of the elementary school—history, geography, economics, law and government (civics), and the other social sciences: psychology, sociology, and anthropology. And that's just the social studies curriculum! Good teachers are learners themselves.

Teachers who continue to develop their knowledge are better able to plan and teach lively and challenging units. The deeper a teacher's knowledge of the American Revolution, for example, the better the chance he or she knows about the revolutionary committees of correspondence of the 1770s, which used letters to unite colonists in taking action against England; the better he or she can orchestrate teams of students to role-play these committees, write biographies of key revolutionaries, such as Jefferson and Washington, and read the letters and pamphlets of Patrick Henry and Abigail Adams; the better he or she can introduce children to reading and writing their own historical narratives of key events, for example, of Paul Revere's ride, remembered years later by Longfellow:

> Listen, my children, and you shall hear
>
> Of the midnight ride of Paul Revere,
>
> On the eighteenth of April in Seventy-five;
>
> Hardly a man is now alive
>
> Who remembers that famous day and year ...

In other words, teachers' knowledge of subject matter matters.[2] And, the knowledge required to plan and teach a particular unit is daunting:

- General knowledge of history, the social sciences, and the humanities
- Particular knowledge of the topic that will be planned and taught
- Knowledge of the school's and/or school district's curriculum expectations
- Knowledge of assessment and the school's assessment policies
- Knowledge of the children—development, home language, ethnicity and culture, gifts and talents, learning disabilities, hobbies, sensitivities
- Knowledge of teaching strategies—from knowing how to make difficult concepts intelligible to children, to knowing how to conduct an inquiry lesson or

skill-development lesson, or how to help students write original biographies of key historical figures

- Knowledge of resources for the teacher's own study as well as for instruction
- Knowledge of good rules of thumb for planning any social studies unit

Rest assured, no human can possibly possess all this knowledge in relation to every curriculum topic; therefore, knowledge of *resources* stands out as the most important of all. While career-long learning is an inescapable fact of teaching, and one of its most central joys, knowledge of resources helps fill the gap between what we *should* know and what we *do* know now. (See Chapter 10, "Four Great Resources.")

Goals. But teachers' goals are just as important as their knowledge and know-how. No amount of knowledge will change what a teacher does with students if his or her goals don't match. Numerous studies show that, compared to their goals, what teachers know has less impact on what they actually do in the classroom. For example, good history teaching is not simply weaving the facts into a good story. Teaching history requires that students be engaged in *doing* history: gathering evidence from competing sources and producing original interpretations based on evidence. If a teacher's goal is to "tell a good story" of the American Revolution, then no amount of knowledge of competing accounts or of how to help students puzzle through these accounts and produce their own, based on evidence, will suffice. Rather, the teacher's goal needs to change—from covering content and telling good stories to teaching students to *do* history.[3]

 # PLANNING THE UNIT

The unit plan is a long-range instructional plan that covers a period of three to eight weeks, during which the class studies some broad topic on an ongoing basis. The unit plan is a way of organizing resources, lessons, activities, and assessments for such an extended study. How units are planned, taught, and assessed varies greatly from one teacher to another. "The art of teaching . . . consists precisely in resisting formulas," writes Howard Gardner.[4] Still, rules of thumb are needed. What follows is a description of the essential components for planning a comprehensive unit, boiled down to three:

1. Study the curriculum guide and talk about it with colleagues
2. Frame learning objectives (determine desired results of study)
3. Determine assessments

Study the Curriculum Guide and Talk About It with Colleagues

Begin by studying the school or school district curriculum guide for social studies. And talk with others about it to compare your interpretation to theirs. This will help you get the lay of the land, the big picture, and give you the background knowledge you need to frame the unit's objectives. In the curriculum guide, you will probably find a grade-level social studies topic along with unit topics or themes. Recall that typical unit topics for each grade were given in Chapter 1. This chapter will provide a preview of what you will find in social studies curriculum guides, show how they differ in specificity and approach, and use them to frame learning objectives.

| EXAMPLE 1 | GRADE 3, COMMUNITIES NEAR AND FAR, NOW AND THEN |

Looking back at Chapter 1, we see that for grade 3 the grade-level topic is likely to be "Communities Near and Far, Now and Then." This suggests a *comparative* study of the communities where people live, integrating both geography ("near and far") and history ("now and then"). We might find six units, lasting roughly five weeks each, with titles like these:

Rural and Urban Communities   Community Workers
Oldest and Newest Communities   Our City's Government
Washington, D.C.: Our Capital   Beijing: China's Capital

A teacher employed by the school district located next door to this one may find that its curriculum guide gives the same grade-level topic, but rather than unit titles, gives curricular themes. Note that these themes are drawn from the curriculum standards from the National Council for the Social Studies (NCSS). (See the standards *Sampler* that accompanies this textbook.) Each theme in this district is followed with focus questions that suggest more specifically what the children should study. Note that the comparative study of communities centers on the children's own community and two of its sister cities in other countries:

Culture. How do the customs and beliefs of people living in our community differ from those of the people living in our sister cities in Japan and Kenya?

Time, Continuity, and Change (History). What were the turning points in our community's history and in the history of our sister cities in Japan and Kenya?

People, Places, and Environments (Geography). Why is our community located where it is, and why are our sister cities located where they are?

| EXAMPLE 2 | GRADE 5, AMERICAN HISTORY |

Let us turn to another grade and again compare a topical curriculum guide to a thematic one. For grade 5, where the general topic is American history, we might find 10 unit topics arranged chronologically with a suggested time frame of 3 weeks each:

The American Land   Creating a New Nation
The Native Americans   The Civil War
European–American Encounters   Westward Expansion
The American Colonies and Slavery   The Industrial Revolution
War for Independence   The Civil Rights Movement

In the school district next door we may find the same general grade-level topic, American history, but this time with themes instead of unit-by-unit topics. This district specifies four of the NCSS themes:

1. *Culture.* What cultures have lived on the American land and how are they alike and different? When has there been cooperation among them? When has there been conflict?

2. *Time, Continuity, and Change.* What were the turning points in American history? Why are they "turning points"?
3. *People, Places, and Environments.* What are the major regions of the United States and in what ways are they different from each other?
4. *Civic Ideals and Practice.* Who was eligible to vote at the time the Constitution was ratified? Who won the right to vote later; when and how?

| EXAMPLE 3 | GRADE 6, WESTERN HEMISPHERE |

For our final example, we narrow in on a particular unit. We will consider a sixth-grade end-of-the-year unit on Canada. In school district *X*, the curriculum guide is short and sweet:

District X. Grade 6: Western Hemisphere, Unit 10: Canada. This unit should provide children with a thorough understanding of the geography of Canada.

On the one hand, this is not very helpful to the teacher who must flesh out a unit with hardly any guidance on the details; on the other, the teacher is left with lots of freedom to flesh out the unit as he or she sees fit. The one-sentence description focuses on geography (as opposed to, say, the history and government of Canada), and then leaves it to the teacher to select and organize subject matter within this broad topic.

I believe this teacher would be wise to go directly to the five themes of geography (see Chapter 4). Recall that these five themes were identified by a committee of educators and professional geographers. They have helped legions of elementary and middle school teachers and children achieve, as the district *X* guide states, "a thorough understanding" of the geographic characteristics of places around the globe. The themes, again, are Movement (migration and transportation), Regions, Human–Environment Interaction, Location, and Place (MR. HELP).

Meanwhile, in school district *Y* the curriculum guide also calls for a unit on Canada to culminate the sixth-grade social studies curriculum. District *Y*'s curriculum guide provides more detail, however, and calls for a comprehensive study—not only the geography of Canada, but its history, culture, government, and economy, too.

District Y. Grade 6: Western Hemisphere, Unit 10: Canada. This unit should provide students with a comprehensive view of Canada as it is today. The study is to be interdisciplinary with an emphasis on contemporary life and social problems. The unit should treat Canada as a whole rather than focus on a particular small sample of Canadian life and culture. Whereas the similarities between the United States and Canada should be studied (both modern, both culturally diverse, both regionally diverse, both capitalistic, both democratic, both with many natural resources), it is important to present Canada as a unique nation among nations and a close friend of the United States.

The central ideas that should emerge from the study of Canada are:

1. *Culture.* Maintaining an ethnic identity is important to most members of any cultural group. (NCSS theme 1)
2. *History.* Turning points in the early history of a country often help to explain its current problems and way of life. (NCSS theme 2)
3. *Geography.* The physical features of an area influence human settlement patterns and transportation. (NCSS theme 3)
4. *Economy.* The use of available resources depends on the nature of the economic system, the values of the people, and their level of technological development. (NCSS theme 7)

5. *Government.* Democracies come in all shapes and sizes (some even have monarchs), but they share important attributes that make them all democracies. (NCSS theme 6)
6. *Civic Participation.* In democracies the people themselves must take responsibility for the common good. (NCSS theme 10)

How does the teacher select subject matter about Canada that will accord with the comprehensive study suggested by this curriculum guide? Just one of the six central ideas in district *Y*'s unit refers to the entire focus of the district *X* unit. To select subject matter for such a broadly focused unit, the teacher, as before, needs to do some research and talk with colleagues. This work needs to span the social sciences and the closely related NCSS curriculum themes. Help is available! The NCSS themes can be studied online, and there are numerous teaching resources linked to each theme. And, don't forget the *Sampler* of these NCSS themes that accompanies this book. Also, each of the social sciences was introduced in Chapter 4, and the history, civics, economics, and geography curriculum standards, with linked resources, can be found online. Much material will be found on Canada in the school and public library, the children's sixth-grade textbook, and online.

The long-term advantage of preparing a comprehensive unit of this sort on Canada is that much of the study and preparation a teacher does for Canada will transfer to planning integrated units on China, Egypt, Russia, Kenya—all other countries. For example, the six themes listed by district *Y* are the same ones that guide students' teamwork in Lesson Plan 9, "A Nation in the News," found in Chapter 6 of this book: culture, history, geography, economy, government, and civic ideals. When a curriculum guide requires teaching and learning about a *place*, whether a country or a community, these are six powerful doorways.

Frame Learning Objectives (Determine Desired Results of Study)

The curriculum guide may or may not state the learning objectives for your unit. As we have seen, school and school district curriculum guidelines may not be written as objectives, but as topics or themes or questions. Or they may be written as objectives but are too broad or too narrow in scope to serve as a reasonable and measurable target for teaching and learning. Or, you may wish to add a particular emphasis. At any rate, most likely you will have to write or modify some of the unit objectives yourself.

Just what are learning objectives? They are statements of ends, not means. They are the desired results of study, the targets. They make clear what students are supposed to learn—what they should know and be able to do as a consequence of the unit of study. (As we saw in Chapter 1, they are also called curriculum standards.) Well-stated learning objectives enable both teachers and learners to see more clearly the purposes of teaching and learning. Insufficient thoughtfulness about objectives is likely to lead to students being involved in activities that have no clear purpose or that have purposes that are not sufficiently worthy of their time and energy. Poor objectives also can undermine assessment of student progress because the teacher and students are not clear about *what* is being assessed or because the objectives are not framed in terms that are measurable. Accordingly, teachers should plan the objectives first, then the assessments. That is, decide on the desired results of instruction, then determine what evidence you'll need to observe in students' work to indicate that the objective has been achieved.

Learning *objectives* are narrower and more focused than learning *goals*. The two overarching goals of social studies instruction, which you may recall from Chapter 1, are social understanding and civic efficacy. Social understanding is knowledge of human beings' social worlds drawn from history, geography, the other social sciences, and the humanities.

Civic efficacy is the readiness and willingness to assume citizenship responsibilities and the belief that one can make a difference. Learning goals cannot be achieved over the course of just one or even several units. Rather, they define what we want students to learn over one or more *years* of schooling. Teachers need to know the goals and keep them in mind because learning objectives should be aligned with them.

Writing Objectives

Looking back at the unit guidelines on Canada, we see that neither district *X* nor district *Y* provides learning objectives that can serve as a solid and measurable target of instruction. District *Y*'s six central ideas are headed in the right direction, but they are too broad: they could apply to any country. And, they are not readily measurable.

Suppose that a teacher takes district *Y*'s central ideas and specifies them for a unit on Canada. He puts them in column 1 of a planning chart and in column 2 lists the specific concepts that students will need to understand if they are to draw these conclusions themselves, as shown in Table 8–1. Each of the main ideas in the chart can serve as a learning objective simply by adding the phrase "Students will learn that...." Accordingly, for the first idea: "Students will learn that Canada is a multiethnic country with three predominant language groups (First

TABLE 8–1	Planning chart for a unit on Canada: Main ideas and concepts.
Main Ideas	**Concepts**
Culture. Canada is a multiethnic country with three predominant language groups (First Nations, English, French) and many religions.	Ethnic group Language group Religious diversity
History. Canada was originally a land of diverse native peoples. With immigration and conquest, it became a colony in the British Empire and later a constitutional democracy.	Natives and immigrants Colonization Constitutional democracy
Geography. Canada is a huge country with a unique northern location and diverse regions and landforms that have influenced settlement patterns and transportation.	Location (absolute, relative) Region Landforms (bay, archipelago) Settlements Transportation Urbanization
Economy. Canada is a wealthy, highly industrialized, technologically advanced country with a market economy.	Capitalist economy Rich/poor nations Industrialization
Government. Canada is a democratic nation with an elected parliament, a queen, and a federal system of government.	Constitutional monarchy Parliamentary system Federalism
Civic Participation. Citizens in Canada must cooperate to decide what to do about numerous controversial public issues.	Civic cooperation Decision making Controversial public issue

Nations, English, French) and many religions." Each of the concepts can serve as a learning objective too, simply by adding a phrase such as "Students will develop and apply the concept. . . ." For the first concept in the list: "Students will develop and apply the concept *ethnic group*."

Skills. But what about skills, attitudes, and values? Three kinds of skills need to be taught in the social studies curriculum if its two broad goals are to be achieved. Recall from Chapter 1 that these are the skills of democratic participation, the skills of study and inquiry, and intellectual skills (higher-order thinking). Here are two objectives for each of the three kinds of social studies skills:

Democratic participation skills

- Students will learn how to deliberate controversial public issues with others, whether or not they are friends.
- Students will learn how to locate the names and addresses of elected officials and newspapers for the purpose of mailing persuasive letters.

Study and inquiry skills

- Students will learn how to find and interpret information on maps and globes.
- Students will learn how to find and interpret primary and secondary sources that are relevant to their research questions.

Intellectual skills (Higher-order thinking)

- Students will learn how to test hypotheses and draw conclusions based on evidence.
- Students will learn how to apply concepts through classifying.

Note that when writing a learning objective that is focused on a skill, the opening phrase shifts from "Students will learn *that*" to "students will learn *how to*. . . ."[5] Of course, the phrases that begin an objective can vary. "Students will learn *that*" and "Students will learn *how to*" are default phrases for knowledge and skill objectives, but different language certainly can be used. Looking at the Lesson Plan samples in this book, readers will find an interesting variety of phrases. Consider the following:

Students will . . .

- "form an initial concept of what historians call *primary* and *secondary sources* and learn how to interpret conflicting primary sources." (Lesson Plan 4 in Chapter 4)
- "develop an initial sense that they live on Earth, and that Earth is moving." (Lesson Plan 6 in Chapter 5)
- "develop some familiarity with concepts relating to the globe. They will begin to gain an appreciation for, and a desire to care for, Earth." (Lesson Plan 7 in Chapter 5)
- "learn how to formulate hypotheses and then revise them as new information is encountered and how to draw conclusions based on evidence." (Lesson Plan 12 in Chapter 9)
- "learn how to use a newspaper's directory and then apply the skill to finding information in several different newspapers." (Lesson Plan 13 in Chapter 9)
- "learn how to use high-quality websites to locate themselves on the planet where they live and on the continent, nation, state, county, neighborhood, and so on, right down to their street address." (Lesson Plan 16 in Chapter 10)

- "understand that (a) descriptions of events depend to some extent on who is describing them and (b) people can interpret events differently depending, in part, on their social positions (e.g., race, gender, class)." (Lesson Plan 19 in Chapter 12)

Virtues.   As for attitudes and values, recall that six democratic virtues were outlined in Chapter 3. Virtues are dispositions. They summarize a person's attitudes and values. Individual responsibility, for example, is the habit of fulfilling one's obligations to family, friends, teachers, and others in one's community, nation, and world. Civility is the habit of treating other persons courteously and respectfully, regardless of whether one likes them, agrees with their viewpoints, or shares their culture. Every unit you teach may feature these virtues as objectives. Since virtues are shown or displayed in our behavior, the opening phrase shifts from "Students will learn that" in the case of content objectives and "Students will learn how to" in the case of skill objectives to "Students will routinely" followed by the targeted virtue. For example:

Democratic virtues

- Students will routinely take responsibility for sharing the workload fairly in small-group work.
- Students will routinely treat other students and adults courteously and respectfully.

Concluding Advice: Priorities, Targets, and Scope

This section on framing learning objectives concludes with three general pieces of advice gleaned from many years of teaching and working with beginning and experienced teachers. First, it is easy to become distracted with the form of objectives at the expense of their content. But what really matters about objectives is that they focus on worthy learning. From the universe of possibilities, to which objectives should we devote our units and spend time teaching and assessing? The school or school district curriculum guide should help; however, these documents are often written by committees whose members include every topic under the sun. Talk with colleagues to find out how they are sorting through the guidelines. Find out what the district and state assessments are emphasizing, and cultivate your own wisdom to know what matters most.

Second, remember that objectives should not describe learning activities (means), but the purposes (ends) of having children engage in activities. For example, the following are not appropriate instructional objectives because they simply describe activities that will be done by the children presumably to learn something that remains undefined:

The children will view a film.

The class will create a newspaper.

Students will work in teams of three or more.

Teams will make progress reports.

The children will draw a map of the playground.

Children will construct a model of a harbor.

Children will role-play workers in a factory.

Third, aim to write objectives that are neither too small nor too great in scope. An objective's scope is the amount of subject matter (content, skills, attitudes and values) it includes. Experienced classroom teachers know that there are hundreds of objectives that their students need to achieve and that it is simply impossible to keep track of whether their students are achieving all of them. One assessment specialist, James Popham, put it succinctly: "If you are preparing to be a classroom teacher, you'll soon discover that dozens and dozens of instructional objectives will overwhelm you."[6]

What to do? Because you want learning objectives to help your teaching rather than hinder it, strive to frame them broadly enough that they will organize and direct a sizable chunk of teaching and learning while making sure they are still measurable (assessable). Recall principle 1 from Chapter 7: Assessment is an integral part of curriculum and instruction, not an afterthought. It must be woven into the fabric of curriculum and instruction. This means that instructional objectives should always be framed with assessment in mind, and vice versa. *The broader the objective is, while still measurable, the more useful it will be to you because you can be guided by a realistic and manageable set of targets.* According to Popham, "If you can conceptualize your instructional objectives so that one, broad, measurable objective subsumes a scad of lesser, smaller-scope objectives, you'll have an objective that will guide your instruction more effectively and, at the same time, that will be a big help in deciding what to assess."[7]

To add some flesh to this third rule of thumb, let us consider the Canada unit the teacher in district *Y* was developing (Table 8–1). Recall that the teacher developed six content objectives first by applying the district's guidelines to Canada specifically, then by adding "Students will learn that" to the front of each of them. He also specified several concepts that needed to be learned for each of these objectives, for a total of 27 content objectives for the unit (6 main ideas plus 21 related concepts). Ask yourself, could you keep track of these? Remember that we haven't yet gotten to skill and attitude objectives!

You might also imagine all the still-smaller-in-scope objectives that could be framed. For example, related to the first main-idea objective:

- Students will learn the relative population size of each of the native and nonnative ethnic groups currently living in Canada.
- Students will learn why there are three major language groups (English, French, Native) currently used in Canada.
- Students will learn the customs and beliefs of the religious faiths practiced by Canadians.

Would this be going too far? Yes! Such a list could go on indefinitely and, therefore, would be *unmanageable*.

Moving toward an objective that is broader in scope, but still measurable, we could try this one:

> After studying a country in an age-appropriate way, students will be able to compose a two-part report, in any medium, that (a) summarizes the country's ethnic groups, historical turning points, geographic regions, economy, government, and civic ideals, and (b) presents the student's personal reaction to the idea of living, playing, and working in that country.

This objective is measurable in a number of ways, but it is so broad as to incorporate any country, students of any age, and reporting in any medium—writing, drawing, speaking, music. It may be appropriate for a world geography course, a Western Hemisphere course, or an Eastern Hemisphere course. An additional objective, equally broad in scope, could focus on skills:

> Students will know how to research the various dimensions of a country (ethnic groups, historical turning points, geography, economy, government, ideals), effectively summarize the results of such research, and present personal reactions to the idea of living, playing, and working in that country.

We will revisit the teacher who is planning such a unit below. Meanwhile, what is your own reaction to these two broad, yet measurable, objectives? Are these important learnings? (Is there something more essential?) Second, do these objectives focus on ends or on means? And third, what of their scope? Are they usefully broad yet still measurable? Will they help or hinder your instruction?

Determine Assessments

Ms. Rivera, whom you met at the beginning of the prior chapter, used a paper-and-pencil test and informal questioning, conducted a group interview, and watched while students sketched a map of the United States to find out what they already knew about maps and map reading. Perhaps you will do something quite similar when assessing what your students already know about a targeted learning (*diagnosis*) and then, as the unit goes along, their emerging conceptions and misconceptions (*formative assessment*). As the unit is brought to a close, you will *summatively* find out what they have learned in the unit in relation to the unit objectives.

In the sixth-grade Canada unit, the teacher may very well begin just as did Ms. Rivera, that is, with the geographic dimension of Canada (as opposed to its culture or history) and, accordingly, with a diagnostic assessment of students' ability to read a map of Canada. (See Ms. Rivera's in Figure 7–1.) Can students find north? Can they distinguish a bay from a peninsula, a railroad from a river? The teacher uses classifying questions to find out. He observes whether they pay attention to the compass rose and the lines of latitude and longitude. He tells them that the city of Vancouver is a beautiful port community on the west coast of Canada in the province called British Columbia. He asks if anyone can describe Vancouver's relative location—relative to the rest of Canada; relative to the North and South Poles; relative to the students' hometown. Have any of the students lived there or visited? Can anyone describe its absolute location using degrees of longitude and latitude? Does anyone know the predominant language spoken in Vancouver? The predominant means of transportation? Moving to research skills, do they know how and where to find resources that will give information such as the size of Canada's population and demographic data such as ethnic groups, religions, languages, average life span, per capita income, and type of government?

During this questioning, a student brings up the subject of greenhouse gases and asks, "Is it true that Canada is mostly ice and is melting?" This piques the interest of the class, and the teacher writes on the chalkboard: "Canada: greenhouse gases and climate change. Melting?" "What are greenhouse gases?" he then asks. And later, "What else would you like to know about Canada?" In this way, the diagnostic assessment not only reveals students' prior knowledge and misconceptions about Canada, but what they want to learn more about.

Following this diagnostic phase, the teacher realizes that the geography of Canada, and especially its climate, really interests his students. They are fascinated by its diverse regions, and at least some of them worry about the effects of global warming. From Table 8–1, he takes the earlier geography main idea and refines it into the following objective:

> Students will learn that Canada is a huge country with a unique northern location and diverse regions and landforms. And they will draw conclusions, based on evidence, about the ways human activity is changing greenhouse gases and, consequently, changing the climate of Canada (i.e., global warming).

The teacher decides that the assessment of greatest importance will be to determine whether and how well students can draw these conclusions, taking care to use evidence skillfully and not to generalize across Canada's geographic regions.

Before turning to learning activities and instructional methods, the teacher plans a performance assessment and identifies performance criteria. The assessment will be written, he decides; it will be an inquiry essay. He pulls the cause–effect essay item (see Figure 7–9 in the preceding chapter) and the short-essay scoring guide (Table 7–1) from his files. These are close to what he needs, but not quite right for the objective. So, he develops a different essay item (see Figure 8–2). At the top, he writes the objective, then gives directions and a few "be sure to" reminders.

To further clarify the target, the teacher develops a 3-point scale. A 5- or 6-point scale might provide more helpful performance criteria, but this is the first time he has developed this particular assessment, and he decides that a 3-point rubric will suffice. After he has tested it with his students, the teacher will revise it as needed.

3   **Outstanding inquiry essay.**

- Follows the directions given.
- Always stays on topic.
- Convinces the reader that the conclusion drawn is the best supported by available evidence.
- Convinces the reader that the contrary evidence is not as reliable or as true as the evidence on which the conclusion is based.

FIGURE 8–2   Inquiry essay.

IS GLOBAL WARMING CHANGING CANADA'S CLIMATE?

Objective: Students will learn that Canada is a huge country with a unique northern location and diverse regions and landforms. They will draw conclusions, based on evidence, about the ways human activity in Canada is changing greenhouse gases and, consequently, changing the climate of Canada (i.e., global warming).

Essay question: Is global warming changing Canada's climate?

Directions: Write a four-to-five-paragraph essay that gives the conclusion you have drawn from your inquiry on the question and supports it with evidence.
- Begin the essay by telling readers your conclusion and introducing the essay.
- Next, tell us which evidence most persuaded you to draw this conclusion.
- Next, tell us the best evidence you've found *against* this conclusion.
- Finally, tell readers why your conclusion is strong even though not all evidence supports it.

Be sure to:
1. Describe the evidence clearly.
2. Explain how the evidence supports your conclusion.
3. Remember your audience; help them follow your reasoning.

2   **Good enough inquiry essay.**

- Follows the directions given.
- Stays on topic most of the time.
- Convinces the reader that the conclusion drawn is the best supported by available evidence.

1   **Poor inquiry essay.**

- Does not follow the directions given or not enough.
- Leaves topic or topic is unclear.
- Does not convince the reader that the conclusion drawn is the best supported by available evidence.

0   **No inquiry essay.**

As he thinks ahead to teaching the unit, this teacher decides he will rely on the teaching strategy called *inquiry*, which is detailed in the following chapter. It is designed specifically to accomplish the kind of objective for which students are trying to draw an evidence-based conclusion about something that concerns them. The teacher learns from a colleague that the Canadian government has an interesting website devoted to the subject of climate change. He reasons that it may be biased toward downplaying the threat of global warming, but that it is precisely the sort of thing he wants his students to consider when gathering evidence: examine the source! His mind races ahead to a variety of learning activities.

First, though, the teacher determines how to assess the other unit objectives. For those concerning Canada's culture, government, and economy, he decides to rely on classifying questions, both informally and in paper-and-pencil tests. Classifying questions are well-suited to assessing student understanding of concepts. For the unit objective on Canada's history, he plans to adapt the short-essay item found in Figure 7–9 of the preceding chapter, focusing on the causes of a turning point in Canadian history, and will use the 3-point scoring rubric above.

Summary.   I offered this example to suggest how assessments might be determined in relation to an objective. The use of a planning format such as the one shown in Figure 8–3 can be helpful for coordinating objectives, assessments, and activities. If a careful job is done in completing the four cells in the first row, the task of selecting resources and planning activities will be easier. *Caution*: No format can be "complete" without being completely unreadable and unhelpful. This one might also include, for example, a place for teaching strategies such as WebQuests (Ch. 10, pp. 339–341), virtual field trips (Ch. 10, pp. 331–337), cooperative learning (Ch. 11, pp. 351–374), and Socratic Seminars (Ch. 12, pp. 395–397). But this planning guide emphasizes *planning* rather than *teaching*.

TEACHING THE UNIT

Now, at last, we turn from *planning* to *teaching* the unit. There are three basic phases in teaching any unit: the beginning, the middle, and the end. We will look at each now. What is important to grasp in this section of the chapter is that the first and third phases are not to be ignored or slighted, and that learning activities must be related clearly and directly to the unit objectives.

FIGURE 8-3   Social studies unit planning (integrated).

This planning form can be used in developing unit plans. Note that it contains five components: (1) the various learnings to be achieved; (2) the resources to be used; (3) learning activities; (4) the relationship to the rest of the curriculum; (5) assessments.

Unit Title: _____   Inclusive Dates: _____

Overview (written as though to a substitute teacher):_____

_____

Main ideas to be developed: Key Concepts:	Related skills: a. reading/writing: b. democratic participation:	Related skills: c. study and inquiry: d. higher-order thinking:	Related attitudes and values:
Resources: a. textbook: b. trade books: c. audiovisual: d. Internet sites: e. community:	Activities: a. reading/writing: Formative assessment:	Activities: b. construction and simulation: Formative assessment:	Activities: c. music and drama: Formative assessment:
Summative assessment:		Other curriculum connections (science, math, literature, art):	

Phase 1: Launching the Unit

Poor planners do not plan the unit, mediocre planners plan the middle of the unit, great planners plan the beginning, the middle, and the end; that is, they surround the middle with a thoughtfully constructed opening and closing.

A good beginning launches the unit successfully. Building and sustaining the interest of children in a topic are continuing responsibilities of the teacher, but are especially important when beginning a new unit of study. This involves much more than getting started. It requires arousing the curiosity of students, assessing their present understanding, exploring with them some of the possibilities for study presented by the topic, inviting them to help you plan it, and setting the stage for learning to take place. The students' multiple intelligences should be considered when launching a unit, too. Music might be a good entry point for some students, a story could be better for others, a dramatic reenactment for still others. "The pedagogical decision about how best to introduce a topic is important," Howard Gardner writes. "Students can be engaged or turned off in quick order."[8]

Before the unit is actually undertaken, the teacher should post material in the room to rouse interest and to indicate the relationship of the new topic to previous work. There should be books, photos, and other materials in the room to catch a child's eye and to allow for browsing in free-reading time. A learning center can be placed in the corner of the room to house these books and photos. A map of Canada is there, too, along with the classroom computer with Web addresses for a virtual tour of Canada's major sites. These environmental stimuli, together with dramatic play and construction activities, create interest and will encourage the children to want to learn more about the topic.

Dramatizations and Constructions

Some teachers use dramatic play successfully in the initial stages of the unit. What child has not "been" a firefighter, a teacher, a jet pilot, a basketball champion, a mother or father, a doctor or veterinarian during the fanciful and imaginative play of early childhood? Such objects of imaginative play are cultural, of course; the teacher must know the students' home cultures to know who they imagine themselves to be during dramatic play.

Let us assume that a primary class is beginning a unit on transportation. The teacher suggests that the children show through creative dramatics what the workers at an airline terminal do. The children become excited about this and want to start immediately. Props are improvised. Under the teacher's guidance, they begin to plan, but they soon discover that they do not really know enough about the situation to present it accurately. They do not know who the workers are at the terminal, let alone what each worker does. Now they have identified a problem they can understand and can go about their inquiry with genuine purpose. The children's purpose has to do with getting information in order to do the dramatic play, whereas the teacher's purpose is to have them learn basic ideas about the airport, jobs, division of labor, and the concept of transportation. By involving children in the planning early on, the teacher wisely helped children come to the realization on their own that they needed to know more. Although the example given applies to a primary grade, the procedure is unlimited.

Through dramatic play at the beginning of a unit (in the middle, too), children can be helped to achieve all sorts of social studies objectives. The biographies of famous Americans, for example, can be dramatized with great effect. Kindergarten teacher and writer Vivian Paley, whom you met in Chapter 3, does this masterfully. In one lesson, she gathered the five-year-olds at the rug to act out events in the life of Martin Luther King, Jr. "The story of King's struggle evoked strong feelings among the children," she says. "The indignities of being told where to sit, where to play and with whom, where to go to school, and where to eat seemed to echo some of the children's own complaints."[9] One child, a boy named Wally, wants the class to act out one of King's speeches. In it, King describes the feelings of his young daughter, Yoki, when she was told she could not enter an amusement park. "My mother told me to bring you this record," Wally said. "She says you'll like the speech about the little daughter." Ms. Paley has the children listen and then immediately dramatize this scene. With this beginning, the children are ready (curious, motivated) to study the Montgomery bus boycott. They dramatize it, too.

History lessons should often feature dramatic reenactments. They are engaging and they challenge students to take the perspective of the people they are studying. *(Anthony Magnacca/Merrill)*

Listening to children's dramatization, teachers can assess their understanding of events as well as their sense of history and their ability to empathize. "Which character did you like best? Why?" "How do you suppose that person felt? Have you ever felt that way?" "Can you think of another event that is like this in some way?" "Now, let's place these events in order. Which happened first?" "How long ago was that?"

Drama isn't the only activity with which to launch a unit. Other activities can be used in a similar way to motivate work and to give children reasons for doing the things they do. Construction activities, which will be discussed later, are often used in this way. If an individual or a class is to build something, they have to learn what goes into it, how it works, and how it is or was used. Children can build model bridges or ports, for example, perhaps a new one in their city and an ancient one in Greece—all in preparation for an integrated social studies and science unit, "Mighty Rivers of the World." Such a unit can take students into cultures on every continent of the world and deep into the natural realm of rain, mountains, lakes, and animal habitats. It can also take them to human attempts to control nature: dams, canals, gardens, and water purification systems. But it all has to begin somehow—with a field trip to a local bridge, perhaps, followed by a construction project on bridges. Or a dramatization. Imagine the possibilities.

REFLECTION

Dramatic play can be an involving way to launch a unit, building interest to learn more. What memories do you have of dramatic play as an elementary and middle school student?

Here is the point: The careful teacher *plans* the beginning phase of any unit. Here, at the launch, the children's prior knowledge is activated, curiosity is sparked, purposes are set, and a need-to-know attitude is aroused.

Phase 2: Developing the Study with Learning Activities

The development phase of a unit of study is composed of purposeful learning activities that are sequenced wisely. Good teachers of social studies have developed two habits that are essential to this phase of the unit: framing objectives before selecting activities and involving students in selecting and planning activities.

First, activities are means to ends. They are used to help children learn something that is worth learning. It is imperative, therefore, that the teacher frame objectives before deciding what activities are to be used. This may sound terribly obvious, but anyone who teaches (and is honest about it) will admit to sometimes leading children in activities that were engaging but not purposeful. Hands-on, perhaps, but not minds-on. That is, the activity did not help students achieve worthy objectives. It was busywork—active without being intellectually challenging—perhaps, or interesting without being meaningful. The remedy for this problem is a habit, and that habit is to clarify the learning objectives before selecting activities. The planning format shown in Figure 8–3 is designed to help you form this habit.

Second, good unit development typically provides for the involvement of children in planning instructional activities. This is in keeping with attaining and maintaining student engagement in the unit. Having children participate in planning can do much to overcome the feeling that they are only doing assignments for the teacher, and they may suggest ideas that the teacher could not have imagined.

For example, a third-grade teacher and her class undertook a unit called "Life in Contemporary Indian Villages" as part of the year-long theme, "Communities of the World." One objective concerned learning that there *are* contemporary native villages to counteract the misconception many children have that American Indian peoples existed only in the past; another objective involved learning how contemporary Indian villages are different and similar to one another. The teacher led students in a lengthy decision-making activity to plan the unit. Since the children were unfamiliar with any contemporary Indian villages, she suggested several and characterized them just enough so that students could make choices. They decided to study a Pueblo village of New Mexico because they were fascinated by the adobe dwellings. For comparison, they chose an Inuit village far to the north in Canada's arctic. "Eskimos," one child called them. "Do they live in snow caves?" another asked. "Let's find out," the teacher replied. The class then made a chart, shown in Figure 8–4, that summarized their initial plans, and it was posted on the wall. Note that the children chose not only the two native groups for study but, with help from the teacher, the six dimensions of study. "Should all of us do everything?" the teacher asked. "Or should we divide up some of the work?"

Now let us examine a number of different types of activities. Although children of all ages need many firsthand experiences to extend their understanding of social studies concepts, older children have a greater familiarity with the world of things, words, and people, and can therefore profit from vicarious experiences to a much greater extent than primary-grade children. Furthermore, older children can use reading as a tool for learning in the social studies, whereas young children are less able to do so. The physiological and psychological

MAKING A MAP

In social studies lessons and units, construction activities motivate students' work and serve as powerful hands-on ways to achieve instructional objectives.

Step 1 After learning about your community, decide what to include on your map.

Step 2 Gather your materials.

- carboard
- map of your community
- clay of different colors
- paper
- tape
- markers

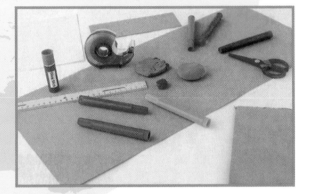

Step 3 Cover the cardboard with a thin layer of clay. Build up the features using different colors of clay.

Step 4 Identify the features with labels. Use toothpicks to place the labels into the clay. Give the map a title.

Source: Banks, Boehm, Colleary, Contreras, Goodwin, McFarland, Parker. *Our Communities*, © 2003 Macmillan/McGraw-Hill. Reproduced by permission of the McGraw-Hill Companies.

INCORPORATING CONSTRUCTION ACTIVITIES

MAKING 3-D GRAPHICS

With folded paper, scissors, glue, and colored pencils, difficult social studies concepts become more graspable for students – vivid and almost tangible. 3-D graphic organizers make great displays on classroom bulletin boards and in the school's showcase, and can also be helpful as formative assessments and study aids.

Here are five hands-on suggestions for social studies construction projects. These simple graphics are easily adapted to fit changing course and content needs.

1. Fold a large sheet of paper into a shutter fold.

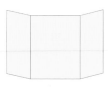

2. Add drawings on the front and label as necessary.

1. Fold a sheet of paper lengthwise, but make one side 1" longer than the other.

2. On the short side, make two cuts equal distances apart to form three tabs.

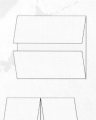

1. Fold a large sheet of paper into a shutter fold.

2. Fold the shutter fold in half.

3. Form four tabs by cutting along the fold lines in the middle of the two long tabs.

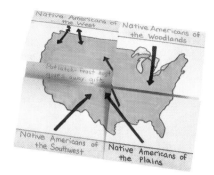

1. Fold a large sheet of construction paper in half.

2. Fold two sheets of white paper in half.

3. Glue the two folded sheets inside the sheet of construction paper.

4. Make two cuts equal distances apart, forming three tabs on the front of each.

---

1. Fold a square piece of paper in half to form a triangle.

2. Fold the triangle in half again, and open to see the square divided into fourths.

3. Cut along one fold line, stopping at the middle.

4. Write titles and draw on three of the triangles.

5. Glue the blank trinagle behind the tab next to it.

Sources: Top illustrations from Banks, Boehm, Colleary, Contreras, Goodwin, McFarland, Parker. *Our Nation*, © 2003 Macmillan/McGraw-Hill. Reproduced by permission of the McGraw-Hill Companies; middle and bottom illustrations from Banks, Boehm, Colleary, Contreras, Goodwin, McFarland, Parker. *Our Communities*, © 2003 Macmillan/McGraw-Hill. Reproduced by permission of the McGraw-Hill Companies.

INCORPORATING CONSTRUCTION ACTIVITIES

MAKING A TIME LINE

Use construction activities often, and remember the four guidelines

1. Clarify with students the purpose of the activity.
2. Plan with students the methods of work.
3. Provide plenty of time each day for beginning and ending work.
4. Use the construction in the unit under study.

- construction paper
- markers
- tape
- scissors
- your notes and sketches

Step 1 Learn about your community's past. Make notes of what you learn.

Step 2 Gather your materials.

Step 3 Make a time line. On the left, write the year your time line begins. On the right, write this year. In between, mark the dates when something interesting happened. Draw pictures to illustrate the events you choose.

Source: Banks, Boehm, Colleary, Contreras, Goodwin, McFarland, Parker. *Our Communities,*
© 2003 Macmillan/McGraw-Hill. Reproduced by permission of the McGraw-Hill Companies.

FIGURE 8–4   Life in two contemporary Indian villages.

Life in Two Contemporary Indian Villages
—Our Class Plan—

- All of us will learn about life in both villages, including location, climate, and history.
- Each of us will specialize in <u>one</u> thing about <u>both</u> villages: food, shelter, or family roles.
- We will organize our findings on a chart like this:

	Pueblo of United States	Inuit of Canada
location		
climate		
history		
food		
dwelling (shelter)		
family roles		

Inuit resources: www. itk. ca (and search for others)
Pueblo resources: www. puebloindian. com (and search for others)

makeup of primary-grade children makes necessary the use of learning activities that involve them actively in firsthand experiences. Ten types of learning activities for all grade levels, along with an example of each, are listed below.

1. **Construction Activities**
   Ms. Kim's class studied contemporary native village life and constructed model dwellings with sticks, rocks, clay, mud, and construction paper.

2. **Dramatic Activities**
   During their study of the Thanksgiving holiday, Ms. Paley's kindergarten class dramatized the story of colonists learning from Wampanoag Indians how to plant corn using fish fertilizer.

3. **Sharing Activities**
   Mr. Johnson's second-graders studied their seashore community and worked on the concepts *natural resources* and *manufactured goods*. Using a sandbox and things that each of them had gathered or collected with their families, they created a model of a seashore. The children talked about what they had brought and where their items had come from. They explained whether the items were natural or manufactured.

4. **Experiments**
   Ms. Womble secured samples of various grains—oats, corn, barley, wheat—while studying food production with her class. The children compared the appearance and taste of each type of grain and then planted some to compare germinating time and appearance of the first shoots.

5. **Music Activities**
   In the Canada unit, students listened to a variety of recordings of Canada's national anthem, *O Canada*. They learned to sing the Canadian folk song, *They Call It Canada (but I Call It Home)*, and compared it to *Home on the Range*.

6. **Discussion Activities**
   Ms. Montoya's sixth-grade class had a regular time set aside for current-events discussion. During the Mexico unit, students decided to collect newspaper articles that reported on U.S.–Mexico controversies and to have discussions in which students took turns taking both sides.

7. **Art Activities**
   A fourth-grade class studying the regions of the United States searched for artworks that captured the essence of each region. Then an art teacher from the high school visited the class to help students compare them.

8. **Field Trips**
   A day was spent at the state fair during the study of their state. Students noticed what products were displayed and grouped them by (a) what region of the state they were from and (b) whether they were natural or manufactured.

9. **Virtual Field Trips on the Internet**
   After searching for the three branches of government in the U.S. Constitution, the class "visited" each one on the Internet. They started with the executive branch and a tour of the White House, then visited the legislative branch, and then the judicial branch with a tour of the Supreme Court.

10. **Processing Activities**
    During a study of preindustrial societies, the class divided into groups to make soap, dip candles, bake bread, churn butter, make dyes, and weave clothing.

Criteria for Selecting Activities

When selecting a social studies activity, the teacher should consider these criteria:

1. The activity is useful in achieving a social studies objective.
2. The time and effort expended can be justified by the learning that occurs.
3. It clarifies, enriches, or extends the meaning of some important concept.
4. It requires children to do careful thinking and planning.
5. It is an accurate and truthful representation.
6. It is within the capabilities of the children.
7. It is reasonable in terms of space and expense.
8. The needed materials are available.

Phase 3: Concluding the Study

As a class nears the end of a unit, the teacher should plan a series of activities that help children summarize what they have learned. Show-and-tell opportunities and writing in response journals will be involved. The end of a unit provides a time to judge the extent to which the overall objectives have been achieved. This is summative evaluation, and both informal and formal evaluation procedures are appropriate at this time. A culminating performance assessment may be planned; portions of the unit test provided by the textbook program may be used as well. As a rule, the learning activities will have resulted in some product (an artifact), and these can be placed in each child's unit portfolio as evidence of learning. It might be a map drawn accurately and with good legends, a team-written biography of a central character in the unit, an annotated list of Internet addresses searched during an inquiry or an evidence-based conclusion that was drawn, or photos of a classroom museum exhibit. In the case of a single product made cooperatively with others, a description of it, perhaps with a photograph, can be placed in each child's portfolio. A sidewalk fair in a local shopping mall could be a good outlet for sharing what has been learned in a comprehensive unit.

What is important about closing a unit of study is the opportunity to teach children to *summarize what has been learned*. It is also the time to identify what children found to be of special interest and to identify areas where additional study is needed. Concluding activities can and should serve as bridges to new studies.

Summary

There are three basic phases to teaching any unit. The first and third phases ensure an effective "launch and landing," and they should not be slighted. Good openings and closings matter tremendously to achieving a unit's objectives because they launch students into the study and help them summarize what happened. Of course, the learning activities during the second phase must be related clearly to the unit objectives; otherwise, the classroom may be filled with activity but not learning. There's a big difference. Things get done, but enduring understandings are not developed. Read again through the letter from parents with which I opened this chapter. They are amazed at both the activities and the learning in Mr. Allison's classroom.

PLANNING LESSONS WITHIN UNITS

Thus far our discussion has been concerned with planning and teaching a unit—a parcel of work that might take several weeks to complete. But day-to-day plans are needed as well. Teachers must extract from the unit plan shorter instructional sequences that may last anywhere from a single day to several days. Usually these are called daily lesson plans. These plans must be complete in every detail, correctly sequenced, with contingencies

This unit on Greece came alive with dramatizations, artwork, and construction activities. *(Barbara Schwartz/Merrill)*

anticipated and accounted for. As the teacher prepares such plans, he or she is rehearsing mentally how the lesson is expected to proceed, step-by-step. This rehearsal is worth its weight in gold.

There are four basic components of plans of this type:

1. The objectives that identify what children will learn
2. The three basic phases of any lesson (a beginning, middle, and end)
3. Assessments: diagnostic, formative, summative
4. Needed instructional materials and resources

The example in Lesson Plan 10 shows how daily plans can be constructed. Other lesson plan samples can be found throughout this text (check the Table of Contents for a full listing). They vary in the ways they attend to the four basic components, but they all attend to each of them. Pay special attention to the excellent plans from Colorado that are featured in the final chapter of this book, "Social Studies as the Integrating Core." Four lessons from a third-grade, integrated social studies–science curriculum called "Explore" are featured. Note that they rely heavily on the teaching strategies of concept formation and inquiry. (Please skip ahead now if you'd like.)

GROUP MEMBERSHIP

Grades	1–2
Time	Two class periods
NCSS Standards	1 (culture) and 5 (individuals, groups, and institutions)
Objectives	In an integrated unit on the concept *group* (e.g., our solar system, flora, fauna), a teacher planned this lesson to help children develop an initial understanding of the concept *human group* and become aware of reasons people are grouped together.
Lesson Development	Display five pictures of groups. (Ideas: soccer team, birthday party, family, class, scout troop) Underneath each, write what type of group is represented, and prompt the children to notice details in each picture.

1. Looking at the similarities across these examples, generate a simple definition of *human group*.

2. Ask the class to think of one word that describes all the pictures. Elicit the words *human group*.

3. Have children think of the names of several more groups. Suggest that they include groups to which they belong. Write these on the chalkboard.

4. Lead a class discussion on "What are the reasons people are grouped together?" Place students' ideas on a chart as follows:

Human groups

What are some groups that we know about?	Why are these people grouped together?
family	love, help each other
team	to play games
class	to learn
birthday party	for fun
scout troop	camping, making things, helping others

5. Discuss ways that groups can be identified. Look at the five original pictures for clues. Some clues might be clothing/uniforms, symbols/mascots, official names, special songs, distinguishing looks, or languages.

Summary	Bring the concept of human group into the children's immediate experience by asking the following questions: Is this class a group? How do you know? Why are we grouped together? What are the reasons for being a member of this group?
Assessment	(Classifying) Have old magazines available and ask children to cut out a picture of a human group. Have each child tell something about what the group is doing. As they make their presentation, have them finish this sentence: "I think that these people make a group because. . . ." Use the pictures to make a collage on the bulletin board.
Materials	Five pictures of different groups for display purposes. White butcher paper and felt pen to make chart. Old magazines or newspapers that have pictures of groups. Option: camera.
Follow-up	Have children bring from home photos of other groups of all sorts—groups to which they belong or that they find in newspapers and magazines—and share them with the class. Take a photo of the class group and post it on the classroom door and at the classroom website. Print it in miniature on classroom stationery students use when writing letters to public officials, thank-you notes to guest speakers, etc.
Integration	Groups are key to the science curriculum, too. Among fauna, there are herds of cattle, flocks of birds, and schools of fish. Among flora, there are also groups and groups within groups (vegetables, trees, shrubs, evergreen, etc.). In the universe, there are groups of stars (e.g., the Milky Way) and planets (solar systems).

An experienced teacher sometimes will brag to a student teacher that "I don't use a lesson plan." The beginning teacher should not be confused by such claims. Most likely, this teacher has internalized the four components of the lesson plan. In this case, the teacher most definitely does use a lesson plan, but does so automatically. The plan is held firmly in mind rather than on paper. (Another possibility, of course, is that the teacher making this claim mistakes activity for learning.)

It is important to grasp that the basic idea of a lesson plan is to help the teacher and students progress through the three phases of any instructional sequence: beginning, middle, and end. Accordingly, each class period should provide for three objectives-related instructional movements: (1) getting ready, (2) work-study, and (3) summary and assessment. Teachers usually begin the social studies instructional period with the entire class in one group. At this time, the previous day's progress is reviewed, plans for the day's work are outlined, and work objectives are clarified. A reading lesson focused on a selection from the textbook; a letter, speech, or other primary document may follow for the purpose of providing needed information for the work-study period to follow. The children then turn to their various tasks while the teacher moves from one child to the next or from one group to another, guiding, helping, clarifying, encouraging, and suggesting. The teacher will terminate the work period sufficiently early to assemble the entire group once again to discuss progress, to assess learning, and to identify tasks left undone that must be continued the next day.

As the children complete their various work projects and are ready to share them with the class, time will be arranged for them to do so. On some days, the children may spend the entire period sharing, giving reports, discussing, and planning. Other days may be spent entirely in reading and research or, judiciously, on worksheets the teacher has prepared or taken from the textbook program. And on other days, part of the group may be reading while others are preparing a mural and still others are planning a panel discussion, television news program, or musical.

The class needs to take time at the end of the work period to review what has been accomplished. Clearly understanding the objective or purpose of a learning activity and having knowledge of progress made go hand in hand. Unless the teacher spends some time crystallizing what has been learned, the children may work for days without feeling that they have learned anything or that they are getting anywhere. Some teachers find it worthwhile to place these daily summaries on charts that serve as a visual log of the unit work as it progresses. Such logs may also be useful in assessment activities associated with the unit.

Judging the Adequacy of a Lesson Plan

Teachers are never as well prepared as they might have been given more time, more resources, and more knowledge. Lesson planning is an open-ended process. Many teachers can recall, as student teachers, staying up half the night preparing a half-hour lesson to be taught the next day. Although such effort is commendable, it cannot be sustained for any length of time. At some point, the teacher must decide that the lesson is good enough and then be able to turn to other matters with a clear conscience.

It is not always easy, especially for beginning teachers, to know when they have reached the point of diminishing returns in lesson planning. The checklist in Figure 8–5 can be useful in deciding whether all-important aspects of the lesson have been given appropriate attention in the planning process.

FIGURE 8–5 Lesson plan checklist.

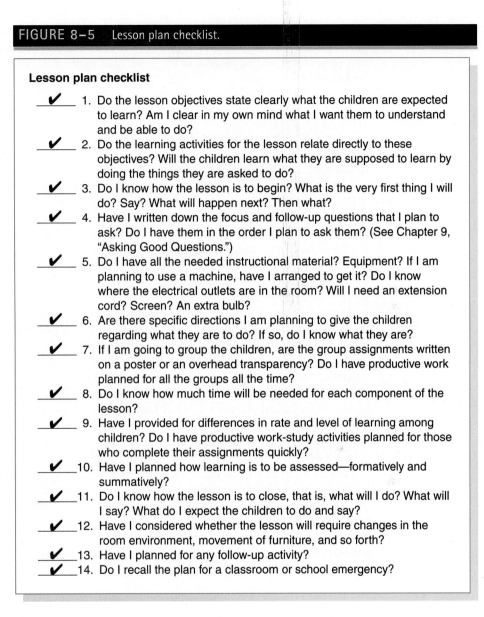

Lesson plan checklist

✔ 1. Do the lesson objectives state clearly what the children are expected to learn? Am I clear in my own mind what I want them to understand and be able to do?

✔ 2. Do the learning activities for the lesson relate directly to these objectives? Will the children learn what they are supposed to learn by doing the things they are asked to do?

✔ 3. Do I know how the lesson is to begin? What is the very first thing I will do? Say? What will happen next? Then what?

✔ 4. Have I written down the focus and follow-up questions that I plan to ask? Do I have them in the order I plan to ask them? (See Chapter 9, "Asking Good Questions.")

✔ 5. Do I have all the needed instructional material? Equipment? If I am planning to use a machine, have I arranged to get it? Do I know where the electrical outlets are in the room? Will I need an extension cord? Screen? An extra bulb?

✔ 6. Are there specific directions I am planning to give the children regarding what they are to do? If so, do I know what they are?

✔ 7. If I am going to group the children, are the group assignments written on a poster or an overhead transparency? Do I have productive work planned for all the groups all the time?

✔ 8. Do I know how much time will be needed for each component of the lesson?

✔ 9. Have I provided for differences in rate and level of learning among children? Do I have productive work-study activities planned for those who complete their assignments quickly?

✔ 10. Have I planned how learning is to be assessed—formatively and summatively?

✔ 11. Do I know how the lesson is to close, that is, what will I do? What will I say? What do I expect the children to do and say?

✔ 12. Have I considered whether the lesson will require changes in the room environment, movement of furniture, and so forth?

✔ 13. Have I planned for any follow-up activity?

✔ 14. Do I recall the plan for a classroom or school emergency?

FIVE WAYS TO ENRICH ANY UNIT

We turn now to five ways to enrich units of study. Briefly, these are reminders to use social studies units to improve students' reading and thinking abilities and to engage them in meaningful *learning by doing*. It is essential to make social studies learning active and involving: hands-on and minds-on.

As you begin to draft a unit plan using the guide in Figure 8–3, return to this section of the chapter. Review the five ways and build two or more into the plan. Remember, unit planning involves the writing process: draft, revise, draft again, and, eventually, "publish" it by implementing it.

1   Incorporating Reading Instruction

Information searches are at the core of most social studies units. This alone makes reading and writing skills central concerns. This is why nearly any social studies unit is an integrated unit: Reading and writing instruction must be incorporated. *Previewing* and *skimming* before reading, and *summarizing* and *note taking* after reading are key skills for these information searches. Learning to preview a text chapter before slogging through it is a powerful comprehension strategy. Previewing is looking before you leap—always a good practice. To follow previewing with skimming for information and main ideas further aids the reader. It builds up additional prior knowledge before reading any portion of the text word by word.

At the other end of reading is the enormously powerful (and difficult) skill of summarizing what has been read. Summarizing requires prioritizing and condensing. Readers must sift through the information that's been gathered to determine which is more or less important and which is more or less encompassing. These are difficult judgments because they require background knowledge and experience, more than the reader may have available on the topic at hand. What to do? Teach summarization slowly but continually. The teacher can build summarization practice into every lesson as part of the closing phase. In the case of Canada: "What information do you have that persuades you that global warming is harming Canada and Canadians?" About the American Revolution: "Complete this sentence: The colonists decided to declare independence from England because _____."

Chapter 12 of this book discusses previewing, skimming, and summarizing at some length. The point now is to encourage you to think of social studies units as homes for reading and writing instruction. They must occur here for two reasons: (1) because many children will not be capable of doing this kind of reading and writing without instruction and practice, and (2) because reading and writing—literacy—cannot properly be developed without challenging subject-matter applications. One can't read reading or write writing, after all.

2   Incorporating Higher-Order Thinking Skills (HOTS)

A second way to enrich any unit is to increase the quality of the intellectual work you will ask students to do. Like reading and writing, higher-order thinking skills (HOTS) do not develop spontaneously. They develop because children need them in the ongoing work of the class and because children are taught what they are and helped to use them well. Occasional special lessons on HOTS are necessary, but they are not sufficient for the proper development of these intellectual skills; they must be *used* in activities that invite them and nurture them.

As we have seen in previous chapters and will see in subsequent chapters, too, several thinking skills are particularly necessary to the subject matter of social studies. Any of them can be brought to the heart of social studies units, lessons, and activities.

Deliberation (Should we donate half our lunch money to hungry people?)

- Identifying and weighing alternatives
- Understanding the perspectives of other persons
- Listening to arguments with which we disagree
- Making decisions

Concept Formation (migration, democracy, transportation)

- Organizing information on data-retrieval charts
- Summarizing similarities across examples of a concept
- Classifying (applying a concept to new material)

Inquiry (Is global warming threatening Canada?)

- Forming hypotheses
- Gathering relevant data and evidence
- Determining the credibility of sources of information
- Hypothesis testing (judging whether hypotheses are supported by evidence)
- Drawing conclusions based on evidence

Interpretation (What does it mean to *pledge allegiance*?)

- Reading between the lines of a print or artwork, taking clues from what's there
- Making meaning from conflicting evidence

Of course, not every higher-order thinking skill will be required by every social studies lesson. But across one or two units, one should see balanced and systematic attention being given to them. In a unit involving inquiry, children naturally will be making and testing hypotheses; to extend concepts, they will be classifying; to decide on the fairest classroom procedures, they will be engaged in deliberation; to read powerful texts with understanding, they will be interpreting.

3 Incorporating Construction Activities

Most children love to make things. They build villages and castles in the sand at the beach, make boats to float in the pond and creek, sew clothing for dolls, and make birdhouses to hang near a window. These natural, sensory–motor, kinesthetic play activities are valuable for children in and of themselves. They give countless opportunities for imagining, thinking, and planning as well as for creative expression, socialization, making and using tools, physical activity, and the development of coordination. Children need many experiences of this type. In social studies, however, these values are only incidental to the chief purpose, which is to extend and enrich meaning of some aspect of the topic being studied. The excellence of the final product is, likewise, not a major concern. What is important is the learning that has occurred as a result of the construction activity.

Construction activities enrich learning. Here, Harrison builds a model of a Luiseño village. *(Suzanne Weinberg)*

It is possible to use construction activities to motivate children's work and to establish more clearly children's purposes for doing things. For example, the teacher of a primary grade is conducting a study of the dairy farm as part of a unit called "Food Around the World." She might suggest that the class construct a model dairy farm in the classroom. Naturally, the children will want to make their model as authentic as possible; therefore, a considerable amount of research will be necessary as they proceed with the building of the farm. In fact, they cannot even begin unless they know what they want to do. This gives them a genuine need for information. The children's purpose in this case may be to learn about the dairy farm to be able to build a classroom model of it. The teacher's purpose, however, is to have children form accurate concepts and understandings of a dairy farm and the foods (some) people eat from them; the construction activity is being used as a vehicle to achieve that objective.

In the sixth-grade Canada unit discussed earlier, the teacher might tap into students' Web skills by asking if they want to construct a classroom website on the effects of global warming on Canada's climate. Perhaps they will want to call it "Is Canada Melting?" On quite a different tack, teams of students can plan and make three-dimensional maps of different places within Canada using clay and other materials. Even third-grade children can do this quite well with assistance. Third-grade children in New York constructed an impressive model of their own community using small and large milk cartons, cardboard tubes and boxes, paint and other materials.[10] A third-grade girl in Seattle is shown with the map she made, along with the directions for the activity, in the full color insert in this chapter.

There is no limit to the items that students can make in projects related to the social studies. The following have been used successfully by many teachers:

Maps (physical, political, crop, wall, floor)
Books
3-D graphic organizers made from paper (see examples on color pages)
Charts and graphs
Musical instruments
Simple trucks, airplanes, boats
Websites
Puppets, marionettes, and paper-bag dolls
"Computer" with paper-roll WWW sites
Looms for weaving
Hats, crowns, and headdresses
Candles and soap
Baskets, trays, bowls
Preparation of foods (making tamales, jelly, butter, ice cream)
Ships, harbor, cargo
Grocery store
Scenery and properties for stage, dioramas, panoramas
Decorations for holidays around the world
Pottery, vases, dishes, cups
Covered wagons
Post office
Hospital
Fire station
Dairy farm and buildings
Pyramids (Egypt, Mexico)
Model communities: their own community and those they are studying
Murals
Production of visual material needed in the unit, such as pictorial graphs, charts, posters, displays, bulletin boards

The following four suggestions should help the teacher use construction activities in teaching social studies. In brief:

1. Clarify the purpose of the activity with the children.
2. Plan methods of work with the children.
3. Provide plenty of time each day for beginning and ending the work.
4. *Use* the construction and relate it to the unit under study.

Clarify the Purpose of the Activity with the Children

The practice of having children make stores or maps without knowing why they are performing these activities is open to serious question. At the beginning of such an activity, therefore, the reasons for planning it should be discussed and understood by all. Also, the purposes for the construction should be reviewed from time to time during the activity.

Plan Methods of Work with the Children

Construction activities involve working in groups, using tools, perhaps hammering and sawing or other noisy activities, and somewhat more disorder than is usually found in classroom work. This means that rules and standards concerning the methods of work need to be established and understood. The teacher and the children should discuss and decide what the rules of work are to be. Group discussions and decision making about rules that will be binding on all constitute citizenship education at its best. These rules concern:

1. How to get and return tools and construction materials.
2. Use of tools, cameras, and equipment, including safe handling.
3. Things to remember during the work period: talking in a conversational voice, good use of materials to avoid waste, sharing tools and materials with others, doing one's share of the work, asking for help when needed, and giving everyone a chance to present ideas.
4. Procedures for cleanup time. Establish a "listen" signal to get the attention of the class. It can be playing a chord on the piano, turning off the lights, or ringing a bell. When the listen signal is given, children should learn to stop whatever they are doing, cease talking, and listen to whatever announcement is made. In this way, the teacher can stop the work of the class at any time to call their attention to some detail or get them started on cleanup.

Provide Plenty of Time Each Day for Beginning and Ending the Work

Before work on the construction activity is begun each day, time should be spent in making specific plans. This will ensure that everyone has an important job to do and that the children know their responsibilities. This time also allows the teacher to go over some of the points the class talked about during its previous day's assessment. "You remember yesterday we had some problem about which group was to use the tools. Which group has the tools today?"

During the work period, the teacher will want to move from group to group observing, assisting, suggesting new approaches, helping groups in difficulty, clarifying ideas, helping children find materials, and supervising and guiding the work of the class. The teacher will identify children who need help in getting started, who are not working well together, who seem not to be doing anything, or who may be having difficulty. The teacher will keep an eye on the time and stop the work of the class in time to ensure a thorough cleanup.

An important part of each period is the assessment that occurs after the work and cleanup. During these times, the teacher will want the class to evaluate its progress on the construction as well as the way children are working with each other.

"What progress did we make in building our farm today?"

"Did anyone see signs of unsafe handling of tools today?"

"I wonder if the mountains aren't too high on Julie's group's map. Did you check that against the picture in your book?"

Some attention should be given to progress on the construction, methods of working together, and problems that need attention the next day.

Use the Construction and Relate It Clearly to the Unit Under Study

When constructed objects are completed, they should be put to good use. A market in the classroom, for example, gives the children an ongoing opportunity to play customer, grocer, checkout person, delivery person, and various community officials—health inspectors, fire and safety advisers, and the tax authority. By rotating these roles, every child gets the opportunity to make change, to make decisions about supply and demand, to see firsthand the interdependence of the store and the community, and even to practice interviewing and preparing a resume for different jobs.

Folded Three-Dimensional Graphic Organizers

One of the most imaginative, fun, and deceptively simple construction activities involves paper, scissors, glue, and colored pencils. It is continually useful as students manipulate, organize, and display information. What is it? Students make simple folds and cuts in paper, then write and draw, to represent the concept or event they are studying. Take, for example, the concept *transportation*. As we will see in Chapter 9, concepts are, by definition, abstract ideas—they exist only in our heads—but examples of concepts are concrete. The concept *transportation* is abstract, as are the two basic kinds of transportation: *animal-powered transportation* and *machine-powered transportation*. Examples, however, are concrete: horse and buggy, sled dog, and pack mule on the animal side; steamboat, airplane, and electric car on the machine side. Manipulating this idea with paper and scissors can be accomplished by folding a piece of standard copy paper almost in half lengthwise, leaving one side one inch longer than the other, then cutting the short side in half, creating two flaps. Students write *animal-powered* on one flap and *machine-powered* on the other. On the one-inch tab, they can write the name of the concept, *transportation*. Inside, on each flap, they can draw and label examples. In this way, the idea is made graphic—vivid. It becomes "real" in a way that helps the children see and feel the concept.

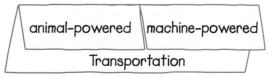

The same can be done with all kinds of concepts: *resources*—manufactured and natural; *states*—northern and southern; *governments*—democracies and dictatorships; *pyramids*—Egyptian and American; *products*—goods and services; *maps*—physical and political. And when the concept divides better into three, four, or five parts rather than two, students can cut the short half of the paper into that many parts: *governments*—local, state, and national; *time*—past, present, and future; *branches of government*—executive, legislative, judicial; *land forms*—islands, peninsulas, and continents; *water forms*—oceans, lakes, rivers, and bays; *religions*—Judaism, Islam, Christianity, Buddhism, Hinduism.

Additional folded-paper graphic organizers can be constructed: three-sided pyramids (showing a country's farming, manufacturing, and trade on each side); four-sided towers (showing the four "sides" of a country—its history, geography, government, and economy); accordion books (for illustrated time lines, autobiographies, and biographies); pie graphs (showing proportions); and four-door books (see the full-color pages in this chapter).

Current and historical events, too, can be made more vivid for children with paper manipulatives. A folded pyramid can depict life before, during, and after the event. An illustrated time line can show many more details. The basic two-tab fold shown in the *transportation* illustration can represent two competing hypotheses about what caused the event. For example, on the one-inch tab they write the inquiry question, "What happened to the Anasazi at Mesa Verde?" On one flap they write, "Hypothesis 1: drought." On the other, they write "Hypothesis 2: warfare." Inside, they elaborate each hypothesis. Younger children make a drawing with an explanatory caption, and older children write a complete paragraph explaining the hypothesis.

Whatever the form, these three-dimensional graphics are favored by children and often selected by them for placement in their permanent portfolios. They can be *used* by students as study guides, and they make great displays on classroom bulletin boards and even the school's showcase. Observers enjoy them, too, for they can see and touch the ideas students are constructing—literally and figuratively! For this reason, these organizers are helpful as formative assessments. Take a minute to examine the examples shown in full-color pages in this chapter. Also, look back to the paper pie graph in Figure 5–11 toward the end of Chapter 5.

A terrific teacher and teacher educator named Dinah Zike boosted my appreciation for all that can be done with folded-paper graphic organizers.[11]

Storyline and Storypath

Another imaginative construction activity—more elaborate and comprehensive than making 3-D graphics from paper—originated in the elementary schools of Scotland and has children create a story together. Called Storyline,[12] the procedure builds on children's prior experience and their love of storytelling, scissors, paper, and glue. There are four interlocking parts. First, a curriculum-related setting for the story is created. In a unit called "Our Community's Needs," the teacher might tell children about a fictitious community in the American southwest that is facing another year of water rationing. Working with the children, the teacher adds sufficient detail so that a shared visual image of the community is created. Second, characters for the story are created. Children are placed in small groups to cut and paste paper-doll families who live in the community. Responding to the teacher's questions (How large are the families? What are their physical characteristics? What kinds of homes do they live in?), the children decide what kind of families to create. Written descriptions of the families are posted with the paper dolls on the classroom wall, thus creating a vivid and highly personal mural representing the families in this community.

Third, the teacher suggests a number of curriculum-related episodes with which the small groups must cope. The teacher tells the groups, for example, that a young child who lives in the community the children have created wants to know what the rules are so that he or she doesn't get into trouble accidentally. Now the small groups create the community's laws—its constitution—and post them on the mural. Next, the teacher tells the class that an exchange student will be joining each family. The small groups decide where the visitor is coming from—someone from a similar climate elsewhere in the world, for example—and then gather information about that country and its region, and decide what the visitor will be most eager to see in their own community. Next comes the water-rationing problem. What are the community's priorities? Should larger families get more water? Should the golf course be closed? The swimming pool? By whom should these decisions be made? Finally, the teacher might introduce the concept of trade, asking the families what goods they will produce and which goods must be imported and purchased with money, which is kept in the bank, which is robbed. The police and courts get involved, and so on.

Once children are engaged in the storyline in this way, they are ready and willing to deepen their understanding of its place, topic, and key ideas and issues. At this point, children have the curiosity to dig deeper—to invest in the research process. This is the fourth phase.

Finally, the children invite an audience, perhaps their own families, to come to class and experience the narrative they have created, with its evolving mural on the classroom wall. After the presentation, a committee of students tells the audience what the class learned from the experience—what objectives were achieved. This requires several planning sessions and discussions with the rest of the class. But it is worth the effort because parents, like the Montoyas in their letter that began this chapter, will want to see that exciting activities result in learning. Storyline is a long-term construction activity. To assure that the time is well spent—to assure that learning occurs—careful planning is required so that the setting and episodes around which the children build this imaginary world are related directly to challenging curriculum objectives.

Margit McGuire brought Storyline to the United States and has developed a good number of highly imaginative storyline units under the name Storypath. For the primary grades, two of my favorite units are *Celebrating Cultural Diversity: The Parade* and *Safari to Kenya: The Land and the People*. For intermediate grades, favorites are *State Studies: The Visitors' Center* and *Democracy in Action: Communities Make Decisions*. These units are very much like simulations and involve role-playing, so let us take up this topic next.

4   Incorporating Simulations and Role-Playing

A fourth way to enrich any unit is to plan a simulation that will deepen students' understanding—through experience—of one or more of the unit's main ideas. In Chapter 4, classroom simulations were suggested for history, geography, economics, anthropology, and sociology. Here is an example of a classroom simulation, one that deals with the economic concept *production*.

A fifth-grade class was studying the concept of assembly-line production in its unit on the growth of industry in the United States. In the discussion, the children contrasted assembly-line production with custom-made, individually built products. The class listed the strengths and limitations of each method of production:

Assembly Line

Strengths	Weaknesses
1. It is faster.	1. Sameness makes for an uninteresting product.
2. Every product is the same.	2. Production can be slipshod because no one person is responsible for it.
3. Can be produced at low cost.	3. The sameness of the work makes for a boring job.

Custom Built

Strengths	Weaknesses
1. One-of-a-kind product. 2. Product made to fit needs of buyer. 3. Work is less boring to the workers.	1. Buyers cannot be sure of the product's quality because each is different. 2. Fewer people can afford to buy the product. 3. It takes longer for workers to become skillful in doing all the tasks needed to make the product.

The teacher pointed out to the class that each of the items they listed could serve as a hypothesis that they might be able to test. "Is it really true," he asked, "that assembly-line production is faster? Do workers on an assembly line become bored more quickly than those who make the whole product themselves? Do workers take greater pride in their product if they do it all themselves and sign their name to it? How could we test the truth of these statements?" The teacher and the children decided they could test their hypotheses by using a simple simulation involving the manufacture of envelopes.

The class was divided into two groups: one group would be assembly-line workers; the other group would be custom workers. The teacher provided cardboard templates, or patterns, of an outline of an envelope, scissors, paste, and used ditto paper that would be needed to manufacture envelopes. After the pattern was placed on a piece of paper, its outline could be traced and could then be cut, folded, and pasted to make the finished product. The assembly line was arranged according to a division of labor as follows:

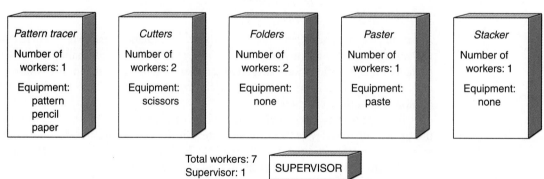

ASSEMBLY LINE

Pattern tracer	Cutters	Folders	Paster	Stacker
Number of workers: 1	Number of workers: 2	Number of workers: 2	Number of workers: 1	Number of workers: 1
Equipment: pattern pencil paper	Equipment: scissors	Equipment: none	Equipment: paste	Equipment: none

Total workers: 7
Supervisor: 1   SUPERVISOR

The custom workers consisted of seven individuals (the same number as on the assembly line) and a supervisor. Each of the seven workers had his or her own pattern, paper, pencil, scissors, and paste and was required to do all the steps necessary to make an envelope. These children would be required to put their own name on each envelope they produced and were encouraged to personalize their own product.

All children in both groups took turns, and all participated in the activity. The supervisor from each group could make changes and substitutions as needed. Three children served as a quality-control panel that would accept or reject finished products in terms of their quality.

CUSTOM CRAFTSPERSONS

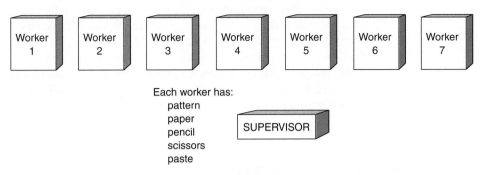

Each worker has:
    pattern
    paper
    pencil   SUPERVISOR
    scissors
    paste

When all preparations were completed, the teacher gave the signal to start, and both groups began manufacturing envelopes. After a half hour, production was stopped, and the debriefing took place. Children were able to test their hypotheses in terms of the data they generated through the simulation.

We have here an example of a simple simulation. It is a strategy designed to reconstruct as closely as possible some of the essential characteristics of the real thing. Simulations are enthusiastically accepted by those teachers who pursue innovative approaches to social studies teaching. The simulation may be a simple one devised by the teacher, as described here, or it may be one of the growing number of commercially prepared simulations and games now available from companies such as Interact. A search of its website should generate a good number of ideas.

Sharon Pray Muir provides an annotated list of nearly 200 simulations appropriate for use in grades K–6 that deal directly with social studies concepts and processes.[13] Muir's collection is a treasure, and finding a copy today may take some digging. Hopefully the university library subscribes to the journal, *Simulation and Gaming*, in which it was published. To accommodate the typical classroom, Muir's collection concentrates on simulations that can be played with large groups. Included are the title, recommended grade levels, and bibliographic information so readers can readily locate or order each simulation. Some appear in journals, newsletters, and magazines, which can be read in libraries for free; others can be purchased. Muir also indicates the social science discipline with which the simulation is associated.

Popular, powerful, and fun simulation games for computers are *Where in the World Is Carmen Sandiego?* (profiled in Chapter 5) and *The Oregon Trail*. The latter has been a favorite for many years for ages 9 and up, and some of your students may have it at home. Users need to make lots of decisions as their wagon train makes its way to Oregon's Willamette Valley in the mid-1800s. Money is limited, but needs are many: food, supplies, repairs, medicine, weapons. They read maps to plan their route; they must avoid buffalo stampedes, cross treacherous rivers, and deal with foul weather and sickness. Decisions have to be made, and the stakes are high. A poor decision can have disastrous consequences for the entire party. Readers can preview both of these at www.learningcompany.com. Popular commercial simulations involving citizenship decision making are *Decisions, Decisions* (for grades 5 and above) and *Choices, Choices* (K–6) from Tom Snyder Productions.

The great value of simulation games is that they are socially interactive, imaginatively playful, and often completely involving. Best of all, they are focused on *learning*. Moreover, these activities provide multiple entry points to curriculum objectives. This is a powerful combination that can make simulations deeply *educative*. Students inhabit roles (e.g., detectives, family members on a wagon train, assembly-line workers, civil-rights marchers, Lewis and Clark, Sacagawea) and with them the perspectives, social positions, and historical contexts of the people they are pretending to be, the events they are pretending to live out, and the decisions they are actually making to move forward within the game's universe.

5   Incorporating Music and Drama

Music activities not only enrich social studies learning, but also contribute to the school's music program. Singing, listening, dancing, and playing musical instruments from cultures near and far add meaning and firsthand experience to social studies learning.

For almost any social studies unit, the teacher will find appropriate songs for children to sing. Singing gives the child an emotional feeling for the material not likely to be obtained in any other way. Like construction activities and simulations, singing allows children to shine in different ways, and it allows some children to shine perhaps for the first time. (See the discussion of multiple intelligences in Chapter 2.) Through singing, the child senses the loneliness of the cowboy, the relief and happiness of a frontier housewarming, the tragedy of slavery and the bravery of slave revolts, or the sadness of a displaced people longing for their homeland. Folksongs can be springboards to the study of a period in history, of the lifestyles of minority (and majority) ethnic groups, and of central themes such as human–environment interaction (sailing and hiking songs, fishing songs), civic ideals (hopeful, protest songs), production (workers' songs), and nationalism (patriotic songs). Singing is an experience that can broaden children's appreciation of people everywhere. In the study of communities around the world, the teacher will want to use the songs of various national groups. This provides opportunities to learn more about a culture through the language of music. (See Figure 8–6.)

"Music from different cultures can offer us an entry point to understanding a people who may have lived thousands of years ago or thousands of miles from us," writes Doug Selwyn in *Living History in the Classroom*.[14] The African American gospel tradition is inseparable from the history of enslavement. "Oh Freedom" and "We Shall Overcome," for example, are synonymous with the Civil Rights movement. Listening to Native American flute and drumming, children of all backgrounds can appreciate that pitch and harmony are not universally applicable attributes of the concept *music*. Contemporary folksongs such as "Little Boxes," "This Land Is Your Land, This Land Is My Land," "Detroit City," and "Sittin' on the Dock of the Bay" convey powerful social messages. Cowboy songs such as "I Ride an Old Paint," "The Night Herding Song," and "Git Along Little Dogie" have both lyrics and melodies that are hauntingly reminiscent of the lonely life of this American folk group. "The Yellow Rose of Texas," "When Johnny Comes Marching Home Again," and "Over There" are associated with significant conflicts of this nation (Texas independence, the Civil War, and World War I, respectively).

And drama? I am so enthused about the possibilities of dramatizations in social studies units that I could say it all again. But instead, let me simply refer you back to the section "Launching the Unit," where I recommended dramatic play as a promising way to begin a unit.

FIGURE 8-6 Culture and music.

Lyrics of "O Canada!"
O Canada!
Our home and native land!
True patriot love in all thy sons command.
With glowing hearts we see thee rise,
The True North strong and free!
From far and wide,
O Canada, we stand on guard for thee.
God keep our land glorious and free!
O Canada, we stand on guard for thee.
O Canada, we stand on guard for thee.

Lyrics of "The Star Spangled Banner"
Oh, say can you see, by the dawn's early light,
What so proudly we hailed at the twilight's last gleaming?
Whose broad stripes and bright stars, through the perilous fight,
O'er the ramparts we watched, were so gallantly streaming?
And the rockets' red glare, the bombs bursting in air,
Gave proof through the night that our flag was still there.
O say, does that star-spangled banner yet wave
O'er the land of the free and the home of the brave?

Conclusion

Unit planning is a lengthy and involved matter. It seems to sprawl every which way. This chapter presented rules of thumb for planning the unit, followed by rules of thumb for teaching the unit. The latter included activity selection. Then came the lesson planning section, followed by five ways to enrich any unit.

At one point, readers were asked to look ahead to the final chapter of this book, which builds directly on the present one. It is an extension of this chapter. Two ambitious unit plans will be found there, and they are presented in full detail. One integrates language arts and social studies to help children read and write original biographies, in this case, of the 19th-century abolitionist and women's rights advocate Sojourner Truth. The other, called "Explore," is a four-lesson unit plan that integrates social studies and science to help students develop the idea that the decisions made by human beings influence the survival of other living things. Both plans deserve your study. Both should stretch your thinking about unit planning, teaching strategies, tying learning activities to unit objectives, lesson planning, and curriculum integration. Just as important, both are doable: They are feasible for beginning teachers who are willing to spend time planning. They are, in short, good models that build on the foundation laid down in this chapter.

In closing, look again at the last paragraph of the parent letter to the school principal with which this chapter began:

When we asked [Mr. Allison] how he did it, he looked sideways as though telling a secret. "Planning," was his reply. "Planning, planning, planning." We would have said it was charm or charisma or that he was a natural born teacher. But he set us straight.

Discussion Questions and Suggested Activities

Go to MyEducationLab and select the topic "History," then watch the video "First Person Presentation" and complete the activity.

1. Look back at the three phases any unit should have and at your response to the question about dramatic play in the *Reflection* sidebar. Find out who in your class has memories of dramatic play, simulations, role-playing, and the like *at school as part of instructional units?* Second, how can dramatic play extend and enrich children's understanding of written language. Is it indispensable?

2. Select a country other than Canada (e.g., Mexico, Afghanistan, China) that would be appropriate for a grade of your choice. Then, adapting the plan of the Canada unit in this chapter, identify three or four main ideas that could be developed in the unit. Complete a unit planning chart such as the one shown in Figure 8–3. Think creatively about using drama to launch the unit, and then incorporate reading, construction, simulation, and/or music in the development phase.

3. Demonstrate for your classmates how you would proceed with a construction activity of some type (e.g., making butter, creating a model Inuit village) during the development or concluding phase of a unit.

4. NCSS Standards *Sampler*. Examine the K–2 classroom vignette for standard #7 on page 19 of the standards *Sampler* that accompanies this book. How does that cookie-making simulation compare to the envelope-making simulation in this chapter?

Selected References

Brown, Victoria, & Pleydell, Sarah. (1999). *The dramatic difference: Drama in the preschool and kindergarten classroom*. Portsmouth, NH: Heinemann.

Cole, Bronwyn, & McGuire, Margit E. (2005). Using Storypath to give young learners a fair start. *Social Studies and the Young Learner, 18* (2), 20–23.

Duckworth, Eleanor. (1996). *The having of wonderful ideas and other essays on teaching and learning*. New York: Teachers College Press.

Lindquist, Tarry, & Selwyn, Douglas. (2000). *Social studies at the center: Integrating kids, content, and literacy*. Portsmouth, NH: Heinemann.

McKean, Barbara. (2006). *A teaching artist at work: Theater with young people in educational settings*. Portsmouth, NH: Heinemann.

McTighe, Jay, & Wiggins, Grant. (2005). *The understanding by design handbook* (2nd ed.). Alexandria, VA: Association for Supervision and Curriculum Development.

Muir, Sharon Pray. (1996, March). Simulations for elementary and primary school social studies: An annotated bibliography. *Simulation and Gaming: An International Journal of Theory, Practice, and Research, 7*, 41–73.

Obenchain, Kathryn M., & Morris, Ronald V. (2006). *50 Social studies strategies for K–8 classrooms* (2nd ed.). Upper Saddle River, NJ: Prentice Hall.

MyEducationLab is a collection of online tools for your success in this course, your licensure exams, and your teaching career. Go to www.myeducationlab.com to utilize these extensive resources including videos from real classrooms, Praxis and licensure preparation, a lesson plan builder, and materials to help you begin your teaching career.

Three Great Teaching Strategies

CHAPTER NINE

MAIN IDEA

Three time-honored, field-tested teaching strategies are presented. Each is tailored to a particular kind of social studies subject matter: concepts (e.g., village, democracy), inquiry (e.g., What happened to the people who lived at Mesa Verde? What really caused the *Titanic* tragedy?), and skills (e.g., map reading, newspaper reading). Each is a powerful strategy for providing high-quality teaching and learning, and each relies on the teacher's skillful use of questions.

PICTURE THIS

The central theme of Dylan Coulter's third-grade integrated curriculum is the concept community. *He uses the concept-formation strategy to teach this concept to his students. The examples they study are their own community, its sister cities in Canada and Mexico, and three communities that are detailed in the social studies textbook: Mesa Verde, Washington D.C., and Los Angeles. After students have formed the concept, Mr. Coulter uses the inquiry strategy to help them determine their community's most pressing controversial issue. After hypothesizing, they gather data by taking a poll of parents, and then draw conclusions based on this evidence. Next, Mr. Coulter uses a skill-teaching strategy to help students learn how to take and defend a position on any controversial community issue. Finally, students write editorials for the classroom newspaper on the issue that emerged from their inquiry.*

Why a separate chapter on teaching strategies? After all, teaching strategies can be found in every chapter of this book. Chapter 6 alone has several for teaching current events and controversial issues, and Chapter 13 presents two methods of curriculum integration. The reason for a chapter on strategies is to introduce readers to three *classic* strategies. These are popular and time-honored instructional methods that are matched to core social studies subject matter. Subject matter, recall, is education jargon for the what (not the how) of teaching and learning—the curriculum, which includes knowledge, skills, attitudes, and values. In social studies, the core subject matter includes facts, of course, and concepts, the social science method called inquiry, skills, and democratic values and attitudes. The three strategies presented in this chapter are tailored to concepts, inquiry, and skills (see Table 9–1).

These strategies are powerful instructional tools with which you can help children learn much of the essential subject matter of social studies. You can think of them as *scaffolds*, [1] without which students probably will not learn as much or as well or be introduced to ways of thinking that will make them stronger learners. Scaffolds were defined in Chapter 2 as adjustable frameworks that lift children up to where they can reach a higher level of performance than otherwise would be possible. Because scaffolds are adjustable, different learners can be lifted more or less, as needed, and the structure can be taken down when learners can perform well without it.

That last point is important. These teaching strategies not only teach subject matter, but they also empower students as learners. In a school where the faculty is committed to empowering students as learners, students not only know more each year, but improve each year in their ability to know. They gradually become better researchers, questioners, and thinkers. Esmé Raji Codell, in her witty and irreverent book about her first year of teaching in Chicago, writes: "The difference between a beginning teacher and an experienced one is that the beginning teacher asks 'How am I doing?' and the experienced teacher asks 'How are the children doing?'" [2]

 TEACHING CONCEPTS

In everyday speech, the term *concept* is used to mean "idea," as when someone says, "My concept of a happy marriage is not the same as yours." In social studies the meaning is the same: Concepts are ideas. Social studies concepts often embody an elaborate meaning that

TABLE 9–1	Matching teaching strategies to subject matter.
Subject Matter	**Teaching Strategies**
Concepts	Provide examples and help students grasp the attributes common to each.
Inquiry	Have students test hypotheses with data and draw conclusions.
Skills	Break the skill into its parts, explain and model each part; provide plenty of practice and application opportunities.

evolves with experience and learning over many years. Sometimes a child's initial understanding of a concept includes misconceptions that in later years must be corrected. Consider a kindergartner's concept of *transportation*, for example, or *family* or *freedom* or *money*, compared to an 8th-grader's or a 12th-grader's or yours. Let us explore briefly what concepts are and then turn to a great way to teach them.

What Are Concepts?

If asked to tell what a village is, most adults would probably say something along this line: "A village consists of a group of persons living in a rural area in a cluster of homes smaller than a city or a town." For most purposes this is an adequate definition to make communication possible. But *village* had a much more elaborate meaning for the native peoples of Canada's British Columbia, as explained in Margaret Craven's novel *I Heard the Owl Call My Name*. On the boat trip north, the young priest, Mark Brain, recalls what his bishop had told him about the village:

> The Indian knows his village and feels for his village as no white man for his country, his town, or even for his own bit of land. His village is not the strip of land four miles long and three miles wide that is his as long as the sun rises and the moon sets. The myths are the village and the winds and the rains. The river is the village, and the black and white killer whales that herd the fish to the end of the inlet the better to gobble them. The village is the salmon who comes up the river to spawn, the seal who follows the salmon and bites off his head, the Bluejay whose name is like the sound he makes—"kwiss-kwiss." The village is the talking bird, the owl, who calls the name of the man who is going to die, and the silver-tipped grizzly who ambles into the village, and the little white speck that is the mountain goat on Whoop-Szo.
>
> The fifty-foot totem by the church is the village, and the cedar-man who stands at the bottom holding up the eagle, the wolf and the raven! And a voice said to the great cedar tree in Bond Sound, "Come forth, Tzakamayi and be a man," and he came forth to be the cedar-man, the first man-god of the people and more powerful than all others. [3]

This is a superb example because it illustrates the richness and depth of meaning that can be signaled by a single word: in this case, *village*. It also illustrates how vital personal experience is in developing such meanings. It is doubtful if anyone who did not actually grow up in the village culture of these people could understand and appreciate the full meaning of village as they conceptualize it.

Again, concepts are ideas. This is an important point for teachers to understand because it suggests how concepts can (and cannot) be taught. Ideas are abstract categories or classes of meaning, "abstract" because they are removed from concrete examples. Ideas, therefore, cannot be observed (seen, heard, touched, tasted, smelled). For instance, *island* is the name for a geographic phenomenon whose attributes are (a) land (b) completely surrounded by water. Kauai is one specific example of such attributes. *Island*, the idea, cannot be observed; but *Kauai*, the example, most definitely can. There are thousands of other specific examples of the concept *island*. But to know that Kauai is an example of *island* (that is, a body of land completely surrounded by water) is not to know very much about that beautiful outcropping of land in the Pacific. Concept definitions, therefore, tell us only about those qualities or attributes that all examples have in common, not about the unique features of particular examples. The concept (the idea) refers to the attributes shared by all examples. And that is the most concise definition of *concept:* the critical (important) attributes shared by all examples. Put a little differently, concepts are "categories into which we group phenomena within our experience."[4] Concepts (e.g., *island*) help us group the phenomena in our world into meaningful categories, but they are meaningful only to the extent we deeply understand the examples to which they refer (e.g., *Kauai*).

Concepts may deal with concrete places, persons, objects, institutions, or events or with ways of thinking, feeling, and behaving. Here are a few more concepts and some examples of each that would be appropriate for study in the third grade.

Justice (fairness)
Taking turns
Writing down the rules
Applying rules equally to everyone

Public Issue
Should adults be required to vote?
Should zoos be allowed?
Should we have a new class rule: "You can't say 'you can't play' "?

Mountain
Mt. Everest
Pikes Peak
Mt. Fuji
Mt. Kilimanjaro

Migration
Oregon Trail
Ellis Island immigration
The Great Migration
Angel Island immigration

Technology
Steamboat
Morse code
Airplane
Computer chip

Island
Kauai
Cuba
Singapore
Angel Island

Community
Mesa Verde
Washington, D.C.
Los Angeles
Tokyo

Holiday
Cinco de Mayo
Thanksgiving
Memorial Day
Yom Kippur

Note that each of the 10 curriculum standards developed by the National Council for the Social Studies (see the standards *Sampler* that accompanies this text) is a concept or a group of two or three concepts:

1. Culture
2. Time, Continuity, and Change
3. People, Places, and Environments
4. Individual Development and Identity
5. Individuals, Groups, and Institutions

6. Power, Authority, and Governance
7. Production, Distribution, and Consumption
8. Science, Technology, and Society
9. Global Connections and Interdependence
10. Civic Ideals and Practice

Similarly, the five themes of geography described in Chapter 4 are concepts:

1. Movement
2. Region
3. Human–environment interaction
4. Location
5. Place

As teachers become more familiar with what concepts are (so that "they know one when they see one"), they can teach more effectively: Recognizing that a curriculum objective centers on a concept, teachers can then reach into their toolbox of strategies for one that is tailored to concepts.

The following section presents the time-honored strategy for teaching concepts called *concept formation*. It begins by helping students experience multiple examples of the concept to be learned; then it helps them grasp the critical attributes that all the examples have in common. In other words, students begin by studying three or four examples of the concept to be learned, and then the teacher helps them see the similarities across these examples. When these similarities are established in students' minds, they form the concept. This, in a nutshell, is the key to teaching concepts: help students to explore several examples and then to see clearly the similarities across them.

After considering concept formation, we will turn briefly to two variations: a concept-teaching strategy called "list, group, and label" and another called "concept attainment." If you have time to learn only one, however, "concept formation" is it.

Concept Formation

A fifth-grade class will be learning the concept *democracy*. It is one of the central concepts for understanding United States history, which is the subject-matter emphasis of the fifth grade. The teacher, Kenneth Bailey, has assessed his students' preinstruction understanding of this idea by asking a few diagnostic questions:

What is democracy?

Is the United States a democracy? Why?

Are our weekly classroom meetings democratic? Why?

Can you think of another example of democracy?

In this way, Mr. Bailey learned that his students have no concept of democracy, save vague notions of voting and elections. With this information in hand, he builds an introductory concept-formation lesson.

First, he assembles three or four examples of democracy that will be the building blocks of the concept. He decides to use the governments of the United States, Mexico, and Canada because the textbook has information on them. For the fourth example, he wants something less bookish, more experiential. He selects the democratic classroom meeting his students have each Monday afternoon.

Using the concept-formation strategy, students will build an understanding of democracy from the bottom up (inductively) by studying each example, comparing and contrasting them, and then summarizing how they are alike. Remember, the similarities among examples are the critical attributes of the concept (they are the things that make these examples of the same concept). The critical attributes common in the United States, Mexico, Canada, and Mr. Bailey's classroom meetings are these: the majority rules (laws are made by all citizens or their representatives), minority rights are protected, and laws are written down. These are the three attributes students eventually should summarize under the name *democracy*. Is the resulting concept as complex as the one formed by college political science majors? Of course not, but it would be quite an achievement for fifth-grade children. Lesson Plan 11 shows the teacher's plan for achieving this result.

Classifying

"Whoa! Pluto's dead," said an astronomer at the California Institute of Technology in Pasadena. He was watching a webcast of the vote. "There are finally, officially, eight planets in the solar system." [5] The vote had been taken at an August 2006 meeting of the International Astronomical Union (IAU), the scientific group that decides such things. What happened? Had the *concept* of planet changed so that poor Pluto was no longer a member of that category? Or had something about Pluto changed so that it no longer fit the definition?

It was a little of both. Since Pluto was discovered in 1930, causing subsequent generations to memorize the sun's planets in terms of their nine-ness, more and more has been learned about Pluto—its shockingly small size, for example (smaller even than Earth's moon), and its own shockingly large moon, Charon, at half the size of Pluto. This new knowledge caused questions to be raised about Pluto's membership in the category *planet* by the end of the 20th century. But in 2006 the IAU, meeting in Prague, came at it from the other direction, too, remodeling the concept *planet* such that Pluto could no longer be included unless its moon also counted as a planet, placing the planetary number at 10 and opening the cosmic door to many more "dwarf planets," as they are now called. Not only was Pluto too small relative to its moon, the IAU committee said, but it did not dominate its neighborhood—its orbital region in the solar system—in another key way: From here on out (or until the concept's attributes are again revised), planets must have clear orbits that are swept clear of other astronomical bits and pieces thanks to the planet's own superior force. Pluto's orbit is anything but swept clear, more like a forest road with branches and pine cones strewn about than an interstate freeway.

In sum, Pluto used to be a planet—it used to be classified as a member of the category or class called "planet"—but no longer. Not only did Pluto itself change, so to speak, as scientists' knowledge of it improved, but the critical attributes of the concept *planet* were revised. The new definition, says astrophysicist Alan Boss of the Carnegie Institution, "is much more scientifically palatable." Consequently, Pluto has gone from being an "example" of *planet* to being a "nonexample" because it lacks some key attribute(s) that examples must possess.

What the case of Pluto illustrates for us about social studies teaching and learning is twofold. First, ideas, whether *planet, village,* or *democracy,* are social constructs (to say they are "constructs" is to say they are constructed: made by humans, not found in nature).

Lesson Plan 11

DEMOCRACY: A CONCEPT-FORMATION LESSON

Grades	4–8
Time	Two to four class periods
NCSS Standards	6 (power, authority, and governance) and 10 (civic ideals and practices)
Objectives	Students will form the concept *democracy* and then apply it (reinforcing and revising it as needed) by determining whether additional items are or are not examples of democracy (classifying).
Interest Building	Remind students of a recent classroom meeting in which a vote was taken to resolve a class or school issue. Lead a discussion on the question, "Is majority rule always fair?"
Preassessment	Tell students that you have heard people say that in this country we live in a democracy. Ask them what they think that means. Have them jot down ideas in their response journals, and circulate to see what they are writing. Ask questions as needed to find out what they think a democracy is. For example, "You wrote *president*. Does that mean a democracy can't have a queen?"

Lesson Development

Step 1

Studying multiple examples. Create a data-retrieval chart that contains the four examples down the left column and focus questions across the top. These questions focus students' attention on the critical attributes.

A Data-Retrieval Chart for the Concept Democracy

FOCUS QUESTIONS

Examples	Does the majority rule? How?	Are minority rights protected? How?	Are the laws written? Where?
United States			
Canada			
Mexico			
Class meeting			

Direct students to use this chart to record information they find on each example. Provide time in class to find the information in their textbooks and complete the chart. Direct them to finish the chart as homework. Suggest that they look for regular elections in response to the first question and push them to find out who can and cannot vote.

Step 2

Noting differences. The next day, verify that all the needed information on the four examples has been gathered and recorded. Then ask students, "In what ways do these four governments differ?"

Step 3

Noting similarities. Ask, "In what ways are these four governments all alike?" Record students' responses on the chalkboard for use in the next step. (*Note:* This is the phase of the lesson when students themselves identify the critical attributes of the concept *democracy*, which are the similarities across the examples.)

Step 4

Summarizing. Direct students to "take a few minutes now to jot down a summary of these similarities in one complete sentence. Let's begin the summary with, 'These are all ways of governing that. . . .'" Now students compose their own definition of the concept, working with the list of similarities still on the chalkboard from Step 3. Allow time for sharing and listen carefully to the concepts they have formed. Provide feedback and correction as needed. Students then compose a second draft, taking more care to include all the critical attributes of democracy in their summaries.

Step 5

Labeling. Ask, "What is a word you might use to describe governments like these? Be creative—invent a word if you like. Make sure it captures the essence of this kind of government." After eliciting several nicknames, tell students that the conventional label for this kind of government is *democracy.* Then use your desk dictionary to read aloud the etymology of this Greek term.

Step 6

Application: Classifying. Now that students have built a rough idea of democracy, it is time to reinforce and extend it to the application activity called classifying.

Classifying type 1. Ask students to read the brief description of the Plymouth Colony in their textbooks and then to decide whether it was a democracy. Ask for a show of thumbs (thumbs up for "Yes, it was a democracy"; thumbs down for "no"; thumbs sideways for "not sure"). Then ask for reasons.

Classifying type 2. Give students information about two or three other governments (China's, Denmark's, Japan's) and ask them to decide which of them, if any, is a democracy. This time have them write down their reasons. Then call on several students to share their decisions and reasons.

Classifying type 3. Form teams of three to four students and direct each team to brainstorm a fictional example of a democracy. Have them imagine themselves shipwrecked on an island with no chance of rescue; hence, they must create a society from scratch. Remind them to look back at their summaries to be sure the example they create has each of the attributes all examples of democracies must have. Have the teams share their fictional examples and tell why they are democracies.

Classifying type 4. Tell students that you will describe an organization that is not an example of democracy. The students' task is to describe the changes that would be needed to make it into a democracy. (Describe a modern military dictatorship or a Little League baseball club.)

Summary Ask a sample of students to review the critical attributes of democracy.

Assessment Any of the four types of classifying in Step 6 will serve as a precise assessment of the extent to which students have formed the concept. The proof is not in the decisions they reach (thumbs up; thumbs down), but in the reasons they give.

Materials Copy of data-retrieval chart for each student. Textbook section on Plymouth Colony and other examples and nonexamples as required.

Integration *Literature.* Voting captures the essence of democracy for young children, and children's trade books on voting are plentiful: *The Ballot Box Battle* by Emily Arnold McCully (Dragonfly, 1998), about women winning the right to vote in the United States, or *The Day Gogo Went to Vote* by Elinor Batezat Sisulu (Little, Brown, 1996), about a Black woman voting in South Africa for the first time in 1994.

Math. Voting in class meetings provides an opportunity to work with fractions and proportions (e.g., "two thirds of us were for the playground rule; one third were against it"). Have students make pie graphs from two round sheets of different-colored paper, each with its radius cut, to display these proportions. See Figure 5–11 in Chapter 5.

Second, ideas change. In other words, concepts are social agreements, and these agreements change as human thinking about the world changes *and* as power relations shift. Here is the classic example: During Galileo's time, early in the 17th century, priests were still deciding what was what, as they had for centuries. They had the authority and the power to back it up. The clergy based their decisions on church doctrine, not observations and experiments. Accordingly, when Galileo wrote that he observed through his new telescope that Earth's moon was not perfectly round and smooth but had mountains and valleys, and that he agreed with Copernicus that Earth moved while the sun stood still, he was brought before the Inquisition, tried for heresy, forced to recant, and put under house arrest. Now, four centuries after the "scientific revolution," the IAU, not the Pope, decides on Pluto.

Healthy diet is another great example. The definition until the 1950s, influenced in no small way by the meat and dairy industries, included lots of animal products containing loads of saturated fats, which by the end of the century were considered harmful, not healthy. The meat-centered "square meal" was replaced by the U.S. Department of Agriculture's "food pyramid" as the icon of healthy eating.

Classifying, then, is an integral part of the concept-formation procedure. It is the method by which students *apply* the concept they have formed. Classifying is a type of thinking that requires students first to recall the critical attributes of a concept and then to determine whether those attributes are present in a new situation. This new situation is bound to be different from the examples studied initially to form the concept; accordingly, students need to think about the differences, and then decide if any of them really matters as far as that concept is concerned. In Pluto's case, a celestial body that once fit the definition of *planet* no longer did. The reason was that Pluto changed (well, not really, but scientists' ability to observe it changed), making it no longer fit the attributes, *and* the critical attributes of the concept changed at the 2006 meeting of the group that is in charge of specifying them.

There are four basic forms of classifying. Each is used in Step 6 in Lesson Plan 11, and every teacher of every age of student needs to know them and would be wise to use them frequently:

Four types of classifying

1. Deciding whether a new item is an example
   (The teacher asks, "Is this an example?")
2. Distinguishing examples from nonexamples
   (The teacher asks, "Which of these are examples?")
3. Producing examples
   (The teacher directs, "Find or make an example.")
4. Correcting nonexamples
   (The teacher asks, "What changes are needed to make this an example?")

The four types of classifying can be used both before and after concept instruction. When used before, it is for the purpose of assessing the extent to which students have already formed and can apply a particular concept. A teacher may be thinking that a class needs a concept formation lesson on *peninsula*. But, not wanting to waste their time, he or she first assesses their understanding. Let us say the teacher decides to use the first type of classifying. Pointing to Florida on the wall map of the United States, the teacher says, "I'm curious. Who can tell us whether this piece of land here in the state called Florida is a *peninsula*? Why don't you take a minute to think about it. Then give a thumbs-up if you think it is, a thumbs-down if you think it isn't, and a thumbs-sideways if you're not sure. Remember, 'not sure' is an honorable position to take if you indeed are not sure." In a class of 25, the teacher sees 2 thumbs-up, 2 down, and 21 sideways. The teacher then elicits their reasons, for without hearing the reasons the teacher has learned almost nothing. "Those of you with your thumbs sideways, what makes you unsure?" Some say they've "never heard that word before." Another thinks a peninsula "is more like a lake." And so forth. The two thumbs-up actually don't know the concept, it turns out. They're claiming Florida is a peninsula, but for all the wrong reasons. The two thumbs-down think it is not a peninsula, but their reasons reveal they haven't thought carefully about the concept either. Hence, the teacher decides to work up a concept-formation lesson.

When classifying is used *after* instruction on a concept, it is for the purpose of strengthening the concept and providing students the opportunity to *use* it—to apply it to new items, as was done at Step 6 of Lesson Plan 11. Of course, if students haven't formed the concept, they will be unable to apply it.

Incorporating Cooperative Groupwork

At Step 1 in concept formation, students can be placed in cooperative teams of four students each. Each member of the group takes responsibility for gathering information on one of the four examples. Sherry takes Mexico, Jim takes Canada, Mie takes the classroom meetings, and Reno gets the United States. (Or, in the case of the peninsula lesson, one takes Florida, another takes the Olympic peninsula, etc.) Because one member of every team is studying the same example, these students get together in an "expert group" to work on their example together (see Chapter 11 for details). Every team member thus leaves his or her team to work with other students responsible for the same example. Eventually, experts return to their teams, where they teach their example to teammates. In this way, everyone studies all examples—which is crucial for concept formation because a concept is a summary of attributes *shared by all examples*.

For Steps 2 through 5, it is a good idea to work with the whole class as Mr. Bailey did. But for classifying, teams can again be convened to complete the application work.

Variation 1 on Concept Formation: List, Group, and Label

I would be remiss not to share a delightful and often usable variation on concept formation called "list, group, and label." Imagine a primary-grade class that has just returned from a field trip to a supermarket. Back in the classroom, the teacher asks the children to list as many things as they can remember having seen in the supermarket. As they name items, the teacher writes them on the whiteboard—for example, eggs, bread, beans, meat, butter, checkout person, stock clerk, watermelons, candy, store manager, dog food, cat food, ice cream, and so on.

After listing the things they saw, the teacher asks them to examine their list to see if certain things seem to go together. "Can these items be put together in groups that have something in common?" They catch on quickly, and soon they are suggesting which items can be placed in the same group. Dog food and cat food are put together.

Having placed items that seem to go together in the same group, children are then asked to think of names or labels for these groups. In the foregoing example, a name for the group

FIGURE 9–1   List, group, and label

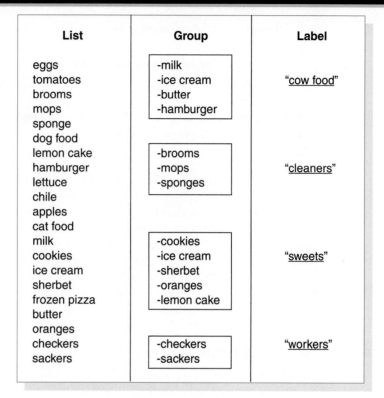

List	Group	Label
eggs	-milk	
tomatoes	-ice cream	"cow food"
brooms	-butter	
mops	-hamburger	
sponge		
dog food		
lemon cake	-brooms	
hamburger	-mops	"cleaners"
lettuce	-sponges	
chile		
apples		
cat food		
milk	-cookies	
cookies	-ice cream	"sweets"
ice cream	-sherbet	
sherbet	-oranges	
frozen pizza	-lemon cake	
butter		
oranges		
checkers	-checkers	"workers"
sackers	-sackers	

would probably be "pet food." The children should develop a name or label for each of the groups. Figure 9–1 provides a sample.

The list, group, and label strategy can be used in many ways to teach concepts in social studies. It can also be played as the game called "Things You See _____" (at the zoo, at the mall, at the swimming pool, in the neighborhood). As students gain more practice, they begin to more skillfully note similarities among items. Consequently, they group and regroup items in more interesting and more subtle ways, using the same item in more than one group. One student can create a group and ask the others to guess the common attribute on which it was formed. For example, can you identify the similarity on which the following group was formed?

Apples

Oranges

Eggs

Ice cream

Possible responses include: each is a food (to produce this response, students would be focusing on the meaning of the words); each begins with a vowel (to produce this response, they would be focusing not on the meanings but the symbols—the alphabet).

Here now are a few additional questions that call for listing, grouping, and then labeling. Each builds geographic awareness.

- Suppose a visitor from another country spent a day at our school. What would he or she see?
- What did you see on our walk through the neighborhood?
- What are all the ways you have seen goods and people being moved from one place to another?
- How many things can you list that are manufactured in our state?
- What are some landforms in North America?
- What natural resources do we depend on in our everyday life?

Grouping is a cultural as well as an individual process. It is important for teachers to keep an eye peeled for cultural influences among students' grouping suggestions. In *The Geography of Thought* (2003), Richard Nisbett reports on a number of studies in which Chinese and European (or European American) students tended to group items differently in ways that reflected different ways of perceiving the world. When children were asked to group pictures of a chicken, a cow, and grass, the European children grouped the chicken and cow together because both were animals. The Chinese children grouped the cow and grass together because the cow eats grass. Attention to *context* may explain the difference.

Variation 2 on Concept Formation: Concept Attainment

There is another variation on concept formation, which is less inductive and more direct; less student-centered and more teacher-centered, but still powerful. This approach is sometimes called "concept attainment" to distinguish it from "concept formation." [6]

Let us say that a sixth-grade class has been studying the economic development of nations in Latin America. The teacher, Ms. Rush, wants her students to develop the concept *modernization* and helps them do so in the following way. Note that she does not first give them examples to study and then lead them to a discovery of the concept based on the examples' shared attributes, as in concept formation. Rather, she explicitly *tells* them the attributes and then provides examples and nonexamples, and helps students distinguish between them. She begins by writing the concept label and critical attributes on the chalkboard.

Modernization involves

1. The use of technology to control nature's resources
2. The use of inanimate (nonanimal) sources of power and energy
3. The use of tools to multiply the effects of human energy

Ms. Rush then explains the meaning of each of the three attributes by using large pictures. She shows the class specific examples of modernization—situations in which technology is applied to the control of resources, where nonanimal power and energy sources are used (i.e., no beasts of burden), and where tools multiply human energy. She calls these "examples" and makes the presence of all three attributes clear in each of them. Children's questions are discussed and problems are clarified. Ms. Rush then provides the class with a series of pictures in which modernization, as defined by the particular attributes, is not evident. She calls these "nonexamples" of modernization and tells

Preparations are made to deeply teach the concept *village* in a unit called "Village Life Around the World." *(Anthony Magnacca/Merrill)*

students they need to understand why they are not examples of modernization. Each photo is explained, and the missing critical attributes are discussed. Questions are encouraged and answered carefully.

Having satisfied herself that the children have a basic understanding of the attributes of modernization, Ms. Rush presents the class with another set of pictures, but this time the students themselves must distinguish examples from nonexamples and explain their decisions (this is classifying type 2). These pictures are discussed in detail, and any misunderstandings are corrected. The teacher then provides the class with back issues of *National Geographic* and asks them to find photo examples and nonexamples of modernization and to tell why each is or is not an example (classifying type 3). Again, she provides feedback. Finally, the teacher double-checks the children's understanding of the concept by showing them a new picture of a nonexample (e.g., a horse pulling a plow) and asking them what changes would need to be made to turn it into an example (classifying type 4).

This variation on concept teaching has the teacher provide the attributes of the concept in advance rather than having learners construct them as they would at Steps 3 and 4 of the concept-formation strategy. In summary, concept attainment has seven steps:

1. Teacher tells students the label for the concept ("modernization").
2. Teacher lists and explains the critical attributes of the concept.

3. Teacher provides examples (each has the attributes) and explains why they are examples.
4. Teacher provides *non*examples (each is missing one or more attributes) and explains why they are *non*examples.
5. Teacher presents more examples and nonexamples, but now has the children decide which is which and explain why (classifying type 2).
6. Teacher has children find examples and nonexamples on their own (classifying type 3).
7. Teacher presents a new nonexample and asks children what changes would need to be made for it to become an example (classifying type 4).

Making Concepts Graphic

Students can make their conceptual understandings graphic in a number of ways. One way is to create a virtual museum, as did Liz Ricketts and her students at Washington Elementary School in Montebello, California. Shown in Figure 9–2, their work with the

---

FIGURE 9–2   Making the concept *transportation* graphic.

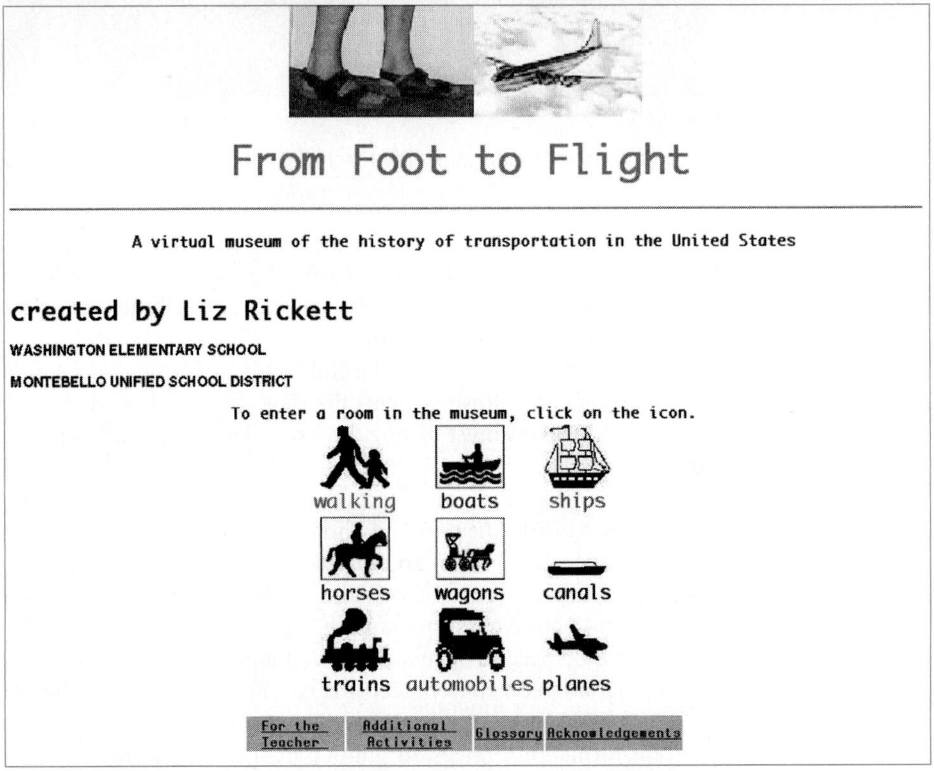

From Foot to Flight

A virtual museum of the history of transportation in the United States

created by Liz Rickett

WASHINGTON ELEMENTARY SCHOOL

MONTEBELLO UNIFIED SCHOOL DISTRICT

To enter a room in the museum, click on the icon.

walking   boats   ships

horses   wagons   canals

trains   automobiles   planes

For the Teacher   Additional Activities   Glossary   Acknowledgements

Reprinted by permission of Margaret Hill, SCORE: http://score.rims.k12.ca.us/

concept *transportation* includes nine examples, each of which can be visited at their on-line virtual museum. Another, more kinesthetic approach is to direct students to make a three-dimensional paper graphic as described in Chapter 8. Doing so helps them sharpen their understanding and allows the teacher to determine whether there is any misunderstanding. A concept pyramid can show one example on each of the three sides. Or, as shown here, a standard piece of copy paper folded almost in half allows the concept name to be written at the bottom; then examples are represented behind each "door." Or, on a three-door Venn-diagram fold, one example can be inside each of the outside doors and their similarities can be listed in the center. See the colorful examples in Chapter 8.

Summary

Concept formation and its two variations help children learn multiple examples of the concept to be learned and grasp the critical similarities among all the examples. This is the heart of concept teaching. In concept attainment, the children do less of the construction work themselves; the teacher does more for them. It is therefore a somewhat easier strategy to use, and you may wish to try it before trying the others.

What About Facts?

Before we leave the subject of teaching concepts, we should address one question that may be on your mind: What about *facts* in concept teaching? When we teach concepts to children, does that mean we are not teaching facts?

Facts are data or information. Facts can be observed using the senses. A child can see that a pueblo home is made of pinkish mud. He or she can feel the straw sticking out of the adobe brick, hear the slow beat of the drum, taste the fry bread, and smell the burning sage. These are facts. There are millions of facts that students could be asked to learn.

Concepts, on the other hand, are ideas. Ideas exist only in our minds. They cannot, therefore, be observed using the senses. They are made up of examples, and examples are bundles of facts. The fact that adobe is used to make pueblo dwellings, that it is made from the soil found in some parts of the southwestern region of what is now the United States, that an adobe home feels remarkably cool inside though the sun shines bright and hot overhead—these facts together make one example of the concept *human–environment interaction*. The Lakota Sioux portable shelter made of buffalo hide is another, and the Woodland Iroquois longhouse is yet another. Figure 9–3 shows the relationship of facts, examples, and concepts.

You can see, then, that concept learning certainly involves the learning of facts. Concepts comprise of examples, which comprise of facts.

FIGURE 9-3   The relationship of facts, examples, and concepts.

CONCEPT: Island

Example 1: Kauai

Facts about: shape
location
population
climate
government
economy
cultures
history
religions

Example 2: Singapore

Facts about: shape
location
population
climate
government
economy
cultures
history
religions

Example 3: Cuba

Facts about: shape
location
population
climate
government
economy
cultures
history
religions

TEACHING WITH INQUIRY

The inquiry process is also called the scientific method or problem solving and, in the field of history, historical interpretation or historical reasoning (see Chapter 4). Call it what you will, it is the chief method used by historians and social scientists to develop new knowledge and correct old, mistaken knowledge. Even young children can learn inquiry; their incessant "why" questions show that the motivation to inquire is fully present. Teachers can help children become more skillful inquirers by engaging them in inquiry often, both as part of daily classroom life and as a way of learning social studies subject matter.

Children who have developed their inquiry abilities are able to draw conclusions based on evidence and judge whether conclusions drawn by others are supported by evidence. This is the essence of inquiry.

When they learn to inquire skillfully, students learn to explore historical (and other social studies) problems by making an educated guess about the problem and then searching

If inquiry is this important, it should be happening frequently and systematically in the school curriculum. Do you agree that it not only cultivates knowledge and the intellect but democracy too? If so, how?

for evidence that would justify one conclusion over another. More specifically, they learn to hypothesize, search for evidence, draw conclusions, and evaluate the strength of conclusions. For this reason, the inquiry process is exalted as the highest form of higher-order thinking or critical thinking. Students learn that evidence varies in its credibility and that there are usually competing accounts of any one event. Their teacher is forever pestering them with the questions "How do you know that's true?" and "Do your sources agree?" And, "If not, how did you decide?" Gradually, thanks to such teachers, students will come to ask these questions themselves. They will develop a healthy respect for facts, a steadfast aversion to jumping to conclusions, and an eagerness to spot prejudices and root them out. These are habits that are among the most valued *cognitive* goals that we have for children's learning, but also they are among the most valued *democratic citizenship* goals. Why? Democracies rely on citizens who can think well: who can distinguish between evidence and opinion, between good arguments and good stories, between well-researched conclusions and outright lies. For these reasons, even beginning teachers should make it a priority to involve children in inquiry experiences.

The general inquiry procedure is this: The teacher engages students' interest in the problem for study and has the children pose hypotheses about it. Then the teacher designs activities in which the children gather information (evidence) and compare it to these hypotheses. As they do the comparisons, the children learn to discard, add, and revise hypotheses, as the facts require. Eventually, they draw conclusions. Let's look at the process step-by-step.

1. The teacher engages students in a problem related to a curriculum objective. This is accomplished using a few photos, a newspaper headline, a film clip, a compelling story, or some other interest-building technique. The problem is usually decided by the teacher, because he or she is trying to address a key curriculum objective or standard; but students also can be involved in deciding on the problem.

Problem	Curriculum Topic
Who really "discovered" America?	First peoples of the Americas
What happened to the Anasazi at Mesa Verde?	Pre-Columbian civilizations in America; human–environment interaction
Did the American colonists really want independence from England?	Revolution, Constitution, and the new nation
Why did the *Titanic* tragedy occur?	Transportation; social life during the Industrial Revolution
Why did the Pony Express end suddenly?	Inventions; communication technology
Why is there poverty in rich nations?	Comparative economic systems; social class
Why do so few adults vote in the United States?	Comparative political systems; citizenship rights and responsibilities
Who benefits from advertising?	Media literacy; production and consumption; needs and wants

2. The teacher elicits hypotheses (reasonable guesses) from students about the problem and records them on the chalkboard or butcher paper taped to the wall.

   A teacher might say to students, "We know that the *Titanic* hit an iceberg, but why do you think this great 'unsinkable' ship did that?" He or she draws hypotheses out of students and writes them in large print on butcher paper taped to the wall:

> HYPOTHESES:
> The Titanic hit the iceberg because there was no radar.
> There was poor visibility that night.
> The lookouts were asleep or at a party.
> The ship was bombed by the other ship company, lost control,
>   and hit the iceberg.
> Competition between companies made the captain speed.
> Overconfidence made him reckless.

3. Students gather information (evidence, data) through reading, oral reports by classmates, field trips, guest speakers, interviews and surveys, the Internet, CDs and DVDs, paintings, teacher read-alouds and presentations, and the like. This data gathering could take anywhere from a day to a few weeks, depending on the amount of data available and the amount the teacher wants students to gather, organize, and analyze. This research should involve multiple information sources and, if possible, both primary and secondary sources.

4. Students organize and interpret the information and draw conclusions. The most efficient way to do this is to organize the information around the hypotheses. That is, students evaluate the hypotheses using the information that has been gathered and draw conclusions as to which hypotheses are best or least supported by the evidence. As with any scientific study, there will be disputes among the researchers. This is good! Challenging one another's claims and conclusions is central to the activity called "science." At this point, students can be directed to make a two-door graphic featuring the two hypotheses they believe are best supported by the evidence.

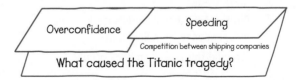

5. The conclusions are published—they are made public. Whether in the classroom newsletter, a report to the school principal or town mayor, or a presentation to younger students, the results of scientific inquiry are always shared. The audience members can then accept or reject the conclusions presented based on their own interpretation of the evidence. This is how knowledge is constructed, corrected, and reconstructed over time.

There follow two quite different examples of inquiry teaching. The differences display the breadth of approaches possible within the concept *inquiry;* however, they share the critical attributes necessary to be called inquiry lessons. The first involves a third-grade class that has been studying the concept *advertising.* Notice how this teacher has students assemble numerous examples, elicits their hypotheses about the value of advertising, and then has them search for information that confirms or denies these hypotheses. The second is an inquiry lesson plan on the causes of the *Titanic* tragedy. It is one of my favorite plans, and I have used it many times. Both examples adhere to the inquiry model just presented.

For additional examples of inquiry teaching in a unit plan alongside concept formation, readers can skip ahead to Chapter 13 and study the integrated third-grade science–social studies unit called "Explore."

Inquiry Example 1: Who Benefits from Advertising?

A third-grade class has been introduced, using the concept-formation strategy, to the concept *advertising.* Sensing that the children's understanding is still quite weak, the teacher selects the following inquiry strategy to strengthen it.

First, children are asked to search for as many different examples of advertising as they can find. This search uncovers newspaper and magazine advertisements, classified ads, radio and television commercials, billboards, signs on transit buses, pop ups on webpages, direct mailers, catalogs, and others. These various methods of advertising are discussed in terms of (a) their purpose; (b) the audience to which they are directed; (c) the extent to which they are local, regional, or national; and, perhaps most important, (d) the nature of the appeal. To help students perceive and think about the appeal, the teacher asks: "How does the 'Marlboro Man' appeal to boys? How does the outdoorsy, four-wheel-drive sports-utility vehicle commercial on television appeal to people who drive mainly in urban and suburban areas? How do slender clothing models appeal to girls?" It should be noted that anthropologists are hired by advertising companies to study a segment of society and advise how a product can be made to appeal to that group. The teacher might videotape advertisement examples from Saturday morning children's programs and bring them to class for scrutiny by the class.

These activities will surely generate student interest. Now, the teacher moves toward the inquiry question. Maybe this one: "Who benefits from advertising, and how do they benefit?" In response, the children develop the following hypotheses that they record on butcher paper and post on the wall:

> HYPOTHESES:
>
> 1. Advertising helps consumers because it informs them about new products and their prices.
> 2. Effective advertising makes people want things whether they are needed or not. It benefits only the sellers.
> 3. Local advertising has a more direct effect on sales in local stores than does national advertising.

The children begin searching for information that would support or reject these hypotheses. Much of their information gathering relies on interviews conducted outside school with consumers and local merchants and conducted by telephone and email with representatives of advertising agencies. This process forces them to explore related subconcepts, such as needs and wants, promotion, audience, client, market, layout, theme, and sales appeal. In time, they are able to form some tentative conclusions.

Inquiry Example 2: What Caused the *Titanic* Tragedy?

The teacher shows students the headline in the local newspaper dated April 15, 1912. It reads, " 'Unsinkable' Greyhound Sinking Off Newfoundland." She tells her students that the headline is referring to the sinking of the luxury ocean liner, the *Titanic*. Due to the hugely popular 1997 film by James Cameron, some students bubble with recognition. She asks them why they think such ocean liners were called "greyhounds" and why the present tense, "is sinking," was used. Then she shows them a 10-minute film clip from the Cameron film of the *Titanic* tragedy and another from the earlier (1958) film *A Night to Remember,* or from one of the several documentaries now available. This accomplishes Step 1—engaging their interest in the inquiry. Then she has students hypothesize about the causes of the tragedy. She selects the inquiry's focus question: "Why did the *Titanic* tragedy occur? We know it hit an iceberg, but why?"

Lesson Plan 12 presents the lesson plan she used. Notice that the teacher in this lesson provides the information to students rather than having them conduct research themselves. Why? She wants to familiarize them with the basic inquiry process, using a highly motivating topic. In the next unit, she plans to help them to use the inquiry process again, following the same five-part plan used with the *Titanic* inquiry, only then they will add considerable Internet and library research. In this way, they gradually build their inquiry skills throughout the year.

Note also that in the *Titanic* plan the teacher provides information a little bit at a time—in chunks, or data sets. This way, children can be helped to evaluate their hypotheses and draw tentative conclusions after each chunk of data. This is a highly effective strategy with younger and older children alike. It is a vivid way to give children a memorable experience of the power of data, a little at a time, for they see hypotheses vanish from the whiteboard as a new chunk of data is considered.

TEACHING SOCIAL STUDIES SKILLS

One of the main causes of poor skills among children—whether cooperative skills, thinking skills, reading and writing skills, research and study skills, or whatever—is, not surprisingly, lack of instruction. The systematic and sequential development of skills is of utmost importance to children because skills are among the tools with which they continue their learning. Inadequately developed skills tend to retard learning in many areas of the elementary and middle school curriculum, particularly in the social studies. Inadequate achievement in the social studies can, in many cases, be traced to poorly developed reading skills, inquiry skills, discussion skills, inability to read maps and globes, poor work–study skills, and inability to

CAUSES OF THE *TITANIC* TRAGEDY: AN INQUIRY

Grades   4–8

Time   Two to four class periods

NCSS Standards   2 (time, continuity, and change) and 8 (science, technology, and society)

Objectives   Students will learn how to formulate hypotheses and then revise them as new information is encountered, and learn how to draw conclusions based on evidence.

Interest Building   Show a 1912 headline of the sinking of the *Titanic* and a clip from a documentary or fiction film of the tragedy, or photos of the *Titanic* gathered from magazine articles about the sinking of the ship and recent expeditions to explore it at the bottom of the Atlantic. Tell students the story of the *Titanic*—that it was billed as luxurious and unsinkable but, nonetheless, hit an iceberg and sank in the cold northern Atlantic on its first voyage.

Lesson Development

1. Ask students why they think a ship this great with a captain so skilled might have hit an iceberg on its maiden voyage. What caused the tragedy? List their reasons on the board under the title "Hypotheses." If needed, suggest some possibilities: captain was asleep, terrorism, lookouts were at a party, crew was not expecting icebergs in those waters at that time of year, captain was overconfident, design flaws in the ship.

2. Ask each student to jot down the hypothesis that he or she thinks might be true. Then ask everyone to share his or her favored hypothesis with the class.

3. Give students more information, one chunk (5 to 10 minutes) at a time. Begin with a set of information on the ship's design; then move to such things as the weather conditions that night, the captain's experience taking new ships across the Atlantic, the *Titanic*'s sister ships, the way ships communicated and received warnings in those days, icebergs, social life aboard the ship, the lifeboats, the ship's cargo, and the competition between the two shipping lines, Cunard and White Star.

   Important: Between each set of data, pause and ask students to examine the list of hypotheses on the board. Have them remove, add, and revise hypotheses in light of the information they are getting. This is the core activity of the lesson.

4. Draw the inquiry to a close. Ask students to return to the hypotheses they jotted down at the beginning of the lesson. Have them revise these as needed to reflect what they now believe to be true. These new statements are conclusions that are based on data. Have them begin their conclusions as follows: "I conclude that the main reasons the *Titanic* tragedy occurred are. . . ." Encourage them to build multiple causes, not just one, into their conclusions.

Summary   Tell the class that this process of revising conclusions ("changing our minds") in light of new data is the essence of science. It is the meaning of *open-minded* and it is the opposite of jumping to conclusions. Now ask students what information they can imagine that would cause them to revise their conclusions yet again.

Assessment   (a) Collect and read the conclusions students wrote at Step 4 and evaluate them on the extent to which they were based on data gathered in Step 3. Invite students to place these conclusions in their portfolios and to begin a subsection called "inquiries." (b) It will also be interesting to find out what students now perceive to be the meaning of such phrases as "jumping to conclusions" and "closed-minded." Also, see if they can write down the inquiry sequence they experienced in this lesson (see list below). Listen to their responses and provide assistance as needed.

1. Become familiar with the problem.
2. Develop hypotheses.
3. Gather and organize information.
4. Use the information to test each hypothesis.
5. Draw conclusion based on the information gathered.

Follow-up   Repeat the inquiry sequence with other, more specific questions that will surely arise: Why were there not enough lifeboats? What was the last music played by the band? Why did rescue ships not arrive sooner? What difference did social class make and why? Begin to teach students ways to evaluate the quality of information: What was the source? Did the author have an agenda? Is information on the *Titanic* found in *National Geographic* equivalent to information found in *National Enquirer?*

Materials   *Titanic* websites (e.g., www.encyclopedia-titanica.org), the textbook, encyclopedias, magazine articles, books about its sinking and the expeditions to find it, film clips from *A Night to Remember* (1958) or the more recent James Cameron film, *Titanic.*

Integration   *Music.* The heroism of the eight band members who kept playing to calm the passengers as the ship foundered is a study in itself. The funeral of their leader, Wallace Hartley, was attended by 30,000 mourners in his home town of Colne, Lancashire (England). A mystery remains: What was the final music they played? Primary sources disagree. The contenders are "Autumn" and "Nearer, My God, to Thee." Invite a music teacher (or a parent who is a musician) to visit the class and help students listen to recordings of both.

Literature. There are many trade books, fiction and nonfiction, narrative and expository, on the *Titanic* tragedy. See *Titanic: The Disaster That Shocked the World*, by Mark Dubowski (DK, 1998) for younger children and, for older children, *Titanic: Destination Disaster* by John Eaton and Charles Haas (Norton, 1987). The latter deals with the music question in detail.

Films: As mentioned above.

---

use reference materials. Therefore, a well-balanced program in the social studies needs to provide for systematic instruction to ensure the development of these skills.

Skill implies proficiency: the capability to do something well. Skills are commonly classified as motor, intellectual, and social. This book does not address motor skills, but social and intellectual skills are considered throughout. Social skills include forming small groups for cooperative work and functioning well within them. Social skills also include citizenship skills, such as discussion and decision making. Such skills are the subject of Chapters 3, 6, and 11. Intellectual skills are dealt with in nearly every chapter of this book. Reading and making maps, globes, time lines, and graphics are the skills discussed in Chapter 5. Numerous reading skills are discussed in Chapter 12.

In the present chapter we have encountered the intellectual skills needed to form concepts and conduct inquiry:

Intellectual Skills in Concept Formation

- Gathering data on each example
- Organizing information on data-retrieval charts
- Noting differences and similarities across examples
- Summarizing similarities
- Classifying (applying the concept in new situations)

Intellectual Skills in Inquiry

- Hypothesizing
- Gathering and interpreting data
- Evaluating hypotheses in light of data
- Drawing conclusions

Students test their hypotheses by gathering data from a website.
(*Scott Cunningham/Merrill*)

All skills have two characteristics in common: they are developmental, and they require practice and feedback if they are to be mastered. To speak of skills as being developmental means that they are learned gradually over a period of years and transformed again and again as the individual's mind and body mature. Furthermore, they are never really learned to completion, although there usually comes a time when the learner has mastered them sufficiently for most purposes; however, one could continue refining these skills through-out one's lifetime. Thus, teachers should not assume that skills are taught and learned only once in some particular grade. All teachers need to assume some responsibility for the teach-ing and maintenance of social studies skills.

The basic skill-teaching procedure is fairly clear-cut. Learners should first understand what is involved in the skill, how it is used, and what it means. Providing a good model of its use is helpful at this point. Second, the learners need to work through a simple applica-tion of the skill, step-by-step, under careful teacher guidance. This is essential to verify that they understand what is involved and are making a correct response. Third, they need to actually use the skill in a purposeful way. This application of the skill should be kept very simple. It is a good opportunity to assess their understanding of the skill and provide feed-back. Fourth, the learners need additional guided practice, only now the level of difficulty can be increased a little. Continue to assess and provide feedback. Fifth, students need con-tinued practice in using the skill in various functional settings. Gradually increase the com-plexity of the tasks in which students use the skill and encourage improved use of the skill.

Sixth, continue to provide practice opportunities intermittently. These steps, along with an example of their application, are provided in Lesson Plan 13. Remember that no amount of explanation alone will make children proficient in skills.

In the ordinary study of a topic there will be numerous opportunities to practice skills in the daily work–study activities of the class. In this way, the children improve their skills as they develop their understanding of concepts and subject matter.

This bears repeating. Skills are learned more effectively when they are closely related to actual situations in which they will be used. This connection is most obvious in the case of work–study skills such as finding information; arranging information in usable forms; using maps, globes, and graphics; and organizing information. Such skills have no purpose outside a functional setting where they are used to learn about peoples and places, form or extend concepts, conduct inquiries on problems, develop democratic dispositions, and meet other valued curriculum goals. This applies to intellectual skills and groupwork skills as well. Higher-order thinking processes, such as summarizing, classifying, inquiry, and decision making, must be put to work as tools for content learning if they are to be taught with integrity and authenticity. Accordingly, teachers should not set out to teach these important processes without giving ample consideration to the subject matter in which they are to be applied. Teaching the needed skills explicitly, using a lesson plan such as the classic one provided here, and then *using* them—that is the proper approach.

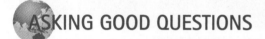ASKING GOOD QUESTIONS

The teaching strategies presented in this chapter all rest squarely on good questions. Each of these three teaching strategies (five, if you count the two variations on concept formation) assumes that the teacher is a skillful question asker. *Asking good questions is not a separate teaching strategy so much as it is a component of any good strategy.* Looking back at concept formation, we see that the teacher's questions compose the scaffold students stand on at each step. At the noting-similarities step, the teacher asks, "In what ways are these four governments all alike?" At the next step, another question invites students to summarize these similarities into a single statement. At the next, a question elicits the concept's label, which is a label for this summary. Each question initiates a particular kind of intellectual work, in a particular sequence, culminating in the formation of a concept and then testing and extending it with still more questions—classifying.

Looking back at inquiry earlier in this chapter, a carefully placed question invites students to hypothesize about causes or consequences of a historic event. This is the essential question for the whole inquiry process. Another question initiates data gathering and another elicits conclusions. Or, looking back to Ms. Paley's rule-posing question in Chapter 3, a classroom rule is proposed, and then Ms. Paley asks two very precise questions: "Will the rule work?" and, "Is it fair?" The same goes for teaching skills, teaching current events, and so on. *Questions are the teacher's constant companion and the handiest and most powerful of tools. They direct the intellectual work of students.* This is not to suggest that questions replace love, patience, and curiosity—these are not replaceable. But whether the subject matter is a concept, such as democracy or shelter; an inquiry on global warming in Canada or the causes of the *Titanic* tragedy; a skill, such as map reading; or, more likely, a combination of these in a unit of study, a toolbox of good questions is arguably the teacher's best friend.

USING A NEWSPAPER DIRECTORY: A SKILLS LESSON

Grades   3–8

Time   Two to three class periods

NCSS Standards   8 (science, technology, and society), 9 (global connections), 10 (civic ideals and practices)

Objectives   Children will learn how to use a newspaper's directory and then apply the skill to finding information in several different newspapers.

Interest Building and Preassessment   Engage students in a brief discussion of a controversial issue in the news, something pertinent to them. Then ask a few questions to determine what they know about the location in newspapers of related news stories, editorials, and political cartoons. Then produce a class set of the day's newspaper.

Lesson Development

Step 1

Make sure children understand what is involved in performing the skill. Show them how it is used. Provide them with a good model of the skill in operation.

For example, for a lesson on using a newspaper directory, hold up the newspaper and show how difficult and time-consuming it is to find some bit of information if one has to leaf through the entire paper to find it. Have children try their hand at finding items without using the newspaper directory. Show how easily one can find information with the aid of the directory.

Step 2

Break the skill into components and arrange them sequentially. Develop the teaching sequence step-by-step, having the children do each component as it is presented and explained. Supervise carefully to make sure their responses are correct.

The following are some ways you might develop a lesson on using a newspaper directory:

- Acquaint children with various sections of the newspaper: general news, classified ads, sports, editorials, letters to the editor, weather, and so on.
- Teach children the specialized vocabulary associated with the newspaper: vital statistics, obituaries, market quotations, headline, byline, dateline, syndicated, and so on.
- Teach children what items are included in the various categories listed in the directory and how they are arranged. For example, what is included in the arts and entertainment section? How are the classifieds organized?
- Provide a newspaper for each member of the class and have the children locate easy items using the directory. Such items might include the television schedule, sports, and the comics. Supervise to make sure everyone is performing the skill correctly.

Step 3

Have children perform a simple variation of the skill under your close supervision. This will ensure that they are performing the skill correctly.

For the lesson on using a newspaper directory, follow Step 2 immediately with an exercise requiring children to locate items using the directory. Supervise and assist as needed. Check responses.

Step 4

After it is established that the children are performing the skill correctly, provide for supervised practice, using simple variations that ensure success.

For the lesson on using a newspaper directory, assign children to find information in the next day's newspaper. This should be done on their own without teacher supervision. Check responses.

Step 5

Gradually increase the complexity of the variation of the skill and begin having children apply the skill in situations in which it is useful. Continue this procedure until the desired level of proficiency is achieved.

For the newspaper directory lesson, bring to class copies of different newspapers from the one used thus far in which slightly different directory formats appear. Assign children to find information in these papers without teacher assistance to see if they can transfer and modify their skill from one situation to another. Check responses. (This can be done in trios, one paper per group.)

Step 6

Follow-up Continue to have students practice the skill at regular intervals, largely through functional application to maintain and improve performance.

For the newspaper directory lesson, have children continue to use the directory to locate needed information. Observe the accuracy and extensiveness of use of the directory. For example, when teaching a current event, have students locate relevant articles, editorials, and letters to the editor.

Summary Review the name of the skill. Then have several students demonstrate it.

Assessment Note the informal assessment that was part of the opening "Interest Building." Following the skill lesson and using a different newspaper (e.g., the next day's), observe students as they locate "as quickly as you can" the following sections: movies, sports, editorials, editorial cartoon, television schedule, national news, local news, classifieds, obituaries, and help wanted section in the classifieds.

Materials A local newspaper for each student

Local newspaper website homepage showing on the classroom computer

Integration *Reading:* This lesson infused reading instruction into the social studies curriculum. Capable newspaper reading also requires the reading skills of previewing and skimming (see Chapter 12). Social studies is the ideal base for reading instruction, with its wide spectrum of content and genres: narrative, informational text, biography, argument, and multiple perspectives.

Purposes of Asking Questions

Questions serve five purposes. They assess, they focus attention, they guide thinking, they follow up on students' responses, and they facilitate participation. A good understanding of these purposes is the first step to asking good questions; therefore, sample questions are given in relationship to each purpose.

Assessment

Ashby and Lee write, "In the end, it is more interesting listening to pupils and trying to understand why they see things as they do than it is to hear one's own voice trying to push them into giving the right answer." [7] Questions help curious teachers listen to students and, thereby, learn how and why they see things as they do. In other words, questions help teachers know children and ascertain their understanding of concepts, inquiry, and skills. They also help teachers assess whether students understand what they are to do and their reactions to demonstrations or explanations. Examples:

- Are playground games *democratic?* Should they be?
- People all over the world eat *food.* Is that just because they like to, or do they need food? Why? What does food do for us? [8]

- Before beginning, let's review the instructions. What are you to do first? Keesha? Michael?
- What did you learn from that demonstration? What would you have done differently?

Focus Attention

"What proves to be effective is not telling the child the right answer, but guiding him or her towards the right considerations." [9] Teachers use questions to focus students' attention on a particular topic, that is, to guide their thinking to certain subjects and objects and not others. This is done in a moment-to-moment fashion during instruction, such as when the teacher shifts students' attention from noting differences to noting similarities during the concept-formation sequence: "Now that we have identified some of the differences among the examples, how are they all alike?" Questions also figure centrally in planning, such as when a teacher plans one question that will guide an entire two-week inquiry unit: "Why did the *Titanic* tragedy occur?" or "Who benefits from advertising?" Reflecting on the teaching strategies addressed in this chapter, focus questions played a key role. For example, here is one focus question per strategy:

- *In concept teaching:* "What is a word you might use to describe governments like these? Be creative—invent a word if you like. Make sure it captures the essence of this kind of government."
- *In inquiry teaching:* "What caused the *Titanic* tragedy? We know it hit an iceberg, but why?"
- *In skill teaching:* "How can the directory be used to locate information in the newspaper?"

Promote Thinking

Different questions promote different kinds of thinking. Research conducted over the past several decades on classroom questions reveals that teachers use a high percentage of questions that stimulate only recall of information that has been read or discussed in class. These questions are lower-level questions because they involve simple memory rather than higher-order thought processes that require some manipulation of information, such as application, analysis, synthesis, interpretation, or evaluation. Lower-order questions can be easily identified because they often begin with *who, what, when*, and *where*. These questions are important, to be sure; we have already discussed the importance of facts. The problem is that they are overused, with a corresponding decreased use of questions that prompt higher-order thinking. Questions that prompt higher-order thinking help children achieve higher levels of understanding and skill: being able to construct and apply concepts, distinguish examples from nonexamples, test hypotheses, draw conclusions, and use skills in contexts different from those in which they were initially practiced.

- *Lower (memory):* "Describe majority rule in Canada and Mexico."
- *Higher (compare and contrast):* "How are these governments alike and different?"
- *Higher still (classifying/application):* "Create a fictional democracy that is different from those we've studied, though still possessing all the attributes of a democracy." [10]

Follow Up

Questions elicit responses. What to do with those responses, how best to respond to them, brings us to the fourth use of questions: following up on students' responses. Generally speaking, the most powerful follow-up questions are those that cause students *to go further with their initial response*. There are four main types of follow-up questions:

- *Clarify:* "What do you mean by _____?" (a term the student has used)
- *Elaborate:* "Tell us more about _____." (something the student has said)
- *Verify:* "How do you know that is true?" (asking for evidence)
- *Variety:* "Who has a different idea?" (broadening the array)

But such questions do more than the term *follow up* may imply: They create and extend a *conversation*. When a teacher is having a conversation with students, it is typically not a "bull session" where there is no particular purpose beyond visiting and chatting. Rather, the teacher is trying to help students understand something or to deepen their understanding or, going back to assessment, trying to understand a student's understanding. Eleanor Duckworth conveys this purpose nicely:

> To the extent that one carries on a conversation with a child as a way of trying to understand a child's understanding, the child's understanding increases in the very process. The questions the interlocutor asks in an attempt to clarify for him/herself what the child is thinking oblige the child to think a little further also. . . . What do you mean? How did you do that? Why do you say that? How does that fit with what was just said? I don't really get that; could you explain it another way? Could you give me an example? How did you figure that out? In every case, those questions are primarily a way for the interlocutor to try to understand what the other is understanding. Yet in every case also, they engage the other's thoughts and take them a step further. [11]

In this way, a teacher's follow-up questions both promote and assess a child's evolving understanding.

Participation and Inclusion

Questions can help teachers increase student participation in the lesson and include all students.

- *"Talk with your partner about your response to that question, and in a moment I will ask several of you to share with the whole class."* The teacher lets the children know they will be held accountable for responding, thus causing more of them to attend to the task. Also, the sharing technique gets all children involved and allows sufficient time for the children to think. The teacher can roam around, giving feedback, praise, and correction as needed.
- *"How many of you think that advertising benefits mainly the consumer? Show one finger if you agree, two if you disagree. Then I'll ask several of you for your reasons."* All students are involved in the decision because of the finger-voting technique, and all know they could be asked to give reasons.
- *"Thanks, Nathaniel. How did some of you others respond?"* The teacher uses this question to acknowledge one student's response and invite other children to speak.

Improving Questioning Skills

All skills require practice if proficiency is to be achieved; asking good questions is no exception. A teacher is in a position to practice question asking daily, and colleagues can be invited to observe and provide feedback. One way to begin such practice is to write out the main (focus) questions for a lesson and carry them on a clipboard during class. Also written on the clipboard are the standard follow-up questions (Figure 9–4). These are clarify, verify, elaborate, and variety. They are taped to the clipboard because they are used to follow up regardless of the focus question. No matter the topic, teachers should encourage students to elaborate and clarify their understandings and be able to back up their conclusions and beliefs with evidence and sound reasoning.

Here now are several specific suggestions for improving your questioning skills.

1. Reduce the proportion of factual recall (literal) questions you ask and increase the number of questions that require students to use higher-order thinking. Also, use and teach the vocabulary of higher-order thinking—terms such as *classify, analyze, hypothesize, summarize,* and, of course, *think.*

2. Don't confuse instructional questions with management directions. When you mean to give a direction, such as "sit down," say "sit down." Indirect commands given as questions ("Are you ready to sit down now?") can be confusing to children, especially

FIGURE 9–4   Use a clipboard to improve your questions.

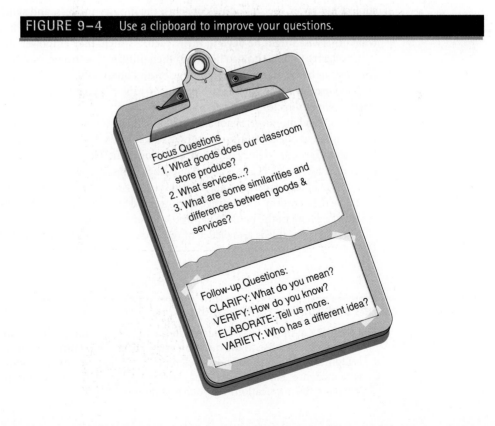

Focus Questions
1. What goods does our classroom store produce?
2. What services...?
3. What are some similarities and differences between goods & services?

Follow-up Questions:
CLARIFY: What do you mean?
VERIFY: How do you know?
ELABORATE: Tell us more.
VARIETY: Who has a different idea?

those who are culturally different from the teacher or who are not native English speakers.

3. Match questions to the purposes they are to serve. Questions that call for yes–no responses are not appropriate when an elaborate response is desired. Discussion questions should not be used for homework or independent study.

4. Provide adequate time for children to respond. Rather than calling on a child and then asking a question, ask the question *before* calling on any child to respond and tell all students to take time to think. This accomplishes two things: first, it requires *all* children to form their own response; second, it gives them all time to collect their thoughts.

5. Vary the way you acknowledge responses. In addition to "uh-huh," "all right," and "okay," ask a follow-up question: "Tell us more about that" or "What do you mean by _____?" Avoid always acknowledging responses with positive evaluations such as "right," "great," or "very good." Using these terms less often gives them more credibility with students.

Conclusion

Teaching strategies can be found in every chapter of this book. Why, then, a separate chapter? To introduce you to three classic strategies that are tailor-made for some of the core subject matter of social studies: concepts, the inquiry process, and skills.

These strategies lift up, or scaffold, students into ways of thinking, knowing, and doing what otherwise might be beyond their reach. As such, they empower students as learners. When a learner knows how to form and then think with concepts, test hypotheses and draw conclusions based on evidence, and develop and hone skills—that's power. *And note that the skills required by concept formation and inquiry are the very skills to which the skills-teaching strategy can be directed.*

Asking good questions is not a separate teaching strategy. Rather, skillful question-asking is a component of each of the other three strategies. Whether the subject matter is a concept (e.g., *democracy*), an inquiry (e.g., on the sinking of the *Titanic*), or a skill (e.g., using the newspaper directory), a repertoire of good questions that serve different purposes is indispensable.

If this chapter were expanded from three to "six great teaching strategies," the additions would be deliberation, cooperative learning, and Socratic Seminar. Yet, these are amply discussed elsewhere in the book (Chapters 3, 11, and 12, respectively).

Also indispensable is knowledge of resources. We take up this topic in the next chapter.

Discussion Questions and Suggested Activities

1. Look back at the *Reflection* sidebar in the Inquiry section of the chapter and think about your response to the question asked there. The claim made there is that the development of both the mind and democratic society rely on individuals' ability to work with evidence. Find out how your classmates are making sense of this. Do you agree? What are the implications for your teaching?

Go to MyEduca-tionLab and select the topic "Teaching Strate-gies," then read the article "Projects that Power Young Minds" and com-plete the activity.

2. Interview individually two or three children from a grade in which you have a special interest to assess their understanding of two or three social studies concepts. Use a straightforward procedure and everyday concepts. For example, you might ask, "What is an *island?* Can you name some islands?" What makes them islands? (or use *democracy, long ago, the future,* or other geographical concepts such as *stream, volcano, map projection, globe,* or *rain forest*). These interviews will provide you with firsthand knowledge of what it means to transform an otherwise complex idea into a form that is sensible for elementary school children. Before the interview, reread the long quote from Eleanor Duckworth about "understanding children's understanding" on page 316. Afterward, write up your findings to share with classmates and potential employers.

3. Using the lesson plan for teaching a skill, apply each step to a map-making or map-reading skill of your choice for a grade in which you have a special interest. Share your example with others in class.

4. NCSS Standards *Sampler*. Examine the seventh-grade classroom vignette for standard #9 on page 43 of the standards *Sampler* that accompanies this book. To what extent is it an example of inquiry strategy presented in this chapter?

Selected References

Beck, Terence A. (1998). Are there any questions? One teacher's view of students and their questions in a fourth-grade classroom. *Teaching and Teacher Education, 14* (8), 871–886.

Bransford, John, et al. (2000). *How people learn: Brain, mind, experience, and school.* Washington, DC: National Academy Press.

Harpaz, Yoram. (2007). Approaches to teaching thinking: Toward a conceptual mapping of the field. *Teachers College Record, 109* (8), 1845–1874.

Hicks, David, Carroll, Jeff, Doolittle, Peter, Lee, John, & Oliver, Brian. (2004). Teaching the mystery of history. *Social Studies and the Young Learner, 16* (3), 14–16.

Joyce, Bruce, & Weil, Marsha. (2004). *Models of teaching* (7th ed.). Boston: Allyn and Bacon.

May, Wanda T. (1993). Teaching as a work of art in the medium of curriculum. *Theory Into Practice, 32* (4), 210–218.

National Council for the Social Studies. (1994). A vision of powerful teaching and learn-ing in the social studies: Building social understanding and civic efficacy. In *Curriculum standards for social studies* (pp. 155–177). Washington, DC: Author.

SCORE: History/Social Science. An impressive collection of online resources, including virtual museums and field trips, at score.rims.k12.ca.us/.

Taba, Hilda, Durkin, Mary D., Fraenkel, Jack E., & McNaughton, A. H. (1971). *A teacher's handbook to elementary social studies: An inductive approach.* Reading, MA: Addison-Wesley.

MyEducationLab is a collection of online tools for your success in this course, your licensure exams, and your teaching career. Go to www.myeducationlab.com to utilize these extensive resources including videos from real classrooms, Praxis and licensure preparation, a lesson plan builder, and materials to help you begin your teaching career.

Four Great Resources

Chapter Outline

Key Concepts

- Multimedia approach
- Guest speakers
- Field trips
- Virtual field trips
- Web-based inquiry

MAIN IDEA

Many different kinds of resources for teaching social studies exist, and a multimedia approach is best. Teachers are encouraged to use a wide range of instructional resources because inquiry and concept formation require extensive information searches and because not all children learn in the same way. Also, different resources may provide competing viewpoints on the same subject; and there may be biases and inaccuracies that go undetected when a single source is used.

PICTURE THIS

Ms. Santana, a veteran second-grade teacher, says to her students on the second day of class: "Welcome again, children. Today, we're going to learn to learn. Because you are Ms. Santana's students, you will become experts at finding needed information quickly in our library, our community, on the Internet, and in our textbook. Did you know that many people cannot find their way around in these resources? They are like blind mice unable to find the cheese. Not you. You will become experts."

The first problem with resources is getting access to them. The second is losing control of them in such a way that the resources use the teacher, rather than the teacher using the resources. The latter is the problem of "the tail wagging the dog"—a saying reserved for situations where ends and means have become confused. This chapter identifies four sets of resources that can be of enormous benefit to teachers and students, but in each case the dog must wag the tail, not the other way around.

I encourage a multimedia approach to teaching and learning in which a wide range of instructional media are used. The reasons are straightforward:

1. Not all children learn in the same way; different media appeal to the personalities and home cultures of different learners.
2. Each medium has peculiar strengths and limitations in the way it communicates a message.
3. Different sources may provide different perspectives on the same subject; there will be biases, inaccuracies, and omissions that go undetected if a single source is used.
4. Teaching strategies that stress inquiry, concept development, and problem solving require extensive information searches and, therefore, a range of resources.
5. The impact of a message is likely to be stronger if more than one sensory system is involved in receiving it.
6. The reading range among children in most classrooms is great, averaging 3 to 5 years in the lower grades and 5 to 10 years in the middle and upper grades.
7. The use of a variety of media is engaging and motivating.

The four sets of resources featured in this chapter are both mundane and exotic. The underused school **library** (also known as the media or resource center) is presented first as a way of reminding readers of its potential and its strange wonder for a child who is just emerging from the private books, magazines, DVDs, and computer setup at home to the wider and less familiar range of public resources—even a librarian!—at school. It may be ordinary for us, but it can be extraordinary for children. The lesson plan on "orienteering" in this new space emphasizes both the importance and the exploratory fun of getting one's hands and mind around this bundle of resources. Next comes the vast possibilities of the **community** as resource. Two approaches are emphasized: taking children to the community and bringing the community to the classroom. Next comes the **Internet**. Here, two avenues are traversed: virtual field trips organized with clear before, during, and after phases, and web-based inquiries. Fourth, we turn to the resources in the social studies **textbook**. The key here is orienting children to what a textbook is and what it contains, plus using it as a resource for teaching nonfiction reading skills.

THE SCHOOL LIBRARY (MEDIA/RESOURCE CENTER)

The collection of resources in the school library makes it one of the teacher's best friends when it comes to social studies teaching and learning. The wide variety of reference materials there (such as almanacs, atlases, and encyclopedias), combined with the historical fiction collection, biographies, and picture books, make it a treasury of information, ideas, and, in the case of historical fiction, sympathetic journeys into the lives of people long ago and far away.

But one teacher's oasis is another teacher's desert. I am continually surprised at the number of teachers who do not realize the library's potential as an instructional aid. Often the reason is simple lack of familiarity with its materials combined with personal lack of experience actually using library materials. Sometimes the reason is just the opposite: Anything this ordinary can't be good. But it is imperative that new teachers explore the school library themselves and help their students do the same.

The best way to accomplish this is to make library exploration an adventure in orienteering. Orienteering is a timed cross-country, territorial competition in which participants begin at point A and try to reach point B using a compass and a map. What a fitting analogy for exploring the library! Lesson Plan 14 on the next page provides an example of how a teacher might use orienteering for second- or third-graders.

COMMUNITY RESOURCES: GUEST SPEAKERS AND FIELD TRIPS

It is in the local community that the teacher should sow the seeds of a lifetime study of human society. Here the social processes that function a thousand times over in communities around the world may be observed firsthand. In the local community, the child is introduced to geographical concepts, to the problems of group living, to government in operation, to the production and distribution of goods and services, and to the migrations, struggles, and stories of the peoples who live there. In most U.S. communities, the child can see evidence that it is possible for persons of varied backgrounds, nationalities, religious faiths, and races to live and work together harmoniously, not by overcoming their differences, but by living with one another respectfully with their differences intact. In most communities, too, the children can see the unsolved problems of poverty and homelessness, crime and vandalism, social class divisions, and ethnic strife.

The teacher may use local community resources in two basic ways. One is to bring some portion of the community to the classroom; the other is to take the class out of the school to some place of educational significance in the community. Either way, the children are interacting with and gathering information from the community. With guidance from the teacher, children can incorporate this information into inquiries they are conducting and concepts they are building.

Teachers also use community resources when children bring materials from home for bulletin boards or for their construction projects. Here is yet another way to help children acknowledge and respect family-to-family diversity. Children who have immigrated from another country or moved from another state or city will have lots to say about the geographic themes *movement* and *place*. Children whose home language is different from the language of the school can be encouraged to bring for show-and-tell items that bear writing in the home language.

Teachers also use community resources when they obtain books from the public library. The teacher should seize such an opportunity for map study. Have students locate on a map the library from which the books were borrowed and find out the location of the library closest to where each student lives. (Here is a chance to practice with relative location; see Chapter 5. "Is your home south of the public library or north? Is it near or far from it? How far?") A librarian can be invited to the class to talk about the public library or libraries in town: their locations, collections, and similarities and differences.

ORIENTEERING IN THE LIBRARY (MEDIA/RESOURCE CENTER)

Grade 2 or 3

Time Three class periods

NCSS Standards 3 (people, places, and environments) and 8 (science, technology, and society)

Objectives To "break the ice" with the library and librarian (i.e., to orient children to the school library, to help them feel comfortable there, to get accustomed to interacting with the librarian) and to learn the contents of the school library.

Interest Building Tell the children about orienteering competitions in your area—perhaps across a forested area or a plateau, depending on local geography. Show them a map and pass around a compass and help them imagine the challenge of finding their way across a strange new territory using these two tools. Then draw the analogy to the school library. Ask who knows this territory and what they know about it. Tell them that, with your help, they are going to become the school's library experts, familiar with each nook and cranny, each plateau and canyon.

Preassessment Ask students to brainstorm a list of what they'll find in the library. Then use the list, group, and label strategy (Chapter 9) to help them think more deeply about the items on the list. This will build prior knowledge (both conceptions to extend and misconceptions to correct) for the trip to the library.

Lesson Development Brief the librarian on the following activity and make an appointment to bring the class to the library. Secure the librarian's permission to post the cardinal directions in the library: a sign saying "north" on the north wall, another saying "south" on the south wall, etc.

Divide the class into teams. Ask each team to choose an interviewer who will ask questions of the librarian. Have them also decide on two questions for the interviewer to ask: one "where" question about the location of something in the library (e.g., Where is the biggest dictionary? Where is information about the Pony Express?), and one "how" question about how to locate something without asking the librarian (e.g., How can we find out where Pony Express information is located without asking you?). Then have the interviewers practice asking the two questions with teammates playing the role of the librarian.

Take the class to the library at the appointed time. Have the children sit in teams. Direct each interviewer to ask the team's questions. After all the questions have been answered, give teams the opportunity to actively experience the answers they received (e.g., go to the dictionary and open it up; load the CD with the Pony Express information).

Back in the classroom, lead the class in a list, group, and label activity dealing with the information provided by the librarian. If there were five teams with two questions each, there will be a list of at least 10 items. Ask children to group this information together based on similarities they see (e.g., electronic databases, biographies, books on the north wall, posters on the south wall).

Assessment/ Summary Distribute grid paper and ask students to sketch from memory a map of the library showing the locations of various references. Have them put a *compass rose* on their maps showing the cardinal directions. Collect and observe these. On the next day, hand the maps back unmarked and take the class to the library to revise the maps as needed. Then, distribute new grid paper on which students draw a revised map of the library to place in their map portfolios.

Materials Grid paper for each child, map and compass for displaying.

Integration *Outdoor sports. Orienteering* is also a term for an increasingly popular outdoor game in which participants use maps and a compass to navigate their way through a predefined terrain. Ask if any of your students are involved in organized orienteering events. (There are special programs for children: www.us.orienteering.org.) Invite a parent *orienteer* to the class to show students how orienteering can apply to finding one's way around the school's media center.

Guest Speakers

The teacher must select with care the persons who are invited to spend time with the class for instructional purposes. The teacher should plan to spend some time with the visitor sufficiently far in advance to brief the guest on the activities of the class, the purpose of the visit, and the points to be discussed and stressed. The guest should be encouraged to bring visuals of some sort: slides, photos, charts, or maps. A pilot can bring flight maps or aerial photographs of Earth. A mail carrier can bring a route map. Likewise, the children must be prepared for the visitor, listing questions they would like to ask and reviewing general courtesies that should be extended to classroom guests. Handled in this way, persons from the community can make a significant contribution to the instructional program in the social studies. Those who might be invited include:

- Persons with special skills: weavers, potters, jewelry makers
- Exchange students
- Persons with interesting hobbies
- Members of the local historical society
- Newspaper reporters, editors, staff writers
- Members of service organizations
- People who produce and distribute food
- County agents (especially in rural, agricultural communities)
- Representatives of environmental and conservation groups
- 4-H and other club leaders
- Professional persons: rabbis, pastors, doctors, software developers
- Members of the local business community: bankers, shop owners
- Labor leaders
- Representatives of local industries (docks, timber, farming, manufacturing)
- Travel agents (think of them as "applied geographers" who can help children understand maps, travel brochures, eco-travel, etc.)
- Recent immigrants and other newcomers to the community
- Artists who work on public murals or public sculptures
- Commercial pilots (more "applied geographers"!)
- Community helpers: firefighters, police officers, librarians
- Government officials representing the three branches
- Judges (municipal court, federal court)
- Legislators (city council members, state legislators)
- Executives (the mayor, the county commissioner)
- Lawyers (Bringing a lawyer to the classroom to talk about law and government is a great way to introduce students to the concept of law as well as to a "real, live person" who deals with the law every day. The American Bar Association will help you contact a local lawyer who is both willing and prepared to visit your classroom.)

The key to hosting a successful visit to the classroom by a community member is to plan well the three phases of the visit: before, during, and after.

Paralegal Amy Williams helps children understand the law using terms they already understand. *(Courtesy of Street Law, Inc.)*

Before the Guest Arrives

Before the guest arrives, the teacher and students need to prepare to get the very most out of the visit. Before a visit by a city council member, for example, they build background knowledge by reading about the structure of city government in the textbook, dramatizing a city council meeting, and following newspaper accounts of council decisions. They also practice interviewing and plan the interview questions. The Welcome Committee that meets the guest at the main office is appointed and plans what they will say.

During the Visit

During the visit, the teacher helps students demonstrate courtesy and curiosity while enacting the interview or other planned activity.

After the Visit

After the visit, the information and experiences are reviewed and organized, and a full report is published—whether prepared in cooperative teams and published in the classroom newspaper or written individually and placed in student portfolios. A follow-up committee writes a thank-you letter telling of the class's plan to publish a report on the guest's visit and promising to send a copy when it is completed.

Field Trips

Field trips are different from simply going somewhere as a class. Field trips are educational adventures. They are connected explicitly to the planned curriculum, and students are active learners—actively pursuing an instructional objective.

As a matter of principle, it is advisable to take elementary school children into the community only for experiences that cannot be duplicated in the classroom. For example, it is usually better to arrange to have a person bring photographs of early life in the community to the school and speak to the children there than it is to take a class of 20 or 30 children to a home. On the other hand, the process involved in canning fish or cranberries or tomato juice cannot be observed in the classroom; the children must be taken to the cannery if this process is to be observed firsthand. There they will see vivid examples of the economic concepts they are learning in class: production, distribution, division of labor, and cooperation. The same can be said for museums, memorials, monuments, government offices, the water treatment plant, a battlefield, a dairy farm.

Whenever children are taken off the school site, the teacher must attend to several important details. As with guest speakers, attention must be paid to the three phases of a field trip: before, during, and after.

Adequate planning will help the teacher anticipate some of the problems that may arise in connection with the field trip and will help make the trip educationally worthwhile. Poorly planned field trips are worse than none at all, for they lack purpose, may jeopardize the safety of the children, and may cause poor public relations between the school and community. Although the field trip should be pleasant for everyone (including the teacher), it is first of all an educational experience, and its primary objective is not that everyone have a joyous outing, but that everyone have an educational one. Good planning will ensure that the trip will be both pleasant and educational. The following suggestions will be helpful in achieving that goal.

Every community has places that can be visited by classes and thereby can contribute to the enrichment of history, geography, and all of social studies. These will differ from place to place, but any of the following could be used. As we saw in Chapter 2, it is important that teachers not restrict field trips to places in their invisible "knapsacks" of personal and ethnic experience. A note home asking parents to make suggestions should provide additional field trip ideas.

State historical society displays	Aquarium
Historical sites, monuments	Library
Floodplain, eroded areas, dam sites	Refinery
Razing of a building	Fish hatchery
Hospital	Museum
Weather bureau	Public health department
Warehouse	Local stores
Airport	Legislative body in session
Railway station	Art gallery
Assembly plant	Fire station
Post office	Newspaper printing facility

Television or radio station
Courthouse
Factory
Farm
Urban planning commission
Greenhouse
Dairy
Shopping center management office

Bakery
Observatory
Canal lock
Harbor
Police station
Cannery
University
Water purification plant

PLANNING A FIELD TRIP

Preparing for the field trip

1. Clearly establish the purposes of the trip and make certain that the children understand the purposes, too. The excursion should provide opportunities for learnings that are not possible in the classroom.

2. Obtain administrative permission for the field trip and make arrangements for transportation. As a matter of policy, it is better to use a public conveyance or a school bus than it is to use private automobiles. In using private cars, the teacher is never sure if the driver is properly insured, is competent behind the wheel, or even has a valid operator's license.

3. Make all necessary preliminary arrangements at the place of the visit. This should include the time for the group to arrive, where the children are to go, who will guide them, and so forth. It is recommended that the teacher make the excursion prior to visiting with the children. This will alert the teacher to circumstances and situations that should be discussed with the children before leaving the classroom. Make sure that the field trip guide is aware of the purposes of the field trip.

4. Delve into informative resources on the subject. No teacher should approach a field trip unprepared. This knowledge will later be valuable in helping prepare children for the field trip and in initiating follow-up and study activities.

5. Obtain written permission from each parent or guardian for the child to go on the trip. Do not take children who cannot or do not return signed permission slips. Although this action does not in itself absolve the teacher of responsibility or liability in the event of an accident, it indicates to the teacher that the parent or guardian knows of the field trip and approves of the child's going. Most schools have forms for this purpose that are filled out by the teacher and sent home with each child for the parent's signature.

6. Prepare the class for the field trip. The easiest way is to conduct a KWL activity: "What do you already Know about this? What do you Want to find out?" And afterward, "What did you Learn?" A more ambitious preparation is often desirable, however, something that will help children observe more keenly, question more knowledgeably, and absorb more thoroughly the whole experience. It is helpful, therefore, if the field trip fits into an inquiry the class is conducting or provides a rich example for concept formation. A trip to the airport, rather than merely a sight-seeing visit, becomes an example to be studied thoroughly in a unit centered on the concept *transportation*. A trip to the dairy farm or to a grocery store becomes a data chunk (as in the *Titanic* inquiry example) in an inquiry on the

(continued)

PLANNING A FIELD TRIP (continued)

question, "Where does our food come from, and who and what are involved?" Accordingly, in place of or in addition to KWL's "What do you want to find out?" we have "What hypotheses are we testing?" and "What questions do we want to be sure to ask the guide?"

Through careful planning the teacher helps children to be more observant and makes a genuine research activity out of the field trip. The children probably will be taken to places to which many of them have been before. Depending on the economic class of the students you are teaching, most of them have been to the airport, some have been to the harbor, and all have been to a filling station. Why, then, should the school take children to such places on field trips? The answer is that different purposes exist for the field trip than for incidental visits. The children are prepared to look for things they would not otherwise see. Discuss with the children how they will record the information obtained on their trip. If they are to take notes, teach the needed note-taking skills. Will each of them need a clipboard? (A class set of clipboards, which are brought out only for such occasions, are aids to note taking and question asking, and they have a symbolic value as well: They symbolize that field trips are a special way to learn.)

The class should establish standards of conduct for the trip before leaving the school. Children are quick to accept the challenge that the responsibility for a good trip rests personally with each member of the group. Time spent on this part of the preparation for the excursion will pay

dividends when the trip is under way. Nothing is more embarrassing for the teacher, more damaging to school–community relations, or more devastating to the educational purpose of the field trip than a group of rude and unruly children. This situation often happens when the children have been inadequately prepared for the trip.

7. If the trip is to be long, make arrangements for lunchroom and restroom facilities. Take along a first-aid kit.

8. Have an alternative plan in case the weather turns bad or something interferes with your plans.

Conducting the trip

9. Take roll before leaving the school grounds and "count noses" frequently during the trip to make sure that none of the children have become lost or left in some restroom along the way. It is a good idea to put young children in pairs because a child will know and report immediately the absence of a partner. To assist with supervision of the children and to help ensure a safe trip, the teacher should arrange for other adults to accompany the group.

10. Arrive at the designated place on time, and have children ready for the guide. Be sure to introduce the guide to the class. Supervise children closely during the tour to prevent accidents or injury. Before leaving, check again to make sure all children are with the group.

11. Make sure that time is allowed for answering children's questions.

12. Make sure that each child can see and hear adequately. Be sure to summarize the experience before the trip is concluded.

Evaluating the trip

13. Engage the class in appropriate follow-up activities. This should include writing a thank-you note to the place and to the adults who accompanied the class. In the primary grades, the children should dictate such a letter to the teacher, who writes it on the chalkboard or a computer projected onto a screen for all to see. Individual children then copy the letter, and one may be selected to be sent, or in some cases, they may all be sent. The children's letter can be sent using email, but a paper letter is always appreciated because of the extra time and care needed.

14. The teacher and children will also want to evaluate carefully the extent to which the purposes of the trip have been achieved. "Did we accomplish what we set out to do? Did we get the answers to our questions? What did we learn that we didn't know before? What are some other things we will want to find out?" The teacher and children should evaluate the conduct of the class in terms of the standards set up before the trip was made. This evaluation should always include some favorable reactions as well as ways in which the group might improve on subsequent trips. A list of these suggestions for improvement may be saved for review just before the next trip.

15. Discuss enrichment projects in which children may engage for further study, such as construction activities, original stories, reports, dramatic plays, and diaries. Survey other resources available in the community for study.

Singapore's "Fieldwork"

Among the best school field trips in the world are surely those that are conducted routinely in the Southeast Asian island-nation of Singapore under the name "fieldwork." Elementary school students regularly venture out of the school on fieldwork excursions into the community, and as the photos on the next page display, they "locate and extract information at the site by conducting surveys and interviews, doing simple experiments, observing and gathering relevant information, sketching the site, etc."[1] Furthermore, they are taught to record the data appropriately, so that they can work with it during the post-fieldwork phase of the project—organizing and collating it, making inferences, and shaping it into suitable presentations and publications: travel guides, historical interpretations, electronic slide shows, scripts, and stories.

The children pictured attend Rosyth School, where a sequence of fieldwork is planned so that the children study the community systematically from grades 1 through 6. Singapore is a multiethnic society—the primary languages are Malay, Tamil, Mandarin, and English—and all students in school study their "mother tongue" plus English. Accordingly, key fieldwork is done in the historic ethnic heritage centers of the city so that students learn the history and culture of each of the main ethnic populations of Singapore.

Fieldwork in Singapore. *(Raymond Bong, Rosyth School, Singapore)*

COMPUTER RESOURCES: VIRTUAL FIELD TRIPS AND WEB-BASED INQUIRIES

Let's turn from actual field trips to virtual or electronic field trips using computers and the Internet. Then we will examine two other computer resources: WebQuests and online museum and library collections. But first, some general comments about computers in social studies education are necessary.

The use of computer technology in education has been promoted—and debated—vigorously. Today, the absence of computers in a classroom or school is thought by many to symbolize poor education. Computers in the classroom have come to symbolize, for some in the community, a school curriculum that is up-to-date and instruction that is benefiting from the latest technology. This is, of course, a silly leap of faith. Both curriculum and instruction can be very good without the latest technology, and, conversely, the presence of computers in no way indicates good curriculum or instruction. The quality of the intellectual work students are helped to accomplish, the importance of the subject matter they are asked to study, and the power and reach of the understandings they are helped to construct are far more important criteria than the presence or absence of this or that hardware or software. In brief, the presence of computers in the classroom is widely misunderstood as an end, when in truth computers are means. Their presence matters only to the degree they enter sensibly into curriculum and instruction.

In the social studies, the contribution of computer-assisted instruction falls into the following three categories:

1. *Using the Computer to Build Knowledge*—especially to gather examples needed in concept formation and evidence needed for inquiry, to visit places far away in time and space,

and to be involved in simulations and other learning games. In other words, computers need to be used mainly for *learning*, not productivity. Technologist Sebastian Foti laments that, today, as distinct from the earlier days of the computer-assisted instruction movement, "schools use computers primarily for productivity tasks (e.g., making presentations, drafting and editing reports) rather than as learning machines."[2] One reason for this strange state of affairs is the wide availability of productivity software (e.g., Word, PowerPoint, iMovie), but another reason is the popular conviction that children are computer "experts." Foti continues:

> The students do seem to know how to handle productivity software, and they spend a great deal of time "on the computer." For those of us who work with computers in education, it is clear that, while students aren't afraid of software tools, they don't have a very good understanding of how computers work, how they are controlled, or even how they communicate. This is because they don't have to. Software exists for almost any productivity task. . . . The computer is now a tool that allows them to be productive and access information, including live streams of information."

What has been lost, he concludes, is using computers not for displaying what children already know, but for boosting their *learning*. If displaying is confused with learning, learning is doomed—rather like the discussion participant who always talks but never listens.

2. *Using the Computer to Practice and Apply Social Studies Skills*—especially the skills needed to build knowledge: map reading, making and interpreting graphs and charts, gathering information from multiple perspectives, classifying, forming and testing hypotheses, drawing evidence-based conclusions.

3. *Using the Computer to Communicate*—especially to revise and edit reports and essays for the classroom newspaper and to communicate with epals or cyberpals in another community in the state or a sister city across the sea. Using "iChat," digital movie-making, and other technology, children around the world can see one another as well and engage in written exchanges.

Now let's turn to virtual field trips and web-based inquiries for social studies teaching and learning.

Virtual Field Trips

Thanks to the Internet, children can visit places virtually. In other words, they can venture far from home electronically and capture some aspects of a distant place. While obviously not as richly textured a learning experience as an actual field trip to this place, an electronic visit nonetheless may help set imaginations afire and provoke additional research. This is our hope when leading virtual field trips.

With virtual field trips, as with actual ones, the recommended approach is to plan the three phases of the trip: before, during, and after. Resources are available to help with the planning. Several virtual field trips are available at the WebQuest website (discussed next) at www.webquest.org. Furthermore, a Maryland organization called Thinkport features several virtual field trips at www.thinkport.org and a link to research showing that the use of virtual field trips can help reluctant readers achieve. Also, a company called Tramline has produced TourMaker Software (www.field-trips.org), which teachers and students can use to design their own trips. At these three sites, readers can sample virtual field trips and develop ideas about creating their own.

Take some time now to think through the sample virtual field trip suggestions below, followed by the culminating Lesson Plan 15: a virtual field trip to public monuments, called "Choosing to Remember."

- The White House
- China and Egypt
- Holiday Celebrations in Other Lands
- The Seven Wonders of the Ancient World
- Plymouth
- Abraham Lincoln's Home
- The Constitution and Declaration of Independence
- U.S. Capitol
- United Nations
- Public Monuments and Memorials

Bon Voyage! But first, a caution: Websites change frequently. While I sometimes identify particular web addresses in the examples that follow, it is important for readers to use a good search engine to identify the best sites for a virtual field trip.

A Virtual Field Trip to the White House

To set the unit context, let us say that this field trip takes place in a third-grade unit called "Countries and their Capitals." Its aim is to help students develop the concepts *nation* and *national capital.*

Before.   Students use their textbooks and other reference material to learn how Washington, D.C., became the capital of the United States. The teacher helps them distinguish between state and national capitals, and then reads them a story about Benjamin Banneker, who drew up the plans for the new capital, and another about Abigail and John Adams, the first occupants of the new White House in 1800. (Children's literature can be found on each.) Then, students should learn that the White House, as the home to the president, is part of the executive branch of government. Following this White House tour, children may want to visit the other two branches of government, legislative and judicial, with trips to the Congress and the Supreme Court.

During.   Students set off for the White House. They begin at the White House home page for kids at www.whitehouse.gov/kids/, where they navigate their way to the virtual White House tour for children. Each administration revises this website, and the children's tour is often led by one of the White House pets.

After.   With this background knowledge, students are ready to compare Washington, D.C., and the White House to a capital city and first residence in another nation. Perhaps London, England, and 10 Downing Street. Or Dakar, Senegal, and its Presidential Palace.

A Virtual Field Trip to China, Then Egypt (Comparative Perspective)

This is a comparative study because there are two places to visit. And the teacher decides to use *cooperative learning,* a special kind of groupwork that is detailed in the next chapter. First, the teacher provides an overview of the activities that take place in each of the three phases—before, during, after—to the entire class. She asks them to decide whether to begin with China or Egypt. Whichever they choose, the teacher will use the first country to develop her students' skills at searching for social studies information on the Internet, then expect them to apply those skills during the second phase of the study. Let's assume they decide on China.

Before.   Students are assigned first to "home teams" and then to "expert groups" (see "Jigsaw" in Chapter 11). There is one expert on each home team for each of six categories. Students decide to use the categories they have already learned in their "Nation in the News" unit (see Lesson Plan 9 in Chapter 6: (1) culture, (2) history, (3) geography, (4) economy, (5) government, and (6) civic ideals).

Expert groups search their social studies textbook chapter on China as their initial data source, gathering whatever information is there about their topic. Note-taking procedures need to be established. Then, *after* they have this initial information, they set off on a virtual field trip to China to gather *additional* information on their assigned topic. (Why this sequence? Because the Internet is very difficult to search intelligently when students have no background knowledge of the topic they are searching.)

Numerous Web addresses could provide useful text and images (maps, artifacts, photos, etc.). The teacher demonstrates a Web search, thinking aloud and modeling a healthy skepticism for many webpages and tentative interest for some, until a number of promising China sites have been located. First, the teacher demonstrates what she calls a blind search, or "shooting in the dark." She types "China" into the search box of her favorite search engine and, presto, gets 1/2 million (!) possible sites or hits. Next, she types "China geography" and gets 30,000 hits. She tells students to pay attention to the domain: some are *.org*, others are *.com* or *.edu* or *.gov* (see Figure 10–1). When she arrives at a promising website (which

FIGURE 10–1   Internet domains.

Domain	Type	Example	Source
.com	Commercial organization	*prenhall.com*	Prentice Hall Publishing Company
.edu	Educational institution	*howard.edu*	Howard University
.org	Professional organization	*ncss.org*	National Council for the Social Studies
.gov	Government organization	*census.gov*	U.S. Census
.uk	Country	*ox.ac.uk*	Oxford University
.int	International organization	*nato.int*	NATO
.net	Network organization	*aera.net*	American Educational Research Association

Source: Adapted from M. J. Berson, B. C. Cruz, J. A. Duplass, and J. H. Johnston, (2007). *Social Studies on the Internet* (3rd ed.). Upper Saddle River, NJ: Merrill/Prentice Hall, p. 2.

she has prescreened), she says, "This looks promising. Let's explore it." When in doubt, this teacher begins with the World Factbook website of the Central Intelligence Agency (follow the links at www.cia.gov) and selects a country. The first image is a good map of the country, followed by key facts and figures (e.g., population, climate, government, and a very brief history).

During.   Assuming there are six computers available, one for each expert group, group members gather around to investigate this site for information related to their assigned topic, each student recording notes. Then, they compile their notes, discuss their "visit," and prepare together an oral report (see Chapter 11). One expert group's oral report is called "History of China"; another's is "Culture of China," and so on through the six topics. Each expert group member will give the report to members of his or her home team. The team will compile a data-retrieval chart like the one shown in Figure 10–2.

After.   (a) The teacher leads a debriefing of the China trip and asks whether students wish to deepen their knowledge of China before going to Egypt or after. They are eager to get moving. (b) The teacher reassigns home teams and expert groups (see Chapter 2 on flexible grouping), and the class now prepares for a trip to Egypt. Again, there are before, during, and after phases. Before the teacher leads students in a collective search for promising websites, she delegates more of the decision making to students, for she is eager for them to become skillful. "No blind searches, please," she says. "Be skeptical." Students are helped to seek information on the same six topics. After the visit to Egypt, the teacher leads the class in comparing and contrasting China and Egypt across the six categories. A challenging follow-up would be to add the United States to the list.

A Virtual Field Trip to a Holiday Celebration

Children are attracted to holidays for all the obvious reasons: fun, food, vacation. But their understanding of holidays can be superficial and ethnocentric (they know only a few holidays, and these are holidays celebrated by their own ethnic group). The idea in this virtual field trip is to visit other countries during their holiday celebrations. By visiting many holiday examples, students will construct a vigorous concept of holiday and will be introduced to cultural diversity around the world.

Before.   Ask students to list all the holidays they can think of that are celebrated in their community. Remind them of holidays not on their list (e.g., religious holidays such as Good Friday, Hanukkah, and Buddha's birthday; secular holidays such as Chinese New Year,

FIGURE 10–2   Data-retrieval chart for comparative field trip.

	Culture	History	Geography	Economy	Government	Civic Ideals
China						
Egypt						

Veterans Day, Kwanzaa, Independence Day, Cinco de Mayo, etc.). Then use the list, group, and label strategy (see Chapter 9) to help them think about the similarities and differences among the holidays on their list (some are religious, some are governmental, some are local only). Ask students if they think any of these are celebrated in other nations, too. Ask if any holidays celebrated in other nations are not celebrated in the United States. Take a straw poll: "How many say yes? No? Not sure?" Then, "Let's find out. . . ."

During. Since 1994, students from all over the world have been not only visiting but *contributing* to a website called KIDPROJ Multi-Cultural Calendar (search for it on your favorite search engine). Here, children can click on a month or a country and find a long list of holidays to explore. Clicking on "country," then China, we find six holidays. Clicking on Egypt, we find eight. Clicking on "month" and then "March," we see many entries for "girls' day" in Japan and "women's day" in China and Italy. Sometimes there is more than one entry for a single holiday, meaning that more than one child has written a description.

Help children browse and then select a holiday to investigate further. Begin by having students locate on the classroom map where their holidays are celebrated and place index cards with brief descriptions of the place and the holiday, written by your students. Also, appoint a student committee to find out what holiday books are held in the school library. For example, a series of books for the primary grades is called *Holidays Around the World* from National Geographic Children's Books. Consider *Celebrate Ramadan* and *Celebrate Diwali*.

After. Create a classroom calendar depicting the holidays selected by students. Ask students to choose a good name for the calendar, for example, "International Holidays," "Our Multicultural Calendar," or "Holidays of the World." Finally, the class can select one or two of the holidays to celebrate in the classroom, making decorations and holiday snacks.

> **REFLECTION**
>
> A recent study of gender differences in education found that "girls have narrowed some significant gender gaps, but technology is now the new 'boys club' in our nation's public schools." Do your own observations and experience support this finding?

Additional Virtual Field Trip Suggestions

The Ultimate Field Trip: The Seven Wonders of the World

Children are typically introduced to world history in a systematic way in grade 6, and this is often the first grade in which they have a textbook dealing specifically with world history. My favorite way to kick off this mind-expanding subject is with a field trip to the Seven Wonders of the Ancient World. *Who* chose them? *What* kinds of places are they? *Where* are they? *When* were they built? *Why*? Buckle your seatbelt and find one of the numerous websites that present them. Then, compare the ancient wonders to the "new" wonders. That's right, the new seven wonders.

An organization at thenew7wonders.com conducted a worldwide Internet contest to nominate and then, by voting, select seven additional, contemporary "wonders" of the world. In July of 2007, the results were announced. The organization's website is well worth a visit, and the National Geographic News website has a vivid slide show of both the old and new wonders.

Ancient Wonders	New Wonders
Great Pyramid of Giza, Egypt	Colosseum, Rome
Colossus of Rhodes, Greece	Petra, Jordan
Lighthouse of Alexandria, Egypt	Machu Picchu, Peru
Statue of Zeus at Olympia, Greece	Chichén Itzá, Mexico
Hanging Gardens of Babylon, Iraq	Taj Mahal, India
Mausoleum of Halicarnassus, Turkey	Christ the Redeemer Statue, Rio
Temple of Artemis, Turkey	Great Wall of China

A Virtual Field Trip to Plymouth

In the week leading up to the Thanksgiving holiday, students can visit what is today Plymouth, Massachusetts—the "Plimouth Plantation" in 1627—site of Plymouth Rock and the first permanent European settlement in southern New England. At www.plimouth.org, click on "Education Programs," and you will find a field trip guide plus an award-winning online learning center. Here, students from across the United States have used the "becoming a historian" material to peel away misconceptions about the "First Thanksgiving." There is also an audio feature, "Talk Like a Pilgrim," where students can listen to how these colonists said hello and goodbye, and instructions and visuals for making a simple Wampanoag toss-and-catch game and the colonists' "fox and geese" game.

A Virtual Field Trip to Abraham Lincoln's Springfield Home

In the week leading up to Presidents' Day, students can visit the homes of several U.S. presidents. For example, Abraham Lincoln's home in Springfield, Illinois, is featured on the National Park Service's website at www.nps.gov/liho. This is not the famous log cabin where Lincoln was born, but the house where he lived with his family just before he became president. From his home, the field trip can continue to numerous additional Lincoln sites: the courthouse where he worked as a lawyer, the U.S. Capitol where he served as a legislator, and the Gettysburg Address site (also a national park).

A Virtual Field Trip to See the U.S. Constitution, the Declaration of Independence, and the Bill of Rights

Constitution Day is September 17th, marking the day in 1787 when the U.S. Constitution was signed by thirty-nine delegates. Leading up to this day, and building a citizenship theme early in the school year, students can tour the National Archives in Washington, D.C., and see the Constitution itself along with two additional founding documents of the United States. Find the "educators and students" page for related teaching activities. Additional activities for Constitution Day can be found at www.constitutioncenter.org/constitutionday/.

A Virtual Field Trip to the U.S. Capitol and the Woman Suffrage Sculpture

Students can take a virtual tour of the Capitol in Washington, D.C., by going to the U.S. Senate webpage (www.senate.gov). And, Wikipedia (the online encyclopedia) has good visuals of the rotunda, including the frieze of American history, historical paintings, and the eight-ton sculpture honoring the Woman Suffrage movement. From that movement, which won women the right to vote in 1920, three leaders are portrayed: Elizabeth Cady Stanton (1815–1902), Susan B. Anthony (1820–1906), and Lucretia Mott (1793–1880). Students will see the sculpture itself. Then have them click on "rotunda" to see where it is located in the Capitol building.

A Virtual Field Trip to the United Nations

Students can visit the United Nations in New York City. This large, information-intensive site will be helpful for older students who want to learn about the UN's current projects as well as crisis spots around the globe. Click on the "cyber schoolbus" site for teachers and students.

A Virtual Field Trip to the Public Monuments at the National Mall in Washington, D.C.

Students can tour the Washington Monument, then go to the memorials to Presidents Jefferson, Lincoln, and Roosevelt. Next come the World War II, Korean, and Vietnam War memorials. Lesson Plan 15 presents an online concept lesson using this site. Notice that this lesson achieves its power by helping students go far beyond merely looking at the monuments to *thinking* about what a monument is—actually *forming the concept*—and peering into the values behind it.

Web-Based Inquiries

A web-based inquiry, like any inquiry, follows the five-step inquiry process discussed in Chapter 9.

1. *Engagement.* Children are helped to become interested in the problem on which the inquiry will be conducted. This is typically accomplished using photos, an artifact, a current event in the news, or a film clip. Recall that in Chapter 9 two problems were demonstrated: *Who benefits from advertising?* and *What caused the Titanic tragedy?*
2. *Hypotheses.* The children offer hypotheses about the problem and these are recorded. For example, "only the sellers benefit from advertising because they make the money," and "the captain didn't know there were icebergs at that time of year."
3. *Evidence.* They are helped to gather information that will help them test the hypotheses.
4. *Conclusions.* They draw conclusions (what historians call a "thesis" and social scientists generally call a "claim"). This conclusion states the result of the inquiry: the students' decisions about which hypothesis(es) is best supported by the evidence.
5. *Publish.* Their conclusions are made public—they are "published." This is how science—both natural science and social science—normally proceeds. Results are made public so that audience members can judge for themselves the strength of the conclusion and the evidence on which it is based.

How does a web-based inquiry differ? The information/evidence students gather at step 3 results from searching the Internet. With younger children, the teacher has prescreened and selected the websites, of course, and has placed them on a webpage. With older students, more independent searching is gradually allowed.

Web-based inquiries (like virtual field trips) require that the teacher spend a good deal of time in preparation, and there are two basic reasons. First, young children cannot be turned loose on the Internet to search for relevant websites by themselves. It simply is not safe. Consequently, as with virtual field trips, the teacher needs to take the time to pre-identify the websites that children will visit for the purposes of gathering information at step 3. Second,

CHOOSING TO REMEMBER

Lesson Plan 15

Grades	4 and up
Time	Two class periods on successive days
NCSS Standards	2 (time, continuity, and change) and 10 (civic ideals and practices)
Objectives	Students will build an initial understanding of the concept *public monument* through *national* examples, and then deepen their understanding with a *local* example. They will begin to know the difference between *public* and *private* because these are public, not private, monuments and memorials. Also, students will able to tell what a group of people values by what it wants to honor and remember.
Interest Building	Using a computer projector that can project these images onto a large screen for all students to see, click on the National Mall website of the National Parks Service, www.nps.gov/nama/. Click on the "Washington Monument" and tell students that it is a monument to the "father of our country," our first president, George Washington. There is additional information at the "in depth" button, and by clicking on "experience the monument," then "view," you can show students several views of the National Mall in Washington, D.C., from the top of the Washington Monument.
Lesson Development	1. Use the basic concept-formation strategy outlined in Chapter 9, Lesson Plan 11, to help students form the concept *public monument*. Choose three examples from the National Mall website in addition to the Washington Monument. You will find the Jefferson, Lincoln, and Roosevelt Memorials and three war memorials to soldiers who fought in World War II, Korea, and Vietnam. Draw information from each monument in turn. Noting the similarities across these four examples, students should conclude something like this: *A public monument is a structure built in memory of (for the purpose of reminding us of) an event or person who was very important to the people who built it. It is owned and maintained by the public (all of us together; "we the people") rather than by a private person, a business, or religious group.* "We" pay for it with our taxes because it is a valuable reminder to "us." As you go, use a data-retrieval chart like this:

Examples	Describe the structure	Describe its location	Who owns and maintains it?	Who/what does it honor and remember?	Why? (What do we value?)
Monument 1					
Monument 2					
Monument 3					
Monument 4					

2. Homework consists of asking adults for additional examples of public monuments and memorials located in other places in the United States or in other countries.

3. On the following day, ask students to share their additional examples. After listing them on the chalkboard, *group* them into national monuments (owned and operated by the national government) and local monuments (owned and operated by state or city governments). Select some of the public monuments suggested by students and find their websites on the Internet. Help students distinguish between these two levels of government (i.e., the concept *federalism*).

Summary and Assessment

1. Ask students to open their response journals and conclude this sentence: "A public monument is _____." Prompt them to remember to include all the things that make *any* public monument a

public monument. That is, what does every example have to have? Walk around and read what students are writing and assess the concept they are forming.

2. Read to students from the National Park Service website the "The National Park Service cares for special places saved by the American people so that all may experience our heritage." Ask, "Why do we save some places and not others?" Draw out the values that steer these decisions.

Follow-up

1. Take a field trip to a local public monument. Add it to the data-retrieval chart above and compare and contrast it to the other monuments on the chart.

2. Ask students if they would like to find and learn about additional public monuments. If so, ask them to deliberate whether this should be done individually or in small groups. Then, you could take a vote.

3. Some students may wish to study the history of the National Park Service generally or the National Mall in Washington, D.C., especially. This information is available at the websites.

4. After studying National Monuments, students may wish to study National Parks—again working on the distinction between *public* ("we the people" acting together through our government) and *private* (individual, corporate, religious).

Materials

- Internet access.
- Computer and computer projector for showing a website on a large screen for all to see.
- Websites bookmarked for easy access during the lesson or stored on the class's webpage.

Integration

Art. Public monuments and parks are often the subject of paintings and photographs, many of which can be viewed and interpreted on the websites associated with the monuments and parks (e.g., Thomas Moran's paintings of Yellowstone along with William Henry Jackson's photographs at www.nps.gov/history/museum/exhibits/moran/gallery1.htm).

Literature. Gary Paulsen's book, *The Monument,* will be the perfect follow-up book to recommend to older children and/or better readers who are intrigued by the idea of public memorials and monuments. Paulsen captures, through the characters of an adopted teenage girl named Rocky, her faithful dog, and her small town's visiting artist, Mick, the emotional turmoil of a townspeople who must decide how and what to remember.

young children will not be able to know which problems are worth studying or which curriculum objectives are being served by studying them. Sometimes, of course, students can suggest their own inquiries, particularly when the current events curriculum is making them curious about what is happening across the nation and around the globe. But generally, teachers are developing a curriculum-related inquiry question and planning the inquiry to achieve one or more curriculum objectives. Please look back to Chapter 9 to see the sample inquiry problems and their related curriculum topics.

To make the process easier, Bernie Dodge at San Diego State University developed WebQuest, and thousands of teachers have since created their own WebQuests and used others they find at www.webquest.org. A WebQuest is a teacher-created webpage that students use to conduct an inquiry using Internet resources. The emphasis, thankfully, and true to *inquiry*, is on using information, not simply looking for it.

Templates are available at the WebQuest website that teachers can use to create their own WebQuests, and a protocol for adapting existing WebQuests is provided. The latter is needed because at the website is a search tool that allows users to enter a subject and grade level and find WebQuests developed by other teachers. Under "Social Studies for grades K–2," you will find dozens of ready-to-use WebQuests, and the same goes for the higher grade levels. In addition to searching at the WebQuest site, teachers can use a search engine to enter "webquest" plus a curriculum topic such as a concept (e.g., river, tsunami), place (e.g., Egypt, Jamestown), or event (American Revolution, Columbus's voyage).

What follows is the basic WebQuest template. For each part of the pattern a brief description is provided. Additionally, here I give an example excerpted from Christine Lee's WebQuest called *Discovering Singapore River* (www.hsse.nie.edu.sg/webquest/SS/singaporeriver.htm). This historic river runs through the city of Singapore, and Lee and her colleagues Kho Ee Moi and Chang Chew Hung have worked closely with the WebQuest model in the elementary social studies curriculum. As readers can see in the brief excerpts below, history, geography, and language arts are seamlessly integrated in this Singapore River WebQuest.[3] Also, collaborative teamwork skills are developed and assessed.

Introduction	This is written to the students and introduces them to the quest they are about to undertake. Its purpose is to both prepare and engage the reader.
	Singapore River... There is so much history along that little stretch of water. One needs only to stand in front of a colonial building like Parliament House and face the old 'godowns' along South Boat Quay as they stand dwarfed by modern skyscrapers to realize that this river basin has seen much comings and goings. If only Singapore River could talk, the tales it could tell.... We would like your team to retell these tales to your classmates.
Task	This describes clearly what the end result will be: a product to be designed, a mystery to be solved, etc.
	The task of your team is to find out what Singapore River was like (a) during the time of the founding of Singapore in 1819, (b) during the time of bustling trade in the 1950s, (c) after the River Clean-Up in the 1970s, and (d) today. After you have done your research, you will tell a story of Singapore River during that time period. Tell your tale from the viewpoint of... (different roles are given for each time period).
Process	This tells which steps the learner will proceed through. (And when other teachers read this, they will know how to conduct this quest with their students.) Typically, these are the websites students are to visit to gather the needed information to complete the task, but they also may be stories to be read and reference books or maps to be consulted.
	First, you will be assigned to a "home team" of four students, each with a different role. Your team will need to make a decision as to which time period to study.... Create a folder, "Singapore River," on your desktop. This is where you will place your findings from the Internet. Select only the information that is relevant to the time period your team has chosen.... After you have done your team research on a particular time period, move away from your home team and form a new group. Share your team's findings with classmates from other teams.... Come back together as a home team and plan how to present your story....
Evaluation	This is a scoring rubric that describes to learners how their performance will be evaluated.
	A scoring rubric on collaborative teamwork is presented. Students earn scores on three dimensions: contribution to the team, acceptance of responsibility, and valuing others' viewpoints.

Conclusion	A few sentences summarize the learning and suggest follow-up tasks.
	After the teams have told their tales, you will have an idea of how Singapore River has changed over the years. Ask yourself these questions: Do you like the change? Is change inevitable? What parts of Singapore River remain relatively unchanged? What would you like the river to be like in the future?
Credits	A bibliography of sources used and acknowledgments of help received in designing the WebQuest.

Please set this book aside and examine the WebQuest site at www.webquest.org. Note, however, that all the teacher-designed "quests" to be found at this site are not necessarily *inquiries* as we have defined them in our five-step process. Some are more like recitations, where the teacher asks questions and students answer them, only now by finding the answers at preselected websites. Others are more like virtual field trips. Genuine inquiries, recall, involve students in actually using information, not simply finding it. Specifically, they involve students in hypothesizing and hypothesis-testing. Information is not gathered simply to answer questions; rather, it is gathered in order to test a hypothesis and draw an evidence-based conclusion. WebQuests, of course, can be designed to be genuine inquiries, but do not expect that all the quests found at the WebQuest website are examples.

Online Museum and Library Collections

When creating their own virtual field trips and web-based inquiries, or adapting those created by others, teachers will want to take advantage of several of the better online museum and library collections—nationally, locally, and internationally. These collections often have kids pages that can be extremely helpful for guiding children through a particular set of paintings or artifacts. Here are five of my favorites:

1. *The Smithsonian Institution.* The Smithsonian is the world's largest museum complex—a collection of museums on the National Mall in Washington, D.C. Browse the museums, and find the pages geared to students and teachers, as well as children and parents. Teachers of grades 4–8 will want to pay special attention to a new online exhibit called "Jamestown, Québec, Santa Fe: Three North American Beginnings." Here is an opportunity to provide a comparative perspective—and in three languages—on the colonization of the North American continent—a sort of three-pronged "unsettling" of the continent in 1607, 1608, and 1609, respectively. "The year is 1600," the exhibit begins, "and everything is about to change."

2. *The National Museum of the American Indian.* This is one of the museums at the Smithsonian. Its "education" page is quite good, and one of the recent offerings to teachers and students is a traveling exhibit and companion website called "Native Words/Native Warriors." Here we learn how American Indian soldiers in World Wars I and II developed codes that America's enemies were unable to crack. Called "code talkers," these soldiers will help students break their stereotypes of "Indians" as warriors with spears on the high plains of the American West.

ONE LAPTOP PER STUDENT?

The Liverpool, NY school board decided that after seven years of trying "there was literally no evidence that laptops had any impact on student achievement—none. The teachers were telling us that when there's a one-to-one relationship between the student and the laptop, the box gets in the way. It's a distraction to the educational process." (*New York Times*, May 4, 2007). The letters to the editor that followed the decision allow us to peer into the spread of public opinion on the value of this costly technology in schools.

"The process of education . . . is all about leading students on paths to knowledge. Those who are shipping off laptops to students in this country and beyond should understand more about that process."

"It will be a tragedy if your article influences other schools not to invest in technology. While other countries are investing in laptops for their students, the U.S. is in danger of moving backward. We live in an information age, and it is time for the U.S. to infuse computing and technology into every aspect of learning."

"Saying that a one-to-one laptop program has no impact . . . misses the point. These programs were not set up to improve test scores; they were set up to make sure students were comfortable with the ever growing use of technology."

"At all levels of education we need to shift our focus from technology to pedagogy to ensure that teachers and students are able to use computers and the Internet in educationally effective ways."

"Schools and parents must get back to teaching our children the basics instead of resorting to technology to revive our failing education system."

3. *The Birmingham Civil Rights Institute.* Located in Birmingham, Alabama, the Institute is a wonderful place to visit in person. Across the street is the 16th Street Baptist Church where four girls were killed in a racially motivated bombing in 1963. At the Institute's Online Resource Gallery, students can hear and see clips of movement activists reminiscing about the events of that period. Elementary school teacher Jessie Champion, for example, tells of his run-in with the Birmingham police in 1963. He was later fired for challenging police abuse of a Black youth.
4. *The Mariner's Museum.* This museum is in Newport, Virginia. The online collections are stunning. Your students can see a life vest from the *Titanic* and a collection on the transatlantic slave trade; there is also a section on the development of maps called "Changing View of the World."

5. *The American Memory at the Library of Congress.* The Library of Congress is the largest library in the world, the nation's oldest federal cultural institution, and serves as the research arm of Congress. American Memory is a set of collections at this library. It provides free access to written and spoken words, audio recordings, photos and films, prints, maps, and sheet music that document the American experience. Users can browse by topic (e.g., literature, cities), or by time period (e.g., 1400–1699, 1970–today), place (e.g., Midwest, South), or source type (audio recording, map).

Online Map Collections

Online map collections are equally important to the design of virtual field trips and web-based inquiries. The CIA's "World Factbook" was introduced earlier in the virtual field trip to China and Egypt, and Google Earth was featured in Chapter 5. Lesson Plan 16 was created with these and other map collections in mind, but it begins with an extraordinary journey through space. Students view the Milky Way at 10 million light-years from Earth, and then move toward Earth in successive orders of magnitude (powers of 10). Soon, students will have reached an oak tree in Tallahassee, Florida. After that, they'll begin to move from outer space to inner space—the microscopic world of an oak leaf's cell walls, the cell nucleus, chromatin, DNA, and the subatomic universe of electrons and protons. Please set the book down next to a computer with Internet access and see for yourself what happens in Lesson Plan 16.

THE SOCIAL STUDIES TEXTBOOK

The policy of school districts that calls for furnishing free of charge the same basic textbook for every child in a class is based on the moral and legal principles of equal treatment and equality of opportunity. For this reason, textbooks are widely used and will probably continue to be widely used for years to come. It is apparent from their continued, widespread use that most teachers perceive textbooks as both a valuable and a manageable teaching tool in social studies. New teachers especially find them an important source of support. The textbook program can help the teacher think about instruction and know what to teach. Researcher David Kaufman and his associates reported that teachers without the necessary curriculum resources felt "lost at sea." One teacher said, "You want me to teach this stuff, but I don't have the stuff to teach." The research team concluded:

> For new teachers, learning to teach well is difficult work. Managing a classroom, deciding what skills and knowledge to cover, designing lessons and implementing them effectively, accurately assessing student understanding, and adjusting to student needs are complex tasks; and new teachers need support to develop the necessary knowledge and skills to carry them out. The curriculum and its associated materials are potential sources of this support, and they play important roles in teacher development.[4]

Elementary school social studies textbooks actually are textbook *programs.* They are more than a textbook. They contain an array of resources, some inside the book and some outside. In the textbook are primary documents, artwork, narrative histories, vocabulary

WHERE ON EARTH ARE WE?

Lesson Plan **16**

Grades 2 and up

Time Two class periods on successive days

NCSS Standards 3 (people, places, and environments)

Objectives Students will learn how to use high-quality websites to locate themselves on the planet where they live and on the continent, nation, state, county, neighborhood, and so on, right down to their street address. Meanwhile, the teacher will assess students' current level of understanding of maps and other geographic concepts. (*Note:* The teacher models Internet use for students, moving among four preselected websites. Meanwhile, students learn where they are located in space. The teacher should get the feel of each website in advance so that the lesson can move along at a good pace.)

Interest Building Point to a poster on the classroom wall that shows Earth from space. Ask students to imagine themselves as the astronauts who took this photo. Specifically, have them imagine themselves as the spaceship circles Earth, bringing into view different oceans and continents. Name the continents and oceans as you move your hand across the photo.

Lesson Development
1. Click on http://micro.magnet.fsu.edu/primer/java/scienceopticsu/powersof10/index.html and view the Milky Way at 10 million light-years from Earth. Then move through space toward Earth in successive orders of magnitude. Soon you will have reached a tall oak tree. After that, you'll begin to move into the microscopic world of a leaf's cell.

   Your students will want to view this more than once. After each viewing, ask a few students to summarize what's happening in this film. There may be many concepts that are new to students: *galaxy, solar system, planet, orbit,* and so forth. Do use these terms (because they are used in the film), but there's no need to attempt to explain them in depth. They can be explained very briefly, if desired; then move on.

2. Next, find the exact location of the school on Earth. Enter the school address in the search box at http://www.mapquest.com/. Zoom in and out to help students get a feel for the school's location in a neighborhood or city. You can enter the school's zip code to view a map of all the places within that mailing area. These maps can be printed.

3. Third, zoom back out to a world map at http://plasma.nationalgeographic.com/mapmachine/. Here you can click on different types of maps (topographic, annual temperatures, farming). Distinguish these for students. Assess students' understanding of different kinds of maps. Find out if they can name any of the nations (China and Mexico), then continental landmasses and oceans (Africa; Indian Ocean). Point out the map legend, and show students that it is difficult to decode any map without a key. Zoom into North America, then to the region of the continent where the children live. You can print this map. But the "printer-friendly maps" are better; find that link and you will find yourself at "XPeditions" where, in addition to crisp black-and-white maps, there are lesson plans and activities.

4. Fourth, switch from the flat maps at National Geographic's map machine to the round, global view at Google Earth. As discussed in Chapter 5, this must be downloaded and is free. Enter in the "fly to" box the city or town where the school is located. The children will see the "camera" zoom in from high over Earth to their community. Enter another nearby city or town, and by clicking on Roads the connecting streets or highways will appear. Use the Zoom button for a closer look and the Tilt button for different perspectives.

Summary and Assessment Review with students each of the saved maps. Ask them to explain them. Listening carefully, and asking a few follow-up questions, you can assess their understandings.

Follow-up
1. Students who are have shown special interest in these maps can be formed into a committee to investigate the "terrestrial eco-regions" maps at the National Geographic site,

http://www.nationalgeographic.com/wildworld/terrestrial.html. Scientists divided Earth into nearly 900 distinct eco-regions, and they are represented at this website with ample detail on flora and fauna, including endangered species. The committee's task can be to present a report on eco-regions to the class, defining the concept, zooming in on the eco-region in which the school is located, and comparing it to an eco-region on another continent of the committee's choosing.

2. Depending on students' age and readiness: (a) List the Web addresses used in this lesson on a poster and ask students in small teams to repeat the lesson, practicing zooming in and out and reviewing the distinction between kinds of maps (showing such things as landforms, climate, and political boundaries). (b) Have students create together a map of the classroom with a key. Follow this by having them create individual maps with a key, including a special symbol for the map-maker's own desk.

3. Further assess students' understanding of maps using Ms. Rivera's assessment at the beginning of Chapter 7, "Assessing Student Learning."

Materials
- Poster showing Earth from space.
- Internet access.
- Computer and computer projector for showing a website on a large screen for all to see.
- Websites bookmarked for easy access during the lesson or stored on the class's webpage.

Integration   *Math.* Students who have learned multiplication well enough can be helped to understand the "Powers of 10" film, shown in step 1 of "Lesson Development," in a new, mathematical light.

---

lessons, skill lessons, explanations of all sorts, and questions and activities. Ancillaries are common as well: CDs, videotapes and DVDs, project books, map collections ("atlases"), giant maps that can be spread out on the classroom floor, smaller maps with washable surfaces that are placed on each student's desk, and anthologies of speeches, plays, and short stories. These ancillaries surround the textbook like satellites and are brought into lessons as the teacher sees fit. The *Teacher's Edition,* too, contains a wealth of resources. There are lesson and unit plans, overviews and summaries, focus questions and follow-up questions, additional background information on the subject of the lesson, website suggestions for online Internet activities, reading and writing lessons, connections to the literature curriculum, student projects, guest-speaker and field-trip suggestions, role-playing suggestions, discussion topics, classroom museum ideas, and both formal and informal student assessments. Some teacher's editions even have bar codes that tie into an accompanying videodisk. The teacher simply touches the code with a bar-code reader, and the DVD is cued to a feature related to the reading students are about to do—a tour of modern-day Mesa Verde perhaps, the Taos Pueblo, or the Alamo.

A textbook program, then, is a *resource of resources* that beginning teachers otherwise would have to gather on their own. Considering all that teachers must do in a day, the social studies textbook program is an indispensable aid to teaching and learning. It doesn't have to be the constraining shackle that some make it out to be; instead, it is often a scaffold that helps the teacher teach well.[5] Without it, social studies tends to be slighted. It is moved to the end of the day, the end of the week, or the end of the year. A busy teacher cannot easily assemble the rich stew of primary documents, explanations, examples, charts and maps, narratives, and artwork and the lesson plans for using these things.

Yet, clearly, a textbook is only a resource. A teacher should be its master, not its servant.

FIGURE 10–3 Organizational structure of social studies textbooks.

USING YOUR TEXTBOOK

CONTENTS

TABLE OF CONTENTS
Lists all parts of your book and tells you where to find them

Your textbook contains many special features that will help you read, understand, and remember the people, geography, and history of the United States.

THE **POW WOW**
by
Clifford E. Trafzer

Life has changed a great deal for
Americans since the 1500s...

TRADITIONS
Lessons that will give you a deeper insight into the history and culture of the United States and its neighbors

REVIEWING MAPS & GLOBES

REVIEWING MAPS AND GLOBES
Reviews skills that will help you use the maps in your book

5 FUNDAMENTAL THEMES OF GEOGRAPHY

What is Geography?

Key Vocabulary
geography   region
environment

Many people immediately think of maps and globes when they hear the word geography (jē-ág-rəfē). Others think of mountains, valleys, and deserts. Although geography is all of those things, it is also much more. Geography is the study of the earth and the way people live on it and use it. It includes the earth's land, bodies of water, weather, and plant and animal life. Geography also includes how the earth is used and changed by people.

How do geographers study such a broad subject? One way in which geographers organize their work is by using the Five Fundamental Themes of Geography. You can think of these themes as clues that will help you ... out geography. These ...

Location
One of the five themes of geography is location. Everything on the earth has an exact position, or absolute location. This position can be measured and expressed through numbers like an address. You will read more about absolute location in the Geography Skills lesson on latitude and longitude on pages 30–31.

Relative location or the relationship of one area's location to another is also important to geographers. For example, North Carolina is farther from the equator than Georgia is. This information helps to explain why Georgia is warmer year-round than North Carolina is.

Description of Place
Place is also a theme of geography. Place explains what an area is like by comparing its natural features and human-made features to those in other areas. Look at the photograph of San Francisco Bay ... describe the ... were ...

FIVE FUNDAMENTAL THEMES OF GEOGRAPHY
Introduces important themes of geography that will help you to compare, to contrast, and to understand the regions and people you will study

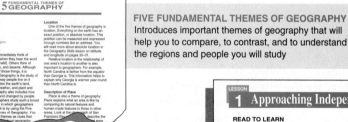

LESSON
1 Approaching Independence

READ TO LEARN

Key Vocabulary	**Key People**	**Key Places**
Second Continental Congress	Benedict Arnold	Fort Ticonderoga
independence	Ethan Allen	
Patriot	William Howe	
Loyalist	Henry Knox	
mercenary		

Read Aloud

"Let them hear the cannon roar," said an English lord, and they will run "as fast as their feet will carry them." King George III declared that once they "have felt a small blow, they will submit."

Both men were talking about the colonial rebels. They were sure that such "ragtag" troops could not match the king's well-trained soldiers. They soon saw how wrong they were.

Read for Purpose
1. **WHAT YOU KNOW:** Why did fighting break out between the colonists and the British soldiers?
2. **WHAT YOU WILL LEARN:** How did the colonists drive the British out of Boston?

LESSON OPENER

Important vocabulary, people, and places introduced in the lesson

Lesson introduction

Asks you to think about what you already know from previous lessons or your own experience

Questions you should keep in mind as you read the lesson

REFERENCE SECTION

ATLAS

Maps of the United States and the world

DICTIONARY OF GEOGRAPHIC TERMS

Definition and pronunciation of major geographic features

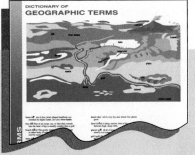

BIOGRAPHICAL DICTIONARY

Identification and pronunciation of important people discussed in your book and page where each is introduced

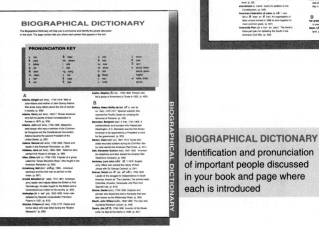

GAZETTEER

Location and pronunciation of the major places discussed in your book and page where each is shown on a map

GLOSSARY

Definition and pronunciation of all Key Vocabulary and page where each is introduced

INDEX

Alphabetical list of important people, places, events, and subjects in your book and pages where information is found

Teaching the Organization of the Textbook

Skillful readers have learned to investigate the organization or structure of a textbook before diving into the first page of the first chapter. In fact, this investigation (the skill called previewing or surveying) is one behavior that distinguishes the more from the less skillful readers of expository (informational) texts—whether elementary-grade students or graduate students. Rather than turning to the first page of the first chapter, utterly in the dark about the way the book is put together, the skillful reader first stands back and takes in the whole scene. He or she surveys the table of contents in front, studies the chapter titles, finds the index at the back of the book, locates a large reference section near the back containing a glossary, atlas, and dictionary of geographic terms. The skillful reader finds that the book's main sections are called units and that these are subdivided into three chapters, each having three lessons. He or she discovers that there are chapter and unit study aids (e.g., overviews and summaries), that pictures have explanatory captions beneath them, and that key vocabulary words are listed at the beginning of each lesson and reviewed in each chapter review. Knowing these things in advance boosts comprehension. A lesson plan for teaching the skill of previewing (Lesson Plan 18) appears in Chapter 12.

Left unguided, a child is not likely to investigate a book's structure. Consequently, students should be taught to do this. Previewing a text is a skill; as such, the teacher can use the skill-teaching strategy presented in Chapter 9. Figure 10–3 illustrates the organizational components that are commonly found in social studies textbooks. In Chapter 12, teaching with the textbook will be considered again.

Conclusion

A variety of resources for teaching social studies are available, beginning with the school library or resource center. The late Hilda Taba, an educator whom I greatly admired, insisted that expensive excursions away from the school were too often lost on children who hadn't actually learned yet to observe the environments and use the resources that are near at hand—namely, the school. The children will need the resources located there, both print and electronic, and they need to feel connected to the librarian, too, and able to call on him or her for help.

Teachers are encouraged to use a wide range of instructional resources because inquiry, concept formation, and skill development require extensive information searches and because not all children learn in the same way. Also, different resources will often provide different viewpoints on the same subject. Biases and inaccuracies will go undetected when a single source is used.

On the next page is a summary chart. Working with a partner, take some time to compare and contrast the resources discussed in this chapter according to the purposes that can be achieved by using the resource, the role students are placed in while using the resource, and planning difficulties and issues that must be considered by the teacher who decides to use the resource in instruction. This will make a good review. Readers may wish to add a fourth dimension of particular concern.

Resource	Purpose	Student's role	Planning concerns for the teacher	?
School library/resource center				
Community: Guest speakers				
Community: Field trips				
Web: Virtual field trips				
Web: Web-based inquiries				
Social studies textbook				

Discussion Questions and Suggested Activities

Go to MyEducationLab and select the topic "Technology," then read the article "Tools for the Mind" and complete the activity.

1. Look back at the in the *Reflection* sidebar in the "Computer Resources" section of this chapter. The study cited there is *Gender Gaps: Where Schools Still Fail Our Children,* by the American Association of University Women (available online, search for the title). The gender gap is only one dimension of what is commonly called the "digital divide," which refers to the unequal access of students to educational technology and computer-related instruction. With a group of classmates, reflect on the schools you have visited and your own education experiences. How deep is the divide, and do you believe it matters? Maybe technology is not so important. Do other resources matter more?

2. Develop a social studies lesson plan using Google Earth or National Geographic's XPeditions. Think carefully about the lesson's objective, and be sure to use the software to help achieve the objective (not the other way around).

3. Visit WebQuest at www.webquest.org, and use one of the templates provided to create a social studies quest for students in a grade level of your choosing. In the "introduction" phase, be sure to tell readers what *kind* of quest it is. Is it actually an inquiry, complete with hypothesis-testing? Or a virtual field trip? Concept formation? Something else?

4. NCSS Standards *Sampler.* Examine the sixth-grade classroom vignette for standard #8 on page 41 of the standards *Sampler* that accompanies this book. What value does it add to the virtual field trip to the Seven Wonders that was featured in this chapter?

Selected References

Bennett, Linda, & Berson, Michael J. (Eds.). (2007). *Digital age: Technology-based K–12 lesson plans for social studies.* Silver Spring, MD: National Council for the Social Studies.

Berson, Michael J., & Bolick, Cheryl M. (Eds.). (2007). Technology and the social studies. *Theory and Research in Social Education,* special issue, *35* (2), 150–332.

Braun, Joseph A., Fernlund, Phyllis F., & White, Charles S. (Eds.). (1998). *Teaching social studies with technology.* Wilsonville, OR: Franklin, Beedle & Associates.

Glenn, Allen D., & Kaviani, Khodidad. (2006). Political socialization, technology, and schools. *International Journal of Social Education, 21* (1), 1–17.

Hickey, M. Gail (2002). Planning a successful field trip. *Social Studies and the Young Learner, 14* (3), 18–21.

Liu, Ping. (2002). Developing an e-Pal partnership: A school-based international activity. *Childhood Education, 79* (2), 81–88.

Salinas, Cinthia, & Robinson, Cecil. (2002). Finding multiple voices through the Internet. *Social Studies and the Young Learner, 14* (3), 31–32.

Shaffer, David W. (2006). *How computer games help children learn.* New York: Palgrave Macmillan.

MyEducationLab is a collection of online tools for your success in this course, your licensure exams, and your teaching career. Go to www.myeducationlab.com to utilize these extensive resources including videos from real classrooms, Praxis and licensure preparation, a lesson plan builder, and materials to help you begin your teaching career.

Cooperative Learning in Social Studies

CHAPTER ELEVEN

Chapter Outline

- Creating a Positive Climate for Human Relations
- Getting Started with Cooperative Groups
- Managing Cooperative Groupwork
- Identifying and Teaching Groupwork Skills
- Teaching and Using Discussion Techniques
- Conclusion

Key Concepts

- Cooperative learning
- Positive interdependence
- Individual accountability
- Hidden curriculum
- Jigsaw
- Structured Academic Controversy
- Discussion

MAIN IDEA

Cooperative groupwork is aimed both at cooperating and learning. It involves more than placing students in groups and giving them a task. Teachers who orchestrate groupwork effectively create a positive classroom climate, and they work up to groupwork gradually. They use different small-group frameworks for different purposes. Most important, they teach groupwork skills directly rather than merely wishing students had already formed them.

PICTURE THIS

Ms. Cassady expects the children to get lots of work done in their small groups. The task, therefore, is always challenging and requires more heads than one. "The task has to be one that actually requires a group," she always says. "That's the key." She makes it a point to become so familiar with each student's talents that by November, she can purposefully mix them in small groups. A student who likes to draw is placed in each group as well as someone who can help the others search for reliable information on the Internet. She also tries to place a strong mediator in each group—someone with good interpersonal skills.

The process of group interaction is "enormously interesting" to children, observed the late, great sociologist, Elizabeth Cohen. Dr. Cohen's research in schools centered on managing groupwork in diverse classrooms. There's something about group interaction, she observed, that is almost magical. Yet it is not magic; children can learn procedures that enable them to learn and to cooperate successfully. They act as a team, caring for one another while accomplishing an engaging task. She wrote,

> Students who usually do anything but what they are asked to do become actively involved with their work and are held there by the action of the group.[1]

What causes this dynamic? First, face-to-face interaction helps children pay attention because it requires a response. Second, children care deeply about the judgment of their peers, and this only increases as children move into adolescence. Third, children get assistance from one another in their groups; the teacher, therefore, is not the only "coach" in the classroom. The importance of this last point cannot be overestimated: Students who do not understand the task at hand become quickly disengaged from it, and disengagement from schoolwork is precisely what teachers and parents want very much to avoid. And for good reason: It can be the proverbial straw that breaks the camel's back for a child who is a member of a language or ethnic minority or for any child who is at risk of school failure.

Groupwork is important for other reasons, too. Democratic citizenship is certainly one of them. Societies that are organized under democratic ideals place special demands on their school systems. Children in these societies need to be educated to be the kind of citizens who can and will share in popular sovereignty. Most basically, the work of democracy requires (as does the world of work) people who can cooperate in task-oriented groups. These may be planning groups, study groups, decision-making groups, or production groups. *These are different from play groups, where one has chosen one's playmates and there is no task per se.* Task-oriented groups have work to do, often solving a problem or building or creating something, and their members are mutually dependent on one another for planning the work, making in-process decisions, and getting it done successfully. Their members may not be fond of one another, and they may be ethnically different from one another, but they have to accomplish something together.

But why is a whole chapter on cooperative learning needed in this textbook? There are three strong rationales. As we saw in Chapter 2, the population of North America is rapidly becoming more diverse racially, ethnically, and linguistically. Such diversity requires students to overcome initial prejudices quickly, to learn to cooperate with people who are culturally different, and to build healthy, working relationships. Second, the transnational corporate community is increasingly demanding employees who can function on cross-cultural teams—together identifying problems, setting priorities, planning, integrating diverse ideas, dividing the workload, and building on one another's contributions. Third, the complexity of world problems—war, religious fundamentalism, global warming, the spread of infectious disease—demands "world citizens" capable of functioning on global problem-solving teams. With globalization, a new era of cooperation is upon us. The two goals of social studies education, recall, are civic competence and social knowledge. Cooperative learning is integral to both.

CREATING A POSITIVE CLIMATE FOR HUMAN RELATIONS

An emotionally supportive atmosphere is one characterized by trust and by evidence that individuals care about each other. When a child volunteers, "Robin's group had more to do than the rest of us. They should have more time to finish," the observer senses that he or she is in a caring environment. Or when a minor classroom accident results in damage to material or broken equipment and the teacher treats the incident as an accident, one concludes that the teacher values human beings more than things. Teachers who develop comfortable classroom environments are concerned with a broad range of educational outcomes, including those that relate to the emotional and social development of children, in addition to attending to subject matter and skills goals. The classroom conditions that establish the context in which children learn the basics of human relations is sometimes referred to as the *hidden curriculum.*

A Caring Environment

The most significant characteristic of a desirable classroom climate is the absence of hostility between the children and the teacher and among the children themselves. Put positively, a desirable classroom atmosphere is one in which caring, kindness, encouragement, and support are fully present. This cannot be assumed; it must be deliberately created. How? Many things are involved, of course, but it includes modeling for children what it looks and sounds like to care for others—children, adults, and pets alike. It means helping children to see that classroom rules originate in caring. As well, it means *attributing the best motive* to children—assuming that a child's intentions are good even when she or he does something bad. Making this assumption is a basic act of kindness on the teacher's part, and generally it should be communicated to the child directly. For example, the teacher might take aside a student who has cheated, beginning not with a reprimand or punishment, though these may well come, but with caring, saying, "I know you want to do well." Likewise, a student who has called another student a cruel name can be taken aside, and the conversation can begin with, "I know you mean to treat others as you want to be treated yourself . . . .[2]

Every schoolteacher has the responsibility to protect and nurture children. As we saw in Chapter 2, it is vitally important that teachers not ignore name calling, whether racial or sexual slurs or other forms of humiliation and ethnocentrism. When teachers are silent in the presence of bigotry, students keenly notice. A teacher's silence conveys a message: "This behavior is okay. Sometimes, we can be cruel." Silence is not neutral; it quietly condones the behavior. Deeply entrenched injustices, such as racism and sexism, are reproduced at school when teachers look the other way.

To clarify these ideas further, consider the eight sets of contrasting teacher behaviors in Figure 11–1.

GETTING STARTED WITH COOPERATIVE GROUPS

Committee work or small-group enterprises are effective instructional procedures in the social studies and have many values for children. In the small group, children get experience with and develop skills in group processes. These experiences should begin in a limited way

FIGURE 11–1   Dimensions of the hidden curriculum.

Practices and Procedures That Tend to Increase Hostility in a Classroom

1. *Excessively competitive situations.*   Fair competition in classrooms is highly desirable. It can stimulate good work, motivate children to do their best, and help children learn the graces associated with winning and losing. It becomes undesirable when it is of the "dog-eat-dog" variety where each child is pitted against every other child whether the competitive situation is fair or unfair.

2. *Negative statements by the teacher.* Ridicule, sarcasm, criticism, and negative and tension-producing statements made by a teacher to children invariably lead to hostility, emotional disturbance, selfishness, fear, and criticism of others. Examples:

> "I wish you would start acting like fourth-graders instead of kindergartners."
>
> "Someone is whispering again, and I guess you all know who it is."
>
> "Most fifth-grade classes could understand this, but I am not sure about you."
>
> "Why don't you listen when I give directions? None of you seems to know how to listen."

3. *Disregard for individual differences.* Classrooms where some children are made to feel "this place is not for me" contribute much toward breeding hostility in children. Such rooms are characterized by one level of acceptable performance applied to all, uniform assignments, one system of reward, and great emphasis on verbal, intellectual performance.

4. *Rigid schedule and pressure.*   A rigid time schedule and constant pressure associated with "hurry up," "finish your work," "you will be late," or stopping lessons exactly on time whether completed or not can create insecurity in children that leads to hostility. A class that is always "one jump behind the teacher" is likely to be one in which children blame others for their failure to finish, invent excuses for themselves, and seek scapegoats.

Practices and Procedures That Tend to Decrease Hostility in a Classroom

1. *Positive interdependence.*   The teacher often structures learning activities so that "students believe that they can reach their learning goals if and only if the other students in the group do too. It is the most basic element of cooperative learning, and it helps children learn to care about and support one another's progress.

2. *Positive statements by the teacher.* Friendly, constructive statements by the teacher tend to reduce tension and hostility in the classroom. Examples:

> "We will all want to listen carefully in order not to miss anything Sue is going to tell us."
>
> "All of us did our work so well yesterday during our work period. Do you suppose we can do as well today?"
>
> "It is really fun for all of us when you bring such interesting things for sharing."
>
> "It's nice to have Jason and Kendra back with us again. The boys and girls were hoping you would come back today."

3. *Recognition of and response to individual differences.*   In such classrooms, all children are challenged at a level commensurate with their abilities and in ways that are mindful of cultural and linguistic differences. The teacher strives to see *all* children's gifts and talents.

4. *Relaxed, comfortable pace.*   Good teachers working with young children maintain a flexible schedule and will not place undue pressures on children. They will have a plan and a schedule, yet will not be compulsive in adhering to it. They will deviate from their plan now and then in the interests of the needs of the boys and girls they teach.

Practices and Procedures That Tend to Increase Hostility in a Classroom

5. *Highly directive teaching practices.* Teachers who must make every decision themselves, give all the assignments, and allow for very little participation on the part of children in the life of the classroom may encourage feelings of hostility.

6. *Lack of closeness between teacher and children.* Some teachers feel they must "keep children in their places," meaning they must remain socially distant from them. This leads to a cold relationship between the children and the teacher, causing the children to feel that the teacher lacks affection and warmth for them.

7. *Lack of satisfying emotional experiences.* Some classrooms do not provide opportunities to express positive affect. Everything is deadly serious business—work, work, work. Even music, art, story time, or dramatic activities are made to seem like work. Little time is spent on teaching children to enjoy one another, feel the inner joy that comes from a good poem or music selection, or express their feelings in some art medium.

8. *Rules are about obeying.* Some teachers have elaborate systems for dealing with violations of classroom rules, but fail to capitalize on them to teach children about caring. Obedience, rather than understanding the purpose of the rule, becomes the sole aim.

Practices and Procedures That Tend to Decrease Hostility in a Classroom

5. *Student involvement in planning and managing the class.* Giving children some opportunity to plan and manage the affairs of the classroom does much to develop feelings of "we-ness" of a democratic community. Children under such circumstances are less inclined to want to think of ways to disrupt the teacher's orderly room and instead will work hard to make "our" room a good place to work.

6. *Warm and friendly relationship between teacher and children.* One of the basic needs of children is that of love and affection. They need it in their homes, in their play groups, and in their schools. The feeling that children will not respect the teacher who is friendly with them is incorrect. They are likely to respect the teacher more whom they feel is a human being capable of warm personal relationships with others. This is a professional relationship, however, and teachers are advised *against* trying to develop a *peer* relationship with the children they teach.

7. *Many opportunities for pleasurable emotional experiences.* Teachers can reduce tensions that build up in children during the course of classroom life by providing opportunities for the release of these tensions through various emotional experiences. Children have the opportunity to express their feelings orally, in writing, or through art forms. They talk together and enjoy one another's company. They prepare skits, do creative dramatics, and role-play situations to help get the feelings of others. All these activities tend to reduce feelings of hostility.

8. *Rules are about caring.* Teachers can use rule violations to help children appreciate that we have rules because we care for one another. We do not call other children names because it hurts their feelings; we don't write on desks and tables out of respect for others who use them; we tell the truth because others deserve sincerity, not lies; we try to be punctual because we care for those who are waiting.

even as early as kindergarten. In block play, for example, the teacher can allow some children to choose the things they wish to build with blocks. Some will want to build an airport; some, a house; others, a post office; others, a supermarket; and so on. The teacher can let each child choose two other children to help build the project. The children proceed with the building and, when it is completed, tell the class or their teacher a story about their building. Early experiences in such block play will consist mainly of parallel play—three children may be building an airport, but each is working independently of the other two. As the year progresses, there will be more evidence of cooperative endeavor. Children become more conscious of what others in their group are doing and will plan their own contribution in terms of the other children and the group goal.

A good way to familiarize primary-grade children with small-group work is to have committees responsible for various housekeeping duties in the classroom. José's committee has the responsibility of keeping the library table neat, Paul's committee is in charge of the game shelf, Long's committee is responsible for the care of the aquarium, and Denisha's committee keeps the coat corner orderly. Membership on these committees can be changed from time to time to include all the children in the class. Such experiences will help prepare children for the committee work that is done as part of the instructional program.

Small-group enterprises in the primary grades need careful supervision and direction. The goals or purposes of the group should be well defined, concrete, and easily understood. Materials needed for the group to do its work must be immediately at hand. Rules and responsibilities of working on committees should be discussed, explained, and posted conspicuously in the room. Groupwork skills develop slowly and gradually and require practice, as do any other skills. The skills of groupwork can be learned only by working in groups.

In grades 4 and 5, small-group work becomes an increasingly greater part of the social studies program. At these grade levels, each group member can be given an assigned task to help the group achieve its goal. Small groups are used to prepare reports; discuss issues; plan activities; do construction, art, or dramatic activities; write plays, biographies, and short stories; gather resources for the class; interview community resource persons; and so on. Through instruction and experience, children will learn that the success of the group depends on the initiative and cooperation of individuals within the group.

The class will be divided into small work groups on many occasions. These groups are task oriented; they are formed to do things that really need doing. In this way, groupwork can avoid artificiality. Groups are not formed merely to have children practice cooperative groupwork; *they are formed to get some sort of work done.* (This may be the most widely misunderstood element of cooperative learning!) Groupwork, therefore, can be relatively short lived. A committee may be assigned to find out how bridges are built or to create a map of a nearby river system. When the committee has completed its task and reported to the larger group, it can be dissolved.

When attempting for the first time to organize small-group work, the teacher may find the guidelines in the box "Forming Academic Committees" helpful. Note that it is not necessary to place all students in small groups at the same time, at least not when the teacher is just learning to manage small-group instruction. Instead, a gradual, diagnostic approach is recommended. This approach permits the teacher and students to get their feet wet little by little, with the teacher all the while observing group dynamics and strengths and weaknesses in the children's cooperative behaviors.

FORMING ACADEMIC COMMITTEES

1. Defer small-group work until the management of the class has been well established and the work habits, interpersonal skills, and special needs of individual children are known.

2. Select children who already have good interpersonal skills for your first academic committee. Keep the group small—never more than five children.

3. Assign the committee an academic task that is simple and well defined, one that the group is certain to accomplish successfully.

4. Have the remainder of the class engage in individual assignments while you are giving guidance and direction to the small group. Either designate a leader for the small group or have the children choose a leader. Explain the nature of their assigned task and begin to discuss some of their special responsibilities when working in a small group.

5. Have resource materials available for the children. Later on, as they become accustomed to working in groups, they will be able to secure needed materials themselves.

6. Meet with the small group every day for a few minutes before they begin work and again at the end of their work period to make sure things are moving along as planned. If possible, have them make a progress report to the other larger group during the summary and evaluation that should come at the close of each social studies period.

7. Give students specific help and suggestions in how to organize their work and how to report what they are doing.

8. Have their report to the class be short, concise, and interesting. Have members of the group explain to the class how they did their work as a group. Begin calling attention to some of the responsibilities of persons working collaboratively in small groups.

9. Follow the same procedure with another group of children as soon as possible. Gradually include other children, selecting some who have had previous experience in groupwork and some who have not. Observe carefully the children who need close supervision and those who are responsible and work well in groups.

10. After all the children have had an opportunity to work in a small group under close supervision, more than one group can work at a time. Eventually, the entire class should be able to work in small groups simultaneously. When this is attempted, precede the work with a review of the standards of groupwork and a clear definition of objectives. A careful evaluation should follow.

How might these guidelines look in action? In the following example, a teacher appoints a committee to help introduce and question a classroom guest.

The children in Mr. Shigaki's fourth-grade class have been involved in a career awareness study and are going to have resource persons visit their classroom. The children have indicated careers they would like to have included. Mr. Shigaki has asked four children to meet him in the rear of the classroom and is now speaking to them.

"Because the four of you are particularly interested in learning about computer science careers, I am asking that you take responsibility for introducing Ms. Timms tomorrow. You will have to select one person to do the introducing. The others can help by suggesting things that should be said about her in the introduction. Also, all of you should help develop some questions to ask her after her presentation. Remember one of our objectives is to find out what kind of training and skills computer scientists need and what opportunities there are in that field. Is there anything else you think you will need to prepare to be the host group tomorrow?"

One member of the group asks if they are to thank the visitor for coming.

"Yes. Good point! I'm glad you thought of that, Mark. You will need to select someone to thank Ms. Timms. Anything else?" (No further suggestions are offered.)

"I guess you are ready to begin your work then," says Mr. Shigaki. "Lisa, would you act as the group leader and report to me when your group is finished planning?"

Mr. Shigaki then leaves the group to its task and supervises the remainder of the class, who have been working on individual assignments.

MANAGING COOPERATIVE GROUPWORK

Let us turn from forming the occasional committee that accomplishes one or more tasks to simultaneous involvement of all children in small-group instruction. First, we consider goals, then group size, group composition, and alternative small-group structures.

Goals

It would be reasonable to assume that if children are given instruction and have several guided experiences in cooperative groups, they are likely to develop group interaction skills and the disposition to be cooperative. But do cooperative learning strategies also affect a child's overall academic achievement? The answer is a confident "Yes!" Results indicate that cooperative learning experiences tend to promote higher achievement than do competitive and individualistic learning experiences.[3] These results apply to all age levels and subject areas and for all sorts of academic tasks, from simple retention to concept learning and problem solving. Kristin Gruber, a third-grade teacher in Minnesota, tells this success story:

> Andy, a low-achieving student who received LD (learning disability) services, was failing social studies, health, and language early in the year. He needed constant supervision just to stay on task, paid little attention to classroom discussions, and seldom completed assignments. With a cooperative group to support and encourage him, however, Andy completed many assignments during class and brought back homework consistently. . . . By mid-February, he was passing every subject; and he was able to maintain his grades for the rest of the year.[4]

Why is this so? Researchers look to the main ingredients of cooperative learning: positive interdependence and individual student accountability. *Positive interdependence* means that group goals cannot be attained unless each member of the group does his or her part; *individual accountability* means that the group's success depends not only on group members doing their parts but also on learning. Indeed, they will be held accountable for learning: grades go to individual students, not groups. Add to these another attribute of cooperative learning: discussion. *Discussion* is a rich stew of face-to-face talking, listening, responding, paraphrasing, and questioning. Positive interdependence makes all this necessary. Putting thoughts into words requires students to think about the task at hand and to

Positive interdependence means that each member of the team does his or her part.
(David Young-Wolff/PhotoEdit Inc.)

clarify what they mean; trying to understand what others mean involves still more talking, thinking, and clarifying. Further, discussion often produces disagreements—healthy social and academic conflicts—which, when managed skillfully by the teacher and students, promote deeper levels of both academic learning and interpersonal development. *Controversies* and *disagreements* flourish in democratic civic life; students must learn to deal with them productively.

Closely related to discussion and controversy is still another reason cooperative learning improves academic achievement—it promotes what researchers call *engaged time* or *time on task*. Cooperative groupwork generally helps children to be more engaged in the task (more attentive and involved) than does seatwork. The main drawback of seatwork is that children are working on their own with little or no guidance, which allows them to drift far from the assigned task or to attempt it without understanding its purpose and without using helpful strategies. This is especially unfortunate when we consider that seatwork often consumes over half the available instructional time in both primary and intermediate grades and, ironically, is prescribed most often to children who already are doing poorly in school! Elizabeth Cohen sums up this problem:

> Choosing a method of classroom organization that leaves the student who rarely succeeds in schoolwork quite alone may indeed be the root cause of the observed disengagement on the part of low-achieving students in seatwork settings. These students are receiving very little information on the purpose of their assignment, on how to complete it successfully, on how they are doing, or on how they could be more successful. The tasks themselves are rarely sufficiently interesting to hold the students' attention.[5]

Cooperative learning promotes active student involvement in learning and therefore helps teachers to spend wisely the most valuable aid they have—time.

Group Size and Composition

The size of a small group affects its achievement both of academic knowledge and of cooperative skills. If groups are too large, there may be duplication of responsibilities, less opportunity for individuals to carry their share of the group effort, difficulty achieving face-to-face interaction, and a tendency for some members to fade out of the group activity. Also, the larger the group, the more skillful group members must be with cooperative behaviors. On the other hand, if groups are too small, there may be insufficient division of labor to warrant groupwork and too few opportunities to cooperate. In general, however, groups should be kept small—from two to five children, with four or five as the optimal size. When teaching groupwork skills, teachers often begin by placing children in pairs to practice particular skills, such as using names, making eye contact with the speaker, and asking for help. Pairs can then be combined into groups of four.

Group size influences the sort of academic work that can be accomplished. Structured Academic Controversy, discussed later in this chapter, requires two pairs of children in groups of four; meanwhile, STAD (also discussed later) has no required group size. The number of students in a Jigsaw group determines the number of topics that can be studied or, when writing original biographies, the number of chapters in the book students produce (see Chapter 13).

Just now, our discussion of goals emphasized learning cooperative behaviors and academic achievement. Let us consider a third goal, which bears particularly on group composition: positive intergroup relations among students of different ethnic and racial backgrounds in integrated classrooms. Anyone who has visited a desegregated school knows that friendships across racial and ethnic groups do not automatically follow the placement of diverse children together in the same school or classroom. To the contrary, especially in the upper grades, children of the same racial or ethnic group often stay together, playing together at recess and eating together in the cafeteria.[6]

A good deal of research shows that when diverse groups of youngsters work together to attain a group goal, positive feelings are generated: They begin to like and trust one another, more often choose to be with one another during free time, and in general grow in their respect for one another. Of course, a teacher cannot expect these results as a consequence only of placing diverse students together in a small group and structuring a cooperative task for them; rather, students must be prepared for groupwork. They must learn the skills and norms of cooperation. But placing them in diverse groups is a precondition—it at least provides the *opportunity* to tackle the goal of positive intergroup understanding.

Thus, the cardinal principle of group composition is to achieve the greatest mix possible given the student population. A teacher should achieve this mix using whatever student differences are available—academic record, interpersonal skill, gender, ethnicity, disability, language, race, and social class. In this way, small groups are as heterogeneous as the whole class. Ability grouping is ruled out (as far as this third goal is concerned) because it minimizes rather than maximizes the mix. There is a time and place for ability grouping, of course, as we saw in Chapter 2, but not when the goal is positive intergroup relations.

The teacher may use one or more of several methods to form heterogeneous student groups:

1. *Work, not play.* Do not allow friends to choose one another for small-group work. Friends tend to play rather than work when placed in the same group, and groupwork should be thought of in terms of work rather than play.

2. *Random assignment.* With a brand-new class, a teacher might randomly assign students to small groups of four to five students each. Forming groups alphabetically is a good way, and it should result in mixed groups. Look over the resulting lists of group members and make any adjustments needed to achieve a greater mix of gender and ethnicity.

3. *Purposeful mixing.* Once a teacher is more familiar with students' work habits, interpersonal skills, and past academic achievement, groups can be purposefully mixed. Some teachers have good success simply by mixing within each group students who are strong and weak on each of these characteristics. Students with poor interpersonal skills and/or poor academic records should not be placed together any more than friends or highly successful students should be placed together.

4. *Special helper.* A variation on purposeful mixing is to select one or more students for each group who will serve as a special helper. The help needed will depend on the kind of work the teacher has structured for the groups. For example, if groups are to construct a papier-mâché map of the United States, each working on a different region, the teacher might identify students who are good with paper products (mixing, gluing, painting) or at creating map legends. One of these helpers is placed in each small group. If the teacher has decided that groups of four children are to write a book of historical fiction about Harriet Tubman or Gandhi, with each student working on a different chapter, it will help to have someone who likes to sketch in each group. It will also help to have a strong planner in each group—someone who can help the group decide on four different chapter topics.

   In general, social and academic skills that can come in handy are reading, writing, planning, decision making (comparing alternatives), note taking, brainstorming, operating tape recorders or cameras, observing detail, using the library, creating time lines, using reference books, finding websites on the Internet, loading software on the computer, using creative dramatics, assisting students with disabilities, interviewing, building with cardboard, drawing, taking surveys, and so on.

5. *Index cards.* Write the name of each student on an index card, a strip of construction paper, or a popsicle stick. Decide on the task each group will tackle and identify the special help that will be needed. Identify the special helpers, putting at least one in each group, and sort the other students into each group. Aim for the greatest mix possible with regard to interpersonal skills, ethnicity, language, academic achievement, gender, and so on. (The teacher can use a random method, such as shuffling the deck of name cards, once special helpers have been selected.)

6. *Duration.* A cooperative group exists until the cooperative task is completed. Rather than re-forming groups for the next group task, the same group usually remains together for the purpose of further developing its cooperative skills. Groups should stay together long enough to make progress on the interpersonal problems that inevitably arise. While the group remains the same, the task, of course, changes (e.g., from making maps to writing a biography). A new task is an opportunity for the

teacher to select a different set of special helpers. The teacher should keep searching for everyone's special talents.

Alternative Frameworks for Cooperative Tasks

There are many different ways to structure groupwork, all with positive interdependence, individual accountability, face-to-face interaction, and discussion. Teachers often invent their own ways and share them with one another. Teachers just beginning to experiment with cooperative learning may prefer STAD (Student Teams Achievement Division). When teacher and students are ready, they can experiment with Jigsaw or Structured Academic Controversy. I describe each in turn.

STAD

Student Teams Achievement Division has the students listening to the teacher present information—except that a cooperative task is tagged onto the end.[7] Students are placed in groups before the lesson begins. First, the teacher explains the purpose and rationale of the lesson and presents needed information. (In a lesson on map legends, for example, the teacher takes 20 minutes or so to display three different maps, explaining the design and function of the legend on each.) Second, the teacher gives the groups one handout with questions and another handout with answers. Each group receives only one copy of each so that group members must share materials. Each group is given 20 minutes to accomplish their task: to understand *why* the answers are correct. Third, students are given a short quiz on the questions and answers, and the group with the highest average score (or that shows the greatest improvement over the last quiz average) is rewarded with special certificates and honorable mention in the class newsletter. This constitutes one round of STAD.

STAD is a sleeper—it has more power than you might imagine. I have seen student teachers use STAD effectively in all sorts of situations. Small-group review for a quiz is probably the most common. What teacher doesn't wish for a concise yet powerful strategy for helping students review?

Jigsaw

We encountered Jigsaw, developed by Elliot Aronson,[8] in Chapter 9 where it was incorporated into the teaching strategy *concept formation*. In that example, students were members of two groups—the usual group of four or five students, which in Jigsaw serves as students' "home team," plus an additional "expert group." Typically, the teacher divides a complex task—whatever it is—into four or five parts. In concept formation, each part is one example of the concept children are to form. Or the task might be to prepare a report on the geography of a continent, say, Asia, and that task is divided into four or five parts: perhaps five geographic regions on that continent or the five themes of geography (Chapter 4). Or the task might simply be to comprehend a difficult chapter on Native Americans in the textbook, and the parts are the chapter's four or five lessons. Whatever the task, each member of the home team is assigned to work on one of the four or five parts, but he or she is not alone (see Figure 11–2). All students from the different home teams who are assigned to the same part join together to work in expert groups (called this because, relative to their

FIGURE 11–2   Jigsaw group assignments.

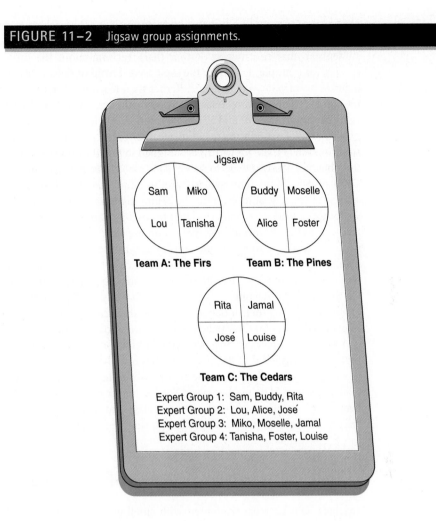

teammates, they become experts on this one part). The goal of working together in expert groups is very simple: to learn their part of the task better than they would working alone. This may require anywhere from 30 minutes to a week or more, depending on the task. Eventually, experts return to their home teams, where they serve as the teacher for their teammates, helping them learn all about the part they studied in the expert groups. Following this, student understanding of the *whole* task (all the parts) is assessed. The teacher rewards the home team that has the highest average score, or that has improved the most, or the one that demonstrated the best use of cooperative skills. This is one round of Jigsaw.

Structured Academic Controversy

We would not want to let the opportunities afforded by cooperative learning to restructure the ways we teach social studies cause us to ignore the chance it provides to reconsider *what* we teach in social studies.[9] Structured Academic Controversy, developed by Roger and

David Johnson, provides just this opportunity.[10] It asks teachers to perceive the academic controversy in whatever social studies knowledge they want students to learn and to engage students in that controversy. Rather than teaching about the protection of endangered species, for example, as though the topic were devoid of debate, teachers can help their students to *participate in that debate*. Rather than teaching about the American Revolution as though the colonists were destined to declare their independence, teachers can help students relive the arguments for and against separation. At election time, students can tackle the key problem of voter apathy by deciding whether or not citizens should be *required* to vote. The study of each of these topics can be designed so that the disagreements at their core are made the object of study. *Doing so boosts both the intellectual rigor as well as the excitement of social studies lessons.* The two go hand in hand. Structured Academic Controversy makes such study manageable, even for the beginning teacher and for very young students.

First, the teacher assigns students to four-person teams. Second, the teacher helps the teams gather background information on the topic, for example, on the American Revolution. The textbook may provide ample background, and supplementary resources, such as primary documents and children's literature, can also be assembled. In the third phase, each four-person team is divided into two pairs, and each pair is assigned to one side of the debate. On the American Revolution, one pair would study the arguments that eventually led to the colonies declaring their independence, and the other pair would learn Loyalist arguments. Fourth, pairs present their perspectives to one another. Fifth, as a test of their listening and questioning, the pairs reverse perspectives, giving now the argument of the other pair until that pair is satisfied that its perspective has been heard and understood. In the final phase, genuine discussion begins as the two pairs join together for the purpose of striving for a team consensus. The teacher says, "You no longer need to represent the assigned position. Feel free to change your mind." Tell the class that in 15 minutes, a spokesperson for each team will report on the team's progress toward consensus.

IDENTIFYING AND TEACHING GROUPWORK SKILLS

Teachers who have experimented with small-group instruction and found it frustrating commonly feel that groupwork breaks down either because some children within the group do most of the work or because the children waste time and accomplish little or nothing. Such responses indicate that the children have not yet developed the prerequisite skills for successful cooperative endeavors. If children are only given the *opportunity* to work in groups without being *prepared* to do so, there is little reason to expect them to function effectively in these groups. (As we saw in Chapter 2, high expectations are an important teaching tool, but without the accompanying instruction only those students who *already* have achieved the objective will succeed. This is not fair and only perpetuates inequality.)

Children need to be taught how to behave during cooperative groupwork so that they can function reasonably well without the teacher's direct supervision. Of course, this is not only a matter of teaching the needed interpersonal skills; group members also need the appropriate academic skills for completing the assigned task. If group members are expected to write a report together, they will require instruction on report writing and some general writing experience. This instruction does not need to occur in advance; providing it when it is needed is sometimes more effective because children immediately see the need for it.

Children need to be taught how to behave in cooperative groups. (© Ellen *B. Senisi/Ellen Senisi)*

The next section offers suggestions on which skills need to be taught and strategies for teaching them. Two kinds of skills are highlighted—skills for getting started as a cooperative group and skills for functioning in a cooperative group.

Skills for Getting Started

Tell children both the purpose and rationale for having them learn to work cooperatively in small groups. Teachers have found it helpful to provide examples of real-world situations, both civic and job related, where people need to function well in groups with others who not only are not their friends, but may even be strangers (town meetings, juries, fire departments, fast-food restaurants, hospital emergency rooms, and so on); in such groups, whether members are strangers or not, disagreements are common.

Children typically need to be taught behaviors that help them to do the following:

- Move into groups efficiently
- Stay with the group during group time
- Use quiet voices
- Make everyone feel welcome
- State and restate the assignment
- Set or call attention to the time frame

Skills for Functioning in Small Groups

When groups are practicing the skills of getting started, it is especially important that the task be short and simple. Once some progress is made in these skills areas, the teacher should instruct the class on some of the behaviors crucial to a group working well together when the task is more complex. These should be posted in the room and referred to often. Examples include:

- Plan how best to proceed
- Encourage everyone to participate
- Use one another's names
- Face the speaker and make eye contact
- Avoid putdowns
- Ask for help when you need it
- Ask questions
- Be a good sport
- Offer to explain, clarify, or summarize
- Listen carefully when others are speaking
- Paraphrase another's statements
- Talk openly about disagreements
- Criticize ideas, not people
- Cheerfully take the jobs the group wants you to do
- Suggest new ideas when the group's motivation is low

Teaching Cooperative Skills

Practicing any cooperative skill requires that learners *understand* the skill. Otherwise, they are not really practicing anything. For this reason, knowledge and skill are said to be interdependent. One effective skill-teaching procedure was given in Chapter 9. The T-chart (Figure 11–3) is another popular method for helping children understand a cooperative skill.[11] The teacher writes the name of a skill on the chalkboard and creates two columns beneath it, one for a group of adjectives describing what the skill *looks* like, another for phrases that exemplify what the skill *sounds* like. Children are then asked to generate a list for each.

Once a skill is understood well enough to make practice worthwhile, practice should begin in earnest. Some teachers find role-playing to be a valuable technique in teaching the skills needed in small-group work. By selecting four to five children to serve as group members, the teacher can demonstrate to the class what it means to "help everyone become a part of the group" or any of the skills that have been discussed. When the role-playing is completed, the remainder of the class can analyze the situation to determine why the group was functioning well or poorly. It is helpful to have children observe certain specific elements in the situation to be presented. For example, they might try to answer such questions as these:

1. What did individual members do to help the group do its job? What did members do that did not help the group?
2. What did the leader do to help the group get its job done?

FIGURE 11–3   A sample T-chart used to help children understand a cooperative skill.

SKILL: Encouraging Participation

Looks Like	Sounds Like
smiles	"What is your idea?"
eye contact	"Excellent!"
thumbs up	"That's a good idea!"
pat on the back	"I'd like to hear what you think."

3. How did the group find out exactly what it was to do?
4. Did the group use good resources in solving its problems?
5. Did the group seem to be working together as a team? Why or why not?
6. How can we help the group do its job better?

Following the role-playing, the class can discuss the situation in terms of the specific points being observed. It may then be helpful to replay all or a portion of the situation to help children appreciate the forces at work in group situations. With young children it may be desirable to have an older group demonstrate such things as a domineering leader, an uncooperative group member, a member who wants only the fun tasks, the noncontributor, the member who must always have his or her own way, the member who talks too much,

REFLECTION

Is ability grouping in reading and math instruction an example of cooperative learning? Why or why not?

and so on. In teaching groupwork skills, the teacher will want to do more than talk about what should or should not be done. Children really need an opportunity to see and experience how it works, as well as an opportunity to experiment and try their hand at doing productive groupwork. Role-playing can do much to sensitize them to the various subtleties and forces that come into play in small-group situations.

Video cameras can be useful in teaching cooperative skills. The teacher can film a group role-playing certain skills needed for productive small-group work. The film can then be used for feedback and analysis. This procedure is widely used in teaching dancers and athletes, and greater use could be made of it in classrooms today.

Rewarding Groupwork Appropriately

Part of the reason that groupwork is at times ineffective is because it is not rewarded as generously as are the academic aspects of classroom work. This stems from the teacher's attitude toward the value of group activities. If the rewards (recognition, praise, reports to parents, grades) go only to those who do well on tests and other paper-and-pencil activities, children rightly conclude that group activities and cooperation do not count much in the entire scheme of things. Groupwork will be enhanced if the teacher (a) regards it as an important part of the instructional program, (b) teaches and assesses the skills of groupwork, and (c) rewards appropriately the children who have done commendable work in group endeavors.

Debriefing

While rewarding good skill use is necessary, it is just as important to talk in detail with students about the progress they are making. All groupwork should involve the deliberate practice of one or more cooperative skills; therefore, all groupwork sessions should be followed by a debriefing in which students are asked to reflect on how often cooperative skills were used, how well they were used, and what skills especially need attention. This is important, but surprisingly rare. Quite common mistakes in cooperative groupwork are first, not helping students identify and clarify just which cooperative skills need to be practiced during a particular groupwork session, and second, forgetting to debrief the session.

Giving Oral Reports

Teams and expert groups will be giving oral reports to the entire class from time to time in the normal course of groupwork. Structured Academic Controversy, recall, ends when a spokesperson for each team reports to the class on the team's attempt to reach a consensus on the issue at hand. Oral reports also are commonly used to share information obtained through individual research and study. Whether the report represents work done as part of a group or inquiry conducted individually, it serves the purpose of bringing to the group the information and ideas that were acquired, as well as teaching children how to organize, plan, and present a report.

Lesson Plan 9, "A Nation in the News," in Chapter 6 involves groupwork and oral presentations. Look back to it to see the scoring guide for the presentations.

It is the teacher's responsibility to take an active part in helping the child prepare the report. This includes suggesting suitable topics, suggesting references, helping with its organization, and suggesting visual devices to use. The teacher should find a few minutes a day or two before the presentation to sit down with the youngster and review what is to be included in the report. Once prepared, the child should be left alone while the report is being given unless help is specifically requested.

Only a few reports should be scheduled on the same day. It is impossible for children to sustain any degree of interest if they must listen to 5 or 10 reports consecutively. A better procedure is to have 2 or 3 reports given at a time and to spread the reporting over a period of several days.

The following are suggested as alternatives to the traditional oral and written reports.

1. Dramatize an incident, sequence, or situation relating to the topic and incorporate essential data to be communicated in the dramatization.
2. Use children's own drawn illustrations, charts, and graphs as the basis for a presentation along with illustrations found in newspapers, magazines, or other sources.
3. Pretend to be a tour guide taking the class through the area studied. Different children report on different "stops" on the tour.
4. Use the overhead projector for visual aids in a presentation or a computer projector for a PowerPoint presentation.
5. Interview a classmate who is role-playing the part of an expert on the topic under study.
6. Use artifacts as the basis for a report.

7. Prepare and explain a bulletin-board display or diorama.
8. Do an original narration for a film or videotape with the sound turned off.
9. Write news stories that might have been appropriate to a particular period or prepare and publish a single issue of a newspaper that might have appeared in some historical period.
10. Tape-record a presentation for playback to the class, which frees the speaker to point to parts of a chart or model or to show photos or slides. In this way, the child is accompanying himself or herself.

TEACHING AND USING DISCUSSION TECHNIQUES

We saw in Chapter 3 that discussion generally and deliberation particularly (which is discussion aimed at making a decision on a controversial issue) are fundamental democratic processes. We have seen in this chapter that discussion is a key ingredient in cooperative learning. Its value lies chiefly in the fact that it represents a type of intellectual teamwork, resting on the principle that the pooled knowledge, ideas, and feelings of several persons have greater merit than those of a single individual. Without discussion, a student may never grasp the fact that there are multiple points of view and opinions on a problem, not just his or her own. Furthermore, the student may never have the opportunity to practice the most fundamental work of popular sovereignty—talking with others about common problems and reaching a decision about what to do. *In this section, we look more closely at discussion, concentrating on large-group, roundtable and panel discussions, and buzz groups. In the next chapter, "The Literacy–Social Studies Connection," we will look at a powerful literature-oriented discussion method called Socratic Seminar.*

Involving Every Child

Because the strength of discussion is obtained from the information and viewpoint of many members of the group, it is necessary that most members of the class participate. It is a thinking-together process that breaks down if one member or group dominates it. It is the teacher's responsibility to encourage the more reluctant children to participate. Although there cannot be a single answer to the question of what to do with the child who dominates the discussion, skillful teachers usually take care of the matter with a statement such as "Jack, you have given us so many good ideas today, and I know you have many more good suggestions, but we want to find out what some of the others think would be a good way to. . . ."

Another strategy for dealing with students who dominate discussions is to use student observers. One or two children are asked to observe the day's discussion. Their task is straightforward: to keep track of who talks and how much. Because student observers learn a good deal about discussion, the domineering student can purposefully be placed in this role. One first-grade teacher placed such a student in the role of student observer, instructing him to gather data without talking. He gathered data on who talked and did a good job, noting that one student had done quite a bit of talking in the group while another had talked very little. The next day, when he was back in the group and no longer the observer, he started to talk, clamped his hand over his mouth, and glanced at the new observer. He knew what behavior was being observed, and he didn't want to be the only one with marks for talking. The teacher said he may have listened for the first time all year.[12]

Roundtable Discussions

A roundtable discussion usually involves a small number of persons, no fewer than three and no more than eight. It requires someone to serve as a moderator to introduce the members of the discussion group, present the problem to be discussed, and keep the discussion moving. The leader's role is to guide the group rather than to dominate it. A relaxed atmosphere needs to prevail, and the presentations are conversational rather than oratorical.

Roundtable discussions are difficult for young children (and adults!) because they are, essentially, a conversation held in front of an audience. They can be used in the intermediate and middle grades (4–8) by having a group of children discuss a problem in front of the rest of the class or by dividing the class into several small discussion groups that function without an audience. It is perhaps best to use this procedure with one group at a time, either with or without an audience, until the children have learned how to participate in discussions of this type. It will be necessary for the teacher to introduce the procedure to the class and to explain and demonstrate its purposes and the way it works. Such points as the following need to be emphasized. They can be posted on the wall for all to see during the teacher's explanation of each point.

1. *Responsibilities of the moderator*—to be informed on the topic to be discussed; introduce the topic; keep the discussion moving; avoid having the group become sidetracked; ask members to explain more fully what they mean; avoid having members quibble over irrelevancies; and summarize periodically.
2. *Responsibilities of members of the discussion group*—to be well informed on the topic to be discussed, especially some phase of it; stay with the topic under discussion; address one another; have sources of information available; back up statements with evidence; and help the group summarize its conclusions.
3. *Responsibilities of the audience*—to listen attentively; withhold questions until the presentation is completed; ask for clarification of ideas; ask for evidence on questionable statements; confine remarks to the topic under discussion; and extend customary audience courtesies to members of the roundtable.

Roundtable discussions may be used for any of the following purposes:

1. Discuss plans for a major class activity, such as a construction project or the best way to present the work of the class to the parents on Parents Night.
2. Evaluate the results of a class activity, the merits of a film, a school assembly, or a decision of the student council.
3. Discuss a current event.
4. Make decisions and recommendations to the class. (The student council, for example, wants to know how the class feels about a new play schedule. A committee of five children discusses this matter and presents its findings and recommendations to the class.)

Panel Discussions

A panel discussion is similar to a roundtable discussion in many respects, but there are important differences. The responsibilities of the moderator are approximately the same as they are for the moderator of the roundtable, as are those of the participants. The procedure, however, is more formal than that of the roundtable. It usually begins with a short statement by each discussant before the panel is opened for free discussion by members. Panels are more audience-oriented than are roundtables, and frequently some provision is made for audience questions or participation at the end of the panel's presentation. A greater responsibility is placed on participants to prepare themselves well for their particular part on the panel, for each panelist is considered more or less an expert.

One sixth-grade teacher used a panel-discussion format in the following way. The topic for the panel to discuss was a community problem involving the conversion of a military base into a community resource. Various special-interest groups were competing for the use of the newly acquired property. In class, the teacher asked children to volunteer to represent one of the following special-interest groups:

1. City planner
2. Golf enthusiast
3. Representative of the local community service club
4. Condominium builder
5. Representative of a local Native American nation
6. Moderator

The children were provided planning time in which to prepare a three- to five-minute statement explaining their point of view regarding the future of this property. Each panelist had a name card that included the name of the group he or she represented. Time was allowed for questions to clarify points made in the presentations or to raise other issues.

Buzz Groups for Brainstorming

The following is an example of a buzz group in operation. The members of Ms. Kryzinski's class viewed in class a television special dealing with homelessness in the United States. They were eager to discuss the program and even more anxious to do something about the problem it portrayed.

"What can we do, Ms. K, to help other kids in our school know about some ways they can help the homeless?" one child asked.

"Why don't you decide?" Ms. Kryzinski responded. "You are already arranged in small groups, so why don't you take the next 10 minutes and come up with some ideas? Be prepared to give us two or three that would be possible for us to carry out in our school."

After about 10 to 15 minutes, the children's attention was refocused, and each group presented some ideas. There was no attempt to evaluate suggestions at that time.

All the suggestions were listed on the board and discussed. The class then voted on the list to determine which one they would implement.

We have here a brief description of a buzz-group or brainstorming technique. It is an informal consideration of ideas or problems where the chief purpose is to solicit the suggestions, feelings, or ideas of the members participating. In brainstorming for ideas and

CHARACTER TRAITS OF PROMINENT PEOPLE

Grades	4–5
Time	Three to five class periods
NCSS Standards	4 (individual development and identity) and 10 (civic ideals and practices)
Objectives	Children will develop the skills of working cooperatively in buzz groups, develop an awareness of the character traits of prominent people, and learn what a biography is.
Interest Building	Place children in buzz groups of three or four and ask them to review the following rating scale. Ask different students to clarify the meaning of each point. Introduce today's lesson and indicate that you will ask each of them to assess their own participation in the small-group work using this rating scale:

	Always	Sometimes	Very rare
1. Focuses on the task	☐	☐	☐
2. Listens to what is said	☐	☐	☐
3. Considers what others say	☐	☐	☐
4. Gives own ideas	☐	☐	☐
5. Takes turns	☐	☐	☐

Lesson Development

Ask the buzz groups to brainstorm as many names of famous people—living or dead—as they can think of in 5 to 10 minutes. Have the recorder from each group list the names. Next, ask the groups to examine their lists and categorize the people on them based on what they did that made them famous (possible categories: musicians, sports figures, politicians, businesspersons, scientists, artists, social activists, television stars). Ask the children to try to think of missing categories and to generate names for them. Have the recorders list their groups' categories on the board. Ask the whole class to eliminate duplicates and then try to think of categories still missing (e.g., painters, religious leaders, dancers, inventors). Ask the children to discuss why the individuals listed on the chalkboard became well known, whereas most of their contemporaries did not. Tell the class that over the next few days, they will study the qualities and character traits of famous people more carefully.

Follow-up

Have a wide selection of biographies of prominent people available for children. (Prominent means well known, but not necessarily for good or ill.) Ask each child to choose one biography to read. Tell them what a biography is. The books are to be read in the next week, and the children are to write in their response journals answers to the following three questions:

1. What, if anything, do you admire about the person?
2. What qualities (character traits, dispositions) did the person have that made him or her come to the attention of others?
3. What did the person do that made him or her famous?

At the completion of the assignment, have children return to their small groups and share their responses. Help each group create a data-retrieval chart with the names of their prominent persons listed down the left side and the three questions across the top. This serves as an organizer plus a guide for their sharing. After each child has shared, ask the groups if any character traits were common to all of the persons about whom they read (there may be none). Have each group choose a representative to give a brief oral report on its findings to the entire class.

Summary

Have the class generate a list of character traits that (1) applied to all; (2) applied to some; (3) applied to a few; and (4) applied to none. Ask the children if prominent persons necessarily have admirable character traits and why it might be that they do or do not. Ask them if famous people are necessarily good people and work to clarify this distinction.

Assessment	1. Have students assess their own participation in the small groups using the rating scale shown in "Interest Building" and then share their assessments with you. (You may want them to do this in writing or in private conferences.)
	2. Following the summary, ask the class to take out their response journals. Each child is to identify his or her favorite prominent person and state the qualities he or she believes make this individual prominent. Collect and read the journals.
	3. Ask the class, "What is a biography?" and listen to as many responses as time allows. Provide feedback and correction as needed.
Materials	Biographies of prominent persons at suitable reading levels for the class, to be secured from the school resource center. Get additional ideas from three websites: the Giraffe Heroes Project, My Hero, and the Smithsonian's "Spotlight Biography."
Integration	*Literature:* Biography is a genre in its own right and plays a crucial role in historical understanding. Because many biography examples are present in this lesson, students can be helped to build the concept of biography—what it is, its role in literature and history, and how it differs from autobiography.

suggested solutions to problems, it is important not to evaluate each one at the time it is offered. If each is discussed, the list will not be very long. *The objective of brainstorming is to get as many ideas to the surface as possible, no matter how outlandish they may seem.* Only *after* the complete list has been generated should time be taken to evaluate each suggestion and select the best ones by consensus. It is usually best for the group to have a designated leader and recorder.

Talking things over in a buzz session can be helpful in getting a broad sampling of opinion and feeling, obtaining a wide and creative variety of suggestions and ideas, and getting children to participate who might be reluctant or fearful in a more structured discussion situation. The teacher needs to establish standards that are clearly understood beforehand. Lesson Plan 17 incorporates buzz groups, individual work, oral reports, and whole-class discussion.

Conclusion

Many of us remember small-group experiences in our K–12 and college years. Unfortunately, these were not always planned in such a way that learning—both social learning and academic learning—would be increased. This chapter has stressed that more goes into planning small-group experiences than placing students in groups and giving them a task. Teachers who orchestrate cooperative groupwork successfully create a positive classroom climate, and they work up to groupwork gradually. They plan work tasks that *require* a group—that require more heads than one. Teachers also *teach* the skills of groupwork rather than wishing students had already formed them. Moreover, they use different small-group frameworks—Jigsaw, committees, panels, buzz groups, and so on— for different purposes. In all, positive interdependence and individual student accountability are the guiding principles. Managing cooperative groupwork requires a good deal of thought and planning, not to mention observation of skilled colleagues and reading about the experiences of others.

Discussion Questions and Suggested Activities

Go to MyEducationLab and select the topic "Geography," then watch the video "Salt Maps" and complete the activity.

1. Look back at the "Reflection" sidebar in the section "Teaching Cooperative Skills." Take a few minutes to share your response to the question with a partner, and then reflect on what *kind* of question it is. Certainly it is a classifying question (see Chapter 9), but which of the four types?

2. Adapt the skills-teaching strategy (the third of the "three great strategies" in Chapter 9) to teach one or more cooperative groupwork skills.

3. Examine the dimensions of the hidden curriculum given in Figure 11–1 and add examples from your own experience that tend to increase the level of care and community in a classroom or decrease the level of hostility.

4. NCSS Standards *Sampler.* Examine the fourth-grade classroom vignette for standard #5 on page 15 of the standards *Sampler* that accompanies this book. Try remodeling this lesson into one using Jigsaw.

Selected References

Cazden, Courtney B. (2001). *Classroom discourse* (2nd ed). Portsmouth, NH: Heinemann.

Cohen, Elizabeth G. (1994). *Designing groupwork* (2nd ed). New York: Teachers College Press.

Cohen, Elizabeth G., Lotan, Rachel A., Abram, Percy L., Scarloss, Beth A., & Schultz, Susan E. (2002). Can groups learn? *Teachers College Record, 104* (6), 1045–1068.

Cohen, Elizabeth G., & Lotan, Rachel A. (1997). *Working for equity in heterogeneous classrooms: Sociological theory in practice.* New York: Teachers College Press.

Johnson, David W., Johnson, Roger T., & Shane, Mary B. (2000). *Cooperative learning methods: A meta-analysis.* Available at www.co-operation.org.

Larson, Bruce E. (2000). Classroom discussion: A method of instruction and a curriculum outcome. *Teaching and Teacher Education, 16* (5), 661-677.

Noddings, Nel. (2006). *Critical lessons: What our schools should teach.* New York: Cambridge University Press.

Pettigrew, Thomas F. (2004). Intergroup contact: Theory, research, and new perspectives. In James A. Banks & Cherry A. McGee Banks (Eds.), *Handbook of research on multicultural education* (2nd ed., pp. 770–781). San Francisco: Jossey-Bass.

MyEducationLab is a collection of online tools for your success in this course, your licensure exams, and your teaching career. Go to www.myeducationlab.com to utilize these extensive resources including videos from real classrooms, Praxis and licensure preparation, a lesson plan builder, and materials to help you begin your teaching career.

The Literacy–Social Studies Connection

CHAPTER TWELVE

Chapter Outline

- Literacy and Content-Area Learning
- Reading Skills Essential to Social Studies Learning
- Using Textbooks as Study Aids
- Locating and Using Reference Materials
- Building Social Studies Vocabulary
- Improving Text Comprehension: Making Sense
- Socratic Seminar: Interpretive Discussion
- Using Children's Trade Books for Multiple Perspectives
- Conclusion

Key Concepts

- Literacy apprenticeship
- Practical, informational, and pleasurable literacy
- Text comprehension
- Interpretive and genuine questions
- Multiple perspectives

MAIN IDEA

The idea that children learn to read in the basic reading program and then read to learn in the social studies program is not quite right. Actually, the two are connected. Children improve their reading ability—expanding and deepening it—as they read to learn social studies material: primary documents, charts and graphs, maps and globes, narratives and informational text. In social studies units, with good coaching, children's reading ability will develop in ways that will rouse their minds and empower them for the rest of their lives.

PICTURE THIS

Ms. McKean was determined that her fourth-graders read lots of social studies material. This was, therefore, the subject area in which she would provide most of her language arts instruction. She didn't want them reading only narrative writing, whether fiction or nonfiction. That was "too limiting," she said. "I am educating future judges and senators, and they have to know how to read more than stories." She taught them to preview and skim as a way of giving them a leg up on complex nonnarrative material. "I want you to read and understand the Constitution, the Declaration of Independence, and Lincoln's Gettysburg Address. I want you to know your way around the atlas, the almanac, and public records. For that, you'll need to learn to take a helicopter ride first— get above the material. This is called 'previewing.'"

Schools can become "sites for true literacy apprenticeships," writes Lauren Resnick,[1] but this requires ample school activities in which students use and develop reading and writing skills as they pursue practical and informational goals, as well as pleasure. Among other things, this means that reading and writing skills must be taught and used in the content areas. This is the main idea of Chapter 12.

This chapter focuses on two additional ideas. First, reading and writing are best thought of as a common enterprise rather than as distinct endeavors. Readers make meaning when they comprehend text in much the same way that writers make meaning when they compose text. Skillful teachers attend to this similarity by paying special attention to the *meaning-making* process itself, whether situated in reading or in writing. Briefly, children construct meanings in relation to what they already know. Children will do this in rigorous and empowering ways or in mediocre ways, depending on the presence of a stimulating environment and skillful coaching and guidance. That's where the teacher and the curriculum come in.

Second, children do not make meaning in a vacuum; children read and write to *accomplish goals*. In social studies, for example, they read and write to investigate the disappearance of the Pony Express, to follow rivers to the sea, to grasp how the Aztecs could possibly have been conquered, and to figure out why there are homeless people and what can be done about it. They read and write, then, to build and express social studies understandings.

LITERACY AND CONTENT-AREA LEARNING

If teachers regard the teaching of reading as something that is done only during the reading instruction block and ignore the reading needs of children during the remainder of the school day, they can expect children to have many frustrating experiences reading social studies material. The feeling that children *learn to read* in the basic reading program and then *read to learn* in the social studies, for example, is not an entirely correct understanding of the relationship. Actually, the two occur simultaneously; children improve their reading ability as they read to learn. Children can extend and improve their reading skills and abilities far beyond the basic reading program as they use reading for a variety of purposes.

This view of literacy education and content learning sees each situated in the other—mutually dependent. It sees the central work of the skillful teacher as creating *apprenticeships* for children in which they are gradually helped to achieve expertise in both. By apprenticeship, I mean a learning situation with at least three characteristics: (1) learners learn as a consequence of being coached into higher levels of capability by adults or more capable peers; (2) practice occurs as learners work to accomplish all or part of a worthwhile task with the guidance and support of the coach or coaches; and (3) the coaching gradually decreases as the learner's capability increases (this is otherwise known as scaffolding).[2]

In the classroom, the head coach is the teacher. Sometimes, the teacher orchestrates situations in which peers who are more capable at a task will support students who are less capable on that task. In the cooperative groupwork strategy called Jigsaw (see Chapter 11), learning is fashioned so that every student serves as a more capable coach to other students and is in the same way helped by other students. This should be familiar to every parent who has had an older child teach a younger one to wash dishes.

Three literacy practices deserve the attention of elementary school teachers, and each requires its own form of apprenticeship. First is the practice of reading or writing texts in order to function in everyday life. This is *practical* literacy: reading in order to complete a task. Examples include reading food labels and bus schedules, following instructions for

TABLE 12–1 Literacy apprenticeships in social studies.		
Perform a Task	**Gain Information**	**Literary Experience**
Reading the ballot	Studying the candidates' positions	Enjoying a biography of the pharaoh Ramses
Reading directions to the polls	Reading the president's speech	Arranging political cartoons about the president in a collage
Reading the procedure at a classroom learning center	Finding Lewis and Clark's route on a map	Reading historical fiction

videotaping a television program or assembling a bookshelf, completing job applications and other forms. Most of this apprenticeship occurs within families with the guidance and modeling of parents and older siblings.

The second literacy practice is reading or writing to get information about the world. This is *informational* literacy. Typical examples are reading newspapers and weekly news magazines, studying campaign literature, reading and writing letters to the editor, taking notes at lectures, consulting an online encyclopedia to find out Katrina's size in relation to other hurricanes, finding Tibet on Google Earth, and reading about Gandhi in a history textbook or on a website. These information searches can be hugely enjoyable, but that is not really their point. For much of this information-driven learning, but certainly not all, we depend on the school curriculum.

The third form of apprenticeship concerns reading for "literary experience." Here the purpose is *pleasure*. The group charged with monitoring the nation's literacy through an assessment called "the nation's report card" describes this literacy as follows: "Readers explore events, characters, themes, settings, plots, actions, and the language of literary works by reading novels, short stories, poems, plays, legends, biographies, myths, and folktales."[3] This is an apprenticeship in literary appreciation. It occurs at home when children are read to by parents and taken to plays; at churches, temples, and mosques when children study scriptures and dramatize events; but also (and for numerous children, mainly) at school when literature is read aloud to children and then dramatized, or when children read engaging stories themselves and then discuss them with other children or use them as springboards for writing original works of literature. Table 12–1 shows these three practices in relation to one another.

READING SKILLS ESSENTIAL TO SOCIAL STUDIES LEARNING

Most elementary schools provide time during the school day when a major effort is made to teach basic reading skills. In this developmental reading program, children acquire a basic reading vocabulary and learn to use various word-recognition techniques along with other skills and abilities that characterize the flexible, independent reader. They learn to identify words, create hypotheses about the meaning of a selection, and revise their hypotheses as they read, write, and reread. But even a strong basic reading program will not meet all the reading needs of children because each area of the school curriculum requires reading tasks that are somewhat unique to that special area.

The special reading skills needed to make sense of social studies material may be identified by examining the sorts of reading tasks children will confront in a genuine social studies program. The most important point to be made is that this material is neither all fiction nor all narrative. Much of it is expository, where a story is not being told but, instead, information and explanation are being given. It may be a cause–effect explanation (history), or a thick description of cultural life in east Asia (anthropology) or of human–environment interaction on the Horn of Africa (geography). In many primary documents, we find neither narrative nor exposition. It may be a letter home from a Civil War soldier on the eve of the battle at Gettysburg or a diary entry of a midwife in the American colonies. It may be a speech, a map, a chart, or a graph. An examination of this material will suggest reading skills such as those given in Figure 12–1.

Some of the skills on this list may never be used if children are reading only fiction narratives. Skimming is a good example. If you skim a fiction story, you may find out what happens, which would spoil the story. Nobody wants that! But skimming a nonfiction essay or chapter in a biography or textbook is an extremely intelligent thing to do—not so that you can avoid reading it, but so that you can comprehend it better once you do. (Please take a minute to skim ahead in this chapter now. Find the sections on previewing and skimming.)

The teacher's responsibility regarding reading instruction in the social studies is twofold. First, those special reading skills unique to social studies must be taught in relation to the subject matter under study. These include the skills listed in Figure 12–1. The teacher's second responsibility is to help children learn how to use reading as a tool to gain needed information. Of course, reading should not be the only means through which children encounter new social studies information. Throughout this text, the idea is stressed repeatedly

---

FIGURE 12–1   Social studies reading skills.

In social studies, the capable reader:
- Reads flexibly
- Uses chapter and section headings as aids to reading
- Uses context clues to suggest meanings
- Talks with classmates about possible meanings
- Adjusts reading speed to purpose
- Hypothesizes cause–effect relationships
- Uses reference material freely to understand vocabulary
- Investigates the author of primary documents (who, when, why, where)
- Seeks data in maps, charts, pictures, and illustrations, and interprets data and symbols found there
- Uses various parts of a book (index, table of contents, introduction, etc.) as aids to reading
- Previews the selection to become familiar with text structure and to hypothesize general meaning
- Skims to locate facts and hypothesize main ideas
- Compares one account with another
- Recognizes and seeks topic sentences
- Uses library and Internet skills to find needed material
- Uses the newspaper directory to locate articles, letters, arts, comics, and editorials

that a multimedia approach (what Howard Gardner calls multiple "entry points"[4]) is vital to inspired teaching of social studies. But in the broad spectrum of media and activities potentially available to children today, reading remains undoubtedly the most important and, in the long run, the most critical to their success in learning social studies.

USING TEXTBOOKS AS STUDY AIDS

In contrast to reading a storybook simply for enjoyment, much of the reading in social studies involves a search for information in sources that bear no resemblance to storybooks. Social studies textbooks are written to be used as information sourcebooks and are not intended to become the social studies curriculum. They can be used in a variety of ways, and individual children may make different uses of the same book. Similarly, different teachers may choose to make different uses of the same book, depending on their skill, experience, and method of teaching. One may mine it for primary documents, another may use it all as the basis for reading and writing instruction, and another may rely on its maps and other visuals. We encourage teachers to make differential use of textbooks rather than to cover the content uniformly and require children to master every bit of it.

Recall from our discussion of textbooks in the "Resources" chapter of this book that social studies textbooks are textbook *programs*. They contain an *array* of resources that teachers otherwise would have to gather on their own. There are primary documents, artwork, explanations of all sorts, narrative histories, maps, map-skills lessons, vocabulary lessons, thinking-skills lessons, and questions and activities. Ancillaries are common as well: CDs, videotapes and DVDs, giant maps that can be spread out on the classroom floor, smaller maps with washable surfaces that are placed on each student's desk, and anthologies of speeches, plays, and short stories. The *Teacher's Edition* also contains a wealth of resources: lesson and unit plans, overviews and summaries, additional background information on the subject of the lesson, website suggestions for online activities, links to the literature curriculum and other curriculum-integration ideas, student projects, guest speaker and field trip suggestions, role-playing suggestions, discussion topics, classroom museum ideas, and both formal and informal student assessments.

Social studies print materials almost always present problems of reading difficulty. This is true of textbooks, too, even though they are written at a level that is suitable for the average reader. The reason for this inherent difficulty is that these books are designed to deal with substantive content, and this means that the terms and concepts relating to that subject matter must be used in explaining the ideas presented or explained. For example, a teacher and students are immersed in a unit on Canada (or any other place). A *place* cannot be meaningfully presented without using core geographical terms such as *landform, climate, culture, region, longitude,* and *latitude.* If such terms are eliminated from a reading selection to simplify the reading task, it is no longer a reading about the geography of Canada! The complexity and frequency of concepts often make reading social studies textbooks difficult, and there is no way to overcome this problem entirely. (The same is true in science textbooks.) The purpose of a good social studies text is to provide information, explanations, charts, documents, and challenging ideas rather than to be a simple storybook.

In other words, it is important *not* to try to overcome the inherent difficulty of reading content-oriented textbooks by changing the content. As we saw in Chapter 2, this happens again and again to children who are already at risk of school failure, and it causes some

Children read and write to accomplish goals. *(Anne Vega/Merrill)*

What are the advantages and disadvantages of changing the content to make reading less difficult for some or all students?

Latino and African American children and children whose home language is not English to fall behind their same-age peers. It is a lowering of expectations. The answer to the problem is not changing from "Canada," or "Our Nation's Government," or "Human–Environment Interaction," or whatever the topic, to "What I Did Over Summer Vacation," "Sports Stars," "Circuses," "Kite Flying," or some other content that is easier to read about because the terms and content are already familiar to children. *Doing so would be miseducative and disabling.* The answer, instead, is to apprentice children into social studies reading—make it a goal of the classroom community and help them to be successful.

Good news: The design of a social studies textbook provides many aids to make the job of reading easier. The teacher cannot assume, however, that children will use such aids unless they are taught to do so. The skills associated with the use of study aids must be taught, reviewed, and retaught each year throughout the elementary school grades. Here are the most basic teaching suggestions, each of which is discussed in turn:

1. Using the parts of a book
2. Using the organization of the book
3. Using pictures to aid comprehension

Using the Parts of a Book

The parts of a book should be taught as aids to getting information. Sara, for example, was studying famous women in American history. She had heard that a native woman assisted Lewis and Clark, and she wanted to know more. How would she find more information?

She had learned that the table of contents was usually very general, so she turned instead to the index. She couldn't look under the woman's name, though, since she didn't know it; so she looked under Lewis and Clark and found the following:

Legislative branch, 345, 356–357

Leirich, Julie, 253, 571

Lewis, Meriwether, 371–372

Lexington, Massachusetts, 300

Liberator, The, 420

She turned to page 371 and noted a boldfaced section heading near the bottom of the page that read, "The Lewis and Clark Expedition." She skimmed the sentences that followed it. Nothing. She turned the page, skimming quickly, and found it. In the second column on page 372 she read:

The expedition spent the winter with the Mandan Indians beside the great bend of the Missouri River. There Lewis and Clark hired a French-Canadian fur trapper as their guide. They also invited the trapper's wife, Sacagawea, a Shoshone, and her newborn son to accompany them. Lewis and Clark believed that if they traveled with this woman and her baby, the Indians whom they met would understand that the explorers were a peaceful group.

Thus, in a matter of moments, Sara was able to find precisely the information she sought. Contrast this with the boy sitting next to her, who needed the same information but, lacking an efficient way of finding it, went through the book page by page looking for a picture or a clue that would reveal the name of that famous Shoshone woman. Without an index lesson from the teacher or Sara, he might never have found what he was looking for.

Rather than teaching parts of a book in a didactic way, the teacher should use exercises that require children to apply these skills. Often such exercises are included in the book itself. Here is one example:

LEARNING THE PARTS OF A BOOK

Directions: In the right column are listed the parts of your book. In the left column are listed some things you might want to find out. For each item in the left column, tell what part of the book you would turn to first to get the information.

You Want to Know:	Parts of Your Book:
the number of chapters in the book	title page
the meaning of *treaty*	copyright page
how to say the word *Iroquois*	preface
when the book was published	table of contents
the population of various states	list of maps
the date Geronimo was captured	list of illustrations
what a sod house looks like	glossary
the route of Marco Polo	atlas
anything about Canada	index

Variations of this exercise are possible. For example, the right column can be omitted, and students can be asked to find and supply the information. Or the child can be asked to indicate the specific page on which the information appears.

Naturally, the complexity of activities of this type should be appropriate to the age and maturity of the learners. Even in the first grade, children learn that books have titles and authors and that pages are numbered. They also learn that sections of their chapter books have titles. In the second and third grades, they can begin to use the table of contents to find a particular story. In the third and fourth grades, they can learn to use the index.

Using the Organization of the Book

Units, chapters, section heads, and subheads; study aids at the end of sections, chapters, and units; maps and charts; picture captions; introductory and concluding questions—all of these make sense to the mature reader who uses them as valuable aids to comprehending a nonfiction book. But left unguided, a child is not likely to make good use of them. In fact, a child is likely to lose sight of the forest for all the trees. Knowledge of how a text is organized is a significant factor in children's being able to negotiate the text and comprehend and recall what they have read.

Please look back at Figure 10–3 in Chapter 10. It shows a very typical "Using Your Textbook" feature that can be found in the front of most student textbooks. Students whose teachers help them master this structural information about the book—how it is put together, its parts and features—have the advantage of viewing the "forest" from above.

Using Pictures to Aid Comprehension

The most widely used of all visual aids are paintings, photographs, cartoons, and illustrations. Publishers invest huge sums of money to provide them in social studies textbooks. These are used to add visual imagery to the printed words, to add realism, to clarify ideas, to recall the real object, and, in short, to give meaning to learning. It is well known that words cannot convey meanings as vividly or quickly as pictures.

Paintings, photos, and illustrations elaborate concepts presented in the narrative but usually do not repeat exactly what is said in the text. Neither do picture captions simply tell what would be obvious to the reader only by looking at the picture. Thus, captions should call attention to some element or relationship in the picture or illustration that might be missed by the casual viewer. Often this is done by using a question or series of questions. In this way a photo or illustration can provide the reader with a wealth of information. In teaching children how to use pictures and illustrations, teachers will find questions such as these appropriate:

- What is being shown in the picture?
- What kind of picture is it? A photo? Painting? Illustration?
- When was this picture made?
- Does the picture illustrate something we discussed in class?
- What causes or effects can be detected in the picture?
- What does the picture show that illustrates the roles of men, women, and children in that society?

- What can you say about the geography of the area shown by the picture?
- What conversation might be going on between the persons in the picture?

LOCATING AND USING REFERENCE MATERIALS

Children should use a wide variety of reference material in studying social studies topics. The value of such references depends not only on their availability, but also on the ability of the children to make use of them. The teacher's responsibility in this respect is, therefore, twofold: teaching children (1) which references to use for various purposes and (2) how to use the reference efficiently once it is found. These are continuing responsibilities of the social studies program and cannot be completely taught in any one grade or any one year. A beginning will be made in the primary grades, but the child will continue to extend and refine the ability to use references throughout high school and college and in later life. Instruction usually begins as soon as the child develops a degree of independence in reading. The reference materials used in the social studies may be grouped as shown in Figure 12–2.

FIGURE 12–2 Types of social studies reference materials.

Books
Textbooks
Picture books
Biographies
Historical fiction trade books

Primary Documents
Letters
Diaries
Journals
Recordings
Speeches
Photos
Posters
Newspapers
Police records
Obituaries
Editorials
Essays

**Special References
(paper and electronic)**
Encyclopedias
Movie reviews
Maps and globes
Online museums (the Smithsonian)
   and libraries (the Library of Congress)

Atlases
Dictionaries
World Almanac
Charts and graphs
Constitution of the United States
Yearbooks
Legislative manuals
Internet
C-SPAN
CNN

Reference Aids (paper and electronic)
Library catalog
The Reader's Guide
Bibliographies

Miscellaneous Materials
Advertisements
Magazines and periodicals
Weather reports
Manufacturers' guarantees
   and warranties
Money, checks, receipts
Music reviews
Book reviews
Government documents

Much of the instruction given on the use of references will have to be specific to the particular resource used. For example, one uses the Internet and the *World Almanac* differently than one uses an atlas or an encyclopedia. Moreover, the references may be used at varying levels of sophistication. The library may be used by primary-grade children under teacher guidance to check out books and CDs, to look at magazines, or to have stories read to them, whereas upper-grade children should be able to use the library independently, making use of the online catalog and locating references themselves. The use of the various references should be taught as the need for them arises in the social studies.

The skills students need for using references can be practiced and learned on an individual basis or by children in pairs using task cards, as illustrated in Figure 12–3.

BUILDING SOCIAL STUDIES VOCABULARY

The vocabulary density of social studies reading material is one of the major causes of the difficulties associated with text comprehension in social studies. Even with the careful attention that authors might give to word difficulties and text structure, social studies vocabulary is challenging. Although a degree of simplification is possible, some specialized vocabulary cannot be avoided. The same situation exists in other areas of the curriculum; the child must learn the language associated with mathematics, science, art, music—all of which have their own peculiar words, terms, or phrases. Figure 12–4 shows a sample of words that are peculiar to social studies.

The teacher should anticipate likely word difficulties *before* asking children to read a social studies selection. Two types of word problems must be expected. One is the inability to recognize the word in print; the other is not knowing the meaning of the word once it is recognized.

Vocabulary development should be conducted in relatively short, fun spurts. Having children look up a long list of terms in the dictionary prior to reading a selection is not productive. No expert reader does this. A better strategy is to write the key terms from a selection on the chalkboard, or write them on cards that are posted on the wall or bulletin board, and discuss their spelling and meaning. These should be the few terms that in the teacher's judgment are critical to student comprehension of the selection. Better still, the sentence in the text in which the word or term appears can be selected for study.

It is essential for the teacher to model curiosity about new words. Teachers should encourage children to use the specialized social studies vocabulary in their discussions and writing. They should also from time to time encourage children to create new words or nicknames for old ideas. During a concept-formation lesson (Chapter 9) on *culture*, the children may be encouraged to think of a term other than culture that might more powerfully convey the meaning of the concept—*lifeway*, for example. Creating new words puts children at the inventing end of language, rather than always being at the receiving end, which can be an enlightening change of vantage point.

Moreover, the teacher may want to involve students in word games. Devising riddles, providing synonyms or antonyms, making or completing crossword puzzles, or participating in spelling bees can increase students' interest in wordplay. Bulletin-board displays and other classroom exhibits can feature new words encountered in social studies.

FIGURE 12-3 An example of teacher-prepared task cards.

SIDE ONE

Find Out for Yourself

(If you cannot do any one of these, look for a clue on SIDE TWO of this card.)

1. Find the article on "Safety" in the *World Book*.
2. Into how many sections is the article divided? _____
3. Skim through the article to find these two facts:
   a. Where do most accidents happen? _____
   b. What do the letters *UL* on electrical wiring and appliances stand for?
      _____

4. Suppose you heard that someone had been killed in an accident in his or her home but you did not know what kind of an accident it was. You would be right most of the time if you guessed that the accident was a
   _____ or _____ or _____

5. Suppose you questioned the accuracy of this article. What is there about the article that might renew your confidence in its authority?
   _____

SIDE TWO

CLUES

1. Select volume *S–Sn*. Look for the article according to the alphabet.
2. See the "Outline" at the end of the article.
3. a. Look under the section "Safety/Home."
   b. Look under "Safety with Electricity."
4. What does the article say about the major causes of accidental deaths in the home?
   _____
   _____
   _____

5. What group critically reviewed the article?
   _____
   _____
   _____
   _____
   _____

FIGURE 12–4 Terms needing special attention in social studies.

Technical terms—Words and expressions peculiar to history and the social sciences and usually not encountered when reading selections from other fields of knowledge. *Examples: veto, meridian, frontier, latitude, longitude, legislature, polls, franchise, temperate, plateau, projection, landform, balance of power, capitalism, democracy, nationalism, civilization, century, ancient, decade, pueblo, fjord.*

Figurative terms—Expressions that are metaphorical; having a different connotation from the literal meaning usually associated with the word. *Examples: political platform, cold war, closed shop, Iron Curtain, pork barrel, open door, hat in the ring, domino theory, Sun belt, Bible belt.*

Words with multiple meanings—Words that have identical spelling but whose meaning is derived from context. *Examples: cabinet, belt, bill, chamber, mouth, bank, revolution, fork, court, assembly, range.*

Terms peculiar to a locality—Expressions peculiar to a specific part of the country that are not commonly used elsewhere. *Examples: truckfarm, meeting, borough, gandy, draw, right, prairie, section, run, butte, arroyo, geoduck, goobers, grits, potlatch, bayou, haul cane road.*

Words easily confused with other words—Words that are closely similar in general configuration. *Examples: continent for country, alien for allies, principal for principle, longitude for latitude, executive for execution, conversation for conservation.*

Acronyms—Words that are abbreviated expressions. *Examples: NATO, NASA, OPEC, NAFTA, NOW, UNICEF, AIDS, MADD.*

Quantitative terms—Words and terms signifying amounts of time, space, or objects. *Examples: shortly after, century, fortnight, several years later, score, millennia.*

Teaching how known words can be used to construct new words can help students recognize new words and understand their meanings. Among the simplest variations are compound words or the addition of prefixes or suffixes. Some examples are these: construct, construct*ed*, construct*ing*, construc*tion*; consume, consume*r*, consume*d*; loyal, *dis*loyal, loyal*ist*; dictate, dictat*or*, dictator*ship*, republic, republic*an*, democracy, democr*at*.

IMPROVING TEXT COMPREHENSION: MAKING SENSE

Reading with comprehension means that readers are able to make sense of what they are reading and come away from the selection with mental pictures of essential facts and ideas. Through discussion with the teacher and classmates, writing, dramatization, and returning to the selection perhaps numerous times, children can check the sense they made with the sense made by others, perhaps revise their interpretation, and, in this trial-and-error way, come to some negotiated understanding about what the author meant to say.

It is obvious that the child who brings the most to a reading situation will receive the most in return. Researchers call this the Matthew effect (see Chapter 1). What the child brings that will enhance social studies reading the most are intellectual aptitude, a storehouse of experience and ideas (prior knowledge), knowledge about reading, and motivation. A teacher cannot do much to increase children's intellectual aptitude, but a great deal can be done about the other four elements. Teachers can capitalize on the knowledge and cultural experience children bring to the reading situation, they can build children's knowledge of important components of the reading process itself, and they can establish clear purposes for reading tasks. To help children want to comprehend, teachers can make connections to students' interests and goals, and they can make sure that the reading tasks they give students to accomplish are meaningful, that is, that they are not mere busywork, nor are they the sort of thing that has no larger purpose. (Drill-and-practice activities are often off the mark on both counts.) Rather, tasks should be related to a worthy challenge. Children are not just practicing writing sentences, for example, but they are writing sentences in the biographies they are producing about people who work to protect the environment from polluters. In these ways, children can be helped to perform nearer to their full potential.

Perhaps the most important general rule of thumb used by good readers is one that seems mundane: read flexibly. This means that readers vary their speed and the skills they use depending on the selection they are reading. Expert readers do this routinely; poor readers do it rarely; mediocre readers do it unevenly. Apprenticing children into the routine practice of flexible reading should be a daily goal in social studies teaching and learning.

Because reading comprehension varies according to the particular topic and selection, *previewing* may be the most important single comprehension strategy other than rereading. It means, essentially, looking before you leap. Good readers use previewing because it tells them what lies ahead, providing a general picture of the terrain. Looking ahead indicates whether familiar or strange material is at hand and, consequently, which additional strategies, such as skimming, may be required. Previewing in this way builds prior knowledge on the spot.

A simple narrative account of a girl who must survive on her own during the American Revolution, for example, may be relatively easy to understand for many children. They can read accounts of this type without much difficulty because they rely on motivating story lines, familiar story structures (e.g., problem–solution), and well-known words. On the other hand, the child may encounter in the textbook a selection called "Democracy, Not Monarchy." This is a complex idea that may be difficult for many young children. Not only is its vocabulary specialized (separation of powers, civil rights, limited government, and so on), but its place in children's experience will be marginal. Yet it is easily one of the most important topics in the social studies curriculum.

What's to be done? Several strategies have been shown to be effective in improving reading comprehension. Let's look at four that are especially powerful:

1. Activate prior knowledge.
2. Preview.
3. Skim for ideas and related details.
4. Summarize.

Activate Prior Knowledge

Just as the rich get richer, the knowledgeable get more knowledgeable. What we know before coming to a learning task influences, often greatly, the kind and amount of learning we will accomplish once we get there. Learners who have more background knowledge about the topic of the text they are about to read, all things being equal, will better comprehend that chapter than learners who know little or nothing about it. Minimally, they will comprehend it differently, making better sense of it than their less knowledgeable counterparts. Over the long term, therefore, schools should do everything possible to contribute to the prior knowledge of students. Extensive use of field trips to construction sites and factories, study trips to museums, exposure to films of historical events and faraway places, assemblies, plays and pageants, projects, pictures, guest speakers, displays, artifacts—all will assist the child in comprehending the ideas encountered in reading.

But there is a problem. When the next learning task is here, staring them in the face, learners will not necessarily use the prior knowledge they have. Ask any teacher! The knowledge they have built up over the years, even in last week's lesson, may lie dormant and untapped in today's lesson. How can a teacher "activate" this prior knowledge so that students can use it to make sense of the reading selection? A popular strategy is helping children make a visually vivid image called a *semantic map* or *web*.

Semantic mapping provides a graphic representation of a key concept that the teacher (or student) has chosen from the reading selection. Consider a teacher who has chosen "Exploring North America" as the central theme for a fourth-grade social studies–language

This class creates a *semantic map* to activate prior knowledge about immigrants.
(Anne Vega/Merrill)

arts curriculum. Developing in-depth knowledge of each region of the United States is the content focus, and the Lewis and Clark expedition has been selected as the first unit. Before having students read a selection from the textbook on Lewis and Clark, the teacher decides to activate the whole array of ideas and information students associate with the concept *exploration.* The procedure follows.[5]

1. The teacher writes the term *exploration* on the chalkboard and asks students to jot down individually any words they can think of related to this theme. They may think of words such as *Columbus, Marco Polo, past, future, time machine, explorers, ships, astronauts, underwater exploration,* and so on.
2. Next, the teacher identifies or elicits from students major category labels related to the theme, prompting students to think of categories they may overlook. These are arrayed graphically around the concept term, which serves as a hub (see Figure 12–5).
3. Now the teacher asks students to generate additional ideas under each category. The teacher can also suggest items and ask students to decide under which category label they belong. Figure 12–6 shows two sample categorization exercises.

Preview

Good readers of informational text have a general idea of what the material is about before starting to read it. How do they get it? By previewing. Comprehension is significantly increased because previewing sheds some light on the subject; consequently, the reader does not have to proceed totally in the dark. It is a method for acquiring prior knowledge on the spot.

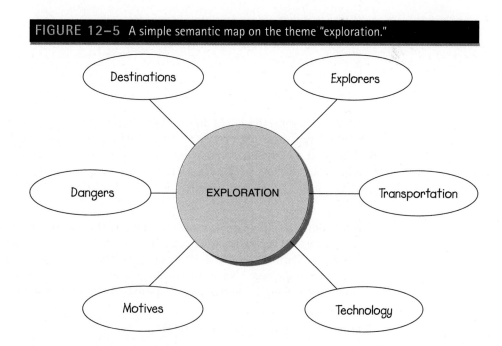

FIGURE 12–5 A simple semantic map on the theme "exploration."

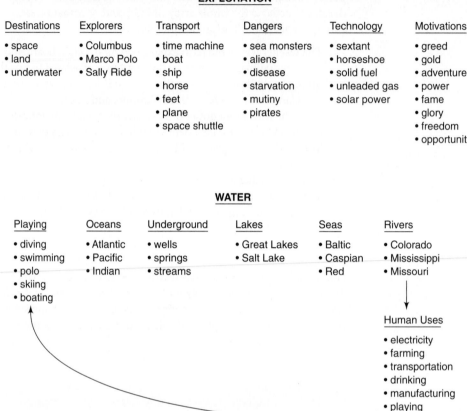

FIGURE 12–6   Expanded semantic maps on the themes "exploration" and "water."

EXPLORATION

Destinations	Explorers	Transport	Dangers	Technology	Motivations
• space	• Columbus	• time machine	• sea monsters	• sextant	• greed
• land	• Marco Polo	• boat	• aliens	• horseshoe	• gold
• underwater	• Sally Ride	• ship	• disease	• solid fuel	• adventure
		• horse	• starvation	• unleaded gas	• power
		• feet	• mutiny	• solar power	• fame
		• plane	• pirates		• glory
		• space shuttle			• freedom
					• opportunity

WATER

Playing	Oceans	Underground	Lakes	Seas	Rivers
• diving	• Atlantic	• wells	• Great Lakes	• Baltic	• Colorado
• swimming	• Pacific	• springs	• Salt Lake	• Caspian	• Mississippi
• polo	• Indian	• streams		• Red	• Missouri
• skiing					
• boating					

Human Uses

• electricity
• farming
• transportation
• drinking
• manufacturing
• playing

Previewing generally will be directed by the teacher, who typically introduces this strategy to children and helps them learn it. But children should develop the habit of previewing material themselves; if instruction goes as planned, the teacher's coaching should gradually diminish as students begin to assume responsibility for previewing. Let us say that a class is about to read a portion of a new chapter entitled "The World of Carmelita and José."

Teacher: Boys and girls, for the next few days we will be reading from our social studies books. I would like to introduce you to two children we will visit in this unit whose names are Carmelita and José. Please open your books to page 86. (The children take time to find the page.) Notice that the large print says, "The World of Carmelita and José." Just looking at this page, what do you think this unit is about?

Frieda: Mexico.

Teacher: Why did you say Mexico, Frieda?

Frieda: Because Carmelita and José are Mexican names. Besides, it shows their pictures, and they are dressed in Mexican clothes. We learned that when we studied the community in Texas. . . .

David: That doesn't mean they are from Mexico. They could be from New Mexico, even Iowa or Vermont, and have names like that.

Teacher: Those are both good ideas. Perhaps if we page through this unit, we can discover the country it talks about. Turn to the map on page 88. . . .

It is established that the unit is, indeed, about Mexico, and the teacher continues:

Teacher: As you look at these pages, what do you suppose you will be reading about in the world of Carmelita and José?

Eric: Well, it looks like . . . uh . . . it tells like . . . what they do every day . . . in school . . . at home.

Lisa: It shows how they do many of the same things we do.

Teacher: What do you mean?

Lisa: Well, we have homes and families, we go to school, we go shopping, and things like that, and they do, too.

The discussion concludes after the teacher is satisfied that the children are oriented to the material to be read. Previews should accomplish the following:

1. Help the reader get the general idea of the selection
2. Help the reader understand how the material is organized
3. Help the reader understand how pictures relate to the subject matter to be read

Skim for Ideas and Related Details

Once children have previewed the selection they intend to read, it is a good idea to skim it for ideas and related details. The teacher begins:

Teacher: Now that you have some general ideas about what you will be reading, let's take some time to become still more familiar with it. We will be using a strategy good readers use called *skimming*. What do you think skimming means?

Mei: It means taking something off the top, like skimming off the bugs at the swimming pool. I see them do it because we go early.

Eddy: Yeah, and it means going really fast.

The teacher helps the children define skimming and then directs them through the following steps:

1. Students are given 30 seconds to thumb through the selection, noticing as best they can what is on every page.
2. The teacher asks what they noticed and takes responses.
3. The teacher directs students to read the questions under the last heading, "Review." Students are asked if, based on those questions, they want to revise what they earlier said the selection was about. The teacher elicits revisions. For example, a student

responds: "Well, it must not be only about Carmelita and José. I mean, it's also about the country because the second question asks about the climate."

4. The teacher directs students' attention to the other section headings and asks students to skim again to find the number of sections and the topic of each.

5. Next, students are directed to quickly read the first few sentences under each section head. After just one minute or so, the teacher asks them what they found.

Teaching students to preview and skim nonfiction material, whether a primary document or a textbook chapter, should improve their comprehension. Lesson Plan 18 approaches this goal in a somewhat different way, employing a powerful analogy.

Summarize

As indicated in Chapter 8, "Planning Units, Lessons, and Activities," summarizing what has been read is both powerful and difficult. The skill of summarizing takes a lifetime to learn because it depends intimately on prior knowledge and judgment. "While good summarizers are invariably older, poor summarizers may be found at any age."[6] The key skill in summarizing is deciding what is important in a text. Summarizing requires readers to sift through the material to determine what will be included and what will be excluded. The writer must also decide how to reword and whether to reorganize the information. This is challenging work.

What to do? Teachers who are serious about summarizing work at it slowly and continually. One way they do this is to build summarization practice into nearly every lesson as part of the closing phase: "Now, let's summarize what we learned today. What information that you gathered today might be most important to our objective?" In the case of the Constitution: "Who will summarize for us how the Constitution is organized?" In the case of Canada: "What information have you found that best helps you predict whether or not Canada will remain unified?" About the American Revolution: "Who can summarize the reasons the colonists decided to declare their independence from England?"

A second, more formal, way to teach summarizing is to follow the two guidelines below, which are derived from the research on teaching summarization.

- *Choose a short text excerpt.* Even grown-ups will have difficulty summarizing the entire Constitution. Summarization practice should therefore be geared to short excerpts. Students might try summarizing just the Preamble. It is important that they hear one another's attempts at summarization (e.g., "It gives six reasons why these people felt they needed a constitution"). A good follow-up question is, "What do the rest of you think? Does that capture what is important in the Preamble?" After this work, students can try summarizing the seven articles.

Teacher: Gina, what do you think this section is about?
Gina: I think it tells how our country is organized.
Teacher: Thanks, Gina. Let's work with that. What do you others think?
Lorraine: I'd say government, not country.
Brad: Doesn't our summary need to include something about the branches?
Teacher: Let's try those revisions.

PREVIEWING AND SKIMMING THE U.S. CONSTITUTION (OR OTHER NONFICTION TEXT)

Grade	4 or 5
Time	One class period
NCSS Standards	2 (time, continuity, and change), 6 (power, authority, and governance), and 10 (civic ideals and practices)
Objectives	Students will become familiar with the structure and, very generally, the contents of the U.S. Constitution. They will learn how to preview and skim a primary document (or other informational text) to build background knowledge before reading.
Interest Building	Ask students to imagine they are about to go on a cross-country hike together to explore a forest that none of them has even seen before. Everyone packs a day pack for the trip with the usual supplies: lunch, poncho, emergency supplies. A bus picks them up at school and takes them on a two-hour trip across the plain to the forest. It stops at the edge of the forest, where helicopters are waiting. Groups of students climb into them and are flown high above the forest. From this perspective, they can see the land below them. The forest appears to be ring-shaped, and in the middle are two lakes and marshland. The helicopters return our explorers to the ground, where the children see motor scooters awaiting them. Their teacher instructs them to use the scooters to "get a feel for this territory. See it all but don't linger in any one place. Keep moving. The purpose is to decide where you want to hike. Set your watches. Return in no more than 30 minutes." Two by two, the kids jump on the scooters and off they go. Thirty minutes later they return bursting with information about the two lakes, the marsh (which turned out to be not so marshy after all), the forest pines, a few deer sightings, and a ton of rabbits and mockingbirds. After this, they set out on foot, in pairs, with instructions to return in two hours. Some head straight for the northernmost lake for a swim, others for the pine forest, and others for the not-so-marshy marsh for a game of soccer. When they return, they gather in a circle and excitedly share their experiences.
Lesson Development	1. *Explain the analogy.* Exploring a complicated reading selection is like the imaginary adventure they just had: They don't know where to go until they have familiarized themselves with the territory. Knowing the territory gives hikers and readers a huge advantage. Once familiar with the lay of the land, they can get on their scooters and quickly visit the places they saw from the air, getting a close-up view but not so close that they stop to linger. Their purpose then is to move quickly through the whole territory so they will know where to linger later. Reading something complicated has the same phases: before, during, and after. The "before" has two parts: the helicopter view from above, called *previewing,* and the quick scooter trip on the ground, called *skimming.* What we learn from quickly previewing and skimming lets us know where we are during reading. These activities keep us from getting lost. Later, after reading, as after hiking, we share to find out what experiences each of us had.
	2. *Tell students about the U.S. Constitution.* Explain the document's importance to all of us as the rule book for our society. Read aloud and discuss an excerpt from Jean Fritz's: *Shh! We're Writing the Constitution* (Putnam, 1987).
	3. *Previewing.* Demonstrate how to flip back and forth through the pages, also known as thumbing through the pages. (This is important for both previewing and skimming, and it is something we almost never do when reading a story.) Guide the students through a preview of the Constitution. For example; "Let's get into the helicopter. You'll have to flip the pages back and forth, because I'll give you just two minutes and I don't want you lingering anywhere. Find out how long it is, how many parts it has, the names of those parts, and whether there are pictures of any sort." Call time in two minutes and ask students to share what they found. (There are three parts: a preamble, 7 articles, and 27 amendments, in that order.)

4. *Skimming.* Now guide the students through skimming the Constitution. For example, "Now hop on your scooters to get a close-up view of each of these three main parts. There'll be lots of new words, but just speed on past them. In 10 minutes, I'll ask you to describe very generally what each part seems to be about. Remember to keep moving; don't get stuck." Call time in 10 minutes and ask students what each part seems to be about. Help students treat every response as a hypothesis that can be checked in the next phase.

5. *Reading.* "Now let's go through the Constitution on foot." Ask students to choose which of the three parts they want to find out more about. Have the three groups cluster in different corners of the classroom to read silently, then talk with one another about the contents of that part. "Change your purpose from getting to know the overall territory to really getting to know one area—the area you chose."

6. *Sharing.* Ask members of each group to share with the whole class what their part is about. Keep track on the chalkboard of the new vocabulary. Encourage different interpretations of the same part (e.g., "Who thought this part was about something different?")

Summary and Assessment   Review the analogy. Then, ask for a definition of *previewing* and *skimming*. Provide correction as needed. Ask students to jot down a summary of the three parts of the Constitution and then ask several to read theirs aloud. Use what you find out as you plan the follow-up study of the Constitution.

Materials

1. A copy of the U.S. Constitution for each student (such as the one provided in Chapter 3 of this text and typically included in fifth-grade social studies texts).

2. Artwork: a painting of the signing of the Constitution by Howard Chandler Christy (search online).

3. *Shh! We're Writing the Constitution* by Jean Fritz (1987).

Integration   *Reading:* This lesson teaches two powerful reading skills, previewing and skimming, needed to comprehend social studies material.

Literature: Following this lesson, use the textbook and Jean Fritz's book to help students learn the story of the U.S. Constitution: what it is; why it is important; who wrote it; and where, when, and why its predecessor (the Articles of Confederation) failed. In many cities, the American Bar Association will provide an attorney to come to your class as a guest speaker on law and the Constitution.

- *Choose an easy kind of text.* The U.S. Constitution is not an easy kind of text, so it is a very difficult place to begin. It is better to begin summarization work with narrative writing that students can readily understand. Jean Fritz's story about the Constitution used in Lesson Plan 18 will serve well. But don't leave your students on this lower rung of the ladder; be sure to scaffold them up to more difficult kinds of text.

Remember that summarizing is a set of skills and that the first step in any skills teaching is modeling (Chapter 9). This means that the teacher needs to demonstrate summarizing for the children often. The most common way to do this is to think aloud as you summarize a short excerpt of text. For example:

Teacher: When I look at the third part of the Constitution, where all those things called amendments are, I think to myself, "Self, these are really 27 of the same kind of thing, and that thing is called an amendment." Then I remember from our discussion that amendment means change. So, my summary might be this: "The third part of the Constitution is a long list of the changes that have been made to the Constitution."

SOCRATIC SEMINAR: INTERPRETIVE DISCUSSION

A fifth strategy for improving text comprehension deserves a section of its own. Called Socratic Seminar, Paideia Seminar,[7] or simply seminar, this is a method for bringing children together to *interpret* texts through *discussion*—to talk with one another about the ideas, issues, and values in them. Although comprehension-boosting strategies such as activating prior knowledge, previewing, skimming, and summarizing are important and necessary, they certainly are not sufficient. They are not reasons to read. They don't motivate a true literacy apprenticeship. Children and adults alike read for purposes beyond these—to function in daily life ("Am I on Bailey or Ash Street?"); to get information ("Did the first Americans really come here via the land bridge at the Bering Strait?"); and to entertain themselves ("I can't wait to see what happens next."). Earlier, we called these literacies *practical, informational,* and *pleasurable.* Socratic Seminars attempt to rouse children's minds toward the latter two, toward the life of the mind—grappling with ideas, issues, and values that speak to who we are, to who we want to be, to our imaginations, and to the problems of living together.

The life of the mind? Indeed. One of the most thoughtful and even-handed contributors to the literacy debates is Richard Allington. He notes that if we can see our way through the standards-and-assessment frenzy of recent years, we will, if we are lucky, be left with a more thoughtful approach to literacy.

> The new national and state standards for proficient reading target a more thoughtful literacy than has traditionally been expected of school reading programs. What I mean is that the latest assessments of reading proficiency typically include extended response items that often require (1) that students actually think about what they have just read and (2) that they explain or describe this thinking. Being asked to think about the text you've just read is different from being asked to recall the text you've just read. And quite different from being asked to simply copy information from the text into a blank on a worksheet or to match information in the text with answer stems on a multiple-choice test.[8]

Seminars may seem to some teachers and parents to be developmentally out of range for primary-grade children, but recall how vehemently Ms. Paley's kindergarten students participated in her discussion of the classroom rule "You Can't Say 'You Can't Play'" (Chapter 3). Playtime was an enormously important *idea* to them, changing the rules of playtime was a hugely controversial *issue,* and all this went directly to their *values.* Is it right to exclude others from your play? Why? Is it ever wrong? Is it always wrong? A worthy text that's developmentally appropriate for the child and right for his or her skill level, plus skillful scaffolding by the teacher, is the needed combination.

In a seminar, the teacher tells students that the purpose of gathering for a discussion is to "tackle some of the ideas in this story" or "to deepen our understanding of what is going on here" or "to figure out why" so and so did such and such. The teacher's main responsibilities are to choose a text worth talking about with others, explain the purpose of the discussion to students, clarify expectations for their seminar behavior, preteach seminar skills as needed, and pose a question that is both interpretive and genuine. During the seminar, the teacher mainly listens, but he or she also asks follow-up questions to clarify, asks for elaboration, invites others into the discussion, summarizes, and so forth. With younger children, the teacher is more active during the seminar; with older children who have more seminar experience, the teacher can be less active, encouraging students to address one another, not the teacher.

Choose a Worthy Text

Not every text has ideas, issues, and values that all the children in a classroom will want to talk about and that all of them are challenged by. Still, that is the goal in text selection. The texts selected by the authors of the school's reading program have been chosen because they help children develop phonemic awareness, build fluency and vocabulary, and, hopefully, because they also contain mind-expanding ideas. But not every text can do all of this; consequently, teachers need to build *great classroom libraries.* Although no book alone can do everything, a library collection can come much closer. And don't forget folktales. Rich in vocabulary, ideas, and social values, such as justice and equality, they often make terrific seminar texts. *Jack and the Beanstalk, The Little Red Hen,* and other folktales from around the world are widely used in primary classrooms. Shel Silverstein's *The Giving Tree* has become a classic, justifiably. In the fourth grade, students are involved in seminars on the Pledge of Allegiance (they may have memorized it, but we can be almost certain that they haven't plumbed its meanings) and the poetry of Langston Hughes (e.g., "Mother and Son"). In the fifth grade, they are discussing the Declaration of Independence and the Preamble to the Constitution of the United States. As a springboard into the geographic theme of *place,* there may be no better book than Judith and Herbert Kohl's *The View from the Oak* (New Press, 2000).

Explain the Purpose

Students need to know that a seminar has a purpose that distinguishes it from other kinds of group talk. A seminar's purpose is to challenge all participants with difficult yet worthy reading, interpretations of which are worked out together in discussion. A seminar is always a reading exercise. With middle school students and higher, the purpose might be stated as follows: "The purpose of today's seminar is to deepen our understanding of the ideas, issues, and values in (the text)." With younger students, the purpose might be stated in terms of figuring out what is happening the text—something that provokes the children.

State and Clarify Expectations

"Be courteous to one another" is a good prompt to primary children. "Be interested in what one another says." "Wait until other children have stopped talking before you start." But it is important to know that the goal of such expectations is to enable students to have civil and insightful discussions with one another of powerful ideas, issues, and values. Toward that end, teachers try to wean children from raising their hands (which forces the teacher into the "traffic cop" role of calling on students) so that they can address one another. A rather standard set of seminar expectations for the intermediate and middle grades might be

- Don't raise hands; have a conversation
- Address one another, not the teacher
- Back up opinions with evidence from the text

Preteach or Postteach Needed Skills

A seminar is a kind of cooperative learning. Cooperation is necessary because the reading is difficult yet worth the trouble. Younger children especially are learning how to have a literature-based discussion as much as they are exploring the issues, ideas, and values in the text. All sorts of skills may need to be taught. Some might be taught in advance of today's seminar; others are taught afterward once the need for them has become apparent. Look back at the T-chart for skill teaching in Chapter 11 (Figure 11–3) and at the skills-teaching strategy in Chapter 9.

Ask an Interpretive, Genuine Question

The teacher opens the seminar, after setting the purpose and expectations, by posing a question. It should be both interpretive and genuine.

An interpretive question requires students to dig into the text but, unlike a literal question, it has no one correct answer. Interpretations are based on judgment, and one will differ from the other, but not all are of equal quality. *A better interpretation can be backed up with evidence from the text.* A good interpretative question for the Pledge of Allegiance might be: "To what are we pledging our allegiance when we recite this pledge?" And for *Jack and the Beanstalk,* "Why did Jack go up the beanstalk the third time?" or "What would make a better title?" For the Declaration of Independence, "Why do the signers think it's their duty to change their government?"

A genuine question is one that the teacher is curious about, puzzled about. When teachers ask genuine questions, they are curious about what children will say since they are themselves interested in the question. The teacher can say, honestly, "I'm puzzled by something and I wonder if you are, too. Why did Jack go up that beanstalk a third time? He already was rich." In this way, true to the Socratic standard set more than 2,000 years ago, teachers leading a seminar don't have the answer; rather, they have the question. The seminar leader tries to sting children with the same sense of thoughtfulness and curiosity that he or she feels personally.

Moves

Once teachers have opened the seminar with an interpretive and genuine question, their job is not over. With younger children, the teacher will need to be quite active during the seminar; with older children, a little less so. Follow-up questions and other moves will be needed, but the leader must be judicious about when and what. In Chapter 9, in the section called "Asking Good Questions," I suggested that questions are the teacher's constant companion and the handiest and most powerful of tools because they direct the intellectual work of students. Here are five that are particularly useful in a seminar:

- *Clarify:* "What do you mean by _____?" (a term the student has used)
- *Elaborate:* "Tell us more about _____." (something the student has said)
- *Verify:* "How do you know that is true?" or "Where does it say that in the text?"
- *Participation:* "What do some of you others have to say about that?"
- *Summarize:* "Let's see what we've said about that so far."

USING CHILDREN'S TRADE BOOKS FOR MULTIPLE PERSPECTIVES

Children's trade books have always been popular curriculum resources in elementary social studies education. For 30 years, one of the most interesting and active committees of the National Council for the Social Studies has been a joint committee of the NCSS and the Children's Book Council, called the NCSS-CBC Joint Committee. A major project of the committee is the annual production of an annotated bibliography, "Notable Social Studies Trade Books for Young People." The list is eagerly awaited, appearing each spring in an issue of the NCSS journal, *Social Education,* and is also downloadable from the NCSS website.

The books selected for this annual list, in the words of the committee, "(1) are written for children in grades K–8, (2) emphasize human relations, (3) represent a diversity of groups and are sensitive to a broad range of cultural experiences, (4) present an original theme or a fresh slant on a traditional topic, (5) are easily readable and of high literary quality, and (6) have a pleasing format and, when appropriate, illustrations that enrich the text."

But the question remains: What is the unique contribution of children's trade books in social studies curriculum and instruction, apart from the role they play in fostering the love

Launching a unit by dramatizing characters in a trade book helps create a "need to know."
(KS Studios/Merrill)

and skill to read? Perhaps their most important purpose in social studies is (a) helping to launch a unit in a highly engaging way and, (b) once in the unit, helping children gather information about and from *multiple perspectives.*

Launching

You may recall from Chapter 8 that much hinges on how a new unit begins. Effectively launching a new unit means arousing the curiosity of students, assessing their present understandings, exploring with them some of the possibilities for study presented by the topic, and, in general, setting the stage for learning to take place. Children's trade books can help, especially when used in combination with dramatization. According to one of the most accomplished teachers I know, Paula Fraser of the Bellevue, Washington, schools, "Literature is a way to entice and engage students initially so they are motivated to discover the substance and the facts."[9] Another terrific teacher, Tarry Lindquist, whom we met in Chapter 3, uses Scott O'Dell's *Sarah Bishop* (Houghton Mifflin, 1980) to launch a study with her fifth-graders of colonial life and the American Revolution. Tarry writes:

> I like this book because both boys and girls find it engaging. It does a good job of bringing out multiple perspectives about the Revolutionary War and provides a setting for the more historically driven information the students will need later to understand the Constitution and the Bill of Rights.[10]

Tarry integrates a good literature activity here. She has students create a storyboard about the novel. Each student divides a 12-by-18-inch piece of white construction paper into eight rectangles. She directs them to express their interpretation of the story by writing and drawing in each box, working in pairs, talking as they go.

Title and student's name	Main character
Setting (time and place)	Conditions before the problem
The problem/antagonist	Conflict
Resolution	Denouement, wrapping up loose ends

As pairs share their work, interpretations are juxtaposed; consequently, students' understandings are challenged and deepened. As Tarry says, "The hook is in, the kids care. Ready now to gather more factual information, we move to the textbook and other resources."

Multiple Perspectives

Children's literature can play a crucial role in teaching students about multiple perspectives. How? First, let's understand these terms.

We all live our lives from one social position and perspective or another; none of us is "positionless" or "perspectiveless." Everyone is born into a particular language, set of customs, historical circumstance, social class, gender, and so on. These elements add up to one's "home base," and everyone's view from home base is unique. While this is one of the central ideas of the social sciences, and we discussed it in Chapter 2 as something teachers need very much to understand, it is a difficult idea for children and many adults. Why? All of us have only a limited ability to see outside our perspective, and the groups to which we belong and with whom we share a perspective may or may not value or encourage it. Members of some groups are actually trained *not* to see the world from others' perspectives or they are trained to view their own perspective as superior.

Beginning in kindergarten, children should be exposed to and helped to grapple with multiple viewpoints. This way, they learn that (a) there are different perspectives—different ways of perceiving and judging—on the same topic; (b) even well-informed people (whether average citizens or specialists on the topic) often disagree about what happened, why something happened, or what will happen next; (c) there may be biases or inaccuracies or omissions that go undetected when we rely on a single viewpoint; and (d) we have no choice but to learn to negotiate and weigh these competing viewpoints and draw defensible conclusions. Of course, a kindergartner in Ms. Paley's class (Chapter 3) will not be able to think about multiple perspectives in the same way as a second-grade child, or a fifth- or eighth-grade child. Biological and social development govern this ability.

Sometimes, a single children's book can successfully show children how life is lived from a perspective different from their own. When a nonfiction book does this especially well, it becomes a candidate for the Carter G. Woodson Award of the National Council for the Social Studies. This annual award "encourages the writing, publishing, and dissemination of outstanding social studies books for young readers that treat topics related to ethnic minorities and race relations sensitively and accurately." Here are several books that have received the award recently.

Elementary Level

- *Let Them Play* by Margot Theis Raven, illustrated by Chris Ellison (Sleeping Bear Press, 2006)
- *Jim Thorpe's Bright Path* by Joseph Bruchac, illustrated by S. D. Nelson (Lee and Low Books, 2005)
- *Sacagawea* by Louise Erdrich, illustrated by Julie Buffalohead (Carolrhoda, 2004)

Middle Level

- *Cesar Chavez: A Voice for Farmworkers* by Barbara Cruz (Enslow, 2006)
- *Voice that Challenged a Nation: Marian Anderson and the Struggle for Equal Rights* by Russell Freedman (Clarion Books, 2005)
- *Power of One: Daisy Bates and the Little Rock Nine* by Judith Bloom Fradin and Dennis Brindell Fradin (Clarion Books, 2005)

Better than a single book with a single perspective, however, is bringing together two children's stories on the same topic. In this way, multiple perspectives are provided. Children are helped to see events, both historical and current, from more than one social position, more than one vantage point. When multiple perspectives are examined routinely, as part of studying any event, a compare-and-contrast method of teaching and learning becomes a common classroom experience. Encouraged in this way, children will form the habit of looking at events from more than one angle. Our aim is that they become students who regularly ask, without prompting, "Have we examined all the viewpoints? Is there someone we are ignoring? Are we getting all the perspectives?"

This strategy has two important advantages over the single-perspective approach. First, any one perspective is prevented from being put forward uncritically as *neutral*. When the English colonists' perspective on the American West is the only viewpoint that is studied, for example, then it does not seem to children like a perspective at all; rather, it seems to them to be simply "the truth"—the way it happened. Actually, different things happened, depending on whom we talk with. If we were to talk to a conquered Apache Indian or the conquering U.S. cavalry general, we would get two very different interpretations of what the Europeans might call the "discovery of the New World." This is true of *any* event, from the Pilgrims landing at Plymouth in the 17th century to the U.S. soldiers landing in Baghdad in the 21st. Readers may recall the surprise event that was staged in Lesson Plan 4 on primary sources (see Chapter 4). The objective of that lesson was for students to learn that there will be multiple perspectives on a single event if there are multiple persons witnessing it.

The second advantage of teaching with multiple perspectives is that children begin to do the work of historians—making sense of competing accounts. When children are apprenticed into this form of historical inquiry, they "begin to understand and appreciate," in the words of the NCSS curriculum standards, "differences in historical perspectives, recognizing that interpretations are influenced by individual experiences, societal values, and cultural traditions."[11]

One children's trade book often represents one perspective quite well, sometimes brilliantly, providing rich contextual detail. When teachers use two (or even three) of these books, in combination with background information, primary sources, and maps, multiple perspectives can easily be brought to bear on the event. Through creative activities such as role-playing, readers' theater, and simulation games, children will deepen their understanding of each perspective.

The possibilities are as endless as there are curriculum topics. In a unit on Native American peoples, children could compare the perspectives of two native men: the legendary Squanto, depicted in Bulla's *Squanto: Friend of the Pilgrims* (Scholastic, 1990), and the native at the center of Speare's *Sign of the Beaver* (Yearling, 1983). The latter is neither "savage" nor "friendly," and children learn something of his culture. These books could then be used as springboards for in-depth study on the two native cultures presented. Who were these people? Where exactly did they live? How did the women live? Children? What kinds of a places were they? How did they differ from other native groups in the same geographical region? What was their language? religion? legal system? medicine? family structure? shelter? food? education? economy?

In a unit on Explorers generally or the expedition of Christopher Columbus specifically, children could compare the perspectives in Greene's *Christopher Columbus: A Great Explorer* (Children's Press, 1989), Liestman's *Columbus Day* (Carolrhoda, 1991), and Yolen's *Encounter* (Harcourt, 1992). This is what Mary Beth Henning and her colleagues did in a fourth-grade unit described in their article, "Listening to Children Think Critically about Christopher Columbus." They write:

> Some children and their families embrace Christopher Columbus as a hero. Columbus embodies the virtues of bravery, calculated risk-taking, persistence, and leadership. . . . (But) after reading *Rethinking Columbus* and *Lies My Teacher Told Me*, it would be difficult to teach about Columbus from an exclusively positive or admiring vantage point.[12]

The books they refer to in the quotation[13] are popular with teachers who labor to present historically accurate portrayals of events rather than only embracing one perspective and calling it "the truth." Using multiple books with multiple perspectives, then, teachers don't have to choose between "in 1492, Columbus sailed the ocean blue" and "in 1493, Columbus stole all that he could see." By exploring several different children's books about Columbus, Hennings and her colleagues conclude, "we hoped to create a more meaningful unit that would offer students a balanced approach to Columbus's encounter with the New World."

A teacher who wishes to use trade books to help students wrestle with multiple perspectives might implement the following general procedure:

- Select a historical or current event that is related to curriculum goals.
- Browse trade books to assemble two or three perspectives on the event.
- Read aloud or assist students in interpreting and discussing the stories using semantic mapping, storyboards, the Socratic Seminar, and other reading comprehension strategies.
- Incorporate dramatizations and other activities to boost children's comprehension of the perspectives.
- Use a data-retrieval chart or a three-dimensional graphic organizer as shown in Chapter 8 to help children compare and contrast the perspectives on the event.

Lesson Plan 19 shows one way to organize such a lesson. It features two popular books by the Collier brothers, *My Brother Sam Is Dead* and *War Comes to Willy Freeman*. Let's assume that the teacher has planned a unit for fifth-grade students on the American Revolution. Broadly, the unit is an inquiry that is centered on the question "Did the American colonists really want independence from England?" The teacher knows that many colonists did, but that many did not, and that the conflict between Loyalists (to England) and Patriots (the rebels wanting independence) was intense and sometimes violent. The Patriots eventually prevailed, writing the Declaration of Independence, fighting a war for independence, and forming a new nation.

The teacher wants to feature these two perspectives on the American Revolution, but she is confident that the lesson can go further by including also the perspectives of race and gender. Accordingly, she plans this extended lesson.

Conclusion

Reading and writing are best thought of as a joint enterprise. Readers make meaning when they comprehend text in much the same way that writers make meaning when they compose text. The skills involved in summarizing probably make this point most clearly, for to write a summary of a reading selection has as much to do with reading carefully as with writing carefully. And both are steeped in thinking. Meanings are constructed by the child's own intellectual labor—his or her own construction activity. The quality of this labor will depend on the child's own intellectual resources working in combination with a skillful, knowing, and caring coach—a teacher—and a well-planned curriculum.

Children do not make meaning in a vacuum; children read and write to accomplish goals. That's where the social studies curriculum comes in. Here they read and write to build and express social studies understandings, to participate in civic life, and to improve their ability to read and write. It sounds circular because it is. These things are interdependent.

We will turn our attention more directly to writing in the next chapter, which presents a rich and engaging way to integrate reading and writing instruction with social studies subject matter. Working in teams, children create an original, multichapter biography of a pivotal historical figure.

THE AMERICAN REVOLUTION: TWO PERSPECTIVES FROM LITERATURE

Grade	5
Time	Two weeks
NCSS Standards	2 (time, continuity, and change), 4 (individual development and identity), and 6 (power, authority, and governance)
Objectives	Children will understand that (a) descriptions of events depend to some extent on who is describing them and (b) people can interpret events differently depending, in part, on their social positions (e.g., race, gender, class). Also, they will enrich their knowledge of the American Revolution with the personal narratives of a fictional boy and girl: one Black, one White; one free, one enslaved. Also, they will form an initial concept of historical fiction.
Literature	*Historical fiction:* James Lincoln Collier and Christopher Collier, *My Brother Sam Is Dead* (Scholastic, 1974) and *War Comes to Willy Freeman* (Dell, 1983).
Viewpoints	These two near-classics of historical fiction present very different perspectives on the American Revolution. Sam's brother Tim tells Sam's story. Both Sam and Tim are European American boys. Their father is against Sam joining with the American Patriots to drive out the British. Younger Tim is torn between his father and Sam. Willy, on the other hand, is a young girl who has to disguise herself as a boy because she is alone and separated from her family. Soldiers are everywhere. Also, she is African American; it doesn't make much difference to her which side wins. Her father, unlike Tim's, joins the Patriots and, before many pages are turned, is killed defending a Patriot fort.
Interest Building	Engage students' interest in the idea that perspective makes a difference. Use Lesson Plan 4 in Chapter 4 on primary and secondary sources in which students themselves are eyewitnesses to a surprise event.
Lesson Development	1. Teach the two books as you normally would, using your favorite strategies. Students should write in their response journals, engage in role-playing and other dramatizations, and participate in numerous interpretive discussions while reading these books.
	2. To work specifically with the concept of "perspective," have students construct a three-door Venn-diagram folded graphic such as the one shown for "democracy" in Chapter 9 (p. 306). "Perspective" can be written across the bottom, "Sam's perspective" on the left door, "both" on the middle, "and Willy's perspective" on the right door. Inside the folds, students can write details about each perspective and, in the middle, their similarities. Alternatively, as shown in the full-color pages in Chapter 8, using the pyramid graphic, three perspectives can be represented. Students can be invited to choose the third: Tim's? Willy's father? Sam's father?
	3. The culminating activity is to have students themselves write a new piece of historical fiction in which Tim and Willy meet. They learn of one another's experiences and perspectives on this war. Before students begin this work, however, use the two texts they have read as the examples in a concept-formation or concept-attainment lesson (see Chapter 9) on the concept *historical fiction.* That way, the example they produce will be an application of their understanding of this concept.
Summary and Assessment	Have several students share their original stories and help the audience evaluate each story on two criteria: the story itself (as taught in literature) and the degree to which Tim's and Willy's perspectives were effectively represented. After revision, have the original stories placed in students' social studies portfolios.
Integration	*Literature:* Children's literature is infused here to help children achieve important social studies objectives. Also, thanks to the concept lesson on historical fiction, they learn about a particular literary genre.
	Writing: Writing in response journals builds literacy skills. Writing an original story in which Tim and Willy meet gives students the opportunity to apply their concept of historical fiction.

Discussion Questions and Suggested Activities

Go to MyEducationLab and select the topic "Literature Connections," then watch the video "The Supply Chain" and complete the activity.

1. Look back at the "Reflection" sidebar in the section on "Using Textbooks as Study Aids." The question raised there is connected to the problem of lowering expectations for students when difficult material is encountered, which in turn is entangled with the achievement gap between Latino, African American, and White students, and between middle-class and working-class students. Discuss the matter with classmates and try to clarify the issues that are involved.

2. Select a social studies topic for a grade of your choice (see scope-and-sequence suggestions in Chapter 1) and search the "Notable Social Studies Trade Books for Young People" at the NCSS website along with books that received the Carter G. Woodson award. Identify two or three trade books that, together, would bring different perspectives to bear on that topic. Reread Lesson Plan 19 and then sketch a lesson plan of your own using these books.

3. Locate a recently published children's social studies textbook for a grade level of interest to you, and examine it and the teacher's guide to find examples of instruction on reading skills. Think about how you can use social studies materials to teach and refine children's reading and writing skills.

4. NCSS Standards *Sampler.* Examine the eighth-grade classroom vignette for standard #2 on page 29 of the standards *Sampler* that accompanies this book. Compare it to Lesson Plan 19, "The American Revolution: Two Perspectives from Literature," in this chapter.

Selected References

Gallavan, Nancy P., & Kottler, Ellen. (2007). Eight types of graphic organizers for empowering social studies students and teachers. *The Social Studies, 98* (3), 117–128.

Hoyt, Linda. (2003). *Make it real: Strategies for success with informational texts.* Portsmouth, NH: Heinemann.

Notable social studies trade books for young people. (yearly). Available online from the National Council for the Social Studies.

Raphael, Taffy E., & Au, Kathryn H. (2005). QAR: Enhancing comprehension and test taking across grades and content areas. *The Reading Teacher, 59* (3), 206–221.

Routman, Regie. (2003). *Reading essentials: The specifics you need to teach reading well.* Portsmouth, NH: Heinemann.

Sandmann, Alexa L., & Ahern, John F. (2002). *Linking literature with life: The NCSS Standards and children's literature for the middle grades.* Silver Spring, MD: National Council for the Social Studies.

Woodson, Carter G. Book Award. (yearly). Available online from the National Council for the Social Studies.

MyEducationLab is a collection of online tools for your success in this course, your licensure exams, and your teaching career. Go to www.myeducationlab.com to utilize these extensive resources including videos from real classrooms, Praxis and licensure preparation, a lesson plan builder, and materials to help you begin your teaching career.

Social Studies as the Integrating Core

CHAPTER THIRTEEN

Chapter Outline

- Making Sense of Curriculum Integration
- Example 1: Composing Cooperative Biographies
- Example 2: Understanding Living Things
- Understanding the Two Examples
- Conclusion

Key Concepts

- Curriculum intregration
- Scholarly disciplines
- Strategy (means)
- Goal (end)
- Biography
- Unifying generalization

MAIN IDEA

This is the second unit-planning chapter in the book, and it focuses squarely on curriculum integration. Two exemplary integrated units are presented. One brings language arts to the service of social studies by involving children in reading and writing original biographies of historical figures. The other involves children in constructing a big idea called a "generalization," which, in this example, brings together social studies and science. Each of the two examples is fully illustrated; accordingly they are effective both as capstones for this book (because they rely on and review material in the preceding chapters) and as models for the reader's own unit planning (because they set high standards).

PICTURE THIS

Mr. Larson wanted his third-grade students to understand something very important, that the decisions made by human beings influence the survival of other living things. This idea was so rich and generative that, if it were not to be treated superficially, it would require the integration of two of the third-grade subjects at his school: science and social studies. This was the only big idea-construction project he would attempt before the winter vacation, so he pulled out all the stops and developed a unit using his most powerful teaching strategies: concept formation, inquiry, and decision making.

This is the second unit-planning chapter in the book and an extension of Chapter 8. Placed directly after that one, however, this chapter would have been incomprehensible, for this one relies on the intervening chapters on teaching strategies (9), resources (10), cooperative learning (11), and the literacy–social studies connection (12), as well as the earlier assessment chapter (7). Integrated education, done well, is challenging for the teacher because there are serious pitfalls to be avoided. Accordingly, this is a culminating chapter. Its contents integrate much of the material presented in the preceding chapters.

MAKING SENSE OF CURRICULUM INTEGRATION

In Part One of this book, social studies education was defined as the integrated study of the social sciences to promote civic competence. Helping children construct powerful social understandings and step up to the responsibilities of democratic citizenship are the basic goals of social studies education. A vision this important to society and this basic to the well-being of our students can easily serve as an integrating core for much of the teaching and learning that goes on in elementary and middle schools.

We begin by clarifying the concept *curriculum integration* or, as it is often called, *interdisciplinary education* or *integrated education*. These terms mean different things to different teachers. Compare the following.

- By integration, some teachers mean that their reading and writing, literature, and art and music instruction are focused on social studies subject matter. When they teach students to use context clues as aids to comprehension, for example, they are using a primary document, such as the journals of Lewis and Clark or the Declaration of Independence, or they are using the social studies textbook or a selection of historical fiction. When they teach literary concepts such as plot, theme, character, narrative, fiction, poem, and biography, they are using social studies materials. When they teach composition (persuasive writing, journaling, report and letter writing), the subject matter is drawn from the social studies curriculum. They teach color, value, and shape in paintings that represent the historical era or geographic place under study. The same goes for the rhythm, melody, and lyrics of songs. In this way, social studies objectives are the sun in the solar system; they are the curricular center of gravity pulling all the other objectives toward the same integrating core.

- Others mean that a powerful theme—usually a *concept*—such as exploration (or borders or equality), has been selected as the centerpiece of the curriculum, for a unit or perhaps the entire year. The teacher then orients social studies, science, language arts, and math toward this concept. Explorers of new places (Marco Polo, Meriwether Lewis, Sally Ride) are studied alongside explorers of new ideas (Confucius, Galileo, Jefferson) and perspectives (Leonardo da Vinci, Virginia Woolf, Picasso). Reading and writing instruction, art and music, and drama are infused into these studies. Mathematics may be included as well.

- For still others, integration means that a different kind of theme—not a concept, but a *generalization*—has been selected as the centerpiece. Generalizations are larger than concepts for they *combine and synthesize concepts.* For example, *animals adapt to their environments* (from biology) or *the family is the fundamental social environment in most cultures and the source of the most basic socialization* (from sociology), or the *decisions of human beings influence the survival of other living things* (from both social studies and science). Generalizations are abstract; they refer to a wide variety of specific cases. Therefore, a large amount of subject matter, often drawn from more than one school curriculum area, and a good amount of intellectual labor and guidance are needed to construct them.

These three meanings do not exhaust all the possibilities of curriculum integration, but they help display the variety of examples within this concept. In this chapter, two model units are featured, and they exemplify the first and third of these three meanings.

Definitions

To understand curriculum integration (integrated or interdisciplinary education), one must first understand the idea of the *scholarly disciplines*. These are fairly distinct bodies of knowledge and methods of inquiry. Anthropology, for example, is the discipline concerned with accumulating a body of knowledge (facts, concepts, generalizations, and issues) about people's culture and customs. Anthropologists' preferred method of building this knowledge is ethnographic fieldwork. Biology, sociology, political science, literature, history, and archaeology are other distinct bodies of knowledge and methods.

The disciplines, according to psychologist Howard Gardner, "represent the formidable achievements of talented human beings, toiling over the centuries, to approach and explain issues of enduring importance."[1] The disciplines are, he stresses, "indispensable in any quality education," and he urges educators not to abandon disciplinary education in the name of integrated education. "The disciplines represent our best efforts to think systematically about the world, and they are prerequisite to competent interdisciplinary work," Gardner continues.[2] Integrated education is not better, therefore, than nonintegrated education any more than a shovel is better than a hammer. It all depends on the goal to which these tools are put. Compare these definitions:

Discipline

An integrated body of teachable knowledge with its own key concepts and generalizations, issues, and methods of inquiry. Quoting Howard Gardner again, "The scholarly disciplines represent concerted efforts by individuals (and groups) over time to address essential questions and answer them."[3]

Interdisciplinary or Integrated

A curriculum approach that purposefully draws together knowledge, perspectives, and methods of inquiry from more than one discipline to develop a more powerful understanding of an issue, person, event, or big idea. The purpose is not to eliminate the individual disciplines but to use them in combination. Wise teachers do not hide the disciplines from students any more than farmers hide their seeds, shovels, and plows from their apprentices. Quite the opposite, they call the disciplines by their proper names and teach children about them—their ideas and methods of inquiry.

Pitfalls

Integrated education has numerous shortcomings that must be understood if they are to be avoided. These range from causing confusion (rather than providing clarity and power), to trivializing learning (turning teachers' and students' attention to unimportant topics) and treating important topics superficially. Mindful of these pitfalls, teachers can steer integrated education clear of the extremes and toward high standards of quality.

Ends and Means

The greatest pitfall regarding curriculum integration is to treat it as a goal. Curriculum integration is a strategy, not a goal. To treat it as a goal is, as the saying goes, to let the tail wag the dog (see Chapter 10). Like a pencil, curriculum integration is a tool that has little value in itself; what matters is how, when, and where it is used. In other words, curriculum integration is not an end in itself; it is neither good nor bad on its own. It may be good, but this depends on the worthiness of the goal toward which it is directed. It may be a skill or process goal, such as learning and applying the inquiry method. It may be a content goal, such as learning why American colonists rebelled against England or understanding that the decisions made by human beings influence the survival of other living things. "The most basic of all principles is goal relevance," write two scholars who have closely examined social studies learning activities. "Each activity should have at least one primary goal that, if achieved, will represent progress toward one of the major social education goals that underlie and justify the social studies curriculum."[4]

Either/Or Thinking ("Putting All the Eggs in One Basket")

This error involves the assumption that either a discipline-based curriculum or an interdisciplinary curriculum is the right thing to do. Neither is true. Both are needed, but at different times and for different purposes. It is important to exercise professional judgment, using each when appropriate. This is the eclectic approach—the middle way between extremes—and it is often the best course.

Trivializing Learning

While discipline-based education compartmentalizes knowledge for the purpose of studying it, thoughtful teachers know that interdisciplinary education can create its own problems. It is particularly susceptible to trivializing the curriculum. This occurs when unimportant content is selected for instruction simply because it can be integrated easily with other content. Meanwhile, important content that may not lend itself to integration goes untaught, and, soon, integrated education is associated in the public's mind with low-quality education. *The point to remember is that a learning activity that crosses disciplinary boundaries is not necessarily worthwhile.* What makes an activity worthwhile is that students are forming or extending a powerful understanding or skill. As psychologist Jerome Bruner said, "The first object of any act of learning, over and beyond the pleasure it may give, is that it should serve us in the future. Learning should not only take us somewhere; it should allow us later to go further more easily."[5]

Confusion

Interdisciplinary education needlessly confuses learners when teachers require them to study simultaneously topics that more fruitfully could be examined separately. Imagine students trying to study three cultures' customs, literature, art, and scientific achievements all at the same time. The loss in analytic clarity and the increased difficulty would not justify the gains hoped for by integrating social studies, literature, art, and science. Experts in a field—craftspersons and connoisseurs and scholars and gifted readers and the like—do not attempt to tackle a problem by focusing their attention on all its parts at once. That would make the problem a tangled knot. John Dewey advised wisely that we limit a topic for study in such a way as to avoid what he called "the great bad." This is "the mixing of things which need to be kept distinct."[6] Experts limit the problem they are working on; they analyze it and break it into its component parts. They do this to understand the big picture better and, therefore, to know where they most profitably might begin chipping away at the problem.

We should not train students to study a topic by making a jumbled mess of it. Readers may remember the clear plastic overlay illustrations found in good biology textbooks. These make it possible to achieve a sort of layered understanding of the human body. Readers are permitted to focus only on the skeletal system, or only on muscle tissue or major organs, and then to lay these systems on top of one another to examine the big picture and the interaction of parts. Similar transparent overlays are found in some student atlases. Children can look at the African continent with only the national boundaries marked in or overlay that with a physical map showing the deserts, savannas, and mountain ranges. Then they can add another overlay showing major cities.

*Dis*integration, then, can be helpful. Knowing how and when to separate topics to clarify them, and knowing, on the other hand, when to integrate them is a major achievement of skillful teaching.

A Little Bit of This, a Little Bit of That

Closely related to the pitfalls of trivializing the curriculum and confusing the learners is what one expert calls "the potpourri problem,"[7] which occurs when a unit is composed of bits of information from each discipline. If the subject is the Mayan civilization, for example, we could find a bit of history, a bit of art, a bit of science, a bit of math, but not the proper depth in any of these to make the study meaningful, powerful, and coherent. Better to help children dig into Mayan history in depth than to "superficialize" learning in the name of integrated education.

If the pitfalls are to be avoided, what is to be done? Let us examine in detail two exemplary integrated curriculum units. In both cases, purposes are paramount (the tail is not wagging the dog), highly important subject matter is at the heart of the unit (the learnings are not trivial), and things that need to be kept separate for clarity's sake are kept separate: Dewey's "great bad" is avoided and the promise of curriculum integration is realized.

The first example is a popular integrated unit used successfully by teachers across the United States and Canada to help children read and write, not alone but with teammates, original biographies of major historical figures: great citizens, social activists, heroes, villains, scientists, artists, poets, inventors, kings and queens, explorers, revolutionaries, labor leaders, and presidents. The essence of this approach to curriculum integration is that reading and writing skills are applied to social studies objectives. The second is a unit that joins social studies and science curricula to help children build a generalization. The generalization in the sample unit is: *The decisions of human beings influence the survival of other living things.* The essence of this approach is that two subjects are fused so that a big, overarching idea can be constructed.

EXAMPLE 1: COMPOSING COOPERATIVE BIOGRAPHIES

Reading and composing biographies is an elegant and authentic way to put language arts and literature in the service of the history curriculum. The reading of biographies is what we called "absorbing" or "learning about" history in Chapter 4. (Recall the two wings of the airplane: absorbing treasured historical stories is one wing of the history-learning airplane, and creating such stories oneself, from primary and secondary sources and artifacts—*doing* history—is the other wing.) In this cooperative biography unit, students will both absorb biographies of the selected historical figure and then *compose,* with teammates, an original biography of this same figure.[8] In this way, they are using historical reasoning, interpreting sources, wrestling with competing eyewitness accounts, and deciding what story to tell about this person's life and times. They are *being historians.*

Our example will feature Sojourner Truth, the 19th-century social activist who fought against the racist institution of slavery and then against the sexist institution of patriarchy. Ample biographical material about her can be found in most school libraries, social studies textbooks, and the Internet, which makes it feasible for teachers to teach children about her and help them to write original, brief narratives of her life and times.

Sojourner Truth was first sold when she was nine years old, probably in the year 1807. She had been born into slavery in New York to a Dutch man named Hardenbergh, so that became her name, too—Belle Hardenbergh. When she was nine, John Neely became Belle's new owner. He paid $50 and got both the Dutch-speaking African girl and 100 sheep. Two years later, after learning some English and suffering beatings at the hands of the Neely family, she was sold again, this time for $105 to Martin Schryver, who had a farm near the Hudson River. In 1810, Belle was sold yet again. Her new master, Mr. Dumont, wrote in his ledger, "For $300, Belle, about 13 years old, six feet tall." Years later, with the help of Quakers, Belle won her freedom and chose the name Sojourner Truth. It was a good handle for the life she was about to live, as a seeker and speaker of truth.

Her speeches attracted great crowds and are today among schoolchildren's favorites. For example, in May of 1851, she attended a women's rights convention in Akron, Ohio. Before she or any of the other women could speak, Protestant ministers—all male—dominated the proceedings. They derided the women who wanted social reform. Francis Gage later wrote this eyewitness account of what happened after the ministers were finally through:

> Then, slowly from her seat in the corner rose Sojourner Truth, who, till now, had scarcely lifted her head. She moved solemnly to the front, laid her old bonnet at her feet, and turned her great speaking eyes on me.
>
> There was a hissing sound of disapprobation above and below. I rose and announced, "Sojourner Truth," and begged the audience keep silence for a few moments.
>
> The tumult subsided at once, and every eye was fixed on this almost Amazon form, which stood nearly six feet high, head erect and eyes piercing the upper air like one in a dream. At her first word there was a profound hush. She spoke in deep tones, which, though not loud, reached every ear in the house and away through the doors and windows:
>
> "Well, children, where there is so much racket, there must be something out of kilter. That man over there says women need to be helped into carriages and lifted over ditches—and to have the best place everywhere. Nobody ever helps me into carriages or over mud-puddles—or gives me the best place at the table!"

Raising herself to her full height, and lifting her voice to a pitch like rolling thunder, Sojourner asked, "And ain't I a woman? Look at me! Look at my arm!" She bared her right arm to the shoulder, showing her tremendous muscular power. "I have ploughed and planted and gathered into barns, and no man could get ahead of me! And ain't I a woman?

"I could work as much and eat as much as a man—when I could get it—and bear the lash as well! And ain't I a woman?

"My mother bore ten children and saw them sold off to slavery, and when I cried with my mother's grief, none but Jesus heard me! And ain't I a woman?

"Then that little man in black says women can't have as many rights as men. If the first woman God ever made was strong enough to turn the world upside down all alone, these women together" (and she glanced over the platform) "ought to be able to turn it back and get it right side up again! And now that the women are asking to do it, the men better let 'em."

Long cheering greeted this. "I'm obliged to you for hearing me," she concluded, "and now old Sojourner hasn't got nothing more to say."[9]

Truth had much more to say. When she wasn't speaking for women's rights, she was speaking against slavery. And after President Lincoln ended slavery, Truth worked in Washington, D.C.—what she called "Mr. Lincoln's city"—to overcome the remnants of slavery: virulent racism and deeply entrenched prejudice. She tried to help freed Africans find work and homes, and she worked for a time as a nurse in Freedman's Hospital. These were chaotic, heartbreaking times. The Civil War, in which her son fought in the famous 54th Massachusetts Regiment, became a slaughter on both sides. And just as it ended, Lincoln, whom she had met and much admired, was killed by an assassin.

Still, she was not defeated. One of my favorite biographers writing for children, Jeri Ferris, writes of yet another of Truth's efforts to right wrongs:

One afternoon as Sojourner walked back to the hospital with an armful of blankets, she was so tired she just couldn't walk any more. Horsedrawn streetcars clanged up and down the road, filled with white folks. Sojourner waited for a car to stop, but none did. Finally, as yet another car passed her, she called out, "I want to ride!" People crowded around, the horses stopped, and Sojourner got on. The conductor was furious and demanded she get off. Sojourner settled back in her seat. "I'm not from the South," she said firmly. "I'm from the Empire State of New York, and I know the law as well as you do."

The next day she tried to ride another streetcar. Again the conductor would not stop. Sojourner ran after the car and caught up with it. When the horses stopped, she jumped on. "What a shame," she panted, "to make a lady run so." The conductor threatened to throw her off. "If you try," she said, "it will cost you more than your car and horses are worth." He didn't.

The third time Sojourner tried to ride a streetcar, she was with a white friend. "Stand back," shouted the conductor to Sojourner, "and let that lady on."

"I am a lady too," said Sojourner, and she stepped aboard with her friend.[10]

Writing About Historical Figures

I provide this brief sketch of the life and times of Sojourner Truth so that readers can better follow the procedure outlined for guiding children to produce biographies themselves. The creation of an original biography is a splendid way to invite children to read, write, and discuss their way into an in-depth understanding of a historical figure. Not only are their horizons expanded and their historical reasoning encouraged by this exposure to lives different from their own, but their skills in reading, writing, revising, planning, and cooperating are developed along the way.

The names of the historical figures on the list that follows are a small sample of the persons whose lives and times warrant in-depth study by elementary and middle school children. Readers might notice that the persons listed could all serve as examples of the concept *democratic citizen*. In the spirit of the teaching strategy called concept formation (Chapter 9), teachers can select three or four persons who together would help children to form this concept. The class could write three or four biographies during the school year, keeping track of the similarities among these citizens—similarities that make them all examples of the concept *democratic citizen:*

- They knew that popular sovereignty is the bedrock of democracy and that this means taking personal responsibility for the common good.
- They took time from their private lives to be active in civic life.
- They understood the difference between complaining and proposing solutions.
- They understood, within the constraints of their times, that democracy means majority rule and minority rights.
- They exhibited courage on behalf of these principles.

Biographies of Democratic Citizens

James Madison	Abraham Lincoln
Susan B. Anthony	Jane Adams
Rosa Parks	Mary McLeod Bethune
Benjamin Franklin	Gordon Hirabayashi
Eleanor Roosevelt	Patrick Henry
Cesar Chavez	Martin Luther King, Jr.

Democratic citizen is not the only concept around which subjects can be selected for biographies, though it is one of the most important. Other central ideas are *explorers, inventors, scientists, champions of the poor, friends of nature, leaders, dictators, revolutionaries,* and *heroes.* Recall that the discussion of concept learning in Chapter 9 emphasized multiple examples. Here this means that a teacher might orchestrate children's biographical studies around one of these themes, having them produce, over a year's time, three or four biographies on that theme rather than one each on different themes. This approach should help children build an in-depth understanding of the theme. On the other hand, teachers might want to cover more ground; accordingly, they would mix the kinds of subjects about whom their students write, for example, choosing a hero (Crazy Horse or Harriet Tubman), an inventor (Benjamin Franklin or Eli Whitney), a scientist (Galileo or Newton), and a great citizen (Sojourner Truth or George Washington). Figure 13–1 suggests several themes and related subjects.

Procedure for Producing Biographies

The teacher will need to plan the several phases of the biography project:

1. Decide on the learning objectives.
2. Select the person about whom children will write their biographies.
3. Introduce the project to students, clarifying the objectives, rationale, and audience.

FIGURE 13–1 Examples of conceptual clusters of persons suitable for cooperative biographies.

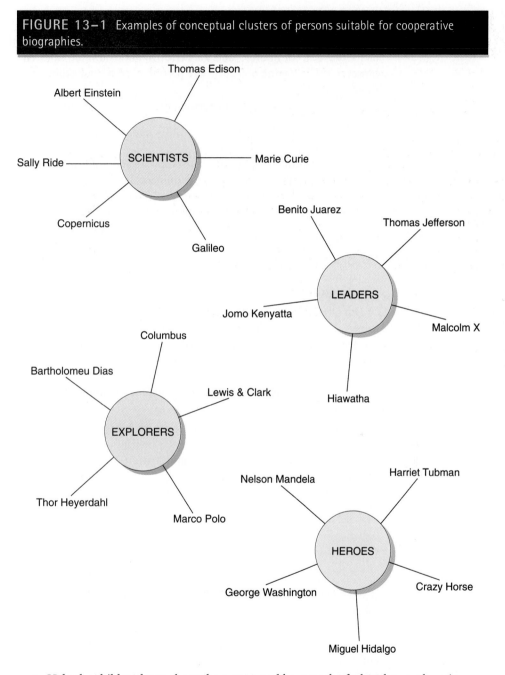

4. Help the children learn about the person and keep track of what they are learning.
5. Help children reflect on the person's life and times and identify key events in the person's life.
6. Orchestrate the cooperative production of biographies in small groups.
7. Conclude the project.

Objectives

The learning objectives for this project will vary with the curriculum, the teacher, the students, the local community, and the person about whom the children will write. Generally, however, the following objectives are pertinent. Note that skills, knowledge, and habits of mind are targeted.

As a result of producing a historical biography with teammates, the students will learn

1. That a person's life is shaped by history and sometimes shapes the history into which the next generation is born
2. How to use the writing process to compose and publish a biography
3. That biography is a distinct genre of literature
4. How to work cooperatively in small groups to which they have been assigned
5. That a variety of reference sources are needed to assemble an understanding of the life and times of a person because different sources—both "primary" and "secondary"—provide different information and perspectives
6. How to make sense of competing accounts of a person or event and compose a fair-minded account
7. How to construct time lines of a person's life

Not all of these objectives need to be addressed to the same extent. The class may have achieved some before the project begins; others may come in a subsequent biography project. Teachers should select objectives that are developmentally appropriate for the children in the class and that can feasibly be achieved given the constraints of time and available materials. Still, this list displays the impressive array of objectives for which the biography project is suitable. Teachers may wish to include the following objectives as well. Students will learn

8. That only some events in a person's life are *turning points* (milestones, pivotal events)
9. That a person's geographical setting(s) may influence his or her life
10. That every person has dilemmas and struggles
11. How to make books
12. How to illustrate a section of narrative using charcoal pencil

Selecting a Subject

Several criteria guide the selection of subjects for children's biographies. Most important is that the person chosen brings children into contact with powerful ideas of history, government, geography, economics, and other social studies disciplines. This study can bring children to the heart of social studies and build firm foundations for further learning.

Another criterion for selecting a good subject for biographical study is the likelihood that children will be captivated by the person's life. It may help some children become more interested in the person if information is available on his or her childhood. Ben Franklin's early troubles with his brother James, for example, or James Madison's illnesses as a child and Sojourner Truth's harrowing childhood all seem to fascinate children, broadening their experiences by giving them access to other children's lives—lives that are different but reassuringly similar, too. Learning a great deal about a person can itself make that person captivating to the young biographer. As this third-grade student quite wisely reported, one cannot know for certain what makes a subject interesting. He seems to conclude, however, that familiarity breeds interest, not contempt. In other words, knowledge breeds enthusiasm:

> Everyone else was interested in Hiawatha but I wasn't because the things I knew about him were boring. But the more I found out—the way they learned to hunt and live together in the long house, plus the magic—made it interesting. Now I know him a lot.

A third criterion is the availability of materials. The "snapshot biography" method outlined here requires students to learn a great deal about the subject.[11] If the subject is obscure, chances are good that neither the textbook nor the school library will have ample books, primary documents, narrative biographies, or other materials.

Consider how Ms. Brem, a fourth-grade teacher, selects biographical subjects. She has decided to weave a yearlong study of *leadership* through the state history curriculum her school district requires in that grade. She wants her pupils to study and eventually write biographies of three state leaders. She wants the leaders to be culturally diverse, and she wants them to expose students to different historical periods and geographical areas of the state. Now Ms. Brem begins her materials search. A booklet she received last year from the state arm of the League of Women Voters provides information on several civic leaders, and she asks a committee of students to select one for the class to study. The social studies education office at the state capital publishes material on the state's governors; Ms. Brem selects the state's first governor. Now she has selected two of the three subjects she needs. Since they are both European Americans, Ms. Brem wants the third leader to be a Native American or a member of another non-White group.

Unaware of who this might be or where materials can be obtained, she appoints another student committee to go to the school librarian for help. The librarian refers them to information on a civic leader who helped to organize the early Chinese American community in the state. Now the class has a set of three leaders and is ready for the reading-and-writing approach to biographical study.

Introducing the Project

On the day the biography project is introduced, the teacher should accomplish five tasks with students: assess, activate prior knowledge, provide purpose, provide rationale, and identify the audience. First, the teacher will need to diagnose what the children already know about biographies and what sense they make of the notion of a person's life and times. A few informal assessment questions should accomplish this task (see Chapter 7's opening example with Ms. Rivera). It is assumed here that the teacher has previously assessed the children's reading and writing ability and knows something of their home cultures, special needs, and prior experiences. Second, based on this brief diagnostic assessment, the teacher can further draw out the children's knowledge and experience. A semantic map (Chapter 12) might be created on the chalkboard, and the school librarian can be invited to discuss biographies with the children.

Third, the teacher should reveal clearly the objectives or targets of the project. These may be posted on the bulletin board and explained. Fourth, the teacher should help the children understand *why* these targets need to be reached—why they are important. For example, it is important to study historical biographies because they can introduce us to amazing new worlds and help us avoid mistakes made in the past. It is important to learn to cooperate in small groups to which one has been assigned because this mirrors realities in the workplace and civic life. Finally, the teacher should help the children identify an audience for their biographies. For example, if they have recently visited the residents of a rehabilitation center, they may wish to write the biographies for this audience and take them personally to the center. Or they may wish to write them to members for the city council, encouraging them to be wise and fair-minded leaders.

Learning About the Subject of a Biography

Before children can begin to write about a biographical subject, they need to learn something about that person's life. Let us be clear, however, that the learning sequence is not read, then write. Rather, it is write a little, drawing on prior experience, and then find out a little by reading, viewing a film, or listening to taped speeches. Write some, learn a little more, write some more, and so on. *Teachers do not have to provide all the facts before asking students to think.* The advice instead is to integrate data gathering and reflection; the revision process is used to correct prior errors as the writing and learning proceed. The teacher should concentrate student attention on the higher-order task, in this case, production of the biography, which in turn motivates gathering facts about the subject and interpreting his or her life.

Accordingly, students begin learning about the subject, such as Sojourner Truth, by finding out a little something about her. Perhaps the teacher begins by reading aloud for just 20 minutes from Jeri Ferris's book, concentrating on the beginning of the story when Truth is taken from her mother and sold to Mr. Neely at the age of nine. Then the teacher asks the children to discuss this passage—the idea of buying and selling persons, in this case, a child. He asks them to imagine the feelings of Belle on the auction block and the feelings of her mother and father. He may ask them what they have learned elsewhere about the enslavement of people. Perhaps some of them will talk about the Jews in Egypt in biblical times. Some may have seen the movie about Spartacus. Some children may know quite a bit about the capture and subsequent ownership of Africans through books they have read or lessons they have had in prior grades or in church. The discussion will provide the teacher with diagnostic information about children's current knowledge of slavery while activating the students' prior knowledge.

Now the teacher can ask students to bring out their journals and begin to write. He may ask them to write about the same things he previously asked them to talk about, which should be the easiest for them. Then he might ask them to predict what will happen to Truth in her new master's home. This should make them want to gather more information. Where will they get it?

The teacher knows that Truth's life with Mr. Neely is documented in the textbook. So, the next day, he has children take out their journals to remind themselves of the predictions they wrote yesterday. Then they are given 20 minutes to read the pertinent section in the text and return to their journal to write what really happened. Next, the teacher turns student attention to the map of the Northeast in the textbook and, based on clues given in the passage read aloud yesterday and the text passage today, helps them to find the state where Truth first was bought and sold (New York). In their journals, he has them enter the date and sketch a map of New York under the title, "Where Sojourner Truth's Story Begins."

Now that they know where the story began (the geographic theme *location*), students are helped to get a feel for New York (the geographic theme *place*). Their teacher has them go to their cooperative teams and, working with the textbook, answer these questions:

1. What states, countries, and bodies of water border New York?
2. Is the geography of New York all the same, or are there different landforms? If there are, what are they?
3. If Truth were able to fly away from the Neely farm, which route would have the fewest mountains to fly over?

The teacher then tells students to sketch all of this on a blank outline map of New York, which he has distributed, including a legend so readers can understand their symbols. He then has them examine one another's maps, and asks them to create a second draft on a new blank handout. (The revision process applies to map writing every bit as much as it does to other kinds of writing.)

The next day, the teacher reads aloud Virginia Hamilton's retelling of the folktale *The People Could Fly*. A wonderfully hopeful tale, though at the same time tragic, it tells of enslaved people literally flying from bondage to freedom:

> They say the people could fly. Say that long ago in Africa, some of the people knew magic. And they would walk up on the air like climbin' up on a gate. And they flew like blackbirds over the fields.[12]

But when the people were captured for slavery, we learn in the tale, they shed their wings. The slave ships were too crowded for wings. A few, however, kept the power. "Toby" did, and he used it to help the others escape. One day Sarah was hoeing and chopping as fast as she could, a hungry baby on her back, but the baby "started up bawling too loud." The Overseer hollered at Sarah to keep the baby quiet, but Sarah fell under the babe's weight and her own weakness. The Overseer began to whip her. "Get up, you black cow," he called. Sarah looked to Toby: "Now, before it's too late," she panted. "Now." Toby raised his arms and whispered the magic words to her. "Kum . . . yali, kum buba tambe."

> Sarah lifted one foot on the air. Then the other. She flew clumsily at first, with the child now held tightly in her arms. Then she felt the magic, the African mystery. Say she rose just as free as a bird. As light as a feather.[13]

Afterward, students return to their journals to reflect on this new material. The teacher continues over the next two or three weeks to read aloud from biographies and other accounts of Sojourner Truth, as well as from related stories and reference material. Student committees are sent to the library to gather data on people, places, events, and issues raised in the teacher's readings that students want to find out more about. The teacher also assembles some material for the students to read themselves—material in the textbook on Lincoln's decision to free the slaves and material on influential abolitionists: Frederick Douglass, who escaped from slavery in the South; William Lloyd Garrison, who published *The Liberator,* an abolitionist newspaper; and the Grimké sisters, Angelina and Sarah, who moved north after having been raised with captive Africans on a South Carolina plantation. This information helps to elaborate the children's understanding of Sojourner's life, as well as her civic missions, and should lead to their producing much stronger, richer biographies.

For this reason, information on the women's movement of the 1800s also needs to be gathered, such as material on the Seneca Falls Convention convened by Lucretia Mott and Elizabeth Cady Stanton in 1848. This is the same movement Sojourner Truth jolted with her "Ain't I a Woman?" speech, delivered three years later at a second women's rights convention.

The setting for all this information needs also to be grasped; consequently, students should study the geography of New York, Ohio, and Michigan—the three states where Truth spent much time working, speaking, and living. In this way, students learn about the subject of their biography and gradually piece together in their minds a model of Truth's life and times.

Setting Priorities

After several weeks of reading, writing, and mapping their biographical subject's life, children are ready to reflect on this life and its times and places and to select key events. A few of these events will become the focal points of the chapters in the book students will write together. The following procedure is recommended.[14]

1. *Opening.* The teacher announces that today the class will begin to pull together all they have learned about the person and informs students of what is to come.

2. *Brainstorming.* The teacher puts students in buzz groups to brainstorm all the events in the subject's life that they found interesting, all the events they believe were pivotal in the subject's life, all the events they figure made the subject the most and least proud, and so on. The point here is to get a long list of varied events in the subject's life. Here are just a few of the events in Sojourner Truth's life that students have suggested.

   - The time she was separated from her mother
   - The second time she was sold
   - The third time she was sold
   - Confronting Mr. Dumont
   - Rescued by Quakers
   - Names herself Sojourner Truth
   - "Ain't I a Woman?" speech
   - Meeting President Lincoln
   - Working as a nurse in Washington, D.C.
   - Confronting the trolley conductor
   - Meetings with Garrison and Douglass

   When the brainstorming slows, the teacher has the buzz groups share their lists so that a whole-class list can be put on butcher paper or smart board. Students might then take a break—go to recess, clean the room, do something physically active. When they return, they open their journals and search for other events to add to the list. They come up with more:

   - Being born in captivity
   - Coping with racism throughout her life
   - Speaking out for women's rights
   - Becoming an abolitionist
   - Living in New York
   - Traveling by buggy in Ohio

3. *Selecting.* The class is now asked to select four or five of the key events brainstormed earlier. These might be the four events that interested students the most, or the teacher might direct them to use other criteria. For example, if the teacher previously has worked with children on constructing and interpreting time lines, he or she might have them divide Sojourner's life into four equal segments and choose one event from each segment. Or, the teacher might have them choose one event in each of several categories that make particular sense with the person being studied. In the case of Sojourner Truth, these categories might be life in slavery, meetings with remarkable people, and life as an abolitionist. Still another criterion would have students select events that are turning points—pivotal events. *The point is that they must make selections and set priorities.* This is what every historian has to do. "No historian tries to write a 'complete' account and no one would have time to read one," observe Linda Levstik and Keith Barton.[15] Children, who are beginning historians and beginning writers, definitely should not try to do more than an experienced writer-historian would attempt.

Once the key events have been selected, the children are placed in cooperative groups of four or five members. Each group is directed to divide the events among themselves, each choosing one event. Dividing the events—and thus the labor—is crucial to the upcoming task: producing an original biography.

Writing and Illustrating

The students are now ready to write and illustrate a biography of their subject. Each cooperative group will produce a biography on the same subject, Sojourner Truth. Some teachers have each group use the same biography title, "The Life and Times of (Sojourner Truth)." Others let each group create its own variation on this title.

Each person on the team is responsible for one chapter. The chapter's topic is the key event selected before. If the teacher wishes, he or she can use the cooperative groupwork technique called Jigsaw (see Chapter 11). One member of each small group is working on the same key event as one child on each of the other groups; consequently, these children can meet together to work on their chapter, discussing, sharing, and revising one another's drafts. Thus, the book may shape up like this:

Title: The Courage and Conviction of Sojourner Truth

Chapter 1: "Sold for 50 Dollars!"

Chapter 2: "New Name, New Life"

Chapter 3: "Ain't I a Woman?"

Chapter 4: "The Trolley Incident"

About the Authors

Bibliography

The child on each team who is responsible for Chapter 1 joins with other children from other teams also working on "Sold for 50 Dollars!" Meanwhile, the child on each team responsible for Chapter 2 joins with the other 2s, and so on. These are *expert groups.* Together they discuss what they will write and draw, read one another's drafts, and provide feedback.

This is advisable with younger children who are just beginning to write early versions of paragraphs; the group support is helpful, and the teacher can more easily monitor and coach the four expert groups than every child in the room writing on a different topic.

Whether the teacher uses the Jigsaw technique or not, the children's work has two parts: they write a description of the key event for which they are responsible, and they draw an accompanying illustration. The least experienced writers may produce only a one- or two-paragraph description and may fit their illustration on the same page. The teacher may press more experienced writers, however, to produce a two- or three-page description. The illustration is embedded in the text somewhere, as in published biographies. Skillful teachers are able to boost their children's confidence about both writing and drawing by encouraging them to "just get started, get something on paper, pull something together from your journal, whatever; we'll go back and polish it later." (Teachers and children who play the board game *Pictionary* understand that illustrating is very different from producing realistic drawings. Virtually anyone can illustrate.)

Each team thus produces the rudiments of a biography: a title and four chapters. But real biographies have more, and so should these. The following parts of a book make a more complete biography, and even the youngest children generally can do them all:

Title Page

Title plus complete publication information, for example, *The Life and Times of Sojourner Truth* (see Figure 13–2).

Foreword

Written by someone other than the four authors, for example, a parent, another teacher, a school board member, a bus driver. Instruct the Foreword writer to write no more than one page and to address two matters:

1. Tell readers some ways you feel you can relate personally to the person about whom the biography was written.
2. Tell readers something about the book.

Introduction with Time Line and Map

The introduction should contain a brief message to readers telling them the subject of the book. Who is the subject? Where and when did he or she live? What, in a nutshell, did he or she do? Why? It is also considerate to tell readers the topic of each chapter. A helpful way to portray the *when* is to sketch a time line of the subject's life. The *where* should be illustrated with a map, physical, political, or both, with a legend to help readers understand the symbols.

Chapters 1–4

Each chapter needs a title and author name. Its body is a written description of a key event in the subject's life, with an illustration that captures the key event.

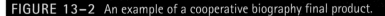

FIGURE 13–2 An example of a cooperative biography final product.

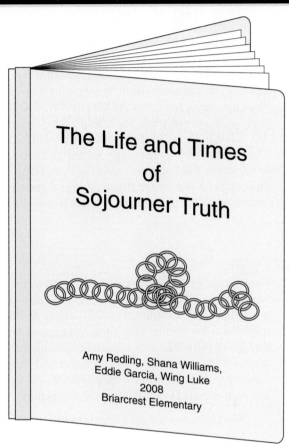

About the Authors' Page

Ask each child to write a sentence or paragraph about himself or herself. The teacher might ask each group to decide how long the author statement should be. Children can be prompted to tell readers their full name, the name of the city or town where they live, their age, and something they like to do:

> Wing Luke lives in Denver, Colorado, with his family. He is 9 years old and loves to play soccer. He wrote Chapter 4, "The Trolley Incident."

Bibliography

At whatever level of sophistication the teacher has taught and expects to see, students should list the resources they have used to develop their section of the biography.

Dealing with Bias

Students in the upper elementary and middle school grades need to begin to work earnestly on the sixth learning objective stated earlier: Students will learn how to make sense of competing accounts of a person or event and compose a fair-minded account. In preparation to *write* a biography, students will have *read* several, and this provides a good opportunity to compare how different biographers portray the same person and events. Students can be helped to do this comparison by creating a data-retrieval chart listing the multiple biographies they have read down the left and dimensions for comparison across the top. In their study of Sojourner Truth, for example, students may have to complete a chart such as the one shown in Figure 13–3 to compare different biographers' work on the same subject. Here is an opportunity to encourage children to attend not simply to the beauty of illustrations or the power of narrative, but also to *evidence* (What facts does the author share with readers?), *focus* (What is the author attending to and ignoring?), and *goal* (Is the biography more an inquiry or an act of admiration—a work of exposition or a paean?).

Concluding the Project

Time should be set aside for drawing the biography project to a close after the books have been completed. The biographies need to be copied so that one can be placed in each child's portfolio. A self-assessment checklist, similar to the one shown in Figure 7–11 (Chapter 7), might be completed by each child and clipped to his or her copy. Details concerning the delivery of the books to the audience identified at the beginning of the project need to be discussed. A committee could be appointed for this purpose. A concluding discussion focusing on the objectives of the project should follow. Focus questions such as the following, each matched to an objective, will be helpful:

1. What have you learned about how history shaped Sojourner Truth's (or name of other person studied) life, and about how her life shaped the history into which the next generation was born?
2. What have you learned about writing?

FIGURE 13–3 Comparing biographies for bias.

	Evidence	Focus	Goal
Ferris, *Walking the Road to Freedom*			
Claflin, *Sojourner Truth and the Struggle for Freedom*			
McKissack, *Sojourner Truth, Ain't I a Woman?*			

3. What is a biography? Whom would you like to read about next?
4. At which cooperative skill do you excel?
5. What have you learned about locating resources in the library?
6. What was difficult about writing a fair-minded account?
7. How would you describe a time line to a younger student?

Summing Up: The Changing Concept of Literacy

Biography writing applies literacy instruction and practice to the social studies curriculum. By embedding literacy instruction in social studies content and cooperative groupwork, the teacher creates the kind of social context that can support in-depth learning. Reading comprehension and writing instruction become much more than plodding through new vocabulary and learning sentences and paragraphs in a vacuum; literacy comes to mean problem solving, competing interpretations, conversation, provocation, writing, and rewriting to find out what one thinks is true and what one believes ought to be done, and experimenting with new possibilities that exist now only in the imagination. This is high literacy.

Reading and writing are processes—more precisely, *crafts*—that evolve through trial, error, instruction, and support from those more accomplished. This process-oriented notion of literacy learning is different from what researchers told us only a generation ago.[16] Then, it was quite common to define literacy as a finished product: you either had it or you didn't; you were literate or illiterate (see Figure 13–4).

This emphasis on process is changing the way skillful teachers orchestrate literacy instruction. They understand that an individual's reading and writing skills grow and change over time. And, they understand that any child's literacy development depends on that child's social context—his or her literacy community. All of us belong to one sort of discourse community or another, and that membership socializes us into one or more patterns of using our minds—of reading, writing, and talking.[17]

The biographical approach is only one way to enrich history and literacy instruction all at once, but it is a feasible and powerful one—feasible meaning that it is doable: Busy teachers and underprepared students can accomplish this. And powerful because it introduces students to a literacy community that for most of them (and us) is novel: the community of biography writers. The noted biographer Milton Meltzer observed that the biography

---

FIGURE 13–4 Literacy research emphases, then and now.

Early Research Emphasis	Current Research Emphasis
Reading and writing instruction are separated.	Reading and writing instruction are integrated.
Both are separated from content learning.	Both are developed within content learning.
Reading and writing are fixed abilities that, like muscles, are the same everywhere.	Reading and writing ability evolves like a craft and mirrors the local literacy community.
Reading and writing are finished products.	Reading and writing are complex processes.

approach is a vehicle for developing children's natural curiosity about people and the world around them to the point where they themselves investigate a particular life and, through the artful use of language, tell that human story to others.[18]

EXAMPLE 2: UNDERSTANDING LIVING THINGS

We turn to a second example of curriculum integration. Now, two subject areas are fused together because the construction of a particular "big idea"—a *generalization*—requires it. The idea in the following example is that *living things are interdependent.* Put differently, and narrowing the focus, *the decisions made by human beings influence the survival of other living things.*

A generalization is defined as a big idea that meaningfully links two or more smaller ideas: concepts. The main concepts we address in the unit that is presented here are *decision making, living things,* what living things need for *survival,* and the *scientific method (inquiry).* Both the generalization and the concepts that compose it are made stronger by reference to subject matter that is conventionally found in the science curriculum and the social studies curriculum. These subject matters are fused in this unit so that the big idea can be developed.

This unit is part of an integrated social studies–science curriculum called "Explore."[19] It is a K–6 program. Accordingly, there are many units like the one featured here—similar, that is, in the way that subject matters are fused to help children build a powerful idea. "Explore" was developed by curriculum specialists and teachers working in the Northglenn, Colorado schools, along with Sydelle Seiger-Ehrenberg, a renowned curriculum planner in the Hilda Taba tradition[20] and a specialist in concept formation. Concept formation, recall, is one of the three "great" teaching strategies featured in Chapter 9. Working with Seiger-Ehrenberg was elementary school principal, Dr. Pat Willsey. The two believed that integrated units of this kind could help children form complex ideas by engaging them in higher-order thinking. Without higher-order thinking, children would not be able to integrate the concepts and thereby construct the big generalization.

Planning a Fusion Unit: Ingredients and Procedure

Teachers who wish to plan a unit that fuses together two subject areas will find this unit from "Explore" a helpful model. Notice that it:

- Sets high expectations for achievement
- Engages students in *inquiry* and *concept formation* so that subject matter and higher-order thinking are integrated
- Provides assessments that are challenging and geared to what was taught
- Incorporates citizenship education: decision making, values, and community action
- Expects children to use the textbook as a data source
- Includes carefully planned focus and follow-up questions
- Fuses important material from two subject areas to help children construct a powerful and unifying idea

When a field trip, such as this one to a park, is placed inside an inquiry unit, such as *Explore*, the students are not merely visiting the park, they are gathering data and testing hypotheses. *(Anthony Magnacca/Merrill)*

The procedure for planning a fusion unit is not etched in stone. What follows is a very basic procedure that should help teachers get started. The planning form shown in Figure 8–3 (Chapter 8) may be helpful.

1. *Identify a unifying concept or generalization that is important and powerful.* "Kites are colorful and ride the wind" is a unifying generalization that could potentially integrate science (aerodynamics) and social studies (production, consumption, and distribution), but it probably is not important or powerful enough to warrant much school time. The prior chapters of this book, the work of curriculum standards committees, and teachers' own subject matter expertise will suggest generalizations that are critically important for children to develop. In the following unit example, the unifying generalization is *The decisions made by human beings influence the survival of other living things.*

2. *Identify the component concepts.* The teacher needs to examine the unifying generalization and identify the concepts that compose it. For example, in the following unit, the key concepts are *decision making, living things,* and *survival.* Another key concept is the *scientific method (inquiry process)* because this is how children will build the unifying idea.

3. *Plan a sequence of learning activities that will help children construct the unifying generalization.* Each lesson plan should have an objective and a focus question that anchor the activity to the overall unit goal, which is to help children build the generalization. For example, in the following unit, the objective and focus question are given at the beginning of each of the four lessons.

4. *Select teaching strategies that will help children achieve lesson objectives.* Concepts are sure to be the focus of one or more lessons because generalizations are composed of concepts. Therefore, one or more concept-teaching strategies will be relevant (see Chapter 9). Likewise, because the scientific method is featured, strategies for teaching children to inquire scientifically will be relevant (again, see Chapter 9). In the following unit, the concept-formation and inquiry strategies are the chief, though not the sole, teaching strategies.

What follows are the four lesson plans in Unit 1 of the third-grade "Explore" curriculum.

1. The first lesson introduces children to the scientific way of learning, that is, the inquiry method. Note that the assessment asks children to classify a number of activities, selecting the ones that represent the *scientific method.*
2. The second lesson helps children form the concept *living things.* Note the use of the data-retrieval chart, the concept-formation procedure, and classifying.
3. The third lesson helps children form the concept *survival needs of living things.* Again, a data-retrieval chart and the concept-formation procedure are deployed.
4. The fourth develops the decision-making and social action component of the unit. Students become aware of and committed to individual and group actions that help living things meet their needs and reach their potential.

The overall desired result is that children will construct an initial understanding of this unifying idea: *The decisions made by human beings influence the survival of other living things.*

UNDERSTANDING THE TWO EXAMPLES

Let us take some time to identify similarities and differences between these two exemplary units. The principal similarity, of course, is that each brings together knowledge and skills conventionally found in separate school subjects. In the cooperative biography unit, we saw language arts material (e.g., the genre of biography, the writing process) brought to the service of social studies objectives (e.g., learning to *do* history; understanding that the way people lead their lives shapes the history into which the next generation is born). In the Explore unit, we saw science material (e.g., the concept *living things;* the scientific method or *inquiry*) fused with social studies material (the concept *decision making*); the scientific method or *inquiry.*

Additional similarities are the very attributes that we have identified as the key ingredients for powerful curriculum integration:

- Purpose is paramount (curriculum integration is not treated as an end in itself but a means to help students achieve worthy learning objectives).
- Highly important subject matter is at the heart of the unit (the learnings are not trivial).
- Things that need to be kept separate for clarity's sake are kept separate (Dewey's "great bad" is avoided).

There also are some interesting differences. Obviously, the content of the two examples is different—the life and times of Sojourner Truth in the one and the impact of human beings on other living things in the other. *But the two examples also represent different approaches*

EXPLORE: UNIT 1, LESSON 1: WHAT IS THE SCIENTIFIC WAY OF LEARNING?

Grades	3–6
NCSS Standards	2 (time, continuity, and change) and 8 (science, technology, and society)
Objective	Students will become aware of the general inquiry procedure they will be following this year to study science and social studies topics.
Focus Question	What is the scientific way of learning?
Lesson Development	Students are told that this year they will be studying science and social studies "as if all of you were scientists." They are then placed in pairs to discuss the question, "From what you know, what does it mean to be a 'scientist'? What does a scientist do?"

As students share their responses, the teacher often poses *verification* questions, especially the central question of science, "How do you know that's true?" This becomes an essential question throughout the unit. Eventually, the teacher presents the following four-step procedure on a chart.

The Scientific Way of Learning

Step 1—Question

Step 2—Hypothesize, Predict

Step 3—Investigate

Step 4—Analyze/Evaluate Data, Conclude

The teacher then puts the following list on the board:

Some Things Scientists Investigate

What plants need to grow
What the stars and planets are made of
How people in communities get along with each other
What the dinosaurs looked like
How people lived long ago
How people live now
What happens when you mix certain chemicals
How we know about weather and climate

After making sure that the class understands each item on the list, the teacher asks students what they know about each topic *as a result of scientists' investigations.*

The teacher then asks the students to go back over the list and name the kind of scientist that investigates some of these things. For example, "What do people call a scientist who investigates stars and planets? Life in human communities? How people lived long ago? Dinosaurs?" It is not important that students learn all the names of scientists, but that they realize, first, that there are different types of scientists, and, second, that social studies stems from the work of *social* scientists.

To review, the teacher then says, "As you study science and social studies this year, you will be working just like the scientists we have been talking about. What does that mean? What will you be doing? What are the four things we said all scientists do?"

Assessment 1   The teacher displays a list of activities related to airplanes and says to students: "Suppose we were going to study airplanes and how they fly, and I told you that you would be working like scientists. Which of the things on this list would you expect to be doing?"

1. Make up a story about airplanes.
2. Find some facts about airplanes and how they fly.
3. Ask questions about airplanes and how they fly.
4. Draw a picture of an airplane.
5. Describe a trip you took on an airplane.
6. Try to think of possible answers to your questions about airplanes and how they fly.
7. Build a model of an airport.
8. Keep looking for more facts about airplanes to see if the answers to your questions are right.

Assessment 2   The teacher reviews the four-step procedure and then shows students a rock, a leaf, a shell, or a similar item, giving them this task: "Suppose you were a scientist and had never seen anything like this before. What would you do to investigate it? Be prepared to tell us what you would do, how, and why."

---

to curriculum integration. The essence of the first approach, exemplified in the cooperative biography unit, is that one subject, here language arts, is brought to the service of social studies objectives. The essence of the second approach, exemplified in the Explore unit, is that two subjects are fused, here science and social studies, so that a big, overarching idea—a generalization—can be constructed. In the first approach, one subject is in a supporting role: language arts supporting social studies. In the second approach, two subjects are supporting one another. They are fused together so that a bigger idea can be developed. We could call the two approaches to curriculum integration *supportive* (or assisted) integration and *fusion* (or synthetic) integration.

Supportive integration is by far the most common kind of curriculum integration. One or more objectives in one subject area are achieved thanks to material borrowed from another. Usually, this means that reading and writing skills are brought to the service of social studies goals. Skillful teachers of social studies link literacy instruction to social studies goals and in this way give literacy skills purpose and meaning while helping to achieve social studies goals. Children cannot read reading or write writing, after all; reading and writing are means to many ends, but they are not ends themselves. Rather, they are used to help achieve valued content goals.

Examples of the supportive approach can be found throughout this text. Turn back, please, to the Table of Contents and find the list of Lesson Plans. Turn to Plans 1–19 and locate the "Integration" heading at the end of the plans. There you will find examples of supportive integration. Most often, language arts (literature in particular) is used to enrich one or more social studies objectives. Sometimes it is art or music that is helping; at other times it is science or mathematics. But *helping* is the role. When you look at the objectives at the beginning of these lesson plans, you will see that they are social studies objectives.

Here are additional examples of this supportive role.

- Use the concepts *plot* and *character* from children's literature to better understand a social event, such as the American Revolution, the Underground Railroad, the Civil Rights movement, or a current event in the children's hometown.
- Use *art* to enrich social studies. For example, historical paintings along with concepts drawn from the fine arts can be used to study major events in American history, such as Howard Chandler Christy's depiction of the signing of the

Lesson Plan
21

EXPLORE: UNIT 1, LESSON 2: WHAT IS TRUE OF ALL LIVING THINGS?

Grades 3–6

NCSS Standards 3 (people, places, and environments) and 8 (science, technology, and society)

Objective Students will develop the concept *living things* in terms of both the characteristics common to all living things and those that distinguish living things from nonliving things.

Focus Question What is true of all living things that distinguishes them from nonliving things?

Lesson Development

1. *Question.* The teacher introduces the lesson: "First we are going to study living things and how they are alike. Since we're going to work as scientists, what is the first thing we need to do to study living things?" The teacher then reviews the chart, "The Scientific Way of Learning," now focusing on the topic "Living Things and How They Are Alike."

2. *Hypothesize.* Student attention is focused on the question, "How do we know whether something is or is not alive?" The teacher points to the second step in the four-step procedure and asks students what they need to do after they have asked a question: "Come up with possible answers." Then the teacher repeats the question, and students hypothesize. The teacher elicits responses, helping students to clarify what they mean, and writes them on a chart:

   We think something is alive if it has these characteristics: _____

   The teacher emphasizes that students should give the information they think is true. Later they will investigate to find out which of their ideas are correct. After a few characteristics are placed on the chart, students work in pairs to come up with additional responses.

3. *Investigate.* The teacher helps children move to Step 3 of the scientific procedure: "As scientists, what is our next step?" Students should respond that they need to investigate, that is, find new information to check the accuracy of what they have put on the chart and find out what else belongs on it. They may ask, "How can we find the kind of information we need?" At this point, "Explore" takes students through a detailed introduction to their textbooks and other references where relevant information might be found. This amounts to teaching students how to use their textbooks as an information source (see Chapter 12).

   Once students are familiar with information sources, they are ready to investigate, to test the characteristics they have listed on their charts. "Explore" uses the concept-formation strategy discussed in Chapter 9. The teacher says, "To test our ideas, let's investigate several living things and find out whether the things we have listed are true of all of them." Each child is given a data-retrieval chart (see Figure 13–5).

   In pairs, using the reference books they just studied, students gather the information each question requires for each living thing on the chart. Pairs then report their work to the whole class, and the teacher uses a class-size retrieval chart to record their work. A transparency of the student chart placed on an overhead projector works well.

4. *Analyze data/conclude.* The teacher guides students through the concept-formation strategy as a way of making sense of all the data by drawing it together into a concept. "Let's see what all this information tells us about all living things. First, what do you see is true of some living things but not of others?" Here the teacher is eliciting differences among the examples. Then students are directed to focus on similarities. "What do you find is true of all living things, regardless of what kind?" After this, students are asked to compose a conclusion, or summary.

   We know something is a living thing if it: _____.

Writing a Conclusion Students write a paragraph explaining what living things are, giving examples, and telling how they differ from nonliving things.

FIGURE 13–5 Data-retrieval chart: Living Things.

LIVING THINGS

List from chart	Bird	Tree	Fish	Cactus	Person
Moves? How?					
Grows? For how long?					
Changes? In what ways?					
Reproduces others like self?					
Needs food? What kind? From where?					
Needs air?					
Needs water?					

Classifying Continuing the fourth step in "The Scientific Way of Learning," students are helped to push their understanding of the concept still further. The teacher has them test their conclusion and at the same time identify the characteristics that distinguish living from nonliving things by having students inspect a nonliving thing—a cloud, an airplane, popcorn, fire, or a balloon.

The teacher says, "Let's consider something nonliving, like a cloud. What answers do we get to each question on our chart when we ask it about a cloud?" Later, "Based on the information we now have about a cloud, what about it could make it *seem* like a living thing?" and, "What is true of all living things that is not true of a cloud and proves it is not a living thing even if it moves?" This classifying activity is repeated with an airplane, popcorn, fire, and a balloon.

Labeling Students should be introduced to the term scientists use as a synonym for a living thing: organism.

Review Students are helped to review how they learned what distinguishes living from nonliving things.

Assessment The teacher prepares a bulletin board with two sections, one marked "Living Things," the other "Nonliving Things." Students are directed to bring in a magazine picture or drawing of something that belongs in each section. Each student should be prepared to tell the class the characteristics that make each item belong to one category or another.

EXPLORE: UNIT 1, LESSON 3: WHAT DO ALL LIVING THINGS NEED TO SURVIVE?

Grades	3–6
NCSS Standards	3 (people, places, and environments) and 8 (science, technology, and society)
Objective	Students will develop the concept *needs of living things*.
Focus Question	What do all living things need to survive and develop as they should?

Lesson Development

Now that the children have developed the concept *living things*, this next lesson is designed to help them build another idea at the heart of the unit generalization: *the needs of living things*. Again, the concept-formation strategy and a data-retrieval chart are used. The same living things are listed across the top of the chart as in the prior lesson (see Figure 13–6), but point out to students that the questions running down the left side of the chart have changed.

Numerous library resources and the science and social studies textbooks are used by children to gather this information. Using the concept-formation strategy, the teacher helps them draw all the data together into a concept. "Let's see what all this information tells us about the needs of all living things. First, what do some living things need but others do not?" Here the teacher is eliciting differences among the examples. Then students are directed to focus on similarities. "What do you find that all living things need, regardless of what kind?" After this, students are asked to compose a conclusion, or summary:

We know that all living things need: _____.

The teacher helps them conclude that the needs of living things include

- Proper nutrition
- Clean air and water
- Sufficient light and warmth
- Protection from enemies and disease
- Opportunity for the organism to reach its potential

Writing a Conclusion

Students write a paragraph explaining what the needs of living things are, giving examples.

Assessment

The teacher and class listen as several students read their conclusions aloud. The teacher clarifies and asks for revisions as needed.

FIGURE 13–6 Data-retrieval chart: Needs of Living Things.

NEEDS OF LIVING THINGS

Question	Bird	Tree	Fish	Cactus	Person
1. Does the organism need *food* to live? What kind? Where and how does it get its food?					
2. Does the organism need *water* to live? What has to be true of the water? Where and how does it get water?					
3. Does the organism need *air* to live? What has to be true of the air? Where does it get air?					
4. Where does the organism usually *live?* What other organisms live there? How do the organisms live together?					
5. What can *harm* the organism? How does the organism stay safe from harm and disease?					
6. What is the organism *able to do?* What sometimes prevents the organism from doing this? What helps the organism do all that it is able to do?					

EXPLORE: UNIT 1, LESSON 4: WHAT DECISIONS DO PEOPLE HAVE TO MAKE?

Grades 3–6

NCSS Standards 8 (science, technology, and society) and 10 (civic ideals and practices)

Objective Students will develop an awareness of and commitment to individual and group action that ensures that living things can meet their needs for survival and development.

Focus Question What decisions and plans do people have to make to see to it that living things have what they need to survive and develop?

This lesson moves children from conceptualizing the attributes of living things (Lesson Plan 21) and what they need to thrive (Lesson Plan 22) to *human action on their behalf*.

Lesson Development There are two learning activities in this lesson.

The first activity has students consider cases where threatening conditions are putting living things at risk by making it difficult or impossible for them to get what they need. Students are then helped to suggest courses of action that might improve the situation.

Sample situations:

1. There has been a very heavy snowfall. All the food and water for birds and deer have been covered with snow for several days, and the animals can't get to any.

2. It has not rained for weeks. The farmers are worried because their crops are not getting enough water.

3. People who picnic near the lake have been throwing junk into it for years. Much of this junk is harmful to the fish, insects, birds, and plants that live in or near the lake.

Students discuss these situations in small groups of three and recommend courses of action. Two focus questions guide their work on each case:

1. Which living things would have trouble surviving if no one did anything to change the situation? Explain why they would have trouble surviving.

2. What could people like you and me do so that the living things in this situation could survive? Explain how each suggestion would help the living things survive.

The second learning activity has children gather data on situations in which the needs of living things are threatened *and* in which people took specific actions that helped living things meet their needs. The teacher assembles reading materials about such people and invites them to class from the community. After gathering and recording data about them, students use the concept-formation strategy to compare and contrast these people and their specific actions. Finally, they return to the courses of action they suggested in the first part of the lesson, revising and adding ideas for action based on the information they gathered about real situations.

Assessment The children make posters summing up what they have learned. Each poster addresses three questions, and children are encouraged to address them however they want.

1. What are living things?

2. What do living things need?

3. What have humans done to help other living things meet their needs?

U.S. Constitution or Jacob Lawrence's paintings of the migration of African Americans from the south to the north after World War I (see Lawrence's *The Great Migration: An American Story*, 1995).

- Use concepts and skills from *mathematics*, such as proportions to make the 3-D paper pie graphs that display social phenomena, as shown in Chapter 5.

Fusion integration can be a somewhat more ambitious approach because two or more subject matters are joined together—synthesized—in such a way that a *new, unified idea can be formed.* There is no sense, as in the supportive model, that subject matter A is simply helping subject matter B; rather, A and B are fused to produce something new: C. C is a powerful idea (usually a *generalization*) that requires for its proper development information from more than one subject area. *Living things,* for example, is an idea that is strengthened when it includes human beings as well as what the science curriculum calls flora and fauna (plants and animals). Similarly, the concept *communities* is strengthened when comprising not only human communities around the world—Tokyo, Rome, and the children's home town, for example—but plant and animal communities as well, such as old-growth forests, ant colonies, and schools of fish, even the communities of planets called solar systems and the communities of stars called galaxies.

Generalizations are bigger and more complex ideas than concepts. Generalizations, as we have seen, are two or more concepts combined into a meaningful statement. The generalization *the decisions of human beings influence the survival of other living things* links several concepts together: decisions, human beings, influence, survival, and living things. Because generalizations are relationships between two or more concepts, they are summarizing statements that have wide applicability. Generalizations are *generally* true: Scientific investigation has proven that in most cases the statement is not contradicted by the facts. To learn a generalization, teachers and students often have to draw information and concepts from more than one subject. That was clearly the case with the generalization featured in the Explore unit: *The decisions of human beings influence the survival of other living things.*

Another terrific example of the fusion approach concerns the voyages of Columbus. A unified understanding of these voyages can help children understand this historic event as a turning point in human *and planetary* history that is more complex and important than the story of a single explorer and his brave and bloody conquests. The exchange of plant life, animal life, and diseases between the Eastern and Western Hemispheres that resulted from the Columbian expeditions changed the world forever. Cultures and customs were exchanged, to be sure, but so were seed packages (called *biota* by biologists). Smallpox and horses were brought from Europe to America; corn and sugar were taken from America to Europe. "Seeds of Change" is what the Smithsonian Institution called the event, and to appreciate that title one has fuse the social studies and the science content of the event.

As the two fusion examples—living things and seeds of change—show, the objective of the fusion approach is to help children build big, complex ideas that cannot be built adequately without joining together two or more subject areas. The big understanding children are helped to construct is a *unifying whole* that has a character and significance that stretch beyond the sum of its parts.[21]

Still, the fusion approach is not superior to the supportive approach. More is not better. Just because subject areas *can* be integrated is no reason to do so. The joining of subject matters is not even the goal. Rather, as "Explore" illustrates, the goal of the fusion approach is to help children build a unifying idea.

Conclusion

Two exemplary units were presented to show what curriculum integration can do when it is made relevant to curricular goals that are vitally important and empowering for children. Biographies are at the center of the humanities, those academic disciplines that explore the human condition. When children learn to compose biographies themselves, their natural curiosity about people and the places they inhabit can be ignited along with the belief that individuals actually do shape history. As well, they are learning history by doing it. The scientific method, featured in the second example, is at the center of both the natural sciences ("science") and the social sciences ("social studies"); it does not belong more to one than to the other. The "Explore" unit, developed for the third grade, teaches this concept to children while helping them to *apply* it to the study of the interdependence of living things.

With the two approaches to curricular integration presented in this chapter, supportive and fusion integration, teachers have two promising tools with which they can launch integrated units of their own. One is not better than the other. It all depends on the goal at hand, the school curriculum, society's needs, and the teacher's and students' passions.

Discussion Questions and Suggested Activities

Go to My-Education-Lab and select the topic "Government/ Citizenship" then watch the video "Sunnyville" and complete the activity.

1. Look back at the "Reflection" sidebar in the biography section of the chapter and your response to the question asked there. Contrast that to the idea of an entire social studies curriculum being based on the second integrative model, fusion, where all units would be aimed at helping children develop the big, unifying ideas called "generalizations." Brainstorm some problems and possibilities of both suggestions.

2. Design an array of biography book formats. What form could first-graders' books take? How about fifth-graders'?

3. Review the "Explore" unit, then add a fifth lesson plan that follows logically from the four presented.

4. NCSS Standards *Sampler*. Examine the third-grade classroom vignette for standard #8 on page 21 of the standards *Sampler* that accompanies this book. What modifications would it require to fit sensibly into the "Explore unit" presented in this chapter?

Selected References

Alleman, Janet, & Brophy, Jere. (1993, Oct.). Is curriculum integration a boon or a threat to social studies? *Social Education, 57,* 287–291.

Gallavan, Nancy P. (2001). Four lessons that integrate math and social studies. *Social Studies and the Young Learner, 13* (3), 25–28.

Hinde, Elizabeth R. (2005). Revisiting curriculum integration: A fresh look at an old idea. *Social Studies, 96* (3), 105–111.

Lindquist, Tarry, & Selwyn, Douglas. (2000). *Social studies at the center: Integrating kids, content, and literacy.* Portsmouth, NH: Heinemann.

Valencia, Sheila V. & Lipson, Marjorie. (1998). Thematic instruction: A quest for challenging ideas and meaningful learning. In Tafy E. Raphael & Kathryn H. Au (Eds.),

Literature-based instruction: Reshaping the curriculum (pp. 95–122). Norwood, NJ: Christopher Gordon.

Wineburg, Sam, & Grossman, Pamela L. (Eds.). (2000). *Interdisciplinary curriculum: Challenges to implementation.* New York: Teachers College Press.

Zarnowski, Myra. (1990). *Learning with biographies: A reading and writing approach.* Washington, DC: National Council for the Social Studies/National Council of Teachers of English.

Zarnowski, Myra. (2003). *History makers: A questioning approach to reading and writing biographies.* Portsmouth, NJ: Heinemann.

MyEducationLab is a collection of online tools for your success in this course, your licensure exams, and your teaching career. Go to www.myeducationlab.com to utilize these extensive resources including videos from real classrooms, Praxis and licensure preparation, a lesson plan builder, and materials to help you begin your teaching career.

Notes

Chapter 1: Social Studies Education: What and Why

1 National Council for the Social Studies, *Expectations of Excellence: Curriculum Standards for Social Studies* (Washington, DC: Author, 1994), 54–55.

2 National Council for the Social Studies, *Expectations of Excellence*, 3.

3 Some scholars classify history along with the humanities rather than the social sciences because it has so much in common with literature. This makes some sense. But I prefer to place it with the social sciences for two reasons: because its method of inquiry emphasizes argument and evidence, and because historians search for the truth of the matter as opposed to only trying to tell a "good story" (see Chapter 4).

4 Task Force on Standards for Teaching and Learning in the Social Studies, *A Vision of Powerful Teaching and Learning in the Social Studies: Building Social Understanding and Civic Efficacy* (Washington, DC: National Council for the Social Studies, 1992). Reprinted as a supplement to *Expectations of Excellence*, 157.

5 E. D. Hirsch, Jr., *Cultural Literacy: What Every American Needs to Know* (New York: Vintage, 1988).

6 National Council for the Social Studies, *Social Studies Curriculum Planning Resources* (Dubuque, IA: Kendall/Hunt, 1990), 25–29.

7 Herbert J. Walberg and Shiow-Ling Tsai, "Matthew Effects in Education," *Educational Research Quarterly, 20* (1983), 359–373.

8 In 1995, the curriculum standards for the field of history were met with criticism by talk-show hosts and politicians, who charged they were written by a "secret group" of "liberal" and "ultra-feminist" historians. These accusations are unfounded. The history standards are politically middle-of-the-road, and they are charged with being overly conservative by an equal number of critics. For a conservative criticism of these standards, see John Fonte, "The Naive Romanticism of the History Standards," *The Chronicle of Higher Education* (June 9, 1995), A48. For a liberal defense, see Gary B. Nash and Ross E. Dunn, "History Standards and Culture Wars," *Social Education, 59* (January 1995), 5–7.

9 Lynn Olson, "Standards Times 50," *Education Week,* special report (April 12, 1995), 15.

10 Jonathan Kozol, *Savage Inequalities* (New York: HarperPerennial, 1992). See also Gary Orfield's *Schools More Separate: Consequences of a Decade of Resegregation* (Cambridge, MA: Harvard Civil Rights Project, 2001). Resegregation is caused mainly by macroeconomic policies in the United States, such as housing policy, union-busting, corporate welfare, federal minimum wages, and school funding through local property taxes. According to the analysis presented in Jean Anyon's book, *Radical Possibilities* (New York: Routledge, 2005, p. 93), "housing segregation produces the educational segregation of urban Blacks and Latinos into schools where the vast majority of students are poor. Such schools are notoriously underresourced and unsuccessful in promoting high achievement."

11 Claudia Meek, "Classroom Crisis: It's About Time," *Phi Delta Kappan, 84* (8) (April 2003), 593.

12 Center on Education Policy, *NCLB: Narrowing the Curriculum?* (Washington, DC: Author, 2005).

13 *Education Week,* May 16, 2001, pp. 1, 2. (Retrieved from *www.edweek.org* on June 15, 2007.)

14 National Academies of Science, Engineering, and Medicine. *Rising Above the Gathering Storm: Energizing and Employing America for a Brighter Economic Future* (Washington, DC: National Academy Press, 2005).

15 Martin Luther King, Jr., "I Have a Dream" in *A Call to Conscience: The Landmark Speeches of Dr. Martin Luther King, Jr.,* ed. Clayborne Carson and Kris Shepard (New York: Time Warner, 2001), 81–82.

16 For the earlier eras, see Charles W. Knudsen, "What Do Educators Mean by 'Integration'?" *Harvard Educational Review, 7* (1937), 15–26, and *The Integration of Educational Experiences, The 57th Yearbook of the National Society for the Study of Education,* ed. Nelson B. Henry (Chicago: University of Chicago Press, 1958).

17 Howard Gardner, *The Disciplined Mind* (New York: Simon & Schuster, 1999), 219.

18 Courtney B. Cazden, *Classroom Discourse* (Portsmouth, NH: Heinemann, 2001).

Chapter 2: Knowing the Children We Teach

1   National Center for Education Statistics, *The Condition of Education, 2007* (Washington, DC: U.S. Department of Education, 2007); Beth A. Young, *Characteristics of the 100 Largest Public Elementary and Secondary School Districts in the United States: 2000–01* (Washington, DC: National Center for Education Statistics, U.S. Department of Education, 2002).

2   Lisa Delpit, *Other People's Children: Cultural Conflict in the Classroom* (New Press, 1995), 120.

3   Gloria Ladson-Billings, *The Dreamkeepers: Successful Teachers of African American Children* (San Francisco: Jossey-Bass, 1994), 33.

4   Ibid., 31.

5   Lisa Delpit, *Other People's Children.*

6   Christine I. Bennett, *Comprehensive Multicultural Education: Theory and Practice,* 6th ed. (Boston: Allyn & Bacon, 2006), 259.

7   Luis C. Moll et al., "Funds of Knowledge for Teaching: Using a Qualitative Approach to Connect Homes and Classrooms," *Theory into Practice, 31* (2), (1992), 131–141.

8   Geneva Gay, *Culturally Responsive Teaching* (New York: Teachers College Press, 2000), 29.

9   Kathryn H. Au, *Literacy Instruction in Multicultural Settings* (Orlando: Harcourt, 1993), 12–13. And see the excellent "Culturally Responsive Instruction" (Chapter 7) in her new book, *Multicultural Issues and Literacy Achievement* (Mahwah, NJ: Lawrence Erlbaum, 2006).

10 Gloria Ladson-Billings, *The Dreamkeepers,* 19.

11 James A. Banks, *Cultural Diversity and Education: Foundations, Curriculum, and Teaching,* 5th ed. (Boston: Allyn & Bacon, 2006), 217.

12 Peggy McIntosh, "White Privilege: Unpacking the Invisible Knapsack," *Peace and Freedom* (July/August 1989), 10–12.

13 For elaboration on social position and perspective, see Chapter 5 in my book *Teaching Democracy: Unity and Diversity in Social Life* (New York: Teachers College Press, 2003).

14 Howard Gardner, *The Disciplined Mind* (New York: Simon & Schuster, 1999), 188.

15 See Marguerite C. Radencich and Lyn J. McKay, *Flexible Grouping for Literacy in the Elementary Grades* (Boston: Allyn & Bacon, 1995).

16 James M. Jones, *Prejudice and Racism* (New York: McGraw-Hill, 1997), 441.

17 David C. Berliner, "Our Impoverished View of Educational Research," *Teachers College Record, 108* (2006), 951.

18 David Gilbert, *The American Class Structure in an Age of Growing Inequality,* 6th ed. (Belmont, CA: Wadsworth/Thomson, 2003), 20.

19 Carol Mukhopadhyay, Rosemary C. Henze, and Yolanda T. Moses, *How Real Is Race? A Sourcebook on Race, Culture, and Biology* (Lanham, MD: Roman & Littlefield, 2007).

20 See *How the Irish Became White,* by Noel Ignatiev (New York: Routledge, 1995), and *How Jews Became White Folks and What That Says About Race in America,* by Karen Brodkin (New Brunswick, NJ: Rutgers University Press, 1998).

21 American Association of University Women, *Harassment-Free Hallways: How to Stop Sexual Harassment in Schools* (Washington, DC: Author, 2002).

22 Myra Sadker and David Sadker, *Failing at Fairness: How America's Schools Cheat Girls* (New York: Charles Scribner's Sons, 1994), 42.

23 Ibid., 43.

24 American Association of University Women, *Hostile Hallways: Bullying, Teasing, and Sexual Harassment in School* (Washington, DC: Author, 2001).

25 Kimberly S. Palmer, "Let's Talk About Sexual Harassment in Middle School," *Middle Level Learning, 17* (May/June 2003), M2.

26 Barrie Thorne, *Gender Play: Girls and Boys in School* (New Brunswick, NJ: Rutgers University Press, 1993), 111.

27 Stephen J. Thornton, "Heteronormativity in the Social Studies Curriculum," *Social Education, 67* (4) (2003), 226.

28 Quoted in Herbert Grossman, *Special Education in a Diverse Society* (Boston: Allyn & Bacon, 1995), 145.

29 Ibid., 189.

30 For example, Lisa Delpit, *Other People's Children.*

31 Herbert Grossman, *Ending Discrimination in Special Education* (Springfield, IL: C.C. Thomas, 2002), 3–6.

32 Howard Gardner, *Multiple Intelligences: The Theory in Practice* (New York: Basic Books, 1993).

33 Carol Ann Tomlinson, *How to Differentiate Instruction in Mixed-Ability Classrooms,* 2nd ed. (Alexandria, VA: Association for Supervision and Curriculum Development, 2001).

34 Howard Gardner, *Multiple Intelligences,* 9.

35 Howard Gardner, *The Disciplined Mind* (New York: Simon & Schuster, 1999), 188.

36 For thoughtful criticisms of learning styles and multiple intelligences literature, see Steven A. Stahl, "Different Strokes for Different Folks? A Critique of Learning Styles," *American Educator* (Fall 1999), 27–31; and Branton Shearer, "Multiple Intelligences Theory after 20 Years," *Teachers College Record, 106* (2004), 2–16.

Chapter 3: Democratic Citizenship Education

1 This is Michael Walzer's interpretation in *What It Means to Be an American* (New York: Marsilio, 1992), which I develop in my book *Teaching Democracy: Unity and Diversity in Public Life* (New York: Teachers College Press, 2003).

2 Thomas Jefferson, *Notes on the State of Virginia* (New York: Norton, 1954; originally published in 1787), 148.

3 James Baldwin, "A Talk to Teachers," in *Multicultural Literacy,* ed. Rick Simonson and Scott Walker (Saint Paul, MN: Graywolf Press, 1988), 4.

4 Polly Greenberg, "How to Institute Some Simple Democratic Practices Pertaining to Respect, Rights, and Responsibilities in Any Classroom," *Young Children, 47* (July 1992), 10–17.

5 Ethel Sadowsky, "Taking Part: Democracy in the Elementary School," in *Preparing for Citizenship: Teaching Youth to Live Democratically,* ed. Ralph Mosher, Robert A. Kenny, Jr., and Andrew Garrod (Westport, CT: Praeger, 1994), 153.

6 Quoted in Richard J. Ellis, *To the Flag: The Unlikely History of the Pledge of Allegiance* (University Press of Kansas, 2005), 82.

7 Ibid., 137.

8 Martha C. Nussbaum, *For Love of Country* (Boston: Beacon, 2002), 14.

9 In 2002, a federal appeals court ruled the "under God" clause unconstitutional because it violated the separation of church and state. The resulting (and preceding) controversy is nicely examined in Ellis's *To the Flag.*

10 Quoted in Thucydides, *History of the Peloponnesian War,* trans. R. Warner (London: Penguin, 1972), 147.

11 Tarry Lindquist, *Seeing the Whole Through Social Studies* (Portsmouth, NH: Heinemann, 1995), 35.

12 Vivian Gussin Paley, *You Can't Say You Can't Play* (Cambridge, MA: Harvard University Press, 1992), 4.

13 Ibid., 16.

14 Ibid., 21.

15 Ibid., 18–19.

16 Ibid., 63.

17 The seminal work on this was done by Jean Piaget, *The Moral Judgment of the Child* (New York: Free Press, 1965); and then F. Clark Power, Anne Higgins, and Lawrence Kohlberg, *Lawrence Kohlberg's Approach to Moral Education* (New York: Columbia University Press, 1989).

18 For additional details, see David Harris, "Classroom Assessment of Civic Discourse," in *Education for Democracy: Contexts, Curricula, and Assessments,* ed. Walter C. Parker (Greenwich, CT: Information Age, 2002), 211–232.

19 From a speech given May 17, 1957, reprinted as "Give Us the Ballot" in *A Call to Conscience: The Landmark Speeches of Dr. Martin Luther King, Jr.,* ed. Clayborne Carson and Kris Shepard (New York: Warner Books, 2001), 47–56.

20 Quoted in Walter C. Parker, *Teaching Democracy: Unity and Diversity in Public Life* (New York: Teachers College Press, 2003), 85.

21 *The Kids Guide to Social Action: How to Solve the Social Problems You Choose, and Turn Creative Thinking into Positive Action* (Minneapolis, MN: Free Spirit Publishing, 1991), 87.

22 Edward A. Wynne, "The Great Tradition in Education: Transmitting Moral Values," *Educational Leadership, 43* (December 1985/January 1986), 4. The most comprehensive resource book for character education is Thomas Lickona's *Educating for Character* (New York: Bantam, 1991).

23 J. P. Mayer, ed., *Democracy in America,* trans. George Lawrence (Garden City, NY: Anchor Books, 1969), 540.

24 Huston Smith, *The Illustrated World's Religions* (New York: HarperCollins, 1991), 13.

25 Quoted in Chapter 1, "The Roots of Religious Liberty," *Rights of the People* (www.usinfo.state.gov/products/pubs).

Chapter 4: History, Geography, and the Social Sciences

1   Quoted in Charlotte Crabtree, "Returning History to the Elementary Schools," in *Historical Literacy,* ed. Paul Gagnon and the Bradley Commission on History in the Schools (New York: Macmillan, 1989), 176.

2   *National Standards for History for Grades K–4: Expanding Children's World in Time and Space* (Los Angeles: National Center for History in the Schools, 1994), 1.

3   Martin Luther King, Jr., *Stride Toward Freedom* (New York: Harper & Row, 1958), 85.

4   Stewart Brand, *The Clock of the Long Now: Time and Responsibility* (New York: Basic Books, 1999), 2. Visit the website, and read about the 10,000-year clock project: www.longnow.org/projects/clock/.

5   *Technology Tools in the Social Studies Curriculum,* ed. Joseph A. Braun, Jr., Phyllis Fernlund, and Charles S. White (Wilsonville, OR: Franklin, Beedle & Associates, 1998), 93.

6   *U.S. History Framework for the 2006 National Assessment of Educational Progress* (NAEP) (Washington, DC: National Assessment Governing Board), vi–vii.

7   Linda S. Levstik and Keith C. Barton, *Doing History: Investigating with Children in Elementary and Middle Schools,* 2nd ed. (Mahwah, NJ: Lawrence Erlbaum Associates, 2001), 5.

8   Vivian Gussin Paley, *Wally's Stories* (Cambridge, MA: Harvard University Press, 1981), 112.

9   Adapted from Linda S. Levstik and Keith C. Barton, *Doing History,* 111–112.

10 Dava Sobel, *Longitude* (New York: Penguin, 1995), 13.

11 James D. Laney and Mark C. Schug, "Teach Kids Economics and They Will Learn," *Social Studies and the Young Learner, 11* (November/December 1998), 13–17. See also Mark C. Schug and Eric Hagedorn, "The Money Savvy Pig™ Goes to the Big City: Testing the Effectiveness of an Economics Curriculum for Young Children," *The Social Studies, 96* (2005), 268–271.

12 Polly Kellogg, "Ten Chairs of Inequality," in *Rethinking Globalization,* ed. B. Bigelow and B. Peterson (Milwaukee, WI: Rethinking Schools Press, 2002), 115–117.

13 Laney and Schug, note 11, and see John D. Hoge's excellent description of classrooms deeply involved in microsociety programs: "Try Microsociety for Hands-on Citizenship," *Social Studies and the Young Learner, 10* (September/October 1997), 18–21.

14 Adapted from Laney and Schug, note 11, and Marilyn Kourilsky, *Mini-Society: Experiencing Real-World Economics in the Elementary School Curriculum* (Addison-Wesley, 1983). See also Sheryl Dunton, "Building a Microsociety," *Educational Leadership, 63* (8), (2006), 56–60.

15 Clifford Geertz, *The Interpretation of Cultures* (New York, Basic Books, 1973), 19.

16 "Latino Connections," *Social Studies and the Young Learner, 9* (September/October *63 (83)*, 1996), 20–32.

Chapter 5: Powerful Tools: Maps, Globes, Charts, and Graphics

1 From "Letters to the Editor" in *Sunburst, 24* (May 1999), 5.

2 "What Is Geography" at www.ncge.net.

3 I am grateful to The Barrie School in Silver Spring, Maryland—one of the oldest Montessori schools in North America—where headmasters Tim and Donna Seldin wrote *The World in the Palm of Her Hand: Geography and History for the Young Child, the Montessori Approach* (Silver Spring, MD: The Barrie Press, 1986), from which this plan is adapted.

4 Eui-kyung Shin and Marsha Alibrandi, "Online Interactive Mapping: Using Google Earth," *Social Studies and the Young Learner, 19* (2007), P1.

5 Ward Kaiser and Denis Wood, *Seeing Through Maps: The Power of Images to Shape Our World View* (Amherst, MA: ODT, Inc., 2001), 4.

6 See Fuller's influential book, *Operating Manual for Spaceship Earth* (New York: Dutton, 1969).

7 From Sarah W. Bednarz, Gilian Acheson, and Robert S. Bednarz, "Maps and Map Learning in Social Studies," *Social Education, 70* (2006), 398–404.

8 For a helpful review of *Carmen Sandiego,* see Terry Carroll et al., "Carmen Sandiego: Crime Can Pay When It Comes to Learning," listed in Selected References.

Chapter 6: Current Events and Public Issues

1 Buckminster Fuller, *Critical Path* (New York: St. Martin's Press, 1981), xxxviii.

2 This three-part typology of controversies is part of the Public Issues Model. Learn more about it in Laurel R. Singleton's "Following a Tragic Event: A Necessary Challenge for Civic Educators," *Social Education, 65* (2001), 413–418.

3 Walter C. Parker, Janet E. McDaniel, and Sheila W. Valencia, "Helping Students Think About Public Issues," *Social Education, 55* (January 1991), 41–44, 67.

4 Quoted in Sandy Cullen, "School's Anti-War Effort Canceled," November 23, 2005, Wisconsin State Journal, A1.

Chapter 7: Assessing Student Learning

1 Howard Gardner, *Multiple Intelligences: The Theory in Practice* (New York: Basic Books, 1993), 174–175.

2 National assessments are developed and administered by the National Assessment of Educational Progress (NAEP).

3 National Council for the Social Studies, "A Vision of Powerful Teaching and Learning in the Social Studies: Building Social Understanding and Civic Efficacy," in *Curriculum Standards for Social Studies* (Washington, DC: Author, 1994), 167.

4 National Center for History in the Schools, *National Standards for History for Grades K–4: Expanding Children's World in Time and Space* (Los Angeles: Author, 1994), 52.

5 California Department of Education, *A Sampler of History-Social Science Assessment, Elementary* (Sacramento: Author, 1994), 30.

6   Ibid.

7   Vivian Gussin Paley, *Wally's Stories* (Cambridge, MA: Harvard University Press, 1981).

8   "Quick! Name Togo's Capital, *Time* (July 10, 1990), 53. The project is fully described in David Smith's *Mapping the World by Heart* (Tom Snyder Productions, 2003).

9   Backward design is elaborated in Grant Wiggins and Jay McTighe, *Understanding by Design,* 2nd ed. (Alexandria, VA: Association for Supervision and Curriculum Development, 2005).

10 Grant Wiggins (1990), "The Case for Authentic Assessment," *ERIC Digest,* ED328611 (ericae.net/db/edo/ED328611.htm).

11 Janet Alleman and Jere Brophy, *Social Studies Excursions, K–3: Food, Clothing, and Shelter* (Portsmouth, NH: Heinemann, 2001), 34, 160, 240.

12 Robert E. Slavin, *Student Team Learning: A Practical Guide to Cooperative Learning,* 3rd ed. (Washington, DC: National Education Association, 1991).

13 Steven L. McCollum, *Performance Assessment in the Social Studies Classroom: A How-to Book for Teachers* (Joplin, MO: Chalk Dust Press, 1994), 24.

14 Sheila Valencia, *Literacy Portfolios in Action* (Fort Worth, TX: Harcourt Brace, 1998).

Chapter 8: Planning Units, Lessons, and Activities

1   See John Dewey's marvelous essay, *The Child and the Curriculum* (University of Chicago Press, 1902). It has helped generations of teachers make peace between the child-centered and the subject-centered impulses within them.

2   The seminal research on this point was done by Lee Shulman. See his article, "Those Who Understand: Knowledge Growth in Teaching," *Educational Researcher, 15* (1986), 4–14.

3   See the superb article on the relationship between teachers' goals and knowledge by Keith Barton and Linda Levstik, "Why Don't More History Teachers Engage Students in Interpretation?" in *Social Education, 6* (October 2003), 358–361.

4   Howard Gardner, *The Disciplined Mind* (New York: Simon & Schuster, 1999), 209.

5   Catherine S. Taylor and Susan B. Nolen, *Classroom Assessment: Supporting Teaching and Learning in Real Classrooms,* 2nd ed. (New York: Prentice Hall, 2008).

6   W. James Popham, *Classroom Assessment: What Teachers Need to Know* (Boston: Allyn & Bacon, 2002), 98.

7   Ibid.

8   Howard Gardner, *The Disciplined Mind,* 186.

9   Vivian Gussin Paley, *Wally's Stories* (Cambridge, MA: Harvard University Press, 1981), 108.

10 Alice K. Mikovch and Eula E. Monroe, "Gingerville: A Study of Community," *Social Studies and the Young Learner, 15* (November/December 2002), 15–16.

11 Dinah Zike calls these folded 3-D graphics "Foldables." See her website, www.dinah.com, where you can view her popular how-to books.

12 Margit E. McGuire, "Conceptual Learning in the Primary Grades: The Storyline Strategy," *Social Studies and the Young Learner, 3* (January/February 1991), 6–8. Also, see the description at www.wikipedia.org.

13 Sharon Pray Muir, "Simulation Games for Elementary and Primary School Social Studies: An Annotated Bibliography," *Simulation and Gaming, 27* (March 1996), 41–73.

14 Douglas Selwyn, *Living History in the Classroom: Integrative Arts Activities for Making Social Studies Meaningful* (Chicago: Zephyr, 1993), 150.

Chapter 9: Three Great Teaching Strategies

1   A scaffold helps students reach higher and learn more—to perform closer to the ceiling of their abilities. See James Wertsch, *Voices of the Mind: A Sociocultural Approach to Mediated Action* (Cambridge, MA: Harvard University Press, 1991).

2   Esmé Raji Codell, *Educating Esmé* (Chapel Hill: Algonquin, 1999), 191.

3 Margaret Craven, *I Heard the Owl Call My Name* (New York: Doubleday, 1973), 19.

4 Peter H. Martorella, "Knowledge and Concept Development in Social Studies," in *Handbook of Research on Social Studies Teaching and Learning,* ed. James P. Shaver (New York: Macmillan, 1991), 370–384.

5 Quoted in Mason Inman, "Pluto Not a Planet, Astronomers Rule," *National Geographic News,* August 24, 2006 (www.news.nationalgeographic.com).

6 See Hilda Taba et al., *A Teacher's Handbook to Elementary Social Studies: An Inductive Approach* (Reading, MA: Addison-Wesley, 1971), and Bruce Joyce and Marsha Weil, *Models of Teaching,* 7th ed. (Boston: Allyn and Bacon, 2003).

7 Rosalyn Ashby and Peter Lee, "Children's Concepts of Empathy and Understanding in History," in *The History Curriculum for Teachers,* ed. Christopher Portal (London: Falmer, 1987), 86.

8 Janet Alleman and Jere Brophy, *Social Studies Excursions, K–3: Food, Clothing, and Shelter* (Portsmouth, NJ: Heinemann, 2001), 34.

9 Rosalyn Ashby and Peter Lee, "Children's Concepts," 86.

10 A system for asking higher-order questions called Bloom's Taxonomy was widely used by teachers in the decades after its publication in 1956 and is still used by many. It has fallen somewhat from favor in the past 10 years, however, following the cognitive revolution in educational psychology. This movement focuses less on the kind of question students are being asked than on the quality of the task they are being helped to perform. Forming a concept, conducting an inquiry, and applying a skill are three terrific constructive–intellectual tasks, the accomplishment of which necessarily involves students in higher-order thinking. See Benjamin S. Bloom et al., *Taxonomy of Educational Objectives. Handbook I: Cognitive Domain* (New York: David McKay, 1956). For a concise criticism, see Richard Paul's chapter, "Bloom's Taxonomy and Critical Thinking Instruction: Recall Is Not Knowledge," in his book *Critical Thinking,* (FT Press, 2002) 421–428.

11 Eleanor Ruth Duckworth, *The Having of Wonderful Ideas and Other Essays on Teaching and Learning* (New York: Teachers College Press, 1996), 96.

Chapter 10: Four Great Resources

1 Jasmine Sim, Ivy Tan, and Hwee Hwang Sim, "Exploring the Use of Inquiry-Based Learning through Fieldwork," in Christine Lee and Chang Chew Hung (eds.), *Primary Social Studies: Exploring Pedagogy and Content* (Singapore: Marshall Canvendish International, 2005), 35.

2 Sebastian Foti, "Technology: Did We Leave the Future Behind?" *Phi Delta Kappan* 88 (9), (2007), 647, 714–715.

3 Lee's WebQuest is featured in a chapter by Christine Lee and Kho Ee Moi, "Integrating the Internet into Social Studies Lessons: The Potential of WebQuests," in Christine Lee and Chang Chew Hung (eds.), *Primary Social Studies: Exploring Pedagogy and Content* (Singapore: Marshall Canvendish International, 2005), 63–65.

4 David Kaufman, Susan M. Johnson, Susan M. Kardos, Edward Liu, and Heather G. Peske, "Lost at Sea: New Teachers' Experiences with Curriculum and Assessment," *Teachers College Record, 104* (2), (2002), 273.

5 Sheila W. Valencia, Susan Martin, Nancy Place, and Pamela L. Grossman, "Curriculum Materials for Elementary Reading: Shackles and Scaffolds for Beginning Teachers," *Elementary School Journal, 107* (1), (2006), 93–121.

Chapter 11: Cooperative Learning in Social Studies

1 Elizabeth G. Cohen, *Designing Groupwork,* 2nd ed. (New York: Teachers College Press, 1994), 3.

2 Nel Noddings, *Caring: A Feminine Approach to Ethics and Moral Education* (Berkeley: University of California Press, 1984).

3   David W. Johnson, Roger T. Johnson, and Edythe J. Holubec, *The New Circles of Learning: Cooperation in the Classroom and School* (Arlington, VA: Association for Supervision and Curriculum Development, 1994). Also, David W. Johnson, Roger T. Johnson, and Mary B. Shane. *Cooperative Learning Methods: A Meta-Analysis* (available at www.co-operation.org).

4   Dianne K. Augustine, Kristin D. Gruber, and Lynda R. Hanson, "Cooperation Works!" *Educational Leadership, 47* (4), (December 1989/January 1990), 4–7.

5   Elizabeth G. Cohen, *Designing Groupwork,* 21.

6   Beverly Daniel Tatum, *Why Are All the Black Kids Sitting Together in the Cafeteria?* (New York: HarperCollins, 1999).

7   Robert E. Slavin, *Using Student Team Learning* (Baltimore, MD: Johns Hopkins University, 1986).

8   Elliot Aronson, *The Jigsaw Classroom* (Beverly Hills, CA: Sage, 1978).

9   Mara Sapon-Shevin and Nancy Schniedewind, "Selling Cooperative Learning Without Selling It Short," *Educational Leadership, 47* (4), (December 1989/January 1990), 63–65.

10 David W. Johnson and Roger T. Johnson, "Critical Thinking Through Structured Controversy," *Educational Leadership, 45* (8), (May 1988), 58–64.

11 David W. Johnson and Roger T. Johnson, "Social Skills for Successful Group Work," *Educational Leadership, 47* (4), (December 1989/January 1990), 29–33.

12 David W. Johnson, Roger T. Johnson, and Edythe J. Holubec, *The New Circles of Learning, Cooperation in the Classroom and School* (Arlington, VA: Association for Supervision and Curriculum Development, 1994).

Chapter 12: The Literacy–Social Studies Connection

1   Lauren B. Resnick, "Literacy in School and Out," *Daedalus, 119* (Spring 1990), 183.

2   See the definition of "scaffold" in Chapter 2 of this book. For elaboration, see the groundbreaking study by Annemarie Sullivan Palinscar and Ann L. Brown, "Reciprocal Teaching of Comprehension Fostering and Monitoring Activities," *Cognition and Instruction, 1* (2), (1984), 117–175. A helpful article focusing specifically on social studies is Patricia G. Avery and Michael F. Graves, "Scaffolding Young Learners' Reading of Social Studies Text," *Social Studies and the Young Learner, 9* (4), (March/April 1997), 10–14.

3   "What Does the NAEP Reading Assessment Measure?" *National Assessment of Educational Progress (NAEP): The Nation's Report Card, Reading.* (Available on the Internet. Search for the title.)

4   Howard Gardner, *The Disciplined Mind* (New York: Simon & Schuster, 1999), 188.

5   A classic on vocabulary instruction is William E. Nagy, *Teaching Vocabulary to Improve Reading Comprehension* (Urbana, IL: ERIC Clearinghouse on Reading and Communication Skills, National Council of Teachers of English, and International Reading Association, 1988).

6   Valerie Anderson and Suzanne Hiki, "Teaching Students to Summarize," *Educational Leadership* (January 1989), 26–28.

7   The National Paideia Center has a helpful website at www.paideia.org. See also the Great Books Foundation's K–12 program at www.greatbooks.org.

8   Richard A. Allington, *What Really Matters for Struggling Readers* (New York: Addison-Wesley, 2001), 87.

9   Quoted in Tarry Lindquist, *Seeing the Whole Through Social Studies* (Portsmouth, NH: Heinemann, 1995), 89.

10 Tarry Lindquist, *Seeing the Whole Through Social Studies,* 89.

11 National Council for the Social Studies, *Expectations of Excellence: Curriculum Standards for Social Studies* (Washington, DC: Author, 1994), 22.

12 Mary Beth Henning, Jennifer L. Snow-Gerono, Diane Reed, and Amy Warner, "Listening to Children Think Critically About Christopher Columbus," *Social Studies and the Young Learner, 19* (2), (2006), 19.

13 Bill Bigelow and Bob Peterson, eds., *Rethinking Columbus: The Next 500 Years* (Milwaukee, WI: Rethinking Schools, 1998). James W. Loewen, *Lies My Teacher Told Me: Everything Your American History Textbook Got Wrong* (New York: Simon & Schuster, 1996).

Chapter 13: Social Studies as the Integrating Core

1 Howard Gardner and Veronica Boix-Mansilla, "Teaching for Understanding in the Disciplines—and Beyond," *Teachers College Record, 96* (Winter 1994), 199.

2 Howard Gardner, *The Disciplined Mind* (New York: Simon & Schuster, 1999), 54.

3 Ibid., 217.

4 Janet Alleman and Jere Brophy, "Is Curriculum Integration a Boon or a Threat to Social Studies?" *Social Education, 57* (October 1993), 290.

5 Jerome Bruner, *The Process of Education* (Cambridge, MA: Harvard University Press, 1960), 17.

6 John Dewey, *The Public and Its Problems* (Chicago: Swallow, 1927), 83.

7 Heidi Hayes Jacobs, ed., *Interdisciplinary Curriculum: Design and Implementation* (Alexandria, VA: Association for Supervision and Curriculum Development, 1989), 2.

8 Myra Zarnowski, *Learning with Biographies: A Reading and Writing Approach* (Washington, DC: National Council for the Social Studies/National Council of Teachers of English, 1990).

9 Francis Gage's account was published in an antislavery journal and is reproduced in many biographies of Truth. For example, see Edward Beecher Claflin, *Sojourner Truth and the Struggle for Freedom* (New York: Barron, 1987), 81–82.

10 Jeri Ferris, *Walking the Road to Freedom: A Story About Sojourner Truth* (Minneapolis, MN: Carolrhoda Books, 1988), 53, 55.

11 Myra Zarnowski, *Learning with Biographies,* Chapter 4.

12 From *The People Could Fly,* retold by Virginia Hamilton. In *Cricket, 15* (February 1988), 21–26.

13 Ibid.

14 Adapted from Myra Zarnowski, *Learning with Biographies,* Chapter 4.

15 Linda S. Levstik and Keith C. Barton, *Doing History: Investigating with Children in Elementary and Middle Schools,* 2nd ed. (Mahwah, NJ: Lawrence Erlbaum Associates, 2001), 5.

16 Glynda Ann Hull, "Building an Understanding of Composing," in *Toward the Thinking Curriculum: Current Cognitive Research,* ed. Lauren B. Resnick and Leopold E. Klopfer, *1989 ASCD Yearbook* (Alexandria, VA: Association for Supervision and Curriculum Development, 1989), 104–128.

17 James P. Gee, *An Introduction to Discourse Analysis: Theory and Method,* 2nd ed. (New York: Routledge, 2005).

18 Milton Meltzer, Foreword to Myra Zarnowski, *Learning with Biographies,* x.

19 *"Explore" Curriculum,* developed and written jointly by Sydelle Seiger-Ehrenberg and School District no. 12, Adams County, Northglenn, Colorado, 1990.

20 Hilda Taba's work on concept development at San Francisco State University and in the Contra Costa school district is featured in Hilda Taba et al., *A Teacher's Handbook to Elementary Social Studies: An Inductive Approach* (Reading, MA: Addison-Wesley, 1971).

21 Jerrold Coombs, *Thinking Seriously About Curriculum Integration* (Simon Fraser University, Burnaby, British Columbia: Tri-University Integration Project, 1991), 2.

Index